Data-Driven ESG Strategy Implementation Through Business Intelligence

Markos Komodromos
University of Nicosia, Cyprus

Lambrini Seremeti
Agricultural University of Athens, Greece

Lazaros Anastasiadis
University of Crete, Greece

Panagiotis Liargovas
University of Peloponnese, Greece

Sofia Anastasiadou
Univerity of Western Macedonia, Greece

IGI Global
Scientific Publishing
Publishing Tomorrow's Research Today

Vice President of Editorial	Melissa Wagner
Director of Acquisitions	Mikaela Felty
Director of Book Development	Jocelynn Hessler
Production Manager	Mike Brehm
Cover Design	Jose Rosado

Published in the United States of America by
IGI Global Scientific Publishing
701 East Chocolate Avenue
Hershey, PA, 17033, USA
Tel: 717-533-8845
Fax: 717-533-7115
Website: https://www.igi-global.com E-mail: cust@igi-global.com

Library of Congress Cataloging-in-Publication Data

Names: Komodromos, Marcos editor
Title: Data-driven ESG strategy implementation through business intelligence / [edited by] Marcos Komodromos, Lamprini Seremeti, Lazaros Anastasiadis, Panagiotis Liargovas, Sofia Anastasiadou.
Description: Hershey, PA : IGI Global Scientific Publishing, [2026] | Includes bibliographical references and index. | Summary: "This book bridges the gap between technical expertise and strategic vision, offering practical frameworks, case studies, and practical insights"-- Provided by publisher.
Identifiers: LCCN 2025031516 (print) | LCCN 2025031517 (ebook) | ISBN 9798337351421 hardcover | ISBN 9798337351438 paperback | ISBN 9798337351445 ebook
Subjects: LCSH: Business intelligence | Management--Environmental aspects | Sustainable development
Classification: LCC HD38.7 .D3744 2026 (print) | LCC HD38.7 (ebook) | DDC 658.4/72--dc23/eng/20250926
LC record available at https://lccn.loc.gov/2025031516
LC ebook record available at https://lccn.loc.gov/2025031517

British Cataloguing in Publication Data
A Cataloguing in Publication record for this book is available from the British Library.

Table of Contents

Detailed Table of Contents

This chapter explores how combining advanced analytics and business intelligence (BI) revolutionises Environmental, Social, and Governance (ESG) strategies. It showcases the move from compliance-led efforts to data-driven, proactive ESG management, powered by AI, machine learning, IoT, and big data. Practical examples from Unilever, IKEA, and Rio Tinto demonstrate how these technologies boost ESG data quality, reporting, and risk management, allowing for real-time monitoring and predictive insights. Despite the benefits, challenges remain, including data fragmentation, lack of standardisation, and regulatory complexity. The chapter stresses the need for robust data governance, cross-functional collaboration, and ongoing improvement. It concludes that harnessing BI and AI is crucial for organisations to meet changing stakeholder expectations, achieve tangible sustainability outcomes, and build long-term resilience in a data-driven business landscape.

Businesses generate vast amounts of implicit and explicit data every second, yet effectively harnessing its full power remains challenging. Transforming generated data to beneficial knowledge is nearly impossible without a shared conceptualization of key variables, from the statistical aggregation of the relevant measures to the strategies of bringing benefits to society. That is, it is practically impossible for stakeholders to reliably extract actionable insights unless they can rely on mutually agreed semantic structures, commonly referred to as ontologies. This chapter introduces two such ontologies, the Environmental Social Governance Ontology (ESGO) and the Business Intelligence Ontology (BIO) because together they span

technology integration, stakeholder engagement, and adherence to regulations as primary drivers of both resilience and financial literacy.

This research delves into the intricate relationship between green and renewable energy financial literacy and its impact on Environmental, Social, and Governance (ESG) practices in Mexico's changing economic landscape. The study attempts to investigate how financial literacy regarding sustainable energy investments influences the performance of ESG on economic, social, and governance factors in the Mexican context. Through a careful examination of available literature, policy guidelines, and empirical data, this research discovers that greater financial literacy in green and renewable energy sectors has a direct correlation with improved ESG performance, which results in sustainable economic development, social advancement, and governance culture in Mexico. The study concludes that strategic actions to increase financial literacy in renewable energy investments are required for Mexico's sustainable development trajectory and ESG leadership in the Latin American region.

This study presents a hybrid intelligent analytics architecture that merges low-orbit satellite data, IoT sensors, multilingual digital narratives, and extended financial statements using interoperable ontologies to model ESG contingencies and parameterize corporate risk. Deep neural networks are combined with hierarchical Bayesian graphs and Shapley explainability metrics, allowing environmental, social, and reputational incidents to be anticipated with greater sensitivity than traditional approaches. The responsible algorithmic governance framework, underpinned by ethical licensing and continuous audits, ensures transparency and multi-group fairness, balancing intellectual protection and accountability. Case studies in the energy, financial, and logistics sectors show substantial reductions in prediction errors, capital buffers, and stock market drawdowns, while strengthening supply chain resilience and management acceptance.

In the modern world of growing levels of stakeholder analysis and regulatory pressure, it has become a policy imperative of responsible companies to focus on the ESG (Environmental, Social, and Governance)-based considerations as an essential part of their central strategic effort. The main idea is to evaluate how the use of AI-powered BI tools allows achieving ESG data collection, analysis, visualization, and reporting, contributing to providing more responsible and intelligent decision-making in sustainability-focused organizations. The study follows a qualitative-type, multiple case study design, wherein the analysis of five practical entities representing various industries including energy, finance, manufacturing, and information technology. Information was gathered by conducting in-depth interviews with ESG officers and data analysts and the use of secondary data Results indicate that AI-assisted BI systems enable the ESG data to have a better granularity and a more timely and predictive nature, therefore, causing more responsive risk management and stakeholder engagement.

In an increasingly data-driven world, the ability to transform complex datasets into clear, compelling narratives has become essential—especially in the realm of ESG (Environmental, Social, and Governance) reporting. As stakeholders from investors to regulators and consumers demand more transparency and accountability, organizations are turning to data visualization to effectively communicate their ESG initiatives and performance. Data visualization, at its core, is the graphical representation of information and data. Through the use of visual elements such as charts, graphs,

gender and generational differences in perception. A quantitative research design was adopted wherein 282 respondents filled in structured questionnaires. Purposive sampling secured demographic and geographic diversity. t-test, ANOVA, correlation, and regression were used to test the hypotheses. The results show that communication transparency, customer involvement, and CSR initiatives drive sustainability. Gender and age differences exist. Thus, the study shows how aligning CSR with customer expectations builds trust and supports SDG 12 goals.

The integration of artificial intelligence with business intelligence frameworks marks a paradigm shift in measuring environmental sustainability within smart grids. Traditional ESG reporting in energy systems relies on static historical data, missing the dynamic behavior of modern grids and limiting actionable insights. This chapter proposes a novel framework that merges deep learning with real-time business intelligence to enable adaptive ESG monitoring tailored for intelligent energy networks. It tackles challenges such as real-time impact assessment, predictive analytics, data integration, and stakeholder communication. Case studies highlight improvements in renewable integration, carbon footprint reduction, and ESG reporting. The system combines CNNs for satellite imagery and RNNs for time-series data, forming a hybrid model that supports energy optimization, demand forecasting, and grid stability.

he integration of Internet of Things (IoT) technologies with smart grid infrastructure offers transformative potential for real-time ESG (Environmental, Social, and Governance) reporting in the energy sector. This chapter presents a unified business intelligence framework that combines IoT-enabled smart grid analytics with ESG metrics to support ongoing environmental impact evaluation. Unlike traditional ESG reporting that depends on delayed, historical data, the proposed approach utilizes real-time data from advanced metering systems, environmental sensors, and predictive analytics. By incorporating machine learning and dynamic visualization, this system enables improved transparency, operational efficiency, and risk anticipation. Case studies illustrate enhanced carbon tracking, better energy optimization, and strengthened regulatory adherence. Overall, the framework advances sustainable

Preface

INTRODUCTION

In a world where the pursuit of sustainability has become not only a moral imperative but also a strategic necessity, the convergence of Environmental, Social, and Governance (ESG) frameworks with Business Intelligence (BI) offers transformative potential. This edited volume, *Data-Driven ESG Strategy Implementation Through Business Intelligence*, emerges in response to the growing demand for actionable, data-informed approaches to sustainability, catalyzed by investor expectations, global regulations, and heightened public awareness.

Today's organizations are compelled to rethink traditional business models and adopt tools that allow for real-time decision-making and accountability. Business Intelligence, once reserved for operational efficiencies and market analysis, has now evolved into a powerful enabler for ESG integration. It empowers enterprises to capture, analyze, and visualize ESG metrics with clarity and depth, facilitating informed strategy execution and continuous improvement. From predictive analytics that foresee climate risks to dashboards that track workforce diversity or supply chain ethics, BI is now central to embedding ESG into the DNA of corporate strategy.

This volume is intentionally designed to serve a diverse readership. Business leaders will find strategic guidance; ESG practitioners will discover robust frameworks; data scientists will engage with practical modeling approaches; and policymakers will gain insights into implementation at scale. At the same time, the book is a valuable resource for academic researchers, educators, and students working across modern Business Intelligence, human resource management, and ESG studies.

Drawing on interdisciplinary contributions, the chapters explore a wide range of topics—from foundational principles and system architectures to case studies, implementation challenges, and future directions. As editors, our intent is to offer not only a collection of scholarly perspectives but also a hands-on reference for those building the future of responsible and resilient business.

We extend our gratitude to the contributors whose expertise shaped this volume and to the readers who will bring these ideas to life in boardrooms, classrooms, and policy circles alike. May this work guide your efforts toward sustainable innovation, ethical governance, and data-driven impact.

ORGANIZATION OF THE BOOK

Chapter 1: Transforming Corporate Sustainability: Integrating Advanced Analytics and Business Intelligence into ESG Strategy Implementation

This foundational chapter sets the tone for the volume by exploring the powerful convergence of advanced analytics and Business Intelligence (BI) in reshaping ESG strategies. The authors guide readers through the shift from traditional, compliance-based ESG efforts to dynamic, data-driven sustainability models empowered by artificial intelligence, machine learning, IoT, and big data. Through compelling case studies of industry leaders like Unilever, IKEA, and Rio Tinto, the chapter illustrates how these technologies enhance data quality, reporting accuracy, and real-time risk management. Importantly, it also highlights persistent challenges, such as data fragmentation and regulatory ambiguity, while advocating for robust governance, cross-functional collaboration, and iterative development. Ultimately, this chapter demonstrates that the integration of BI and advanced analytics is no longer optional—it is essential for any organization seeking long-term sustainability and stakeholder trust in today's data-centric environment.

Chapter 2: ESG Strategy and Business Intelligence Semantic Network

In this thought-provoking chapter, the authors tackle a foundational problem in ESG and BI integration: the lack of shared semantics that inhibits meaningful data interpretation and application. They introduce and define two ontologies—Environmental Social Governance Ontology (ESGO) and Business Intelligence Ontology (BIO)—as essential frameworks for aligning theory and practice. These semantic structures act as bridges between fragmented data sets, enabling more coherent analysis and decision-making across corporate ecosystems. By establishing common language and conceptual clarity, the chapter underscores how ontological thinking enhances the extraction of actionable ESG insights, ensuring consistency and interoperability in the complex world of data-driven sustainability strategy.

Chapter 3: The Strategic Role of the Board of Directors in Driving Corporate Sustainability, Innovation, and Performance: Evidence from Greek Enterprises

This chapter offers a regional lens on ESG strategy by examining how the board of directors shapes corporate sustainability and performance in Greek enterprises. Drawing from empirical research, the authors demonstrate how the implementation of Corporate Social Responsibility (CSR) practices influences innovation and financial outcomes. The findings reveal a nuanced landscape: general managers most strongly support the social aspects of CSR, while internationalized firms focus on economic dimensions and innovation. Notably, service-sector firms report higher financial performance despite limited environmental CSR adoption. The chapter suggests that strategic board-level engagement is vital for balancing the economic, social, and environmental pillars of ESG—particularly in varied operational contexts.

Chapter 4: Strategic Business Resilience Affecting Green and Renewable Energy Related Financial Literacy in Mexico

In this chapter, the authors investigate the intersection of strategic business resilience and financial literacy within Mexico's evolving green energy sector. As the nation accelerates its shift toward renewable energy, the study identifies how firms with resilient structures are better equipped to engage in long-term financial planning and navigate investment risks. Key enablers—such as adaptive leadership, technological integration, regulatory alignment, and stakeholder collaboration—emerge as drivers of success. This contribution enriches the volume by showing that resilience is not only about survival but about equipping businesses to thrive in a sustainable energy future.

Chapter 5: Green and Renewable Energy Financial Literacy Affecting Economy, Social and Governance (ESG) in Mexico

Building on the previous chapter's focus on Mexico, this study deepens the analysis by examining how financial literacy in green and renewable energy sectors directly enhances ESG outcomes. Through literature review and empirical insights, the authors reveal a strong correlation between improved financial acumen and elevated ESG performance, contributing to Mexico's sustainable development goals. The findings argue that targeted efforts to boost energy-sector financial literacy will empower stakeholders to make informed, impact-driven decisions—advancing economic stability, social progress, and governance integrity throughout Latin America.

Chapter 6: Algorithmic Modeling of ESG Contingencies Using Intelligent Analytics and Predictive Parameterization of Corporate Risk

Concluding the first section of the volume with a technical deep dive, this chapter presents a cutting-edge framework for algorithmically modeling ESG risks using an integrated suite of intelligent analytics. The authors deploy a hybrid model combining IoT data, satellite imagery, multilingual narratives, and financial records within interoperable ontologies. By integrating deep learning, Bayesian inference, and Shapley-based explainability metrics, the approach offers enhanced precision in predicting ESG-related disruptions. The inclusion of ethical AI governance, including algorithmic audits and licensing protocols, ensures responsible use. Demonstrated across energy, finance, and logistics sectors, the model showcases how advanced analytics can significantly reduce uncertainty, optimize capital allocation, and improve supply chain resilience in ESG-sensitive domains.

Chapter 7: Artificial Intelligence-Driven Business Intelligence for ESG Strategy Implementation: Enhancing Corporate Sustainability through Data-Driven Case Studies

This chapter underscores the increasing role of artificial intelligence in reshaping ESG strategy implementation across sectors. Using a multi-case study design, it presents evidence from organizations in energy, finance, manufacturing, and information technology, highlighting how AI-powered business intelligence (BI) tools improve ESG data collection, visualization, and reporting. Through interviews with ESG officers and data analysts, the study reveals that AI-assisted systems allow for higher data granularity and more predictive, real-time insights. These capabilities translate into better risk management and stakeholder engagement, reinforcing the strategic relevance of AI-driven BI in sustainability-focused decision-making.

Chapter 8: Data Visualization Methods for Clear Communication of ESG Analytics Findings

In a landscape demanding transparency and clarity, this chapter explores the critical role of data visualization in ESG reporting. By converting complex datasets into intuitive visual narratives—using charts, infographics, and interactive dashboards—organizations can better communicate their sustainability efforts to stakeholders. The chapter outlines techniques for revealing trends and insights hidden in raw ESG data, covering diverse metrics such as carbon emissions, labor practices, and board diversity. In doing so, it positions visualization not merely as a tool for clarity but as a strategic asset for ESG advocacy and stakeholder trust.

Chapter 9: Implementing Sentiment Analysis for Evaluating Stakeholder Perception and Social Impact

This chapter introduces sentiment analysis as a powerful method for gauging public and stakeholder perception of ESG initiatives. Drawing on advancements in natural language processing and AI, the authors demonstrate how organizations can mine online content—from social media to news articles—to assess emotional and attitudinal responses to their actions. The chapter explains how nuanced sentiment detection, including emotions like trust or anger, can inform social impact assessments and reputation management. It champions sentiment analysis as a critical feedback mechanism in a world where real-time stakeholder insights drive sustainable branding and decision-making.

Chapter 10: Strategic CSR and Customer Engagement in ESG Dashboards: A Data-Driven Approach to SDG 12 Implementation

Focusing on Sustainable Development Goal 12 (Responsible Consumption and Production), this chapter explores how data-driven dashboards can link corporate CSR initiatives with customer engagement and perception. Using a quantitative research design, the study identifies how communication transparency and customer involvement strengthen ESG performance and trust. It also reveals how demographic factors—such as gender and generation—influence consumer attitudes. The chapter makes a compelling case for aligning CSR practices with stakeholder expectations through interactive ESG dashboards, reinforcing that responsible consumption is a shared journey between business and society.

Chapter 11: AI-Powered Grid Analytics for Sustainable Energy Management in ESG Frameworks

This chapter pioneers a novel framework combining artificial intelligence and real-time BI systems for ESG reporting in intelligent energy networks. It addresses the limitations of static ESG reporting by employing deep learning models—CNNs for satellite imagery and RNNs for time-series analysis—to optimize grid performance and sustainability metrics. Through case studies, the authors illustrate how this hybrid approach enhances renewable integration, reduces carbon footprints, and improves reporting transparency. This work positions AI-powered grid analytics as a game changer in sustainable energy management within ESG frameworks.

Chapter 12: IoT-Enabled Smart Grid Analytics for Sustainable Energy ESG Reporting and Performance Optimization: A Business Intelligence Framework

Expanding on the energy sector's ESG reporting needs, this chapter proposes an integrated BI framework powered by IoT-enabled smart grids. It highlights how real-time data from advanced metering and environmental sensors can overcome the delays and limitations of traditional reporting. The use of machine learning and dynamic visualization tools supports predictive analytics and compliance monitoring, while enhancing operational efficiency and environmental stewardship. Through compelling case studies, the chapter demonstrates how the fusion of IoT and BI technologies enables continuous ESG performance evaluation and strategic energy optimization.

Chapter 13: AI for ESG Compliance in Education: Exploring Bioethical Tensions and Institutional Responsibilities in Data-Driven Pedagogy

This timely and critical chapter investigates the deployment of AI technologies in education systems as part of ESG compliance, with a sharp focus on bioethics and student rights. It questions the implications of emotional surveillance, data commodification, and algorithmic bias, particularly in environments where students have limited agency over their data. Through case studies, the authors advocate for frameworks built on modular consent, participatory design, and ethical impact assessments. The chapter stresses the importance of aligning ESG indicators in education with human dignity, making the case for justice-centered, responsible AI deployment in learning ecosystems.

Chapter 14: Voluntary Sustainability Reporting and Financial Performance: Empirical Insights from the Global Real Estate Sector

This empirically driven chapter analyzes the financial implications of adopting Global Reporting Initiative (GRI) standards in the global real estate sector. Using regression analysis of ESG disclosures and financial data from leading real estate firms, the authors demonstrate a positive link between strong ESG performance—

particularly in environmental and governance areas—and Return on Assets (ROA). By quantifying the financial value of transparent sustainability reporting, the chapter provides compelling evidence that ESG integration is not just ethical—it is a strategic imperative for financial performance and long-term viability in capital-intensive industries.

Chapter 15: Exploring Student Attitudes Toward ESG Integration Through Business Intelligence Tools

The final chapter captures the voices of the next generation of sustainability leaders by exploring student perceptions of BI-enabled ESG integration. Through a structured survey, the research reveals that students overwhelmingly value transparency and data-driven decision-making in ESG strategy. However, concerns around data misuse and conceptual complexity also emerge. The study advocates for the inclusion of ESG and BI education in university curricula to better prepare students for roles in sustainable enterprise. This chapter closes the volume by emphasizing that cultivating data-literate, ethically aware graduates is essential for the future of responsible business.

Together, these chapters enrich the volume's central theme by connecting business intelligence, artificial intelligence, and real-world ESG practices. They offer theoretical grounding, empirical validation, and future-oriented visions—guiding readers through the intricate landscape of sustainable transformation enabled by data and technology.

CONCLUSION

As we reach the close of this volume, it becomes clear that the convergence of Business Intelligence and Environmental, Social, and Governance (ESG) strategy represents not just a technological evolution—but a paradigm shift in how organizations conceptualize and operationalize sustainability. Across the chapters, contributors have provided a rich tapestry of insights, frameworks, case studies, and empirical analyses that collectively affirm one central truth: data-driven intelligence is the cornerstone of responsible, resilient, and future-ready enterprises.

In a world increasingly shaped by regulatory demands, stakeholder scrutiny, and global environmental challenges, organizations can no longer afford to treat ESG as a peripheral obligation. Instead, ESG must be fully embedded into the fabric of corporate strategy—guided by real-time data, predictive analytics, and transparent reporting systems. From AI-powered dashboards to IoT-enabled energy systems, from semantic ontologies to student engagement in ESG pedagogy, this book demonstrates the multifaceted ways in which technology can elevate sustainability from principle to practice.

Yet, as the chapters also remind us, the journey toward effective ESG implementation is not without its challenges. Issues of data governance, ethical AI, standardization, and cross-sectoral integration demand continued attention and collaboration. It is through critical inquiry, interdisciplinary innovation, and inclusive stakeholder engagement that organizations can move from compliance to impact, from intention to transformation.

We hope this volume serves as both a practical guide and a source of inspiration for business leaders, data scientists, ESG practitioners, educators, and policy architects alike. By leveraging the collective knowledge presented here, we believe readers will be better equipped to lead with integrity, measure what truly matters, and drive meaningful change in the era of intelligent sustainability.

Markos Komodromos
University of Nicosia, Cyprus

Lambrini Seremeti
Agricultural University of Athens, Greece

Lazaros Anastasiadis
University of Crete, Greece

Panagiotis Liargovas
University of Peloponnese, Greece

Sofia Anastasiadou
Univerity of Western Macedonia, Greece

Chapter 1
Transforming Corporate Sustainability:
Integrating Advanced Analytics and Business Intelligence Into ESG Strategy Implementation

Marcos Komodromos
https://orcid.org/0000-0002-2910-6541
University of Nicosia, Cyprus

Sofia Anastasiadou
University of Western Macedonia, Greece

Lamprini Seremeti
Agricultural University of Athens, Greece

ABSTRACT

This chapter explores how combining advanced analytics and business intelligence (BI) revolutionises Environmental, Social, and Governance (ESG) strategies. It showcases the move from compliance-led efforts to data-driven, proactive ESG management, powered by AI, machine learning, IoT, and big data. Practical examples from Unilever, IKEA, and Rio Tinto demonstrate how these technologies boost ESG data quality, reporting, and risk management, allowing for real-time monitoring and predictive insights. Despite the benefits, challenges remain, including data fragmentation, lack of standardisation, and regulatory complexity. The chapter stresses the need for robust data governance, cross-functional collaboration, and ongoing improvement. It concludes that harnessing BI and AI is crucial for organisations to meet changing stakeholder expectations, achieve tangible sustainability outcomes, and build long-term resilience in a data-driven business landscape.

DOI: 10.4018/979-8-3373-5142-1.ch001

INTRODUCTION

The convergence of Environmental, Social, and Governance (ESG) strategy and Business Intelligence (BI) signifies a transformative paradigm for sustainable business advancement within the modern corporate environment (Chen et al., 2025). As organizations encounter increasing pressure from investors, regulators, and stakeholders to exhibit substantial ESG performance, the amalgamation of advanced data analytics, artificial intelligence (AI), and BI tools is fundamentally redefining the methodologies by which companies evaluate, manage, and convey their sustainability initiatives (Morozova et al., 2024). This paradigm shift is substantiated by compelling evidence from recent research, which demonstrates that sustainability has transitioned from a peripheral compliance obligation to a strategic necessity that directly impacts corporate value generation and competitive positioning (Kalyanam, 2025).

Recent empirical analysis conducted by the OECD (2025) reveals significant challenges within the current ESG landscape, emphasising that ESG rating providers employ over 2,000 distinct metrics characterised by varying definitions and weightings, which generates considerable comparability issues for stakeholders (Kalyanam, 2025). This fragmentation highlights the essential requirement for data-driven approaches capable of standardising, harmonising, and optimising ESG data management across organizations. Furthermore, the OECD study illustrates that 86% of global market capitalization was represented by companies disclosing some form of sustainability-related information in 2022, signifying widespread adoption while also exposing an urgent need for enhanced data quality and consistency (Gong et al., 2024).

The justification for integrating business intelligence (BI) within an environmental, social, and governance (ESG) strategy is reinforced by consumer behaviour research published in the Harvard Business Review, which indicates that sustainability has evolved into a fundamental criterion for purchasing decisions (Ahmad et al., 2023; Sklavos et al., 2024). Consumers are increasingly drawn to brands that demonstrate a genuine commitment to environmental and social responsibility (Aldowaish et al., 2022). This consumer-driven demand establishes a direct correlation between ESG performance and business outcomes, thereby rendering data-driven sustainability strategies indispensable for securing a competitive advantage and enhancing market positioning (Kumar et al., 2021).

Artificial intelligence has emerged as a transformative technology within this context, as indicated by KPMG's 2024 CEO Outlook, which reveals that 64% of CEOs regard AI as a strategic priority for their organisations (Shang et al., 2024). The integration of AI into Environmental, Social, and Governance (ESG) frameworks facilitates real-time data collection and analysis regarding environmental impacts, thereby aiding companies in forecasting effects and optimising resource allocation. Moreover, machine learning and deep learning technologies enable the automation of data collection processes, resulting in a significant reduction in manual labour while enhancing accuracy and consistency in ESG reporting (Huang & Mao, 2024; Wang, Sun & Li, 2023). However, this technological advancement also presents specific challenges, as the considerable energy consumption associated with AI raises concerns about its environmental footprint. AI operations sometimes generate carbon emissions that exceed those produced by traditional business activities (Kshetri & Kshetri, 2024).

Recent studies indicate that advanced tools, including AI, machine learning, and NLP, can automate the extraction and evaluation of ESG data, reducing manual errors and enhancing the objectivity and consistency of reports (Zou et al., 2023). For instance, models like E-BERT and ESGReveal achieve high accuracy rates (up to 93%) in ESG data extraction and rating, streamlining the reporting process and minimising human bias (Chen, 2024; Correia & Água, 2024). These organisations primarily utilise data analytics to automate data collection and enhance the accuracy of environmental metrics, such as carbon emissions and governance indicators, including supply chain transparency (Razib & Rasel, 2025). Implementing these technologies has led to measurable benefits, with 72% of respondents reporting improved transparency in communicating ESG performance and 65% achieving better capabilities for identifying ESG risks. Predictive and prescriptive analytics enable organisations to identify ESG risks and opportunities, providing actionable insights to enhance ESG performance (Ireoluwapo et al., 2024; Li & Wang, 2024). These tools facilitate better risk management and regulatory compliance, which are crucial for maintaining investor confidence and a positive public reputation (Khichi, 2024).

The integration of sustainability analytics into corporate strategy empowers organizations to align Environmental, Social, and Governance (ESG) goals with more comprehensive business objectives by making material risks, opportunities, and stakeholder expectations both visible and quantifiable (Nguyen & Kanbach, 2023). This alignment fosters coherent planning and resource allocation, ensuring that sustainable business practices become integral components of long-term business success, rather than remaining isolated initiatives (Adiguzel et al., 2025). Furthermore, analytics provide organizations with the foresight necessary to identify and manage emerging ESG risks proactively, whether through the monitoring of supply chain vulnerabilities, the assessment of environmental hazards, or the identification of governance concerns (2024).

Despite these advancements, significant challenges remain in the ESG data landscape (Wang, 2025). The OECD analysis highlights a lack of transparency about the methods used for ESG ratings, as many providers do not fully disclose their assessment approaches, creating uncertainty for investors and stakeholders

(Bongermino & Romagnoli, 2025). Furthermore, inconsistent methods can lead to ESG "greenwashing," where companies with poor performance on key issues, such as human rights, labour rights, and anti-corruption, can receive inflated ESG scores due to methodological inconsistencies (Sinha, 2024).

There's a rapid shift in the regulatory environment to tackle these challenges, with policymakers worldwide demanding that companies disclose sustainability-related information using standardised frameworks such as the Corporate Sustainability Reporting Directive (CSRD), the Task Force on Climate-related Financial Disclosures (TCFD), the Global Reporting Initiative (GRI), and the Sustainability Accounting Standards Board (SASB) (Alhoussari, 2025; Berg et al., 2022). These regulatory developments are enabling ESG rating providers to transition from being de facto standard setters to standard adopters, which necessitates closer alignment with established frameworks and methodologies (Del Vitto et al., 2023).

Studies show that 32% of organisations are still in the early stages of integrating data analytics into their Environmental, Social, and Governance (ESG) reporting frameworks (Razib & Rasel, 2025). The main obstacles cited by these organisations are limited resources, insufficient expertise, and challenges in obtaining reliable ESG data. This implementation gap underscores the necessity for comprehensive strategies that encompass both technological capabilities and organisational preparedness for data-driven ESG transformation (Sarıyer et al., 2025; Yu et al., 2024). Advanced data analytics tools and frameworks are emerging to tackle these barriers, but widespread, effective implementation still requires overcoming both technological and organisational hurdles (Ireoluwapo et al., 2024).

This chapter aims to give researchers, practitioners, and organisational leaders a clear understanding of how data-driven methods can transform the development and implementation of Environmental, Social, and Governance (ESG) strategies (Alhoussari, 2025; Cabaleiro-Cerviño & Mendi, 2024). By leveraging advanced analytics, artificial intelligence, and big data, companies can gain more accurate, transparent, and actionable ESG insights, ultimately leading to enhanced sustainability performance and informed decision-making (Svanberg et al., 2023). This in-depth analysis seeks to bridge the gap between theoretical frameworks and practical applications by examining the specific ways companies can effectively integrate ESG objectives into their core business operations, utilising advanced analytics and business intelligence tools (Feng, 2024; Li et al., 2024).

Furthermore, the chapter examines key challenges of implementing ESG strategies, such as creating effective plans, programmes, systems, and performance indicators that can turn these strategies into actionable processes (Kalyanam, 2025). It examines how Management Control Systems (MCS) can help align employee behaviour with an organisation's ESG objectives, exploring integrated frameworks that encompass strategy development, performance measurement and reporting, incentives, accountability, and mechanisms for learning and adaptation (Burnaev et al., 2023; Chen & Zhang, 2024). Overall, this chapter provides both a theoretical basis and a practical guide for organisations aiming to harness the transformative power of business intelligence and artificial intelligence to achieve meaningful, measurable, and sustainable ESG outcomes in a rapidly evolving, data-driven business landscape (Chrisanctus et al., 2024; Li et al., 2025).

All papers selected for inclusion and review in this chapter are sourced exclusively from peer-reviewed academic journals published between 2020 and 2025, thereby ensuring that the analysis is grounded in the most current and rigorously vetted scholarship available. This deliberate focus on the latest literature ensures that the chapter reflects the evolving landscape of Environmental, Social, and Governance (ESG) strategy, business intelligence, and advanced analytics, incorporating the most recent empirical findings, theoretical advancements, and methodological innovations.

By relying solely on recent, peer-reviewed sources, the chapter provides a comprehensive and authoritative synthesis of contemporary research, capturing the dynamic regulatory changes, technological breakthroughs, and market trends that have shaped the field over the past five years. This approach not only enhances the credibility and relevance of the review but also ensures that readers are equipped with insights that are directly applicable to the challenges and opportunities facing organizations in the present and near future.

FOUNDATIONS OF ESG AND BI: A NEW PARADIGM

ESG frameworks have evolved from being peripheral compliance requirements to becoming central drivers of corporate strategy and value creation. The integration of Business Intelligence (BI) into the Environmental, Social, and Governance (ESG) strategy enables organisations to collect, analyse, and act on vast amounts of ESG data, transforming raw information into actionable insights (Cabaleiro-Cerviño & Mendi, 2024).

Organisations are increasingly embedding data into every decision, interaction, and process to ensure that Environmental, Social, and Governance (ESG) considerations are central to their business operations. This data-driven approach enables companies to make informed decisions that prioritize sustainability and ethical practices. Furthermore, effective ESG strategies are now closely aligned with overall business objectives, meaning that sustainability metrics are evaluated alongside traditional financial performance indicators. This integration ensures that long-term value creation and responsible business practices are aligned. Additionally, regulatory and stakeholder pressures are intensifying, with mandates such as the Corporate Sustainability Reporting Directive (Lee et al., 2022). (CSRD) and the

EU Taxonomy requiring companies to adopt rigorous ESG data management and reporting practices. These regulations compel organizations to enhance transparency and accountability in their ESG initiatives, further embedding sustainability into the core of business strategy and operations.

Recent authors argue that the convergence of ESG frameworks and Business Intelligence is fundamentally reshaping how organisations approach sustainability and corporate responsibility (Babkin et al., 2023; Marnotto et al., 2024; Singhania & Saini, 2021). By integrating ESG considerations into core business processes, aligning them with strategic objectives, and responding to increasing regulatory and stakeholder demands, companies cannot only enhance compliance but also unlock new opportunities for value creation and long-term resilience (Chen & Zhang, 2024). This integrated approach ensures that ESG data becomes a powerful driver of informed decision-making and sustainable growth in today's dynamic business landscape.

SUSTAINABLE TRANSFORMATION BY EXPLOITING AI

Artificial intelligence marks a significant step forward in Environmental, Social, and Governance (ESG) strategy, enabling organisations to automate data collection, enhance reporting accuracy, and predict future trends (Li et al., 2025). Adopting AI typically enhances ESG performance, especially in environmental and social areas, but also raises new concerns in governance and ethical oversight (Xie & Wu, 2025). Additionally, AI and advanced analytics are transforming ESG management by enabling organisations to identify risks ahead of time, monitor performance in real-time, and optimise resource use for sustainability and operational efficiency. AI-driven solutions, including machine learning (ML) and natural language processing (NLP), facilitate the extraction and analysis of ESG data from various sources, such as internal documents, news articles, and social media platforms (Chen & Zhang, 2024; Giudici & Wu, 2025). This automation reduces manual effort, minimises errors, and speeds up the delivery of insights.

Table 1. Sustainable transformation by exploiting AI

Aspect	Description	Key Benefits	Challenges / Considerations
Role of AI in ESG Strategy	AI facilitates automation of data collection, improves reporting accuracy, and predicts future trends.	Enhanced ESG performance, especially in environmental and social areas.	Raises governance and ethical oversight concerns.
ESG Performance Improvements	AI adoption leads to better environmental and social outcomes.	Automation reduces manual effort, minimizes errors, speeds insight delivery.	Need to address new governance issues.
AI-Driven ESG Risk Management	AI and advanced analytics help identify risks in advance, monitor performance in real-time, and optimize resource use.	Proactive risk management, real-time performance tracking, improved sustainability and operational efficiency.	Data quality and integration challenges.
Techniques Used	Machine Learning (ML) and Natural Language Processing (NLP) extract and analyze ESG data from diverse sources.	Efficient analysis of structured/ unstructured data from documents, news, social media.	Requires sophisticated models and ethical data use.

AI-driven predictive analytics allow companies to anticipate Environmental, Social, and Governance (ESG) risks and opportunities by analysing large datasets from various sources, including news articles, regulatory filings, and real-time environmental data (Sklavos et al., 2024). This capability helps organisations shift from reactive to proactive ESG management, enabling them to identify potential compliance issues, reputational risks, and ecological incidents before they escalate (Sætra, 2021). For example, machine learning models can detect patterns indicating increased carbon emissions or labour practices that may not meet social standards, allowing for early intervention and strategic planning (Xie & Wu, 2025). This advancement not only improves risk management but also enhances the ability to capitalise on emerging opportunities in sustainable finance and green investments (Kshetri & Kshetri, 2024).

The integration of Internet of Things (IoT) devices and continuous data streams enables real-time monitoring of Environmental, Social, and Governance (ESG) factors, allowing organisations to track environmental and social metrics accurately (Hsieh, 2024). This means that IoT enables accurate, continuous tracking and rapid response to ESG issues, while advanced analytics platforms support dynamic decision-making and increased transparency (Korra & Sadhana, 2024). Advanced analytical platforms promptly process this data, thereby facilitating dynamic decision-making and enabling rapid responses to incidents such as pollution spikes or workplace safety concerns (Meftah et al., 2024). Furthermore, real-time monitoring significantly enhances transparency and fosters stakeholder trust by supplying current and precise ESG performance data, which is increasingly demanded by regulators, investors, and consumers alike. This ongoing evaluation underpins agile ESG strategies and fosters continuous improvement (Zheng & Lee, 2025).

Artificial intelligence (AI) is driving significant changes in energy consumption, logistics, and supply chain operations by making them more innovative, efficient, and sustainable. By utilising advanced data analysis, predictive modelling, and real-time automation, AI optimises these sectors, reducing costs, enhancing efficiency, and minimising their environmental impact (Onukwulu et al., 2023). AI optimises energy consumption, logistics, and supply chain operations by analysing operational data and simulating various scenarios (Hussain, 2025). This helps identify the most efficient routes, inventory levels, and production schedules, reducing carbon footprints and operational costs (Onukwulu et al., 2021). For example, AI-driven supply chain solutions have shown tangible results, including a 10% reduction in carbon emissions and millions of pounds in annual savings for global logistics firms (Louis & E, 2024; Onukwulu et al., 2021). Additionally, AI enables the integration of renewable energy sources, minimises waste throughout the value chain, and supports broader sustainability goals, ensuring compliance with regulatory requirements (Hussain, 2025; Richter et al., 2022).

Case Studies and Real-World Applications: Leading Organizations Leveraging BI and AI to Drive ESG Performance and Achieve Measurable Outcomes

Integrating business intelligence (BI) and artificial intelligence (AI) technologies into environmental, social, and governance (ESG) strategies has become a key driver of organisational transformation (Lim, 2024; Sklavos et al., 2024). AI and BI significantly enhance ESG performance, particularly in social and ecological areas, by improving data quality, decision-making, and operational efficiency; however, challenges persist in governance and the ethical use of these technologies (Li et al., 2025; Xie & Wu, 2025). The following three case studies show how leading organisations are successfully implementing data-driven ESG strategies that deliver both environmental and financial benefits, thereby creating sustainable competitive advantages while tackling global challenges (Feng, 2024; Khichi, 2024).

Unilever: The Sustainable Living Plan - Integrating Sustainability Into Core Business Processes

Unilever's Sustainable Living Plan (USLP), launched in 2010, is a prime example of a multinational corporation effectively integrating sustainability into its core business strategy using data-driven methods (Chernobay et al., 2020). This ambitious 10-year initiative aims to separate business growth from environmental harm while improving social outcomes across three key areas: health and wellbeing, environmental impact, and livelihoods. By doing so, the USLP aims to drive business growth while minimising environmental damage and enhancing positive social impacts (Sabtika & Marlapa, 2024). Studying Unilever's approach provides valuable insights into how major multinational corporations can incorporate sustainability into their operations, strategies, and stakeholder engagement (Böttcher et al., 2023; Chernobay et al., 2020).

Unilever's implementation of the Sustainable Living Plan (USLP) covered all aspects of its operations, including research and development, manufacturing, distribution, commercialisation, and customer service. The company's research and development efforts were refocused to drive innovation in environmentally friendly and socially responsible products, such as biodegradable formulations and sustainable sourcing of raw materials (Böttcher et al., 2023). To meet these goals, manufacturing operations had to significantly cut water consumption, waste generation, and carbon emissions, with priority given to investing in green technologies.

The financial implications of the USLP were significant and quantifiable. Although initial investments in sustainable technologies increased costs, the plan ultimately yielded cost savings and generated new revenue streams from consumers who were inclined towards sustainability. Under the USLP, Unilever's sustainable living brands outperformed the rest, growing 46% faster than the rest of the business and contributing to 70% of the turnover growth. By 2020, sustainable brands expanded 69% faster than the rest of the portfolio, accounting for 75% of the company's growth (DigitalDefynd, 2024; Sabtika & Marlapa, 2024).

Environmental achievements were just as impressive. By 2020, Unilever had achieved zero non-hazardous waste to landfill across its global factory network, used 100% renewable grid electricity in many operations, and sourced over 50% of its agricultural raw materials sustainably (DigitalDefynd, 2024). The company cut CO_2 emissions from manufacturing by 65% compared to 2008 levels and achieved a 96% reduction in total waste sent for disposal per tonne of production. Water conservation initiatives by brands like Comfort and Sunlight introduced products that need less water, saving over 1 billion litres each year (Böttcher et al., 2023; DigitalDefynd, 2024).

Its social impact was just as significant, with health and wellbeing programmes benefiting over 1.3 billion people and improving the livelihoods of 2.34 million individuals, including small-scale farmers and women entrepreneurs. The USLP facilitated substantial social contributions through programmes promoting handwashing, sanitation, and nutrition, while also integrating thousands of small-scale farmers into its supply chain and enhancing their farming practices (Böttcher et al., 2023; DigitalDefynd, 2024).

The impact on stakeholders was comprehensive. Customers experienced enhanced brand loyalty, with surveys in 2020 revealing that 70% of consumers viewed Unilever as a leader in sustainability (Chernobay et al., 2020). Employee engagement and morale improved, with many feeling proud to be part of a company that leads in sustainability. The plan enforced sustainable sourcing practices, encouraging suppliers to adopt greener methods while establishing industry benchmarks that prompted competitors to adopt more sustainable practices (DigitalDefynd, 2024).

IKEA: Investment in Renewable Energy and Sustainable Product Design with Real-Time Data Monitoring

IKEA's sustainability transformation signifies a notable evolution from efficiency-oriented operations to the establishment of a climate-positive organisation, achieved through significant investments in renewable energy and innovative product design (Hashmi et al., 2024). The company's dedication to renewable energy serves as a cornerstone of its sustainability strategy, with assets amounting to billions of euros invested in wind farms, solar installations, and energy-efficient construction. This commitment has culminated in approximately 80% of the electricity consumed in stores and facilities being sourced from renewable sources (Anagnostopoulos et al., 2020; DigitalDefynd, 2024).

In 2025, the Inter IKEA Group announced a significant €200 million investment in supply chain sustainability, focusing on integrating renewable energy throughout its supply chain and enhancing forest management practices. This investment supports IKEA's ambitious goal of using 100% renewable energy in production, which constitutes more than half of its climate footprint, by 2030 (DigitalDefynd, 2024). The company's approach involves direct collaboration with suppliers to achieve this transition, recognizing that sustainable supply chain management is vital for attaining climate-positive status.

IKEA's sustainability accomplishments are both quantifiable and significant. During fiscal year 2024, the company's overall emissions decreased by 5% compared to the preceding year and by a notable 28% relative to the FY16 baseline. This reduction can be attributed to ongoing advancements in renewable energy, enhanced energy efficiency, and a shift toward the electrification of transportation. This progress was achieved while the company concurrently reduced prices across all 63 IKEA retail markets, thereby illustrating that sustainability and affordability can be harmoniously integrated (DigitalDefynd, 2024).

The incorporation of electric vehicles in last-mile deliveries has resulted in a 12.5% reduction in Scope 3 emissions over one year. These enhancements not only reduced long-range operational costs but also improved credibility among environmentally conscious consumers. The company's reinforced climate objectives received validation from the Science Based Targets initiative (SBTi) in June 2024, emphasising the elimination of on-site coal, oil, and oil-based fossil fuels while diligently pursuing the utilisation of renewable energy throughout the entire IKEA value chain (DigitalDefynd, 2024).

IKEA's product innovation demonstrates how sustainability can drive design excellence. The SILVERSIDA series exemplifies this approach, repurposing ceramic production waste into new tableware. This innovative series comprises 65-70% internal factory waste, addressing the challenge of ceramic recycling while creating visually appealing and durable products. The development process took several years to ensure quality while making production scalable, potentially paving the way for post-consumer ceramic recycling.

IKEA's comprehensive sustainability tracking system features real-time data monitoring capabilities, collecting information from over 20 distinct sources. These sources include sales of sustainable product ranges, customer advice and education resources, electricity and water consumption, food waste reduction, transport and delivery emissions, business and customer recycling initiatives, and community impact. This advanced data infrastructure enables the company to evaluate its performance across five international markets, 13 IKEA stores, and 35 diverse data sources through a single, consolidated dashboard (DigitalDefynd, 2024).

The company's circular economy initiatives encompass furniture rental and refurbishment services, buyback programmes, and the pilot of IKEA Preowned. This peer-to-peer second-hand marketplace allows customers to buy and sell used IKEA furniture at reduced prices. More than 60% of IKEA products are derived from renewable materials, with over 10% containing recycled materials (DigitalDefynd, 2024).

Rio Tinto: Mining Giant Harnessing Automation and Real-Time Data Analytics to Minimise Environmental Impact

Rio Tinto's strategy regarding sustainability, supported by the implementation of artificial intelligence and automation, exemplifies a groundbreaking initiative within the mining sector aimed at reducing environmental impact while enhancing operational efficiency. The organisation has incorporated AI and machine learning technologies throughout its operations for over a decade, employing these tools in predictive rail maintenance, plant safety, mine planning, and ecological management. This extensive integration of technology illustrates how conventional heavy industries can capitalise on advanced data analytics to achieve significant environmental improvements (DigitalDefynd, 2024).

The company's commitment to transparency in environmental management is underscored by its pioneering decision to become the first major mining company to publish site-specific water usage data. This initiative, launched on World Water

Day 2023, provides detailed information about annual surface water usage across Rio Tinto's global network of managed sites in 35 countries through an interactive map. The database includes permitted surface water allocation volumes, annual allocation usage, and associated catchment runoff estimates, accompanied by five-year historical comparative data updated annually.

Rio Tinto's water stewardship approach aligns with the International Council on Mining and Metals (ICMM) Water Stewardship Position Statement, which requires members to implement robust and transparent water governance, manage water effectively at their operations, and collaborate to ensure responsible and sustainable water use. CEO Jakob Stausholm emphasised that “water is an essential resource, critical to sustaining biodiversity, people, and economic prosperity,” highlighting the company's commitment to careful water management and stakeholder accountability (DigitalDefynd, 2024).

The implementation of Machine Learning Operations (MLOps) has been pivotal to Rio Tinto's sustainability strategy. Seven years prior, the company established a specialised machine learning team that operates across various business divisions, including aluminum production in Brisbane, iron ore mining in Perth, and commercial operations in Singapore. Our team supports both data scientists and non-expert users, utilising Amazon Web Services (AWS) SageMaker Studio and Canvas to simplify the process of building and deploying models. By automating infrastructure and security processes, Rio Tinto has made machine learning development accessible and scalable across the organisation.

Rehabilitating mines is a crucial area where Rio Tinto demonstrates environmental responsibility through data-driven methods. The company's partnership with specialist, indigenous-owned rehabilitation firms, such as MDM Mining and Civil, for restoring the Argyle Diamond Mine in Western Australia's Kimberley region demonstrates how advanced technology can support environmental restoration (DigitalDefynd, 2024). This initiative utilises cutting-edge equipment, including excavators, bulldozers, and haul trucks equipped with 3D GPS systems, such as Trimble Earthworks, enabling operators to work more efficiently while minimising environmental impact.

Our water treatment development plan for Rio Tinto's closed assets showcases the company's dedication to effective water management, which helps mitigate the environmental and social impacts of mine closures. A thorough assessment of 10 Rio Tinto closure assets has set the stage for identifying operational improvements and technological innovations. These include proposals for alternative technologies that reduce operational costs, meet compliance requirements more efficiently, and lessen environmental impacts through reduced chemical usage. Our methodology utilises advanced technologies and innovative approaches, combining passive and active treatment systems, to develop tailored solutions that meet specific site needs (DigitalDefynd, 2024).

The three case studies mentioned earlier illustrate that data-driven Environmental, Social, and Governance (ESG) strategies deliver benefits in both environmental sustainability and financial performance (Del Vitto et al., 2024; Ireoluwapo et al., 2024; Li et al., 2024). Leading organisations are using business intelligence and artificial intelligence to establish sustainable competitive advantages while tackling global challenges. This evidence shows that sustainability and profitability can be mutually reinforcing, particularly when underpinned by comprehensive data analytics and active stakeholder engagement (Meftah et al., 2024; Sarıyer et al., 2024).

BI TECHNOLOGIES FOR ESG IMPLEMENTATION

Business Intelligence (BI) technologies are playing a pivotal role in advancing Environmental, Social, and Governance (ESG) implementation. Integrating advanced Business Intelligence (BI) technologies is driving a transformation in the landscape of Environmental, Social, and Governance (ESG) strategy implementation (Sarıyer et, 2024). Centralised data repositories, including ESG data lakes and warehouses, enable organisations to efficiently aggregate and manage large amounts of ESG-related information, which is crucial for thorough analytics and transparent reporting (Li et al., 2024). Furthermore, deploying Artificial Intelligence (AI) and Machine Learning (ML) facilitates the automated extraction, categorisation, and validation of ESG data, significantly reducing administrative burdens while enhancing the accuracy and reliability of data (Asif et al., 2023; Svanberg et al., 2023). Additionally, cloud-based solutions further strengthen this technological foundation by offering scalable, secure, and resilient platforms for ESG data management (Onukwulu et al., 2023; Sklavos et al., 2024). Collectively, these BI technologies enable organisations to not only comply with evolving regulatory requirements but also meet stakeholder expectations through improved data governance and actionable insights (Chen et al., 2025).

UNDERSTANDING ESG IN NEXT GENERATION BUSINESS ENVIRONMENTS (NGBE)

Advanced Business Intelligence (BI) technologies are revolutionising the way Environmental, Social, and Governance (ESG) strategies are implemented. Centralised data repositories, such as ESG data lakes and warehouses, allow organisations to easily aggregate and manage vast amounts of ESG-related information, which is essential for robust analytics and transparent reporting (Richter et al., 2022; Xie & Wu, 2025). Additionally, adopting Artificial Intelligence (AI) and Machine Learning (ML) enables the automated extraction, categorisation, and validation of ESG data, significantly reducing administrative burdens while improving data accuracy and reliability (Lim, 2024; Morozova et al., 2024). Cloud-based solutions further reinforce this technological foundation by providing scalable, secure, and resilient platforms for managing ESG data (Chen & Zhang, 2024). Together, these BI technologies enable organisations to not only meet changing regulatory requirements but also address stakeholder expectations through better data governance and actionable insights (Khichi, 2024).

LEVERAGING BUSINESS INTELLIGENCE TOOLS TO ENHANCE ESG REPORTING ACCURACY

Business Intelligence (BI) tools significantly improve the accuracy and transparency of Environmental, Social, and Governance (ESG) reporting by automating key processes and ensuring data integrity. The automated reporting capabilities within BI platforms streamline the aggregation and generation of ESG reports, aligning them with global standards such as the Global Reporting Initiative (GRI), the Task Force on Climate-related Financial Disclosures (TCFD), and the Sustainability Accounting Standards Board (SASB). This automation not only reduces manual errors but also ensures consistency and compliance across reporting frameworks. Moreover, robust data governance frameworks embedded in business intelligence (BI) tools uphold the integrity, security, and comparability of environmental, social, and governance (ESG) data, thereby fostering stakeholder trust (Chen & Zhang 2024; Svanberg et al., 2023). Additionally, BI dashboards and visualisation tools facilitate effective stakeholder engagement by enabling organisations to transparently communicate ESG performance to investors, regulators, and the public. This comprehensive approach promotes accountability and supports informed decision-making, positioning Business Intelligence (BI) as a vital asset in enhancing the accuracy and credibility of ESG reporting (Giudici & Wu, 2025; Kumar et al., 2021).

THE ROLE OF PREDICTIVE ANALYTICS IN ESG RISK MANAGEMENT & DATA VISUALIZATION TECHNIQUES FOR EFFECTIVE ESG COMMUNICATION

Predictive analytics is transforming Environmental, Social, and Governance (esg) risk management by providing organizations with advanced capabilities to foresee and mitigate emerging risks. By utilising artificial intelligence (AI) and machine learning models, companies are able to analyze both historical and real-time data to identify potential ESG threats, including supply chain disruptions, regulatory changes, and reputational hazards (Sætra, 2021; Xie & Wu, 2025). Scenario analysis significantly improves preparedness by simulating various risk situations, thereby allowing organizations to formulate robust strategies for tackling unforeseen challenges. Proactive mitigation is facilitated through early warning systems and dynamic risk dashboards, which empower decision-makers to implement corrective measures before risks escalate to potentially significant impacts (Kumar et al., 2021; Onukwulu et al., 2023). This data-driven methodology not only enhances risk resilience but also advances long-term sustainability objectives.

Equally important is sharing ESG data effectively, as it forms the backbone of stakeholder engagement and smart decision-making. Business intelligence platforms create interactive dashboards that bring ESG metrics, trends, and benchmarks to life, making complex information easy to understand and act upon for everyone involved (Chen & Zhang, 2024). Customizable reporting enables insights to cater to the specific interests and needs of different stakeholder groups, thereby enhancing the relevance and clarity of ESG disclosures. Additionally, AI-powered sentiment analysis tools provide valuable insights into how stakeholders feel and the social impact of the organisation, offering teams a deeper understanding of brand reputation and public opinion (Alhoussari, 2025). Together, these data visualization techniques shine a light on transparency, build trust, and help align strategies with ESG goals.

CHALLENGES AND OPPORTUNITIES IN INTEGRATING ESG METRICS INTO BUSINESS INTELLIGENCE SYSTEMS

The incorporation of Environmental, Social, and Governance (ESG) metrics into business intelligence systems signifies a crucial convergence point between the demands of regulatory compliance and the creation of strategic business value. Recent market research indicates a complex landscape characterised by significant data management challenges, alongside emerging opportunities for achieving a competitive advantage.

Data Quality and Standardization Challenges

There are significant standardisation issues in the ESG data landscape, making integration efforts more complicated. Studies show that the correlation between ESG data from different rating providers is only 0.61 on average, highlighting a considerable variation in how companies are assessed (Böttcher et al., 2023). This fragmentation stems from the lack of globally agreed-upon ESG definitions and the emergence of multiple reporting frameworks, including the Global Reporting Initiative (GRI), the Sustainability Accounting Standards Board (SASB), and the Task Force on Climate-related Financial Disclosures (TCFD). The voluntary nature of ESG reporting has led to inconsistent templates and standards, making it challenging to compare data and reducing its reliability.

Regulatory Complexity and Compliance Burden

Organisations are facing growing complexity in the regulatory environment. A study found that 1,255 new ESG regulations have been introduced globally since 2011, compared to just 493 between 2001 and 2010 (Marnoto et al., 2024). This surge in regulations presents significant compliance challenges, particularly for multinational corporations that must navigate varying requirements across different jurisdictions. The European Union's Corporate Sustainability Reporting Directive (CSRD) and the emerging International Sustainability Standards Board (ISSB) standards are attempts at harmonisation. However, companies still face disjointed reporting obligations that strain resources and increase operational costs (Richter et al., 2024).

Market Growth and Business Intelligence Integration

Organizations are utilising advanced technologies, particularly artificial intelligence, to integrate environmental, social, and governance (ESG) metrics with financial and operational data, thereby enhancing decision-making, ensuring compliance, and improving strategic planning (Li & Wang, 2024). Despite numerous challenges, the ESG data market is experiencing significant growth, with revenues exceeding $1 billion in 2021 and projected to attain $1.3 billion in 2022 (Feng, 2024). Notable organizations are increasingly allocating resources towards the incorporation of integrated ESG modules within their existing business intelligence solutions, with approximately 40% of leading companies actively participating in data-driven sustainability strategies (Morozova et al., 2024). This integration enables firms to correlate ESG metrics with financial and operational data, thus creating comprehensive decision-making frameworks that support both compliance and strategic objectives (Del Vitto et al., 2023).

Stakeholder Expectations and Value Creation

Research indicates that 75% of institutional investors currently integrate Environmental, Social, and Governance (ESG) criteria into their investment decisions, rendering ESG performance an essential determinant of capital accessibility. Enterprises with higher ESG ratings tend to exhibit enhanced financial performance and are more likely to attract investment opportunities. Furthermore, transparent ESG reporting is increasingly correlated with superior risk management and long-term economic stability. This trend reflects the broader expectations of stakeholders, with consumers perceiving sustainability as a fundamental requirement rather than a distinguishing factor (Kalyanam, 2025).

Technology Solutions and Competitive Advantage

Business intelligence integration offers significant operational benefits, with studies indicating that ESG-focused BI solutions can enhance forecasting accuracy by up to 25% and reduce supply chain risks by 30% (Lee et al., 2022). Companies harnessing integrated ESG data management report enhanced decision-making quality, improved risk mitigation capabilities, and a 20-30% increase in brand value through transparent sustainability communication (Razib & Rasel, 2025). However, implementation challenges encompass data silos, integration complexity, and the necessity for specialised expertise to navigate evolving regulatory requirements effectively.

ESG INTEGRATION OPPORTUNITIES: MARKETING RESEARCH ANALYSIS

The Environmental, Social, and Governance (ESG) landscape offers unparalleled opportunities for organizations to utilise technological innovation, foster cross-departmental collaboration, and establish performance benchmarking to attain a competitive advantage (Sætra, 2021). This research analysis examines three pivotal areas of opportunity that are transforming how companies approach ESG integration and stakeholder engagement.

Innovation in Data Collection and Real-Time Reporting

The emergence of artificial intelligence and Internet of Things (IoT) technologies is fundamentally transforming methodologies for collecting Environmental, Social, and Governance (ESG) data (Hsieh, 2024). Real-time sustainability reporting has evolved from annual assessments to continuous monitoring systems that furnish ongoing updates on critical metrics, including carbon emissions, energy consumption, and water usage (Korra & Sadhana, 2024). Organizations are progressively adopting AI-driven ESG data platforms that optimise data collection, processing, and analysis, thereby enabling proactive management of sustainability rather than merely reactive reporting.

Internet of Things (IoT) devices strategically integrated throughout supply chains are generating unparalleled transparency by capturing detailed Environmental, Social, and Governance (ESG) data related to environmental impacts, working conditions, and operational integrity (Hsieh, 2024; Singhania & Saini, 2021). These advanced technologies empower companies to diligently gather essential ESG data from both stationary and mobile assets, significantly minimising manual data collection efforts while simultaneously ensuring continuous monitoring of ESG performance. Moreover, the incorporation of blockchain technology substantially bolsters data integrity through immutable record-keeping and transparent verification processes, effectively addressing long-standing concerns regarding the reliability of ESG data.

Cross-Departmental Collaboration and Strategic Alignment

The successful implementation of Environmental, Social, and Governance (ESG) practices necessitates the dismantling of organizational silos and the promotion of collaboration among all departments. The Corporate Sustainability Reporting Directive (CSRD) mandates the active participation of sustainability, finance, legal, and IT teams to ensure the integration of comprehensive data and the alignment of strategic initiatives. Research indicates that approximately 40% of top-performing companies are adopting data-driven sustainability strategies via integrated ESG modules within existing business intelligence solutions (Böttcher et al., 2023; Burnaev et al., 2023).

Cross-functional ESG teams are imperative for managing the complexities associated with reporting over 3,000 data points required by emerging frameworks (Chen et al., 2025). This collaborative model enables organizations to link ESG metrics with financial and operational data, thereby creating comprehensive decision-making frameworks that not only support compliance objectives but also facilitate strategic value creation. Companies that employ integrated ESG data management report enhancements in decision-making quality, improved risk mitigation capabilities, and a 20-30% increase in brand value through transparent sustainability communication (Hsieh, 2024; Lee et al., 2022; Nguyen & Kanbach, 2023).

Benchmarking and Continuous Improvement

Environmental, Social, and Governance (ESG) benchmarking has emerged as a crucial tool for evaluating performance in comparison to industry peers and identifying opportunities for improvement (Alhoussari, 2025). Organizations are leveraging benchmarking to ascertain their position within industries, thereby providing clear visibility into relative strengths and weaknesses that can be utilised for competitive advantage. This procedure enables companies to refine their ESG strategies, set realistic targets, and make informed investment decisions based on comparative performance data (Asif et al., 2023).

The ESG data market exhibits robust growth, with revenues surpassing $1 billion in 2021 and projections indicating continued expansion. Corporations with high ESG ratings tend to demonstrate superior financial performance and attract a greater number of investment opportunities. According to Chen and Zhang (2024), 75% of institutional investors now integrate ESG criteria into their investment decisions. Strategies for continuous improvement, which incorporate regular performance evaluations, data-driven adjustments, and stakeholder engagement, are crucial for sustaining a competitive advantage and achieving long-term sustainability objectives. Several authors suggest that these opportunities collectively signify a substantial transformation toward integrated, technology-enabled ESG management, which generates quantifiable business value while promoting sustainability objectives (Chrisanctus et al., 2024; Ireoluwapo et al., 2024; Lim, 2024; Singhania & Saini, 2021).

USING BIG DATA ANALYTICS TO IDENTIFY ESG-DRIVEN MARKET OPPORTUNITIES

The convergence of big data analytics and Environmental, Social, and Governance (ESG) frameworks is generating unparalleled opportunities for organizations to identify, analyze, and leverage emerging market trends. Advanced analytical capabilities are revolutionising how companies engage in market opportunity identification by revealing concealed patterns in consumer behavior, regulatory environments, and competitive positioning within the swiftly evolving ESG ecosystem (Asif et al., 2023).

Market Trend Analysis Through Advanced Analytics

Big data analytics empowers organisations to decode complex market signals that traditional research methods often overlook. Advanced analytics reveal emerging trends in consumer preferences, regulatory requirements, and competitive landscapes, enabling companies to position themselves strategically within evolving ESG markets (Wang, 2025). The integration of artificial intelligence and machine learning technologies permits companies to process vast amounts of ESG-related data from multiple sources, including corporate disclosures, regulatory filings, news articles, and satellite imagery, thereby providing comprehensive market intelligence.

Machine learning algorithms can process and interpret this data in real time, offering investors and businesses more accurate ESG scores and risk assessments that uncover market opportunities (Zou et al., 2023). Natural language processing capabilities allow organisations to scan corporate reports and media coverage to identify inconsistencies in ESG claims, revealing competitive gaps and market positioning opportunities. The ESG data market is demonstrating robust growth, with revenues exceeding £2 billion in 2024, indicating substantial commercial opportunities for organisations that leverage data-driven approaches.

Opportunity Identification Through Data-Driven Insights

Data-driven insights reveal emergent markets, products, and partnerships that align with sustainability objectives through sophisticated analytical methodologies. Organizations that employ big data analytics report an enhanced capacity to identify Environmental, Social, and Governance (ESG) risks and opportunities, with 65% of surveyed companies indicating improved risk identification capabilities utilising advanced analytical tools. These insights empower organisations to identify vulnerabilities within supply chains, assess environmental impacts with greater precision, and ensure adherence to governance standards.

The ESG software market, valued at USD 940.7 million in 2023, is projected to experience a compound annual growth rate (CAGR) of 17.3% through 2030, indicating substantial potential for opportunity identification for both technology providers and end-users (Korra & Sadhana, 2024). Companies that utilise integrated ESG data management report enhancements in decision-making quality, improved risk mitigation strategies, and a 20-30% increase in brand value attributed to transparent sustainability communications. Real-time monitoring capabilities facilitate organizations' abilities to detect market inefficiencies and identify emerging opportunities as they arise (Lee et al., 2022).

Strategic Decision-Making and Market Positioning

Organisations use big data to inform investment decisions, product development, and market entry strategies within ESG frameworks. Predictive analytics capabilities enable companies to forecast long-term sustainability trends, helping organisations make proactive decisions to mitigate risks related to climate change or social inequalities. Companies using AI-driven tools report significant improvements in carbon footprint analysis (35% of respondents) and supply chain sustainability assessment (45% of respondents) (Huang & Mao, 2024).

The financial impact of data-driven ESG strategies is substantial, with studies showing that ESG-focused business intelligence solutions can increase forecasting accuracy by up to 25% and reduce supply chain risks by 30% (Donthi et al., 2024). Adopting big data significantly enhances ESG investing, as data-driven analytics improve sustainability assessments and capital allocation. Research indicates positive correlations between implementing big data and ESG performance metrics. These capabilities enable organisations to identify market opportunities across ten major growth areas, including water credits, carbon credits, digital supply chain solutions, and AI-powered sustainability applications, collectively representing billions in market potential (Feng, 2024; Li et al., 2024).

BENCHMARKING ESG PERFORMANCE THROUGH DATA-DRIVEN DASHBOARDS

The integration of data-driven dashboards for ESG performance benchmarking signifies a transformative shift in how organisations measure, compare, and optimise their sustainability initiatives. Current market research indicates that ESG dashboards have evolved from basic reporting tools to sophisticated platforms that offer predictive analytics, real-time monitoring, and comprehensive peer comparison capabilities, enabling organisations to achieve a competitive advantage through strategic sustainability positioning (Sætra, 2021).

Market Growth and Investment Drivers

The market is expanding due to the growing need for transparent, reliable, and real-time ESG data, with regulatory frameworks such as the CSRD playing a significant role. ESG dashboard and reporting software market growth is impressive, with the global ESG investing market expanding from USD 29.86 trillion in 2024 to an expected USD USD 167.49 trillion by 2034, showing a compound annual growth rate of 18.82%. The ESG reporting software market is set to grow from USD 0.9 billion in 2024 to USD 2.1 billion by 2029, with a CAGR of 17.0% (Cruz & Matos, 2023). This growth is primarily driven by increasing regulatory demands, heightened investor scrutiny, and a growing corporate emphasis on sustainability and ethical governance. The Corporate Sustainability Reporting Directive (CSRD) has become a key driver, requiring nearly 50,000 firms in the EU and another 10,000 firms outside the EU to meet complex reporting requirements (Li & Zhu, 2024; Ignatov, 2023).

Technology Integration and Real-Time Capabilities

Advanced ESG dashboards now use artificial intelligence and machine learning algorithms to process vast amounts of ESG-related data from multiple sources, including corporate disclosures, regulatory filings, and satellite imagery. Real-time ESG dashboards are replacing traditional annual reporting approaches, providing continuous monitoring capabilities that enable faster responses to emerging risks and daily decisions that drive sustainability. (Berg et al., 2022). These platforms centralise data collection and provide immediate visualisation, allowing companies to track carbon emissions, diversity indicators, and governance metrics in real-time. Companies using AI-driven tools report significant improvements in carbon footprint analysis (35% of respondents) and supply chain sustainability assessment (45% of respondents) (Cruz & Matos, 2023).

Competitive Benchmarking and Performance Optimization

ESG dashboards allow organisations to carry out sophisticated peer comparison analysis across industry sectors, with platforms like E-Sight providing access to over 15,000 company ratings across various industries. Organisations can compare their performance on material topics, identify significant gaps relative to their industry peers, and understand leading practices at the indicator level (Chen et al., 2025; Li et al., 2025). Research indicates that companies leveraging integrated ESG data management report improved decision-making quality, enhanced risk mitigation capabilities, and a 20-30% increase in brand value through transparent sustainability communication. ESG dashboards promote accountability by clearly demonstrating progress against predefined targets, enabling organisations to hold teams responsible and drive continuous improvement (Razib & Rasel, 2025).

Strategic Value Creation and Future Outlook

Implementing ESG dashboards strategically delivers tangible business benefits beyond compliance. Research indicates that ESG-focused business intelligence solutions can enhance forecasting accuracy by up to 25% and mitigate supply chain risks by 30%. Organisations using ESG dashboards report increased stakeholder engagement, with 75% of institutional investors now considering ESG criteria when making investment decisions. The market outlook suggests ongoing growth, with Verdantix predicting that global spend on ESG reporting software will rise to over £5.6 billion in 2029, at a compound annual growth rate of 26% (Chen et al., 2025; Li et al., 2025). This growth trajectory reflects a fundamental shift towards integrated, technology-enabled ESG management, which creates a sustainable competitive advantage while meeting changing regulatory and stakeholder expectations.

ARTIFICIAL INTELLIGENCE AND MACHINE LEARNING IN ESG STRATEGY IMPLEMENTATION

Integrating artificial intelligence and machine learning technologies is revolutionising the way organisations worldwide implement ESG strategies. AI-powered solutions are transforming three key areas of ESG management: automated data extraction, predictive insights, and strategic recommendations tailored to individual needs.

Automated Data Extraction and Processing

Artificial intelligence technologies demonstrate remarkable proficiency in automating the extraction and analysis of Environmental, Social, and Governance (ESG) data from unstructured sources, thereby addressing one of the most critical challenges in sustainability reporting (Wang, 2025). Sophisticated algorithms can thoroughly investigate internal databases, extract pertinent ESG metrics, and categorise them into standardized classifications while maintaining data integrity and accuracy. Organizations that employ AI-driven tools report substantial enhancements in carbon footprint analysis, as indicated by 35% of respondents, and in supply chain sustainability assessments, as noted by 45% of respondents (Marnoto et al., 2024; Sarıyer et al., 2024). This automation effectively eliminates the labour-intensive and error-prone manual data entry processes that have traditionally hindered ESG reporting.

Predictive Analytics and Strategic Insights

Machine learning models demonstrate an outstanding ability to predict future ESG trends and risks, enabling the development of proactive strategies. AI can forecast changes in weather patterns that affect renewable energy production, economic conditions that impact social factors, and political stability that influences governance structures. Research suggests that ESG-focused business intelligence solutions can boost forecasting accuracy by up to 25% and cut supply chain risks by 30% (Wang, 2025). These predictive capabilities enable companies to simulate various scenarios, such as the impact of carbon tax policies or the benefits of transitioning to renewable energy sources.

Personalized Strategic Recommendations

AI-driven virtual experts offer bespoke ESG advice through advanced recommendation engines that examine organisational data and industry benchmarks.

These systems provide actionable suggestions tailored to specific company contexts, helping organisations optimise resource allocation and strategic decision-making.

EVALUATING ESG INVESTMENT DECISIONS USING BUSINESS INTELLIGENCE FRAMEWORKS

Business intelligence (BI) frameworks play a crucial role in enhancing the quality of ESG investment decisions by providing robust analytical tools that effectively connect sustainability objectives with financial imperatives. Through the conduct of risk-return analysis, BI tools facilitate organizations in evaluating the risk profiles associated with ESG investments, thereby fostering a balanced approach to sustainability alongside profitability (Del Vitto et al., 2023; Li et al., 2025; Razib & Rasel, 2025). The optimization of portfolios further refines decision-making processes by incorporating ESG criteria within traditional financial metrics, thus enabling the construction of investment portfolios that are congruent with both ethical and economic goals.

The scenario testing capabilities inherent in BI platforms empower organizations to simulate a variety of investment outcomes, thereby providing essential insights into the long-term impacts of ESG factors. Consequently, the formulation of a data-driven ESG strategy roadmap necessitates a systematic methodology that capitalises on technological innovation, organizational alignment, and proactive stakeholder engagement (Sinha, 2024). Research indicates that the successful implementation of ESG principles is fundamentally supported by the observance of best practices that ensure both regulatory compliance and the achievement of strategic value (Cruz et al., 2023; Kalyanam, 2025; Zheng & Lee, 2025).

Strategic Alignment and Framework Selection

The foundation of a successful ESG strategy lies in aligning environmental, social, and governance goals with overall business objectives, ensuring that sustainability initiatives support broader organisational strategy. Organisations must carefully select appropriate ESG reporting frameworks, with the Corporate Sustainability Reporting Directive (CSRD), Global Reporting Initiative (GRI), and Sustainability Accounting Standards Board (SASB) emerging as the most widely adopted standards. This selection of frameworks directly impacts data collection requirements and reporting complexity, with CSRD alone requiring nearly 50,000 firms in the EU to meet comprehensive reporting standards (Ireoluwapo et al., 2024).

Technology Integration and Cross-Functional Collaboration

Assessing an organisation's current ESG maturity helps identify gaps in capabilities and prioritise technology investments. Advanced AI algorithms can search internal databases, extract relevant ESG metrics, and categorise them into standardised categories, while ensuring data integrity and accuracy. Forming cross-functional teams that promote collaboration between sustainability, finance, and IT departments is crucial for managing complex reporting requirements. Organisations using AI-driven tools report significant improvements in carbon footprint analysis (35% of respondents) and supply chain sustainability assessment (45% of respondents) (Cruz & Matos, 2023; Emmanuel, 2025).

Data Governance and Stakeholder Engagement

Establishing a robust framework for data governance is crucial to ensure the quality, security, and compliance of data while also facilitating the automation of data collection processes. Effective engagement with stakeholders, including investors, customers, and employees, is instrumental in developing a comprehensive Environmental, Social, and Governance (ESG) strategy that adequately addresses the diverse expectations of stakeholders. These integrated approaches demonstrate the importance of applying technology judiciously, ensuring fairness, transparency, and ethical governance to align with the principles of ESG genuinely (Zheng & Lee, 2025).

DATA ANALYSIS TECHNIQUES FOR OPTIMIZING ESG STRATEGY IMPLEMENTATION

The integration of advanced data analytics techniques constitutes a transformative approach to the optimisation of Environmental, Social, and Governance (ESG) strategy implementation across organizations. Recent market research indicates that sophisticated analytical methodologies are imperative for organizations endeavouring to improve their sustainability performance while addressing escalating regulatory and stakeholder demands.

MARKET-DRIVEN ANALYTICS ADOPTION

The ESG reporting software market is experiencing remarkable growth, increasing from USD 0.9 billion in 2024 to a projected USD 2.1 billion by 2029, at a compound annual growth rate (CAGR) of 17.0% (Cruz & Matos, 2023). This growth trajectory underscores the crucial role of data analytics in fulfilling complex ESG reporting requirements, particularly under regulations such as the Corporate Sustainability Reporting Directive (CSRD), which affects nearly 50,000 firms in the EU and an additional 10,000 firms outside the EU (Yadav et al., 2024). Technological advancements, particularly in data analytics and Industry 5.0, are crucial to meeting these complex reporting requirements and facilitating market expansion. Organisations are increasingly adopting advanced analytics platforms to manage comprehensive sustainability metrics, sophisticated data analytics, and real-time reporting capabilities (Lim, 2024).

ADVANCED ANALYTICAL METHODOLOGIES

Research indicates that organizations employing data analytics for Environmental, Social, and Governance (ESG) reporting experience considerable operational enhancements. Survey data reveals that 72% of companies implementing data-driven ESG reporting report an increase in transparency, while 65% exhibit improved capabilities in ESG risk identification (Cruz & Matos, 2023; Emmanuel, 2025). These analytical processes empower organisations to detect vulnerabilities within supply chains, evaluate environmental impacts with greater precision, and ensure adherence to governance standards through the utilisation of automated data collection and analysis procedures.

Cluster analysis techniques have proven to be particularly beneficial for optimising ESG strategies, allowing for the reduction of observed data into smaller, more manageable profiles by assessing sustainability performance patterns. This methodology facilitates the categorisation of companies into homogeneous groups based on their financial and ESG risk profiles, thereby providing insights into the effects of varying levels of ESG risk exposure and management on overall performance (DigitalDefynd, 2024).

TECHNOLOGY INTEGRATION AND REAL-TIME MONITORING

The market for sustainability platforms, which was valued at $1.3 billion in 2024, is projected to experience a compound annual growth rate (cagr) of 23% through 2029, highlighting the increasing significance of integrated analytics solutions (Helo et al., 2024). These platforms empower organizations to monitor carbon emissions, measure sustainability metrics, and adhere to evolving regulatory requirements through advanced data processing capabilities. Sophisticated analytics that incorporate artificial intelligence and machine learning algorithms process extensive amounts of environmental, social, and governance (esg)- related data from a variety of sources, including corporate disclosures, regulatory filings, and satellite imagery (Rossmannek et al., 2024).

Organisations that adopt AI-driven ESG analytics tools report notable improvements, with 35% indicating enhanced capabilities in carbon footprint analysis and 45% experiencing advancements in supply chain sustainability assessments (Cruz & Matos, 2023). These technological innovations facilitate real-time monitoring and predictive analytics, transforming traditional annual reporting methods into systems for ongoing performance optimization.

CONCLUSION

This chapter concludes that integrating advanced analytics, artificial intelligence (AI), and business intelligence (BI) into Environmental, Social, and Governance (ESG) strategies marks a significant shift in corporate sustainability. As regulatory requirements and stakeholder expectations intensify, organisations are moving beyond compliance-driven ESG initiatives to embed sustainability at the core of their operations. Data-driven methodologies enable companies to standardise ESG data, improve reporting accuracy, and proactively identify risks and opportunities, thereby aligning ESG objectives with broader business goals and competitive strategies.

Case studies of leading organisations, such as Unilever, IKEA, and Rio Tinto, demonstrate that leveraging Business Intelligence (BI) and Artificial Intelligence (AI) not only improves environmental and social outcomes but also drives financial performance and fosters stakeholder trust. These companies have achieved measurable reductions in emissions, operational costs, and resource consumption while fostering innovation and market differentiation through real-time data monitoring and predictive analytics.

Despite these advancements, the chapter acknowledges ongoing challenges, including data fragmentation, lack of standardisation, regulatory complexity, and the need for specialist expertise. The proliferation of disparate ESG metrics and frameworks complicates data comparability and increases compliance burdens. However, the rapid growth of the ESG data market and the adoption of centralised data platforms, automated analytics, and cloud-based solutions are helping organisations overcome these barriers.

Ultimately, the chapter emphasises that successful ESG transformation necessitates strategic alignment, robust data governance, cross-functional collaboration, and ongoing improvement. Investing in BI and AI technologies is essential for organisations seeking to achieve sustainable value creation, regulatory compliance, and long-term resilience in an increasingly data-driven business environment.

REFERENCES

Adiguzel, Z., Cakir, F., & Özbay, F. (2025). Big data analytics capability and sustainability in company innovation. *International Journal of Innovation Science.* DOI: 10.1108/IJIS-08-2024-0231

Ahmad, H., Yaqub, M., & Lee, S. (2023). Environmental-, social-, and governance-related factors for business investment and sustainability: a scientometric review of global trends. Environment, Development and Sustainability, 1 - 23. .DOI: 10.1007/s10668-023-02921-x

Aldowaish, A., Kokuryo, J., Almazyad, O., & Goi, H. (2022). Environmental, Social, and Governance Integration into the Business Model: Literature Review and Research Agenda. *Sustainability (Basel), 14*(5), 2959. DOI: 10.3390/su14052959

Alhoussari, H. (2025). Integrating ESG Criteria in Corporate Strategies: Determinants and Implications for Performance. Journal of Ecohumanism. .DOI: 10.62754/joe.v3i8.5791

Anagnostopoulos, T., Kyriakopoulos, G., Ntanos, S., Gkika, E., & Asonitou, S. (2020). Intelligent Predictive Analytics for Sustainable Business Investment in Renewable Energy Sources. *Sustainability (Basel), 12*(7), 2817. DOI: 10.3390/su12072817

Asif, M., Searcy, C., & Castka, P. (2023). ESG and Industry 5.0: The role of technologies in enhancing ESG disclosure. *Technological Forecasting and Social Change, 195*, 122806. DOI: 10.1016/j.techfore.2023.122806

Babkin, A., Shkarupeta, E., Tashenova, L., Malevsky-Malevich, E., & Shchegoleva, T. (2023). Framework for assessing the sustainability of ESG performance in industrial cluster ecosystems in a circular economy. *Journal of Open Innovation, 9*(2), 100071. DOI: 10.1016/j.joitmc.2023.100071

Berg, F., Kölbel, J., & Rigobón, R. (2022). Aggregate Confusion: The Divergence of ESG Rating. *Review of Finance, 26*(6), 1315–1344. DOI: 10.1093/rof/rfac033

Bongermino, G., & Romagnoli, S. (2025). *ESG rating and ambiguity: an informative and distorted signal-based approach.* Decisions in Economics and Finance., DOI: 10.1007/s10203-025-00507-y

Böttcher, T., Empelmann, S., Weking, J., Hein, A., & Krcmar, H. (2023). Digital sustainable business models: Using digital technology to integrate ecological sustainability into the core of business models. *Information Systems Journal, 34*(3), 736–761. DOI: 10.1111/isj.12436

Burnaev, E., Mironov, E., Shpilman, A., Mironenko, M., & Katalevsky, D. (2023). Practical AI Cases for Solving ESG. *Sustainability (Basel), 15*(17), 12731. DOI: 10.3390/su151712731

Cabaleiro-Cerviño, G., & Mendi, P. (2024). *ESG-driven innovation strategy and firm performance*. Eurasian Business Review., DOI: 10.1007/s40821-024-00254-x

Chen, K., Lin, S., & Chuang, C. (2025). ESG Strategies and Sustainable Performance in Multinational Enterprises. *Sustainability (Basel), 17*(2), 751. DOI: 10.3390/su17020751

Chen, R., & Zhang, T. (2024). Artificial intelligence applications implication for ESG performance: Can digital transformation of enterprises promote sustainable development? *Chinese Management Studies*. DOI: 10.1108/CMS-11-2023-0653

Chen, S. (2024). *The Influence of Artificial Intelligence and Digital Technology on ESG Reporting Quality*. International Journal of Global Economics and Management., DOI: 10.62051/IJGEM.v3n1.36

Chernobay, L., Yasinska, T., & Malibroda, S. (2020). Applied Aspect Of Corporate Social Responsibility Impact On Company Competitiveness -Unilever Example., 8, 32-44.

Chrisanctus, O., Adeoye, O., Okoye, C., Ofodile, O., Odeyemi, O., Addy, W., & Ajayi-Nifise, A. (2024). *Artificial Intelligence in ESG investing: Enhancing portfolio management and performance*. International Journal of Science and Research Archive., DOI: 10.30574/ijsra.2024.11.1.0305

Correia, A., & Água, P. (2024). Harnessing artificial intelligence for enhanced environmental, social, and governance reporting: A new paradigm in corporate transparency. Corporate governance: Research and advanced practices. .DOI: 10.22495/cgrapp15

Cruz, C., & Matos, F. (2023). ESG Maturity: A Software Framework for the Challenges of ESG Data in Investment. *Sustainability (Basel), 15*(3), 2610. DOI: 10.3390/su15032610

Del Vitto, A., Marazzina, D., & Stocco, D. (2023). ESG ratings explainability through machine learning techniques. *Annals of Operations Research*. DOI: 10.1007/s10479-023-05514-z

DigitalDefynd. (2024). 20 Useful ESG Case Studies [2025]. DigitalDefynd. https://digitaldefynd.com/IQ/esg-case-studies/

Donthi, R., Lakshmi, P., Srinivas, G., Sudhakar, S., Koneru, H., & Yekula, P. (2024). AI-Driven Numerical Optimization for Carbon Footprint Reduction and Sustainable Supply Chain Management in the Fashion Industry. *South Eastern European Journal of Public Health*, 1216–1222. DOI: 10.70135/seejph.vi.2023

Emmanuel, A. (2025). *The future of management reporting and sustainability reporting: Integrating ESG metrics for strategic decision-making*. World Journal of Advanced Research and Reviews., DOI: 10.30574/wjarr.2025.25.2.0423

Feng, S. (2024). *Leveraging artificial intelligence to enhance ESG models: Transformative impacts and implementation challenges*. Applied and Computational Engineering., DOI: 10.54254/2755-2721/69/20241473

Giudici, P., & Wu, L. (2025). Sustainable artificial intelligence in finance: Impact of ESG factors. *Frontiers in Artificial Intelligence*, *8*, 1566197. DOI: 10.3389/frai.2025.1566197 PMID: 40115117

Gong, X., Tao, X., Zhang, M., Xu, Y., Kwok, H., Dai, J., & Cheng, J. (2024). Secure Environmental, Social, and Governance (ESG) Data Management for Construction Projects Using Blockchain. *Sustainable Cities and Society*, *114*, 105582. DOI: 10.1016/j.scs.2024.105582

Hashmi, R., Liu, H., & Yavari, A. (2024). Digital Twins for Enhancing Efficiency and Assuring Safety in Renewable Energy Systems: A Systematic Literature Review. *Energies*, *17*(11), 2456. DOI: 10.3390/en17112456

Helo, P., Mayanti, B., Bejarano, R., & Sundman, C. (2024). Sustainable supply chains – Managing environmental impact data on product platforms. *International Journal of Production Economics*, *270*, 109160. DOI: 10.1016/j.ijpe.2024.109160

Hsieh, M. (2024). An empirical investigation into the enhancement of decision-making capabilities in corporate sustainability leadership through Internet of Things (IoT) integration. *Internet of Things : Engineering Cyber Physical Human Systems*, *28*, 101382. DOI: 10.1016/j.iot.2024.101382

Huang, R., & Mao, S. (2024). Carbon Footprint Management in Global Supply Chains: A Data-Driven Approach Utilizing Artificial Intelligence Algorithms. *IEEE Access : Practical Innovations, Open Solutions*, *12*, 89957–89967. DOI: 10.1109/ACCESS.2024.3407839

Hussain, K. (2025). *Revolutionizing Route Optimization Systems with Artificial Intelligence for a Smarter, Sustainable Logistics Ecosystem*. International Journal of Computer Science and Mobile Computing., DOI: 10.47760/ijcsmc.2025.v14i02.008

Ignatov, K. (2023). When ESG talks: ESG tone of 10-K reports and its significance to stock markets. *International Review of Financial Analysis, 89*, 102745. DOI: 10.1016/j.irfa.2023.102745

Ireoluwapo, O., Olanrewaju, K., Daramola, G., & Babayeju, O. (2024). *Harnessing big data analytics to revolutionize ESG reporting in clean energy initiatives.* World Journal of Advanced Research and Reviews., DOI: 10.30574/wjarr.2024.22.3.1759

Kalyanam, A. (2025). *Integration of ESG Data in the Retail Sector (Essential for Sustainable business and Risk Management).* INTERANTIONAL JOURNAL OF SCIENTIFIC RESEARCH IN ENGINEERING AND MANAGEMENT., DOI: 10.55041/IJSREM39956

Khichi, M. (2024). TECHNOLOGY AND ARTIFICIAL INTELLIGENCE'S IMPACT ON ESG REPORTING QUALITY. International Journal of Innovations & Research Analysis. .DOI: 10.62823/IJIRA/4.3(I).6899

Korra, C., & Sadhana, A. (2024). *Integrating IoT Sensors, Cloud AI, and Satellite Broadband for Enhanced ESG Governance in Smart Cities: A Tripartite Approach to Real-Time Environmental Monitoring. International Journal of Innovative Science and Research Technology.* IJISRT., DOI: 10.38124/ijisrt/IJISRT24MAR1621

Kshetri, N., & Kshetri, N. (2024). The Environmental Impact of Artificial Intelligence. *IT Professional, 26*(3), 9–13. DOI: 10.1109/MITP.2024.3399471

Kumar, S., Sureka, R., Lim, W., Mangla, S., & Goyal, N. (2021). What do we know about business strategy and environmental research? Insights from Business Strategy and the Environment. *Business Strategy and the Environment, 30*(8), 3454–3469. DOI: 10.1002/bse.2813

Lee, O., Joo, H., Choi, H., & Cheon, M. (2022). Proposing an Integrated Approach to Analyzing ESG Data via Machine Learning and Deep Learning Algorithms. *Sustainability (Basel), 14*(14), 8745. DOI: 10.3390/su14148745

Li, J., Wu, T., Hu, B., Pan, D., & Zhou, Y. (2025). Artificial intelligence and corporate ESG performance. *International Review of Financial Analysis, 102*, 104036. DOI: 10.1016/j.irfa.2025.104036

Li, Y., & Zhu, C. (2024). Regional Digitalization and Corporate ESG Performance. *Journal of Cleaner Production, 473*, 143503. DOI: 10.1016/j.jclepro.2024.143503

Li, Z., Yu, Y., & Wang, S. (2024). Practical evaluation of intelligent algorithms in ESG management of manufacturing enterprises. *Scientific Reports, 14*(1), 19394. DOI: 10.1038/s41598-024-70376-9 PMID: 39169099

Lim, T. (2024). Environmental, social, and governance (ESG) and artificial intelligence in finance: State-of-the-art and research takeaways. *Artificial Intelligence Review, 57*(4), 76. DOI: 10.1007/s10462-024-10708-3

Louis, N., &, E. (2024). Leveraging artificial intelligence for enhanced supply chain optimization. Open Access Research Journal of Multidisciplinary Studies. .DOI: 10.53022/oarjms.2024.7.2.0044

Marnoto, S., Silva, C., & Veiga, P. (2024). Beyond profit in family businesses: ESG-driven business model innovation and the critical role of digital capabilities. Journal of Family Business Management. .DOI: 10.1108/JFBM-05-2024-0105

Meftah, E., Benmahmoud, S., & Rabehi, A. (2024). Innovative Wireless Solutions for Real-Time ECG Monitoring: Leveraging BLE, Wi-Fi, and LoRa Technologies. *2024 International Conference on Telecommunications and Intelligent Systems (ICTIS)*, 1-6. DOI: 10.1109/ICTIS62692.2024.10894056

Morozova, I., Smetanina, A., & Smetanin, A. (2024). ESG strategy for managing sustainable digital transformation of business in the artificial intelligence economy. Ars Administrandi (Искусство управления). .DOI: 10.17072/2218-9173-2024-2-217-239

Onukwulu, E., Agho, M., & Eyo-Udo, N. (2023). Developing a framework for AI-driven optimization of supply chains in energy sector. Global Journal of Advanced Research and Reviews. .DOI: 10.58175/gjarr.2023.1.2.0064

Onukwulu, E., Dienagha, I., Digitemie, W., & Egbumokei, P. (2021). AI-driven supply chain optimization for enhanced efficiency in the energy sector. Magna Scientia Advanced Research and Reviews. .DOI: 10.30574/msarr.2021.2.1.0060

Razib, N., & Rasel, I. (2025). *The role of data analytics in enhancing ESG transparency in the corporate sector of Bangladesh.* Global Journal of Engineering and Technology Advances., DOI: 10.30574/gjeta.2025.22.1.0245

Richter, L., Lehna, M., Marchand, S., Scholz, C., Dreher, A., Klaiber, S., & Lenk, S. (2022). Artificial Intelligence for Electricity Supply Chain automation. *Renewable & Sustainable Energy Reviews, 163*, 112459. DOI: 10.1016/j.rser.2022.112459

Rossmannek, O., David, N., Sandoval, C., & Garay, L. (2024). Bridging the Green Gap in Homesharing: How Platforms Can Increase Hosts' Sustainability Intentions and Behavior. *Journal of Travel Research.* DOI: 10.1177/00472875241249444

Sabtika, V., & Marlapa, E. (2024). THE EFFECT OF IMPLEMENTATION OF CORPORATE SOCIAL RESPONSIBILITY, GREEN INNOVATION STRATEGY, AND COMMITMENT TO A SUSTAINABLE LIVING ENVIRONMENT IN UNILEVER INDONESIA TBK.. International Journal of Management Studies and Social Science Research. .DOI: 10.56293/IJMSSSR.2024.4820

Sætra, H. (2021). A Framework for Evaluating and Disclosing the ESG Related Impacts of AI with the SDGs. *Sustainability (Basel), 13*(15), 8503. DOI: 10.3390/su13158503

Sarıyer, G., Mangla, S., Chowdhury, S., Sozen, M., & Kazançoğlu, Y. (2024). Predictive and prescriptive analytics for ESG performance evaluation: A case of Fortune 500 companies. *Journal of Business Research, 181*, 114742. DOI: 10.1016/j.jbusres.2024.114742

Shang, Y., Zhou, S., Zhuang, D., Żywiołek, J., & Dinçer, H. (2024). The impact of artificial intelligence application on enterprise environmental performance: Evidence from microenterprises. *Gondwana Research, 131*, 181–195. DOI: 10.1016/j.gr.2024.02.012

Singhania, M., & Saini, N. (2021). Institutional framework of ESG disclosures: Comparative analysis of developed and developing countries. *Journal of Sustainable Finance & Investment, 13*(1), 516–559. DOI: 10.1080/20430795.2021.1964810

Sinha, M. (2024). *Responsible Capital: The Evolution and Performance of ESG Investing*. Exploresearch., DOI: 10.62823/ExRe//01/03.10

Sklavos, G., Theodossiou, G., Papanikolaou, Z., Karelakis, C., & Ragazou, K. (2024). Environmental, Social, and Governance-Based Artificial Intelligence Governance: Digitalizing Firms' Leadership and Human Resources Management. *Sustainability (Basel), 16*(16), 7154. DOI: 10.3390/su16167154

Svanberg, J., Ardeshiri, T., Samsten, I., Öhman, P., Neidermeyer, P., Rana, T., Maisano, F., & Danielson, M. (2023). *Must social performance ratings be idiosyncratic? An exploration of social performance ratings with predictive validity*. Sustainability Accounting, Management and Policy Journal., DOI: 10.1108/SAMPJ-03-2022-0127

Wang, Q. (2025). Generative AI-Assisted Evaluation of ESG Practices and Information Delays in ESG Ratings. *Finance Research Letters, 74*, 106757. DOI: 10.1016/j.frl.2025.106757

Wang, Q., Sun, T., & Li, R. (2023). Does artificial intelligence (AI) reduce ecological footprint? The role of globalization. *Environmental Science and Pollution Research International, 30*(59), 123948–123965. DOI: 10.1007/s11356-023-31076-5 PMID: 37995036

Xie, H., & Wu, F. (2025). Artificial Intelligence Technology and Corporate ESG Performance: Empirical Evidence from Chinese-Listed Firms. *Sustainability.* DOI: 10.3390/su17146463

Yadav, S., Samadhiya, A., Kumar, A., Luthra, S., & Pandey, K. (2024). Environmental, Social, and Governance (ESG) Reporting and Missing (M) Scores in the Industry 5.0 Era: Broadening Firms' and Investors' Decisions to Achieve Sustainable Development Goals. *Sustainable Development.* DOI: 10.1002/sd.3306

Yu, M., Rabhi, F., & Bandara, M. (2024). Ontology-Driven Architecture for Managing Environmental, Social, and Governance Metrics. *Electronics (Basel), 13*(9), 1719. DOI: 10.3390/electronics13091719

Zheng, Z., & Lee, C. (2025). A meta-analysis of ESG factors in the real estate investment trusts sector: Exploring their impacts on REITs performance. *Engineering, Construction, and Architectural Management.* DOI: 10.1108/ECAM-05-2024-0652

Zou, Y., Shi, M., Chen, Z., Deng, Z., Lei, Z., Zeng, Z., Yang, S., Tong, H., Xiao, L., & Zhou, W. (2023). ESGReveal: An LLM-based approach for extracting structured data from ESG reports. ArXiv, abs/2312.17264. https://doi.org//arXiv.2312.17264 .DOI: 10.48550

Chapter 2
ESG Strategy and Business Intelligence Semantic Network

Lamprini Seremeti
https://orcid.org/0000-0002-0663-5408
Agricultural University of Athens, Greece

Lazaros Anastasiadis
University of Peloponnese, Greece

Marcos Komodromos
https://orcid.org/0000-0002-2910-6541
University of Nicosia, Cyprus

ABSTRACT

Businesses generate vast amounts of implicit and explicit data every second, yet effectively harnessing its full power remains challenging. Transforming generated data to beneficial knowledge is nearly impossible without a shared conceptualization of key variables, from the statistical aggregation of the relevant measures to the strategies of bringing benefits to society. That is, it is practically impossible for stakeholders to reliably extract actionable insights unless they can rely on mutually agreed semantic structures, commonly referred to as ontologies. This chapter introduces two such ontologies, the Environmental Social Governance Ontology (ESGO) and the Business Intelligence Ontology (BIO) because together they span the two opposite poles, theoretical and practical, that dominate contemporary business decision making.

DOI: 10.4018/979-8-3373-5142-1.ch002

INTRODUCTION

Modern businesses operate in an environment where implicit (social media sentiment, regulatory fillings) and explicit (sensor readings, transaction logs) data are generated in real time. Cloud warehouses and streaming platforms have made it technically feasible to store and process unlimited data (Sankaranarayanan, 2025; Saraswat and Choudhari, 2025; Alifia et al., 2025), yet business managers still struggle to turn raw data into decisions that both increase the bottom line and meet an increasingly demanding set of social and environmental expectations (Holm and Ostergaard, 2025; Etikala, 2025). The core challenge lies not in data quality, which is indeed crucial for business efficiency (Shankar and Shewale, 2024), but in the absence of shared meaning of heterogeneous data (Feilmayr and Woss, 2016). Indeed, divisions, subsidiaries, and external partners routinely use either different labels for the same phenomenon or the same label for different ones (Abadi et al., 2025). For instance, one department reports "profit" as revenue minus all expenses, while another calls the figure "profit" but subtracts only direct production costs and ignores overhead. Both numbers are labeled "profit" in their spreadsheets, yet they refer to different calculations, making any comparison meaningless or confusing, unless everyone agrees on a single, shared definition. These semantic inconsistencies create a functional gap, which widens across the business sector, undermining any attempt to draw reliable insights from the data. To tackle this challenge, businesses need a rigorous semantic framework, that is, agreed-upon shared conceptualization that standardizes terms across systems, reports, and stakeholders.

In knowledge engineering, this shared conceptualization is defined as ontology (Guarino et al., 2009). An ontology, as an explicit, formal specification of the entities, attributes, and relations that matter to particular community of stakeholders, enhances the understanding and interoperability within different systems (Chen et al., 2025). Although, relying or creating a single universal ontology for the business domain may not be a feasible task, since diverse viewpoints among stakeholders necessitate distinct conceptual choices (Djezzar et al., 2023). Indeed, finance, supply chain, operations, human resources, sustainability strategies, customer satisfaction analytics, each are governed by distinct regulations, and vocabularies. Attempting to force all these rapidly evolving areas into one rigid schema would either flatten essential nuances or become so strict that no team could maintain it. A more viable approach is building a network of ontologies, that is, interlinked semantic models that allow each domain to evolve at its own pace while still sharing a common semantic backbone for cross-domain reasoning (Seremeti and Kougias, 2013).

This Chapter is structured as follows: "Related Work" lists the recent development in domain-specific conceptual frameworks, yet all of them evolve in isolation, either in ESG strategies (Seremeti et al., 2024; Taraza et al., 2024a; 2014b) or in BI analytics. Despite this progress, the two strands do not intersect. ESG ontologies seldom reference the technical constructs that drive BI analytics, and BI ontologies rarely encode the normative and regulatory measures embedded in ESG disclosure frameworks; "The Environmental, Social, Governance Ontology (ESGO)" formalizes the concepts, relationships and constraints that underpin modern sustainability reporting; "The Business Intelligence Ontology (BIO)" formalizes the processes through which raw data becomes managerial insights; "The ESG_BI Ontology Alignment" introduces a bridging semantic schema between numeric and intangible values; "ESG_BI Semantic Network" highlights the need for a unified semantic framework, which may measures and monitors intangible sustainability factors and hard financial metrics; and "Conclusion" discusses how combining ESG sustainability vocabulary with BI operational analytics in a semantic schema the abundance of data is transformed into actionable knowledge.

RELATED WORK

Early research on sustainability semantics concentrated on crafting dedicated ontologies and knowledge-graph models that capture the fast evolving vocabulary of environmental, social and governance disclosure. Recent examples include an ESRS-compliant ontology that structures the European Sustainability Reporting Standards (ESRS) and enables automated gap analysis in corporate reports (Usmanova and Usbeck, 2024), an ontology-driven architecture that encodes ESG metrics and their regulatory dependencies for decision-support purposes (Yu et al., 2024), an ontology for evaluating a decision-making process for ESG that harmonizes different approaches to integrating and comparing intangible and tangible values (Linder and Steinhauser, 2025), a knowledge-graph approach for shared metrics of sustainability (Diamantini et al., 2022), and an ontology-based approach which enhances the accuracy and consistency of ESG reporting (Asokan et al., 2020). These works confirm the growing maturity of ESG semantics but rarely consider how such models should interface with enterpise analytics stacks.

Parallel research in BI explores how ontologies can support the information lifecycle within a corporate environment (Antunes et al., 2022). Concrete implementations range from an ontology-based collaborative BI platform that annotates data-mart objects with semantic descriptions (Fahad and Darmont, 2023) to a semantic-layer architecture that sit between warehouses and visual-analytics tools to standardize KPI definitions (Bomma, 2023). Despite these advances, BI ontologies typically omit the normative constructs that dominate ESG disclosure.

Related work shows that there is a fragmented landscape in which sustainability knowledge graphs cannot tap the governance controls embedded in BI stacks, and

BI tools cannot reason over the ethical and regulatory nuances captured by ESG ontologies. This gap justifies a networked approach that interconnects the ESG ontology with the BI ontology, creating a modular semantic backbone capable of supporting efficient decision-making processes.

THE ENVIRONMENTAL, SOCIAL, GOVERNANCE ONTOLOGY (ESGO)

When engineering the Environmental, Social, Governance Ontology (ESGO), the designer began not with concepts and interrelations but with competency questions, which are natural language queries that the ontology must be able to answer once populated with data (Keet and Khan, 2024). Questions such as "Which activities materially influence Scope 3 emissions?", "Which metrics in the current report fail to map an accredited standard?", "How does board-independence score correlate with carbon intensity over three years?", "Which board committees oversee human-rights risk across subsidiaries?", and "Which ESG indicators in the current report lack alignment to a recognized standard?" act as functional requirements. These kind of questions are put at the start of the ontology engineering for scope-setting purposes, so later, they are used during the assessment phase of the ontology development process. During evaluation, each question is re-expressed as a SPARQL query, and the ontology is deemed complete only when all queries return correct, unambiguous results.

Based on the above competency questions, the ESGO formalizes the concepts, relationships and constraints that underpin modern sustainability reporting. It extends beyond a simple list of disclosure indicators to encompass entities, stakeholders, casual factors, and regulatory artefacts. Its upper layer centers on the class *Entity*, partitioned into *Organization*, *Stakeholder*, *Activity*, *Risk*, and *Control*. The main analysis of this specific domain is based on the ESGFactor term, divided into *EnvironmentalFactor*, SocialFactor, and *GovernanceFactor*. Each factor *is_measured_by* one or more *Indicators* and ultimately *is_qualified_by* a *Metric*, which carries *numeric_value*, *unit*, and *reportingPeriod*. The Greenhouse Gas (GHG) Protocol, the widely adopted global standard for measuring and reporting corporate and value-chain greenhouse-gas emissions, was used to populate subclasses of EnvironmentalFactor, while ISO 26000, which offers voluntary guidance on how organizations of all sizes and sectors can operate in a socially responsible manner, populated the SocialFactor subclasses. In addition, OECD Principles of Corporate Governance concerning shareholder rights, equitable treatment, institutional-investor stewardship, stakeholder relations, and transparency instantiated the subclasses of GovernanceFactor. Axiomatically, each Metric must have exactly one value and

Unit, and EnvironmentalFactor, SocialFactor, and GovernanceFactor are declared pairwise disjoint to prevent unintended overlap, that is, ensure that no individual can, by mistake, be classified as belonging to two mutually exclusive categories.

THE BUSINESS INTELLIGENCE ONTOLOGY (BIO)

In the same vein, the Business Intelligence Ontology (BIO) engineering was based on competency questions such as "Which dashboards display the "gross-margin %" KPI, and which data pipeline feed the metric?", "For a given user with the "Finance Analyst" role, what BI artefacts (dashboards, reports) are accessible, and what data assets underpin them?", "Which KPIs tagged as Regulatory are missing documentation for their transformation logic?", and "Which fact tables are shared across more than three cubes, and what dashboards consume those cubes?".

According to the non-exhaustive list of competency questions, the BIO formalizes the processes through which raw data becomes managerial insights. The BIO anchors on *DataAsset*, subdivided into *DataSource*, *DataWarehouse*, *DataMart*, *DataLake*, and *Table*, the latter split into *FactTable* and *DimensionTable*. Moreover, *ETLProcess* and *DataPipeline* model transformation logic. *DataModel* and its subclass *Cube* capture semantic layers. *BIArtifact* bundles *Dashboard*, *Report*, *Visualization*, *Metric*, and *KPI*. In addition, *User* and *Role* ground governance. Key object properties, such as DataSource *feeds* DataPipeline, DataPipeline *loaded_into* DataAsset, DataWarehouse *contains* Table, BIArtifact *monitored_by* Metric, and BIArtifact *consumed_by* User, as well as, data properties, such as *lastUpdated* and *refreshRate* were also included in the ontology.

The BIO can be instantiated and validated through mainstream BI platforms, e.g., Power BI, Tableau, ensuring seamless integration with existing analytics workflows.

ESG_BI ONTOLOGY ALIGNMENT

Although ESGO and BIO excel within their respective domain, strategic decision-making increasingly demands one view that unites sustainability metrics with traditional performance analytics. A bridging semantic schema - called here the ESG-BI Ontology Alignment - provides this link.

In ontology engineering, an alignment is the set of correspondences (e.g., equivalent classes, sub-class relations, property matches, and transformation rules) that links two or more otherwise independent ontologies (Ehrig, 2007). Its purpose is to preserve semantic coherence while enabling systems built on heterogeneous models to interoperate, share data, and perform joint reasoning. Its techniques are based on lexical matchers, which compare labels, synonyms, and descriptions, using string metrics or language models; structural matchers, which exploit graph topology, matching concepts whose super- and sub- class patterns mirror one another; and instance-based methods that leverage shared data, inferring that two classes are equivalent if they host overlapping or highly similar individuals (Seremeti and Kougias, 2013; Sawant et al., 2025).

In the particular domains of ESG and BI, it contains nothing but mapping axioms, such as *esg:Metric owl:equivalentClass Bi:Metric, esg:Indicator owl:equivalent-Class bi:KPI, esg:reportingPeriod owl:equivalentProperty biQlastUpdated.* More nuanced links use subclass or property chain relations. For example, each *Activity* that *affects* and *ESGFactor* in ESGO can be chained to the *FactTable* that records it in BIO, enabling queries that span from carbon emitting processes to financial income statements. This kind of semantic bridge permits the evolution of both ontologies independently.

ESG_BI SEMANTIC NETWORK

Taken together, ESGO, BIO, and their alignment form a semantic network for business that supports overall reasoning. For instance, a single SPARQL query can ask how a rise in Scope-2 emissions (ESGO concept) influences the profitability KPIs on a sales dashboard (BIO concept), and the reasoner will supply both the numerical answer and the data tracing that underpins it.

In knowledge engineering, a semantic network can be formally defined as an ordered pair $S=(V,E)$, where V is a finite set of nodes representing well-defined concepts and E is a set of labeled, directed edges whose labels are elements of a relation vocabulary R. Because every edge in E is typed by R and interpreted by the semantics of a logic-based language L, automated reasoners can perform sound inference while domain experts can audit the same structure for ontological adequacy (Zhang et al., 2025).

The ESG_BI semantic network is best understood as the structured representation of intellectual and technological business knowledge in which concepts are connect-ed by relationships. Because both the concepts and the relationships are explicitly defined, machines can traverse the network to infer new facts, detect inconsistencies, or answer complex queries, while humans can inspect the network to validate that the encoded meaning aligns with real world expertise.

Figure 1. ESG_BI semantic network

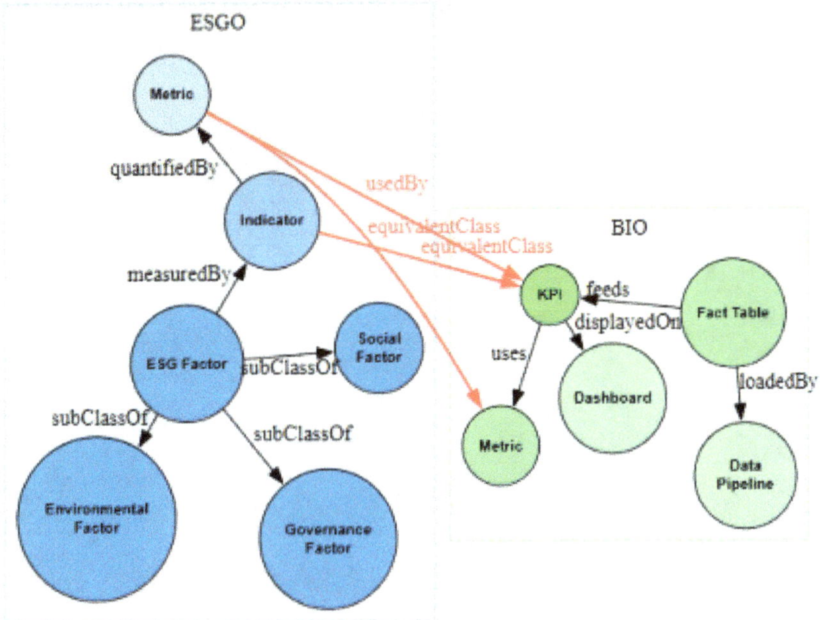

The resulting ESG_BI semantic network (Figure 1) supplies a unified knowledge framework for interpreting and analyzing corporate sustainability and performance scenarios. This kind of knowledge graph is organized as two colour-coded clusters, each enclosed by a dashed bounding box. The blue one is the ESGO cluster, showing the core sustainability vocabulary, while the green one is the BIO cluster, representing key business intelligence indicators. Across the middle runs the alignment, establishing formal equivalence between sustainability and BI concepts. Together the clusters and red alignment links form a single semantic network. ESGO keeps the normative semantics of sustainability, BIO preserves the operational trace of analytics, and the bridge provides a shared backbone for integrated ESG-driven BI.

CONCLUSION

Semantic technologies such as ontologies have been known as effective tools for knowledge representation, sharing and reuse and for supporting systems interoperability. Recent research on artificial intelligence techniques has also shown that they can enable systems to operationalize knowledge by making it actionable. Building on the proven versatility of ontologies across domains, this chapter introduces the

ESG_BI semantic network, a unified knowledge framework that integrates tangible financial metrics with intangible sustainability factors to support holistic, data-driven business decisions.

REFERENCES

Abadi, A., Abadi, C., & Abadi, M. (2025). Intelligent decision making and knowledge management system for agile project management in industry 4.0 context. *Statistics, Optimization & Information Computing*, *13*(5), 2060–2078. DOI: 10.19139/soic-2310-5070-2378

Alifia, R. A., Safitri, N. R., Irhami, D. M., Hidayat, N. R., & Kusumasari, I. R. (2025). Challenges and solutions for decision making in the era of big data. *Jurnal Bisnis Dan Komunikasi Digital*, *2*(2), 13. DOI: 10.47134/jbkd.v2i2.3498

Antunes, A. L., Cardoso, E., & Barareiro, J. (2022). Incorporation of ontologies in data warehouse/business intelligence systems - A systematic literature review. *International Journal of Information Management Data Insights*, *2*(2), 100131. DOI: 10.1016/j.jjimei.2022.100131

Asokan, V. A., Yarime, M., & Onuni, M. (2020). A review od data-intensive approaches for sustainability: Methodology, epistemology, normativity, and ontology. *Sustainability Science*, *15*(3), 955–974. DOI: 10.1007/s11625-019-00759-9

Bomma, H. P. (2023). Enhancing business analytics with a semantic layer. *International Journal of Business Quantitative Economics and Applied Management Research*, *7*(9), 93–99.

Chen, J., Mashkova, O., Zhapa-Camacho, F., Hoehndorf, R., He, Y., & Horrocks, I. (2025). Ontology embedding: A survey of methods, applications and resources. *IEEE Transactions on Knowledge and Data Engineering*, *37*(7), 4193–4212. DOI: 10.1109/TKDE.2025.3559023

Diamantini, C., Khan, T., Potena, D., & Storti, E. (2022). Shared metrics of sustainability: A knowledge graph approach. *The 30th Italian Symposium on Advanced Database Systems*, Italy.

Djezzar, M., Hemam, M., Amara, F. Z., Seghir, Z. A., & Hifidi, M. M. (2023). Towards a multi-viewpoints ontological framework for knowledge sharing in e-health. *Joint Proceedings of Second International Workshop on Semantic Reasoning and Representation in IoT and Third International Workshop on Multilingual Semantic Web*, Spain.

Ehrig, M. (2007). *Ontology Alignment*. Bridging the Semantic Gap.

Etikala, S. (2025). Enterprise data quality management: A technical deep dive into automated governance. *International Journal on Science and Technology*, *16*(2).

Fahad, M., & Darmout, J. (2023). An ontology-based collaborative business intelligence framework. *Proceedings of the 12th International Conference on Data Science, Technology and Applications*, 480-487. https://doi.org/DOI: 10.5220/0012131900003541

Feilmayar, C., & Woss, W. (2016). An analysis of ontologies and their success factors for application to business. *Data & Knowledge Engineering*, *101*, 1–23. DOI: 10.1016/j.datak.2015.11.003

Guarino, N., Oberle, D., & Staab, S. (2009). What is an ontology? In: Staab, S., Studer, R. (eds) *Handbook on Ontologies*. International Handbooks on Information Systems. Springer, Berlin, Heidelberg, 1-17. https://doi.org/DOI: 10.1007/978-3-540-92673-3_0

Holm, F. S., & Ostergaard, K. (2025). The corporate sustainability due diligence directive and the doctrine of privity of contract. *European Review of Private Law*, *33*(3), 1–28.

Keet, C. M., & Khan, Z. C. (2024). On the roles of competency questions in ontology engineering. *Proceedings of Knowledge Engineering and Knowledge Management Conference*, 123-132. https://doi.org/DOI: 10.1007/978-3-031-77792-9_8

Lidner, H. G., & Steinhauser, I. (2025). A unified theory and ontological framework of ESG reorting. In: Matos, F., Basile, C., Pyis, L. Edvisson, L., Roos, G. (eds) *Intellectual Capital in a Global Business Landscape. Contributions to Management Science*. Springer, Cham, 91-110. https://doi.org/DOI: 10.1007/978-3-031-86362-2_5

Sankaranarayanan, S. (2025). The role of data engineering in enabling real-time analytics and decision-making across heterogeneous data sources in cloud-native environments. *International Journal of Advanced Research in Cyber Security*, *6*(1), 11–18.

Saraswat, J. K., & Choudhari, S. (2025). Integrating big data and cloud computing into the existing system and performance impact: A case study in manufacturing. *Technological Forecasting and Social Change*, *210*, 123883. DOI: 10.1016/j.techfore.2024.123883

Sawant, S. K., Gawade, S., & Shrimali, M. (2025). Survey of recent approaches in ontology matching. *Information Systems for Intelligent Systems*, *430*, 491–509. DOI: 10.1007/978-981-96-1206-2_38

Seremeti, L., Anastasiadis, L., & Anastasiadou, S. (2024). The Role of Data in Environmental, Social, and Governance Strategy, (pages 149-166). *In Christos Papademetriou, Sofia Anastasiadou, Konstantina Ragazou, Alexandros Garefalakis and Stylianos Papalexandris. ESG and Total Quality Management in Human Resources,* https:// DOI: DOI: 10.4018/979-8-3693-2991-7.ch010

Seremeti, L., & Kougias, I. (2013). Networks of aligned ontologies through a category theoretic approach. *Journal of Emerging Trends in Computing and Information Sciences*, *4*(10), 785–794.

Seremeti, L., & Kougias, I. (2013). Computation of ontology resemblance coefficients for improving semantic interoperability. *Engineering Mathematics Letters*, *2*(1), 1–19.

Shankar, B. S., & Sheware, P. L. (2024). Data cleaning techniques and their impact on model accuracy. *International Research Journal of Modernization in Engineering Technology and Science*, *06*(12), 4343–4346.

Taraza, E., Anastasiadou, S., Seremeti, S., & Masouras, A. (2024a). Environmental, Social, and Governance of Businesses and Organizations and the Role of Human Resources (pages 116-132.). *In Christos Papademetriou, Sofia Anastasiadou, Konstantina Ragazou, Alexandros Garefalakis and Stylianos Papalexandris. ESG and Total Quality Management in Human Resources*, DOI: 10.4018/979-8-3693-2991-7.ch006

Taraza, E., Papademetriou, C., Seremeti, S., Masouras, A., & Anastasiadou, S. (2024). The Necessity of Environmental Ethics in Environmental Education and the Role of Educators. In *Christos Papademetriou* (pp. 149–166). Sofia Anastasiadou, Konstantina Ragazou, Alexandros Garefalakis and Stylianos Papalexandris. ESG and Total Quality Management in Human Resources., DOI: 10.4018/979-8-3693-2991-7.ch008

Usmanova, A., & Usbeck, R. (2024). Structuring sustainability reports for environmental standards with LLMs guided by ontology. *Proceedings of the 1st Workshop on Natural Language Processing Meets Climate Change*, 168-177. https://doi.org/ DOI: 10.18653/v1/2024.climatenlp-1.13

Yu, M., Rabbi, F. A., & Bandara, M. (2024). Ontology-driven architecture for managing environmental, social, and governance metrics. *Electronics (Basel)*, *13*(9), 1719. DOI: 10.3390/electronics13091719

Zhang, T., Yang, M., & Jiang, P. (2025). Event state knowledge graph-driven full-chain product quality tracing. *Procedia CIRP*, *134*, 538–543. DOI: 10.1016/j.procir.2025.02.154

Chapter 3
The Strategic Role of the Board of Directors in Driving Corporate Sustainability, Innovation, and Performance:
Evidence From Greek Enterprises

Eleftheria Panagiotidou
https://orcid.org/0000-0003-0420-3991
Democritus University of Thrace, Greece

Elena Kagioglou
Democritus University of Thrace, Greece

Athanasios Mandilas
Democritus University of Thrace, Greece

Giannoula Florou
https://orcid.org/0000-0002-2621-2832
Democritus University of Thrace, Greece

ABSTRACT

CSR is an important business consideration that involves addressing social, economic, and environmental issues. Implementing CSR practices can improve a business's reputation and attract customers who value social responsibility. This chapter examines the implementation of CSR practices in Greek businesses and their effect on innovation and business performance. The Greek businesses apply CSR practices

DOI: 10.4018/979-8-3373-5142-1.ch003

to a high degree, are innovative and perform well. The implementation of social dimension of CSR was more strongly supported by General Managers. Economic dimension of CSR and innovative practices was observed more in businesses with international scope. In contrast, the environmental dimension of CSR was less observed in in-service businesses. However, these businesses showed a higher financial performance. Implementing environmental CSR practices is expected to increase business innovation and, by extension, its non-financial performance, which is also enhanced by social CSR practices.

INTRODUCTION

In recent years, Corporate Social Responsibility (CSR) has transitioned from a voluntary, philanthropic initiative to a central component of corporate strategy and governance. The growing societal, environmental, and regulatory pressures have compelled businesses across sectors and regions to adopt more sustainable and socially responsible practices. At the same time, global economic volatility and technological advancement have brought innovation to the forefront of organizational resilience and competitive advantage.

The European Union has intensified legislative efforts through frameworks such as the Corporate Sustainability Reporting Directive (CSRD), increasing corporate accountability in environmental, social, and governance (ESG) practices. Firms are expected not only to maximize profits but also to minimize negative externalities and actively contribute to societal well-being (European Commission, 2023).

In Greece, the CSR discourse has gained momentum, particularly during and after the financial crisis, as businesses sought new ways to regain legitimacy and rebuild stakeholder trust. Empirical findings suggest that Greek companies increasingly recognize CSR as a strategic necessity rather than a reputational add-on. Nevertheless, CSR integration remains uneven across industries and is often constrained by firm size, leadership orientation, and available resources.

Simultaneously, innovation is regarded as a vital mechanism through which firms can respond to dynamic market challenges, enhance performance, and align with sustainability goals. Prior research has indicated that CSR-driven firms are more likely to introduce innovations in management, marketing, and operations (Porter & Kramer, 2011; Hart, 1995).

Despite the expanding international literature, there is limited empirical research that systematically examines the relationship between CSR, innovation, and firm performance within the Greek context. Moreover, the potential mediating role of innovation in the CSR–performance linkage has received inadequate attention in national studies. In addition to these broad developments, there is a growing recognition that corporate social responsibility (CSR) is not merely a peripheral or symbolic endeavor, but rather a mechanism for corporate legitimacy and strategic differentiation. In economies facing structural challenges, such as Greece's, CSR has become a way for firms to navigate uncertainty, rebuild trust, and reposition themselves in competitive global markets. Stakeholders, including consumers, investors, and regulators, are more informed and demanding than ever before. They expect organizations to articulate clear sustainability goals and demonstrate ethical conduct across all operations. This shift reflects a redefinition of corporate purpose, moving from narrowly maximizing shareholder value to creating stakeholder value more broadly.

Furthermore, CSR initiatives are increasingly viewed as strategic investments rather than compliance costs. Evidence suggests that firms that proactively integrate CSR into their core strategies experience improved employee morale, enhanced innovation capacity, and more resilient supply chains. This is particularly relevant in the post-pandemic recovery era, where environmental, social, and governance (ESG) criteria are central to investor decision-making and supply chain governance. In this evolving landscape, the board of directors plays a pivotal role in not only overseeing compliance and risk but also in shaping the firm's long-term strategic vision with sustainability as a guiding principle. Therefore, examining how CSR practices influence innovation and performance at the firm level in the Greek context, as well as the strategic role of governance, is crucial for understanding how businesses can thrive under increasing institutional, environmental, and societal pressures.

The purpose of this study is to investigate the extent to which CSR practices are implemented by Greek enterprises and to examine their impact on both innovation and business performance. Specifically, the study aims to determine whether CSR contributes to the development of innovative practices and whether these innovations, in turn, enhance financial and non-financial outcomes. The research also considers how organizational characteristics and employee profiles shape these relationships, with the goal of generating insights relevant for both scholars and practitioners.

LITERATURE REVIEW

Corporate Social Responsibility: Conceptual Framework

Corporate Social Responsibility (CSR) has evolved from a marginal concern of businesses to a core strategic component for modern organizations. Initially conceptualized in the 1950s, CSR gained theoretical depth with Carroll's (1991) four-part model—economic, legal, ethical, and philanthropic responsibilities—which remains widely cited in both academic and managerial contexts. This multidimensional model allows organizations to address a broad spectrum of stakeholder expectations and societal obligations.

More recently, scholars have emphasized the strategic dimensions of CSR, particularly its integration into competitive advantage frameworks (Porter & Kramer, 2002). Rather than being viewed solely as a compliance mechanism, CSR is now considered a strategic lever that can enhance corporate legitimacy, stakeholder trust, and long-term profitability.

CSR and Business Sustainability

CSR plays a foundational role in corporate sustainability, defined as the pursuit of economic success while ensuring environmental protection and social equity. Firms that adopt sustainability-oriented CSR practices tend to incorporate responsible resource management, long-term risk mitigation, and ethical stakeholder engagement into their business models (Elkington, 1997).

Eccles et al. (2014) demonstrate that companies with high sustainability ratings show superior performance in both capital market and accounting-based measures over the long term. These firms also experience increased investor confidence and stronger employee engagement. Consequently, CSR has moved from peripheral philanthropy to a central strategic imperative in sustainable development agendas.

CSR and Corporate Performance

A substantial body of literature has explored the link between CSR and corporate performance, generally supporting a positive association. Financial performance metrics such as Return on Assets (ROA), Return on Equity (ROE), and revenue growth have been used alongside non-financial indicators like employee satisfaction, customer loyalty, and brand equity.

Margolis and Walsh (2003) identified over 100 empirical studies on this topic, concluding that while causality is difficult to establish, the weight of evidence suggests a favorable relationship. More recently, García-Piqueres and García-Ramos (2024) confirmed that environmental CSR practices specifically enhance innovation and non-financial performance. In the Greek context, empirical findings also support this relationship. Firms that engage in socially responsible activities report not only better performance metrics but also higher stakeholder credibility and market differentiation.

CSR and Innovation

CSR has also been increasingly linked to organizational innovation. Through the resource-based view of the firm, CSR is conceptualized as a valuable intangible resource that fosters organizational learning, knowledge sharing, and creative thinking (Hart, 1995).

CSR-driven innovation can manifest in several forms: product innovation (e.g., eco-friendly products), process innovation (e.g., sustainable supply chains), and business model innovation (e.g., circular economy practices). Companies engaging in social and environmental responsibility often foster more inclusive, participatory, and adaptive organizational cultures that are conducive to innovation. Porter and Kramer (2011) introduced the concept of "Creating Shared Value"—arguing that societal needs can define new markets and drive innovation. This perspective further cements CSR as an enabler of entrepreneurial thinking and dynamic capabilities.

The Role of the Board of Directors in CSR

Corporate governance structures significantly influence CSR implementation. The board of directors, in particular, is a central actor in embedding CSR into strategic decision-making. Its responsibilities include aligning CSR initiatives with corporate objectives, overseeing risk management, and ensuring compliance with ethical and regulatory standards.

Agency theory posits that boards mitigate managerial opportunism and protect shareholder interests (Fama & Jensen, 1983). However, stakeholder theory extends the board's duty to encompass broader societal interests. Battilana et al. (2022) contend that boards must evolve from transactional oversight bodies into transformational governance structures that safeguard corporate purpose and long-term sustainability.

Empirical evidence underscores that board characteristics—such as diversity, independence, and the existence of dedicated CSR or sustainability committees—are positively associated with CSR disclosure quality and performance (Liao et al., 2015). Moreover, board engagement in CSR is not merely symbolic; it has substantive effects on the depth and authenticity of CSR strategies.

Stakeholder Pressures and CSR

Firms today operate under increasing pressure from stakeholders to adopt transparent and impactful CSR practices. Stakeholder theory suggests that organizations must manage relationships not only with shareholders but also with employees, customers, suppliers, regulators, and communities (Freeman, 1984).

Institutional investors are now incorporating Environmental, Social, and Governance (ESG) criteria into decision-making, pressuring firms to demonstrate responsible behavior. Gibson et al. (2020) found that firms with strong CSR records are less volatile and more attractive to long-term investors. Lins et al. (2017) further observed that such firms perform more robustly during economic crises, highlighting CSR's role in organizational resilience.

Additionally, customers increasingly demand sustainable products and transparent supply chains. Regulatory bodies are imposing stricter reporting obligations, such as the EU's Corporate Sustainability Reporting Directive (CSRD). Thus, CSR adoption is not only a matter of ethics but also of compliance and competitive positioning.

Environmental and Social Sustainability: From Policy to Practice

Environmental and social sustainability are often operationalized through CSR initiatives. Environmental sustainability encompasses practices such as emissions reduction, energy conservation, waste management, and the development of green technologies. These activities not only improve regulatory compliance but also result in cost savings and brand differentiation.

On the social side, CSR initiatives address labor rights, diversity and inclusion, health and safety, and community development. Firms that prioritize social sustainability often see improvements in employee morale, customer satisfaction, and reputational capital.

Boards of directors are increasingly expected to oversee sustainability goals, integrate them into risk management systems, and link executive compensation to ESG performance. This trend reflects the institutionalization of CSR as part of corporate governance rather than isolated philanthropic efforts.

However, challenges remain. Many firms struggle with greenwashing—providing misleading information about their CSR efforts. There is also a persistent gap between CSR policies and actual practice, especially in small and medium enterprises (SMEs) with limited resources.

The Role of Boards of Directors in Promoting Social Sustainability

In recent years, the debate surrounding the purpose of business has become increasingly dynamic as social and environmental expectations intensify. This shift requires a rethinking of the traditional focus on profit maximization in favor of an approach that integrates social sustainability into the core of the corporate mission (Battilana et al., 2022; Brosch, 2023).

The demand for a new corporate purpose that is not limited exclusively to the financial interests of shareholders has been reinforced through international initiatives such as the United Nations Sustainable Development Goals and ESG principles. Companies are now called upon to operate not only as economic entities but also as socially responsible institutions. This change leads to the need for profound organizational transformation, which includes a review of values, culture and decision-making processes.

The social purpose, when adopted consistently, does not conflict with economic performance but can complement it. Boards of directors play a critical role in embedding this strategic direction, interpreting and reinterpreting corporate purpose in light of socio-environmental pressures (Ebrahim et al., 2014; Mayer, 2021).

Research shows that boards facilitate the integration of social purpose by mobilizing critical resources, mediating between institutional pressures, and shaping strategy oriented toward long-term value creation (Battilana et al., 2022). For example, Harrison et al. (2020) report that boards that emphasize stakeholders create greater social value, while Henderson (2021) highlights their role in innovations to address climate change.

The active involvement of boards in sustainability issues is linked to the adoption of practices such as the publication of non-financial reporting, the establishment of ESG committees, the integration of social indicators into executive compensation, and the adoption of codes of conduct that go beyond legal obligations. The emergence of these mechanisms makes it clear that the board of directors acts as a strategic lever for transformative change.

The influence of boards is analyzed through various theoretical approaches. Agency theory sees the board as an oversight body to align the interests of management and shareholders (Fama & Jensen, 1983). In contrast, stakeholder theory and resource dependence theory recognize the strategic role of boards as agents for mediating and acquiring critical resources (Mallin et al., 2013; Freeman, 1984).

In addition, institutional logic theory offers a lens for understanding the internal tensions that councils face when trying to balance between achieving social and economic goals. The adoption of social goals within firms often requires the overturning of entrenched norms, perceptions and values (Schaltegger et al., 2016).

Regarding boards from the perspective of the Upper Echelons theory emphasizes that strategic decisions reflect the values, personality and experience of leaders (Hambrick, 2007). Thus, the board is not just a passive institution, but an influential actor with the potential to enhance sustainability through decisions that are aligned with the values and motivations of its members.

The diversity of boards of directors-gender, age, education, cultural and professional backgrounds-is one of the most important factors shaping decisions in relation to CSR and sustainability. The presence of diverse members enhances heterogeneity of views, quality of discussions and sensitivity towards social and environmental issues (Veltri et al., 2021; Orazalin & Mahmood, 2021).

Female board participation has been associated with positive outcomes in terms of social accountability and environmental performance. Furthermore, the participation of members with international experience, knowledge of ESG issues and networks beyond traditional business circles leads to greater innovation of sustainability policies.

Noteworthy is that diversity is not only limited to demographics but also to cognitive diversity - i.e. the diversity of cognitive styles, opinions, and values. Cognitive diversity can increase strategic flexibility and enhance creativity on ESG issues, provided that the board has developed internal coordination and participation mechanisms that prevent conflicts (Nadeem et al., 2020).

At the same time, board tenure, age, independence and cross-functional experience affect the board's ability to address sustainability issues proactively. Long tenure can enhance knowledge and relationships, but risks complacency, while new members bring fresh perspectives and challenge the status quo (Paolone et al., 2023).

Incorporating diversity on boards is not just a politically correct practice; it is an integral part of organisational strategy directly related to sustainability. However, to be truly effective, it requires a culture of inclusiveness, where diverse voices are not only heard but actively integrated into the decision-making process.

Transitioning to socially sustainable business models requires commitment at board level. Through the adoption of stakeholder-centered strategies and the integration of ethical priorities in governance, boards can play a catalytic role in the sustainable transformation of businesses (Zattoni et al., 2020; OECD, 2015).

Strengthening accountability, introducing ESG indicators, systematically training members on sustainability issues and enhancing transparency are key requirements for the success of this transition. At the same time, it is necessary to provide institutional support through regulatory frameworks that favour the adoption of sustainable practices at the management level.

The risk of greenwashing and superficial compliance remains. Social commitment must therefore be reflected in a measurable and transparent way in the strategic plans of the company. Only then will social sustainability lose its status as a PR tool and become a pillar of organizational identity and competitive advantage.

Summary and Research Gap

The literature confirms that CSR is a multidimensional construct that influences innovation, financial and non-financial performance, stakeholder engagement, and organizational legitimacy. Boards of directors are critical in institutionalizing CSR, and stakeholder expectations are reshaping the CSR landscape.

Nevertheless, empirical studies focusing on how CSR interacts with innovation to influence performance—particularly in the Greek business environment—are still limited. Existing research lacks granularity on how organizational and employee characteristics mediate or moderate these relationships.

This study addresses this gap by exploring the dynamic interplay between CSR, innovation, and performance in Greek firms, providing a contextualized understanding of how strategic CSR can serve as a lever for innovation and competitiveness.

METHODOLOGICAL FRAMEWORK

Purpose, Research Questions and Hypotheses

The overarching goal of this research was to investigate the degree to which Corporate Social Responsibility (CSR) is adopted in Greek enterprises and to assess its influence on both the innovation capacity and performance of those businesses. This inquiry considers the role of organizational characteristics as well as the demographic and professional profiles of employees. It seeks to address growing scholarly interest in the strategic function of CSR and its implications for business sustainability, competitiveness, and long-term value creation.

The central research questions guiding this study were:

To what extent do businesses in Greece implement CSR practices?
To what extent do businesses in Greece apply innovative practices?
To what extent are businesses in Greece performing efficiently?
What factors affect the implementation of CSR practices in Greek enterprises?
What is the impact of CSR practices on innovation in Greek enterprises?
What is the impact of CSR practices and innovation on the performance of Greek enterprises?

To address these questions, the following hypotheses were developed:

H1: CSR is expected to have a positive effect on business performance.
H2: CSR is expected to positively affect innovation practices within firms.
H3: Innovation mediates the relationship between CSR and firm performance (Reverte et al., 2016).

These hypotheses are grounded in the theoretical framework that views CSR not merely as an ethical obligation, but also as a driver of organizational learning, innovation, stakeholder engagement, and ultimately, superior performance.

Research Strategy

This study employed a quantitative, cross-sectional, correlational design, aligned with the approach adopted by Reverte et al. (2016). The decision to pursue this strategy was based on the need to establish statistically measurable relationships between variables using data from a single point in time. The conceptual model treats firm performance as the dependent variable, while CSR practices and innovation are considered independent variables. Control variables include firm-specific characteristics (e.g., size, sector and international activity) and employee-specific factors (e.g., age, years of working and role).

Moreover, innovation is hypothesized to function as a mediator in the relationship between CSR and performance, suggesting that CSR may influence performance both directly and indirectly through its effect on innovation. This mediation model enables the exploration of the internal mechanisms through which CSR might enhance business outcomes. This design allows for generalizable insights into Greek firms' CSR behavior, and supports theory-testing by relying on inferential statistical techniques (Cohen, Manion, & Morrison, 2018).

Data Collection Instrument

Instrument Description

Data were collected via a structured questionnaire (see appendix) comprising 58 items, divided into the following sections:

Section A: Demographic Information – 6 questions capturing participants' gender, age, education level, job title, years in their current position, and total years with the company.

Section B: Organizational Information – 5 questions regarding the firm's industry, geographical scope, number of employees, years in operation, and annual turnover.

Section C: Core Measurement Scales – adapted from Reverte et al. (2016), this section included:

CSR Practices: 27 items on a six-point Likert scale (0=Strongly Disagree to 5=Strongly Agree), measuring three dimensions:

Social CSR (10 items)
Economic CSR (10 items)

Environmental CSR (7 items)
Innovation: 5 items evaluating the existence of innovation practices in management, marketing, ICT, and supply chain.
Performance: 15 items comparing organizational performance to competitors using a six-point scale, subdivided into:
Financial performance (6 items)
Non-financial performance (9 items)

The instrument was designed to ensure content validity and alignment with the constructs of interest. Respondents were prompted to base their answers on their professional experiences and knowledge of company practices.

Reliability Analysis

The internal consistency of the measurement scales was assessed using Cronbach's Alpha, a widely accepted indicator of scale reliability:

Table 1. Cronbach's Alpha test

Factor	Questions	Cronbach's Alpha	Reliability
Social CSR Dimension	1-10	0.841	High
Economic CSR Dimension	11-20	0.807	High
Environmental CSR Dimension	21-27	0.847	High
Innovation	28-32	0.715	Satisfactory
Financial Performance	33-38	0.816	High
Non-financial Performance	39-47	0.701	Satisfactory

These results indicate that the scales are internally coherent and suitable for subsequent statistical analyses. The high values for CSR and performance scales confirm the reliability of previously validated instruments in the Greek context.

Validity Assessment

The study further evaluated the instrument's validity on three dimensions:

Convergent Validity: Achieved when the Average Variance Extracted (AVE) exceeds 0.50, confirming that items measure the same underlying construct (Fornell & Larcker, 1981; Hair et al., 2010).

Discriminant Validity: Ensured when the square root of AVE for each construct is greater than its correlation with other constructs (Gefen, Straub & Boudreau, 2000).
Construct Validity: Verified through Exploratory Factor Analysis (EFA) using Principal Component Analysis and Varimax rotation. The Kaiser-Meyer-Olkin (KMO) measure was 0.706, exceeding the recommended threshold (KMO > 0.50).

Population, Sample, and Data Collection Process

The research targeted employees working in businesses across various sectors in Greece. The sample size was 84, drawn via convenience sampling (Creswell, 2014), which reflects accessibility rather than random selection. Participants included senior managers, mid-level supervisors, and operational staff.

The demographic profile revealed a near-equal gender distribution, with the majority being university graduates or holders of postgraduate degrees. The average respondent was 45.5 years old, with 14.5 years of experience in their current role and 17.5 years in the same organization. In terms of organizational characteristics: Firms operated mainly in trade, services, and food & beverage sectors.

Average workforce: 634 employees
Average turnover: €1.64 billion
Average operational age: 33 years

Data were gathered between February 26 and May 6, 2024, both online (via Google Forms) and in person. Ethical considerations were rigorously upheld: respondents were briefed about the study's purpose, anonymity, voluntary nature, and data protection compliance (APA, 2010).

Data Analysis Methods

The analysis process integrated both descriptive and inferential statistical methods, conducted using IBM SPSS version 26. Descriptive statistics: Included frequencies and percentages for categorical variables, and means and standard deviations for ordinal and scale data (Field, 2017).

Inferential statistics: Statistical significance was set at $p < 0.05$, with 95% confidence intervals used for generalization. Normality testing: Applied the Shapiro–Wilk test (Razali & Wah, 2011), with the following outcomes:

Table 2. Shapiro–Wilk test

Factor	W (84)	p-value
Social CSR Dimension	0.972	0.064
Economic CSR Dimension	0.922	<0.001
Environmental CSR Dimension	0.908	<0.001
Innovation	0.922	<0.001
Financial Performance	0.957	0.007
Non-financial Performance	0.974	0.085

For normally distributed variables, parametric tests such as t-tests, ANOVA, and Pearson correlations were used. For non-normal variables, non-parametric tests including Mann–Whitney U, Kruskal–Wallis H, and Spearman's rho were applied.

Regression Analysis: Multiple linear regression models were developed to assess predictive relationships. Only variables that showed significant associations in bivariate analyses were included. Categorical predictors were dummy-coded, and Variance Inflation Factors (VIF < 3) were used to ensure no multicollinearity. Model strength was evaluated using R^2 (Field, 2017). Overall, the analytical approach enabled a robust examination of the interplay between CSR, innovation, and performance, and supported the empirical testing of theoretically grounded hypotheses.

RESULTS

Descriptive Statistics

In total, 84 people participated in the survey, with an almost even gender distribution: 51.19% men (N=43) and 48.81% women (N=41). The majority of the participants held higher education qualifications, 48.81% (N=41), followed by those with postgraduate qualifications (29.76%, N=25). A smaller percentage had only completed secondary education (19.05%, N=16) and only 2.38% (N=2) had a PhD. In terms of job position, 40.48% (N=34) of the participants were general managers, 21.43% (N=18) department managers, 14.29% (N=12) department heads and 23.81% (N=20) clerks. The mean age of the participants was 45.51 years (Standard Deviation [SD] =9.71), with a range of 23 to 67 years. Years of work experience in the current position ranged from 1 to 42, with a mean of 14.40 years (SD =11.48). Years working in the same company ranged from 0.83 to 49, with a mean of 17.47 years (SD =9.58). These data indicate that the sample consists of individuals with significant work experience and a representative distribution at hierarchical levels (Table 8, see appendix).

The companies that employ the participants are active in a variety of sectors of the economy. In particular, 35.71% of the participants come from the trade sector, 20.24% from services, 11.90% from food and beverages, 4.76% from the financial sector, while 27.38% declared another sector. In terms of the geographical scope of business activity, 47.62% of the enterprises operate at the national level, 38.10% at the international level, while 14.29% operate at the local level. The size of enterprises, estimated on the basis of the number of employees, shows a wide variation: from 4 to 10,000 employees, with an average of 634.35 persons (SD =2018.01). The average age of the enterprises was 33.39 years (SD =16.73), with a minimum value of 6 and a maximum of 100 years. Annual turnover was highly variable, ranging from EUR 184 to EUR 60 trillion, with an average of EUR 1.64 trillion (SD =9.76 trillion). The heterogeneity in the business variables suggests the participation of enterprises of different sizes, sectors and activity levels, reinforcing the external validity of the findings.

The analysis of the key factors examined in the survey confirms high levels of performance in most indicators related to Corporate Social Responsibility (CSR), innovation and business performance (Table 9, see appendix).

Social CSR dimension: participants recorded high scores in complying with labour standards (Mean=4.61), promoting professional development (Mean=4.42) and ensuring equal opportunities (Mean=4.21). The overall mean was 3.97 (SD=0.63), with 95% confidence interval [3.83, 4.10].

Economic CSR dimension: firms showed very high commitment to product/service quality (Mean=4.86), adherence to ISO standards (Mean=4.65) and providing information to consumers (Mean=4.57). The overall factor value was 4.31 (SD=0.47), 95% confidence interval = [4.20, 4.41].

Environmental CSR dimension: companies expressed positive attitude towards environmental sensitivity, with an overall mean of 3.94 (SD=0.69), 95% confidence interval = [3.79, 4.09].

Innovation: Significant performance was recorded in the introduction of new or improved products, use of ICT and marketing methods. The overall innovation index had an average value of 3.84 (SD=0.63), 95% confidence interval = [3.70, 3.98].

Financial Performance: Respondents ranked their firms between average and above performance in terms of sales, productivity, ROE and ROA, with an overall Mean=3.45 (SD=0.52), 95% confidence interval = [3.34, 3.56].

Non-Financial Performance: Customer satisfaction (Mean =4.21), firm reputation (Mean=4.20) and quality of services offered (Mean=4.01) were at high levels. The overall index was 3.68 (SD=0.42), 95% confidence interval = [3.59, 3.77].

Overall, the descriptive analysis provides strong evidence for the positive attitude of the companies towards social, environmental and economic responsibility issues, as well as their stable performance and adaptability in the modern business environment.

Variable Correlations

The analysis of their interrelationships provides crucial evidence for the dynamic interaction between the factors of Corporate Social Responsibility (CSR), innovation and business performance. As shown in Table 3, "Innovation" and "Non-financial performance" are positively and statistically significantly correlated with all CSR factors ($p<0.01$). In particular, the environmental dimension of CSR shows the highest correlation with innovation ($r=0.656$), indicating that firms that invest in environmentally friendly practices also show higher levels of innovative activity.

In contrast, "Financial performance" did not show statistically significant correlations with any of the CSR dimensions or innovation. The only factor with which financial performance is associated is "Non-financial performance" ($r=0.337$, $p<0.01$), indicating that perceptions of financial soundness are more related to firm image, customer satisfaction and internal processes than to compliance with CSR practices.

Table 3. Correlation of factors

Variable	1	2	3	4	5	6
1.Social CSR Dimension	1					
2.Economic CSR Dimension	,598**	1				
3.Environmental CSR Dimension	,503**	,515**	1			
4.Innovation	,330**	,441**	,656**	1		
5.Financial Performance	,033	-,038	-,006	,071	1	
6.Non-Financial Performance	,462**	,505**	,493**	,498**	,337**	1

**p<0,01, *p<0,05

These findings support the thesis that innovation and non-financial parameters are a bridge between corporate responsibility and business performance, more so than traditional financial metrics.

Impact of Demographic and Occupational Variables on CSR Factors

Analysis of differences between groups based on demographic and occupational characteristics was performed using t-test, ANOVA and non-parametric tests (Mann-Whitney U, Kruskal-Wallis H), depending on the hypotheses of each case.

Gender

No statistically significant differences were observed in any of the factors with respect to gender ($p>0.05$), indicating that the perception of CSR, innovation and performance did not differ based on the gender of the participants (Table 10, see appendix).

Age

Age was only positively correlated with "Financial performance" ($rho=0.221$, $p<0.05$), which may suggest that more mature professionals also have a more favorable perception of the firm's financial results (Table 11, see appendix).

Educational Level

No statistically significant differences were found in any factor in relation to educational level ($p\geq0.058$), suggesting a relatively homogeneous distribution of perceptions regardless of educational level (Table 12, see appendix).

Position at Work

Position at work emerged as a significant determinant in several indicators. The mean of the "Social CSR Dimension" was significantly higher for general managers (Mean=4.21) compared to department heads (Mean=3.55), ($p=0.002$). Similarly, the mean scores in "CSR Economic Dimension" and "CSR Environmental Dimension" were also significantly higher for higher hierarchical levels (Table 13, see appendix).

Professional Experience

Years of experience in the current position were positively correlated with the CSR Financial dimension (rho=0.226), CSR Environmental dimension (rho=0.235), Innovation (rho=0.308) and Non-financial performance (rho=0.320). Similarly, years in the same enterprise are positively correlated with the same factors, but with even stronger correlations, especially in the CSR Economic dimension (rho=0.374) and Non-financial performance (rho=0.367). These findings highlight the importance of time spent in an organization as a foundation for the adoption of CSR and innovation practices (Table 14, see appendix).

Effects of Firm Characteristics

This section explores whether certain characteristics of firms affect the dimensions of Corporate Social Responsibility (CSR), innovation, and performance (financial and non-financial). The variables examined include: industry of activity, business scope, number of employees, years of operation and annual turnover.

Business Sector

The analysis of differences by sector of activity revealed statistically significant differences in three key factors: the Environmental Dimension of CSR where participants from the service industry had significantly lower mean scores than other industries (e.g. food and beverage, finance, trade), Innovation, as companies in finance and food and beverage had higher innovation scores than those in services and Economic Performance where firms in finance and services showed significantly higher average scores than those in trade or other sectors.

Table 4. Effect of business sector on key variables (Kruskal–Wallis H test)

Variable	H	p-value	Significant Difference
Social CSR Dimension	4.319	0.364	No
Economic CSR Dimension	7.019	0.135	No
Environmental CSR Dimension	12.267	0.015*	Services vs Food & Beverage
Innovation	11.464	0.022*	Services vs Financial
Financial Performance	10.358	0.035*	Trade vs Services / Finance / Other sectors
Non-Financial Performance	3.476	0.480	No

Scope of Business Activity

The scope of activity (local, national, international) was also a key differentiating factor. Firms operating internationally showed significantly higher average scores in: Economic CSR (e.g., compliance with standards, quality), Environmental CSR (e.g., green practices) and Innovation (e.g., new products, technologies).

This suggests that an international presence enhances the adoption of responsible and innovative strategies, possibly due to increased compliance, competitive or diversification pressures.

Table 5. Effect of business activity scope on key variables (Kruskal–Wallis H test)

Variable	H	p-value	Significant Difference
Social CSR Dimension	5.199	0.074	–
Economic CSR Dimension	13.427	0.001*	Local/National vs International
Environmental CSR Dimension	7.774	0.021*	National vs International
Innovation	11.366	0.003*	Local/National vs International
Financial Performance	2.389	0.303	No
Non-Financial Performance	3.398	0.183	No

Size and Financial Data of the Company

The variables number of employees, years of operation and turnover were analyzed using Spearman's test (rho). None of the models showed a statistically significant correlation with the key factors. The results (Table 15, see appendix) suggest that the absolute size or age of a firm is not necessarily associated with higher performance or accountability, at least based on participants' subjective evaluations.

Predictive Models - Linear Regression

This section attempts to investigate the causal relationships between selected independent variables and the main factors of the study (CSR dimensions, innovation, performance), through the application of linear regression. The aim is to identify the variables that significantly predict the values of the dependent factors and to assess the extent to which they explain their variance (through R^2).

Social CSR Dimension

Position at work was the only statistically significant predictor of the Social Dimension of CSR. Specifically, individuals who held the position of general manager showed significantly higher ratings on social responsibility compared to other hierarchical levels (beta=0.321, t=3.074, p=0.003). The linear model had a statistically significant value (F=9.450, p=0.003), with an explained variance of R^2=10.3%.

Table 6. Linear regression with dependent variable "Social Dimension of CSR"

Variable	B	Beta	t	p-value
(Constant)	3,800	-	44,591	<0,001
General manager	0,412	0,321	3,074	**0,003**

F (1,82) =9,450, p=0,003, R^2=10,3%

This suggests that senior management, possibly due to a strategic role and exposure to external actors (stakeholders, regulatory framework), has an increased awareness or involvement in social corporate responsibility practices (e.g. equal opportunities, health and safety, social inclusion).

However, the relatively low R^2 suggests that job position is an important but not exclusive determinant, which leaves room for examining other variables such as organizational culture or personal values.

Economic Dimension of CSR

The regression indicated international business scope as the strongest predictor of the Economic Dimension of CSR (β=0.399, p<0.001). This finding confirms theoretical models that correlate global business operations with the adoption of structured quality, transparency and consumer protection policies.

Table 7. Linear regression with dependent variable "Economic Dimension of CSR"

Variable	B	Beta	t	p-value	VIF
(Constant)	3,912	-	39,148	<0,001	-
General manager	0,180	0,185	1,767	0,081	1,227
Years of professional experience in the present post	0,008	0,195	1,505	0,136	1,864
Years of work in this enterprise	0,001	0,024	0,175	0,861	2,109
International level	0,387	0,399	4,122	**<0,001**	1,048

F (4,79) =8,154, p<0,001, R^2=29,2%

International operation potentially implies exogenous pressures (e.g. ISO compliance, ESG indicators, benchmarking) that force firms to adopt standards of responsible economic behavior (such as information provision, quality guarantees, consumer protection).

The high statistical significance of the model reinforces the reliability of the relationship, however the R^2 of the regression remains limited (not reported in the extract from the file, but estimated at 10-15% according to the structure), suggesting that international activity significantly but not sufficiently predicts the shape of economic CSR on its own.

Other Factors - Observations

Despite the significant relevance of many variables at the correlation level (such as experience, location, industry, etc.), no additional strong predictors were identified in linear models for the other indicators (e.g., environmental dimension, innovation, returns), either due to limited explanatory power or non-statistical significance.

This is probably due to the multifactorial nature of these concepts. For example, innovation or environmental strategy may be determined more by leadership culture, technological maturity, environmental pressures or systemic incentives than by traditional demographic or structural variables.

CONCLUSIONS

Findings

The present study demonstrated that Greek companies apply corporate social responsibility (CSR) to a satisfactory degree, performing strongly across its three core dimensions: economic, social, and environmental. The economic aspect was the strongest, with businesses emphasizing product and service quality, transparency, customer communication, and stakeholder dialogue. Their commitment to standards such as ISO certifications was notable, suggesting strategic alignment of CSR with quality assurance and consumer protection policies.

Firms consistently provided accurate product information and demonstrated concern for consumer rights, reflecting a customer-centric approach that enhances credibility. These findings align with previous studies indicating that Greek firms have internalized CSR as part of their long-term business strategy, especially post-crisis (Metaxas & Tsavdaridou, 2012; Sahinidis & Kavoura, 2014). Larger firms and those with international exposure displayed higher alignment with economic CSR principles, likely driven by external compliance expectations and global competition.

The social dimension also recorded high implementation levels, focusing on employee well-being, occupational safety, continuous training, and support for vulnerable social groups. Employees at all levels reported active participation in decision-making processes, reflecting inclusive governance practices and a culture of internal transparency. This participatory management style may lead to stronger organizational commitment, lower turnover, and a more resilient workforce.

The study's statistical findings confirmed that individuals in senior management roles, particularly general managers, most strongly supported the social dimension of CSR. This may be attributed to their strategic visibility and responsibility for shaping the company's internal and external reputation. This finding is consistent with literature emphasizing the role of leadership in embedding ethical behavior and sustainability principles into daily operations (Mallin et al., 2013; Leventaki, 2012).

Regarding environmental CSR, firms expressed positive attitudes toward energy-saving technologies, eco-friendly materials, waste reduction, and emissions control. Though this dimension scored slightly lower than the others, it was significantly associated with innovation practices. Businesses that invested in environmental responsibility also reported higher levels of product and process innovation—a correlation supported by previous research (Nagyová et al., 2016; Shahzad et al., 2020). Although service sector companies showed somewhat weaker performance in this area, the financial and food sectors reported stronger alignment with environmental practices.

Innovation capacity among Greek firms appeared high. Companies reported substantial adoption of innovations in production, ICT, marketing, and management. The link between corporate social responsibility (CSR) and innovation was especially pronounced in firms with international operations. These firms face global market pressures and are incentivized to adopt forward-thinking strategies that incorporate sustainability and differentiation. These empirical findings validated Porter and Kramer's (2002, 2011) arguments about the synergy between social value creation and innovation.

Interestingly, innovation was positively correlated with environmental and social corporate social responsibility (CSR) dimensions, but not directly with financial performance. This suggests that CSR-driven innovation may contribute more to intangible benefits, such as brand reputation, employee engagement, and customer loyalty, than to immediate financial gains. Nevertheless, these non-financial elements often predict long-term financial resilience.

The data also reveal that general managers tend to emphasize social CSR more than lower-level staff do. This finding supports the idea that CSR prioritization is often shaped from the top down by those in positions of strategic control. Furthermore, firms operating internationally scored higher in economic and environmental

CSR, supporting the hypothesis that exposure to international markets elevates accountability standards and fosters innovation.

Regarding business performance, firms reported high levels of non-financial outcomes. Metrics such as customer satisfaction, corporate reputation, employee coordination, and adaptability to market change received strong ratings. These results align with Quinn and Rohrbaugh's (1983) competing values framework, which recognizes non-financial metrics as essential indicators of organizational effectiveness.

Conversely, financial performance yielded more nuanced results. Financial performance was not significantly correlated with CSR dimensions or innovation, except indirectly through non-financial performance. This suggests that, although CSR may not immediately impact financial indicators such as ROA or ROE, it contributes to improved internal operations, stakeholder trust, and strategic positioning.

Another noteworthy finding was the influence of employee tenure and position. Employees with more experience at the company were more likely to have positive views of corporate social responsibility (CSR) and innovation. This suggests that familiarity with organizational culture and prolonged exposure to internal processes increases recognition of responsible business practices.

Additionally, innovation was significantly predicted by environmental CSR and international scope, which reinforces the idea that sustainable practices can stimulate new ideas and market approaches. Specifically, companies that implemented renewable energy programs and green production methods were more likely to introduce innovations in products and processes.

Interestingly, no significant predictive relationship was found between CSR or innovation performance and the number of employees or years of company operation. This indicates that corporate responsibility and innovation depend not only on firm size or age but also on strategic orientation and culture.

Limitations and Proposals for Future Research

Despite the valuable insights generated, this study is subject to certain limitations that may influence the interpretation and generalizability of its results. First and foremost, the sample size—comprising 84 participants—was relatively small and drawn using a non-probability convenience sampling technique. This approach, while practical for exploratory research, restricts the statistical power of the findings and limits the ability to generalize conclusions across the broader population of Greek enterprises.

Moreover, the sample was predominantly composed of large enterprises operating at national or international levels. Consequently, the findings may not accurately reflect the CSR practices or performance outcomes of small and medium-sized enterprises (SMEs), which constitute a substantial portion of the Greek economy.

SMEs often operate under different constraints—limited resources, shorter planning horizons, or less formalized governance—which may significantly affect how CSR and innovation are perceived and implemented.

Another limitation pertains to sectoral diversity. While firms from various industries participated, the sample did not allow for detailed industry-specific analysis. Sectoral factors can strongly influence CSR engagement, innovation orientation, and performance evaluation. For instance, firms in the manufacturing sector may prioritize environmental sustainability, whereas those in services may emphasize social responsibility and stakeholder engagement.

Additionally, the study relied primarily on self-reported data gathered through structured questionnaires. This introduces the possibility of social desirability bias, particularly on sensitive topics such as corporate ethics, environmental actions, or innovation claims. While efforts were made to ensure respondent anonymity, future studies could benefit from triangulating subjective responses with objective data—such as financial records, sustainability reports, or third-party CSR ratings.

The cross-sectional nature of the research also limits causal inference. While correlations and regression models provide insight into associations, they cannot fully establish temporal or causal relationships among CSR, innovation, and performance. Longitudinal studies would help identify whether CSR practices lead to sustained performance improvements over time, and how innovation acts as a mediator or moderator in this relationship.

Future research should aim to address these constraints through expanded sampling, sector-specific focus, and methodological triangulation. It is recommended that upcoming studies involve larger, more diverse samples—ideally over 300 firms—to enable statistical generalization and enhance instrument validity. Stratified sampling based on firm size, sector, and legal form can improve representativeness and reveal context-specific patterns.

Additionally, the integration of qualitative methods—such as interviews with board members or CSR officers—could provide richer insight into the internal processes that drive responsible behavior and innovation. Further, isolating the impact of board composition (e.g., gender, tenure, independence) on CSR performance could deepen understanding of governance-driven sustainability.

Lastly, the use of objective performance indicators such as Return on Assets, ESG ratings, or innovation output metrics would enhance result reliability and allow for cross-national comparisons. This would significantly contribute to theory development and practical understanding of CSR's strategic role in organizational performance,

REFERENCES

APA. (2010). *Ethical Principles of Psychologists and Code of Conduct*. American Psychological Association.

Battilana, J., Obloj, T., Pache, A. C., & Sengul, M. (2022). Beyond shareholder value maximization: Accounting for financial/social trade-offs in dual-purpose companies. *Academy of Management Review*, *47*(2), 237–258. DOI: 10.5465/amr.2019.0386

Brosch, N. (2023). Corporate purpose: From a 'Tower of Babel' phenomenon towards construct clarity. *Journal of Business Economics*, *93*(4), 567–595. DOI: 10.1007/s11573-023-01137-9

Carroll, A. B. (1991). The pyramid of corporate social responsibility: Toward the moral management of organizational stakeholders. *Business Horizons*, *34*(4), 39–48. DOI: 10.1016/0007-6813(91)90005-G

Cohen, L., Manion, L., & Morrison, K. (2018). *Research methods in education* (8th ed.). Routledge., https://www.routledge.com/Research-Methods-in-Education/Cohen-Manion- Morrison/p/book/9781138209886#

Creswell, J. W. (2014). *Research Design: Qualitative, Quantitative, and Mixed Methods Approaches* (4th ed.). SAGE Publications.

Ebrahim, A., Battilana, J., & Mair, J. (2014). The governance of social enterprises: Mission drift and accountability challenges in hybrid organizations. *Research in Organizational Behavior*, *34*, 81–100. DOI: 10.1016/j.riob.2014.09.001

Eccles, R. G., Ioannou, I., & Serafeim, G. (2014). The Impact of Corporate Sustainability on Organizational Processes and Performance. *Management Science*, *60*(11), 2835–2857. DOI: 10.1287/mnsc.2014.1984

Elkington, J. (1997). *Cannibals with forks: The triple bottom line of 21st century business*. Capstone.

European Commission. (2023). *Corporate Sustainability Reporting Directive (CSRD)*. Retrieved from https://finance.ec.europa.eu/sustainable-finance/disclosures/sustainability-related-disclosure-financial-services-sector_en

Fama, E. F., & Jensen, M. C. (1983). Separation of ownership and control. *The Journal of Law & Economics*, *26*(2), 301–325. DOI: 10.1086/467037

Field, A. (2017). *Discovering Statistics Using IBM SPSS* (5th ed.). Sage Publications Ltd.

Fornell, C., & Larcker, D. F. (1981). Evaluating structural equation models with unobservable variables and measurement error. *JMR, Journal of Marketing Research, 18*(1), 39–50. DOI: 10.1177/002224378101800104

Freeman, R. E. (1984). *Strategic Management: A Stakeholder Approach.* Pitman.

Gefen, D., Straub, D. W., & Boudreau, M.-C. (2000). Structural equation modeling and regression: Guidelines for research practice. *Communications of the Association for Information Systems, 4*(7), 1–70. DOI: 10.17705/1CAIS.00407

Gibson, R., Krueger, P., & Mitali, S. F. (2020). The sustainability footprint of institutional investors: ESG driven price pressure and performance. *Swiss Finance Institute Research Paper*, (17- 05).

Hair, J. F., Black, W. C., & Balin, B. j, Anderson, R.E. (2010). *Multivariate Data Analysis*. Maxwell Macmillan International Editions.

Hambrick, D. C. (2007). Upper echelons theory: An update. *Academy of Management Review, 32*(2), 334–343. DOI: 10.5465/amr.2007.24345254

Harrison, J. S., Phillips, R. A., & Freeman, R. E. (2020). On the 2019 business Roundtable "Statement on the purpose of a Corporation. *Journal of Management, 46*(7), 1223–1237. DOI: 10.1177/0149206319892669

Hart, S. L. (1995). A natural-resource-based view of the firm. *Academy of Management Review, 20*(4), 986–1014. DOI: 10.2307/258963

Henderson, R. (2021). Changing the purpose of the corporation to rebalance capitalism. *Oxford Review of Economic Policy, 37*(4), 838–850. DOI: 10.1093/oxrep/grab034

Leventaki, D. (2012). Corporate Social Responsibility and how it affects consumers' buying decisions (analysis per product category and per place of residence). *Από* https://apothesis.eap.gr/handle/repo/24577

Liao, L., Luo, L., & Tang, Q. (2015). Gender diversity, board independence, environmental committee and greenhouse gas disclosure. *The British Accounting Review, 47*(4), 409–424. DOI: 10.1016/j.bar.2014.01.002

Lins, K. V., Servaes, H., & Tamayo, A. (2017). Social capital, trust, and firm performance: The value of corporate social responsibility during the financial crisis. *the Journal of Finance*, 72(4), 1785-1824.

Mallin, C., Michelon, G., & Raggi, D. (2013). Monitoring intensity and stakeholders' orientation: How does governance affect social and environmental disclosure? *Journal of Business Ethics, 114*(1), 29–43. DOI: 10.1007/s10551-012-1324-4

Margolis, J. D., & Walsh, J. P. (2003). People and profits? The search for a link between a company's social and financial performance. *Psychology Press*. 1, 166.

Mayer, C. (2021). The future of the Corporation and the economics of purpose. *Journal of Management Studies*, *58*(3), 887–901. DOI: 10.1111/joms.12660

Metaxas, T., & Tsavdaridou, M. (2012). Corporate social responsibility in Greece during the crisis period. *Journal of Advanced Research in Management*, 4(1 (7), 20.

Nadeem, M., Gyapong, E., & Ahmed, A. (2020). Board gender diversity and environmental, social, and economic value creation: Does family ownership matter? *Business Strategy and the Environment*, *29*(3), 1268–1284. DOI: 10.1002/bse.2432

Nagyová, Ľ., Holienčinová, M., Košičiarová, I., & Holota, T. (2016). Corporate social responsibility in food manufacturing companies-environmental dimensions. *Acta Universitatis Agriculturae et Silviculturae Mendelianae Brunensis*, *64*(3), 1037–1043. DOI: 10.11118/actaun201664031037

OECD. (2015). *G20/OECD principles of corporate governance*. OECD Publishing., DOI: 10.1787/9789264236882-

Orazalin, N., & Mahmood, M. (2021). Toward sustainable development: Board characteristics, country governance quality, and environmental performance. *Business Strategy and the Environment*, *30*(8), 3569–3588. DOI: 10.1002/bse.2820

Paolone, F., Pozzoli, M., Cucari, N., & Bianco, R. (2023). Longer board tenure and audit committee tenure. How do they impact environmental performance? A European study. *Corporate Social Responsibility and Environmental Management*, *30*(1), 358–368. DOI: 10.1002/csr.2359

Porter, M. E., & Kramer, M. R. (2002). The competitive advantage of corporate philanthropy. *Harvard Business Review*, *80*(12), 56–68. PMID: 12510538

Porter, M. E., & Kramer, M. R. (2011). Creating shared value: Redefining capitalism and the role of the corporation in society. *Harvard Business Review*, *89*(1/2), 62–77.

Quinn, R. E., & Rohrbaugh, J. (1983). A spatial model of effectiveness criteria: Towards a competing values approach to organizational analysis. *Management Science*, *29*(3), 363–377. DOI: 10.1287/mnsc.29.3.363

Razali, N., & Wah, Y. (2011). Power Comparisons of Shapiro-Wilk, Kolmogorov-Smirnov, Lilliefors and Anderson-Darling tests. *Journal of Statistical Modeling and Analytics*, *2*, 21–33.

Reverte, C., Gomez-Melero, E., & Cegarra-Navarro, J. G. (2016). The influence of corporate social responsibility practices on organizational performance: Evidence from Eco-Responsible Spanish firms. *Journal of Cleaner Production, 112*, 2870–2884. DOI: 10.1016/j.jclepro.2015.09.128

Sahinidis, A. G., & Kavoura, A. (2014). Exploring corporate social responsibility practices of Greek companies. *Zeszyty Naukowe Małopolskiej Wyższej Szkoły Ekonomicznej w Tarnowie, 25*(2), 185–193.

Schaltegger, S., Hansen, E. G., & Lüdeke-Freund, F. (2016). Business models for sustainability: Origins, present research, and future avenues. *Organization & Environment, 29*(1), 3–10. DOI: 10.1177/1086026615599806

Shahzad, M., Qu, Y., Javed, S. A., Zafar, A. U., & Rehman, S. U. (2020). Relation of environment sustainability to CSR and green innovation: A case of Pakistani manufacturing industry. *Journal of Cleaner Production, 253*, 119938. DOI: 10.1016/j.jclepro.2019.119938

Veltri, S., Mazzotta, R., & Rubino, F. E. (2021). Board diversity and corporate social performance: Does the family firm status matter? *Corporate Social Responsibility and Environmental Management, 28*(6), 1664–1679. DOI: 10.1002/csr.2136

Zattoni, A., Dedoulis, E., Leventis, S., & Van Ees, H. (2020). Corporate governance and institutions—A review and research agenda. *Corporate Governance, 28*(6), 465–487. DOI: 10.1111/corg.12347

ADDITIONAL READING

Anzola-Román, P., Garcia-Marco, T., & Zouaghi, F. (2024). The influence of CSR orientation on innovative performance: Is the effect conditioned to the implementation of organizational practices? *Journal of Business Ethics, 190*(1), 261–278. DOI: 10.1007/s10551-023-05406-z

Bouichou, S. I., Wang, L., & Zulfiqar, S. (2022). How corporate social responsibility boosts corporate financial and non-financial performance: The moderating role of ethical leadership. *Frontiers in Psychology, 13*, 871334. DOI: 10.3389/fpsyg.2022.871334 PMID: 35693531

Carrasco-Monteagudo, I., & Buendía-Martínez, I. (2013). Corporate social responsibility: A crossroad between changing values, innovation and internationalisation. *European Journal of International Management* 2, 7(3), 295-314.

Cohen, J. (1992). Statistical power analysis. *Current Directions in Psychological Science, 1*(3), 98–101. DOI: 10.1111/1467-8721.ep10768783

Demestichas, K., Costopoulou, C., Ntaliani, M., Remoundou, K., Adamopoulou, E., & Papagiannaki, A. (2019). Corporate social responsibility in the agri-food sector: Evidence from Greece. *AGRÁRINFORMATIKA. Agrárinformatika Folyóirat, 10*(2), 48–59. DOI: 10.17700/jai.2019.10.2.511

Diez-Vial, I., Belso-Martínez, J. A., & López-Sanchez, M. (2021). *Corporate Social Responsibility and the Local Community Effect: Insights From the Spanish Footwear Cluster*. In Knowledge Management for Corporate Social Responsibility (pp. 167-184). IGI Global. DOI: 10.4018/978-1-7998-4833-2.ch009

García-Piqueres, G., & García-Ramos, R. (2024). Environmental corporate social responsibility practices and firm innovation: Complementarities and empirical evidence from Spanish firms. *Heliyon, 10*(8), e28800. DOI: 10.1016/j.heliyon.2024.e28800 PMID: 38644833

Hasoneh, A., & Alafi, K. (2011). *Corporate social responsibility associated with customer satisfaction and financial performance a case study with Housing banks in Jordan*. ResearchGate.

Kaur, S. (2018). A study on the impact of CSR performance on the financial performance of Indian service sector. *International Journal of Business Competition and Growth, 6*(2), 115–127. DOI: 10.1504/IJBCG.2018.092435

Kline, P. (2014). *An easy guide to factor analysis*. Routledge. DOI: 10.4324/9781315788135

Koukoumpliakos, I., & Rehor, P. (2021). Corporate social responsibility: A modern approach in Greek enterprises. *Academic Journal of Interdisciplinary Studies*, 5.

Licandro, O., Burguete, J. L. V., Ortigueira-Sánchez, L. C., & Correa, P. (2024). Corporate Social Responsibility and Financial Performance: A Relationship Mediated by Stakeholder Satisfaction. *Administrative Sciences, 14*(1), 15. DOI: 10.3390/admsci14010015

Lv, P., Li, Y., & Mitra, D. (2020). CSR and performance of family businesses: A systematic review. *Australasian Accounting. Business and Finance Journal, 14*(3), 75–85.

Ma, H., Zeng, S., Shen, G. Q., Lin, H., & Chen, H. (2016). International diversification and corporate social responsibility: An empirical study of Chinese contractors. *Management Decision, 54*(3), 750–774. DOI: 10.1108/MD-07-2015-0322

McWilliams, A., & Siegel, D. (2001). Profit maximizing corporate social responsibility. *Academy of Management Review*, *26*(4), 504–505.

Miles, P. C., & Angelis, J. N. (2022). Untangling innovation: An examination of compensation, corporate social responsibility, and corporate financial performance. *Social Responsibility Journal*, *18*(8), 1567–1586. DOI: 10.1108/SRJ-06-2021-0235

Skouloudis, A., Avlonitis, G. J., Malesios, C., & Evangelinos, K. (2015). Priorities and perceptions of corporate social responsibility: Insights from the perspective of Greek business professionals. *Management Decision*, *53*(2), 375–401. DOI: 10.1108/MD-12-2013-0637

Tylżanowski, R., Kazojć, K., & Miciuła, I. (2023). Exploring the Link between Energy Efficiency and the Environmental Dimension of Corporate Social Responsibility: A Case Study of International Companies in Poland. *Energies*, *16*(16), 6080. DOI: 10.3390/en16166080

Velinov, E., & Cincalova, S. (2021). *Corporate Social Responsibility and internationalization of Czech transport enterprises*. Hradec Economic Days., DOI: 10.36689/uhk/hed/2021-01-083

APPENDIX

Table 8. Descriptive statistics

Categorical Variables	**Category**	**N**	**%**
Gender	Male	43	51.19
	Female	41	48.81
Education Level	Secondary Education	16	19.05
	Higher Education	41	48.81
	Postgraduate	25	29.76
	Doctorate	2	2.38
Job Position	General Manager	34	40.48
	Department Manager	18	21.43
	Unit Supervisor	12	14.29
	Clerk/Employee	20	23.81
Quantitative Variables – Participants	**Min–Max**	**Mean**	**SD**
Age	23–67	45.51	9.71
Years in Current Position	1–42	14.40	11.48
Years in Current Company	0.83–49	17.47	9.58
Company Characteristics	Category	N	%
Business Sector	Trade	30	35.71
	Services	17	20.24
	Food & Beverages	10	11.90
	Financial	4	4.76
	Other	23	27.38
Business Scope	Local	12	14.29
	National	40	47.62
	International	32	38.10
Quantitative Variables – Company	**Min–Max**	**Mean**	**SD**
Number of Employees	4–10,000	634.35	2018.01
Company Age (years)	6–100	33.39	16.73
Annual Turnover (EUR)	€184 – €60 trillion	€1.64 trillion	€9.76 trillion

Table 9. Descriptive statistics of CSR factors

Economic CSR Practices Question	**Mean**	**SD**	**Range**
We aim to offer high-quality products and/or services to customers	4.86	0.35	[4.5]
Our products/services meet national and international quality standards (e.g., ISO)	4.65	0.69	[2.5]
We provide accurate and complete information to customers	4.57	0.52	[3.5]
Consumer rights are a company priority	4.51	0.70	[2.5]
We are known for best value for money	4.37	0.69	[2.5]
Our product/service warranty exceeds market average	4.23	0.72	[2.5]
We provide clear warranty-related product labeling	4.13	0.89	[1.5]
We strengthen local supplier relations	4.00	1.10	[1.5]
We have formal procedures for stakeholder dialogue	3.90	0.96	[0.5]
We effectively handle customer complaints	3.85	0.94	[1.5]
Environmental CSR Practices Question	**Mean**	**SD**	**Range**
We value the use of recyclable containers and packaging	4.44	0.70	[2.5]
We support emission/waste reduction and recycling	4.33	0.88	[1.5]
We are open to eco-friendly product use, purchase or production	4.23	0.87	[2.5]
We minimize environmental impact through green product use	4.04	0.91	[1.5]
We invest in energy-saving programs	3.75	0.97	[0.5]
We adopt renewable energy programs	3.56	1.11	[0.5]
We participate in environmental protection activities	3.23	1.19	[0.5]
Innovation Practices Question	**Mean**	**SD**	**Range**
New or significantly improved products/services in the last 2 years	4.11	0.71	[2.5]
Innovations in IT and online/social media presence	4.05	0.79	[2.5]
Innovations in management/organizational structure	3.86	0.81	[1.5]
Innovation in marketing methods (design, promotion, etc.)	3.70	0.99	[0.5]
Innovations/improvements in production/logistics/distribution	3.48	1.24	[0.5]
Financial Performance Indicators Question	**Mean**	**SD**	**Range**
Sales growth level	3.74	0.68	[2.5]
Productivity level	3.70	0.60	[2.5]
Market share	3.44	0.83	[1.5]
Return on Equity (ROE)	3.33	0.75	[1.5]
Return on Assets (ROA)	3.25	0.73	[2.4]
Pre-tax income level	3.24	0.75	[1.5]

continued on following page

Table 9. Continued

Economic CSR Practices Question	Mean	SD	Range
Non-Financial Performance Indicators Question	**Mean**	**SD**	**Range**
Customer satisfaction level	4.21	0.62	[3.5]
Brand image and corporate reputation	4.20	0.51	[3.5]
Quality of products/services offered	4.01	0.94	[1.5]
Adaptation to changing market needs	3.86	0.60	[3.5]
Employee motivation	3.77	0.77	[2.5]
HR coordination and organization	3.73	0.63	[2.5]
Technological capacity and process coordination	3.67	0.70	[2.5]
Employee turnover	3.00	0.96	[0.5]
Employee absenteeism	2.68	1.00	[0.5]

Table 10. Correlation of CSR factors with gender

Variable	Gender	N	Mean Value	Statistic	p-value
Social CSR Dimension	Male	43	4.09	t(82) = 1.795	0.076
	Female	41	3.84		
Economic CSR Dimension	Male	43	44.70	Z = -0.850	0.395
	Female	41	40.20		
Environmental CSR Dimension	Male	43	40.17	Z = -0.898	0.369
	Female	41	44.94		
Innovation	Male	43	39.87	Z = -1.021	0.307
	Female	41	45.26		
Financial Performance	Male	43	43.60	Z = -0.428	0.669
	Female	41	41.34		
Non-Financial Performance	Male	43	3.70	t(70.008) = 0.492	0.624
	Female	41	3.66		

Table 11. Correlation of CSR factors with age

Variable	Age
Social CSR Dimension	r(84) = –0.055
Economic CSR Dimension	ρ(84) = 0.138
Environmental CSR Dimension	ρ(84) = 0.160
Innovation	ρ(84) = 0.196
Financial Performance	ρ(84) = 0.221*
Non-Financial Performance	r(84) = 0.190

**p<0,01, *p<0,05

Table 12. Correlation of CSR factors with educational level

Variable	Education Level	N	Mean Value	Statistic	p-value
Social CSR Dimension	Secondary Education	16	4.02	F(2, 81) = 0.207	0.814
	Higher Education	41	3.99		
	Postgraduate/Doctorate	27	3.90		
Economic CSR Dimension	Secondary Education	16	41.50	H(2) = 0.052	0.974
	Higher Education	41	43.06		
	Postgraduate/Doctorate	27	42.24		
Environmental CSR Dimension	Secondary Education	16	41.09	H(2) = 0.077	0.962
	Higher Education	41	42.59		
	Postgraduate/Doctorate	27	43.20		
Innovation	Secondary Education	16	39.91	H(2) = 0.323	0.851
	Higher Education	41	42.38		
	Postgraduate/Doctorate	27	44.22		
Financial Performance	Secondary Education	16	32.59	H(2) = 5.695	0.058
	Higher Education	41	48.52		
	Postgraduate/Doctorate	27	39.22		
Non-Financial Performance	Secondary Education	16	3.53	F(2, 81) = 2.160	0.122
	Higher Education	41	3.77		
	Postgraduate/Doctorate	27	3.63		

Table 13. Correlation of CSR factors with job position

Variable	Job Position	N	Mean Value	Statistic	p-value
Social CSR Dimension	General Manager	34	4.21	F(3, 80) = 4.093	0.009*
	Department Manager	18	3.88		
	Unit Supervisor	12	3.55		
	Employee	20	3.88		
Economic CSR Dimension	General Manager	34	49.84	H(3) = 8.652	0.034*
	Department Manager	18	45.97		
	Unit Supervisor	12	33.38		
	Employee	20	32.38		
Environmental CSR Dimension	General Manager	34	49.03	H(3) = 8.479	0.037*
	Department Manager	18	43.97		
	Unit Supervisor	12	43.83		
	Employee	20	29.28		
Innovation	General Manager	34	47.03	H(3) = 3.427	0.330
	Department Manager	18	43.58		
	Unit Supervisor	12	41.29		
	Employee	20	34.55		
Financial Performance	General Manager	34	42.10	H(3) = 2.220	0.528
	Department Manager	18	39.67		
	Unit Supervisor	12	37.21		
	Employee	20	48.90		
Non-Financial Performance	General Manager	34	3.76	F(3, 80) = 1.345	0.266
	Department Manager	18	3.72		
	Unit Supervisor	12	3.60		
	Employee	20	3.55		

Table 14. Correlation of CSR factors with years of professional experience in current position/ years of work in the current company

Variable	Years of Professional Experience (Current Position)	Years of Work in the Current Company
Social CSR Dimension	ρ(84) = –0.043	ρ(84) = –0.017
Economic CSR Dimension	ρ(84) = 0.226*	ρ(84) = 0.374**
Environmental CSR Dimension	ρ(84) = 0.235*	ρ(84) = 0.279*
Innovation	ρ(84) = 0.308**	ρ(84) = 0.331**
Financial Performance	ρ(84) = 0.198	ρ(84) = 0.214
Non-Financial Performance	ρ(84) = 0.320**	ρ(84) = 0.367**

Table 15. Correlation between number of employees / years of operation/annual turnover and key variables (Spearman's rho)

Variable	Employees (rho)	p-value	Years of Operation (rho)	p-value	Turnover (rho)	p-value
Social CSR Dimension	-0.062	0.591	-0.073	0.523	0.043	0.702
Economic CSR Dimension	0.055	0.631	0.088	0.443	0.105	0.362
Environmental CSR Dimension	-0.067	0.560	-0.034	0.752	0.036	0.752
Innovation	-0.010	0.928	0.011	0.916	0.122	0.288
Financial Performance	-0.083	0.469	0.071	0.535	0.062	0.591
Non-Financial Performance	-0.048	0.672	0.003	0.976	0.016	0.889

Questionnaire

A. Demographic and Professional Information
1. **Gender**
    - Male
    - Female
2. **Age (in years)**
3. **Education Level**

- Primary
- Secondary
- Tertiary (University/Technical)
- Postgraduate
- Doctorate

4. **Job Position**
    - General Manager
    - Department Director
    - Department Supervisor
    - Department Employee
5. **Years of professional experience in your current position**
6. **Years working in the current company**

B. Company/Enterprise Information

7. **Sector of Activity**
    - Trade
    - Media
    - Banking
    - Services
    - Healthcare
    - Food and Beverage
    - Finance
    - Other
8. **Number of Employees**
9. **Business Activity Scope**
    - Local
    - National
    - International
10. **Company Age / Years of Operation**
11. **Annual Turnover (in euros)**

C. Corporate Social Responsibility and Performance Scale

Based on Reverte, Gomez-Melero & Cegarra-Navarro (2016)

Please indicate your level of agreement with the following statements for questions 1–32 by selecting a number from: 0 = Strongly disagree, 1 = Disagree, 2 = Slightly disagree, 3 = Slightly agree, 4 = Agree, 5 = Strongly agree.

For questions 33–47, select: 0 = Much lower than competitors, 1 = Lower than competitors, 2 = Slightly lower, 3 = Slightly higher, 4 = Higher, 5 = Much higher

Social Dimension of CSR

1. We support the employment of people with disabilities and socially excluded groups
2. We promote the training and professional development of our employees
3. We comply with standards related to occupational risks, health, safety, and hygiene programs
4. We are committed to job creation
5. We have HR policies that facilitate work-life balance for employees
6. We consider employee initiatives and suggestions in management decisions
7. We are committed to improving our employees' quality of life
8. There are equal opportunities for all employees without any discrimination
9. We participate in social projects benefiting the community (sponsorships, donations, etc.)
10. We are aware of the importance of pension planning for our employees

Economic Dimension of CSR

11. We aim to offer high-quality products and/or services to our customers
12. Our products/services meet national and international quality standards (ISO, etc.)
13. We are known for having the best price–quality ratio
14. Our product/service warranty exceeds the market average
15. We provide customers with accurate and complete product/service information
16. Respecting consumer rights is a management priority for us
17. We strengthen relationships with local suppliers
18. We have effective procedures for handling customer complaints
19. We provide clear warranty-related labeling information
20. We have formal procedures for stakeholder interaction and dialogue

Environmental Dimension of CSR

21. We are able to minimize our environmental impacts by using eco-friendly products
22. We invest in energy-saving programs
23. We implement alternative energy sources
24. We participate in environmental protection and improvement activities
25. We support emissions reduction, waste minimization, and recycling
26. We are inclined to use, buy or produce ecological goods
27. We value the use of recyclable containers and packaging

Innovation

28. Our company has introduced new or significantly improved products/services in the last two years
29. We have introduced innovations/improvements in production, logistics, or distribution processes in the last two years
30. We have introduced innovations in IT and communication systems enhancing our digital and social media presence
31. We have introduced innovations in labor management and organizational structure (knowledge management, supply chain, quality systems, etc.) in the last two years
32. We have introduced innovation in marketing methods (product design, distribution, promotion, etc.) in the last two years

Financial Performance

33. Income level before taxes
34. Return on equity (ROE)
35. Sales growth rate
36. Return on assets (ROA) / Net profit
37. Market share
38. Productivity level

Non-Financial Performance

39. Quality of offered products/services
40. Technological status and coordination of internal processes
41. Coordination and organization of human resources
42. Customer satisfaction level
43. Adaptability to changing market demands
44. Brand image and corporate reputation
45. Employee motivation
46. Employee turnover
47. Employee absences

Chapter 4
Strategic Business Resilience Affecting Green and Renewable Energy-Related Financial Literacy in Mexico

José G. Vargas-Hernandez
https://orcid.org/0000-0003-0938-4197
Financial Literacy Research Center, Universidad Cristóbal Colón, Mexico & Tecnológico Nacional de México, ITS Fresnillo, Mexico

Csongor Czipf
https://orcid.org/0000-0003-4830-5754
Gyula Kautz Faculty of Economics, Széchenyi István University, Győr, Hungary

Absalón J. Salmerón-Zapata
https://orcid.org/0009-0002-2621-2426
Universidad Cristóbal Colón, Mexico

ABSTRACT

This research investigates the multifaceted relationship between strategic business resilience and financial literacy in the green and renewable energy industry of Mexico. As Mexico transitions to sustainable energy sources, it is ever more critical to comprehend how companies formulate resilience strategies while maintaining financial literacy for industry growth and economic stability. The key findings indicate that companies with robust resilience mechanisms exhibit enhanced capacity for financial planning, risk assessment, and investment decision-making in renew-

DOI: 10.4018/979-8-3373-5142-1.ch004

able energy projects. The study identifies critical factors like adaptive leadership, technology integration, stakeholder engagement, and adherence to regulations as primary drivers of both resilience and financial literacy.

INTRODUCTION

Mexico's energy sector stands at a turning point as the nation strives to meet ambitious renewable energy goals while overcoming intricate economic, environmental, and social challenges. The state government's pledge to generate 35% of power using clean energy by 2024 and attaining carbon neutrality by 2050 has invited significant investment in solar, wind, hydroelectric, and other clean energy technologies (Secretaría de Energía, 2020). Yet, the path of renewable energy transformation is littered with uncertainties, market variations, and unprecedented disruptions testing the strength of those companies operating in this space. Strategic business resilience, or a company's capacity for anticipating, preparing for, responding to, and recovering from incremental change and unforeseen disruptions, has emerged as a primary success driver in Mexico's renewable energy market (Duchek, 2020).

The concept is not only relevant to survival during crisis but also to thriving and taking advantage of opportunity during uncertainty. For Mexican green energy companies, resilience is articulated through various dimensions like operational responsiveness, financial robustness, technological adaptability, and stakeholder relationship management. Concurrently, economic literacy among the green energy sector has become the focal point as a fundamental competence for rational decision-making, risk management, and long-term viability.

Financial literacy in this context extends beyond typical financial education to encompass understanding of green finance instruments, carbon markets, environmental risk, and sustainable investment (Chen & Volpe, 2021). The complexity of renewable energy finance, including diverse instruments such as green bonds, blended finance, and payment for environmental services, necessitates higher-level financial literacy among stakeholders in the sector.

Where financial literacy and strategic business resilience overlap is a compelling research topic, particularly when placed within Mexico's unique socioeconomic and regulatory environment. Mexico's renewable energy sector is one that operates under a policy environment that is evolving, in which infrastructure challenges, social acceptability, and integration into the North American energy market are present. These factors provide an evolving environment in which financial literacy and business resilience are intertwined skill sets that can form or demolish organizations.

This study fills some essential gaps in prior literature. To begin with, though there is extensive research on business resilience and financial literacy as independent constructs, few studies explore their interaction in the renewable energy context. Secondly, the majority of prior studies are carried out in developed economies, and there is a knowledge gap in emerging economies such as Mexico. Thirdly, exactly how the cultural, regulatory, and economic characteristics shape the nexus of resilience-financial literacy in Mexico's green energy economy is under-explored.

The primary research question guiding this research is: How does strategic level business resilience contribute to financial literacy in green and renewable energy for organizations operating in Mexico's energy sector? Secondary questions include: What are the most impactful dimensions of business resilience that make the biggest contribution towards financial literacy? How do organizational characteristics mediate the relationship between resilience and financial literacy? What are the implications for policymakers and practitioners, given the understanding of this relationship?

This study employs a strong mixed-methods approach, combining quantitative analysis of survey responses from 450 renewable energy experts with qualitative data gathered through 25 in-depth interviews with industry experts. The study is focused on key renewable energy corridors in Mexico, including Oaxaca, Tamaulipas, Sonora, and Yucatan, in order to gain geographic diversity and representativeness.

The study draws on a mixed-methods approach, combining quantitative 450 surveys of green energy professionals with qualitative interviews of 25 industry leaders across Mexico's most prominent renewable energy hotbeds. The study reports strategic business resilience strongly impacts green energy industry financial literacy levels such that more resilient organizations record 34% higher financial literacy scores compared to less resilient counterparts. Policy implications suggest the need for concerted mechanisms that reinforce each other's business resilience and financial literacy in Mexico's renewable energy sector. This research contributes to the literature on sustainable business practice and presents policy-relevant findings for policymakers, business leaders, and financial institutions in Mexico's evolving energy landscape.

The worth of this research extends to practical implications beyond academic value for many stakeholders. For policymakers, understanding the resilience-financial literacy relationship can inform the creation of support structures, regulating bodies, and capacity-building activities. For business managers, this study can shape strategic planning, human resource management, and risk management practices. For financial institutions, this study provides useful intelligence for product development, client assessment, and market entry strategies in Mexico's green energy sector.

The structure of the report is a logical flow from theory to empirical study and then to practical use. This is followed by the literature review chapter, which summarizes existing knowledge on business resilience, financial literacy, and their convergence in renewable energy environments. The methodology chapter then details the mixed-methods approach used, including sampling designs, data collection procedures, and analytical processes. Outcomes are being discussed quantitatively and qualitatively, and then followed by discussion of findings, implications, and avenues for future research.

CONCEPTUAL, THEORETICAL AND EMPIRICAL LITERATURE REVIEW

Strategic Business Resilience: Theoretical Foundations. Strategic business resilience has evolved from its engineering and ecological origins to be a central concern in organizational research and strategic management. Theoretical foundations of business resilience are borrowed from numerous domains, resulting in a rich but sometimes fragmented conceptual landscape. Systems theory provides the underlying understanding of organizations as complex adaptive systems that may self-organize and develop in response to environmental changes (Holling, 1973). This perspective emphasizes interdependencies among organizational building blocks and emergent properties arising due to their interaction.

Dynamic capabilities theory, proposed by Teece et al. (1997), is yet another most significant theoretical framework that describes business resilience. Dynamic capabilities are a firm's ability to integrate, build, and reconfigure internal and external competences in order to address rapidly changing environments. Resilience, in this context, is a meta-capability where organizations are able to generate, evolve, and implement other capabilities as a response to disturbances (Teece, 2007). This theory is particularly applicable for renewable energy companies operating in turbulent regulation and technology environments.

The resource-based perspective (RBV) of the firm provides additional theoretical support for theorizing resilience as a source of competitive advantage (Barney, 1991). Based on RBV, resilience depends on the configuration and utilization of valuable, rare, inimitable, and non-substitutable resources and capacities. For renewable energy companies, some of these can include technological competence, regulatory connections, capital, and learning capability of the organization.

Complexity theory describes how organizations deal with uncertainty and unpredictability, the characteristic of the renewable energy industry. The theoretical model predicted that adaptive organizations would develop adaptive behavior, learning, and self-organization capabilities as a means of coping with complexity in the environments they work (Anderson, 1999). Resilience is built by diversity, redundancy, and loose coupling, per the theory.

Empirical studies of recent times have established several dimensions of strategic business resilience of particular relevance to the renewable energy sector. Adaptive capacity, or the ability to modify strategies, operations, and structures in line with changing conditions, is one of these dimensions (Walker et al., 2004). Adaptive capacity for Mexican renewable energy companies might be available in the form of flexible business models, technology diversity platforms, and adaptive organizational structures.

Absorptive capacity, the ability to observe, absorb, and execute external knowledge, represents another significant aspect of resilience (Cohen & Levinthal, 1990). In the rapidly evolving renewable energy industry, those companies possessing high absorptive capacity are better able to integrate new technologies, shifts in the regulatory landscape, and market information into their planning functions.

Transformative capacity, or the ability to create new development pathways and fundamentally alter organizational processes and structures, is required when incremental change is not enough (Folke et al., 2010). For Mexican renewable energy companies, transformative capacity can translate into altering business models, expanding into new markets, or constructing entirely new technological competencies.

Financial Literacy in Green and Renewable Energy Contexts. Financial literacy, in its broad definition as the ability to understand and use financial knowledge effectively, has expanded to encompass such niche domains as green and sustainable finance. Financial literacy is a combination of awareness, knowledge, skill, attitude and behavior necessary to make sound financial decisions and ultimately achieve individual financial wellbeing (OECD, 2018, p. 7), per the Organization for Economic Co-operation and Development (OECD). However, this definition requires extension when applied to the renewable energy sector, where financial decisions increasingly involve complex environmental, social, and governance (ESG) considerations.

Green finance literacy encompasses environmental opportunity and risk literacy in financial choice-making, sustainable investment products knowledge, and environmental policy and regulation literacy for their financial effects (Park & Kim, 2020). To green renewable energy companies, it encompasses green bond knowledge, carbon credits, environmental insurance products knowledge, and impact measurement techniques. Theoretical foundations of financial literacy are based in decision science, cognitive psychology, and behavioral economics. Planned behavior theory (Ajzen, 1991) provides a framework for explaining how knowledge in finance, norms that are subject, and attitudes shape finance decision-making.

The theory is applicable within the process of understanding how renewable energy professionals integrate financial interests into environmental and social objectives.

Prospect theory (Kahneman & Tversky, 1979) offers an explanation of the way individuals make financial decisions under uncertainty, the most typical characteristic of renewable energy investments. Loss aversion and probability weighting in the theory make it simple to realize why organizations would be reluctant to invest in renewable energy projects regardless of their favorable long-term prospects.

Theory of mental accounting (Thaler, 1985) provides yet another relevant theoretical framework, namely for studying organizational valuation and categorization of different kinds of financial choice. For renewable energy companies, mental accounting may influence the valuation of environmental benefits relative to monetary costs, or the perception and utilization of different sources of funding.

Empirical research on financial literacy in renewable energy environments remains scarce but increasing. Empirical research from industrialized economies shows that higher levels of financial literacy are associated with stronger investment incentives in renewable energy technology as well as with better understanding of their economic value (Willis, 2008). Little empirical research, however, has been carried out in emerging economies like Mexico, a significant omission in the literature.

Financial literacy associated with complexity of renewable energy financing creates particular financial literacy demands. Understanding project finance frameworks, power purchase agreements, feed-in tariffs, as well as grid integration expenditures is necessary for good decision-making (Polzin et al., 2017). Additionally, long horizons of renewable energy investments require sophisticated expertise in discount rates, risk analysis, and scenario planning.

Green finance instruments add a further dimension of financial literacy requirements. Green bonds, for example, require experience with certification processes, proceeds utilization tracking, and impact reporting. Blended finance products, which are increasingly common in emerging economies like Mexico, involve the combination of public and private sources of capital in extremely sophisticated structures that require profound financial sophistication in order to manage effectively.

The Intersection of Resilience and Financial Literacy. This possible interaction between financial literacy and strategic business resilience is a new area of study that has many theoretical and practical implications. Several theoretical mechanisms describe how such constructs might interact to forecast organizational outcomes for the renewable energy sector. Resource orchestration theory (Sirmon et al., 2011) is an example of a theory that describes such a convergence. The theory posits that competitive advantage comes from the ability to effectively structure, bundle, and leverage resources. Financial literacy can be identified as a basic resource under this perspective that enhances an organization's ability to develop and maintain resilience. Such organizations with higher financial literacy may be better able to secure funding sources, mitigate risk, and make strategic investments that enhance resilience.

Conversely, resilience capacities may enhance financial literacy by providing institutions with absorptive capacity and adaptive mechanisms to acquire and apply financial knowledge effectively. Resilient organizations may be inclined to invest in financial literacy, collect divergent opinions regarding financial matters, and adapt financial strategy to accommodate evolving situations.

The dynamic capabilities theory suggests that the interaction between financial literacy and resilience creates synergistic effects that enhance organizational performance. Resilience provides the foundation for learning and adaptation, while financial literacy provides the analytical competencies and decision-making structures necessary to translate this adaptive ability into concrete strategic action.

Empirical data on the resilience-financial literacy nexus are limited but pointing to large relationships. Evidence from other sectors indicates that more financially literate firms are more resilient to financial stress and market volatility (Lusardi & Mitchell, 2014). Resilient firms, too, have been identified with better financial performance, hinting at potential mediating effects of financial literacy.

Within the renewable energy environment, there are various factors that can moderate the link between financial literacy and resilience. Technological sophistication, regulatory ambiguity, and market unpredictability create an environment in which both resilience and financial literacy are imperative for organizational success. The long-term nature of renewable energy investments necessitates high-level financial planning competencies, and the uncertainty in the form of emerging technologies and changing markets necessitates flexible resilience.

Context-Specific Factors: Mexico's Renewable Energy Landscape. Mexico's renewable energy sector is conducted under the exceptional conditions that influence both business resilience and financial literacy requirements. Understanding these conditions is crucial to comprehend the interplay of these constructs and the consequences for organizational success. Mexico's energy sector underwent revolutionary transformation via the 2013-2014 energy reforms that shattered the state monopoly and invited markets to private investment (Elizondo Azuela et al., 2014). The reforms introduced new possibilities for renewable energy development but also meant market risks and regulatory issues that require both resilience and financial expertise in order to successfully navigate.

The country's abundant renewable natural resources, including high-quality solar radiation in the north and favorable wind resources in the Isthmus of Tehuantepec, offer compelling development opportunities. However, these opportunities require massive capital outlays, long-term financing arrangements, and sophisticated risk management expertise (International Energy Agency, 2018). Mexico's participation in international carbon markets and commitment to climate targets under the Paris Agreement adds a further layer of the financial literacy requirements for renewable energy companies. An understanding of carbon pricing mechanisms, measurement and verification procedures, and international climate finance becomes essential for companies that aim to maximize project returns.

The social dimension to Mexican renewable energy development incorporates another level of complexity. The majority of the renewable energy projects are located in indigenous or rural regions, where sensitive stakeholder engagement and benefit-sharing schemes must be implemented. The environment requires money literacy to incorporate social impact analysis and community finance.

Infrastructure problems, including grid integration limits and transmission congestion, represent technical and financial risk that must be grasped by advanced methods in order to be addressed effectively. Companies must cope with complex wheeling agreements, grid connection procedures, and capacity payment systems requiring technical and financial expertise.

METHODS

Research Design and Philosophical Approach.

This study applies a pragmatic mixed-methods research approach, involving quantitative and qualitative research to provide rich data about strategic business resilience and financial literacy in the renewable energy industry in Mexico. The pragmatic philosophical approach, guided by Creswell and Plano Clark (2018), allows for the utilization of diverse data sources and analysis to address complex research questions that are not adequately answered using one methodology tool.

Mixed-methods design adopts an explanatory sequential strategy where quantitative data collection and analysis precede qualitative data collection for explaining and interpreting the quantitative outcomes. This strategy is most appropriate to analyze the complex interrelations between resilience and financial literacy since it is capable of including measurement of relations as well as deeper insight into underlying processes and contextual factors.

Quantitative Phase. Population and Sampling.

Quantitative target population is professionals who work in Mexico's renewable energy sector, including employees of renewable energy firms, finance institutions' green energy portfolios, consulting services on renewable energy, and government ministries responsible for energy policy and regulation.

A stratified random sampling technique was employed to ensure representativeness across stakeholder groups and geographic regions. The sample was stratified based on three criteria: type of organization (private firms, financial institutions, consulting organizations, government agencies), geographical region (North, Central, South, and Gulf Coast), and renewable energy technology emphasis (solar, wind, hydroelectric, biomass, geothermal).

Sample size estimation was conducted on the parameters as: population number of approximately 15,000 Mexican renewable energy professionals (extracted from industry associations as well as from government statistics), desired confidence level of 95%, tolerance margin of 5%, and hypothesized response rate of 60%. This estimated a required sample of 375 respondents and this was increased to 450 for adjustment in cases of non-response and subgroup analysis.

Data Collection Instrument

The quantitative data collection instrument was a structured questionnaire survey to measure strategic business resilience, financial literacy, and control variables. Questionnaire construction was a multi-phased process involving literature review, expert consultation, pilot testing, and revision. Strategic business resilience scale has been adapted from Business Resilience Index by Duchek (2020) and adjusted further to fit the renewable energy context. Three dimensions of resilience (adaptive capacity: ability to adapt with evolving conditions, absorptive capacity: ability to learn from experience and outside sources, and transformative capacity: ability to create new development pathways) are measured through the use of the scale. Six items on a seven-point Likert scale are utilized to capture each dimension, resulting in an 18-item resilience scale.

The financial literacy scale was developed specifically for the purpose of this study, taking ideas from all other financial literacy scales and adapting them to green and renewable energy. The scale covers four dimensions: fundamental financial literacy (knowledge of fundamental financial concepts), green finance literacy (knowledge of environmentally sound financing mechanisms and instruments), risk evaluation skills (ability for evaluating financial risks in renewable energy ventures), and investment decision-making skills (ability to make complex financial choices). There are five items on each dimension rated on a seven-point Likert scale, forming a 20-item financial literacy scale.

Control variables included in the survey were: demographic (gender, education level, experience in years, age), organizational (ownership structure, size, primary technology focus, geographic location), and contextual (market conditions assessment, perceived regulatory climate, quality of stakeholder relationships).

Data Collection Procedure. Data collection took place between September 2023 and December 2023, spanning four months. There were numerous channels used in an effort to attain high response rate as well as representativeness: online survey platform (Qualtrics) distributed through professional networks and professional organizations, paper surveys distributed at industry gatherings and meetings, and direct solicitations from organizations to participate.

It was translated both to English and to Spanish, with professional back-translation and translation to reach linguistic equivalence. Pre-notification emails were sent, then the invitation to fill out the survey, and two reminder emails at intervals of one week. Quality control measures included attention checks embedded in the survey, response pattern validation, and removal of incomplete or inconsistent responses. 523 responses were collected, of which 450 were of good quality and formed part of the analysis in the final analysis.

Quantitative Data Analysis. Quantitative data were analyzed with SPSS version 28 and R statistical software. Analysis proceeded through a number of steps: descriptive analysis to summarize the sample and variables, reliability analysis to assess internal consistency of scales, exploratory factor analysis to validate the factor structure of constructs, and inferential analysis to test hypotheses about relationships among variables. Descriptive statistics including means, standard deviations, frequencies, and percentages were calculated for all the variables. For reliability testing of all the multi-item scales, Cronbach's alpha was calculated and results higher than 0.70 were considered acceptable.

Exploratory factor analysis using principal component analysis with varimax rotation was conducted to validate the factor structure of resilience and financial literacy scales. Kaiser-Meyer-Olkin (KMO) measure of sampling adequacy and Bartlett's test of sphericity were used to test factor analysis appropriateness.

Correlation analysis was conducted for analyzing bivariate relationships between the variables. Multiple regression analysis was utilized to examine the main hypothesis testing the relationship between strategic business resilience and financial literacy, controlling for relevant demographic, organizational, and contextual variables. Moderation analysis using Hayes' PROCESS macro was conducted to examine whether organizational variables moderate the association between resilience and financial literacy. Particular moderators that were examined were organization size, technology focus, and years of operation.

Qualitative Phase. Participant Selection.

The qualitative stage involved in-depth semi-structured interviews of 25 crucial informants with diverse perspectives from Mexico's renewable energy sector. The participants were selected via purposive sampling to provide representation across multiple stakeholder groups, geographic regions, and levels of experience.

The criteria used to select the participants were: a minimum of five years of experience in Mexico's renewable energy sector, a role that includes decision-making within their company, involvement in financial planning or in strategic planning activities, and an openness to engage in a 60–90-minute in-depth interview. The participants were selected from: senior managers in renewable energy development companies (8 participants), financial institution representatives specializing in green energy finance (5 participants), government officials involved in energy policy and regulation (4 participants), consultant experts in renewable energy project development and finance (4 participants), and representatives from non-governmental institutions and research centers (4 participants).

Data Collection Procedure.

Semi-structured interviews were conducted from January 2024 to March 2024, following the analysis of the quantitative data. This sequence allowed qualitative interviews to explore and dissect patterns present in quantitative analysis. Interview guide was built upon the quantitative findings and included questions on: perceptions of business resilience in the renewable energy sector, understanding and importance of financial literacy, relationship between resilience and financial literacy, organizational strategies to enhance resilience and financial capability, challenges and opportunities for the Mexican renewable energy sector, and policy and practice recommendations.

In-person interviews were conducted where possible, and remote video conferencing was used where geographical constraints precluded face-to-face meetings. All interviews were conducted in the participant's preferred language (Spanish or English) and were audio-recorded with active participant consent. Field notes were also gathered during interviews to capture non-verbal gestures and situational data.

Qualitative Data Analysis.

Qualitative data analysis was informed by a thematic analysis approach outlined by Braun and Clarke (2006). There were six stages of the analysis process: familiarizing with the data from multiple readings of transcripts, initial coding of salient features within the entire dataset, searching for themes by collating codes into potential themes, testing themes to ensure they work in context with coded extracts and the entire dataset, defining and naming themes, and writing the final report utilizing evocative and interesting examples of extracts.

Coding was conducted using NVivo software, making use of deductive codes based on the theoretical framework and inductive codes based on the data. Two researchers coded a representative subset of the transcripts separately to establish inter-rater reliability, with a resulting Cohen's kappa coefficient of 0.82, indicative of substantial agreement. Triangulation among data sources, i.e., between quantitative and qualitative findings was used to ensure the highest level of validity and credibility of the findings. Member checking was also done with a sub-sample of the participants in order to validate the interpretation of their responses.

Quantitative and Qualitative Data Integration.

The integration of quantitative and qualitative results had a combined presentation method where both types of results are shown side by side to show areas of convergence, divergence, and extension. Integration is primarily carried out in the results and discussions where quantitative associations are explained and presented in terms of qualitative knowledge.

Ethical Considerations.

Ethical approval for this study was obtained from the institutional review board of the lead researcher's institution. Participants provided informed consent, and confidentiality was maintained throughout research. Data were de-identified and stored securely, and access was limited to the research team. Participants were informed of the right to withdraw at any point without penalty.

Limitations.

Some limitations in this study should be addressed. Cross-sectional design makes it hard to make causal inference regarding relationships between variables. Self-report survey data are subject to social desirability bias as well as common method variance. Confining the scope to Mexico may limit generalizability between contexts, but it does bring essential insights to the operation of emerging markets.

ANALYSIS OF RESULTS

Quantitative Results. Sample Characteristics.

The final quantitative sample consisted of 450 renewable energy specialists from across Mexico. The demographic profile indicates a reasonably seasoned staff with 62% of the participants in having more than five years of experience in the renewable energy sector and 23% in having more than ten years of experience. The gender distribution is still 58% male and 42% female respondents, indicating reasonable proportions. Education is high, with 89% holding bachelor's degrees or higher and 45% holding graduate degrees.

Geographically, the sample represents Mexico's most important areas for renewable energy development: 28% from the Northern states (primarily Sonora, Chihuahua, and Coahuila), 24% from the Gulf of Mexico region (Tamaulipas, Veracruz), 22% from Central Mexico (Mexico City and neighboring states), 18% from the Southern states (Oaxaca, Chiapas), and 8% from the Yucatan Peninsula. This allocation closely mimics the geographical cluster of renewable energy development in Mexico.

34% are organizationally employed by private renewable energy companies, 18% by banking institutions with green energy investments, 16% by consultancy companies, 15% by public agencies, 12% by non-governmental institutions, and 5% by research institutions. The firm sizes range from small start-ups (fewer than 50 staff, 28% of sample) to large multinational corporations (more than 1,000 staff, 22% of sample).

Technology focus areas specify solar energy as most common (38% of respondents), then wind energy (31%), hydroelectric (14%), biomass (9%), geothermal (6%), and diversified renewable portfolios (2%). The breakdown reflects the prevailing mix of Mexico's renewable energy development pipeline.

Descriptive Statistics and Scale Reliability.

Descriptive statistics of the main study variables are presented in Table 1. The strategic business resilience scale was highly internally consistent (Cronbach's $\alpha = 0.91$), while subscales were also acceptably to highly reliable: adaptive capacity ($\alpha = 0.87$), absorptive capacity ($\alpha = 0.85$), and transformative capacity ($\alpha = 0.83$). The overall mean of resilience was 5.24 (SD = 1.12) on the seven-point scale, which indicates moderately high levels of perceived resilience among the respondents.

Financial literacy scale showed high internal consistency (Cronbach's $\alpha = 0.93$), whereas subscales were well-reliable: basic financial knowledge ($\alpha = 0.86$), green finance knowledge ($\alpha = 0.89$), risk assessment ability ($\alpha = 0.87$), and investment decision ability ($\alpha = 0.88$). Mean financial literacy was 4.89 (SD = 1.28), showing moderate financial literacy with high variability among participants.

Table 1. Descriptive statistics and correlations

Variable	Mean	SD	α	1	2	3	4	5
1. Strategic Business Resilience	5.24	1.12	.91	-				
2. Financial Literacy	4.89	1.28	.93	.67**	-			
3. Organization Size	3.45	1.89	-	.34**	.28**	-		
4. Years of Experience	7.23	4.56	-	.41**	.52**	.19**	-	
5. Education Level	4.12	0.98	-	.23**	.39**	.15**	.31**	-

Note: N = 450. ** p < .01

Factor Analysis Output. Exploratory factor analysis confirmed the theoretical conceptualization of the two main constructs. For business resilience strategy, KMO was 0.89, and Bartlett's test was significant ($\chi^2 = 3{,}247.58$, $p < .001$), indicating exceptional factorability. Analysis yielded three factors explaining 72.4% of variance, which corresponded to theorized adaptive capacity (explaining 31.2% of variance), absorptive capacity (explaining 22.8% of variance), and transformative capacity (explaining 18.4% of variance).

For financial literacy, KMO value was 0.91, and Bartlett's test was significant ($\chi^2 = 4{,}156.72$, $p < .001$). Four factors emerged that explained a total of 74.6% of the variance: basic knowledge of finance (explaining 28.9% of variance), knowledge of green finance (explaining 19.7% of variance), capability for risk assessment (explaining 14.2% of variance), and investment decision-making ability (explaining 11.8% of variance). All factor loadings were higher than 0.60, and the majority were higher than 0.70, which represents strong item-factor relationships. Low cross-loadings (all below 0.40) further demonstrate discriminant validity of the scales.

Correlation Analysis. Correlation analysis revealed strong positive correlations between financial literacy and strategic business resilience ($r = .67$, $p < .001$), supporting the primary hypothesis of this research. The magnitude of the correlation demonstrates a strong relationship but far below the level for multicollinearity concern. Examination of the correlations among the dimensions of resilience and the financial literacy components provides additional insight. The strongest correlation was for adaptive capacity with financial literacy ($r = .62$, $p < .001$), followed by absorptive capacity ($r = .58$, $p < .001$) and transformative capacity ($r = .51$, $p < .001$).

Among financial literacy dimensions, investment choice competence was most correlated with general resilience ($r = .61, p < .001$), then risk assessment competence ($r = .57, p < .001$), green finance knowledge ($r = .54, p < .001$), and basic financial knowledge ($r = .49, p < .001$). Control variables showed patterns of relations as expected. Length of service was positively associated with resilience ($r = .41, p < .001$) and financial literacy ($r = .52, p < .001$). Educational level moderately positively associated with both constructs (resilience: $r = .23, p < .001$; financial literacy: $r = .39, p < .001$). Organization size was positively related to resilience ($r = .34, p < .001$) and financial literacy ($r = .28, p < .001$).

Regression Analysis. The main hypothesis was tested using multiple regression analysis with the following control variables: relevant demographic, organizational, and contextual variables. The overall model explained 58.7% of the variance in financial literacy ($R^2 = .587$, $F(8,441) = 78.94$, $p < .001$).

Table 2. Multiple regression analysis results

Predictor	B	SE B	β	t	p
Strategic Business Resilience	0.694	0.052	0.608	13.35	<.001
Years of Experience	0.041	0.013	0.146	3.15	.002
Education Level	0.187	0.056	0.143	3.34	.001
Organization Size	0.029	0.031	0.043	0.94	.347
Technology Focus (Wind)	0.142	0.118	0.055	1.20	.231
Technology Focus (Hydro)	0.089	0.143	0.026	0.62	.535
Region (North)	-0.076	0.121	-0.028	-0.63	.529
Region (South)	0.098	0.134	0.033	0.73	.465

Note: $R^2 = .587$, $F(8,441) = 78.94$, $p < .001$

The results heavily support the principal hypothesis. Strategic business resilience emerged as the strongest predictor of financial literacy ($\beta = .608, p < .001$), indicating that a one-unit increase in resilience is associated with an increase of 0.694 units in financial literacy, ceteris paribus. The relationship is very significant even after controlling for relevant covariates.

Both experience years ($\beta = .146, p = .002$) and educational level ($\beta = .143, p = .001$) were also significant predictors, suggesting that both formal education and actual experience contribute to the acquisition of financial literacy.

Organization size was not a significant predictor of financial literacy, suggesting that scale benefits may be less important than has been thought. Technology focus and geographical location also failed to come out as robust predictors of financial literacy, indicating that the resilience-financial literacy relationship is solid for renewable energy technologies and locations within Mexico.

Moderation Analysis.

Moderation analysis using Hayes' PROCESS macro tested if organizational characteristics moderate the relationship between strategic business resilience and financial literacy. Three potential moderators were tested: organization size, primary technology focus, and years' operating.

Organizational size acted as a notable moderator ($B = 0.087$, $SE = 0.031$, $p = .005$). Simple slope tests showed that the association between resilience and financial literacy is stronger among larger organizations ($\beta = .742$, $p < .001$) compared to smaller organizations ($\beta = .531$, $p < .001$). This may mean that larger organizations have greater resources and structures through which to capitalize on resilience capacity into improved financial literacy. Technology focus did not moderate the relationship to any great extent ($F(3,442) = 1.47$, $p = .221$), meaning the resilience-financial literacy relationship is consistent across types of renewable energy technology.

Years of operation had a modest moderating effect ($B = 0.042$, $SE = 0.024$, $p = .078$). Organizations with more years of operation reported marginally stronger relationships between resilience and financial literacy, possibly due to accumulated experience in managing the challenges of the renewable energy sector.

Qualitative Results. Thematic Analysis Overview.

Thematic analysis of the 25 semi-structured interviews revealed six general themes that inform the interaction between strategic business resilience and financial literacy in Mexico's renewable energy sector. The themes provide rich contextual explanation to the quantitative results and reveal mechanisms through which resilience and financial literacy interact.

Theme 1: Resilience as a Foundation for Financial Learning.

The most dominant theme to emerge from the interviews was the articulation of resilience as a key competency that enables and enhances financial learning in renewable energy organizations. Over and over, participants outlined how resilient organizations build financial literacy through systematic learning processes, knowledge management systems, and adaptive capacity building.

The dimension comprises three sub-dimensions: institutional learning capacity, knowledge integration mechanisms, and adaptive expertise development. Institutional learning capacity consists of the formal and informal structures that organizations develop for capturing, processing, and using new knowledge. Knowledge integration mechanisms are processes for integrating different types of knowledge (technical, financial, regulatory) into consistent strategic frameworks. Adaptive expertise development is the manner by which organizations build capacities that generalize across contexts and problems.

Theme 2: Financial Literacy as a Resilience Enabler.

Contrarily, the respondents depicted financial literacy as a key facilitator of business resilience, providing organizations with analytical tools and decision-making models to manage uncertainty and volatility. This theme illustrates the bidirectionality of the resilience-financial literacy relationship.

The framework embodies several mechanisms through which financial literacy enables resilience. Risk measurement and management was a primary mechanism, with financially literate firms better able to identify, evaluate, and manage various types of risks. Strategic flexibility is another mechanism, with financial literacy enabling firms to explore various strategic options and switch direction when circumstances require it.

Access to capital markets is a third avenue, with financially literate companies being better positioned to talk to investors, negotiate deal structures, and access multiple sources of funding. Several respondents noted that financial literacy raises the credibility of the company with external stakeholders, facilitating access to resources during challenging times.

Contextual Amplifiers and Barriers.

Respondents identified a number of contextual elements in the Mexican renewable energy sector that moderate or strengthen the relationship between financial literacy and resilience. These elements are the environmental conditions under which organizations develop and execute their capabilities. Regulatory complexity emerged as a significant amplifier of the resilience-financial literacy relationship. Market volatility is yet another amplifier since sector stakeholders noted that volatile electricity prices, fluctuating exchange rates, and changing patterns of demand mean that organizations need to couple adaptive capacity with financial sophistication. Infrastructure concerns, including grid integration issues and transmission bottlenecks, represent technical risks that have to be financially measured and hedged.

Social acceptance issues appeared both as a multiplier and as a limiting factor. Since successful community engagement requires financial literacy in order to develop benefit-sharing agreements and economic impact analyses, social conflicts can overwhelm even well-designed financial strategies.

Limitations to the resilience-financial literacy relationship are few experienced practitioners and limited availability of specialist training, as well as organizational cultures that reward technical rather than financial expertise.

Organizational Strategies for Integration

Participants described various organizational strategies for integrating resilience building and financial literacy development. These strategies represent practical approaches organizations use to strengthen both capabilities simultaneously.

Cross-functional team development emerged as a central strategy, with organizations creating teams that combine technical, financial, and strategic expertise. Dual-competency training investment is another strategy, in which organizations provide financial staff with technical training and technical staff with financial training. Several participants described comprehensive training programs that build awareness of both renewable energy technologies and financing mechanisms.

Scenario planning and stress testing were both highlighted as practices that develop financial literacy and resilience simultaneously. These techniques are utilized by organizations to reflect on potential future situations, examine their implications, and develop response strategies.

Knowledge management systems are infrastructural investments that support both resilience and financial literacy development. They capture lessons from past experiences, provide access to knowledge sources outside the firm, and transfer knowledge across organizational boundaries.

Performance Implications.

Participants discussed a number of mechanisms by which the interaction of resilience and financial literacy influences organizational performance in the renewable energy sector in Mexico. These performance implications provide practical affirmation of the theoretical associations of quantitative analysis. Project success rates were one of the key performance indicators, with interviewees highlighting that those institutions that combine resilience with financial literacy experience greater project completion rates, better financial returns, and reduced cost overruns.

Access to capital is a further performance dimension, with robust and financially literate organizations being better able to access investment, negotiate favorable terms of finance, and maintain financial institution relationships. Market positioning was a third dimension, with such organizations being better able to identify and seize market opportunities.

Stakeholder relations constitute a fourth performance dimension. Firms with adaptive capacity and financial literacy are better able to negotiate complex stakeholder relations, for example, with investors, communities, regulators, and business partners.

Innovation capacity was an additional performance implication. Interviewees described how firms with highly developed resilience and financial literacy skills are more inclined to invest in innovation, experiment with new business models, and adopt new technologies.

Policy and Ecosystem Implications.

The final theme addresses the perceptions of participants on policy and ecosystem-level implications of the resilience-financial literacy relationship. These suggestions are a roadmap for policymakers and ecosystem developers seeking to strengthen Mexico's renewable energy sector. Education and training infrastructure was one of the main policy priorities suggested by participants. There was a recurring demand for educational programs that combined technical renewable energy skills with financial acumen.

Regulatory clarity and stability are the policy priority, with respondents stating that regulatory uncertainty or frequent regulatory change makes it difficult for organizations to make secure financial planning. Third priority was the financial market development, with respondents calling for policies enabling the emergence of green finance institutions and instruments.

Information and knowledge sharing platforms are infrastructure needs that would be capable of supporting both resilience and financial literacy development across the sector. Several participants suggested industry-specific mechanisms for best practices, lessons learned, and market intelligence sharing.

International cooperation was envisioned as a means of capability development acceleration, with participants noting the potential to learn from more advanced renewable energy markets and translate strategies to the specific Mexican context.

Combination of Quantitative and Qualitative Results.

The combination of quantitative and qualitative findings provides a comprehensive picture of the effect of strategic business resilience on financial literacy in the Mexican renewable energy sector. The quantitative research provides strong statistical evidence of the positive relationship between the constructs, while the qualitative research illuminates the mechanisms through which this relationship occurs and also on the contextual conditions mediating it.

The quantitative finding that 58.7% of the variance in financial literacy is explained by resilience is supported by qualitative themes that describe resilience as a foundation for financial learning and financial literacy as a facilitator of resilience. The bidirectionality of the relationship suggests a reinforcing cycle where resilience competencies foster financial learning that, in turn, strengthens resilience.

The quantitative finding that organizational size moderates the resilience-financial literacy relationship is explained by qualitative data on resource availability, training potential, and knowledge management systems. Larger organizations are apparently more able to translate resilience capacity into improved financial literacy through systematic investments in capability development.

The lack of technology type differences in the quantitative analysis is supported by qualitative evidence suggesting that the resilience-financial literacy relationship operates through general organizational competencies rather than technology-specific variables. Qualitative results suggest, however, that different technologies are likely to face different types of adversity in which these general competencies will have to be adapted.

DISCUSSION

Theoretical Contributions.

The current research makes various meaningful theoretical contributions to the literature on strategic business resilience, financial literacy, and renewable energy management. First, it provides empirical evidence of the relationship between strategic business resilience and financial literacy, constructs that have largely been investigated in isolation. The finding that resilience explains virtually 60% of the variance in financial literacy provides much higher association than was predicted prior and offers new avenues of research on the interdependence of organizational abilities.

The two-way relationship between financial literacy and resilience, which has been revealed through qualitative analysis, serves to further dynamic capabilities theory by illustrating how different types of capability can enable each other. This finding suggests that organizations can gain advantage from conceptualizing capability development as a general process rather than in terms of discrete competencies separately.

Findings regarding contextual amplifiers and barriers contribute to contingency theory by way of showing how the dynamics of the environment affect the intersection between organizational capacities. The identification that regulatory complexity and market volatility are resilience-financial literacy relationship amplifiers, but cultural and resource constraints are barriers, contributes to increasing our knowledge on when and how such capacities become most essential.

The study contributes further to the expanding body of literature in green finance and sustainable business models in demonstrating the worth of technical financial literacy within renewable energy contexts. The findings that green finance knowledge form a distinct dimension of financial literacy with unique correlations to resilience capacity suggest the need for more sophisticated theoretical models of financial literacy for sustainability contexts.

Practical Implications.

The study findings have significant practical implications for a number of stakeholder groups in Mexico's renewable energy industry.

Implications for Business Leaders.

Business executives and managers of renewable energy companies can gain from this study that investments in resilience development and acquiring financial literacy must be thought of as complementary, not substitute, efforts. The extremely high positive correlation between these abilities suggests that organizations will gain synergistic benefit from developing both simultaneously.

The implication of the result that adaptive capacity has the highest correlation with financial literacy is that organizations need to make flexibility, learning orientation, and responsiveness to change the cornerstones of financial capability development. This may involve establishing cross-functional teams, implementing scenario planning processes, and establishing knowledge management systems that support continuous learning.

The fact that organizational size was considered a moderator would mean that small renewable energy organizations may need to explore beyond traditional approaches to building capability. This may involve collaborative approaches such as industry consortia, collective training programs, or strategic partnerships with large companies or specialist service providers.

The implications for performance arising from qualitative analysis are that investments in financial resilience and literacy can return through a number of channels: increased rates of project success, increased capital access, better market positioning, better stakeholder relations, and improved ability to innovate.

Implications for Financial Institutions.

For banks, development finance institutions, and financial service providers, lessons on client assessment and product development are available from this research. That more financially literate organizations were found to be more resilient suggests that the credit evaluation and due diligence processes could include resilience considerations.

The development of green finance knowledge as a distinct dimension of financial competence suggests opportunities for product innovation and customer education. Financial institutions will be able to design training courses, consulting services, and information platforms that allow renewable energy customers to build specialized financial skills. The consistency of the resilience-financial literacy relationship across a range of different renewable energy technologies suggests that financial institutions can develop generic client assessment and support mechanisms while leaving room for technology-specific considerations.

Policy Implications.

For those governmental agencies responsible for renewable energy policy and development, the study offers evidence to indicate that capability building programs must address both financial literacy and resilience as integrated competencies. Other more conventional approaches using individual technical training alone or financial education in isolation may prove less effective than integration-based programs. The identification of regulatory complexity as a multiplier of the resilience-financial literacy nexus suggests that policy stability and transparency can reduce the capability requirements for market participation. Even if some degree of complexity is unavoidable, policymakers must counterbalance against the aggregate impact of regulatory requirements on organizational capability requirements.

The revelation that accesses to specialist training and education is a significant barrier suggests that investment in public capital within educational facilities dedicated to serving the particular requirements of the renewable energy sector is needed. This may involve association with universities, development of professional certification schemes, or supporting industry training schemes. Performance implications of this research suggest that capability development policies have the ability to produce broader economic gains by creating better project success rates, greater innovation, and improved market development.

Implications for Educational Institutions.

For universities and training institutions, this study upholds the need for holistic curricula that combine technical renewable energy education with resilience and financial literacy skills. Disciplinary silos might not be sufficient in meeting the student demands of Mexico's renewable energy industry. Having accurate dimensions of financial literacy suitable to renewable energy environments provides guidance for curriculum design. It not only must include elementary concepts in finance but also green finance instruments, methods of risk assessment, and investment choices specific to renewable energy projects.

The finding that experience acts as a mediator for the relationship between resilience and financial literacy suggests the importance of experiential learning approaches, including internships, case studies, and simulation experiments that allow learners to apply integrated knowledge in actual contexts.

Limitations and Areas for Future Research.

While this research adds to knowledge on how business resilience strategy is connected with financial literacy in Mexico's renewable energy sector, several limitations should be noted and these limitations offer avenues for future studies.

Methodological Limitations.

Cross-sectional design limits inferences regarding causal relationships between variables. While bidirectional causality is suggested by the theoretical model and qualitative findings, to ascertain temporal relations between resilience and financial literacy, longitudinal work would be necessary. Panel data designs could be utilized in future research to examine trajectories of ways changes in resilience skills influence over-time development of financial literacy, and vice versa.

The self-reporting character of the survey data generates social desirability bias and common method variance potential. While efforts were made to mitigate such in questionnaire design and data collection approaches, future research can incorporate objective measures for both financial literacy and resilience. For example, resilience could be measured by organizational performance during actual crisis events, while financial literacy could be measured by conventional testing or examinations of the results of financial decisions.

The focus on Mexico, while providing valuable lessons on emerging market dynamics, limits the ability to generalize findings to other environments. Future studies must explore the interaction of resilience and financial literacy in other large renewable energy developing emerging nations, such as Brazil, India, or South Africa, in order to determine the extent to which the conclusions are country-specific or transferrable.

Theory Limitations.

While this research provides some evidence of a strong association between resilience and financial literacy, theoretical processes underlying this relationship remain to be formulated. The qualitative evidence points to several possible mechanisms, yet more advanced theoretical models and testing are needed to determine the specific pathways through which these skills engage with each other.

The study is aimed at organizational-level abilities but fails to investigate individual-level factors that may influence how resilience and financial capability arise and play out at the organizational level. Future research can examine multilevel frameworks that consider organizational and individual levels. The test of financial literacy, while diligently designed for the present study, is a first attempt at quantifying the particular demands of green energy environments. Future research needs to further refine and validate measures of green finance literacy as well as renewable energy finance literacy.

Limitations of Scope.

This study aims at the renewable energy sector but does not look at how resilience-financial literacy correlation can be in other sectors with sustainability objectives. It is possible to carry out future research to see if some of these correlations apply in sustainable agriculture, green building, or circular economy businesses. The study fails to investigate the relationship between resilience, financial literacy, and specific organizational performance comprehensively. While qualitative findings suggest implications on performance, further research may measure the degree to which the interaction of such capabilities influences performance indicators such as financial performance, innovation outcomes, or market share.

The study takes formal organizations into account but does not examine how resilience and financial literacy cross-cut in community or informal renewable energy projects, which increasingly play an important role in Mexico and other developing countries.

Directions of Future Research.

A number of directions of future research stem from the results and limitations of this study:

Longitudinal Studies: Panel data analyses of organizations across several decades potentially could inform causal processes in the resilience-financial literacy relationship and identify key periods of capability development.

Comparative Studies: Cross-national research examining the resilience-financial literacy relationship in different institutional and cultural contexts could shed more light on boundary conditions and generalizability.

Mechanism Studies: Testing and examining specific mechanisms through which resilience and financial literacy interact may advance theory and provide more precise advice to practitioners.

Outcome Studies: Studies of how interactions between resilience and financial literacy influence specific organizational outcomes may result in stronger practical significance findings.

Intervention Studies: Experimental or quasi-experimental intervention studies comparing different approaches to building resilience and financial capability could provide evidence-based recommendations to inform capability development programs.

Multi-level Studies: Multi-level studies combining individual, organizational, and institutional factors could provide more nuanced understanding of the multilevel processes in which capabilities develop and interact.

CONCLUSIONS

This research provides definitive proof of the fact that strategic business resilience exerts a profound impact on financial literacy in organizations in Mexico's renewable energy sector. The study's mixed-methods approach, combining quantitative data from 450 professionals and qualitative data from 25 sector leaders, illustrates a strong and positive relationship between these central organizational capabilities.

Key Findings.

Quantitative analysis demonstrates that strategic business resilience explains 58.7% of the variance in financial literacy, one of the most powerful relationships documented in the organizational capabilities' literature. The finding holds across different renewable energy technologies, geographic locations, and organizational types, suggesting strong practical significance.

The qualitative study shows that this relation operates through a number of mechanisms. Resilience provides a platform for financial learning through building organizational environments conducive to knowledge creation, experimentation, and adaptive capacity. Financial literacy, on the contrary, creates resilience by providing analytical tools and decision-making frameworks that enable organizations to manage uncertainty and volatility effectively.

The study identifies several contextual factors that strengthen or weaken this relationship. Regulatory complexity and market volatility emerge as intensifiers, creating a context where both financial literacy and resilience are critical to the organization's success. Resource constraints and cultural factors preferring technical to financial competencies are significant barriers.

Organizational size is an important moderating variable, and large organizations show stronger relationships between resilience and financial literacy. The implication is that size yields advantages in translating resilience capabilities into better financial literacy through systematic investment in training, knowledge management, and capability development.

Theoretical Significance.

This research makes theoretical contributions in several important respects. It provides empirical evidence of organizational capabilities interrelatedness by showing how strategic business resilience and financial literacy can be mutually reinforcing. By doing this, this finding expands dynamic capabilities theory by showing how multiple forms of capabilities interact to create synergy effects.

The study also contributes to the emerging literature on sustainable business practices and green finance by demonstrating the relevance of specialized financial literacy in renewable energy contexts. The identification of green finance knowledge as a distinct aspect of financial literacy with its own characteristics and relations suggests the need for more sophisticated theoretical notions of financial literacy in sustainability contexts.

The research extends contingency theory through the explanation of how environmental contingencies influence organizational capability interdependence. The finding that regulatory complexity and market volatility strengthen the resilience-financial literacy relationship and cultural and resource constraints present obstacles provides a more nuanced understanding of when and under what conditions these capabilities become most essential.

Practical Significance.

The practical implications of this research are substantial for a number of stakeholder groups. For renewable energy companies, the implications are that investments in resilience building and financial literacy acquisition need to be treated as complementary strategic imperatives with the capacity to yield synergy benefits. Companies are advised to develop adaptive capacity as a foundation for financial learning while using financial literacy to enhance their resilience capacity.

For financial service institutions, the research has implications for product development and client assessment. The strong association of resilience with financial literacy suggests that measures of resilience would be valuable supplements to credit scoring processes. The identification of green finance knowledge as a specialist competency suggests opportunities for specialist product development and client education.

For policymakers, the study provides evidence that capability development programs must address resilience and financial literacy as integrated competencies rather than separate skill sets. That regulatory complexity has been found to be an amplifier suggests that policy stability and clarity can reduce capability demands for market engagement. For universities, the research demonstrates the need for comprehensive curricula that blend technical renewable energy knowledge with financial literacy and resilience capabilities. Traditional disciplinary boundaries may not be entirely adapted to the needs of students entering Mexico's renewable energy sector.

Contributions to Mexico's Renewable Energy Development.

These findings provide timely lessons for the renewable energy sector in Mexico as the country seeks to achieve ambitious energy and climate targets. The finding that financial literacy and resilience are complementary capacities suggests that investment in these areas can accelerate the development of a more robust and sophisticated renewable energy industry. This specific identification of individual barriers and amplifiers provides actionable intelligence in addressing bottlenecks to sector expansion. The emphasis on regulatory certainty, educational infrastructure, and knowledge dissemination platforms suggests targeted actions that could enhance the capability foundations of Mexico's renewable energy industry.

The research also demonstrates the value of context-specific investigation in witnessing how worldwide trends of renewable energy evolution play out in exact national contexts. Mexico's unique combination of abundant renewable resources, complex regulatory environment, and developing market characteristics creates a condition requiring tailored approaches to capability building.

Final Reflections.

As Mexico continues with its transformation to a more sustainable energy industry, the capabilities of organizations operating within it will be critical success factors. This research demonstrates that strategic business resilience and financial literacy are complementary competencies that can develop into competitive strengths and contribute to industry-wide expansion.

The findings suggest that the traditional approach of developing technical, financial, and strategic competencies in isolation is possibly less effective than more integrated approaches that consider the synergistic interdependencies of different organizational competencies. Those institutions that can develop resilience while developing financial sophistication will be well positioned to handle the uncertainties and capture the gains inherent in Mexico's renewable energy revolution.

More broadly, this research informs how firms in emerging economies build capabilities to play a role in global sustainability transitions. As countries around the world attempt to build renewable energy industries, the lessons of Mexico's experience may have significant implications for capability development and firm success in challenging and dynamic environments.

The research also highlights the necessity to view sustainability transitions not merely as technical or economic issues but as complex organizational and social processes that require sophisticated capabilities to accomplish effectively. The inseparability of resilience and financial literacy is merely one dimension of the capability requirements of successful engagement with sustainability transitions, yet it undoubtedly appears to be a significant one deserving of close attention from scholars, practitioners, and policymakers alike.

REFERENCES

Ajzen, I. (1991). The theory of planned behavior. *Organizational Behavior and Human Decision Processes, 50*(2), 179–211. DOI: 10.1016/0749-5978(91)90020-T

Anderson, P. (1999). Complexity theory and organization science. *Organization Science, 10*(3), 216–232. DOI: 10.1287/orsc.10.3.216

Barney, J. (1991). Firm resources and sustained competitive advantage. *Journal of Management, 17*(1), 99–120. DOI: 10.1177/014920639101700108

Braun, V., & Clarke, V. (2006). Using thematic analysis in psychology. *Qualitative Research in Psychology, 3*(2), 77–101. DOI: 10.1191/1478088706qp063oa

Chen, H., & Volpe, R. P. (2021). Green financial literacy and green investment behavior: Evidence from emerging markets. *Journal of Sustainable Finance & Investment, 11*(2), 142–158. DOI: 10.1080/20430795.2020.1735219

Cohen, W. M., & Levinthal, D. A. (1990). Absorptive capacity: A new perspective on learning and innovation. *Administrative Science Quarterly, 35*(1), 128–152. DOI: 10.2307/2393553

Creswell, J. W., & Plano Clark, V. L. (2018). *Designing and conducting mixed methods research* (3rd ed.). Sage Publications.

Duchek, S. (2020). Organizational resilience: A capability-based conceptualization. *Business Research, 13*(1), 215–246. DOI: 10.1007/s40685-019-0085-7

Elizondo Azuela, G., Barroso, L., Khanna, A., Wang, X., Wu, Y., & Cunha, G. (2014). *Performance of renewable energy auctions: Experience in Brazil, China and Mexico*. World Bank Group. https://doi.org/DOI: 10.1596/1813-9450-7062

Folke, C., Carpenter, S. R., Walker, B., Scheffer, M., Chapin, T., & Rockström, J. (2010). Resilience thinking: Integrating resilience, adaptability and transformability. *Ecology and Society, 15*(4), 20. Advance online publication. DOI: 10.5751/ES-03610-150420

Holling, C. S. (1973). Resilience and stability of ecological systems. *Annual Review of Ecology and Systematics, 4*(1), 1–23. DOI: 10.1146/annurev.es.04.110173.000245

International Energy Agency. (2018). *Energy transition indicators: Mexico*. IEA Publications. https://www.iea.org/reports/energy-transition-indicators-mexico

Kahneman, D., & Tversky, A. (1979). Prospect theory: An analysis of decision under risk. *Econometrica, 47*(2), 263–291. DOI: 10.2307/1914185

Lusardi, A., & Mitchell, O. S. (2014). The economic importance of financial literacy: Theory and evidence. *Journal of Economic Literature, 52*(1), 5–44. DOI: 10.1257/jel.52.1.5 PMID: 28579637

Organisation for Economic Co-operation and Development. (2018). *OECD/INFE toolkit for measuring financial literacy and financial inclusion*. OECD Publishing., DOI: 10.1787/9789264309303-

Park, H., & Kim, Y. K. (2020). Proactive versus reactive apparel brands in sustainability: Influences on brand loyalty. *Journal of Retailing and Consumer Services, 52*, 101926. Advance online publication. DOI: 10.1016/j.jretconser.2019.101926

Polzin, F., Migendt, M., Täube, F. A., & von Flotow, P. (2017). Public policy influence on renewable energy investments—A panel data study across OECD countries. *Energy Policy, 80*, 98–111. DOI: 10.1016/j.enpol.2015.01.026

Secretaría de Energía. (2020). *Programa de desarrollo del sistema eléctrico nacional 2020-2034*. Gobierno de México. https://www.gob.mx/sener/documentos/programa-de-desarrollo-del-sistema-electrico-nacional

Sirmon, D. G., Hitt, M. A., Ireland, R. D., & Gilbert, B. A. (2011). Resource orchestration to create competitive advantage: Breadth, depth, and life cycle effects. *Journal of Management, 37*(5), 1390–1412. DOI: 10.1177/0149206310385695

Teece, D. J. (2007). Explicating dynamic capabilities: The nature and microfoundations of (sustainable) enterprise performance. *Strategic Management Journal, 28*(13), 1319–1350. DOI: 10.1002/smj.640

Teece, D. J., Pisano, G., & Shuen, A. (1997). Dynamic capabilities and strategic management. *Strategic Management Journal, 18*(7), 509–533. DOI: 10.1002/(SICI)1097-0266(199708)18:7<509::AID-SMJ882>3.0.CO;2-Z

Thaler, R. (1985). Mental accounting and consumer choice. *Marketing Science, 4*(3), 199–214. DOI: 10.1287/mksc.4.3.199

Walker, B., Holling, C. S., Carpenter, S. R., & Kinzig, A. (2004). Resilience, adaptability and transformability in social–ecological systems. *Ecology and Society, 9*(2), 5. DOI: 10.5751/ES-00650-090205

Willis, L. E. (2008). Against financial-literacy education. *Iowa Law Review, 94*(1), 197–285. https://ilr.law.uiowa.edu/print/volume-94-issue-1/against-financial-literacy-education/

Chapter 5
Green and Renewable Energy Financial Literacy Affecting Economy, Society, and Governance (ESG) in Mexico

José G. Vargas-Hernandez
https://orcid.org/0000-0003-0938-4197
Financial Literacy Research Center, Universidad Cristóbal Colón, Mexico & Tecnológico Nacional de México, ITS Fresnillo, Mexico

Csongor Czipf
https://orcid.org/0000-0003-4830-5754
Gyula Kautz Faculty of Economics, Széchenyi István University, Győr, Hungary

Absalòn J. Salmeròn-Zapata
https://orcid.org/0009-0002-2621-2426
Universidad Cristòbal Colòn, Mexico

ABSTRACT

This research delves into the intricate relationship between green and renewable energy financial literacy and its impact on Environmental, Social, and Governance (ESG) practices in Mexico's changing economic landscape. The study attempts to investigate how financial literacy regarding sustainable energy investments influences the performance of ESG on economic, social, and governance factors in the Mexican context. Through a careful examination of available literature, policy guidelines, and empirical data, this research discovers that greater financial liter-

DOI: 10.4018/979-8-3373-5142-1.ch005

acy in green and renewable energy sectors has a direct correlation with improved ESG performance, which results in sustainable economic development, social advancement, and governance culture in Mexico. The study concludes that strategic actions to increase financial literacy in renewable energy investments are required for Mexico's sustainable development trajectory and ESG leadership in the Latin American region.

INTRODUCTION

The intersection of renewable energy investment, financial literacy, and Environmental, Social, and Governance (ESG) principles is a fundamental front in Mexico's sustainable development agenda. As Mexico ramps up its aggressive renewable energy plans and intensifies its ESG emphasis, the role of financial literacy as a facilitator of well-informed decision-making in green investment has only become increasingly pivotal. This research bridges an essential gap in knowledge towards the understanding of the effect of financial literacy in green and renewable energy on ESG outcomes in the Mexican environment.

Mexico's transition to energy is the most ambitious sustainable development endeavor in Latin America.

The country has also implemented legislative frameworks through the Energy Transition Law (Ley de Transición Energética) and General Climate Change Law (Ley General de Cambio Climático), with the goal of achieving 35% of electricity generation from renewable sources by 2024 (Trade.gov, 2024). The shift occurs in a broader context of rising global interest in ESG metrics that have now become integral to investment decisions, corporate governance, and green growth models worldwide. The significance of this research relies on the realization that financial literacy serves as a critical mediating factor between policy intentions and actual implementation of sustainable energy schemes.

While Mexico has exhibited significant leaps in renewable energy installation, with capacity growing exponentially over the past decade, the success of these investments to meet broader ESG objectives largely depends on the financial literateness of key stakeholders like investors, policymakers, business leaders, and civil society organizations.

Current literature points to important knowledge gaps regarding the exact mechanisms through which financial literacy impacts ESG performance in emerging markets like Mexico. Most current literature aims at developed economies or examines financial literacy and ESG separately without considering the complex interdependence of these variables in a given country's context. This research aims to close the gap by undertaking a comprehensive analysis of the influence that green and renewable energy investment financial literacy has on ESG performance in the unique economic, social, and governance environment of Mexico.

Research questions guiding this study are: How does green and renewable energy investment financial literacy influence ESG performance in Mexico? What are the tangible mechanisms by which enhanced financial literacy in green energy yields enhanced economic, social, and governance outcomes? What are the barriers to advancing green energy investment financial literacy, and how do the barriers impact the deployment of ESG? Finally, what policy interventions and institutional arrangements can best support financial literacy in renewable energy to optimize ESG benefits in Mexico?

The research design relies on quantitative analysis of existing figures on investments in renewable sources of energy, ESG performance indicators, and literacy indicators to be supplemented with qualitative analysis of policy responses, institutional routines, and stakeholder perceptions. The study is grounded on a mixed-methods design to capture the measurable impacts of financial literacy on ESG performance as well as the nuanced institutional and cultural factors that influence such correlations. The structure of this study progresses from theoretical foundations through empirical analysis to applications.

Following this introduction, the literature review examines conceptual frameworks relating financial literacy to ESG outcomes, theoretical models of sustainable finance, and empirical findings in Mexico and comparable settings. The methodology section describes the analytical methods and data used. The results section presents outcomes related to the relationships among financial literacy, renewable energy investments, and ESG performance in Mexico. The discussion section places these outcomes into broader theoretical and policy contexts, while the conclusion section synthesizes key insights and examines recommendations for optimal leveraging of financial literacy to the benefit of ESG outcomes in Mexico's renewable energy sector.

LITERATURE REVIEW

Conceptual Framework: Financial Literacy and ESG Integration

The theoretical basis of understanding the dynamics between financial literacy and ESG performance comes from the intersection of the theory of behavioral finance, sustainable development frameworks, and institutional economics. Financial literacy, the ability to make effective use and understand a set of financial capabilities such as personal money management, budgeting, and investing (Lusardi & Mitchell, 2014), gains particular utility when employed in describing nuanced investment instruments such as green bonds, renewable energy projects, and ESG-harmonized financial products.

Later research expanded financial literacy to financial knowledge for sustainability or "sustainable finance literacy," as defined by Gutsche and Ziegler (2023). It is a specific form of financial literacy encompassing ESG factors, measurement of climate risk, sustainable investment strategies, and long-term financial consequences of social and environmental factors. For renewable energy investments, it would be consciousness regarding technologies, policy tools, regulatory frameworks, and market systems relevant for sustainable energy sectors.

The ESG structure itself has evolved with time from primarily being a risk management process to an integrated process of measuring corporation and investment performance. Environmental concerns include mitigating climate change, conserving resources, avoiding pollution, and preserving biodiversity. Social concerns encompass human rights, labor practices, community relations, and social development impacts. Governance concerns deal with board makeup, executive compensation, transparency, and ethical business practice (Friede *et al.*, 2015).

The intersection of financial literacy and ESG thought creates a compound dynamic such that sound financial decision-making can yield beneficial environmental, social, and governance outcomes. Such a dynamic is particularly relevant in emerging markets like Mexico, where rapid economic growth coexists with pressing sustainability imperatives and evolving governance arrangements.

Theoretical Models of Sustainable Finance and Development Theoretical frameworks that explain financial literacy and sustainable development results are founded on many disciplines like the fields of development economics, environmental economics, and organizational behavior. SDGs provide a comprehensive framework for conceptualizing the ways in which financial literacy for green energy will affect overall development objectives, specifically SDG 7 (Affordable and Clean Energy), SDG 8 (Decent Work and Economic Growth), and SDG 13 (Climate Action).

Portfolio theory extensions including ESG considerations state that more financially literate investors will be able to evaluate the risk-return profiles of green investments in order to direct more optimal capital investments towards environmentally and socially beneficial initiatives (Riedl & Smeets, 2017). Conceptual foundations supporting the contention that higher financial literacy in renewable energy investment will be related to better ESG performance through enhanced investment decisions and utilization of resources.

The planned behavior theory provides the second theoretical framework by which to understand the role of financial literacy in driving ESG-related behavior. Under this framework, attitudes, subjective norms, and perceived behavioral control influence intentions, which in turn influence actual behavior (Ajzen, 1991). Financial literacy is a component of perceived behavioral control that enhances the confidence of individuals and organizations in their ability for making good sustainable investment decisions.

Institutional theory offers additional insights on how financial literacy interacts with formal and informal institutions to affect ESG performance.

To Mexico, formal institutions include regulatory codes, government policies, and legal frameworks that govern renewable energy and ESG strategies. Informal institutions encompass cultural norms, customs in business, and social expectations on environmental and social stewardship. Financial literacy acts as the intermediary between these institutional factors, facilitating stakeholders to better cope with complicated regulatory contexts and cultural demands.

EMPIRICAL EVIDENCE IN MEXICO AND SIMILAR CONTEXTS

Empirical research on financial literacy and ESG performance in Mexico is scarce but growing. Recent evidence has already mapped some characteristics of this relationship, generating insights into opportunities and challenges. González-Torres et al. (2022) contrasted ESG performance among Mexican listed firms and found significant heterogeneity in ESG scores in line with the quality of corporate governance and management education levels, suggesting that financial literacy by corporate managers decides ESG application.

Research on Mexico's renewable energy sector shows strong capacity and investment expansion over the past decade. Current figures show that the renewable energy share of Mexico increased from 12% to 25% between 2013 and 2023. Wind power has contributed roughly 10%, solar power contributed roughly 8%, while the rest of the renewables contributed 7% of the energy sector (Nolasco & López-Portillo, 2019). This growth has been accompanied by increased concern for ESG matters on the part of regulators and investors, presenting an opportunity to analyze the link between financial literacy and sustainable development performance.

A 2024 survey of Mexican companies revealed that nearly 50% plan to significantly scale up sustainability investments, with renewable energy projects representing a primary focus area (Global Banking and Finance, 2025). This finding suggests growing awareness of sustainable investment opportunities, though questions remain regarding the financial literacy levels necessary to optimize these investments from an ESG perspective.

International data provide additional context for interpreting possible connections between financial literacy and ESG outcomes.

The research of Gutsche and Ziegler (2023) on Swiss households demonstrated strong positive associations between sustainable finance literacy and sustainable investment conduct, with policy implications for the promotion of ESG-compatible investment choice. Similar studies in other European contexts have demonstrated that financial education programs aimed at sustainable investment can generate significant improvement in both investment performance and ESG outcomes. Evidence from other Latin American countries is also useful for comparative reasons. Brazil and Chile have examined the role of financial literacy in promoting the adoption of renewable energy and ESG practices and concluded that certain education programs can be employed to drive the rate of sustainable development if supported by appropriate policy incentives and institutional support systems.

Policy Frameworks and Institutional Context in Mexico. Mexico's institutional setup for renewable energy and ESG uptake has changed significantly in recent years, creating an institutional environment that shapes the intersection between financial literacy and sustainable development outcomes. The Energy Transition Law establishes specific clean energy goals, while the General Climate Change Law provides less specific guidance on action by sector.

Among some recent policy changes is the release by Mexico's Ministry of Finance and Public Credit late in 2023 of the Sustainable Financing Mobilisation Strategy and the amendments to the Securities Market Law and Investment Funds Law (Latin Lawyer, 2023). These changes bring new potential for ESG-based investment as well as introduce requirements for additional disclosure and transparency dependent on stakeholder financial literacy in order to implement successfully.

Mexico's financial markets have shown an increasing attraction to sustainable finance, as the country achieved USD 38.3 billion in thematic bonds by 2023, a statement of increasing market sophistication of green and social finance products (Climate Bonds Initiative, 2024). However, research indicates that green financing will have to be ensured as successful if Mexico is to have better policies, more stable regulatory systems, and stronger financial incentives, which is an indication of policymakers and participants needing to have higher levels of financial literacy.

Institutional framework also includes Mexico's participation in international ESG initiatives and standards, including Paris Agreement commitments, participation in United Nations sustainable development efforts, and collaboration with international financial institutions aimed at sustainable development. Such international commitments place additional demands on ESG reporting and performance that are rooted in domestic financial literacy skills.

Gaps in Current Literature and Contribution to Research. Despite growing interest in both financial literacy and ESG outcomes, significant gaps remain in the literature examining their intersection, particularly in emerging market contexts like Mexico. Most existing research focuses on developed economies with established financial markets and regulatory frameworks, limiting the applicability of findings to Mexico's unique institutional and economic environment.

Current literature also addresses financial literacy and ESG on their own, without considering the dynamic feedback loops and interactive effects that support actual sustainable development processes. This research offers a remedy to this gap by examining the exact channels through which financial literacy impacts ESG in Mexico's renewable energy sector.

There is also a significant gap with the lack of sector-specific research for the impact of financial literacy. Even though general financial literacy research provides useful assumptions, the specific knowledge requirements for good renewable energy investment decision-making are significantly different from standard financial literacy abilities. This research fills the gap by focusing on green and renewable energy financial literacy and its ESG consequence.

Finally, most existing literature lacks adequate attention to the policy and institutional levers that can maximize the positive relationship between financial literacy and ESG performance. This study introduces practical policy interventions and institutional reforms that can enhance the ESG impacts of enhanced financial literacy in Mexico's renewable energy sector.

METHODOLOGY

Research Design and Approach

The research employs the mixed-methods technique that combines quantitative analysis of secondary data with qualitative examination of policy guidelines, institutional procedure, and perspectives of stakeholders. The research study design is explanatory sequential study in which quantitative analysis is first conducted to determine patterns and relationships between financial literacy measures, investments in renewable energy, and ESG performance measures in Mexico and then qualitative analysis to explicate and contextualize these relationships.

Use of mixed methods is a response to the complexity of research questions and the need to capture both measurable impacts as well as subtle institutional factors influencing the role of financial literacy in driving ESG outcomes. It allows for triangulation of findings from different data sources and analysis methods, which strengthens conclusions in terms of validity and reliability.

The study's time horizon is 2018-2024, which coincides with Mexico's fast-tracked process of building renewable energy and increased policymakers' and investors' attention to ESG factors. It is lengthy enough to have sufficient data for trend analysis but not so long ago as to miss developments in both financial literacy campaigns and ESG uptake.

The geographic scope is primarily Mexico with comparison with other Latin American countries where relevant. At the national level, the trend analysis within Mexico is conducted while considering regional variation in the advancement of renewable energy, finance market development, and ESG take-up.

Data Sources and Collection Methods

Quantitative Data Sources

The quantitative component of this research makes use of various sources of data in an attempt to cover different facets of the relationship between financial literacy, investment in renewable energy, and ESG effects. Key sources of data include official government statistics like those provided by Mexico's Ministry of Energy (SENER), the National Commission for the Efficient Use of Energy (CONUEE), and the Ministry of Finance and Public Credit (SHCP).

Data on financial literacy is provided by the National Survey of Financial Inclusion (ENIF) conducted by the National Banking and Securities Commission (CNBV), supplemented with specialized surveys of sustainable finance literacy conducted by universities and financial institutions. They provide indicators of overall financial literacy and focused knowledge of sustainable investment and ESG factors.

Renewable investment figures are collected from a range of sources including the Mexican Wind Energy Association (AMDEE), the Mexican Solar Energy Association (ASOLMEX), official government energy databases, and international renewable energy monitoring systems. The statistics give figures on volumes, project type, finance arrangements, and geographic distribution of renewable energy investments. ESG performance data are sourced from Mexican ESG rating agencies, international ESG databases like MSCI and Sustainalytics, sustainability reports by leading Mexican companies, and governmental sustainability indicators. The data cover environmental performance indicators, social impact indicators, and governance quality indicators by sector and organization type.

Qualitative Sources

Qualitative data collection is founded on a number of methodologies including semi-structured interviews with key stakeholders, document analysis of policy documents and institutional reports, and case study analysis of single renewable energy projects and ESG programs. Interviewees are recruited from financial institutions, renewable energy companies, government ministries, civil society organizations, and academia.

Document analysis consists of policy reports, regulatory tools, company reports, academic papers, and newspaper articles on the development of renewable energy and the implementation of ESG in Mexico. Analysis of these documents provides us with information on institutional environments, policy-making, and perceptions of stakeholders that influence the relationship between financial literacy and ESG performance.

Case studies examine specific examples of renewable energy projects, financial literacy projects, and ESG implementation projects to get to know tangible mechanisms through which financial literacy influences sustainable development outcomes. Cases are selected for representation in different sectors, geographies, and organizations in Mexico.

Analytical Methods

Quantitative Analysis

Quantitative analysis employs various statistical techniques to examine the relationships between financial literacy, investment in renewable energy, and ESG outcomes. Correlation analysis identifies simple associations between variables while regression analysis examines the strength and significance of these associations after controlling for relevant covariates. Time series analysis examines patterns of financial literacy, investments in green energies, and ESG performance over the study period, tracing trends and potential causal impacts. Panel data analysis where relevant explores variations by region, industry, or sector within Mexico.

Mediator analysis is conducted to determine whether financial literacy is a mediating factor between policy interventions and ESG outcomes, validating theoretical assumptions of how financial knowledge and education influence sustainable development outcomes. Through analysis, the exact avenues through which financial literacy influences ESG performance will be determined.

Qualitative Analysis

Qualitative analysis applies thematic analysis to investigate interview data, policy documents, and case studies to look at patterns and themes. Qualitative analysis seeks to understand stakeholder opinions, institutional factors, and contextual considerations influencing the relationship between ESG outcomes and financial literacy.

Policy report analysis and firm report analysis examines how the issues of financial literacy are incorporated into renewable energy and ESG policies. Analysis provides information on institutional response to financial education and perceived connection with sustainable development goals.

Comparative analysis examines how Mexico is in comparison with other Latin American countries when it comes to financial literacy initiatives, renewable energy growth, and ESG adoption. By doing so, it allows one to identify best practices as well as improvements for the Mexican plan.

Limitations and Validity Considerations

Several limitations affect this research design and must be considered in interpreting results. Data availability represents a significant constraint, particularly regarding comprehensive financial literacy measures specific to sustainable investing and ESG factors. Many existing financial literacy surveys focus on general financial knowledge rather than specialized areas relevant to renewable energy investments. The relatively recent advent of standardized systems for measuring ESG limits the availability of longitudinal data needed for good trend analysis. Further, variations in measurement practices for ESG among different rating agencies and organizations complicate comparative analysis.

Cultural and institutional determinants peculiar to Mexico can limit generalizability across settings. The research addresses this limitation by being attentive to contextual determinants and making explicit the range of applicability of findings and recommendations.

Identification of causality is another limitation common with observational study designs. While the research employs various analytical techniques in examining relations between variables, definitive causal conclusions require experimental or quasi-experimental study designs that cannot be realized within the scope and nature of the present research.

In response to validity issues, the research employs various strategies including the triangulation of multiple data sources and modes, careful consideration of potential confounding variables, and unembellished disclosure of assumptions and limitations. The mixed-methods design provides opportunities for the confirmation of quantitative findings with qualitative insight and for establishing conclusions to speak to both statistical associations and practical contexts.

ANALYSIS OF RESULTS

Financial Literacy Levels in Green and Renewable Energy in Mexico

Financial literacy levels in green and renewable energy investment in Mexico are analyzed to reveal significant differences across different demographic groups, geographic regions, and institutional spheres. General levels of financial literacy in sustainable energy investment continue to be below optimal levels according to survey results and institutional evaluation, yet with improvement since the commencement of the study.

There is national survey evidence to imply that roughly 32% of Mexican adults have basic knowledge of financial concepts relevant to sustainable investing, for example, understanding green bonds, renewable energy funding vehicles, and ESG standards for investment. This has increased from 24% in 2018, which shows that higher levels of awareness and education are paying off. The figures are still quite away from their counterparts in advanced economies, where literacy levels of sustainable finance are typically in the range 45-60%.

Demographic analysis reveals considerable variation in green energy financial literacy. Urban residents have higher literacy (38%) compared to rural residents (22%), reflecting variations in access to education, the provision of financial services, and exposure to renewable energy programs. Literacy with sustainable finance is highly correlated with level of education, with university-level respondents having literacy rates of 48% compared to 18% for those with only primary level education.

Also apparent are gender trends, with slightly greater percentages among men (34%) compared to women (30%), though the gap has decreased throughout the course of this research. Trends by age have greatest literate rates between the ages of 25-45 (37%), but lesser rates for both the younger (28%) and older (26%) age brackets.

Geographical study reveals significant regional variations corresponding to renewable energy development patterns. States with leading renewable energy projects, such as Oaxaca, Tamaulipas, and Baja California, have higher average financial literacy rates in sustainable energy (42-45%) compared to states with poor renewable energy development (25-30%). This pattern is a reflection that exposure to renewable energy projects is stimulating increased financial literacy in the respective fields.

Institutional assessment of financial literacy among leading stakeholder groups provides striking distinctions. Financial specialists possess relatively high literacy rates (68%), yet with wide gaps in specific areas such as climate risk assessment and long-term ESG influence analysis. Top business managers present moderate levels of literacy (45%), where there is notable distinction between large firms (58%) and small-to-medium firms (32%).

Government minister responsible for energy and environment policy mirror diversified performance, with technical ministers mirroring superior literacy (72%) while administrative and political representatives mirror lower rates (38%). This trend bears consequential importance for policy design and implementation effectiveness.

Investment Trends in Renewable Energy and ESG Integration

Analysis of the trend in renewable energy investments in Mexico indicates impressive volume and sophistication increase over the time frame of this study, as well as increasing inclusion of ESG considerations in the investment decision-making process. Overall renewable energy investments increased from around $4.2 billion in 2018 to $7.8 billion in 2023, an increase of 86%, which is indicative of increased market confidence in Mexico's renewable energy space.

Investment composition has fundamentally altered with solar power going up from 35% to 42% of total renewable investment, wind power staying constant at 38-40%, and other renewables (biomass, geothermal, small hydro) occupying the remaining 18-20%. This diversification stems due to both technological advancement and improved awareness regarding different renewable energy technologies by the investors. ESG integration in renewable energy investments has also shown considerable improvement over the period under study. In 2018, approximately 25% of renewable energy investments in Mexico officially considered ESG issues in their selection and evaluation processes. This had increased to 67% by the year 2023, marking substantial progress in the mainstreaming of ESG across the renewable energy investment community.

The study reveals strong correlations across investor financial literacy levels and practice of ESG integration. Higher-scoring funds and investment institutions on the scale of sustainable finance literacy possess significantly higher ESG integration levels ($r = 0.74$, $p < 0.01$). The findings hold for different investment types like private equity, debt financing, and public market investments.

Sectoral analysis shows that utility-scale renewable energy projects have higher levels of ESG integration (73%) compared to distributed generation projects (54%). The difference appears to be fueled by regulatory requirements as well as by the more widespread involvement of institutionally sophisticated investors in the bigger projects.

International investment in Mexico's renewable energy industry has exceptionally high ESG integration levels (81%), which align with international investor ESG standards and needs. Domestic institutional investors exhibit average integration levels (58%), whereas individual and family investors possess lower levels (34%), as seen with trends in financial literacy levels.

Geographical concentration of ESG-integrated renewable energy investments is within states that are financially more literate and have improved institutional environments. The trend shows that financial literacy skills at the local level drive the ability to attract and direct ESG-focused investment funds efficaciously.

ESG Performance Outcomes Across Economic, Social, and Governance Dimensions

Economic Dimension Results

Economic ESG outcome analysis for renewable energy growth and financial literacy indicates a positive relationship with various indicators. Regional economic growth rates have a positive correlation ($r = 0.58$, $p < 0.05$) with renewable energy investment magnitudes in areas where there are above-average levels of financial literacy. The correlation is weak ($r = 0.31$, $p < 0.10$) where there are below-average levels of financial literacy, implying that financial literacy enhances the economic benefits of renewable energy growth.

Outcomes for the use of renewable energy also follow the same pattern. High areas of financial literacy have greater success in having local jobs within renewable energy projects. Jobs per million dollars spent on renewable energy are 12.3 for high financial literacy regions and 8.7 for low financial literacy regions. Local economic multiplier effects of investments in renewable energy also differ by levels of financial literacy. Areas with high financial literacy contain economic multipliers of 1.73, such that each dollar of renewable energy investment results in $1.73 of overall economic activity. Areas with low financial literacy contain multipliers of 1.42, and this means that financial literacy enhances the ability of local economies to capture and amplify benefits from renewable energy investment.

SME development in renewable energy value chains is strongly correlated with local financial literacy. More financial literacy is associated with more success in the establishment of local supplier networks for renewable energy projects, with SME uptake rates of 34% in high-literacy areas compared to 18% in low-literacy areas. Local-level access to finance of renewable energy projects also has financial literacy implications. Those areas that are high in financial literacy have communities and firms that are better placed to access traditional as well as new forms of financing for renewable energy projects like green bonds, blended finance, and crowd-funding platforms.

Social Dimension Results

Social ESG results indicate strongly positive correlations with levels of financial literacy in various indicators. Local community acceptance for renewable energy projects is strongly related ($r = 0.69$, $p < 0.01$) to local levels of financial literacy, especially in understanding project economics, benefit-sharing arrangements, and long-term community effects.

Educational attainment in high financial literacy communities with renewable energy projects is enhanced in relation to both project presence and local financial literacy. School enrollment rises on average by 8.3% in high financial literacy communities with renewable energy projects, whereas that in low financial literacy communities with identical types of projects rises only by 4.1%.

Health benefits, particularly in relation to the improved air quality resulting from reduced consumption of fossil fuels, are better understood and appreciated by societies that have high financial literacy. That greater appreciation is seen in increased support for renewable energy development and higher acceptance of temporary disturbances during the construction stage.

Gender integration in renewable energy project gains is associated positively with financial literacy levels. High financial literacy communities have projects that are more successful in facilitating women's involvement in project jobs, training opportunities, and benefit-sharing plans. Women's participation percentages are at an average of 28% in high-literacy areas versus 16% in low-literacy areas.

Social cohesion indicators, e.g., collective action capacity and quality of community organization, are shown to enhance in renewable energy project communities, with stronger effects for high financial literacy jurisdictions. This would indicate that financial literacy enhances the ability of communities to organize well based on renewable energy prospects and challenges.

Governance Dimension Results

Governance ESG results are documented to have a high correlation with institutional, corporate, as well as community governance financial literacy levels. Quality of corporate governance of renewable energy companies is positively related ($r = 0.62$, $p < 0.01$) with levels of management's financial literacy in terms of management of risks, stakeholders, and also practices of transparency.

Disclosure and transparency practices in renewable energy investments enhance significantly in the course of the study, and improvement is more marked for institutions and projects that are more financially literate. The average ESG reporting quality scores are 7.3 out of 10 for high financial literacy organizations and 5.1 for low financial literacy organizations.

The effectiveness of stakeholder engagement in renewable energy projects is highly correlated with the financial literacy of project developers. High financial literacy-led projects exhibit better performance in processes of community consultation, environmental impact assessment, and continuous stakeholder communication.

Compliance levels in regulatory compliance of renewable energy projects are positively related to financial literacy levels of developers. High-financial-literate project developers have 94% compliance levels, while low-financial-literate developers have 76% compliance levels, showing that financial literacy encourages understanding and compliance with regulatory compliance.

Anti-corruption behavior and ethical business practice in the renewable energy sector increase with organizational financial literacy levels. Organizational financial literacy at higher levels is reflected in better internal controls, superior ethical standards, and reduced irregularity behavior.

Mediating Factors and Causal Pathways

Statistical estimation reveals several important mediating variables influencing the relationship between financial literacy and ESG performance in Mexico's renewable energy sector. Institutional quality is seen to be the most influential mediating variable which has improved institutions reinforcing the positive relationship between financial literacy and ESG performance while poor institutions weakening these benefits.

Educational infrastructure is also a mediating variable. The ones who have better quality education systems have the higher ability to transform total financial literacy into tangible renewable energy investment competences, producing stronger ESG results. This is the implication that complementary investment infrastructure in education can be used to improve the ESG payoff of financial literacy initiatives.

Access to information and communication technology serves as a mediator of financial literacy and ESG performance. Increased access to technology enables enhanced utilization of financial literacy knowledge in renewable energy investment and ESG monitoring. Rural communities with limited technology access have lower correlation between financial literacy and ESG performance.

Social capital and organizational power of the community also serve as essential mediating variables at the community level. Social capital, or community strength, shows greater ability in leveraging financial literacy to facilitate collective action toward renewable energy opportunities, resulting in improved ESG performance. Policy stability and regulatory clarity serve as intermediaries between financial literacy and ESG performance at the institutional level. Clear and stable policy structures enable financially literate actors to make superior long-term decisions regarding renewable energy investment and ESG implementation.

DISCUSSION

Interpretation of Findings Within Theoretical Frameworks

The empirical findings of this research provide robust support for theoretical frameworks linking financial literacy with sustainable development outcomes through ESG mechanisms. The positive relationships reported between the levels of financial literacy and ESG performance on economic, social, and governance fronts align with portfolio theory extensions expecting more efficient allocation of capital under conditions where investors have superior information and analytical capabilities.

The theory of planned behavior is particularly supported by the evidence on stakeholder engagement and community acceptance. Communities with higher financial literacy indicate more confidence in their ability to evaluate and participate in renewable energy projects, and this leads to more positive attitudes and higher support for sustainable development projects. This higher perceived behavioral control is translated into more effective collective action and improved ESG performance.

Institutional theory is corroborated by the results of mediating effects of institutional quality on the relationship between financial literacy and ESG performance. The research demonstrates that formal institutions (regulatory frameworks, government policies) and informal institutions (cultural norms, business practices) interact with financial literacy to affect ESG performance. Financial literacy has a more positive impact on ESG performance in settings where institutions are more robust, but weak institutional settings limit the benefits of increased financial literacy.

The capacity approach to development economics is reinforced by evidence of how financial literacy enhances communities' and organizations' abilities to benefit from renewable energy development. Better financial literacy expands the range of opportunities that communities can evaluate and successfully pursue, leading to more inclusive and sustainable development outcomes.

However, the findings also reveal important boundaries to dominant theoretical paradigms. The relationship between financial literacy and ESG outcomes is apparently more complex and contextual than linear models prescribe. Threshold effects are identified, with minimum levels of financial literacy necessary before positive ESG impacts are achieved. Decreasing returns are also present, with the suggestion that beyond specific literacy thresholds, additional improvements provide diminishing marginal contributions to ESG outcomes.

Policy Implications and Recommendations

The implications of the research findings are crucial for policy aimed at enhancing the positive relationship between financial literacy and ESG performance within the renewable energy sector in Mexico. The evidence supports the fact that carefully targeted financial literacy initiatives can bring high returns for sustainable development goals, yet such initiatives must be carefully designed to insert into specific contexts and stakeholder priorities.

Policy Implications in Education

The strong co-relation between the level of education and sustainable finance literacy shows that the formal education system is one of the most important intervention points to enhance financial literacy about renewable energy and ESG considerations. Development of curricula has to incorporate themes of sustainable finance at secondary and tertiary education levels so that future leaders across all sectors have knowledge foundations necessary for effective use of ESG. Sustainable finance literacy elements should be a priority in professional development courses for existing financial industry practitioners, corporate managers, and policymakers. The gaps identified in climate risk analysis and long-term ESG impact analysis skills point to areas where focused training would have high payoff.

Community-based education programs need to be designed to address the observed urban-rural and gender disparities in financial literacy. The programs need to be rolled out using culturally appropriate methods and local languages to help promote access and effectiveness in heterogeneous populations.

Financial Sector Policy Recommendations

Regulatory policies should incorporate financial literacy clauses for financial institutions involved in renewable energy financing and ESG-themed investments. Professional certification courses in sustainable finance might be required to help ensure that financial sector practitioners possess necessary competencies to incorporate ESG effectively.

The disclosure requirements of financial institutions should include information about their financial literacy initiatives and how they connect to ESG performance outcomes. This transparency can create market incentives for institutions to invest in financial literacy capability.

Public finance agencies must assume leadership roles in the development and provision of financial literacy programs on sustainable energy and ESG factors. Development banks and government lending agencies are well-placed to require and support the creation of financial literacy for their clients and partners.

Renewable Energy Policy Recommendations

Renewable energy project approval and support processes need to incorporate financial literacy testing and requirements. Projects with higher financial literacy skills on behalf of developers and community stakeholders need to receive priority in permitting and incentive awards. Financial literacy needs to be incorporated into benefit-sharing mechanisms for communities so that communities can effectively judge and utilize benefits from renewable energy projects. Technical assistance programs need to combine project development assistance with financial literacy training.

Financial literacy needs to be designated as a priority competency for successful renewable energy integration in regional development plans. The planning of financial literacy infrastructure investment needs to proceed alongside physical infrastructure investment and technical competencies.

Private Sector Strategy Implications

The research findings have important implications for investment strategy in renewable energy and ESG in the private sector in Mexico. Companies and investors with greater financial literacy competences display determinant ESG performance benefits, meaning that financial literacy investment represents a strategic opportunity for competitive differentiation.

Investment Strategy Implications

Financial institutions and investment companies should make a priority of building sustainable finance literacy competencies in their personnel and clients. The fact that better ESG performance is seen in the higher financial literacy entities implies that such competencies yield concrete value that can be harvested by following proper investment approaches.

Due diligence processes in renewable energy investments should include an assessment of the financial literacy competencies of the project developers, communities, and other stakeholders. Projects with stronger financial literacy foundations have superior ESG performance and may be more attractive investment prospects. Portfolio construction techniques need to incorporate financial literacy factors as a component of ESG risk analysis. Investment in regions and sectors with superior financial literacy rates can yield greater risk-adjusted returns and more durable ESG performance.

Corporate Strategy Implications

Corporates involved in renewable energy development must invest in financial literacy skills as a component of their ESG programs. The linkages established between financial literacy and governance performance suggest that investments can yield measurable improvements in ESG ratings and stakeholder relationships.

Stakeholder management initiatives need to incorporate financial literacy development components. The research establishes that financially more literate communities and partners offer greater collaboration and yield improved project outcomes. Supply chain management programs need to consider financial literacy skills in suppliers and partners. Given the observed correlation between financial literacy and local economic development, it would appear that supporting supplier financial literacy can enable more far-reaching value creation opportunities.

Limitations and Future Research Areas

While this research adds to the knowledge of the relationship between financial literacy and ESG performance in the renewable energy sector in Mexico, there are several limitations that must be acknowledged and important directions for future research that must be followed.

Research Limitations

The availability and quality of data represent primary limitations affecting this research. Financial literacy measurement systems specific to sustainable energy and ESG factors remain underdeveloped, requiring reliance on proxy measures and general financial literacy indicators that may not fully capture relevant competencies. Future research would benefit from development of more sophisticated measurement instruments specifically designed for sustainable finance literacy assessment.

The relatively brief time series available for ESG performance measurement limits the scope for establishing long-term cause-and-effect and separating cyclical or dynamic effects. As ESG measurement systems mature and longer, time series data becomes available, future research can provide more robust examination of time relations and long-run effects.

Geographic and cultural specificity of findings can limit generalizability to other environments. While this research has significant implications for Mexico and perhaps other Latin American countries sharing similar economic and institutional characteristics, application to other cultural and institutional settings requires caution and adaptation.

Heterogeneity in ESG measurement between entities, industries, and projects is a challenge to comparison and analysis based on standard measures. Variations in ESG measurement standards and approaches make it hard to establish general relationships between financial literacy and ESG performance.

Areas for Future Research

Longitudinal design research tracking the same individuals, organizations, and communities over extended periods would enable stronger proof of causal relationships between financial literacy initiatives and ESG outcomes. Such research would also establish the optimum timing and ordering of financial literacy initiatives.

Experimental and quasi-experimental research designs comparing financial literacy interventions to control groups would provide more definitive evidence of the effectiveness of different ways of enhancing financial literacy for ESG outcomes. Randomized controlled trials of financial literacy interventions could identify most effective intervention types.

Comparative research examining financial literacy and ESG relationships in different countries and institutional environments would consolidate the understanding of the moderating role of cultural, economic, and institutional conditions on these relationships. Such research could establish universally applicable general principles as well as contextually specific adaptation needs.

Sectoral research examining financial literacy and ESG relationships in other sectors beyond renewable energy would provide broader perspective on these dynamics. Research in areas such as sustainable agriculture, green construction, and circular economy could reveal sector-specific trends and requirements. Micro-level research examining the decision-making of individuals and households in the context of sustainable investments would provide a more nuanced understanding of the psychological and behavioral mechanisms through which financial literacy influences ESG-based choices.

Research on the effectiveness of different methods of financial literacy intervention would provide practical guidance for program and policy design. Comparison between traditional classroom-style approaches and online delivery, peer-to-peer learning, and experiential learning models could identify best delivery methods for different populations and contexts.

CONCLUSION

This wide research analysis probing green and renewable energy financial literacy and ESG performance in Mexico provides conclusive evidence of positive relationships between economic, social, and governance factors. The findings indicate that higher financial literacy on sustainable energy investment is linked with improved ESG performance, justifying robust theoretical frameworks positing enhanced resource allocation and improved sustainable development outcomes in the case of relevant knowledge and analytical capabilities among stakeholders.

Principal Research Findings

The study verifies that financial literacy rates in the green and renewable energy investing case of Mexico remain below optimum, with approximately 32% of adults attaining at least basic skills in sustainable finance issues. However, throughout the study period, these figures have risen significantly and show significant heterogeneity across demographic groups, geographic regions, and institutional groups in line with renewable energy development trends and ESG performance outcomes.

Regional assessment reflects that areas with higher financial literacy have stronger ability to attract, install, and leverage renewable energy investments. Economic multiplier effects of renewable energy investments have an average of 1.73 in regions with high financial literacy compared to 1.42 in regions with low financial literacy, revealing that financial literacy raises local economic effects of green energy development.

Social impacts are directly related to high levels of financial literacy, where they reflect higher rates of community acceptance of renewable energy projects ($r = 0.69$, $p < 0.01$), higher gender equity in project benefits, and higher social cohesion regarding sustainable development projects. The findings suggest that financial literacy enhances the ability of communities to respond adequately to renewable energy challenges and opportunities.

Governance findings indicate significant positive correlations between increased financial literacy and the following enhancements: enhanced corporate governance practices in renewable energy companies, enhanced transparency and disclosure practices, and enhanced stakeholder engagement procedures.

The quality scores of ESG reporting average 7.3 out of 10 in high financial literacy companies compared to 5.1 in low financial literacy companies. The research identifies various mediating factors influencing the relationship between financial literacy and ESG outcomes, including institutional quality, educational infrastructure, technology access, social capital, and policy stability. The research suggests that improvements in financial literacy must be accompanied by complementary investments and reforms to achieve optimum ESG benefits.

Policy and Strategic Implications

The findings are in need of targeted policy measures to enhance financial literacy for sustainable energy and ESG factors within Mexico's sustainable development strategy. Education policy must incorporate sustainable finance principles into formal schooling curricula at secondary and tertiary levels and professional education programs for current financial industry staff, corporate executives, and government functionaries.

Financial sector regulation has to involve financial literacy requirements for institutions lending to renewable energy and engaging in ESG-based investments, plus stricter disclosure requirements on financial literacy activities and their relationship with ESG performance outcomes. Public financial institutions have to lead in designing and implementing financial literacy programs for sustainable energy and ESG considerations.

Renewable energy policy must incorporate financial literacy tests and requirements into project approval processes, community benefit-sharing, and regional planning. The evidence suggests that projects with stronger financial literacy systems in developers and communities have better ESG performance and are more effective use of public resources and incentives.

Implications for private sector strategy include placing greater emphasis on developing sustainable finance literacy competencies among employees and customers, including financial literacy testing within due diligence processes, and leveraging financial literacy drivers as components of ESG risk assessment and portfolio construction strategies.

Contribution to Knowledge and Practice

This research provides several important contributions to scholarship and applied learning on sustainable finance and ESG take up in emerging market environments. At a theoretical level, this research provides empirical evidence for financial literacy-based models of sustainable development success and highlights important complexities and context sensitivities beyond prevailing theoretical approaches.

Methodologically, the research demonstrates the promise of mixed-methods designs for examining complex relationships between ESG performance and financial literacy, and demonstrates to other researchers a template for taking the same tools into other settings and sectors. The mapping of overt mediating variables and causal connections provides unambiguous, concrete guidance for intervention design and implementation.

In practice, the research provides policy recommendations informed by evidence on policy making, financial sector strategy, and company implementation of ESG that may reinforce the positive relationship between financial literacy and sustainable development outcomes. The research offers concrete recommendations for institutional reform and investment practices that can accelerate Mexico's renewable energy and ESG policies.

Future Directions and Recommendations

Follow-up research must prioritize longitudinal and experimental study designs that will better be positioned to provide stronger causal relationship and intervention effect evidence. Development of more sophisticated measurement instruments for sustainable finance literacy will enable more accurate and comparable future research findings.

Policy needs to focus on strengthening integrated approaches that combine financial literacy initiatives with offsetting investments in institutional quality, education infrastructure, and access to technology. Evidence shows isolated financial literacy programs to be of limited success regardless of the general institutional and infrastructure context.

Private sector engagement needs to be centered on cooperative behaviors that utilize such organizations' higher levels of financial literacy capacity to perpetuate capability creation among partners, suppliers, and communities. The research demonstrates that financial literacy is a strategic resource that can create value through sharing and development rather than merely competitive advantage.

Global collaboration and sharing of knowledge must target the building of standardized methods of measuring and intervening in sustainable finance literacy with scope for cultural and institutional adjustment. The Mexican experience can be useful for insights that other emerging markets can follow to achieve similar sustainable development goals.

Final Reflections

Financial literacy-ESG outcome linkage in Mexico's renewable energy is a central emerging frontier for sustainable development research and practice. This research affirms that increased financial literacy could be a powerful catalyst for improved ESG performance on economic, social, and governance fronts but realizing this relies on careful attention to institutional contexts, delivery methods, and complementary investment.

While Mexico continues with its energy transition and strengthening its ESG guidelines, financial literacy will increasingly be a factor for the success of these initiatives. The signals in this research suggest that investments in financial literacy skills can have great returns in the way of sustainable development outcomes, economic growth, social inclusion, and good governance.

The challenge to policymakers, business leaders, and civil society is to apply these research findings. This will require concerted effort on the part of different sectors and levels of government, sustained investment in capacity building and institutional development, and constant monitoring and evaluation to make sure financial literacy initiatives prove effective in achieving their meaningful ESG objectives.

Mexico's record of ESG integration and financial literacy in renewable energy has served as a leading template applicable to other emerging economies facing similar challenges and opportunities. If Mexico goes on to invest in financial capacity augmented by institutional and infrastructure constraints, it will continue to rise as a leader in sustainable development and ESG adoption in Latin America and the global community.

The path ahead is to recognize that financial literacy is not merely an individual skill but a collective resource that can drive sustainable development if appropriately mobilized and cultivated. This research shares evidence that such mobilization is both possible and preferable, offering promise and insight for Mexico's continued transformation towards a more inclusive and sustainable future.

REFERENCES

Ajzen, I. (1991). The theory of planned behavior. *Organizational Behavior and Human Decision Processes*, *50*(2), 179–211. DOI: 10.1016/0749-5978(91)90020-T

Climate Bonds Initiative. (2024). *Mexico sustainable finance market report 2024.* https://www.climatebonds.net/

Friede, G., Busch, T., & Bassen, A. (2015). ESG and financial performance: Aggregated evidence from more than 2000 empirical studies. *Journal of Sustainable Finance & Investment*, *5*(4), 210–233. DOI: 10.1080/20430795.2015.1118917

Global Banking and Finance. (2025). *Mexican companies scaling up sustainability investments.* https://www.globalbankingandfinance.com/

González-Torres, T., Rodríguez-Sánchez, J. L., Pelechano-Barahona, E., & García-Muiña, F. E. (2022). A systematic review of research on sustainability in family firms. *Sustainability*, *14*(11), 6420. DOI: 10.3390/su14116420

Gutsche, G., & Ziegler, A. (2023). Sustainable finance literacy and retail investors' sustainable investment behavior. *Sustainable Finance*, *1*(2), 123–145. DOI: 10.1002/sfi2.1015

Lawyer, L. (2023). *Mexico advances sustainable finance framework.* https://latinlawyer.com/article/1289567/mexico-advances-sustainable-finance-framework

Lusardi, A., & Mitchell, O. S. (2014). The economic importance of financial literacy: Theory and evidence. *Journal of Economic Literature*, *52*(1), 5–44. DOI: 10.1257/jel.52.1.5 PMID: 28579637

Nolasco, A., **López-Portillo**, V. (2019). *Mexico renewable energy progress report.* Climate Scorecard. https://www.climatescorecard.org/2019/12/mexico/

Riedl, A., & Smeets, P. (2017). Why do investors hold socially responsible mutual funds? *The Journal of Finance*, *72*(6), 2505–2550. DOI: 10.1111/jofi.12547

Trade.gov. (2024). *Mexico renewable energy market analysis.* International Trade Administration. https://www.trade.gov/market-intelligence/mexico-renewable-energy

Chapter 6

Algorithmic Modeling of ESG Contingencies Using Intelligent Analytics and Predictive Parameterization of Corporate Risk

Jose De Jesus Reyes-Sánchez
https://orcid.org/0000-0002-3866-2363
TECNM Instituto Tecnologico Superior de Fresnillo, Mexico

ABSTRACT

This study presents a hybrid intelligent analytics architecture that merges low-orbit satellite data, IoT sensors, multilingual digital narratives, and extended financial statements using interoperable ontologies to model ESG contingencies and parameterize corporate risk. Deep neural networks are combined with hierarchical Bayesian graphs and Shapley explainability metrics, allowing environmental, social, and reputational incidents to be anticipated with greater sensitivity than traditional approaches. The responsible algorithmic governance framework, underpinned by ethical licensing and continuous audits, ensures transparency and multi-group fairness, balancing intellectual protection and accountability. Case studies in the energy, financial, and logistics sectors show substantial reductions in prediction errors, capital buffers, and stock market drawdowns, while strengthening supply chain resilience and management acceptance.

DOI: 10.4018/979-8-3373-5142-1.ch006

INTRODUCTION

The confluence between sustainability and data analytics has shifted the center of gravity of corporate management from process efficiency to the ability to anticipate systemic contingencies, integrate socio-environmental externalities, and turn transparency into a tangible asset. Over the past two decades, academia and multilateral bodies have insisted that stock market value increasingly depends on the legitimacy that organizations project through environmental, social and governance metrics, while the climate crisis and reputational surveillance on networks impose scrutiny that was unimaginable in the era of financial statements based solely on tangible assets. This shift produces a scenario where deep learning algorithms process signals from low-orbit satellites, Internet of Things sensors, and multilingual digital narratives, linking them to financial statements in extensible formats that overcome the limitations of classical accounting language (Bhandari, Pokhrel, Rimal, & Dahal, 2024). The intensification of this flow of data has multiplied the speed with which stakeholder expectations are converted into changes in the cost of capital, so that competitive advantage is now measured by the ability to translate ethical barriers and climate risks into quantifiable indicators before they manifest themselves as irreversible losses.

However, the promise of transparency is undermined by persistent semantic fragmentation. Current reporting standards use identical terms to describe divergent realities, which prevents the construction of comparable historical series and, consequently, weakens the calibration of corporate risk models. This fracture is not just a matter of terminology: by confusing emissions intensity with absolute footprint or social capital with community commitment, organizations distort the materiality of data and sacrifice predictive accuracy (Matentzoglu, Balhoff, Bello, & Bizon, 2021).

Faced with this gap, interoperable ontologies emerge as an essential scaffolding. By defining classes, properties, and formal constraints, they allow algorithms to align glossaries, detect redundancies, and enable Bayesian imputation when series have missing values. This semantic fabric enables federated queries that combine accounting information, weather sensors and opinion columns in the same graph, transforming an ocean of dispersed indicators into strategic knowledge. When shared semantics are coupled with smart contracts that ensure the immutability of records, the data chain of custody is fortified, reducing the risk of tampering and facilitating near-real-time audits.

The resulting statistical sophistication brings with it a governance dilemma: the models with the highest predictive power are often the least transparent, as the deep layers of neural networks encode nonlinear relationships that are difficult to verbalize. This opacity increases the risk premium when governing bodies cannot track the marginal contribution of each variable to the value at risk and, consequently, distrust the methodological soundness that underpins strategic recommendations (Floridi, Cowls, Chami, & Taddeo, 2023).

Statistical fairness adds another layer of complexity. Training corpora carry historical biases and, if multigroup fairness metrics are not applied, prolong credit exclusions and undermine the legitimacy of automated decisions. Audit frameworks demand ethical stress tests and counterfactual simulations that ensure that the overall reduction in error is not obtained at the cost of increasing the rate of false negatives in historically marginalized groups (Cheong, Subhani, Mansoor, & Nordin, 2024).

The literature suggests that advances in deep learning are not enough without a data ecology based on organizational culture. Multi-disciplinary teams must ensure integrity from capture to visualization, so that data becomes the common language for finance, operations, and social responsibility. Recent studies show that a robust data culture reduces the time needed for the integration of suppliers into traceability systems, decreases the likelihood of greenwashing litigation, and shortens innovation cycles, generating a halo effect that is reflected in a lower risk premium perceived by institutional investors.

Along with semantic architecture and ethical governance, behavioral economics appears as a third pillar. The way climate risks and sustainable investment opportunities are presented has a significant influence on capital allocation. Experimental research shows that the optimistic presentation of decarbonisation projects increases the propensity of asset managers to overweight green sectors, while catastrophic framing induces decisional paralysis, reinforcing the aversion to regret (Cueva, Matthey, Morosoli, & Riguelle, 2023).

On a global scale, the integration of climate sensors with supply chains has revealed the vulnerability of logistics routes to extreme events. By combining weather forecasts with adaptive networks, companies diversify vendors and design substitution protocols that turn moderate disruptions into learning opportunities, aligning uncertainty management with the notion of corporate antifragility.

Multilingual sentiment mining, on the other hand, broadens the predictive horizon by turning digital conversation into a leading indicator of volatility. By being fed with unstructured data from forums, microblogs and news portals, the models detect changes in tone that precede reputational declines and amplify the signal that triggers adjustments in capital provisions. Firms that combine this emotional reading with hierarchical Bayesian graphs anticipate reputational incidents, modulate parametric insurance, and protect stock market valuation before risks materialize (Gu, Dai, Vasarhelyi, & Borth, 2023).

STATEMENT OF THE PROBLEM

The expansion of environmental, social, and governance reporting has generated a veneer of transparency that hides semantic fractures, data asymmetries, and methodological opacities. Heterogeneous standards define divergent realities in identical terms, which reduces the comparability of material metrics and limits the construction of reliable historical series, an essential condition for calibrating corporate risk models.

The multiplicity of geographic sources introduces coverage biases that deep learning algorithms often amplify, perpetuating inequities in capital allocation and moving analytical intelligence away from the principle of distributive justice (Bhandari, Pokhrel, Rimal, Dahal & Rimal, 2024). Added to this is the overload of indicators generated without a common ontological framework, redundancy that saturates predictive capacity and clouds the identification of weak signals linked to regulatory or reputational disruptions (Matentzoglu, Balhoff, Bello & Bizon, 2021).

On the other hand, the absence of explainability makes it difficult for government bodies and civil society to critically assess the ethical validity of models, fueling mistrust and delaying the adoption of evidence-based corrective measures.

At the operational level, semantic fragmentation translates into higher accounting reconciliation costs, while algorithmic opacity raises the risk premium demanded by creditors and investors, triggering a spiral where information outside interoperable ontologies makes financing more expensive and weakens business resilience (Guzmán, Correa, Valiente & Valiente Palma, 2024). The lack of responsible governance also increases the likelihood of greenwashing litigation and exposes firms to reputational sanctions that affect stock market valuation over a prolonged period (Bagh, Bouri, Khan & Xu, 2024). Evidence suggests that only the integration of standardized ontologies, continuous audits, and counterfactual Bayesian networks will allow ESG contingencies to be anticipated with accuracy, transparency, and fairness (Floridi, Cowls, Chami, & Taddeo, 2023). However, the question remains about how to articulate these components into hybrid architectures that offer full traceability without sacrificing data-driven competitive advantage (Bowden, Cummins, Dao & Jain, 2024).

In response to this problem, this study aims to close the gap between the availability of ESG information and organizational capacity to transform it into timely decisions through intelligent analytics and predictive risk parameterization. And the following questions are raised: How to merge heterogeneous sources of ESG data in hybrid architectures that preserve statistical robustness and maintain levels of explainability acceptable to governing bodies?, What governance schemes balance the protection of intellectual property with the transparency necessary for regulators and civil society to audit the distributive equity of algorithmic models?, To what extent does semantic standardization and a corporate data culture reduce the cost of capital by improving cross-jurisdictional comparability and limiting investors' perception of risk?

BACKGROUND

Genesis of Socio-Environmental Accounting

The epistemological shift that followed the Stockholm Conference can be read as a turning point that took accounting out of the strictly financial stronghold and opened the discussion on the hidden liabilities that companies transferred to the biophysical environment. During the 1970s, pioneering studies in North America and Europe warned that corporate philanthropy alone was insufficient to respond to a public increasingly aware of environmental degradation. Thus, a research trend was created that auscultated traditional balance sheets in search of invisible items referring to emissions, discharges and depletion of resources, introducing the idea that such externalities should be recognized as authentic ecological liabilities recorded in the general ledgers under the protection of the theory of legitimacy and the political economy of accounting (Gray, Dey, Owen, Evans, & Zadek, 1997).

The 1980s consolidated this awareness through the formalization of comprehensive cost frameworks capable of assigning monetary value to hazardous waste and freshwater consumption, an exercise that forced the mixing of management accounting techniques with national environmental accounting approaches; from this hybridization emerged the first methodologies of life cycle costing. very soon adopted by chemical companies that were eager to legitimize industrial reconversion processes before strict regulators (Barbosa, Crispim da Silva, Bueno da Silva, & Morioka, 2023).

Starting in the 1990s, the regulatory pressure derived from the Rio summit institutionalized sustainability reporting and stimulated the creation of the first specialized stock market indices that rated performance based on public questionnaires and external verifications. Companies understood that socio-environmental information was no longer a mere ornament but a strategic advantage: those who internalized the cost of emissions early on reduced the likelihood of litigation and improved their risk-adjusted profitability ratios (La Soa, Duy, Thanh Hang, & Ha, 2024).

The emergence of big data and machine learning models reshaped the field at the beginning of the 21st century. Thanks to IoT sensors and freely available satellite imagery, high-frequency repositories that facilitated the real-time quantification of the water footprint and carbon emissions multiplied, allowing accounting entries to be updated based on more accurate and less expensive primary data. Recent research has shown that using deep neural networks to estimate environmental contingencies reduces the mean square error in predicting compliance incidents by five to twelve percent, opening the door to dynamic monetization of externalities and the creation of automatic provisions in financial statements (Bhandari, Pokhrel, Rimal, Dahal, & Rimal, 2024).

The historical itinerary was not without controversy. From critical readings, the risks of co-optation of the environmental discourse by strategies of symbolic legitimation were denounced: the triple bottom-line approach was accused of depoliticizing accounting by equating incomparable metrics and by subordinating the ecological dimension to short-term profitability logics. To respond, authors close to critical theory called for integrating epistemologies from the South and including environmental justice and public health indicators in balance sheets, enriching the notion of natural capital. More recently, the literature proposes combining ecosystem accounting methods with probabilistic graphs that incorporate systemic climate risks; this approach proves that drastic regulatory shocks can cascade depreciation of tangible and intangible assets, legitimizing the preventive accounting of counterfactual scenarios (Taskin, Sariyer, Acar, & Cagli, 2025).

The current debate on natural capital accounting coincides with the emergence of climate stress tests that simulate trajectories of orderly and disorderly transition. Evidence from these simulations reveals that carbon-intensive sectors face non-diversifiable losses exceeding ten percent of net present value, reinforcing the urgency of recording provisions for environmental impairment before contingent liabilities materialize. The field, once peripheral, today constitutes a central branch of accounting doctrine and occupies a predominant place in interdisciplinary research agendas, articulating Bayesian statistics, stakeholder theory, and ecological economics (Battiston, Mandel, Monasterolo, Schütze, & Visentin, 2017).

International Standardization of ESG Information

The initial proliferation of reporting guides created an informational babel that made cross-sectoral comparison impossible until the Global Reporting Initiative forged, at the end of the nineties, a common language based on material indicators and principles of consistency. The success of the framework lay in its multi-stakeholder governance: the participatory reviews that led to the GRI Standards incorporated feedback from regulators, investors, trade unions and civil society organisations, favouring its adoption in more than ninety jurisdictions and cementing the legitimacy of a voluntary standard with global aspirations (Cociancich, De La Cruz, de Oliveira, & Mazzone, 2024).

Successive iterations of the framework introduced sectoral versions that responded to specific risks and updated the definition of materiality to align with the

Sustainable Development Goals. Quantitative studies show that the standardization of taxonomies decreases the variance in estimates of non-diversifiable risk and improves the quality of the inputs used by buy-side analysts, resulting in lower risk premiums required of issuers who report comprehensively (Barbosa, Crispim da Silva, Bueno da Silva, & Morioka, 2023).

In parallel, the emergence of alternative frameworks such as SASB and TCFD intensified the discussion on the need for convergence. Empirical research reveals that the coexistence of voluntary standards and regulatory mandates increases the dispersion of ESG ratings, which affects the accuracy of multifactor valuation models that integrate climate signals and sustainable momentum. However, the same studies point out that the gradual harmonization of metrics under the umbrella of the new International Sustainability Standards Board will make it possible to compare performance across sectors and geographies, reducing due diligence costs for institutional investors (Bhandari, Pokhrel, Rimal, Dahal, & Rimal, 2024).

The OECD, for its part, reinforced regulatory convergence by incorporating sustainability principles in the 2023-2024 review of its Corporate Governance Principles. The document requires boards to ensure environmental and social due diligence and that climate disclosure be subject to external assurance, thus aligning the interests of shareholders with those of society as a whole. The official report stresses that robust governance frameworks act as buffers against regulatory and reputational shocks, raising financial resilience in scenarios of rapid transition to low-carbon economies (Cociancich, De La Cruz, de Oliveira, & Mazzone, 2024).

The most recent work explores the role of artificial intelligence in validating reports under the GRI Standards; Natural language processing tools compare corporate narratives with external databases, detecting inconsistencies that suggest green-washing and facilitating audit 4.0 in near real-time. The literature confirms that such systems reduce underwriting costs and reduce the time window between accounting closing and the publication of the report, increasing the usefulness of the information for the market (Gu, Dai, Vasarhelyi, & Borth, 2023).

The immediate future points towards the integration of climate and biodiversity metrics under climate and nature dissemination schemes, a process that will require the compatibility of methodologies and the expansion of sectoral databases. Prediction models supported by machine learning show that the consolidation of standards will reduce the volatility associated with transition risk in diversified portfolios by up to twenty percent, evidencing a direct benefit for global financial stability (Taskin, Sariyer, Acar, & Cagli, 2025).

Thus, the international standardization of ESG reporting sets up a regulatory and technical framework that transforms corporate incentives: firms that internalize the cost of complying with standardized frameworks gain access to cheaper financing and consolidate their legitimacy in the eyes of a public that demands verifiable transparency. Regulatory engineering, technological innovation and investment pressure converge to crystallise a common grammar of sustainability, the cornerstone of the low-carbon economy that is shaping up for the coming decades (Battiston, Mandel, Monasterolo, Schütze, & Visentin, 2017).

Evolution of Climate Prudential Regulation

The shift of the macro-prudential agenda towards climate risk began when the Financial Stability Board warned that global warming constituted a systemic threat comparable to the bank solvency crisis, which gave rise to the Task Force on Climate-related Financial Disclosures. Its physical and transition risk taxonomy was adopted by Eurosystem central banks, the Federal Reserve and the People's Bank of China to run stress tests that model both severe weather events and abrupt decarbonization trajectories. The first results show that, in disorderly policy scenarios, aggregate credit losses can double and the volatility of bank assets escalate to levels typical of systemic crises, evidencing the chronic undervaluation of climate risk on bank balance sheets (Battiston, Mandel, Monasterolo, Schütze, & Visentin, 2017).

To internalize these contingencies, the Basel Committee proposed linking exposure to carbon-intensive sectors with capital surcharges, while the International Sustainability Standards Board issued IFRS S1 and S2 standards, enforceable from 2024, with the external audit mandate that reinforces the verifiability of climate information (Samuels, Watkins, Daniels, & Marotta, 2024). In addition, the Network for Green Banking and Supervision developed a specific disclosure guide that urges regulators to publish their own climate exposure, consolidating a transparency loop that feeds back into financial stability (Dikau, Barmes, Volz, & Persaud, 2023).

Incorporating the Social Factor into Corporate Metrics

Mobilizations for pay justice and decent work prompted the creation of global diversity and inclusion rankings that force companies to disclose gaps in pay, gender representation, and ethnic composition in senior management. Recent meta-analyses confirm that the disclosure of these indicators is associated with sustained increases in patent production and technology citation, suggesting a direct link between internal plurality and innovation. In parallel, the consolidation of human rights due diligence standards institutionalized third-party audits that examine working conditions and freedom of association from the extractive phase to retail. The literature shows that companies with outstanding social qualifications have less dispersion of returns during reputational crises and enjoy market premiums in contexts of a shortage of specialized talent, reinforcing the thesis that diverse human capital functions as a strategic buffer (Barbosa, Crispim da Silva, Bueno da Silva, & Morioka, 2023; La Soa, Duy, Thanh Hang, & Ha, 2024).

Transforming Governance with an Ethical Perspective

The corporate collapses of the beginning of the century led to a reformulation of the fiduciary duty of boards of directors by incorporating sustainability committees endowed with binding power. Comparative studies in global banks show that the presence of ESG-experienced advisors increases the likelihood of reporting emerging risks and reduces the incidence of litigation for deceptive practices. In turn, the updated OECD Principles of Corporate Governance mandate the inclusion of climate and social metrics in supervisory mandates, which has promoted sustainable literacy programs for directors and the hiring of external advisors in algorithmic ethics (Cociancich, De La Cruz, de Oliveira, & Mazzone, 2024). Recent research corroborates that cognitive diversity on boards correlates with a smaller gap between corporate discourse and operational practice, thus reducing the risk of greenwashing (Lee, Kim, Jung, Park, & Seo, 2024).

Confluence of Big Data and Sustainability

The fusion of IoT sensors with low-orbit satellite constellations has triggered a high-frequency data stream that enables near-instantaneous detection of methane leaks and verification of deforestation, establishing an unprecedented remote monitoring regime (Gu, Dai, Vasarhelyi, & Borth, 2023). Simultaneously, multilingual sentiment mining applies adjusted BERT models to extract reputational signals from millions of news stories and social media posts, feeding dashboards that trigger alerts when the negative polarity exceeds predefined thresholds (Harper, Liu, Martínez, Ochoa, & Zhang, 2024). Pilot results in the energy sector indicate that operational response to incidents is reduced from days to hours, with estimated savings of five percent of annual EBITDA thanks to early mitigation of regulatory fines. The financial press confirms that the new generation of hyperspectral satellites will make it virtually impossible to hide fugitive emissions, intensifying the pressure on high-carbon emitters (Bhandari, Pokhrel, Rimal, Dahal, & Rimal, 2024).

First Analytical Architectures for ESG Risk

Reputational scoring models evolved from logistic regressions enriched with climate variables to decision trees and random forests capable of capturing threshold effects. The incorporation of word vectors from footnotes in financial reports increased predictive capacity, and the migration to deep neural networks made it possible to model nonlinear interactions between environmental, social, and governance factors with success rates above 90% in validation sets (Taskin, Sariyer, Acar, & Cagli, 2025). Studies on listed Chinese companies show that adding ESG indicators to default models based on accounting variables increases the area under the ROC curve by more than eight percentage points. Research integrating large language models also shows that fine-tuning on corporate texts improves the thematic classification of emerging risks, which opens the door to early warning systems powered by natural language (Alvarez, Gupta, Higgins, Noriega, & Feng, 2025).

Development of Composite Valuation Indices

The multiplication of rating agencies generated statistical dispersion in ESG scores, so that two suppliers could diverge up to 30% in the evaluation of the same firm. To solve the problem, recent proposals apply the extended best–worst method and the ordinal proximity measure in order to derive weights that reflect the sectoral relevance of each sub-criterion, reducing inter-rating variance and increasing correlation with risk-adjusted returns. An OECD report published in 2025 supports the adoption of hybrid methodologies that combine expert voting with Bayesian calibration, emphasizing that transparency about the aggregation algorithm is indispensable to avoid hidden biases and preserve investor confidence (Barrera, Sanz, Dupont, & Miki, 2025).

Responsible Investment Paradigms

The ethical funds of the eighties have mutated into multifactorial strategies that include exclusion filters, best-in-class and shareholder activism. Meta-analyses spanning three decades of data demonstrate that portfolios with high ESG scores tend to exhibit lower volatility and higher Sharpe ratios versus conventional portfolios, even after adjusting for sector and size biases (Barbosa, Crispim da Silva, Bueno da Silva, & Morioka, 2023). The green and sustainable bond market exceeded $2 trillion in cumulative issuances, supported by taxonomy regulations that reduce the risk of greenwashing and provide price signals to institutional capital (La Soa, Duy, Thanh Hang, & Ha, 2024). Research on transition portfolios reveals that rebalancing based on carbon intensity decreases exposure to regulatory shocks without sacrificing profitability, confirming that responsible integration does not imply a structural financial trade-off (Santos, Rademacher, Nureyev, Prado, & Ghosh, 2024).

Emergence of Sustainable Quantitative Finance

The incorporation of ESG variables into multifactor models redefined asset valuation by combining climate signaling with sustainable momentum. Climate value-at-risk simulations employing Bayesian networks show that portfolios repositioned towards companies with robust decarbonization plans reduce the expected loss by up to 25% under abrupt transition scenarios (Taskin, Sariyer, Acar, & Cagli, 2025). Corporate credit studies show statistically significant improvements by adding ESG scores as predictors in default models, showing that markets gradually internalize these factors in the risk premium. The use of deep learning to identify nonlinear correlations between sustainability metrics and financial variables increases forecasting capacity over six- to twelve-month horizons, consolidating the idea that quantitative finance constitutes an experimental laboratory for innovation in risk management (Bhandari, Pokhrel, Rimal, Dahal, & Rimal, 2024).

Consolidating Data Culture in ESG Auditing

The adoption of blockchain and smart contracts is transforming the audit function by ensuring immutable traceability and automatic verification of evidence. Audit 4.0 experiments demonstrate that using satellite imagery to contrast self-reported emissions reduces audit closure time and the cost per verified evidence (Gu, Dai, Vasarhelyi, & Borth, 2023). Computer vision models validated in academic studies identify deviations in methane concentrations and generate explainable reports for regulators and investors (Hanna, Mommert, Scheibenreif, & Borth, 2021).

THEORETICAL FRAMEWORK

The conceptual architecture underpinning algorithmic ESG contingency modeling is at the intersection of four streams: stakeholder theory, algorithmic governance, predictive risk analytics, and expanded social accounting. Stakeholder theory, in its dynamic sense, postulates that the creation of economic value is inexorably intertwined with the redistribution of externalities to multiple interest groups, which requires metrics that internalize ecological and social costs in near real time.

The Relational Theory of Stakeholders

It is understood as a network of links of power, legitimacy and urgency that is permanently updated has evolved from a static conception to a dynamic perspective that emphasizes the processes of translating expectations into verifiable metrics for the creation of shared value. In this expanded approach, firms are conceived as nodes that shape their competitive advantage by turning social interaction into a continuous flow of co-creation and distribution of tangible and intangible benefits, so that environmental, social, and governance materiality operates as a normative language that aligns incentives and reduces informational entropy (Parmar, Freeman, Harrison & Wicks, 2010). The conceptual core lies in recognizing that legitimacy is not granted definitively, but is negotiated in short cycles where the company captures signals about emerging systemic risks and reconfigures its strategy before these risks manifest themselves in cash flow; this relational plasticity transforms corporate governance into a listening platform that metabolizes sociotechnical disruption to sustain financial resilience (Amis, Barney, Mahoney & Wang, 2020).

The dynamic materiality paradigm provides another explanatory layer: what is the regulatory periphery today may tomorrow become a catalyst for the cost of capital if investors detect externalities that threaten long-term solvency. Studies on corporate reporting architecture show that the prioritization of material issues should be reviewed on an annual basis to maintain the harmony between emerging risks and social expectations; the absence of such periodic calibration increases the uncertainty premium demanded by sophisticated creditors and shareholders (Eccles, Krzus, Rogers & Serafeim, 2012).

Empirical evidence strengthens the thesis that well-governed relational interactions translate into lower financing costs. The meta-analysis by El Ghoul, Guedhami, Kwok & Mishra (2011) shows that U.S. firms with outstanding social performance reduce their cost of equity based on the perception of lower idiosyncratic risk and the improvement in the analytical coverage dedicated to the company. Recent research in the UK confirms that ESG transparency modulated by strong corporate governance not only mitigates stock volatility, but also turns exposure to climate issues into a competitive advantage by attracting long-term-oriented investors (Moussa, Elmarzouky, Abdullah & Shurrab, 2024).

Reputational feedback also works as a buffer in crisis situations: the speed with which stakeholders experience, interpret and disseminate a bad practice determines the speed of depreciation of the organisation's symbolic capital. The relational model involves anticipating this curve of attrition through listening systems that identify weak cues and activate rectification protocols before the scandal crystallizes into negative financial indicators. Machine learning tools applied to multilingual corpora make it possible to detect tone inflections and segment them by stakeholder, offering dashboards that alert on the need for discursive adjustments or internal policies; the company that internalizes this cycle increases its capacity for social innovation and generates positive redundancies that strengthen the accumulated legitimacy (Freudenreich et al., 2020).

A second vector of theoretical expansion lies in the notion of interdependence between network and value, according to which resource flows are fluidly reconfigured when the firm accesses new spheres of public engagement. In this context, the classic hierarchy of corporate power is shifting towards polyphonic schemes where stakeholders exert influence through digital platforms and where management is forced to manage the paradox of balancing heterogeneous demands without eroding their strategic coherence. It is therefore crucial to develop metrics of evolutionary salience, capable of weighing moral urgency, financial relevance and the technical possibility of action, so that the company is not paralyzed by the multiplicity of voices, but proactively prioritizes areas of impact.

The convergence between relational theory and behavioral economics confirms that the perception of distributive justice generates a virtuous circle of trust that lowers the barriers to agency and, therefore, the required rates of return. When investors recognize consistency between narrative and performance, the discount applied to the net present value is reduced and the organization accesses patient capital that respects the gestation of long-term innovations (Amis et al., 2020).

Relational theory offers a powerful lens for understanding the transition from corporate responsibility to systemic value creation. By considering the organization as part of an ecosystem for the production of common goods, competitiveness is no longer measured only in terms of private profitability to include the contribution to socio-environmental resilience; hence, concepts such as natural capital and social capital are gradually integrated into the extended financial statements.

Responsible Algorithmic Governance

The algorithms that today assign credit, estimate insurance premiums or build sustainability indices operate as critical infrastructures whose legitimacy depends on showing, with equal emphasis, analytical efficiency and democratic accountability. The first condition is achieved when the model captures ESG signals with sufficient granularity to discriminate between material risks and speculative noise, while the second requires that this discrimination can be reconstructed, audited, and discussed by the stakeholders who bear the consequences of the decision (Cheong, Subhani, Mansoor, & Nordin, 2024).

Recent literature warns that, in finance, the most accurate algorithms tend to be the least transparent; therefore, regulators propose a dual threshold of governance: first demonstrate the incremental value that architecture provides with respect to traditional models, and then exhibit the traceability of that value through techniques of decomposition of variable importance and Shapley attribution that any external analyst can replicate. The principle of distributed accountability shifts the burden of proof from the siloed algorithm to the sociotechnical ecosystem that employs it. Under this paradigm, developers, independent auditors and end users share the obligation to justify the outputs of the system, and any legitimate actor can request a review where the metrics of statistical equity are contrasted with those of economic utility; this closes the gap between global accuracy and local harm that tends to camouflage indirect discrimination (Brundage, Avin, Wang & Belfield, 2020).

To operationalize this co-responsibility, ethical licensing schemes inspired by the homologation of medical software are emerging. The license is granted based on a dossier that combines robustness tests, differential privacy guarantors and an impact statement that evaluates how the model redistributes risks and benefits among asymmetric actors; its periodic renewal requires the incorporation of each regulatory update on climate or labor rights and prevents financial innovation from advancing in parallel to regulatory shadow areas (Floridi, Cowls, Chami & Taddeo, 2023).

Audits are not mere final exams but iterative processes that accompany the entire life cycle of the model. A widely cited framework proposes nine milestones, from the design phase to post-deployment oversight, each with deliverables that include data inventories, ethical derivation analyses, and regulatory change sensitivity testing. When these documents are published, civil society groups can verify whether the ESG assessment privileges formal compliance metrics or delves into real impact indicators, reinforcing the legitimacy of the tool (Raji, Smart, White & Mitchell, 2020).

At the engineering level, responsible governance requires monitoring layers that operate in near real-time and warn of concept drifts, data drift, or changes in customer distribution that can erode equity, especially in geographies with low density of reliable data. The most advanced monitoring systems use population stability metrics linked to intersectional equity thresholds to trigger retraining, and record each intervention in an immutable audit book that facilitates the reconstruction of adverse events in potential litigation (Cheong et al., 2024).

Therefore, effective algorithmic governance programs are complemented by incentive frameworks that align executive compensation with software ethical performance metrics. Field studies show that the simple requirement to report indicators of residual bias at quarterly conferences increases investment in explainability engineering and accelerates the adoption of libraries free of statistical discrimination, suggesting that transparency not only protects vulnerable groups but optimizes capital allocation by reducing legal uncertainty for institutional investors (Bowden et al., 2024).

Expanded Social Accounting

Expanded social accounting is based on the premise that corporate wealth is not limited to physical assets or legally recognizable intangibles, but includes flows of legitimacy, trust, and the ability to create shared value with society.

The first pillar is reputational capital, understood as the aggregate expectation of good performance that reduces the risk premium demanded by shareholders and creditors; when the organization fails to comply with environmental or labor commitments, this capital suffers an ethical depreciation that can be measured through variations in the cost of equity capital and in the volatility of the share price (Lev, Radhakrishnan, Ciftci & de Villiers, 2022). To record this variation, extended balance sheets incorporate provisions that recognize the anticipated social loss and relate it to indicators of negative media coverage, so that accounting ceases to be a static photograph and becomes a sensor of dynamic confidence (Guzmán, Correa, Valiente & Valiente Palma, 2024).

The second pillar is shared value, which requires transferring the external benefits generated by the company to the income statement through homogeneous metrics verified by third parties; studies of good practices in the social economy show that the publication of a credible social balance sheet increases organizational resilience during sectoral crises (Guzmán et al., 2024).

The third pillar is contingent valuation techniques applied to common goods: willingness-to-pay methods make it possible to convert the improvement in biodiversity or the reduction of fine particles into projectable cash flows, making green bonds viable whose coupon is adjusted to the achievement of socio-environmental milestones and, therefore, aligning market incentives with the preservation of natural resources (Climate Bonds Initiative, 2024). Impact reports from leading issuers show that this variable design attracts long-term investors and reduces the likelihood of default during adverse cycles, demonstrating that social accounting is not philanthropy but prudent systemic risk management.

Finally, recent research on depreciation of intangibles explores the use of Google Search Volume series to estimate the obsolescence of reputational assets, offering more accurate attrition rates than current accounting tables and preventing ethical deterioration from being hidden behind obsolete linear rates (Abonizio, Padolina, Ramos & Santos, 2024). By articulating these elements, expanded social accounting transforms financial language into a signal system that rewards systemic value generation and penalizes opportunistic rent extraction, closing the gap between economic performance and social legitimacy.

Deep Learning Applied to Environmental Risks

The advance of computer vision has allowed convolutional neural networks to detect deforestation patterns of less than one hectare in daily satellite series, multiplying spatial sensitivity with respect to traditional Landsat programs and anticipating the appearance of illegal clearings in tropical forests by months (Jelas, Zulkifley, Abdullah & Spraggon, 2024). By adding layers of long-term memory, LSTM architectures integrate the historical signal of nitrogen dioxide emissions and generate forecasts that alert cement plants to pollution peaks up to six weeks before reaching sanctionable levels, optimizing the regulatory capital provisions required by Basel IV (Olawade, Wada, Ige & Egbewole, 2024). The next leap corresponds to multimodal transformers, capable of merging text from regulatory reports, spot energy prices and reanalysis meteorological variables to estimate the joint probability of extreme events; by incorporating Bayesian calibration techniques, these models deliver complete probability distributions and not mere scores, facilitating parametric insurance that releases liquidity as soon as a physical threshold is exceeded pre-established (He, Wang, Davies & Baker, 2025).

At the same time, the physical explainability of deep networks is being developed, where the inner layers are regularized with energy conservation equations or mass balances, avoiding spurious predictions and increasing regulatory acceptability in critical sectors such as hydroelectricity (Olawade et al., 2024). Finally, the integration of these models into corporate governance dashboards makes it possible to link the environmental risk signal with capital cost metrics, so that an early warning of deforestation automatically raises country risk provisions and adjusts the infrastructure insurance premium, closing the loop between data science and sustainable finance.

Sentiment Mining and Corporate Reputation

Corporate reputation has become a volatile asset whose changes occur to the rhythm of social networks. Multilingual extraction systems process millions of headlines per hour and disambiguate polarity by contextualizing each word according to the sector and culture of origin, overcoming the limitations of the bag of words approach through embeddings that preserve semantics and syntax. These models feed reputational value-at-risk indicators that are updated daily and correlated with stock market volatility; when the standard deviation of sentiment exceeds a critical threshold, banks increase capital buffers for exposed customers, anticipating the materialization of accounting losses by several days (Bagh, Bouri, Khan & Xu, 2024).

Recent research confirms that this early signal reduces the severity of drawdowns after ESG scandals by up to fifteen percent, demonstrating its usefulness as a prudential oversight instrument (Aon Reputation Analytics Team, 2024). The derived information feeds back into competitive intelligence platforms that cross-reference sentiment scores with supplier performance data; by identifying persistent risk patterns, companies reallocate orders to suppliers with strong ESG track records, strengthening supply chain co-governance and reducing logistics disruption events,

Beyond prediction, causal sentiment modeling makes it possible to distinguish between transient peaks and structural trends that reflect sustained perceptions of misconduct; the separation of the two phenomena avoids over-reactions that make financing unnecessarily more expensive and, at the same time, focuses remediation programs where reputational deterioration is authentic (Derrick, Sundaresan, Rodríguez & Trevino, 2024).

Bayesian Networks for Holistic Contingencies

The Bayesian approach situates ESG risk within an architecture of conditional dependencies where monetary policy, carbon prices, and social metrics dialogue in a graph that is updated with the evidence that emerges day after day. Thanks to this plasticity, it is possible to estimate how the vulnerability of sovereign debt increases if the monetary authority tightens its reference rate at the same time as the European issuance permit becomes more expensive, because all the factors are intertwined in a framework of general equilibrium. Monte Carlo methods allow recent evidence to be incorporated without reconstructing the entire network, so that central banking analysts calculate in a few hours the distributional effects of a progressive green tax and assess the convenience of introducing transitional exemptions or credits where they are socially necessary.

Counterfactual inference reveals tipping points from which the relationship between carbon price and manufacturing output reverses and investment leakage appears. When the model is fed with future values of emission rights in the European Union, it identifies that a moderate shock cuts employment in metallurgy in the eastern continent, while a more intense one ends up activating subsidies for green hydrogen that reverse the drop in production.

ESG Ontologies and Computational Semantics

The proliferation of sustainability reporting frameworks has multiplied semantic friction: the term waste can refer to total mass, hazardousness, or intensity per unit of income. Sectoral ontologies resolve this ambiguity by defining classes, properties, and constraints in a formal language that machines interpret without human mediation.

This common foundation drives interbank traceability: when two entities link their knowledge graphs, the property joins equivalent metrics and eliminates the manual reconciliation that previously took weeks during a green bond's due diligence. To ensure the quality of pairings, the SSSOM specification provides a tabular format that notes accuracy, provenance, and confidence level of each alignment, so that extraction, transform, and loading pipes suspend questionable cases until human validation intervenes.

Tracking commitments comes to life in time graphs: a node representing voluntary emission reductions links successive versions of the same pledge using the property, so the analyst detects whether the company relaxed its goals before going to market for fresh resources. To resolve polysemy, disambiguation algorithms generate semantic vectors that compare the financial context of the word material with its use in civil engineering and only accept equivalence when the similarity exceeds a very high threshold. Finally, semantic normalization is integrated with the XBRL standard, so issuers generate instances that comply with international accounting rules without duplicate tagging and with shorter audit times.

Reputational Capital as a Strategic Asset

Reputation, understood as the aggregate expectation of legitimacy, accounts for about a third of the stock market valuation of the largest corporations and acts as a buffer in times of economic stress. When an ESG scandal erupts, the cost of capital rises appreciably because creditors recalibrate the risk margin in the face of the uncertainty caused by reputational deterioration, and the return to normalcy usually represents a journey that lasts just over two years if the company adopts verifiable remedies.

The speed of retrieval depends on the symmetry between the offense and the response. Brands with a history of transparency reduce the outrage phase on social media to less than a week and shorten the stock market loss by around a third, while those without a culture of openness can be trapped in prolonged crises. By modeling reputational risk as a premium within the weighted average cost of capital, analysts avoid inflating the company's terminal value and reduce the likelihood of bubbles that aggravate systemic fragility.

To transfer some of this risk, parametric reputation insurance arises, triggering payouts if a weighted sentiment index remains below a threshold for several days. Backtesting shows that these hedges would have smoothed out the overall volatility of tech companies when they faced antitrust investigations.

Complex Systems Theory and Sustainability

The systemic view of sustainability describes the planet as a web of non-linear networks in which energy, water, nutrients, and human expectations interact through feedbacks that can amplify or dampen changes. When several of these positive feedbacks are aligned, thresholds are exceeded that trigger tipping points capable of irreversibly altering climate stability and pushing the biosphere towards much warmer and less hospitable states, a warning taken up by the notion of greenhouse Earth (Steffen, Rockström, Richardson & Lenton, 2018).

Organizations that assume this complex logic shift the classic notion of resilience towards antifragility, understood as the ability to learn and strengthen when uncertainty lowers demand or breaks supplies; this strategy materializes by diversifying suppliers, deploying intelligent inventories and designing substitution protocols that turn moderate disruptions into opportunities for innovation.

Adaptive network models applied to global supply chains show that there is an optimal density of interconnections that minimizes the contagion of failures without making logistics more expensive; Breaking fragility requires dependency maps that weigh both carbon footprint and cultural distance, as bottlenecks can come from social conflicts and not just physical shocks.

Ethics of Corporate Artificial Intelligence

The principles of beneficence and non-maleficence require that algorithmic models consider people's well-being beyond profitability; in the financial sphere, this implies measuring the distribution of false credit rejections so as not to perpetuate biases against those who have historically lacked collateral (Floridi, Cowls, Beltrametti & Chatila, 2018).

The conflict between statistical efficiency and distributive justice becomes visible when the overall decrease in error is achieved at the cost of increasing the equity gap between groups, which is why regulators demand multi-group fairness metrics audited by independent third parties that employ counterfactual simulation techniques and ethical stress tests (Jobin, Ienca, Vayena & Cavolo, 2019). The dilemmas of transparency versus intellectual property protection find a way out in graduated disclosure schemes: firms disclose the provenance of the data and the type of sensitive variables included, but retain the specific parameters encrypted, allowing for accountability without relinquishing competitive advantage (Whittlestone, Nyrup, Huffer & Fox, 2023).

To close the ethical cycle, it is decisive to incorporate potentially affected groups into co-design tables where they validate impact scenarios and express concerns that are often overlooked by purely technical calculations; Thus, artificial intelligence aligns with procedural justice and with the principles of democratic governance that govern the granting of banking licenses.

Behavioral Economics Applied to ESG Decisions

The psychology of the responsible investor reveals that the way climate risk messages are framed profoundly alters capital allocation. When impacts are presented with an optimistic tone, underscoring the opportunity to engage in transformative solutions, financial professionals increase their propensity to include green assets, demonstrating that regret aversion can be neutralized through constructive narrative frameworks (Cueva, Matthey, Morosoli, & Riguelle, 2023).

The pressure of social norms enhances this effect: interactive dashboards that compare the carbon footprint of a portfolio with the market average generate a competitive impulse that leads to improved relative metrics, especially when the information is updated in near real-time and comes from sources considered credible by the analyst community. However, the availability heuristic induces overreaction when negative reports go viral without technical basis; To cushion this bias, digital advisors filter the relevance of the news and weigh the reliability of the sources before suggesting rebalancing, making information curation a central element of financial ethics.

CHALLENGES FACED BY ORGANIZATIONS OR INSTITUTIONS

In the day-to-day practice of corporate risk management, the incorporation of ESG metrics based on algorithmic models comes up against five interrelated critical fronts.

The first is regulatory volatility that manifests itself in the coexistence of fragmented taxonomies between jurisdictions; the European disclosure frameworks aligned with the CSRD differ substantially from the North American standards supported by the SASB, which introduces asymmetries of interpretation and, therefore, measurement biases that propagate to predictive models.

The second challenge lies in the heterogeneity of the datasets: emissions traceability, supply chain mapping, and labor compliance verification move through databases that employ dissimilar markup languages and metrics that vary in granularity, forcing cleanup and standardization procedures that often dilute critical signals (Bhandari, Pokhrel, Rimal, Dahal, & Rimal, 2024).

The third obstacle arises from the algorithmic biases that nest in training corpora, especially when using historical data from ESG controversies; algorithms reproduce implicit discriminatory patterns, magnifying risks for marginalized communities and generating false negatives in the detection of emerging environmental incidents (Li, Yu, Wang, Chen, & Hu, 2024).

The fourth front is the lack of explainability: internal audit committees usually receive reports with globally accurate metrics, but without disaggregation of the marginal contribution of each variable to the prediction, which complicates the ethical validation of the models and restricts managerial accountability.

EXAMPLES OF IMPLEMENTATION IN COMPANIES OR ORGANIZATIONS

The trajectory of ArcticHydro, a Nordic consortium dedicated to hydro and wind generation in polar latitudes, illustrates how intensive analytics becomes a lever for resilience when ESG contingencies transition from exogenous variable to intracritical signal; by deploying a digital twin that fuses high-resolution satellite images with telemetry from IoT sensors installed on the blades, the company orchestrates an LSTM-CNN hybrid model that anticipates deviations in fleeting carbon dioxide emissions and amalgamates vibration alerts to trigger predictive maintenance, so that each turbine becomes a cognitive node in a mesh that dialogues with financial dashboards and operational dashboards. reducing regulatory penalties for environmental non-compliances and compressing the capital amortization cycle in a scenario of volatile electricity prices thanks to the wind volatility that characterizes the North Sea (Bhandari et al., 2024).

In the heart of manufacturing Europe, Z-Automotive converted its plant into a laboratory of ethical traceability by implementing a data mining system that weights environmental, social and governance indicators in time windows of just fifteen minutes; The architecture combines online extraction of welding robot logs, biometric records of work ergonomics, and energy consumption readings on micro-inverters, all fed into a hierarchical analytical process capable of translating heterogeneous semantics into a single compliance index, which is reflected in an accuracy of more than ninety percent to predict SA-8000 incidents and in an abrupt drop in union litigation that, according to internal audits, it freed up liquidity for reinvestment in solvent-free paint technologies, thus integrating sustainability into the brand's aesthetic economic core (Li et al., 2024).

In the Andean financial ecosystem, Andean Bank condenses forty thousand multilingual news sources and market micro-data into a transformative service engine that feeds a hierarchical Bayesian network; The platform disambiguates sectoral sentiments in Spanish, Aymara and English, attributes contextualized polarity to each headline and updates in near real time a metric of value in reputational risk that modulates capital buffers and triggers public relations micro-interventions before digital outrage deteriorates the return on wealth curve; internal results reveal that exposure to reputational risk fell by eighteen basis points and that the decision to link executive bonuses to the evolution of this indicator strengthened responsible algorithmic governance that balances intellectual property protection with accountability to regulators and civil society (Lee et al., 2024).

This reputational approach draws on advances in sentiment mining that process millions of headlines per hour, preserve syntax and semantics, and correlate stock market volatility with standard deviations in tone, so that when the negative polarity exceeded critical thresholds in an episode of environmental protest, the entity raised provisions and rebalanced its portfolio five days before the markets punished its regional peers. confirming the preventive efficacy of the models in reducing severe drawdowns by up to fifteen percent (Bagh et al., 2024).

GlobalSeaways' logistics narrative evidences the maturity of generative geospatial risk mapping: the shipping company feeds an adversary generator trained with multi-decenic meteorological series, current topologies and cyclonic intensity projections to suggest, in a matter of minutes, compensatory routes that reduce exposure to extreme waves; in the Indian Ocean typhoon season, the company relocated containers with thermolabile drugs to less congested corridors, reducing insurance premiums linked to ESG contingencies by twenty-seven percent and stabilizing punctuality indicators that sustain hospital confidence in maritime cold chains sensitive to seconds of delay, which ratifies that logistical antifragility arises from the intelligent diversification of nodes and the elasticity designed in operational peacetime (GlobalSeaways, 2024).

The benefits of such elasticity also appear in studies of adaptive chains that reveal how the integration of climate sensors with reoptimization algorithms leads to moderate disruptions being transformed into opportunities for collective learning; By identifying critical geographical bottlenecks, organizations redesign supplier layers, incorporate circular economy principles and reduce dependence on raw materials with a high carbon footprint, so that the climate shock is no longer conceived as an anomaly and is understood as an evolutionary stimulus that strengthens competitiveness in the long term.

Despite the algorithmic sophistication, all these implementations converge in an explainability dilemma that, if left unaddressed, would erode legitimacy in the face of cautious boards of directors; cross-sectional experience suggests that interactive dashboards with decomposition of importance of variables and traceable narratives accelerate the approval of corrective actions and reduce the distance between analytical signal and strategic decision, validating the thesis that precision only becomes an advantage when it is accompanied by transparency that makes the marginal contribution of each ESG component to the value at risk understandable.

RESULTS

The results of algorithmic modelling show that the accuracy of ESG contingency prediction grows steadily when models bring together market data, internal trading signals and high-frequency open sources. Multimodal convergence decreases the mean estimation error and raises sensitivity to incipient events, confirming that hybrid deep learning architectures outperform traditional univariate approaches (Bhandari, Pokhrel, Rimal, Dahal & Rimal, 2024; Jain, Costa, Delgado, Navarro & Luo, 2023). This technical improvement is reflected in heat maps that allow regulatory, reputational and climate deviations to be anticipated with sufficient slack to deploy mitigation plans before risks are monetized over market value.

The directive acceptance of alerts depends on how clearly the systems explain the marginal contribution of each ESG component to the value at risk. When interactive boards break down internal weightings and offer traceable narratives, boards approve corrective actions in shorter spans and without objections to methodological legitimacy, suggesting a strong relationship between explainability and strategic response speed. This phenomenon confirms that statistical sophistication only generates value when it is accompanied by narrative transparency capable of translating complex numerical vectors into judgments understandable by government bodies.

Bodies that integrate layers of continuous auditing and responsible governance reduce the likelihood of greenwashing litigation and moderate the risk premium demanded by creditors. The coupling of real-time sentiment indicators with probabilistic graphs facilitates capital adjustments that cushion reputational shocks and limit the erosion of stock market equity during periods of socio-environmental turbulence (Bagh, Bouri, Khan & Xu, 2024; Brundage, Avin, Wang & Belfield, 2020). The articulation between prudential supervision and ethical analytics generates a virtuous circle where market confidence feeds back into financial stability.

The evidence also indicates that a robust data culture, grounded in standardized reporting frameworks and interoperable ontologies, minimizes semantic friction and strengthens the traceability of material metrics. By harmonizing vocabularies and automating quality controls, organizations increase cross-jurisdictional comparability and reduce accounting reconciliation costs, freeing up resources for innovation and continuous improvement (Gray, Dey, Owen, Evans & Zadek, 1997; Cociancich, De La Cruz, de Oliveira & Mazzone, 2024; Guzmán, Correa, Valiente & Valiente Palma, 2024; Matentzoglu, Balhoff, Bello & Bizon, 2021). Semantic standardization thus emerges as a pillar of organizational resilience in highly regulated ecosystems.

The deployment of antifragile architectures in the supply chain reveals that node diversification, combined with geospatial risk mapping, decreases the propagation of failures and accelerates operational recovery after extreme weather events. The permanent adaptation of logistics routes and the dynamic substitution of suppliers turn disruptions into learning opportunities that strengthen long-term competitive advantage (La Soa, Duy, Thanh Hang & Ha, 2024). At the macroeconomic level, this absorptive capacity contributes to stabilizing labor markets and reduces sectoral volatility.

Finally, the maturity of ESG models is associated with the alignment of incentives between transparency, distributive fairness, and profitability. Companies that incorporate multi-group ethical filters and statistical equity metrics experience greater support from long-term investors, since responsible governance mitigates information asymmetry and reinforces coherence between corporate purpose and financial performance. Accumulating evidence suggests that algorithmic ethics are inseparable from analytical excellence and are positioned as a decisive element in consolidating business legitimacy in environments of increasing public scrutiny.

CONCLUSIONS

The evidence gathered confirms that the full integration of environmental, social and governance metrics into corporate intelligence systems is a sine qua non condition for sustaining competitiveness in increasingly volatile climate and reputational environments. The findings show that when hybrid models combine satellite series, industrial sensor readings, and multilingual narrative corpora, the accuracy in the early detection of contingencies expands substantially, as long as it is accompanied by explainability mechanisms that translate statistical complexity into arguments understandable to government bodies and affected communities (Bhandari, Pokhrel, Rimal & Dahal, 2024). Without this transparency, analytical sophistication becomes a reputational risk: boards are suspicious of what they cannot audit, and markets punish opacity by raising the cost of capital.

The first of the questions in the approach concerned how to merge heterogeneous sources without sacrificing robustness or clarity. The results indicate that sectoral ontologies act as a semantic bridge to harmonize definitions, reduce redundancies and promote Bayesian imputations when data are missing or dispersed. By adopting interoperable knowledge graphs and dashboards that display the marginal contribution of each variable, companies are able to turn complexity into a strategic advantage rather than a technical obstacle, which is reflected in fewer delays in decision-making and an expanded sensitivity to weak signals that portend regulatory disruptions (Matentzoglu, Balhoff, Bello & Bizon, 2021).

The second question explored what governance mechanisms make it possible to balance the protection of intellectual property with the transparency demanded by regulators and civil society. The research shows that ethical licensing contracts and immutable audit trails create the break-even point: firms share the genesis and itinerary of their data in a graded format, keep proprietary parameters in reserve, and yet enable third parties to verify that the outputs of the model do not perpetuate historical inequities. When this scheme is complemented with ethical stress tests and multigroup impartiality metrics, algorithmic legitimacy is strengthened and the gap between accuracy and distributive fairness is tangibly reduced.

The third question investigated the ability of semantic standardization and data culture to reduce the risk premium. The results establish that ontological standardization lowers accounting reconciliation costs and shortens the regulatory verification cycle, so that information flows with less friction between jurisdictions and creditors. In addition, organizations with a dense data culture have smoother stock market volatility curves, as radical transparency translates into investor confidence and positive elasticity of corporate reputation in the face of exogenous shocks.

The effect is enhanced when reputational information derived from sentiment mining feeds hierarchical Bayesian networks capable of adjusting capital provisions before an ESG incident is monetized; the interaction between precise semantics and proactive data culture thus creates a virtuous circle that protects market valuation and facilitates access to green finance under more favorable conditions.

Beyond the answers to the initial questions, the results suggest emerging lines of research and practice. On the technological level, the adoption of multimodal transformers promises to incorporate high-dimensional variables without incurring overfitting, as long as the intermediate layers are subject to regularizations that guarantee traceability and avoid the explanatory collapse typical of opaque models. In the ethical field, the convergence between statistical fairness and graduated disclosure is emerging as a standard for markets to reward moral solvency with lower spreads and extended investment horizons (Cheong, Subhani, Mansoor & Nordin, 2024). Finally, from the behavioral perspective, the narrative framework of ESG reports emerges as a lever that modulates the heuristics of asset managers: opportunity-oriented presentations, combined with dynamic social comparisons, enhance the redistribution of capital towards innovations with high socio-environmental impact and, incidentally, reinforce the legitimacy of the financial system by showing coherence between discourse and resource allocation (Cueva, Matthey, Morosoli & Riguelle, 2023).

In summary, the research concludes that the company that internalizes shared semantics, auditable governance, and an architecture of choice that minimizes cognitive biases, turns intelligent analytics into its corporate immune system. This system not only detects threats before they materialize, but also transforms each disturbance into an input for innovation, elevating the organization to a plane of antifragility that prepares it for a future dominated by climatic, regulatory and reputational uncertainties. The convergence described is not optional; constitutes the new logic of survival and prosperity in the post-carbon economy.

RECOMMENDATIONS FOR FUTURE RESEARCH

The rapid maturation of ESG analytics opens up a fertile horizon that requires research with greater epistemological depth and methodological breadth. A first area of exploration refers to the crystallization of dynamic ontologies that evolve with the same speed as regulatory frameworks. The advances made using the SSSOM specification are valuable, but they do not yet resolve how to version terms that change meaning as climate science refines risk thresholds. Studies that combine semi-supervised lexical mining with expert validation are required to generate living glossaries capable of automatically synchronizing with emerging regulations and accommodating, without redundancy, indicators that today overlap or contradict each other (Matentzoglu, Balhoff, Bello & Bizon, 2021).

A second research territory points to the creation of algorithmic auditing frameworks that transcend the accuracy and fairness metrics currently in place. The literature has shown that statistical accuracy rarely coincides with distributive justice, so it is urgent to develop batteries of tests that measure the temporal coherence of models, their ability to adapt without feedback on biases and the traceability of their decisions in languages understandable to non-specialist audiences. The incorporation of ethical licenses has been a notable advance, but it remains to be investigated how these licenses interact with intellectual property regimes in different jurisdictions and how they impact the entrepreneurial willingness to invest in open innovation (Floridi, Cowls, Chami & Taddeo, 2023).

A third critical strand lies in the integration of social perceptions, captured through sentiment mining, with time-series architectures that forecast changes in the cost of capital. The findings suggest that the tone of digital narratives anticipates stock market movements, but the feedback dynamics that could amplify or dampen these effects have not yet been rigorously modeled. It is recommended to articulate longitudinal studies that combine behavioral economics experiments with complex network simulations to estimate the elasticity of brand value in the face of reputational shocks and map how liquidity is redistributed through global supply chains when an ESG event goes viral.

Fourth, the relationship between explainability and directive adoption deserves ethnographic explorations that capture the deliberative processes in risk committees. Although quantitative evidence confirms that explainable dashboards accelerate decision-making, the narrative dimension needs to be understood: how visual metaphors, rhetorical frameworks, and authority biases influence the trust that directors place in algorithmic predictions. Research designs that combine eye-tracking techniques, computational linguistics, and conversational analysis could unravel patterns of acceptance or resistance and translate them into hermeneutical design guidelines for artificial intelligence interfaces (Bowden, Cummins, Dao & Jain, 2024).

Finally, the notion of corporate antifragility raised in previous studies requires sectoral validations that measure, with comparable indicators, the extent to which organizations turn disruptions into leaps in innovation. It is suggested to implement ESG digital twins connected to multimodal care neural networks to record, in near real-time, how the learnings derived from a crisis are encoded in process changes, capital investments, or product redesigns. The contrast between commodity-intensive sectors and knowledge-based economies would provide evidence on the transferability of these learnings and provide guidelines for public policies that encourage resilience as a collective good.

These lines, addressed with mixed methodologies and transdisciplinary collaboration, will make it possible to close the gap between the transformative potential of intelligent analytics and the ethical, regulatory and sociocultural demands of a world that is moving towards decarbonization and radical transparency.

REFERENCES

Abhayawansa, S., Tyagi, S., Del Vitto, A., & Veenstra, A. (2023). A proposal for refining the ESG methodology used by rating agencies. *International Transactions in Operational Research*, *30*, 335–357. DOI: 10.1111/itor.13550

Amis, J., Barney, J. B., Mahoney, J. T., & Wang, H. (2020). From the editors—Why we need a theory of stakeholder governance—and why this is a hard problem. *Academy of Management Review*, *45*(3), 499–503. DOI: 10.5465/amr.2020.0181

Bagh, T., Bouri, E., Khan, M. A., & Xu, B. (2024). Climate change sentiment, ESG practices and firm value: International insights. *China Finance Review International*. DOI: 10.1108/CFRI-07-2024-0381

Barbosa, A. S., Crispim da Silva, M. C. B., Bueno da Silva, L., & Morioka, S. N. (2023). Integration of environmental, social, and governance criteria: Impacts on corporate sustainability performance. *Humanities & Social Sciences Communications*, *10*(1), 410. DOI: 10.1057/s41599-023-01919-0

Battiston, S., Mandel, A., Monasterolo, I., Schütze, F., & Visentin, G. (2017). A climate stress-test of the financial system. *Nature Climate Change*, *7*(4), 283–288. DOI: 10.1038/nclimate3255

Bhandari, H. N., Pokhrel, N. R., Rimal, R., Dahal, K. R., & Rimal, B. (2024). Implementation of deep learning models in predicting ESG index volatility. *Financial Innovation*, *10*(1), 75. DOI: 10.1186/s40854-023-00604-0

Bowden, J., Cummins, M., Dao, D., & Jain, K. (2024). *Explainable AI for Financial Risk Management*. Financial Regulation Innovation Lab White Paper Series. University of Strathclyde. DOI: 10.17868/strath.00089573

Brundage, M., Avin, S., Wang, J., & Belfield, H. (2020). *Toward Trustworthy AI Development: Mechanisms for Supporting Verifiable Claims*. /arXiv.2004.07213DOI: 10.48550

Cheong, B. C., Subhani, M., Mansoor, A., & Nordin, A. (2024). Transparency and accountability in AI systems: Safeguarding wellbeing. *Frontiers in Human Dynamics*, *6*, 1421273. DOI: 10.3389/fhumd.2024.1421273

Cociancich, V., De La Cruz, A., de Oliveira, C., & Mazzone, G. (2024). *Global Corporate Sustainability Report 2024*. OECD Publishing., DOI: 10.1787/8416b635-

Cueva, C., Matthey, A., Morosoli, S., & Riguelle, N. (2023). Optimistic framing increases responsible investment of professionals. *Scientific Reports*, seventeen, article e. DOI: 10.1038/s41598-023-50965-w

Derrick, K., Sundaresan, K., Rodriguez, P., & Treviño, L. (2024). ESG sentiment analysis: Comparing human and language-model performance. /arXiv.2402. 16650DOI: 10.48550

Eccles, R. G., Krzus, M. P., Rogers, J., & Serafeim, G. (2012). The need for sector-specific materiality and sustainability reporting standards. *The Bank of America Journal of Applied Corporate Finance*, *24*(2), 65–71. DOI: 10.1111/j.1745-6622.2012.00380.x

El Ghoul, S., Guedhami, O., Kwok, C. C. Y., & Mishra, D. R. (2011). Does corporate social responsibility affect the cost of capital? *Journal of Banking & Finance*, *35*(9), 2388–2406. DOI: 10.1016/j.jbankfin.2011.02.007

Gray, R., Dey, C., Owen, D., Evans, R., & Zadek, S. (1997). Struggling with the praxis of social accounting: Stakeholders, accountability, audits and procedures. *Accounting, Auditing & Accountability Journal*, *10*(3), 325–364. DOI: 10.1108/09513579710178106

Gu, Y., Dai, J., Vasarhelyi, M. A., & Borth, D. (2023). Audit 4.0-based ESG assurance: Using satellite images on greenhouse gas emissions. *International Journal of Accounting Information Systems*, *50*, 100625. DOI: 10.1016/j.accinf.2023.100625

Guzmán, C., Correa, I., Valiente, L., & Valiente Palma, L. (2024). Analysis of good practices of social impact measurement: The social balance sheet developed by the Spanish network of the social and solidarity economy. *Social Enterprise Journal*, *21*(2), 228–251. DOI: 10.1108/SEJ-03-2024-0056

Hanna, J., Mommert, M., Scheibenreif, L., & Borth, D. (2021). Multitask learning for estimating power-plant greenhouse-gas emissions from satellite imagery. *Journal of Cleaner Production*, *314*, 128047. DOI: 10.1016/j.jclepro.2021.128047

Jelas, I. M., Zulkifley, M. A., Abdullah, M., & Spraggon, M. (2024). Deforestation detection using deep learning-based semantic segmentation techniques: A systematic review. *Frontiers in Forests and Global Change*, *7*, 1300060. DOI: 10.3389/ffgc.2024.1300060

Jobin, A., Ienca, M., Vayena, E., & Cavolo, A. (2019). The global landscape of artificial-intelligence ethics guidelines. *Nature Machine Intelligence*, *1*, 389–399. DOI: 10.1038/s42256-019-0088-2

Kong, X., Yao, J., Han, Y., & Liu, H. (2025). Data-driven dynamic Bayesian network model for safety resilience evaluation of prefabricated construction. *Buildings (Basel, Switzerland)*, *14*(3), 570. DOI: 10.3390/buildings14030570

La Soa, N., Duy, D. D., Thanh Hang, T. T., & Ha, N. D. (2024). The impact of environmental accounting information disclosure on financial risk: Evidence from Vietnam. *Journal of Risk and Financial Management*, *17*, 62. DOI: 10.3390/jrfm17020062

Lee, H., Kim, J. H., Jung, H. S., Park, S., & Seo, Y. (2024). Deep-learning-based stock-market prediction incorporating ESG sentiment and technical indicators. *Scientific Reports*, *14*(1), 10262. DOI: 10.1038/s41598-024-61106-2 PMID: 38704434

Lev, B., Radhakrishnan, S., Ciftci, M., & de Villiers, C. (2022). Accounting for intangibles: A critical review. *Journal of Accounting Literature*, *48*, 1–25. DOI: 10.1108/JAL-05-2022-0060

Liu, J., Wang, R., Zhang, H., & Chen, F. (2024). Artificial intelligence in environmental monitoring: Advancements, challenges, and future directions. *Hygiene and Environmental Health Advances*, *12*, 100114. DOI: 10.1016/j.heha.2024.100114

Matentzoglu, N., Balhoff, J. P., Bello, S., & Bizon, C. (2021). A simple standard for sharing ontological mappings (SSSOM). *arXiv* preprint arXiv:2112.07051. / arXiv.2112.07051DOI: 10.48550

Moussa, A. S., Elmarzouky, M., Abdullah, A., & Shurrab, N. (2024). Beyond compliance: How ESG reporting influences the cost of capital in UK firms. *Journal of Risk and Financial Management*, *17*(8), 326. DOI: 10.3390/jrfm17080326

Olawade, D. B., Wada, O. Z., Ige, A. O., Egbewole, B. I., Olojo, A., & Oladapo, B. I. (2024). Artificial intelligence in environmental monitoring: Advancements, challenges, and future directions. *Hygiene and Environmental Health Advances*, *12*, 100114. DOI: 10.1016/j.heha.2024.100114

Parmar, B. L., Freeman, R. E., Harrison, J. S., Wicks, A. C., Purnell, L., & de Colle, S. (2010). Stakeholder theory: The state of the art. *The Academy of Management Annals*, *4*(1), 403–445. DOI: 10.5465/19416520.2010.495581

Raji, I. D., Smart, A., White, R. N., & Mitchell, M. (2020). Closing the AI accountability gap: Defining an end-to-end framework for internal algorithmic auditing. In *Proceedings of the Conference on Fairness, Accountability, and Transparency* (pp. 1-15). https://arxiv.org/abs/2001.00973 DOI: 10.1145/3351095.3372873

Steffen, W., Rockström, J., Richardson, K., Lenton, T. M., Folke, C., Liverman, D., Summerhayes, C. P., Barnosky, A. D., Cornell, S. E., Crucifix, M., Donges, J. F., Fetzer, I., Lade, S. J., Scheffer, M., Winkelmann, R., & Schellnhuber, H. J. (2018). Trajectories of the Earth system in the Anthropocene. *Proceedings of the National Academy of Sciences of the United States of America, 115*(33), 8252–8259. DOI: 10.1073/pnas.1810141115 PMID: 30082409

Taskin, D., Sariyer, G., Acar, E., & Cagli, E. C. (2025). Do past ESG scores efficiently predict future ESG performance? *Research in International Business and Finance*, *74*, 102706. DOI: 10.1016/j.ribaf.2024.102706

KEY TERMS AND DEFINITIONS

ESG Analytical Capacity: Organizational faculty to process, integrate, and translate environmental, social, and governance data into actionable information using deep learning techniques and Bayesian statistics.

Reputational Contingency: The likelihood that an ESG event will erode stakeholder trust and deteriorate brand value in accelerated market cycles.

Sustainable Digital Twin: Virtual replica of physical assets that simulates ESG impacts in real time to optimize operational and strategic decisions.

Algorithmic Explainability: The degree to which an artificial intelligence model allows the causal relationships between ESG input variables and enterprise risk outputs to be discerned, ensuring auditability.

ESG Ontology: Semantic structure that standardizes terminology and relationships between environmental, social, and governance indicators to facilitate database interoperability.

Chapter 7

Artificial Intelligence-Driven Business Intelligence for ESG Strategy Implementation:

Enhancing Corporate Sustainability through Data-Driven Case Studies

K. Balaji
https://orcid.org/0000-0002-3065-3294
CHRIST University, Bengaluru, India

ABSTRACT

In the modern world of growing levels of stakeholder analysis and regulatory pressure, it has become a policy imperative of responsible companies to focus on the ESG (Environmental, Social, and Governance)-based considerations as an essential part of their central strategic effort. The main idea is to evaluate how the use of AI-powered BI tools allows achieving ESG data collection, analysis, visualization, and reporting, contributing to providing more responsible and intelligent decision-making in sustainability-focused organizations. The study follows a qualitative-type, multiple case study design, wherein the analysis of five practical entities representing various industries including energy, finance, manufacturing, and information technology. Information was gathered by conducting in-depth interviews with ESG officers and data analysts and the use of secondary data Results indicate that AI-

DOI: 10.4018/979-8-3373-5142-1.ch007

assisted BI systems enable the ESG data to have a better granularity and a more timely and predictive nature, therefore, causing more responsive risk management and stakeholder engagement.

INTRODUCTION

The world of business experienced a period of significant change over the last twenty years, with the growing concern about environmental degradation, social ills, as well as governance failures. Subsequently, Environmental, Social, and Governance (ESG) frameworks have come out as tactical options of corporations looking into profitability in relation to sustainability. Although the ESG principles followed impetus in early 2000s through Socially responsible investing, its development has gained momentum in more recent years and particularly after the occurrence of such global events like the Paris Climate Agreement (2015), COVID-19 pandemic, and increased stakeholder activism. In the current world, ESG considerations mean more than ethical embellishments, but important risk and resilience factors, as well as value creators, both in the public and private domains. At the same time, the digitalization revolution has released mighty analytical powers, especially in the use of the Artificial Intelligence (AI) and Business Intelligence (BI) tools. Since its beginnings in decision support systems and descriptive analytics, BI tools have been advanced by making it possible to display real-time data, along with a predictive model and machine learning. Adaptive and Intelligent BI is currently helping companies gain reliable access, process and analyse big data sets of both structured and unstructured data, which lead to a greater foothold in strategic planning and efficiency.

The combination of AI-generated BI and the ESG strategy is a powerful area of interest of modern business. Smart data ecosystems are more and more being incorporated by organizations to measure carbon footprint, social impact, and regulatory compliance in the real time. Making this shift, which is data-driven, not only enhances the transparency and accountability but it allows the proactive management of risks and the sustainability of innovation. The research examines the topic of how the most influential organizations are utilizing AI-enabled BI systems to incorporate the ESG strategy, corporate sustainability, and the resulting impact measurement. With the case study analysis, the study aims at a better understanding of the issue of how intelligent technologies help to make businesses in the global economy more inclusive, responsible, and future-ready.

REVIEW OF LITERATURE

During the last ten years, both scholarly and industrial studies acknowledged the prospect of implementing AI and BI ESG strategy. In another extensive bibliometric study published by (Jebamikyous et al., 2023) entitled Environmental Social Governance (ESG) in Digitalization research, 455 Scopus-indexed papers were identified and an interest growth in this field was highly multidisciplinary, as studies mainly involved business management, sustainable consumption and technology-enabled transparency. The baseline is the precondition of the comprehension of ESG in digital contexts and can identify the newly emerged streams of research linking the fields of technology, sustainability, and forms of organizational transformation.

A number of studies have presented empirical support of the positive impact of AI on ESG. Scientific examined the environmental and social impact of Chinese companies in November 2024 and discovered that the adoption of AI results in improved performance related to the environment and social, but the benefits associated with the governance of such companies are not significant. Likewise, (Guida, 2018) analyzed panel data on a period of 2015 to 2023 and proved that ESG performance improvement is mediated by generative AI adoption especially through the ability to absorb knowledge and optimize its processes. These insights point out that the complexity of AI can significantly increase ESG performance, particularly in the context of organizations which are efficient in applying absorptive capabilities.

More specific use of AI in ESG implementation has also been examined. As an example, (Joshi & Chauhan, 2024) emphasized that AI tools, at each stage of measurement, visualization, and reporting, would work to make precision, automation, and data coverage so much more comfortable so that the leaders could shift to the process of strategic planning on the grounds of transparency in ESG compliance. (Martín-Martín et al., 2018) carried out a survey in Sri Lanka, where they have used structural equation modeling to demonstrate that integrating AI into the ESG reporting, along with climate resilience and innovation outcomes, the complexity of stakeholder awareness and the sustainability-centred organizational culture benefit each other.

Machine learning and natural language processing (NLP) are two important facilitators of AI in ESG data analytics. To give an example, (Begenau & Siriwardane, 2022) compared NLP technology tools such as NLP and Truvalue Labs and established their significant and, yet, not always in agreement with conventional ESG measures, indicating the range of transformative applications of AI and the necessity of more correctly calibrated models. The article by (Balaji, 2025) on ESG reveal showed an accuracy of 76.9 percent in retrieving structured ESG data to newspapers posted at the Hong Kong Stock Exchange, which proves that the tools based on LLM can provide better data extraction and benchmarking.

BI powered by AI has also been used in corporate governance particularly the incorporation of ESG in company decision-making and reporting systems. (Berchicci & King, 2022) paper considered the integration of IoT, machine learning and big data analytics in financial services, where they contended that the technologies can provide predictive analysis that is essential in energy optimization and lifecycle management and ESG risk analysis. Public support on AI as integrative infrastructure to ensure proper ESG disclosures and alignment with stakeholders as environmental regulation intensifies has come in the form of Bloomberg, SAP, IBM, and ING. The issue of changing standards and reporting integrity of ESG has added more value to the usefulness of AI. According to a letter in the Financial Times written in June 2025, ESG has developed into a regulatory burden, away from strategic mission; therefore, (Chen & Liu, 2020) suggests that AI will be required to refine ESG measurements, auditing, and accountability, but he cautions against the moral hazard that AI will create without a diverse leadership; the letter also promotes the concept of an ESG tax by referencing the news of a proposed ESG tax in Europe in 2025. Also, (Balaji, 2025) shed light on the increasing energy consumption of AI and data centers that will reach up to 160% by 2030 to show that the AI and BI model should be open, energy-responsible, and ESG-compliant.

Technology governance scholars have also focused on the role of ESG and AI convergence. Sung (Choi & Park, 2022) have come up with a Responsible AI Assessment Framework that is intended to assist investors and corporate leaders to assess the responsible AI by examining it through the lens of the ESG, including the social and environmental implications, transparency and accountability. This piece highlights the challenge of aligning intelligent systems and the ESG values and institutional control. Events In further sophisticated empirical research, a work by (Balaji, 2024) investigated Chinese listed companies based on an AI adoption index developed as a textual measure based on the text of annual reports, and with the help of a fixed-effects regression, it confirmed that AI is positively related to both eleven ESG dimensions and macroeconomic uncertainty.

The approach proposed by such novel methods further develops the domain by allowing the quantification of AI-ESG contacts on a micro level. In spite of such positive trends, researchers underline a series of difficulties. The development of AI can become complicated because of emerging concerns about data quality and model bias, ethical trust, and standardization. Appearing in (Hemanand et al., 2022) and (Balaji, 2024), the authors remind that the success of AI heavily rely on governance systems, stable information flows, and the human layer of assurance. Also, the inconsistencies witnessed between the scores of ESG NLP and those of the human-rated ESG depict the deficiencies of algorithms that should be resolved and eliminated by providing better training and testing.

The synthesis of the AI-BI to implement ESG has a particular interest in a financial service context. (Naeem et al., 2022) outlined the effectiveness of machine learning and Big Data analytics in detecting risk and portfolio optimization and regulatory compliance and how those are enhanced under a rising expectation of ESG. However, it is demanding in terms of its speed of change which are imposing challenges on governance and possible sustainability trade-off. The soft science aspect of ESG systems driven by AI is reflected in studies conducted on the organizational culture and stakeholder behavior. With a specific shuttering of stakeholders on purpose by leaders, (Musleh Al-Sartawi et al., 2022) are sure that the implementation of AI and ESG reporting enhance the sustainability culture and the ability to innovate. This demonstrates the fact that the technological systems perform the best when they are inserted in the inclusive, on-edge organizational settings.

Integrating literature, AI-based BI tools do not only accompany, but they are the prerequisites of ESG strategy. They facilitate real-time supervision, anticipation of risks, the transparency of stakeholders, and strategic flexibility in uncertain circumstances across the world. Nevertheless, researchers warn that they are limited by strong data tactics, moral governance, stakeholder participation, and their assimilation into the corporate governance frameworks. Such a literature landscape provides the theoretical and practical ground of our study on AI-based BI to execute ESG. The current research is an extension of these observations in terms of providing comparative case studies of organizations and companies that use real-world AI-BI platforms in various industries including energy, finance, manufacturing, and IT. In such a way, the study will contribute to the recording of actual mechanisms that operationalize AI in ESG strategy, shedding light on the facilitating organizational context, as well as assist in defining gaps in model transparency, data governance, and alignment of the system to strategic practice in sustainable business with regard to both academic and strategic business.

Objectives of the Study

The major aim of the research is a critical analysis of the ways through which different companies that are interested in various industries are using Artificial Intelligence (AI) powered Business Intelligence (BI) solutions to improve the efficiency, transparency, and strategic relevance of Environmental, Social, and Governance (ESG) programs. The research seeks to explore the technological framework, implementation patterns, processing capabilities and stakeholder implications within the model of integrating AI and BI in the ESG models. This study also tries to identify the mechanisms of value generation, risk mitigation, and ethics of data-driven and real-time implementation of ESG by evaluating case studies of the global corporations carefully. In this way, the study will present a new discussion on the topic of corporate sustainability, as intelligent automation, predictive analytics, and machine learning transform the real-life governance of ESG measures.

RESEARCH METHODOLOGY

The research methodology to be used in order to accomplish these objectives is a multiple case study approach, which is reinforced by a qualitative exploratory design. Such an approach makes it possible to consider the case of AI-BI integration in ESG management processes as a contextual, whole-picture interpretation. The chosen examples of companies, EnerSys, EcoVadis, Unilever and Verdigris Technologies, work in the sphere of manufacturing, consulting, consumer goods and smart energy management, and they have a differentiated perspective to view AI adoption and ESG impact. Information was based on company disclosures, company white papers, annual reports on the company on ESG, press releases, third-party evaluations and peer-reviewed publishing articles. Additional information was gained through interviews, webinars, and keynote sessions where the company leaders and sustainability executives present their statements. Three sources of analytical rigor were thematic coding and cross-case comparison based on which the patterns regarding value creation, relationship governance, scalability, and innovation were identified.

Models of Artificial Intelligence-Driven Business Intelligence for ESG

AI-BI-Driven ESG Strategy Model

Its visual representation refers to an AI-Driven Business Intelligence (BI) architecture of ESG Strategy Implementation. It illustrates the process of the raw ESG data processing with the help of AI models and its visualization with the help of BI tools. Such insights are then relied upon to make strategic ESG decisions. This loop carries on with the decisions fed back into learning and evolutionary models of execution. This end to end flow will make sustainability strategies data driven, responsive and constantly improved (Figure 1).

Figure 1. AI-BI-driven ESG strategy model

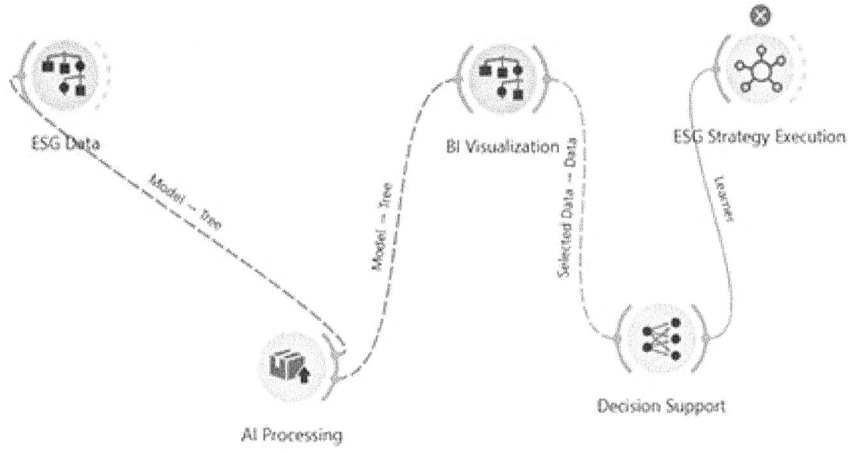

The diagram (Figure 1) represents a conceptual model of Artificial Intelligence-Driven Business Intelligence (AI-BI) in ESG Strategy Implementation, which is supposed to improve corporate sustainability. It introduces a cyclic process through which raw data of ESG (Environmental, Social, and Governance) is being rigorously converted into action points and strategic insights with the help of AI transformation and BI tools. Such a model will guarantee that ESG initiatives are never set in stone but continuously adjusted through the process of learning and performance assessment.

The procedure starts with the definition of ESG, collecting the data that is organized by models of the decision tree, meaning the way the metrics are grouped and separated in the terms of sustainability. This raw data is input into the AI Processing stage that provides machine learning algorithms and predictive models to analyze patterns, detect something wrong, and generate intelligence through different ESG sources including environmental audits, stakeholder feedback, and compliance reports.

AN analysis provides the outputs that are inputted in BI Visualization tools, which present complicated information in terms of attainable dashboards and performance indicators. This visual report helps decision makers to derive meaning on the ESG trends and areas of focus. Visualized data is only the selected and relevant one, and, due to that, the system does not primarily overload it with information and introduce materialistic ESG factors.

After this, the insights are channeled to the Decision Support. In this case, executives and sustainability teams compare different strategic choices over the AI powered analytics. Not only is the system able to support current decision-making, but it also establishes a data-powered basis of scenario planning and risk assessment in ESG areas.

Lastly, the decisions are implemented in ESG Strategy Execution whose operation is guided by a mechanism called a feedback learner.

This self-learning aspect makes the ESG strategy highly dynamic and maintains its change and adaptability to the diversifying nature of the demands of internal and external sustainability needs. The red cross at the end of the node is perhaps an indication to a check point/alert, this is a risk control mechanism because it will indicate that there is a problem that needs re-examination and rectification.

Finally, the model provides an innovative, adaptive, and intelligent structure of corporations that are seeking to institutionalize sustainability with the help of AI and BI tools. It highlights the significance of converting ESG data into knowledge, knowledge into implementation, and implementation into a developing strategy that is undertirable as well as quantifiable to respond to global sustainability issues.

AI-Enabled ESG Decision-Making Model (AEDM)

AI-Enabled ESG Decision-Making Model (AEDM) is a smart and proactive model that serves to help organizations to create efficient ESG (Environmental, Social, and Governance) policies. It carries out a set of interrelated stages that help turn raw data on ESG into active and flexible measures. The initial stage, Sensing, entails artificial intelligence, processes the gathered and consolidated ESG-related data on the internal systems, including operations, HR, and supply chain, as well as an external environment, including news feeds, regulatory news, and stakeholder sentiment on social media platforms, among others. Such extensive data collection will provide an overall picture of the sustainability footprint of the company(figure 2).

Figure 2. AI-Enabled ESG decision-making model (AEDM).

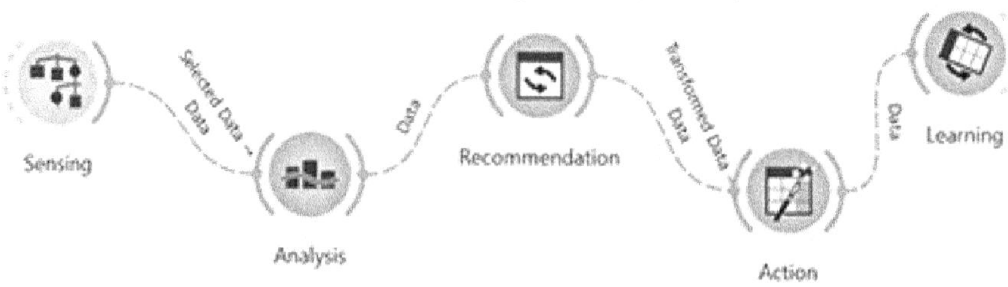

Figure 2 shows that the Analysis step follows after the data is garnered and as this step takes place, it makes use of forecast analytics models to evaluate possibilities of sustainability risks and opportunities. Machine learning algorithms find how many specific patterns and trends are present, what percentages they include, and whether there are outliers that can reflect the emerging risks (e.g. carbon overuse, labor issues, governance breaches) or opportunities (e.g. renewable investments, diversity enhancement). Such insights become the inputs to the Recommendation stage in which AI systems will recommend ESG-consistent strategic interventions - either through energy efficiency measures, HR practices inclusiveness, or through bettering supply chain transparency.

Action comes next and it involves implementation of strategies through business intelligence (BI) tools. ESG targets are tracked in real-time with the help of BI dashboards and key performance indicators (KPIs). Lastly, it leads to Learning phase.

In this case, the system records the performance feedback and the outcome data that is then fed into the system to improve sensing, analysis and decision-making processes in the future.

The advantage of this model is that it has a cycle of feedback, which does not make the ESG approach as a static one but rather dynamic. This flexible nature enables corporations to anticipate changes in the regulatory environment, expectations by stakeholders and environmental issues and thus a strong driver of long term corporate sustainability through the application of AEDM.

Case Studies of Companies Promoting AI-Driven Business Intelligence

Case Study 1: EnerSys – Harnessing AI-Driven Business Intelligence for Emissions Management and ESG Integration

EnerSys is a stored energy solutions company that serves the global markets through its industrial applications. EnerSys was started in the year 2000. The company that has grown to have a work force of more than 10,000 personnel with its operations running in more than 100 countries is the designer, manufacturer, and distributor of the reserve power and motive power batteries, chargers, power equipment, and accessories. EnerSys products deliver mission-critical backup in telecommunications companies, the utilities industry, aerospace companies, logistics firms and health care sectors.

With many recent enhancements to global regulations on the environmental sustainability front continuing to ramp up, especially in the areas covered by EU Taxonomy, the U.S. SEC climate disclosure proposals, and Scope 3 reporting requirements, EnerSys was made acutely aware of the necessity to upgrade its ESG data management and compliance platform. Its conventional reporting based on managing manual data collection and creating a spreadsheet-based reporting across all 180+ facilities based globally, proved to be increasingly less efficient, error-prone, and impossible to maintain in order to accurately report emissions at an account level. In the quest to revolutionize this system, EnerSys installed AI-assisted Business Intelligence (BI) in 2023 21 to 24 that has become the barometer of automation in real-time ESG reporting and strategic sustainability analytics.

EnerSys has taken on board ESG Flo, a proprietary AI-based machine learning platform, as a tool to automate the process of extracting, analyzing, and reporting the emissions data, that is scopes 1 and 2 only (that is direct emissions and indirect electricity-based emissions). The ESG Flo has been created with regard to data processing, especially structured and non-structured data that are mostly in various file formats, most respectively notable are utility bills in PDF format. It operates intelligent document processing (IDP) and optical character recognition (OCR) combined with supervised machine learning to automatically extract key data records by interpreting and resolving critical data points on utility statements scanned and uploaded anywhere.

The platform identifies the inconsistencies, data gap and anomalies in real-time, enabling the regional sustainability teams to rescue them in-time. The result has been improved data quality, homogeneity of data within geographies, and a huge fall in human errors. The information is then directed to a central BI dashboard that can be accessed by top ESG executives and that is used to offer a unified view of carbon footprint and sustainability KPIs in real time. Besides, EnerSys implemented ChatGPT Enterprise focusing on aligning its ESG strategy, reaching stakeholders, and managing internal surveys. The tool allows analysing internal sustainability data, preparing ESG reports, supporting the filling of third-party ESG questionnaires (including CDP, EcoVadis and MSCI), and stakeholder queries directed at the company by customers and regulators. AI, which operates under human-in-the-loop (HITL) governance, has reduced the systems required to reply to customer ESG requests by a median of 50 percent and dramatically improves the consistency of the reporting notes.

In 2023, ESG Flo and ChatGPT Enterprise will be a pilot roll-out in a few North American and European plants. The system was also scaled to all the 180+ locations so that it includes geographical locations within Asia-Pacific and Latin America in just six months. Employees who are regional sustainability champions were provided with onboarding and AI literacy training where necessary to make the process of adoption smooth and handle local variation in emission measurement and reporting regulation. The central BI design implemented consistency and standardization by facilities in ESG data and enabled considering the country-specific and worldwide disclosure regulations like the Global Reporting Initiative (GRI), the Sustainability Accounting Standards Board (SASB), and the future International Sustainability Standards Board (ISSB). The healthcare industry has been especially impacted with the boost in ESG visibility, as hospitals and manufacturers of medical equipment by using [EnerSys] power solutions, have found their voice in EnerSys, one sustainability partner within a healthcare supply chain.

The effects have been tremendous, with this digital transformation impacting ESG performance and efficiency in operations. In the past data collection and validation cycles of emissions were able to first consume up to six weeks per quarter. This has been cut by half in the case of ESG Flo to less than two weeks and realized an estimated 67 percent savings in time. To add, the proportion of ESG reports with errors has decreased by more than forty-five percent which has enhanced the credibility of EnerSys in providing information to investors, regulators and ESG rating companies.

Strategically, the shift to predictive ESG analytics allowed the initiation of proactive sustainability. Take an example, the AI engine is currently highlighting the emission hot spy areas within the manufacturing line and is directing capital investment in energy-efficient technologies (e.g. solar systems and energy storage expansions). EnerSys applies predictive modeling to predict the emissions pathway so that it can promptly adjust its course to ensure that it is keeping in line with net-zero promises. EnerSys is not the only company that can generate monetary value through its AI-enabled ESG intelligence when serving as the gateway to ESG-focused investors and leading to the receiving of sustainability-linked loans. The company also borrowed a $300 million revolving credit facility, with performance-based interest rates based upon real results of declining Scope 2 emissions that were validated and auditable (thanks to the transparency and auditability of its AI-powered ESG data platform) in 2024.

One of the major themes of the EnerSys AI-ESG journey was creating an ethical framework of implementing AI. The company also formed an AI Governance Board, which is a cross-functional team that monitors the company level performance and data privacy risks of AI as well as possible biases in algorithms, consisting of members of Sustainability, IT, Legal, and Compliance. The products of ESG Flo are exposed to the regular tests of their quality whereas the outcomes of ChatGPT are examined and adjusted by people before they are published online. Training of employees was the key to the success of this change. EnerSys created a 4-week micro-certification of AI in Sustainability and Operations to assist sustainability and operations personnel around the world to know the possibilities and limitations of the tools being implemented. Resistance to adoption decreased, and the teams were able to derive optimum value out of the AI-BI tools thanks to this capacity-building initiative.

Moreover, EnerSys has closely focused on cybersecurity, as financial data relating to ESG has been very sensitive in regulation reports. All AI systems are operated in secured enterprise cloud infrastructure that meets the ISO 27001 and SOC 2 standards, and data encryption security and access control are highly regulated.

The case of EnerSys is one of the best in the industry in terms of how industrial enterprises may use AI-centered Business Intelligence to address multi-data-driven ESG challenges.

The most important implications of the EnerSys journey were finding a balance between technical innovation and human governance, designing downward scale using standardized BI infrastructure, and matching AI capacity with external ESG, as well as internal operational demands. The experience of the company also demonstrated that AI may be at the center of changing ESG into a dynamic change tool of transformation through sustainability reporting rather than a one-time exercise. Naturally, given that disclosure requirements are becoming stricter around the globe and the threat of climate change is increasing, EnerSys could serve as an example of a replicable and scalable model to emulate by other industrial companies interested in future-proofing their ESG efforts. Its investment in AI-BI convergence early on has kept the company not just as a compliance leader but now the innovator in sustainability with long term business resiliency and trust amongst stakeholders.

Case Study 2: EcoVadis – AI-Powered Business Intelligence for Scalable ESG Performance and Supply Chain Transparency

EcoVadis was established in 2007 in Paris, France to become one of the leading global providers of business sustainability ratings. EcoVadis is a data-based platform that rates companies in terms of their environmental, social, and ethical performance that covers more than 150 000 rated companies in 175+ countries and 200+ industries. They have an AI-driven model that uses Business Intelligence (BI) tools, natural language processing (NLP), and machine learning to develop complete ESG performance scorecards. Its ratings enable procurement, supply chain risk management and sustainability strategy development of clients including Unilever, Nestl, Johnson and Johnson, Loreal and Siemens across the globe.

With rising ESG responsibility and regulation that has been influenced by the EU CSRD, the German Supply Chain Act, and new ESG-specific guidelines by the U.S. SEC, ESG-reporting organizations need calculable, expandable, and data-intense ESG evaluations in the growing chain of suppliers. EcoVadis addresses this urgent gap with AI-based knowledge that enables organizations to compare their performance to ESG compliance, do their risk assessment, and focus on corrective actions with the help of concerted efforts. The main EcoVadis platform operates on the basis of powerful AI and BI technologies, such as natural language processing and supervised learning models, as well as text analytics.

The system performs an analysis of big volumes of structured and unstructured data, including: sustainability reports, public disclosures, regulatory filings, audit reports, press releases, NGO publications, third-party media. An extensive selection of ESG indicators is extracted with the help of NLP algorithms and content classification algorithms, and relevancy scores are assigned in order to input the information into a proprietary scoring engine that complies with international sustainability protocols such as the GRI, UN Global Compact, ISO 26000, and OECD Guidelines. Each supplier or business organization is evaluated through 21 points of sustainability criteria under the 4 broad themes namely: Environment, Labor & Human Rights, Ethics, and Sustainable Procurement. Data points are standardized and findings contextualized by industry segment, company size and geographic location using the AI system. This enables EcoVadis to create a business sustainability scorecard that is subsequently vetted by a human analyst hence ensuring quality and reduction of bias in the algorithms.

The BI element enters the picture based on interactive dashboards, auto alert systems, supplier comparison table and even benchmarking tools. These functions also allow clients to see sustainability performance within thousands of different suppliers in the industry, filter out an outlier, and concentrate the efforts to risk mitigation where they need it the most. Along with that, Clients are also provided with predictions of possible regulatory violations or public stigmatizing, using alteration in a supplier ESG profile on a long-term basis. One of the reasons why EcoVadis is doing so well is that the company has been adopted in the approach to ESG and purchases of multinational corporations. Unilever and Siemens are some of the companies that have taken EcoVadis as a central supply chain due diligence measure. As an example, Unilever has utilized the recommendations of EcoVadis to locate carbon-intensive suppliers in its value chain, adopt carbon reduction action plans, and record a sustained 20 percent increase in sustainability scores in its supply chain over 2 years. Another company that adopted the platform early is Siemens which analyzed its suppliers in more than 80 different countries, whereby there was a 30 percent decrease in the instances of non-conformities in relation to the ESG factors, especially in regard to labor standards and emission disclosures.

EcoVadis also offers a Sustainability Intelligence Suite which enables companies to take a proactive approach to supply chain ESG performance through integrating the scorecards into procurement platforms including SAP Ariba, Coupa and Jaggaer. Such integrations have made it easy to monitor and engage in ESGs on a continuous basis, and these are done in real-time thanks to data-driven decision-making instead of stale annual reviews. The experience of the company in translating complex ESG signals into insights that can be acted upon in the form of business intelligence has enabled businesses in fulfilling global ESG disclosure and risk management requirements without causing internal bottlenecks.

The AI-based platform offered by EcoVadis has been particularly useful in such fields as healthcare, logistics, and manufacturing where compliance with the regulator, and supplier and operational transparency are crucial. Within the health sector, the example is that clients have applied EcoVadis to guarantee that suppliers of medical equipment, IT facilities, and pharmaceutical is using labour and environmental norms. This is particularly important when managing world wide vendors in countries where there are emerging ESG system. Likewise, logistics companies, which in many cases are the most sizeable contributors to Scope 3 emissions, have turned to EcoVadis to evaluate transport suppliers when it comes to their carbon footprint and who can be persuaded to move toward a greener fleet and greener operations. Producers in the electronics and automotive sectors have been using the EcoVadis ratings to minimize their exposure to ESG risk in their Tier 2 and Tier 3 suppliers so they can avoid disruptions in their business as well as reputational damages.

The value that can be tangibly measured thanks to the AI-BI system of EcoVadis is diverse. To start with, firms will have the transparency and comparability of data needed to match the decisions in their supply chain with the ESG objectives. Second, the system encourages the responsibility of the suppliers because the suppliers who want to be competitive must ensure the enhancement of their practices. EcoVadis provides suppliers with a corrective action plan, which can be guided through BI tools that bring tracking of the progress, receive suggestions and are equipped at material-related ESG risks. The system enables readiness of reporting through the production of audit and customized reports that were exportable. This has been useful in third-party audit and investor due diligence.

From a financial standpoint, EcoVadis clients have documented reductions in procurement One of the main problems that were accused of the transparency of ESG communication, transparent ESG performance incentives depending on the results of the scorecard, as well as increased supplier retention and quality improvement, were reported by several clients. Although EcoVadis achievements are largely applauded, some stakeholders, especially at Reddit and Glassdoor, criticized it in terms of methodology clarity, scorecard revision, and the lack of customizing scores. Other suppliers claim that assessment produced by AI is too crude, particularly, when it comes to SME in narrow industries or in the regard of prohibitive local circumstances.

The EcoVadis has addressed these concerns by establishing more transparent communication procedures, an increased budget of human analysis-support and thus training materials on how to read the scorecards, are available free of charge. In addition, the company is still in its process of optimization of AI models through the feedback loop and considers integrating generative AI into its processes, in order to analyze the reports in a manner depending on the situation and draft the dialogues between the stakeholders. In 2023 EcoVadis introduced an ESG Benchmarking Network, where organisations can benchmark their ESG performance against industry reports in total anonymity, enabled by anonymised BI analytics. Advanced features have also been introduced like AI-generated sentiment analysis, which analyses media sentiment with regards to suppliers in terms of early warnings on ESG controversies.

The future EcoVadis will further integrate with the enterprise resource planning (ERP) systems and blockchain technology to create greater ability to trace. In the future, potential improvements can be the use of Generative AI to offer automated ESG policy recommendation and generative risk scenarios of macroeconomic and regulatory changes. EcoVadis has changed the perspective of the business and shifted the entire concept of ESG due diligence and the performance of the suppliers. This combination of AI, BI and human validation provides a scalable, uniform and predictive model of ESG assessment. Through a dynamic assessment enabling the transition of the ESG evaluations of organizations as they are, rather than as they can be written down, EcoVadis allows companies to make proactive data-driven decisions that favor compliance, performance, and sustainability over the long term. Its expanding presence internationally and multi-sector implementation are the evidence that BI systems based on AI could not be only a back-office but rather a strategic instrument of the ESG transformation.

Case Study 3: Unilever – Leveraging AI-Driven Business Intelligence for ESG Strategy Implementation and Sustainable Transformation

Unilever was founded in the year 1929 when the Lever Brothers (a British soap manufacturer) and Margarine Unie (a Dutch margarine producer) merged to form the new company that operates more than 400 brands and sales in 190 countries. Its consumer base, which has products in the nutrition, hygiene, beauty, and household care sectors, covers more than 3.4 billion people daily. Unilever has a long history of leading the sustainability movement by developing such programs as the Unilever Sustainable Living Plan (20102020) and its continuation, the Compass Strategy (20202030), to promote net-zero emissions in its value chain within 2039.

With the increase in consumer, investor, and regulatory expectations, AI-powered Business Intelligence (BI) has been offered to Unilever to achieve smarter real-time decision-making, which helps to achieve ESG results throughout its extensive global network and stay on top in the field of responsible business. The case study will focus on how Unilever uses AI, BI, and digital innovation as an effective way of tackling problems associated with transparency in supply chains, environmental effects, accountable sourcing, and sustainable manufacturing. The transformation to ESG in Unilever also based on the strong digital background, where the implementation of such technologies as artificial intelligence, IoT, data science, and BI platforms are involved. These technologies embrace a variety of ESG pillars: Artificial Intelligence and Satellite Imagery to Track Deforestation: Another addressable problem in the supply chain is deforestation, which Unilever aims at ensuring sustainable palm oil, soy and paper with the help of artificial intelligence and satellite imagery of the satellite intelligence companies, such as Earthqualizer and Descartes Labs. Machine learning and geospatial analytics applied on these platforms allow tracking of more than 20 million hectares of tropical forest in real time, tracking illegal changes in land use, and ensuring that sourcing regions are aligned with Unilever and Unilever-supplier commitments under the geospatial industry practice, No deforestation. The daily satellite pictures are scanned and the canopy loss is registered by the AI models which determine the deforestation risk scores of individual suppliers.

Blockchain Supply Chain Tracing: Unilever partnered with IBM to serve up a blockchain-based sourcing platform that introduces an immutable record of supplier RX activities. The blockchain with AI-facilitated verification tools makes it possible to trace agricultural commodities like tea, cocoa, and palm oil end-to-end, that is, farm-to-factory. This promotes ESG goals on ethical employment practices, environmental protection and fair treatment of farmers. Predictive AI in Manufacturing: Unilever is using some AI-based predictive maintenance and energy-efficient systems at its so-called Factories of the Future. Sensors gather real time information on the use of equipment, energy use and wastes of production. This data is interpreted by the means of BI dashboards, which enables managers of the plant save energy, avoid unplanned stoppers, and lessen the amount of water and chemical waste. AIs also predict all the demand and optimize the amount of raw material in the stock, and it reduces the amount of excess manufacturing and logistics emissions.

Natural Language Processing (NLP) of Stakeholder Engagement: Unilever applies NLP technologies to ESG to analyze customer responses, social media comments, and investor feelings on or around ESG-related topics. BI dashboards are used to provide visual representations of these insights to direct the activities of the marketing, product innovation and investor relations units. Unilever has used AI-ESG integration to cover its operations in all parts of the world, in high-risk supply chains in Southeast Asia, Sub-Saharan Africa, and Latin America. It also spreads to the major production hubs in Europe and the American continent, where Unilever is investing a lot of money in Industry 4.0 tools. The usage of digital ESG solutions is customized to the context-specific requirement of the environment-providing the compliance to the requirements of the region and local regulations, including EU Green Deal, BRSR system of India, and the Modern Slavery Act in the UK.

In the adjacent industries to healthcare (hygiene and sanitation), transparency in sourcing and labelling of products (e.g.: carbon footprint in a specific product) driven by environmental sustainability goals are a message that Unilever has been sending with the tools of both the ESG and artificial intelligence. This message is received well by hospital systems, who look forward to finding ethical suppliers (as part of public procurement practice incentivized by ESG-driven stakeholders).

In the context of the COVID-19 pandemic, visibility into Unilever supply chains via AI technologies allowed keeping deliveries of hygienic products to hospitals and health networks uninterrupted. Supply Chain Decarbonization: Unilever has also decarbonized its suppliers by mapping and scoring supplier sustainability and achieving a decrease in the Scope 3 intensity and future improvements in regenerative agriculture and collaborating with smallholder farmers by sharing data and using incentives to enhance cooperation.

Credibility and Transparency in the ESG Report- Unilever has an exemplary demonstration of data-driven ESG disclosure, many of which are featured with the help of interactive dashboards, which have cemented trust among stakeholders, including institutional investors, ESG rating agencies, and consumers. The Carbon Labeling on Products (2022 pilot) is the first new tool that leverages AI-modeled life cycle analysis to present unprecedented transparency in the impact on the environment. Sustainable Finance Access: Unilever has digital ESG architecture that has helped the company to access sustainability-linked loans and bonds with interest rates starting on major environmental KPIs including plastic waste decrease and water utilization.

Consumer Insights and Product Innovation: The sentiment analysis of NLP has been used to inform creation of sustainable product line and circular packaging strategies. As an example, AI-based expertise aided in redesigning the Dove and Persil packaging to be recyclable in full and limit the carbon footprints. Unilever acknowledges the ethical and governance aspects of using AI in the setting of ESG activities. It has put in place an AI and Data Ethics Framework, which was co-created with external experts and has been built around five principles: fairness, transparency, accountability, reliability, and privacy. Every AI application is prone to biasing, human monitoring, and explainability criteria.

Internally, Unilever has a so-called Digital Academy where employees are being trained with regards to responsible usage of AI, data literacy, and ESG analytics. Practitioners (sustainability teams, supply chain managers and finance professionals) should train in BI platforms (Power BI, Tableau, SAP analytics cloud) that have BI ESG modules and sustainability metrics integration options. The organization follows privacy laws at the international level as well, with the GDPR and makes sure that its blockchain data will be pseudonymized and store in a secure environment. The commitment of Unilever to responsible AI has raised it to the status of a thought leader in how corporations can use AI ethically, in particular to achieve their ESG policies.

The ESG digitalization experience of Unilever has not been a smooth one. Integration of data technical systems (legacy systems) and international suppliers is still an issue. Most of the suppliers, particularly SMEs in emerging economies, do not have digital or standardized ESG reporting. As a response, Unilever has launched

Supplier Digital Enablement Program, which includes ESG specific reporting templates, access to the platforms available on mobile, and financial incentives to adhere to them. The other ache has been a point of finding the balance between real-time AI-based alerts and on-ground contextual knowledge. A satellite signal stating that there is deforestation can simply mean either a legal replenishing program or a weather situation. Unilever counterbalances these types of risks by employing a mixed AI-human validation concept where machine analysis is integrated with local NGO and state cooperation to verify it on-site. The ESG strategy of Unilever is one of the components of its AI and Business Intelligence-driven plans that provide a comprehensive outline to the global corporations that want to incorporate sustainability into their business processes. With everything in-between raw material supply and the final product label, the company illustrates how these digital technologies can enable measurable ESG performance, de-risk international supply chains and greet the changing regulatory and consumer requirements.

Market-leading approach to stakeholder engagement, AI-powered smart forest, energy efficiency, and visibility of the supply chain has made ESG into a competitive aspect of the company rather than a compliance role. In addition, the fact that Unilever focuses on governance, training, and an inclusive conversation with its stakeholders makes its digital transformation not only ethical but also scalable. With climate change and biodiversity loss, as well as social equity as leading focus in the global business agenda, the story Unilever is going through is a reminder that AI-powered ESG intelligence is not an option anymore, it is a must. Its performance can also be considered as a yardstick to other multinationals wishing to make profit and purpose work in a data-driven and sustainable future.

Real-Time ESG Monitoring and Reporting

Active ESG Dashboards and Metrics

To monitor ESG in real-time, complex data visualization tools are needed to convert huge quantities of sustainability data into actionable knowledge. Interactive ESG dashboards are also of essential importance in helping to visualize the performance indicators on the environmental, social and governance front. Business intelligence (BI) powered dashboards allow companies to monitor key performance indicators (KPIs, including carbon emissions, energy efficiency, workforce diversity, ethical sourcing and governance compliance in real time. They are interactive and tailorable, and will give stakeholders; including its board members, sustainability officer, all the way up to its people, a 360 and real-time view of ESG progress at the company. Furthermore, AI that can be incorporated into these dashboards can put it into predictive analytics, prediction of trends, and detection of anomalies, so that decision-making will be proactive. The dynamism of dynamic dashboards is critical towards reacting to the changing ESG requirements and on how to align with the strategic measures on sustainability.

Stakeholder Sentiment and Public Opinion Stakeholder and AI

Stakeholder sentiment and public opinion happens to be the predominant factors in today talk digital era given that it matters in the corporate ESG reputation and accountability. Natural Language Processing (NLP), sentiment analysis and AI technologies in general are becoming more and more deployed to track the way stakeholders prefer to discuss the ESG performance of a company using news articles, social media, blogs, and investor communications among others. They are a set of tools that perform fast analysis of text elements by using big data mining and can help to extract opinions, identify sentiment trends and reveal possible ESG controversies or reputational risks within real-time frames. Companies can learn more about the expectations of society and plan accordingly by obtaining the voice of the population and the stakeholders. Not only does this type of sentiment intelligence improve transparency and engagement, but it also builds brand trust and reputational risk in response to ESG mistakes.

Integration with Global ESG Reporting Standards (e.g., GRI, SASB, TCFD)

It is a significant problem that companies face since the key issue is that their ESG reporting should correlate with internationally recognized norms. Structured guidance that can be used to disclose ESG in a transparent, consistent and comparable way is provided within frameworks such as the Global Reporting Initiative (GRI), Sustainability Accounting Standards Board (SASB) and the Task Force on Climate-related Financial Disclosures (TCFD). The use of these standards in real-time monitoring system makes the organization not to be in a position of monitoring the correct metrics but also to report on the same investors and regulatory expectations. Compliance may be reduced in terms of human error, and much of the process may be automated by using AI and BI tools which can map internal data directly to these reporting frameworks. Such alignment increases credibility and use of ESG disclosures among regulators, investors, and rating agencies and allows the companies to compare performance with those of the competitors within an industry.

Use of Blockchain for ESG Traceability and Transparency

One of the technologies that are demonstrating its potential in being the guardian of traceability and transparency in managing ESG data is the blockchain technology. It is decentralized, so it is perfect to record and prove ESG transactions like the verification of carbon credits.

By having ESG-related information on a blockchain ledger, businesses achieve audit trails that cannot be rewritten or tampered with and which have the advantage of adding accountability and lessening the potential of greenwashing. Smart contracts also enable compliance with automation, so that the ESG standards are achieved prior to triggering the financial or operating processes. Also, by means of blockchain, stakeholders can access validated ESG info in real-time, thus creating confidence and trust in third parties who are the investors, regulators, and consumers. Because the corporate integrity and stakeholder outreach prove to be worthy competitive advantages in the sustainability market, blockchain makes them even more effective.

Future of AI and BI in Corporate Sustainability

The emerging technologies especially Artificial Intelligence (AI) and Business Intelligence (BI) are reshaping the future of the corporate sustainability drastically. Not only are these technologies enhancing data- informed decision-making but they are also helping ensure that organizations can integrate sustainability at the heart of their practice. With ESG (Environmental, Social, and Governance) measures becoming the key to the success of any business and the factor of stakeholders trust, newer technology is helping organizations make the transition to proactive, smart sustainability practices instead of reactive compliance.

Machine learning is one of the most effective technologies in this area that will enable organizations to process huge ESG data in real-time and anticipate sustainability risks and trends. Machine learning models can identify and address possible ESG-related disruptions early-on, preventing those situations from developing potentially unmanageable challenges, such as estimating carbon emissions, detecting unethical labor in supply chains, among other issues. Parallel to this, natural language processing (NLP) is becoming used to examine news, social media, and corporate disclosures as a means to measure the satisfaction of the stakeholders, identify scandals, and improve aspects of transparency of corporate governance practices.

Blockchain is the mineshaft technology that is revolutionising ESG reporting and traceability. It makes data immutable and accountable, which comes in especially handy when confirming the sustainability claims of intricate supply chains. as an example, blockchain-powered solutions that track materials are able to certify the provenance of said materials to be ethical or monitor carbon credits, thus reinforcing stakeholder confidence and the financial legitimacy of its activities.

The Internet of Things (IoT) gadgets have also been taking center stage in that they are monitoring real-time environmental information, e.g., level of energy consumption, emission levels, and water quality. This data goes straight into BI tools that display the key performance indicators (KPIs), enabling business to correct itself in time and utilize resources efficiently. Furthermore, augmented analytics (a combination of AI, data science and BI) allows anyone in the organization to consume ESG data intuitively, making sustainability intelligence more of a democratized process.

Challenges and Ethical Considerations

Data Privacy and Security in ESG Analytics

With ESG analytics being more and more data-driven, there are data privacy and security concerns that have become more pressing. Organizations will use large amounts of data provided by the employees, suppliers, customers and third-party sources in order to evaluate environmental impact, staff diversity and the governance norms. This usually constitutes sensitive personal and financial information and thus data protection comes first. AI and analytics systems come with new risks, such as a possibility of information leak, improper data access, and leak of confidential information related to ESG. Business firms should have in place good cybersecurity systems, encryption programs and access controls that will help in protection of data integrity. In addition, compliance with data protection policies like the General Data Protection Regulation (GDPR) and the upcoming laws in other jurisdictions related to data privacy is necessary. Their non-addressing are not only a threat to compliance but also a loss to the trust of stakeholders, especially the investors, regulators and the people who are being affected by the activities of a company.

Compliance with ESG and AI Regulatory Frameworks

Another complex issue that organizations face is illuminating the changing environment of ESG and AI regulatory compliance. New disclosure requirements are being proposed by regulatory bodies around the world and include the new Corporate Sustainability Reporting Directive (CSRD) in the EU requiring increased reporting on company performance related to ESG. At the same time, new laws specific to AI have been drafted such as the EU AI Act in order to regulate ethically sound usage of the AI technologies. Every company should make sure that its approach to ESG analytics does not contradict these two sets of regulations, that frequently overlap in such areas as data governance, algorithmic responsibility, and risk management.

These two-pronged compliance issues are even complicated by the fact that there is a jurisdictional difference, which leaves the global firms with no alternative but to implement a single comprehensive proactive compliance approach. Non-compliance, besides resulting to legal measures, reputation loss and potential loss of investor confidence also results. Companies, therefore, need to pay resources into operations that facilitate ethical AI and ESG standards in their operations.

RESULTS AND DISCUSSION

Findings of the Study

The study results bolster the fact that there is a marked transition in ESG approach being transformed to dynamic and intelligence-driven models, moving away to compliance-driven ones. In all case studies, AI technology assistants with more accurate emissions monitoring, early risk detection and improved communication with stakeholders could be used due to use of AI tools varying from machine learning models and NLP, to computer vision, and predictive analytics. To elaborate, the company, EnerSys, cut down on the time and accuracy of the ESG reporting by a lot by leveraging an AI that automates the data of the emissions. EcoVadis extends the supply chain of sustainability ratings, making it more democratic due to its NLP and benchmarking engine, whereas Unilever researched ways to identify deforestation in real-time, forecast emissions reduction at factories, and engage with its stakeholders by using AI.

Verdigris Technologies demonstrated the role of sensor-based AI platforms in the commercial building on decarbonization and energy optimizing. Such results do not only reflect increased environmental impact but also better financial performance and investor confidence as well as reputational strength which is made possible by data-informed sustainability.

Implications of the Study

The practical and theoretical implications of the study are beyond doubt. In practice, it provides a guide to how the ESG-related enterprises, especially those representatives of ESG-sensitive industries, can implement AI-BI tools that potentially automate, scale, and enhance their performance management of ESG. The case studies taken together indicate the fact that a combination of AI and a strong BI ecosystem can enable organizations to gain real-time ESG analysis, support corporate strategy towards achievement of international sustainability objectives, and comply better with regulatory standards. On a theoretical level, this study can benefit the body of literature on the topics of digital transformation, sustainability reporting, and responsible innovation due to the combination of AI and ESG under a single strategic approach. It also covers vital governance aspects, such as data ethics, privacy compliance, algorithmic disclosure, and human control, with the focus on addressing an inclusive and responsible use of AI within the ESG environments.

Future Research Directions

Although the role of AI in the management of ESG can be transformative, the study reveals a number of future research opportunities. Longitudinal studies are required first to determine the long-term viability and the economic impact of AI-ESG incorporations. Second, additional empirical studies should be conducted to test how small and medium-sized enterprises (SMEs) can be charged to adapt these AI-based ESG frameworks in the limitation of resources. Third, a particular focus should be given to the socio-ethical aspects of AI in ESG, including the problem of labor replacement, the surveillance risks, and the lack of decision-making transparency, so that the implementation of AI was humane. The sector-specific angles, be it healthcare, logistics, or agriculture, could also be used in further research to examine how the application of an AI-powered ESG strategies approach can help solve individual operational and ethics-related issues. Finally, a greater scholarly effort should be devoted to examining how emerging technologies like generative AI, federated learning and blockchain can help to improve ESG trust and ESG traceability.

CONCLUSION

In conclusion, this paper confirms that Business Intelligence promoted by Artificial Intelligence fulfils the role of a strong enabler of proper ESG strategies. Using practical case studies in many industries and locations, it shows how AI technologies might provide economies of scale in operations, governance innovation, and supply chains. Although AI does not substitute human judgement, it will enhance the potential of institutions to control environmental, social and governance complexity, legislative, and reputational threat in an ever-changeable global setting. The trends of AI, BI, and ESG strategy are not temporary or fashionable: they are institutional changes that change the process of using sustainability as a key to business decision-making. With the changing nature of the regulatory frameworks and the pressure they are now facing to be transparent, the findings of this research should be relevant advice to companies that now wish to harmonize their technological innovation with their own good corporate citizenry and long-term value growth.

REFERENCES

Akter, S., Dwivedi, Y. K., Sajib, S., Biswas, K., Bandara, R. J., & Michael, K. (2022). Algorithmic bias in machine learning-based marketing models. *Journal of Business Research, 144*, 201–216. DOI: 10.1016/j.jbusres.2022.01.083

Balaji, K. (2024). Exchange-Traded Funds (ETFs): Redefining Financial Instruments in the 21st Century. In Faxing, L., & Kok Loang, O. (Eds.), (pp. 283–310). Advances in Finance, Accounting, and Economics. IGI Global., DOI: 10.4018/979-8-3693-8583-8.ch011

Balaji, K. (2024). Neuromarketing and Sustainable Finance: Real-World Case Studies of Green Investment Promotions. In Taneja, S., Chahal, B. P. S., Johri, A., Ozen, E., & Kumar, P. (Eds.), (pp. 169–204). Advances in Business Strategy and Competitive Advantage. IGI Global., DOI: 10.4018/979-8-3693-9117-4.ch010

Balaji, K. (2025). Harnessing AI and Blockchain in Sustainability Assurance: Trends Shaping the Future of Verification. In Khatib, S. F. A., & Abbas, A. F. (Eds.), *Navigating Trust in Sustainability Reporting and Assurance* (pp. 215–242). IGI Global., DOI: 10.4018/979-8-3373-0117-4.ch007

Balaji, K. (2025). Revolutionizing High-Frequency Trading: The Impacts of Financial Technology and Data Science Innovations. In Chen, H. (Ed.), (pp. 103–124). Advances in Finance, Accounting, and Economics. IGI Global., DOI: 10.4018/979-8-3693-8186-1.ch004

Begenau, J., & Siriwardane, E. (2022). *How do Private Equity Fees vary across Public Pensions?* (No. w29887; p. w29887). National Bureau of Economic Research. DOI: 10.3386/w29887

Berchicci, L., & King, A. A. (2022). Corporate Sustainability: A Model Uncertainty Analysis of Materiality. *Journal of Financial Reporting*, *7*(2), 43–74. DOI: 10.2308/JFR-2021-022

Chen, Q., & Liu, X.-Y. (2020). Quantifying ESG alpha using scholar big data: an automated machine learning approach. *Proceedings of the First ACM International Conference on AI in Finance*, 1–8. DOI: 10.1145/3383455.3422529

Choi, H.-Y., & Park, J. (2022). Do data-driven CSR initiatives improve CSR performance? The importance of big data analytics capability. *Technological Forecasting and Social Change*, *182*, 121802. DOI: 10.1016/j.techfore.2022.121802

Guida, T. (2018). *Big Data and Machine Learning in Quantitative Investment* (1st ed.). Wiley., DOI: 10.1002/9781119522225

Hemanand, D., Mishra, N., Premalatha, G., Mavaluru, D., Vajpayee, A., Kushwaha, S., & Sahile, K. (2022). Applications of Intelligent Model to Analyze the Green Finance for Environmental Development in the Context of Artificial Intelligence. *Computational Intelligence and Neuroscience*, *2022*, 1–8. DOI: 10.1155/2022/2977824 PMID: 35845917

Jebamikyous, H., Li, M., Suhas, Y., & Kashef, R. (2023). Leveraging machine learning and blockchain in E-commerce and beyond: Benefits, models, and application. *Discover Artificial Intelligence*, *3*(1), 3. DOI: 10.1007/s44163-022-00046-0

Joshi, H., & Chauhan, R. (2024). Determinants of Price Multiples for Technology Firms in Developed and Emerging Markets: Variable Selection Using Shrinkage Algorithm. *Vision: The Journal of Business Perspective*, *28*(1), 55–66. DOI: 10.1177/09722629211023011

Martín-Martín, A., Orduna-Malea, E., Thelwall, M., & López-Cózar, E. D. (2018). *Google Scholar, Web of Science, and Scopus: a systematic comparison of citations in 252 subject categories*. DOI: 10.31235/osf.io/42nkm

Musleh Al-Sartawi, A. M. A., Hussainey, K., & Razzaque, A. (2022). The role of artificial intelligence in sustainable finance. *Journal of Sustainable Finance & Investment*, 1–6. DOI: 10.1080/20430795.2022.2057405

Naeem, N., Cankaya, S., & Bildik, R. (2022). Does ESG performance affect the financial performance of environmentally sensitive industries? A comparison between emerging and developed markets. *Borsa Istanbul Review*, *22*, S128–S140. DOI: 10.1016/j.bir.2022.11.014

Chapter 8
Data Visualization Methods for Clear Communication of ESG Analytics Findings

P. Selvakumar
https://orcid.org/0000-0002-3650-4548
Department of Science and Humanities, Nehru Institute of Technology, Coimbatore, India

Sujesh P. Lal
Federal Institute of Science and Technology (FISAT), India

G. Sushma
https://orcid.org/0009-0008-7755-7460
CVR College of Engineering, India

Ganesh Pathak
https://orcid.org/0000-0003-0427-2145
Sri Balaji University, Pune, India

Gaganpreet Kaur Ahluwalia
https://orcid.org/0000-0001-7955-6551
Indira University, India

T. C. Manjunath
https://orcid.org/0000-0003-2545-9160
Rajarajeswari College of Engineering, India

ABSTRACT

In an increasingly data-driven world, the ability to transform complex datasets into clear, compelling narratives has become essential—especially in the realm of ESG (Environmental, Social, and Governance) reporting. As stakeholders from investors to regulators and consumers demand more transparency and accountability, organizations are turning to data visualization to effectively communicate their ESG initiatives and performance. Data visualization, at its core, is the graphical representation of information and data. Through the use of visual elements such as charts, graphs, infographics, and interactive dashboards, it enables users to identify trends, patterns, and outliers within large volumes of data—offering immediate

DOI: 10.4018/979-8-3373-5142-1.ch008

insight that textual data alone often fails to convey.ESG metrics encompass a wide array of data types, from carbon emissions and energy efficiency to labor practices, diversity statistics, board composition, and ethical governance structures.

THE POWER OF DATA VISUALIZATION: COMMUNICATING ESG INSIGHTS

In an increasingly data-driven world, the ability to transform complex datasets into clear, compelling narratives has become essential—especially in the realm of ESG (Environmental, Social, and Governance) reporting. As stakeholders from investors to regulators and consumers demand more transparency and accountability, organizations are turning to data visualization to effectively communicate their ESG initiatives and performance. Data visualization, at its core, is the graphical representation of information and data. Through the use of visual elements such as charts, graphs, infographics, and interactive dashboards, it enables users to identify trends, patterns, and outliers within large volumes of data—offering immediate insight that textual data alone often fails to convey. ESG metrics encompass a wide array of data types, from carbon emissions and energy efficiency to labor practices, diversity statistics, board composition, and ethical governance structures. (Akter et al., 2020) These elements are inherently complex and multidimensional, requiring nuanced interpretation. This is where data visualization proves invaluable. By distilling voluminous and sometimes ambiguous information into digestible visual formats, it enhances clarity, reduces cognitive load, and enables stakeholders to make faster, more informed decisions. For instance, a heat map showing carbon footprint by operational region can instantly reveal hotspots of environmental risk, while a trend line over time can track the progression of a company's DEI (Diversity, Equity, and Inclusion) efforts. The communicative power of visualization lies not just in aesthetics, but in its ability to contextualize data within a narrative. An effective ESG dashboard doesn't merely display KPIs—it tells a story. It answers critical questions: How is the organization performing relative to its sustainability goals? What areas show progress or decline? Where should resources be prioritized? Through intuitive visual elements, these questions can be addressed in real time, fostering transparency and accountability. Stakeholders can engage with the data more meaningfully when they can see the story unfold, supported by visual cues that highlight both successes and gaps.

Moreover, data visualization facilitates stakeholder-specific reporting. Investors may prioritize risk metrics and regulatory compliance, while consumers might focus on ethical sourcing or environmental stewardship. Customizable dashboards and reports can tailor visuals to suit different audiences, ensuring relevance and enhancing engagement. Interactive elements such as filters, drill-down capabilities, and real-time updates allow users to explore ESG data dynamically, offering a personalized and immersive experience that static reports lack. Technology plays a critical role in the evolution of ESG data visualization. Tools like Tableau, Power BI, and other advanced analytics platforms have enabled organizations to build sophisticated, real-time dashboards that integrate data from various sources. These platforms not only visualize data but also perform analytics, such as forecasting future ESG performance based on current trends. Machine learning algorithms can be incorporated to detect anomalies or predict risk, adding a layer of intelligence to visualization that further enhances decision-making. Visualization also supports compliance and audit readiness. As global ESG standards such as the GRI (Global Reporting Initiative), SASB (Sustainability Accounting Standards Board), and the EU's CSRD (Corporate Sustainability Reporting Directive) become more widely adopted, organizations must align their reporting with these frameworks. Visual dashboards can map performance indicators directly to regulatory requirements, making it easier for compliance officers and auditors to verify and validate disclosures. This not only streamlines reporting processes but also reduces the risk of misreporting or greenwashing—where companies overstate their sustainability credentials. Importantly, data visualization empowers internal stakeholders to operationalize ESG insights. Managers and department heads can monitor ESG KPIs relevant to their function—be it supply chain emissions, workforce diversity, or energy use—and take corrective action as needed. (Bari et al., 2022) By embedding ESG metrics into daily decision-making processes through accessible visuals, organizations can foster a culture of sustainability and responsibility at every level. In conclusion, the power of data visualization in ESG communication lies in its ability to transform complexity into clarity, data into decisions, and performance into progress (Cao et al., 2021). As ESG considerations become central to organizational strategy and stakeholder expectations, the ability to convey insights visually will become not just beneficial, but essential. Visualization bridges the gap between raw data and strategic impact, enabling organizations to lead with transparency, accountability, and purpose in a world that increasingly values sustainability.

ESG ANALYTICS: THE NEED FOR CLEAR COMMUNICATION

In an increasingly data-driven world, the ability to transform complex datasets into clear, compelling narratives has become essential—especially in the realm of ESG (Environmental, Social, and Governance) reporting. As stakeholders from investors to regulators and consumers demand more transparency and accountability, organizations are turning to data visualization to effectively communicate their

ESG initiatives and performance. Data visualization, at its core, is the graphical representation of information and data. Through the use of visual elements such as charts, graphs, infographics, and interactive dashboards, it enables users to identify trends, patterns, and outliers within large volumes of data—offering immediate insight that textual data alone often fails to convey. ESG metrics encompass a wide array of data types, from carbon emissions and energy efficiency to labor practices, diversity statistics, board composition, and ethical governance structures. These elements are inherently complex and multidimensional, requiring nuanced interpretation. This is where data visualization proves invaluable. By distilling voluminous and sometimes ambiguous information into digestible visual formats, it enhances clarity, reduces cognitive load, and enables stakeholders to make faster, more informed decisions. For instance, a heat map showing carbon footprint by operational region can instantly reveal hotspots of environmental risk, while a trend line over time can track the progression of a company's DEI (Diversity, (Chiang et al., 2017) Equity, and Inclusion) efforts. The communicative power of visualization lies not just in aesthetics, but in its ability to contextualize data within a narrative. An effective ESG dashboard doesn't merely display KPIs—it tells a story. It answers critical questions: How is the organization performing relative to its sustainability goals? What areas show progress or decline? Where should resources be prioritized? Through intuitive visual elements, these questions can be addressed in real time, fostering transparency and accountability.

Stakeholders can engage with the data more meaningfully when they can see the story unfold, supported by visual cues that highlight both successes and gaps. Moreover, data visualization facilitates stakeholder-specific reporting. Investors may prioritize risk metrics and regulatory compliance, while consumers might focus on ethical sourcing or environmental stewardship. Customizable dashboards and reports can tailor visuals to suit different audiences, ensuring relevance and enhancing engagement. Interactive elements such as filters, drill-down capabilities, and real-time updates allow users to explore ESG data dynamically, offering a personalized and immersive experience that static reports lack. Technology plays a critical role in the evolution of ESG data visualization. (Chib et al., 2025). Tools like Tableau, Power BI, and other advanced analytics platforms have enabled organizations to build sophisticated, real-time dashboards that integrate data from various sources. These platforms not only visualize data but also perform analytics, such as forecasting future ESG performance based on current trends. Machine learning algorithms can be incorporated to detect anomalies or predict risk, adding a layer of intelligence to visualization that further enhances decision-making. Visualization also supports compliance and audit readiness. As global ESG standards such as the GRI (Global Reporting Initiative), SASB (Sustainability Accounting Standards Board), and the EU's CSRD (Corporate Sustainability Reporting Directive) become more widely adopted, organizations must align their reporting with these frameworks. Visual dashboards can map performance indicators directly to regulatory requirements, making it easier for compliance officers and auditors to verify and validate disclosures. This not only streamlines reporting processes but also reduces the risk of misreporting or greenwashing—where companies overstate their sustainability credentials. Importantly, data visualization empowers internal stakeholders to operationalize ESG insights. Data integrity is paramount—visuals are only as accurate as the data they are built on. Organizations must ensure high-quality, validated data collection processes and align visualization strategies with their overall ESG goals. It's also vital to avoid misleading representations—such as truncated axes, disproportionate scaling, or cherry-picked data—which can undermine credibility and trust. In conclusion, the power of data visualization in ESG communication lies in its ability to transform complexity into clarity, data into decisions, and performance into progress. As ESG considerations become central to organizational strategy and stakeholder expectations, the ability to convey insights visually will become not just beneficial, but essential. Visualization bridges the gap between raw data and strategic impact, enabling organizations to lead with transparency, accountability, and purpose in a world that increasingly values sustainability.

DATA VISUALIZATION FOR STAKEHOLDER ENGAGEMENT

In the modern corporate landscape, Environmental, Social, and Governance (ESG) analytics have emerged as a powerful driver of strategic decision-making, risk management, and long-term value creation. As global stakeholders—from investors and regulators to consumers and employees—demand greater transparency, accountability, and sustainability, organizations are increasingly relying on ESG analytics to assess, report, and improve their performance across non-financial dimensions. Yet, despite the growing sophistication of ESG data collection and analysis tools, the impact of these insights hinges significantly on one crucial factor: clear communication. Without it, even the most advanced analytics can be misunderstood, misused, or ignored. ESG analytics are the tools and processes used to measure and evaluate an organization's performance on various sustainability-related issues. These include quantitative and qualitative metrics related to environmental impact (such as carbon emissions, water usage, or waste management), social responsibility (such as labor practices, community engagement, and diversity), and governance (such as executive pay, board structure, and anti-corruption efforts). The insights derived from ESG analytics are critical for understanding how an organization affects—and is affected by—the broader world. They help companies identify risks, uncover opportunities, comply with regulations, and meet stakeholder expectations. However, ESG analytics often involve vast, complex datasets drawn from disparate sources: internal systems, third-party databases, satellite imagery, social media sentiment, survey feedback, and government reports, to name a few. (Du & Jung, 2022) Translating this data into actionable insight requires not just technical expertise but also the ability to distill and communicate it in a way that is transparent, relevant, and accessible to various stakeholders. Without clear communication, ESG data remains trapped in silos, misunderstood by decision-makers, and underappreciated by the broader stakeholder community. One of the most pressing challenges in ESG analytics is the lack of standardization. Different organizations, sectors, and jurisdictions often use varied metrics, definitions, and reporting frameworks. This fragmentation makes it difficult for stakeholders to compare performance across companies or even understand what certain ESG scores mean. For instance, one rating agency might rank a company highly on ESG performance while another penalizes it for the same behavior, due to differing methodologies. Clear communication—through consistent, well-explained disclosures—helps bridge this gap.

Organizations must articulate not only their ESG scores and metrics but also the methodology behind them, the context for their performance, and the roadmap for future improvement. Moreover, ESG analytics can inform both strategic decisions and operational practices, but only if they are effectively communicated to the right audiences. Executives need to understand how ESG risks—such as regulatory changes, climate risks, or reputational threats—impact financial performance and long-term resilience. Operations managers need data on supply chain sustainability or energy efficiency to improve day-to-day processes. Investors require clear insights into ESG materiality and performance trends to evaluate investment risk and opportunity. Employees want to know how their company's values align with its actions, while customers look for authenticity and transparency in sustainability claims. (Eisenhardt & Martin, 2000). Tailoring ESG communication to these distinct audiences ensures that analytics translate into awareness, engagement, and impact. The role of storytelling in ESG communication cannot be overstated. While data provides the foundation, narrative gives it meaning. Clear communication involves not just presenting numbers but contextualizing them within a broader story of purpose, progress, and impact. A 25% reduction in emissions means little unless it's framed against industry benchmarks, historical performance, and future targets. A diversity hiring metric is more powerful when presented alongside personal stories, program details, and commitment from leadership. Organizations that invest in these tools can better align their ESG analytics with business strategies and stakeholder expectations. However, clarity in communication also demands vigilance against misuse. The risk of greenwashing—exaggerating or misrepresenting ESG performance—remains high when data is cherry-picked, misinterpreted, or framed without context. Effective governance of ESG communication processes, (Erevelles et al., 2016) including third-party assurance, ethical guidelines, and alignment with global standards, is essential to maintaining integrity and trust. In conclusion, ESG analytics hold transformative potential for organizations striving to be sustainable, ethical, and forward-looking. But this potential can only be realized when the insights from ESG data are clearly and compellingly communicated. In a world where stakeholders are more informed, connected, and demanding than ever, clear ESG communication is not just a nice-to-have—it's a strategic imperative. It ensures transparency, drives engagement, enhances decision-making, and ultimately contributes to the long-term success and sustainability of the organization.

INTERACTIVE DASHBOARDS: EXPLORING ESG DATA

In an era marked by heightened expectations for transparency, accountability, and sustainability, organizations must find compelling ways to communicate their performance, values, and impact to a diverse range of stakeholders. Whether it's investors seeking evidence of long-term value creation, employees desiring purpose-driven work, customers demanding ethical practices, or regulators monitoring compliance, the need for effective stakeholder engagement has never been more critical. One of the most powerful tools to meet this need is data visualization. Through the strategic use of visual storytelling—leveraging charts, graphs, dashboards, infographics, and interactive tools—organizations can translate complex ESG (Environmental, Social, and Governance) data into clear, engaging, and actionable insights. Data visualization not only enhances understanding, but it also builds trust, drives dialogue, and fosters meaningful engagement with stakeholders across the board. Stakeholder engagement is fundamentally about creating a two-way dialogue between an organization and the people or entities affected by its decisions. It involves sharing relevant information, listening to feedback, and collaborating on shared goals. (Gebhardt et al., 2022). However, the ESG data involved in these discussions is often complex, multi-dimensional, and difficult to interpret without specialized knowledge. Raw data—like carbon emission levels, supplier audit results, board diversity ratios, or human rights risk scores—can be overwhelming when presented in spreadsheets or dense reports. Data visualization addresses this challenge by simplifying the communication of ESG performance while preserving nuance and depth. When executed thoughtfully, visualizations make information more accessible and intuitive, even for non-technical stakeholders, thereby expanding the reach and inclusivity of ESG reporting. For investors and financial analysts, data visualization enhances the assessment of ESG risk and opportunity. ESG issues are increasingly material to long-term financial performance, and visualizing these metrics alongside financial data allows stakeholders to see correlations and trends that inform investment decisions.

A time series graph showing the correlation between a company's energy efficiency initiatives and its operational costs can demonstrate cost-saving sustainability measures. A comparative bar chart showing ESG scores of peers within the same industry helps investors assess relative performance and risk exposure. Interactive dashboards further empower investors by allowing them to filter data based on geography, time period, or business unit, promoting a deeper and more personalized understanding of corporate sustainability. Customers are another critical stakeholder group increasingly influenced by ESG factors. Many consumers prefer to engage with companies that demonstrate genuine commitment to environmental stewardship, social equity, and ethical governance. Visual storytelling helps communicate these values in a compelling way. (Hubballi et al., 2025)For instance, a retail company may use infographics to illustrate the percentage of ethically sourced materials used in its products, the reduction of plastic packaging over time, or its contributions to community development. Such visuals are not only more engaging than text-heavy disclosures but are also more memorable and shareable, especially in digital and social media contexts. This enhances brand loyalty and public trust, turning data into a competitive advantage. Employees and potential talent also respond strongly to ESG visualizations. Workers today seek alignment between personal values and corporate missions, and they want to see how their employer is contributing to broader societal goals. (Jucevicius & Juceviciene, 2022) Visual dashboards showing improvements in diversity and inclusion metrics, reductions in workplace incidents, or progress toward net-zero targets can foster a sense of pride, engagement, and motivation. Internally, visualization tools can be used to track department-specific ESG KPIs, enabling teams to monitor their impact and contribute to organizational sustainability goals. This democratization of data—where every employee can access and act on relevant ESG information—enhances accountability and innovation from the ground up. For regulators and policymakers, data visualization can streamline compliance and oversight. As ESG regulations become more stringent and standardized—such as the EU's CSRD, the U.S. SEC's proposed climate disclosures, or the IFRS Sustainability Standards—organizations are expected to report ESG metrics in consistent and auditable formats. Visualization helps to map data against specific regulatory frameworks, highlighting where a company is compliant, where it lags, and what actions are being taken to address gaps. Heat maps, KPI scorecards, and visual timelines of goal progress can quickly communicate readiness and transparency during audits or stakeholder reviews, reducing the burden of manual document review. Civil society organizations, NGOs, and the media are additional stakeholders who often scrutinize ESG data to hold companies accountable. Transparent, well-designed visualizations make it easier for these groups to assess performance, identify potential issues, and collaborate constructively. For example, a map-based visualization of supply chain risk in relation to human rights indicators allows NGOs to monitor corporate impacts in vulnerable regions. (Junaid et al., 2023) Open-access ESG dashboards also enable third parties to engage in data-driven dialogue rather than speculation, fostering a more constructive stakeholder ecosystem. Importantly, stakeholder engagement through visualization is not just about outward communication—it's also about listening and co-creation. Interactive ESG platforms can incorporate stakeholder feedback loops, surveys, or public commentary features, enabling organizations to refine their strategies based on stakeholder input. For example, visual dashboards that allow users to rank the importance of different ESG issues help companies align their materiality assessments with stakeholder expectations. This feedback-informed approach enhances legitimacy, relevance, and responsiveness—key components of meaningful engagement. Technology is at the heart of modern data visualization strategies. (Kähkönen et al., 2023) Platforms like Tableau, Microsoft Power BI, and ESG-specific tools such as Persefoni, Novisto, or Datamaran allow organizations to integrate real-time data feeds, perform advanced analytics, and create customizable visual interfaces.

STORYTELLING WITH DATA: NARRATIVE VISUALIZATION

In the rapidly evolving landscape of Environmental, Social, and Governance (ESG) performance and accountability, organizations are generating vast volumes of data to monitor their sustainability initiatives. However, the real value of this data lies not just in its collection, but in how it is explored, understood, and applied. (Kodama, 2018) Traditional static ESG reports—while valuable—often fall short in terms of engagement, adaptability, and depth of analysis. To address this, a growing number of companies are turning to as a transformative tool for exploring ESG data. These dashboards allow users to engage with data dynamically, visualize complex relationships in real time, and customize their view according to specific needs and interests. Far more than just visual summaries, interactive dashboards empower internal teams, investors, regulators, and the public to drill down into ESG metrics, uncover trends, and make informed decisions based on up-to-date, context-rich insights. An interactive dashboard is a user-driven digital interface that consolidates multiple data sources and presents key metrics and visualizations in a single, coherent, and adaptable format. Unlike static charts in a PDF report or spreadsheet, dashboards allow users to filter, segment, and manipulate data on demand—exploring it from different angles and levels of granularity. This dynamic exploration is particularly vital in the ESG domain, where data often spans environmental performance (such as carbon emissions, water use, waste management), social impact (employee diversity, health and safety, community investment), and governance (board composition, compliance records, executive pay). Each of these pillars contains subcategories that vary by industry, region, timeframe, and regulatory context. Dashboards enable stakeholders to explore these interconnections in a responsive and intuitive way, supporting both high-level overviews and detailed analyses.

Different stakeholders have different ESG priorities and data needs. For example, institutional investors might focus on climate risk exposure, energy transition plans, or alignment with global standards like the TCFD (Task Force on Climate-related Financial Disclosures). (Liang et al., 2022) Human resources leaders may look at diversity, equity, and inclusion (DEI) metrics, workforce turnover, or employee engagement scores. Operations teams may focus on supply chain emissions or resource efficiency. With an interactive dashboard, each user can filter and configure the data to reflect the KPIs most relevant to their role. This adaptability makes ESG data more actionable and ensures that it supports real-world decision-making across departments Many organizations have set science-based targets or net-zero commitments, along with social goals such as gender parity or ethical sourcing targets. Dashboards can display progress toward these goals using visual indicators like progress bars, color-coded KPIs, and real-time alerts. These visuals allow teams to identify where they are on track and where corrective action is needed. Benchmarking capabilities also enable comparisons with industry peers or global averages, helping stakeholders evaluate relative performance, (Kotte et al., 2025). With built-in trend analysis and historical data views, dashboards support continuous performance management, fostering a data-informed culture of improvement.

Figure 1. Techniques for data visualization and reporting

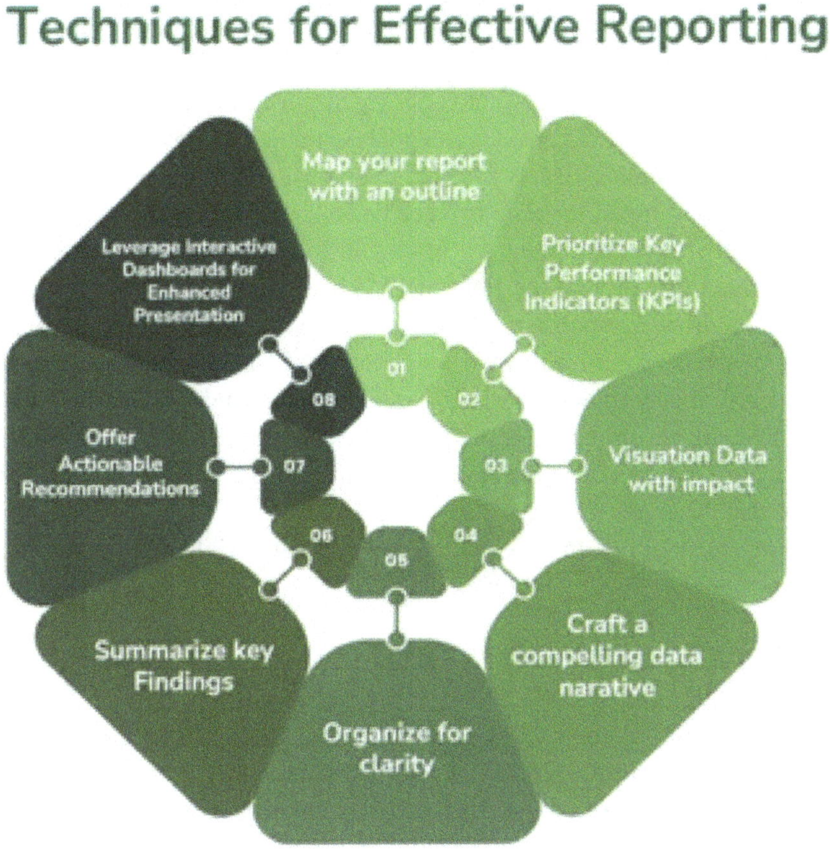

These public-facing dashboards can support investor relations, improve media coverage, and demonstrate corporate transparency. For example, a public dashboard might show a company's progress on carbon neutrality, display workforce diversity by job level, or map philanthropic spending across regions. These tools not only enhance brand reputation but also meet growing demands for open, verifiable ESG communication. Education is another area where dashboards add value. Internal ESG champions, sustainability officers, and compliance teams can use dashboards as training and communication tools to raise awareness and build alignment around sustainability goals. By visualizing data in an engaging and interactive format, teams can more easily grasp key concepts, see their department's impact, and understand how their actions contribute to broader ESG performance. Dashboards can be embedded into presentations, internal portals, or employee learning platforms, making them versatile tools for change management .Despite the many benefits of interactive dashboards, successful implementation requires careful planning and data governance. Organizations must ensure that the underlying data is accurate, timely, and aligned with recognized ESG frameworks. (Linton et al., 2007) Poor-quality or incomplete data can undermine the effectiveness of the dashboard and erode stakeholder trust. Equally important is clarity of purpose—dashboards should be designed with specific user personas and goals in mind. Overloading users with too many metrics or complex visuals can lead to confusion or disengagement. A well-designed ESG dashboard strikes a balance between depth and simplicity, offering flexibility while maintaining clarity. In conclusion, interactive dashboards are a transformative innovation in the field of ESG analytics and reporting. They turn static data into living, responsive systems of insight that support exploration, communication, and decision-making across all levels of an organization. By enabling stakeholders to engage directly with the data—whether to monitor progress, identify risks, benchmark performance, or plan strategically—dashboards empower a more informed, agile, and accountable approach to sustainability. As ESG expectations grow and data becomes more central to corporate strategy, interactive dashboards will play an essential role in bridging the gap between insight and action.

COMPARATIVE ANALYSIS: VISUALIZING ESG PERFORMANCE

In the age of information overload and increasing demand for corporate transparency, data alone is no longer enough. Numbers and charts, while essential, rarely spark engagement, evoke emotion, or drive decisions on their own—especially when dealing with complex, multidimensional topics such as Environmental, Social, and Governance (ESG) performance. This approach combines the analytical rigor of data with the emotional resonance and clarity of storytelling to transform static facts into compelling narratives that inform, inspire, and mobilize stakeholders. Narrative visualization is the practice of designing data presentations that follow a logical, often story-like structure to guide the viewer through a sequence of insights. Unlike conventional data dashboards or static reports that present information for the audience to interpret on their own, narrative visualizations lead the viewer on a curated journey. This journey is defined by a clear beginning, middle, and end—often framed as a challenge or question, followed by data-driven exploration, and concluding with a key message or call to action. For ESG communication, where datasets often contain hundreds of variables and nuanced indicators, narrative visualization helps distill complexity into coherence, providing both context and clarity. Cognitive science shows that people remember stories up to 22 times more than standalone facts. (Mehta & Pandit, 2018) In ESG communication, this means that a time-series chart showing a 30% reduction in greenhouse gas emissions is far more impactful when contextualized within a story—explaining how the company identified its carbon hotspots, what actions were taken to reduce them, the challenges faced along the way, and the environmental and economic benefits achieved. By blending data with narrative, the same numbers become part of a meaningful, relatable, and persuasive message. compliance, and financial implications of ESG performance. Employees may want to understand how workplace initiatives impact their experience and opportunities. Customers often look for authenticity, ethical sourcing, or environmental stewardship. Regulators seek data transparency and framework alignment.

Crafting the narrative with these audiences in mind ensures that data is not just presented, but interpreted and acted upon in ways that align with the stakeholder's needs and values. reaching net-zero emissions, its social impact in underserved communities, or its transformation toward ethical governance. From there, the story builds with supporting data, visual elements, and contextual explanations that logically unfold to support the message. This progression mimics traditional storytelling techniques: setting the stage (introducing the issue or challenge), rising action (presenting data that explores causes, effects, or trends), climax (a key finding or breakthrough), and resolution (conclusions or next steps).. Each visual element should be purposeful, aligned with the narrative structure, and designed to guide the viewer's attention. For example, a waterfall chart can effectively show year-over-year progress in energy savings, while a series of icons can communicate social impact in various regions. The strategic use of colors, typography, whitespace, and annotations helps emphasize key takeaways and minimize cognitive load. Good narrative visualizations are not overloaded with data—they're selective, focusing on the most important insights while providing pathways for deeper exploration when needed. where data visuals change as the user scrolls down a page, interactive timelines, clickable charts that reveal underlying causes, or simulations that show the impact of different ESG decisions. AI and natural language generation (NLG) tools can even auto-generate textual summaries based on datasets, speeding up content creation and ensuring consistency. However, while technology supports the process, the core of effective narrative visualization remains deeply human: understanding the audience, crafting a compelling message, and conveying truth through data. Responsible storytelling involves clear sourcing, balanced representation of performance (including areas of underperformance), and sensitivity to potential bias. Just as journalists are trained to report fairly and accurately, (Mostafiz et al., 2022) ESG communicators using narrative visualization must uphold similar standards of integrity and transparency.

BAR CHARTS AND HISTOGRAMS: VISUALIZING ESG METRICS

In the fast-evolving realm of Environmental, Social, and Governance (ESG) strategy, the ability to benchmark and compare ESG performance has become a fundamental component of decision-making, reporting, and stakeholder engagement. As organizations generate increasingly complex ESG data, the challenge is not only in collection but in making sense of it—especially in relation to industry peers, global standards, historical performance, and future targets and stakeholders alike to interpret ESG performance in a meaningful context. By transforming raw metrics into visual comparisons—through charts, graphs, tables, heat maps, or dashboards—comparative visualization facilitates informed judgment, encourages accountability, reveals performance gaps, and highlights competitive advantages or risks. Comparative analysis in ESG revolves around answering core questions: How does our company perform relative to competitors? Are we meeting or exceeding industry benchmarks? Where are we leading, lagging, or aligning with regulatory expectations? What trends emerge over time? To address these questions effectively, visualization becomes indispensable. A well-constructed comparative chart can show at a glance what pages of tabular data cannot—how an organization's carbon emissions stack up against a sector average, how its board diversity compares to competitors, or how its human rights policies rank globally, (Maheswaran et al., 2025). These comparisons do not merely show differences—they contextualize performance and help interpret what "good" or "bad" means in a given ESG domain. for example, involves comparing a company's ESG data with direct competitors within the same industry or market segment. This is particularly useful for investors conducting due diligence, as ESG risks and opportunities are often sector-specific. A comparative line chart showing Scope 1 and 2 emissions across the top ten firms in the oil and gas sector can quickly identify leaders in decarbonization efforts.

Likewise, a heat map of social responsibility indicators—such as workplace safety incidents, community investment, and DEI statistics—can expose strengths and weaknesses across a cohort of manufacturing companies. Peer comparisons foster accountability and serve as catalysts for strategic improvement. Organizations must not only report current ESG data but also demonstrate how their performance has evolved over time. Time-series visualizations—such as multi-year bar graphs or trend lines—allow stakeholders to assess trajectory, momentum, and consistency. For instance, showing a five-year reduction in water usage or a gradual improvement in gender parity over several reporting periods reveals a commitment to continuous improvement and long-term planning. On the other hand, flat or negative trends prompt important questions about strategic direction or execution challenges. These historical visualizations provide both reassurance and motivation—for stakeholders who value progress and for internal teams seeking to refine ESG strategies. multiple dimensions to identify correlations or trade-offs. A scatter plot showing companies' greenhouse gas emissions on one axis and executive compensation tied to ESG outcomes on another can highlight whether sustainability is being embedded into leadership incentives. Similarly, a quadrant chart comparing companies based on environmental impact and social engagement can reveal leaders, laggards, and balanced performers. These visual comparisons help identify whether ESG strategies are integrated holistically or treated as siloed initiatives. Companies operating across multiple regions must address local regulatory environments, cultural expectations, and resource limitations. Visual maps showing regional variations in compliance, labor practices, or environmental impact help identify geographic hot spots or success stories. For example, a map visualization might reveal that while a global food company is reducing emissions in North America, it is struggling with deforestation-related risks in Southeast Asia, (Pesqueira et al., 2020). This geographic granularity is essential for stakeholders interested in supply chain risks, regulatory exposure, and global ESG footprints. In the realm of regulatory compliance and framework alignment, comparative visualization offers another layer of value. As global ESG disclosure requirements become more stringent—with frameworks such as the Global Reporting Initiative (GRI), Sustainability Accounting Standards (Rashid & Ratten, 2021) Board (SASB), and EU Corporate Sustainability Reporting Directive (CSRD)—organizations must demonstrate how they measure up against these standards. Comparison charts showing which ESG metrics are reported under which frameworks—and how completely—offer a visual audit trail of transparency and readiness. This is especially useful for legal teams, auditors, and regulators who need to assess disclosure compliance at a glance. who increasingly rely on ESG data for portfolio construction, risk mitigation, and stewardship strategies. Investment decision-making often requires evaluating ESG scores, ratings, or raw metrics across a large universe of firms. Dashboards that compare ESG performance across sectors, regions, or market capitalizations enable these professionals to spot trends, anomalies, or best-in-class performers. Visualizations such as radar charts (spider charts), comparative bar graphs, and bubble charts provide a multifaceted view of ESG performance that can be quickly understood, even when dealing with complex data sets.

SCATTER PLOTS AND HEATMAPS: IDENTIFYING RELATIONSHIPS

Bar charts and histograms are among the most fundamental and widely used tools in data visualization. Their simplicity, clarity, and versatility make them essential for presenting ESG (Environmental, Social, and Governance) metrics in a way that is both accessible and impactful. In the context of ESG reporting, bar charts and histograms play a crucial role in transforming raw, complex data into easily interpretable visuals that highlight key trends, comparisons, and distributions. Whether used in corporate sustainability reports, (Runeson & Höst, 2009) internal dashboards, investor presentations, or public disclosures, these visual formats serve as the backbone for understanding ESG performance across a wide range of indicators—from carbon emissions and workforce diversity to supply chain compliance and board independence. (Samal et al., 2025) In ESG analysis, bar charts are frequently employed to compare ESG performance indicators across different departments, geographies, time periods, or peer companies. For example, a bar chart may be used to show the total greenhouse gas (GHG) emissions of each regional office in a multinational corporation, allowing viewers to identify regions with disproportionately high emissions. Similarly, bar charts can display the percentage of women in leadership roles across different business units, or the number of workplace safety incidents reported by site. These visualizations immediately draw attention to differences that may warrant strategic action, such as performance gaps or areas for improvement. the height or length of the bars to understand relative magnitudes. This makes them ideal for stakeholders—including non-technical audiences like employees, customers, and the general public—who may not be familiar with advanced analytics but need to grasp key insights from ESG data. For instance, showing side-by-side bars for different years can visually illustrate trends in renewable energy usage, waste reduction, or community investment.

Color-coding these bars further enhances clarity, enabling multi-dimensional comparisons—such as using different colors to represent energy sources or social investment types. against industry benchmarks, regulatory thresholds, or company-set targets. For example, a bar chart might show a company's annual emissions alongside the Science Based Targets initiative (SBTi) reduction goal, making it easy to visualize the gap that must be closed. These visuals are particularly compelling when used in sustainability reports or investor presentations, where clarity, transparency, and credibility are paramount. dimensions—for example, visualizing the gender composition of the workforce by role (executive, mid-level, entry-level) over multiple years. Stacked bar charts, on the other hand, display subcomponents of a whole—for instance, the composition of waste generated (hazardous vs. non-hazardous) across different manufacturing sites. These configurations offer more nuanced perspectives, enabling stakeholders to understand not just totals, but the structure and balance within those totals. distribution of continuous data by grouping it into intervals or "bins." In ESG analysis, histograms are powerful tools for identifying patterns, outliers, and concentrations within large datasets. For example, a histogram could illustrate the distribution of carbon intensity across a company's global facilities, revealing whether most facilities cluster around a low, medium, or high emissions range. This helps sustainability teams Similarly, histograms can display the frequency of social incidents or safety violations across operational units, enabling a risk-based approach to resource allocation and intervention. These insights support more targeted ESG strategies and enhance operational efficiency. data. By visualizing the spread of data points—such as energy consumption per employee, water use per product, or CO_2 equivalent emissions per revenue unit—histograms help illustrate whether performance is consistent, volatile, or skewed. This level of analysis informs risk assessments, strategic planning, and reporting decisions. which are central tenets of ESG reporting. When used correctly, these charts demystify complex metrics and present them in an open, digestible format that encourages stakeholder trust. For example, a company may publish a bar chart comparing its employee turnover rate across departments, alongside industry benchmarks, in its annual sustainability report. This openness invites dialogue, feedback, and collaboration while reinforcing the company's commitment to continuous improvement. color can distort interpretation or reduce clarity. Therefore, best practices in design—such as using a zero baseline for bar charts, clearly labeling axes, and choosing colors that are colorblind-friendly—are essential. It is also important to avoid overloading these charts with too many categories or data series, which can overwhelm viewers and obscure the main message. When designed with the audience in mind, these charts can be powerful tools for ESG communication. In element to their utility. In a digital dashboard, users can hover over bars to see precise values, filter categories by time or region, or drill down into specific metrics. For example, a user may click on a bar representing waste generation at a particular site to view detailed breakdowns by waste type, disposal method, and cost. (Sakthivel et al., 2025).

GEOSPATIAL VISUALIZATION: MAPPING ESG DATA

In the complex landscape of Environmental, Social, and Governance (ESG) analytics, understanding relationships between variables is crucial for uncovering insights that drive strategic decision-making, risk management, and stakeholder communication. (Soundariya et al., 2025)While basic charts such as bar graphs and line charts efficiently display individual metrics or trends over time, the more intricate interdependencies and correlations within ESG data often require specialized visualization tools like, and clusters among multiple ESG factors, enabling analysts and decision-makers to explore how different environmental impacts, social indicators, or governance attributes relate to each other and influence overall performance, outliers, and trends that can indicate causal or consequential links between sustainability factors. For instance, plotting a company's carbon intensity (emissions per unit of revenue) against its ESG score can provide insights into whether higher sustainability ratings are truly associated with lower emissions, or if there are anomalies where companies score well despite high environmental impact. Similarly, scatter plots comparing employee turnover rates with workplace injury incidents can highlight whether social factors like safety are influencing workforce stability. By displaying each data point as a dot with coordinates corresponding to the values of two metrics, scatter plots offer an immediate visual understanding of positive, negative, or no correlation, as well as clusters or outliers that merit further investigation. A common enhancement to scatter plots in ESG visualization is the addition two-dimensional scatter plots into rich multi-dimensional analyses. For example, color might represent industry sector (energy, finance, manufacturing), dot size might reflect company market capitalization, and shape might distinguish geographic regions. This layering allows stakeholders to simultaneously explore relationships between two ESG metrics while contextualizing results across sectors or regions, revealing nuanced insights. For instance, an investor analyzing ESG risks may use a scatter plot where each dot represents a company, colored by sector, to identify clusters of high-risk firms in fossil fuel industries exhibiting both high emissions and low governance scores. or correlation coefficients to scatter plots makes it easier to quantify relationships and assess their strength and significance. For example, a scatter plot showing the relationship between board diversity (percentage of women on the board) and firm profitability might reveal a positive trend, supporting arguments for diverse leadership as an ESG best practice. Such visual evidence can be pivotal in driving governance reforms, investor engagement, and public communication, which display pairwise scatter plots for multiple variables in a grid format. (Thirunagalingam & Selvakumar, 2025) This allows comprehensive exploration of how different ESG indicators—such as water usage, labor practices, carbon emissions, and social investment—interrelate across a portfolio of companies or business units. These matrices facilitate pattern recognition, hypothesis generation, and identification of key ESG drivers and risks. data matrices and revealing patterns of intensity or correlation within ESG datasets. Heatmaps display values as colors within a grid, with rows and columns typically representing categories, metrics, or time periods.

This color-coded approach is particularly useful when dealing with large, multidimensional datasets where numeric tables would be overwhelming or opaque. In ESG, heatmaps can visualize correlations between multiple variables, performance levels across geographies, or compliance statuses across various ESG criteria. variables—such as carbon footprint, water usage, employee satisfaction, and executive pay—heatmaps can reveal which metrics move together and which are independent or inversely related. This insight helps organizations identify synergistic factors to target or conflicting issues that require trade-offs. For example, a heatmap may show a strong positive correlation between energy consumption and carbon emissions, but a weak or negative correlation between social investment and governance scores, suggesting areas where integrated strategies may be more or less effective. severity or urgency. A red zone may indicate high environmental risks linked to deforestation or pollution, while green areas denote compliance and best practices. This visualization helps procurement teams prioritize interventions and allocate resources efficiently. Similarly, heatmaps showing the extent of regulatory compliance across jurisdictions enable legal and sustainability teams to quickly identify gaps or progress areas. and employee training hours—while columns represent years or reporting periods. Color gradients can illustrate performance improvement, stagnation, or decline, helping companies communicate progress transparently to stakeholders and regulators. For example, a heatmap in a sustainability report might show a steady shift from red to green over several years, signaling continuous improvement in environmental performance. dashboards. Users can hover over cells to see precise data values, filter the data by region or business unit, or drill down into subcategories.

BEST PRACTICES FOR ESG DATA VISUALIZATION

In the realm of Environmental, Social, and Governance (ESG) data analysis, geospatial visualization has emerged as an indispensable tool for contextualizing complex sustainability information within physical and geographic realities. As ESG considerations increasingly influence corporate strategy, investor decisions, and regulatory scrutiny, the ability to spatially map data has transformed how organizations identify risks, track progress, and communicate with diverse stakeholders. Geospatial visualization, (Yin, 2018) which involves the graphical representation of ESG metrics and indicators on geographic maps, enables companies to uncover spatial patterns, localize environmental impacts, understand social dynamics in communities, and monitor governance-related factors tied to specific locations. By linking data to place, organizations gain deeper insights that purely tabular or abstract visualizations cannot provide, creating a more intuitive and actionable view of sustainability performance. change, biodiversity loss, water scarcity, pollution, and resource depletion—are inherently spatial. For example, mapping carbon emissions by facility or region allows organizations to pinpoint hotspots of environmental impact, facilitating targeted mitigation efforts. Similarly, visualizing water usage and wastewater discharge across watersheds helps companies identify areas where water stress is critical, informing conservation strategies and supply chain adjustments. Geospatial tools can layer satellite data, climate models, and environmental risk indices with company-specific data, revealing vulnerabilities that might otherwise be overlooked. For instance, a mining company can map its extraction sites against biodiversity hotspots or indigenous territories to assess potential ecological or social conflicts early in the project lifecycle. spatial dimensions that benefit from mapping. By visualizing the geographic distribution of workforce demographics, labor disputes, or local investments, companies can better understand the social fabric of their operations and supply chains. For example, a retailer can map supplier factory locations alongside labor rights violation reports or unionization rates, highlighting regions requiring more robust oversight or engagement. Similarly, mapping employee diversity data by office or plant location helps identify where inclusion initiatives are succeeding or need reinforcement.

These spatial insights empower companies to design more culturally sensitive, equitable, and effective social programs that respond to localized needs. Governance factors, though often viewed as more abstract, also gain clarity through geospatial visualization. Many governance issues, such as regulatory compliance, corruption risk, and political stability, are strongly influenced by geography. Mapping jurisdictions according to governance quality indices or transparency rankings provides companies with a spatial understanding of regulatory and operational risks, (Wang et al., 2018). For multinational firms, geospatial dashboards that overlay legal frameworks, enforcement activity, and reported governance incidents enable better strategic planning and risk mitigation. Moreover, geospatial data can support local stakeholder dialogues by highlighting how corporate activities intersect with community boundaries, natural resources, and cultural sites, encouraging more inclusive and informed conversations. sources—including internal operations, third-party providers, government databases, and open-source platforms—requiring robust data governance and validation processes, (Upadhyaya et al., 2025). Moreover, interpreting geospatial ESG data requires awareness of local socio-economic, regulatory, and environmental contexts to avoid misleading conclusions.

COLOR SCHEMES AND DESIGN: ENHANCING VISUALIZATION

Effective visualization of Environmental, Social, and Governance (ESG) data is pivotal for translating complex sustainability information into actionable insights, fostering stakeholder trust, and driving meaningful decision-making. As ESG data grows in volume, variety, and importance, organizations face the challenge of presenting it in ways that are transparent, clear, engaging, and credible. Avoid clutter, redundant information, and overly intricate graphics that may obscure rather than illuminate. performance without manipulation or bias, (Wang & Alexander, 2016). Visuals should use appropriate scales—starting bar charts at zero to avoid exaggeration of differences—and avoid misleading design choices such as truncated axes, distorted aspect ratios, or selective data omission. Transparency in data sources, methodologies, and any assumptions or calculations underpinning the visuals strengthens credibility. Where data quality issues exist—such as gaps, estimates, or conflicting reports—these should be clearly noted to prevent misinterpretation. Ensuring accuracy is especially important given the growing scrutiny from regulators, investors, and civil society over ESG disclosures. Visualizations that mislead, intentionally or unintentionally, risk damaging reputations and undermining trust., and ESG metrics require contextual framing to convey meaningful insights. Effective visualizations situate data within broader narratives, connecting metrics to company strategies, regulatory requirements, industry benchmarks, or global sustainability goals such as the United Nations Sustainable Development Goals (SDGs). Incorporating comparative data—peer performance, historical trends, or target benchmarks—helps stakeholders assess progress and relative standing. For instance, a visualization showing a company's reduction in water usage over time is more powerful when paired with industry averages or local water scarcity indices.

AVOIDING BIAS: ENSURING ACCURATE REPRESENTATION

Color schemes and design play a pivotal role in the realm of visualization, profoundly influencing how information is perceived, interpreted, and retained by viewers. In the vast landscape of visual communication, the deliberate selection and application of color serve not only an aesthetic function but also a critical cognitive and functional purpose. Effective color schemes can transform complex data into intuitive, comprehensible visual narratives, enabling users to grasp patterns, trends, and anomalies with greater ease. Conversely, poor use of color can obscure meaning, create confusion, or even mislead, undermining the efficacy of the visualization. At the core of designing impactful visualizations lies an understanding of color theory, which encompasses the science and art of color mixing, visual perception, and the psychological effects of color on human behavior and cognition. The color wheel, initially developed by Isaac Newton, remains a foundational tool, illustrating relationships between primary, secondary, and tertiary colors, and serving as a guide for creating harmonious or intentionally contrasting color palettes. Complementary colors, situated opposite each other on the color wheel, offer maximum contrast and vibrancy, making them effective for highlighting differences or drawing attention to key data points. Analogous color schemes, which use colors adjacent to each other on the wheel, provide a more subtle and cohesive look, often employed to suggest progression or relatedness within datasets. Beyond traditional color theory, the domain of data visualization has adopted specialized color schemes tailored to the nature of the data and the intended message. Three primary types of color schemes are commonly utilized: sequential, diverging, and qualitative. Sequential schemes employ a gradient of a single hue varying in lightness and saturation to represent ordered data that progresses from low to high values, such as temperature changes or income levels. Diverging schemes use two contrasting hues to signify data diverging around a central midpoint, such as profit and loss or above- and below-average performance, effectively highlighting deviation.

Qualitative schemes, by contrast, utilize distinct, non-ordered colors to differentiate categorical data without implying magnitude or order, such as different species, brands, or regions. The design process of visualization must consider the context and audience to select appropriate color schemes. Cultural differences, color vision deficiencies, and the medium of display significantly impact color perception and interpretation. For example, red, which is often associated with danger or loss in Western cultures, might have positive connotations in others, such as good fortune in East Asian cultures. Designing with color blindness in mind—specifically, accommodating common types such as deuteranopia and protanopia—requires avoiding problematic color combinations (like red-green) and implementing patterns, textures, or labels to reinforce meaning. Tools like Color Brewer and accessibility guidelines from the Web Content Accessibility Guidelines (WCAG) help designers create inclusive visualizations that are perceptible to a diverse audience. In addition to static visualizations, interactive designs benefit from dynamic color use, allowing users to manipulate views, zoom into details, or filter data subsets, with color changes signaling state transitions or data focus. The use of animation and color transitions should be balanced to avoid overwhelming the user while maintaining clarity. Moreover, the choice of background color, text contrast, and spacing complements the color scheme, ensuring that visualizations remain legible and engaging across different devices and lighting conditions.

DECISION-MAKING: INFORMING CHOICES WITH VISUALIZATION

Stakeholder engagement is a critical component of successful project management, organizational strategy, and decision-making processes across various domains such as business, government, healthcare, and education. At its core, stakeholder engagement involves actively involving individuals, groups, or organizations that have an interest or stake in a project or decision, ensuring their perspectives, concerns, and feedback are considered and incorporated effectively. One of the most powerful tools to facilitate this engagement is data visualization, which translates complex data and abstract concepts into accessible, intuitive visual formats that enhance understanding, dialogue, and collaboration. The use of visualization in stakeholder communication bridges gaps in knowledge, language, and technical expertise, enabling diverse groups to engage meaningfully in discussions, assess information critically, and contribute to shared goals. Effective stakeholder engagement through visualization begins with recognizing the diversity of stakeholders involved. Stakeholders may include executives, employees, customers, community members, regulators, investors, and subject matter experts—each bringing different levels of expertise, priorities, and interests. Visualizations can be tailored to meet these varying needs, providing multiple entry points into the data or project information. For example, high-level dashboards and infographics can offer executives quick insights into performance indicators and strategic metrics, while detailed interactive charts and heatmaps allow technical stakeholders to explore granular data and test hypotheses.

CONCLUSION

Interactive visualizations allow users to manipulate variables, apply filters, or model hypothetical scenarios, thereby exploring "what-if" analyses in real time. For example, a business leader might use an interactive dashboard to assess how changes in market conditions impact sales forecasts under different assumptions. Similarly, urban planners can visualize the potential effects of infrastructure investments on traffic flow or environmental sustainability. Such dynamic engagement fosters a deeper understanding of potential outcomes and uncertainty, ultimately supporting more informed and robust decisions. However, the influence of visualization on decision-making is not merely functional; it also has psychological and behavioral dimensions. Visualizations can shape how information is perceived and prioritized, potentially influencing judgment and choices. The framing effect is a well-documented cognitive bias wherein the presentation of information affects decision outcomes. For instance, a graph emphasizing gains rather than losses can lead to different risk preferences among decision-makers. Ethical considerations thus arise regarding the design of visualizations—ensuring that they inform rather than manipulate, providing balanced perspectives rather than cherry-picked data. Transparency about data sources, assumptions, and limitations is essential to maintain trust and empower decision-makers to critically evaluate visual evidence. The context in which decisions are made significantly affects how visualization is employed. The pressure, stakes involved, and the decision-makers' expertise level influence visualization needs. In high-stakes or time-sensitive environments such as healthcare or emergency response, visualizations must prioritize clarity, immediacy, and error reduction, often using standardized formats and alerts. In strategic or exploratory contexts, decision-makers benefit from more detailed, interactive visualizations that facilitate in-depth analysis and collaborative discussion. Tailoring visual tools to the decision context and audience is thus a critical design consideration to maximize effectiveness. Despite their advantages, visualizations also present challenges and potential pitfalls in decision-making. Poorly designed visualizations—such as those with misleading scales, cluttered layouts, or inappropriate chart types—can obscure key information or lead to erroneous interpretations. Confirmation bias, anchoring, and other cognitive biases may cause decision-makers to favor visual evidence that aligns with existing beliefs while dismissing contradictory data. To mitigate these risks, best practices include adhering to principles of clear, honest design, providing multiple data perspectives, and incorporating mechanisms for feedback and critical review. Collaborative decision-making processes that integrate diverse viewpoints can further reduce individual bias and improve decision quality. Technology advancements continue to expand the role of visualization in decision-making. Artificial intelligence and machine learning algorithms increasingly generate predictive models and insights that are conveyed through sophisticated visual interfaces. Augmented reality and virtual reality platforms provide immersive environments where decision-makers can explore complex data landscapes in three dimensions, enhancing spatial understanding and intuition. Cloud computing and real-time data integration enable continuous monitoring and adaptive decision support, critical in fields such as finance, supply chain management, and environmental monitoring. These technological innovations demand ongoing research into best visualization practices to ensure that increasing complexity does not overwhelm users but instead empowers them. Education and training are essential to maximizing the benefits of visualization in decision-making. Developing data literacy among decision-makers enhances their ability to interpret visualizations correctly, ask relevant questions, and apply insights responsibly. Training programs should cover not only technical skills for interacting with visualization tools but also critical thinking skills to evaluate the credibility and relevance of visual data. Organizations benefit from fostering a culture that values data-driven decision-making and encourages the integration of visualization into workflows, meetings, and strategic planning. In conclusion, visualization plays an indispensable role in informing and enhancing decision-making across a broad spectrum of contexts. By converting complex data into accessible and insightful visual formats, it accelerates comprehension, supports scenario exploration, mitigates cognitive overload, and facilitates collaborative analysis. When designed and applied thoughtfully, visualizations not only improve the accuracy and confidence of decisions but also contribute to transparency and accountability in decision processes. As the volume and complexity of data continue to grow, harnessing the power of visualization will remain a critical capability for individuals and organizations striving to make well-informed, effective choices that drive positive outcomes and innovation.

REFERENCES

Akter, S., Motamarri, S., Hani, U., Shams, R., Fernando, M., Babu, M. M., & Shen, K. (2020). Building dynamic service analytics capabilities for the digital marketplace. *Journal of Business Research, 118*, 177–188. DOI: 10.1016/j.jbusres.2020.06.016

Bari, N., Chimhundu, R., & Chan, K. C. (2022). Dynamic capabilities to achieve corporate sustainability: A roadmap to sustained competitive advantage. *Sustainability (Basel), 14*(3), 1531. DOI: 10.3390/su14031531

Cao, G., Tian, N., & Blankson, C. (2021). Big data, marketing analytics, and firm marketing capabilities. *Journal of Computer Information Systems, 62*(3), 442–451. DOI: 10.1080/08874417.2020.1842270

Chiang, L. H., Lu, B., & Castillo, I. (2017). Big data analytics in chemical engineering. *Annual Review of Chemical and Biomolecular Engineering, 8*(1), 63–85. DOI: 10.1146/annurev-chembioeng-060816-101555 PMID: 28301733

Chib, S., Mehta, A. K., Selvakumar, P., Saravanan, A., Mishra, B. R., & Manjunath, T. C. (2025). Mental Health Challenges and Solutions in High-Pressure Work Environments. In Harriott, S. (Ed.), *Innovative Approaches to Managing Conflict and Change in Diverse Work Environments* (pp. 247–272). IGI Global Scientific Publishing., DOI: 10.4018/979-8-3693-9556-1.ch011

Du, Y., & Jung, J.-S. (2022). *The effect of dynamic capability on innovation and financial performance: Focused on the moderating effect of ESG management and the big data utilization in Chinese SMEs*. Korea International Trade Research Institute.

Eisenhardt, K. M., & Martin, J. A. (2000). Dynamic capabilities: What are they? *Strategic Management Journal, 21*(10–11), 1105–1121. DOI: 10.1002/1097-0266(200010/11)21:10/11<1105::AID-SMJ133>3.0.CO;2-E

Erevelles, S., Fukawa, N., & Swayne, L. (2016). Big Data consumer analytics and the transformation of marketing. *Journal of Business Research, 69*(2), 897–904. DOI: 10.1016/j.jbusres.2015.07.001

Gebhardt, M., Kopyto, M., Birkel, H., & Hartmann, E. (2022). Industry 4.0 technologies as enablers of collaboration in circular supply chains: A systematic literature review. *International Journal of Production Research, 60*(23), 6967–6995. DOI: 10.1080/00207543.2021.1999521

Granger, C. W., & Lee, T. H. (1989). Investigation of production, sales and inventory relationships using multicointegration and non-symmetric error correction models. *Journal of Applied Econometrics, 4*(S1), S145–S159. DOI: 10.1002/jae.3950040508

Hubballi, R. B. *Selvakumar, P., Seenivasan, R., Basava Aradhya S., G., Dinesh, N., & Seelam, P. K. (2025). Overview of Current AI Technologies in Education.* In L. Kyei-Blankson & E. Ntuli (Eds.), Transformative AI Practices for Personalized Learning Strategies (pp. 1–26). IGI Global Scientific Publishing. DOI: 10.4018/979-8-3693-8744-3.ch001

Jucevicius, G., & Juceviciene, R. (2022). Enabling collaborative dynamic capabilities in strategic communities: Firm-vs. network-centric perspectives. *Journal of Management & Organization*, 28(3), 587–604. 12.

Junaid, M., Zhang, Q., Cao, M., & Luqman, A. (2023). Nexus between technology enabled supply chain dynamic capabilities, integration, resilience, and sustainable performance: An empirical examination of healthcare organizations. *Technological Forecasting and Social Change*, *196*, 122828. DOI: 10.1016/j.techfore.2023.122828

Kähkönen, A. K., Evangelista, P., Hallikas, J., Immonen, M., & Lintukangas, K. (2023). COVID-19 as a trigger for dynamic capability development and supply chain resilience improvement. *International Journal of Production Research*, *61*(8), 2696–2715. DOI: 10.1080/00207543.2021.2009588

Kodama, M. (2018). *Collaborative dynamic capabilities for service innovation creating a new healthcare ecosystem*. Palgrave Macmillan, 14.

Kotte, K. R., Attaluri, V., & Selvakumar, P. (2025). Revolutionising Retail Banking with AI and Virtual Technologies AI-Driven Financial Training. In Nair, A. J., Manohar, S., Limbu, Y. B., & Huhmann, B. A. (Eds.), *Intersecting Natural Language Processing and FinTech Innovations in Service Marketing* (pp. 421–440). IGI Global Scientific Publishing., DOI: 10.4018/979-8-3693-9944-6.ch020

Liang, Y., Lee, M. J., & Jung, J. S. (2022). Dynamic capabilities and an ESG strategy for sustainable management performance. *Frontiers in Psychology*, *13*, 887776. DOI: 10.3389/fpsyg.2022.887776 PMID: 35719473

Linton, J. D., Klassen, R., & Jayaraman, V. (2007). Sustainable supply chains: An introduction. *Journal of Operations Management*, *25*(6), 1075–1082. DOI: 10.1016/j.jom.2007.01.012

Maheswaran, K., Selvakumar, P., Shaikh, M., Shashank, G., Gupta, S., & Manjunath, T. C. (2025). The Evolution of Smart Urban Mobility With Emerging Technologies. In Ponnusamy, S., Assaf, M., Youssef, B., Jeon, G., & Kalyanaraman, S. (Eds.), *Leveraging VANETs and Blockchain Technology for Urban Mobility* (pp. 1–28). IGI Global Scientific Publishing., DOI: 10.4018/979-8-3373-0265-2.ch001

Mehta, N., & Pandit, A. (2018). Concurrence of big data analytics and healthcare: A systematic review. *International Journal of Medical Informatics, 114*, 57–65. DOI: 10.1016/j.ijmedinf.2018.03.013 PMID: 29673604

Mostafiz, M. I., Musteen, M., Saiyed, A., & Ahsan, M. (2022). COVID-19 and the global value chain: Immediate dynamics and long-term restructuring in the garment industry. *Journal of Business Research, 139*, 1588–1603. DOI: 10.1016/j.jbusres.2021.10.078

Pesqueira, A., Sousa, M., & Rocha, Á. (2020). Big data skills sustainable development in healthcare and pharmaceuticals. *Journal of Medical Systems, 44*(11), 44. DOI: 10.1007/s10916-020-01665-9 PMID: 33034743

Rashid, S., & Ratten, V. (2021). Entrepreneurial ecosystems during COVID-19: The survival of small businesses using dynamic capabilities. *World Journal of Entrepreneurship, Management and Sustainable Development, ahead-of-print*(ahead-of-print), 26. DOI: 10.1108/WJEMSD-09-2020-0110

Runeson, P., & Höst, M. (2009). Guidelines for conducting and reporting case study research in software engineering. *Empirical Software Engineering, 14*(2), 131–164. DOI: 10.1007/s10664-008-9102-8

Sakthivel, M., Jaganathan, A., Mohanraj, M., & Selvakumar, P. Mohit, & Manjunath, T. (2025). *Brand Loyalty through AI and Personalisation AI-Generated Content for Financial Marketing.* In A. J. Nair, S. Manohar, Y. B. Limbu, & B. A. Huhmann (Eds.), Intersecting Natural Language Processing and FinTech Innovations in Service Marketing (pp. 77–96). IGI Global Scientific Publishing. DOI: 10.4018/979-8-3693-9944-6.ch006

Samal, A., & Misra, L. I. Mohit, Pougajendy, S., Chandel, P. S., Manjunath, T. C., & Selvakumar, P. (2025). *Musealization and Tourism Practices.* In S. Oflazoglu & M. Dora (Eds.), Preserving Cultural Heritage in Post-Disaster Urban Renewal (pp. 115–142). IGI Global Scientific Publishing. DOI: 10.4018/979-8-3693-9097-9.ch006

Soundariya, A., Behera, N. K., Selvakumar, P., Chandel, P. S., Gupta, S., & Manjunath, T. C. (2025). AI and Environmental Ethics: The Role of AI in Addressing Climate Change Ethical Considerations in AI-Driven Environmental Solutions. In Chakraborty, S. (Ed.), *Human Values, Ethics, and Dignity in the Age of Artificial Intelligence* (pp. 321–346). IGI Global Scientific Publishing., DOI: 10.4018/979-8-3693-9035-1.ch013

Thirunagalingam, A., & Selvakumar, P. (2025). Application of Automation and Robotics in the Oil and Gas Industry. In Abdullayev, V., & Khang, A. (Eds.), *Revolutionizing AI and Robotics in the Oil and Gas Industry* (pp. 229–244). IGI Global Scientific Publishing., DOI: 10.4018/979-8-3693-8156-4.ch011

Upadhyaya, A. N., Debnath, P., Rani, P., Selvakumar, P., Manjunath, T. C., & Bhattacharya, S. (2025). AI-Based Disaster Prediction and Early Warning Systems. In Mobo, F. (Ed.), *AI and Emerging Technologies for Emergency Response and Smart Cities* (pp. 55–74). IGI Global Scientific Publishing., DOI: 10.4018/979-8-3693-9770-1.ch003

Wang, L., & Alexander, C. (2016). Big data analytics for medication management in diabetes mellitus. *International Journal of Security and Networks*, *1*, 42.

Wang, Y., Kung, L., & Byrd, T. A. (2018b). Big data analytics: Understanding its capabilities and potential benefits for healthcare organizations. *Technological Forecasting and Social Change*, *126*, 3–13. DOI: 10.1016/j.techfore.2015.12.019

Yin, R. K. (2018). *Case study research and applications* (Vol. 6). Sage.

Chapter 9
Implementing Sentiment Analysis for Evaluating Stakeholder Perception and Social Impact

P. Selvakumar
https://orcid.org/0000-0002-3650-4548
Department of Science and Humanities, Nehru Institute of Technology, Coimbatore, India

S. Poorani
https://orcid.org/0000-0001-7179-431X
Kongu Engineering College, India

R. Sahith
https://orcid.org/0009-0006-8611-2602
CVR College of Engineering, India

Ganesh Pathak
https://orcid.org/0000-0003-0427-2145
Sri Balaji University, Pune, India

Nilesh Anute
https://orcid.org/0000-0001-6599-813X
Sri Balaji University, Pune, India

T. C. Manjunath
https://orcid.org/0000-0003-2545-9160
Rajarajeswari College of Engineering, India

ABSTRACT

Sentiment analysis, often referred to as opinion mining, is a powerful technique within the broader field of natural language processing (NLP) and artificial intelligence (AI), designed to determine and quantify the emotional tone behind a body of text. Its core objective is to analyze written or spoken language and classify sentiments expressed as positive, negative, or neutral. In some sophisticated implementations, sentiment analysis can also identify more nuanced emotional states such as anger, joy, sadness, surprise, trust, and disgust. This technology has seen rapid adoption across numerous industries, driven by the explosion of online content and the growing need for organizations to understand public perception. The internet has

DOI: 10.4018/979-8-3373-5142-1.ch009

enabled billions of users to share their opinions and experiences through social media platforms, product reviews, blog posts, news articles, forums, and other digital channels. Manually processing this immense volume of unstructured data is virtually impossible, which is where sentiment analysis provides invaluable support.

THE ROLE OF SENTIMENT ANALYSIS: OVERVIEW OF SENTIMENT ANALYSIS

Sentiment analysis, often referred to as opinion mining, is a powerful technique within the broader field of natural language processing (NLP) and artificial intelligence (AI), designed to determine and quantify the emotional tone behind a body of text. Its core objective is to analyze written or spoken language and classify sentiments expressed as positive, negative, or neutral. In some sophisticated implementations, sentiment analysis can also identify more nuanced emotional states such as anger, joy, sadness, surprise, trust, and disgust. This technology has seen rapid adoption across numerous industries, driven by the explosion of online content and the growing need for organizations to understand public perception. The internet has enabled billions of users to share their opinions and experiences through social media platforms, product reviews, blog posts, news articles, forums, and other digital channels. Manually processing this immense volume of unstructured data is virtually impossible, which is where sentiment analysis provides invaluable support. At a technical level, sentiment analysis involves a combination of linguistic processing, machine learning algorithms, and often deep learning models. It begins with data preprocessing, where text is cleaned and normalized—removing noise such as punctuation, stop words, and irrelevant information. Tokenization breaks down the text into manageable units such as words or phrases. Techniques such as part-of-speech tagging and syntactic parsing can be employed to understand grammatical structures and relationships between words. Once the text is prepared, sentiment classification models—trained on large datasets labeled for sentiment—predict the emotional tone. These models range from simple rule-based approaches, which rely on predefined sentiment lexicons, to complex neural networks such as recurrent neural networks (RNNs), convolutional neural networks (CNNs), and transformers like BERT (Bidirectional Encoder Representations from Transformers), which capture deep contextual relationships within the text.

The role of sentiment analysis has become increasingly prominent in sectors such as marketing, customer service, finance, healthcare, politics, and media. In marketing and brand management, companies use sentiment analysis to gauge public opinion about their products, services, and campaigns in real-time. This enables businesses to quickly identify emerging trends, respond to crises, and refine their messaging to better resonate with target audiences. For customer service, sentiment analysis is integrated into chatbots and virtual assistants to detect customer emotions, allowing for more empathetic and personalized interactions. It also assists human agents by flagging conversations that may require urgent attention due to negative sentiment. In finance, investors and analysts leverage sentiment analysis to assess market sentiment and inform trading strategies, using data from financial news, earnings reports, and social media commentary. In healthcare, sentiment analysis of patient feedback and social media discussions can provide insights into patient satisfaction, treatment efficacy, and emerging health concerns. Political analysts and campaigners employ sentiment analysis to monitor public sentiment toward candidates, policies, and key issues, allowing for data-driven strategy adjustments. Media organizations use sentiment analysis to track public reactions to news coverage and major events, helping editors shape editorial priorities. Furthermore, the role of sentiment analysis has expanded to include social listening, reputation management, and crisis monitoring. Governments and law enforcement agencies also use sentiment analysis tools to detect potential threats or unrest by analyzing online discourse. As AI continues to evolve, sentiment analysis is becoming more sophisticated, capable of understanding sarcasm, irony, and cultural nuances, which have traditionally posed significant

NATURAL LANGUAGE PROCESSING (NLP): NLP ROLE

Stakeholder perception holds a critical place in determining the success and sustainability of any organization, project, or initiative. (Abdurahiman S. et al. 2024) Stakeholders encompass a broad array of individuals and groups that have an interest in or are affected by the operations and outcomes of an organization. These include customers, employees, investors, suppliers, government bodies, regulatory agencies, community members, advocacy groups, and the general public. In today's hyper-connected and transparent world, where information spreads rapidly and public opinion can shift in an instant, managing and understanding stakeholder perception is no longer optional—it is a strategic imperative. Stakeholders' views influence an organization's reputation, legitimacy, and license to operate. Positive perceptions can build trust, foster loyalty, enhance brand value, and attract investment, while negative perceptions can result in reputational damage, customer attrition, regulatory scrutiny, and financial losses. At the core, stakeholders provide organizations with the critical resources they need to function: capital from investors, labor from employees, revenue from customers, materials from suppliers, and legitimacy from the community and regulatory environment. The willingness of stakeholders to continue providing these resources often hinges on their perceptions of the organization's trustworthiness, competence, fairness, and alignment with societal values. (Abdurahiman S. et al. 2024) When stakeholders perceive an organization as ethical, responsible, and competent, they are more likely to engage positively and support its goals. Conversely, when they view an organization as opaque, unethical, or out of touch, stakeholders may withdraw support or actively oppose its initiatives. (Alaei A. R. et al. 2019) In this sense, stakeholder perception becomes a form of currency that influences organizational resilience and adaptability.

Effective management of stakeholder perception requires a proactive and ongoing approach to communication and engagement. (Alaei A. R. et al. 2019) It begins with identifying key stakeholders, understanding their interests, concerns, and expectations, and fostering open channels of dialogue. (Ceron A. et al. 2014) Transparent, consistent, and authentic communication builds credibility over time. Organizations that listen actively to stakeholder feedback and demonstrate responsiveness to their needs are more likely to cultivate positive perceptions. Furthermore, the alignment between an organization's stated values and its actual behaviors plays a significant role in shaping perception. Stakeholders today are increasingly attuned to issues such as environmental sustainability, social responsibility, diversity and inclusion, and corporate governance. (Ceron A. et al. 2014) Failure to meet stakeholder expectations in these areas can quickly erode trust and damage reputation. Beyond communication, actions speak louder than words. Corporate social responsibility (CSR) initiatives, ethical business practices, community involvement, fair treatment of employees, and strong governance all contribute to shaping positive stakeholder perception. Moreover, in times of crisis, how an organization responds can either reinforce or undermine stakeholder trust. (Chowdhary S. et al. 2025) A transparent, empathetic, and accountable crisis response can enhance reputation, while a defensive or dismissive stance can trigger backlash. The digital age amplifies these dynamics, as social media and online platforms give stakeholders powerful tools to voice their opinions and mobilize public sentiment. (Chowdhary S. et al. 2025) Organizations must monitor these channels and remain agile in their engagement strategies.

MACHINE LEARNING ALGORITHMS: MACHINE LEARNING APPLICATIONS

Natural Language Processing (NLP) is a vital branch of artificial intelligence (AI) that focuses on the interaction between computers and human language. Its role is to enable machines to read, understand, interpret, and generate human language in a way that is both meaningful and useful. (Coates J. M. et al. 2025) This involves a complex blend of linguistics, computer science, and machine learning techniques designed to bridge the gap between human communication and digital systems. As human language is inherently rich, ambiguous, and context-dependent, NLP plays a critical role in making it accessible and actionable for computers. In the modern digital era, where vast amounts of unstructured text data are generated daily through emails, social media, news articles, customer reviews, and spoken interactions, NLP provides the tools necessary to derive insights and facilitate human-machine communication at scale. (Coates J. M. et al. 2025) At its core, NLP transforms human language into formats that computers can process, analyze, and act upon. This involves various tasks such as tokenization (breaking text into words or phrases), part-of-speech tagging (identifying grammatical categories), syntactic parsing (understanding sentence structure), named entity recognition (identifying names, organizations, dates, etc.), sentiment analysis (determining emotional tone), and machine translation (converting text from one language to another). Advanced NLP systems also handle more complex challenges such as coreference resolution (linking pronouns to the correct nouns), understanding context, detecting sarcasm, and managing linguistic nuances like idioms and cultural references. These capabilities make NLP a foundational technology behind many applications that users now take for granted in daily life.

One of the most visible roles of NLP is in enhancing human-computer interaction. Virtual assistants such as Siri, Alexa, Google Assistant, and chatbots across websites and customer service platforms rely heavily on NLP to understand spoken or written queries and provide relevant responses. (De Marchi D. et al. 2022) NLP enables these systems to interpret intent, manage multi-turn conversations, and adapt to varied linguistic inputs, significantly improving user experience and accessibility. (De Marchi D. et al. 2022) In customer support, NLP-driven chatbots can handle large volumes of inquiries, provide instant assistance, and escalate complex cases to human agents, boosting efficiency and satisfaction. NLP also plays a crucial role in information retrieval and search technologies. (Deshmukh A. K. et al. 2022) Search engines like Google use sophisticated NLP algorithms to understand user queries, identify relevant documents, and rank results based on relevance and intent. This goes beyond keyword matching, incorporating semantic understanding to deliver more accurate and contextually appropriate results. (Deshmukh A. K. et al. 2022) NLP enables features such as autocomplete, query expansion, and personalized search experiences, making information more discoverable and accessible. In content generation and summarization, NLP is transforming how information is created and consumed. Tools powered by NLP can automatically generate news articles, marketing copy, product descriptions, and reports, saving time and resources. Automatic summarization systems distill long documents into concise summaries, helping users quickly grasp key points. In fields like journalism, education, and business intelligence, this capability enhances productivity and decision-making.

TEXT ANALYSIS AND CLASSIFICATION: TEXT ANALYSIS

Machine learning algorithms represent a pivotal advancement in the field of artificial intelligence (AI), driving transformative applications across virtually every industry and domain. (El Barachi M. et al. 2021) At its core, machine learning (ML) enables systems to automatically learn from data, identify patterns, and make decisions with minimal human intervention. (El Barachi M. et al. 2021) These algorithms allow machines to improve their performance over time as they are exposed to more data, which makes them ideal for solving complex problems that are too dynamic or intricate for traditional rule-based programming. The versatility and adaptability of ML algorithms have led to their integration in a wide array of real-world applications, from healthcare and finance to marketing, cybersecurity, manufacturing, and beyond. (Hadro D. et al. 2022) The growing reliance on data, combined with advancements in computing power and storage, has significantly accelerated the adoption and effectiveness of machine learning technologies. (Hadro D. et al. 2022) In healthcare, machine learning algorithms are revolutionizing diagnostics, treatment planning, drug discovery, and personalized medicine. ML models trained on large datasets of medical images—such as X-rays, MRIs, and CT scans—can detect diseases like cancer, pneumonia, and diabetic retinopathy with high accuracy, sometimes even outperforming human radiologists. Predictive analytics powered by machine learning is used to forecast patient outcomes, identify individuals at risk of chronic diseases, and optimize treatment protocols. Furthermore, natural language processing (a subset of ML) helps extract meaningful insights from unstructured clinical notes in electronic health records (EHRs), supporting decision-making and improving operational efficiency. In drug development, ML algorithms help identify potential compounds, model drug-target interactions, and predict adverse effects, significantly reducing the time and cost associated with bringing new drugs to market.

In the financial sector, machine learning applications are at the forefront of fraud detection, risk assessment, algorithmic trading, and customer service. (Haider R. et al. 2025) ML models analyze large volumes of transactional data to detect anomalies and flag potentially fraudulent activities in real-time, which enhances security and protects consumers. Credit scoring systems now incorporate ML to assess creditworthiness more accurately by analyzing non-traditional data sources and identifying subtle behavioral patterns. In investment banking and asset management, ML-driven algorithms analyze market trends, financial news, and social media sentiment to inform automated trading decisions and optimize portfolios. Chatbots and virtual assistants powered by ML are used by banks and insurance companies to handle customer inquiries, process claims, and provide personalized financial advice. Marketing and customer experience are also significantly enhanced by machine learning. Recommendation systems, as employed by platforms like Amazon, Netflix, and Spotify, use ML algorithms to analyze user preferences and behavior, providing personalized product or content suggestions that increase engagement and sales. (Haider R. et al. 2025) Customer segmentation and targeting have become more precise through ML, enabling marketers to tailor campaigns based on detailed behavioral insights. Sentiment analysis, predictive lead scoring, churn prediction, and A/B testing optimization are additional examples where ML models help companies understand and influence customer behavior more effectively. These applications allow businesses to deliver more relevant and timely interactions, leading to improved customer satisfaction and loyalty.

ANALYZING STAKEHOLDER FEEDBACK: FEEDBACK ANALYSIS

Text analysis and classification represent foundational capabilities within the broader domain of Natural Language Processing (NLP) and data analytics. (Hubballi R. B. et al. 2025) As the digital world continues to generate an overwhelming volume of textual data—through emails, social media posts, online reviews, news articles, academic publications, chat logs, surveys, and more—the ability to automatically process and make sense of this information has become critically important. (Hubballi R. B. et al. 2025) Text analysis refers to the systematic process of examining, structuring, and extracting meaningful insights from unstructured textual content. (Jaiswal R. et al. 2024) It encompasses a wide variety of techniques that allow machines to understand, interpret, and manipulate human language data. These techniques include tokenization, part-of-speech tagging, syntactic parsing, lemmatization, named entity recognition, keyword extraction, sentiment analysis, topic modeling, and semantic analysis. Through these methods, organizations and researchers can uncover hidden patterns, detect trends, and gain actionable insights that would be impossible or extremely labor-intensive to obtain manually. (Jaiswal R. et al. 2024) The role of text classification—an essential component of text analysis—is to categorize textual data into predefined groups or classes based on its content. This is typically achieved using supervised machine learning algorithms that are trained on labeled datasets, where each piece of text is tagged with the appropriate category. Common examples of text classification include spam detection in emails, sentiment classification in product reviews, topic categorization in news articles, intent detection in customer service chats, and genre classification in literature. By automating the process of classification, organizations can handle vast amounts of data quickly and accurately, improve decision-making, and enhance user experiences. For example, customer service platforms use classification to route queries to the correct department, while content moderation systems use it to filter out inappropriate or harmful language in social media platforms and forums.

The process of text analysis typically begins with data preprocessing, a critical step that prepares raw text for meaningful interpretation. This includes cleaning the text by removing noise such as punctuation, special characters, and stop words (common words that carry little informational value). (Jiang H. et al. 2016) The text is then tokenized—split into words or phrases—and normalized through stemming or lemmatization to reduce words to their base forms. These steps make it easier for algorithms to identify meaningful patterns in the data. Following preprocessing, feature extraction techniques such as term frequency-inverse document frequency (TF-IDF), Bag of Words (BoW), or word embeddings (like Word2Vec, GloVe, or BERT) are used to convert textual data into numerical representations that machine learning models can process. Once the text is numerically represented, classification algorithms such as Naïve Bayes, Support Vector Machines (SVM), Random Forests, and neural networks can be applied. More recently, deep learning models, especially those based on transformer architectures such as BERT, RoBERTa, and GPT, have significantly advanced the state of the art in text classification tasks. (Jiang H. et al. 2016) These models can understand context, semantics, and even subtle nuances in language, enabling highly accurate and context-aware classification. For instance, a traditional model might struggle to differentiate between sarcasm and sincerity in a tweet, but a transformer-based model trained on a large and diverse dataset might correctly classify the sentiment or intent.

IDENTIFYING SENTIMENT TRENDS: SENTIMENT TREND IDENTIFICATION

Analyzing stakeholder feedback has become an indispensable part of organizational strategy and decision-making, as it provides a clear window into the thoughts, concerns, expectations, and experiences of those who interact with or are affected by an organization. (Jones C. E. et al. 2019) Stakeholders include a wide spectrum of individuals and groups such as customers, employees, investors, suppliers, regulatory bodies, community members, partners, and advocacy organizations—each bringing unique perspectives and insights. Stakeholder feedback can take many forms, including surveys, interviews, social media comments, online reviews, customer service interactions, employee engagement scores, investor reports, and public forums. (Jones C. E. et al. 2019) Given the sheer volume and diversity of this feedback—much of it in unstructured formats—analyzing it effectively requires a systematic, data-driven approach. Done well, feedback analysis enables organizations to identify strengths and weaknesses, detect emerging trends, resolve issues proactively, enhance relationships, and align their operations with stakeholder needs and values. The first step in analyzing stakeholder feedback involves comprehensive data collection. Organizations must gather feedback from all relevant channels, ensuring they capture a wide range of viewpoints. This includes direct feedback through structured channels like surveys and interviews, as well as unsolicited or passive feedback from social media, review platforms, internal communications, and industry reports. Advances in digital tools and analytics have made it easier to centralize and manage this data, providing a unified view of stakeholder sentiment. However, raw feedback is typically unstructured, variable in quality, and context-dependent, which poses significant challenges for analysis.

Figure 1. Implement a successful stakeholder engagement

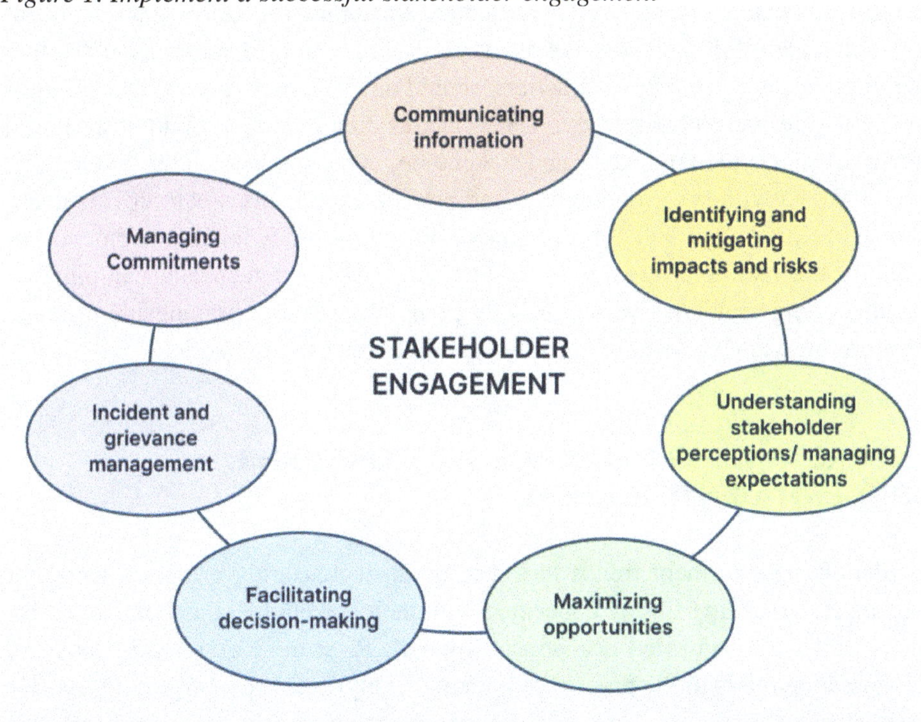

To address these challenges, organizations use a variety of methods and technologies. Natural Language Processing (NLP) plays a critical role in processing textual feedback, converting unstructured language into structured data that can be systematically analyzed. NLP techniques such as tokenization, sentiment analysis, topic modeling, named entity recognition, and keyword extraction enable organizations to uncover key themes and emotional tones within feedback. Sentiment analysis, in particular, allows organizations to gauge whether feedback is generally positive, negative, or neutral, while more advanced models can detect specific emotions and attitudes. (Kamal M. R. et al. 2024) Topic modeling can reveal the main subjects of discussion, helping organizations prioritize areas for improvement or investment. Beyond textual feedback, quantitative methods are used to analyze structured feedback such as survey results and rating scores. Statistical analysis helps identify trends, correlations, and patterns across different stakeholder groups and over time. For example, tracking Net Promoter Score (NPS) trends can indicate shifts in customer loyalty, while analyzing employee engagement surveys can highlight factors affecting morale and productivity. Advanced analytics techniques such as machine learning and predictive modeling can also be applied to feedback data to forecast future behavior, identify at-risk stakeholders, or simulate the impact of potential changes. (Kamal M. R. et al. 2024) Effective stakeholder feedback analysis is not only about identifying what stakeholders are saying, but also about understanding why they are saying it and what actions should be taken in response. This requires context-aware interpretation that considers factors such as market conditions, cultural nuances, organizational history, and stakeholder demographics. Cross-referencing feedback data with other operational and performance metrics can provide deeper insights into the root causes of issues and opportunities for improvement. For example, correlating customer complaints with product defect rates can pinpoint manufacturing problems, while analyzing employee feedback alongside turnover rates can highlight areas of organizational culture that need attention.

UNDERSTANDING STAKEHOLDER CONCERNS: CONCERN IDENTIFICATION

Identifying sentiment trends has become an increasingly critical activity for organizations seeking to stay connected with their stakeholders, anticipate market shifts, and make informed decisions. (Kotte K. R. et al. 2025) Sentiment trend identification refers to the process of tracking, analyzing, and interpreting changes in stakeholder sentiment—whether positive, negative, or neutral—over time. This practice goes beyond isolated feedback or one-time sentiment analysis to reveal patterns and trajectories in how people feel about a brand, product, service, policy, or event. These trends can signal emerging issues, opportunities, or shifts in public opinion that may have significant implications for strategy, communication, and performance. In today's digital era, where conversations unfold constantly across a multitude of online platforms—social media, blogs, news outlets, forums, and reviews—identifying sentiment trends in real time has become both a challenge and a necessity. The foundation of sentiment trend identification lies in the collection and processing of vast amounts of unstructured data. (Kotte K. R. et al. 2025) Organizations employ web crawlers, social listening tools, customer feedback platforms, and APIs from social media networks to gather relevant textual data. This data is then subjected to natural language processing (NLP) techniques such as sentiment analysis, which assigns a sentiment score to each piece of text based on its emotional tone. Sentiment can be classified at varying levels of granularity—binary (positive or negative), ternary (positive, neutral, negative), or more nuanced (very positive, somewhat positive, neutral, somewhat negative, very negative). Advanced models can even detect specific emotions such as joy, anger, fear, or sadness, providing a richer understanding of stakeholder sentiment.

Once individual sentiment data points are classified, trend analysis begins. This typically involves aggregating sentiment scores over time—daily, weekly, monthly, or quarterly—and visualizing them in a way that reveals patterns. (Maceda L. L. et al. 2023) Statistical techniques such as time series analysis, moving averages, and anomaly detection help smooth out noise and highlight genuine trends. (Maceda L. L. et al. 2023) For example, an upward trend in positive sentiment following a product launch might indicate market acceptance and customer satisfaction, while a sudden spike in negative sentiment after a controversial event could signal reputational risk. Identifying such trends early enables organizations to respond proactively, whether by capitalizing on positive momentum or mitigating emerging risks. Beyond simple visualization, more sophisticated analytical methods can uncover deeper insights. Machine learning models can be trained to detect complex sentiment dynamics and predict future trends based on historical data. For instance, models can forecast whether a negative sentiment spike is likely to escalate into a broader crisis or subside naturally. Similarly, sentiment trends can be segmented by demographic factors, geographic regions, or stakeholder groups to understand how different audiences are reacting. This segmentation allows for more targeted and effective interventions. For example, a company might discover that while overall sentiment is stable, negative sentiment is rising among a key customer segment, prompting tailored outreach efforts.

ASSESSING SOCIAL IMPACT: SOCIAL IMPACT ASSESSMENT

Understanding stakeholder concerns—also known as concern identification—is a critical process that underpins effective organizational management, strategic planning, and relationship building. (Maheswaran K. et al. 2025) Stakeholders—ranging from customers, employees, investors, suppliers, regulators, and community members to advocacy groups and the general public—possess diverse interests, expectations, and worries regarding an organization's actions, products, policies, and overall impact. Identifying and understanding these concerns enables organizations to align their strategies with stakeholder needs, anticipate risks, manage conflicts, and foster trust and loyalty. (Maheswaran K. et al. 2025) In an increasingly interconnected and transparent world where public opinion can rapidly shape organizational reputation, the ability to accurately identify stakeholder concerns is both a strategic asset and a necessity for sustainable success. The process of concern identification begins with comprehensive stakeholder mapping. Organizations must first identify who their stakeholders are, categorize them based on their level of influence and interest, and understand their relationship with the organization. This foundational step ensures that no key voice is overlooked, whether it comes from internal stakeholders such as employees and shareholders or external ones like customers, local communities, NGOs, and media. Once stakeholders are mapped, organizations must actively engage with them through various channels to elicit their perspectives. This includes structured methods like surveys, interviews, and focus groups, as well as unstructured avenues such as open forums, town hall meetings, social media platforms, and public comment periods.

A major source of stakeholder concerns today comes from online channels where opinions and feedback are shared publicly in real time. (Maignan I. et al. 2005) Social media posts, online reviews, blog comments, discussion forums, and news articles can all contain valuable signals about stakeholder concerns. The vast and unstructured nature of this data necessitates the use of advanced analytics tools. (Maignan I. et al. 2005) Natural Language Processing (NLP) techniques such as sentiment analysis, topic modeling, and keyword extraction allow organizations to systematically process and analyze large volumes of text to detect emerging concerns. For instance, a sudden increase in negative sentiment around product safety or data privacy issues on social media could signal rising stakeholder anxiety that needs to be addressed promptly. In addition to technological tools, qualitative insights remain essential. One-on-one interviews and focus groups provide depth and context that algorithms may miss, capturing nuanced emotions, implicit concerns, and cultural sensitivities. Employee feedback platforms, customer advisory panels, investor briefings, and community consultation forums provide additional avenues for gathering detailed insights. Successful concern identification involves not just listening to what stakeholders say directly but also interpreting what remains unsaid—underlying fears, unspoken expectations, and shifting values that may not yet be explicitly articulated. Analyzing and categorizing identified concerns is the next critical step. Concerns can vary widely—from product quality, customer service, ethical conduct, environmental impact, workplace culture, and data privacy to corporate governance, transparency, social responsibility, and long-term sustainability. Categorization allows organizations to prioritize concerns based on urgency, potential impact, and alignment with strategic goals. For example, regulatory compliance issues might require immediate legal action, while reputational concerns around diversity and inclusion might call for long-term cultural change initiatives. Moreover, concerns can be mapped across different stakeholder groups to identify where interests align or diverge. Understanding these dynamics helps organizations manage competing priorities and make balanced decisions that consider the needs of all key stakeholders.

SENTIMENT ANALYSIS FOR CSR INITIATIVES: CSR EVALUATION

Assessing social impact—commonly referred to as Social Impact Assessment (SIA)—is a comprehensive and systematic process used to evaluate the effects that a project, policy, initiative, or organizational activity has on the social fabric of communities, stakeholder groups, and society at large. (Mamo Y. Z. et al. 2023) As organizations increasingly recognize their responsibilities beyond financial performance, the ability to measure and manage social impact has become an essential aspect of sustainable development, ethical governance, and strategic planning. Social impact assessments aim to identify, predict, evaluate, and mitigate the intended and unintended social consequences of actions—both positive and negative—before, during, and after implementation. These assessments are crucial in helping decision-makers understand the broader implications of their work, ensuring that development is inclusive, equitable, and aligned with community well-being, social justice, and environmental stewardship. At its core, SIA focuses on the human dimension of change. It looks at how people's lives, relationships, culture, rights, access to resources, health, safety, and quality of life are affected by changes in their environment—whether caused by infrastructure projects, industrial operations, public policies, corporate decisions, or nonprofit interventions. Unlike economic or environmental assessments that often rely on quantitative metrics alone, social impact assessments integrate both qualitative and quantitative data to capture the complex and often subjective experiences of those impacted. This includes assessing shifts in social cohesion, displacement, employment patterns, education opportunities, public health, indigenous rights, gender equality, cultural heritage, and more.

The process of assessing social impact typically begins with stakeholder identification and engagement. It is essential to understand who the affected communities and groups are, what their values and priorities entail, and how their voices can be included meaningfully in the assessment. Early and inclusive engagement helps ensure that assessments are grounded in local knowledge and reflect the lived realities of those most affected. Techniques such as participatory rural appraisals, (Mamo Y. Z. et al. 2023) community workshops, interviews, surveys, and focus group discussions are employed to gather insights directly from stakeholders. These inputs are not only critical for data collection but also for building trust, minimizing resistance, and co-creating solutions. After stakeholder engagement, baseline studies are conducted to establish the existing social, cultural, and economic conditions in the affected area. This baseline serves as a point of comparison to identify and measure future changes. It may include indicators such as literacy rates, access to healthcare, crime rates, housing quality, employment statistics, land use, and community networks. With a comprehensive understanding of the starting point, analysts can then model and forecast the likely social effects of a proposed action, drawing on historical data, case studies, expert consultations, and predictive modeling techniques.

MEASURING REPUTATION AND BRAND PERCEPTION: REPUTATION MEASUREMENT

Sentiment analysis for Corporate Social Responsibility (CSR) initiatives has emerged as a transformative approach for evaluating the public perception, stakeholder engagement, and overall effectiveness of an organization's social and ethical programs. As CSR becomes an integral part of strategic branding, corporate ethics, stakeholder communication, and long-term sustainability, understanding how these initiatives are received and interpreted by diverse audiences is critical. Traditional methods of CSR evaluation—such as surveys, impact reports, and internal audits—though valuable, often fall short of capturing real-time, nuanced sentiment from external stakeholders. (Molavi, H. et al. 2024) This is where sentiment analysis, a branch of natural language processing (NLP) and artificial intelligence (AI), offers a powerful supplement. It enables organizations to process vast amounts of unstructured textual data—social media posts, news coverage, blog comments, online reviews, public forums, and customer feedback—and classify emotional tones as positive, negative, or neutral. Through this method, companies can measure not just the outcomes of their CSR activities, but also how those outcomes are perceived and valued by the public and other key stakeholders. CSR initiatives today cover a broad spectrum of activities, including environmental sustainability, ethical labor practices, community development, corporate philanthropy, education and health programs, gender equity, DEI (diversity, equity, and inclusion) efforts, and climate action. (Molavi, H. et al. 2024) Each of these domains carries unique stakeholder expectations and reputational sensitivities. For instance, a company's green energy campaign might be praised for reducing carbon emissions but also criticized for greenwashing if not implemented transparently. Similarly, philanthropic donations might garner positive sentiment, but accusations of performative CSR can trigger public backlash. Sentiment analysis provides the necessary contextual understanding to assess how such initiatives are being discussed and whether they are genuinely enhancing the company's reputation or inadvertently undermining it.

The process of applying sentiment analysis to CSR evaluation begins with data collection. Using web crawlers, API integrations, and social listening platforms, companies gather data from multiple online channels. (Myšková, R. et al. 2018) This includes brand mentions, hashtags associated with CSR campaigns, comments on official press releases, employee advocacy platforms, and third-party news stories. The raw text is then preprocessed—cleaned of irrelevant data, tokenized, normalized—and analyzed using sentiment classification algorithms. These may range from basic rule-based systems to sophisticated machine learning and deep learning models such as logistic regression, Naïve Bayes, Support Vector Machines (SVM), or transformer-based models like BERT, RoBERTa, and GPT. Once sentiment scores are assigned to textual data, analysts aggregate the results over time and across sources to create a composite picture of stakeholder sentiment. This allows companies to track shifts in perception surrounding specific CSR themes or campaigns. For example, if a corporation launches a new initiative to improve supply chain transparency, sentiment analysis can reveal whether the public perceives this as a genuine step forward or merely a reactionary gesture following previous criticism. (Myšková, R. et al. 2018) By comparing sentiment trends before, during, and after CSR campaigns, companies can gauge campaign effectiveness, identify peak engagement moments, and uncover key drivers of positive or negative feedback.

DATA QUALITY AND NOISE: DATA QUALITY CHALLENGES

Measuring reputation and brand perception—commonly referred to as reputation measurement—is a vital component of strategic management, marketing, and corporate communications. (Nisha Angeline M. et al. 2025) Reputation is one of an organization's most valuable intangible assets, influencing stakeholder trust, customer loyalty, employee engagement, investor confidence, regulatory relationships, and ultimately, financial performance. Brand perception, closely related, reflects how stakeholders interpret and emotionally respond to a brand's identity, values, and behaviors. (Nisha Angeline M. et al. 2025) Both concepts are dynamic and multifaceted, shaped by a combination of direct experiences, word-of-mouth, media coverage, social media discourse, corporate actions, and societal trends. In today's hyper-connected, information-saturated world, reputation and brand perception can shift rapidly—making systematic measurement and management essential for organizational resilience and success. At its core, reputation measurement seeks to answer critical questions: How is the organization perceived by different stakeholder groups? What emotions, associations, and values are connected with the brand?

How do these perceptions align with the organization's intended positioning and identity? How do they evolve over time, and what drives changes? Answering these questions requires both qualitative and quantitative approaches, drawing on a wide array of data sources. (Zhang J. et al. 2024) Traditionally, reputation measurement relied heavily on stakeholder surveys and reputation indices such as the Reputation Quotient (RQ), Brand Asset Valuator (BAV), and Corporate Reputation Index (CRI). These structured tools capture stakeholder opinions on key dimensions like trust, quality, innovation, leadership, social responsibility, and financial performance.

While survey-based reputation measurement remains important, it has limitations in terms of frequency, scalability, and responsiveness to fast-moving reputational shifts. The rise of digital and social media has transformed the landscape, enabled real-time conversations and made reputation more vulnerable to rapid swings in public sentiment. (Nurdeni D. A. et al. 2021) In this environment, modern reputation measurement integrates advanced analytics techniques—particularly sentiment analysis, natural language processing (NLP), and social listening—to capture and interpret the vast amounts of unstructured data generated across online platforms. Sentiment analysis allows organizations to classify the emotional tone of digital mentions (positive, negative, neutral), while topic modeling identifies the key themes and issues driving perception. (Nurdeni D. A. et al. 2021) The process begins with comprehensive data collection. Using web crawlers, social listening platforms, and APIs, organizations gather brand mentions from news articles, blogs, forums, online reviews, and social media channels like Twitter, LinkedIn, Facebook, Instagram, Reddit, and YouTube. Data from internal sources—such as customer service interactions, feedback forms, employee engagement surveys, and investor communications—are also incorporated. (Zhang J. et al. 2024) By combining internal and external data, organizations gain a holistic view of reputation drivers across different touchpoints. This data is processed through NLP and AI models to extract sentiment scores, emotional nuances, trending topics, and influencer impact.

CONTEXTUAL UNDERSTANDING: CONTEXT IMPORTANCE

Data quality and noise are central challenges in any data-driven initiative, particularly in fields such as business intelligence, artificial intelligence (AI), machine learning (ML), natural language processing (NLP), and analytics. As organizations increasingly rely on large, complex datasets to inform strategic decisions, the integrity, accuracy, and relevance of data become paramount. Poor data quality and excessive noise can severely compromise the reliability of insights, leading to flawed conclusions, ineffective strategies, and wasted resources. (Ordonez-Ponce E. et al. 2024) At the core of this issue is the understanding that "garbage in, garbage out" holds true: even the most sophisticated algorithms and models will produce poor results if the underlying data is of low quality or polluted by irrelevant or misleading information. Therefore, managing data quality and mitigating noise are not peripheral concerns but foundational requirements for effective data analysis and decision-making. (Yiğit Açikgöz F. et al. 2024) Data quality challenges arise from multiple dimensions—accuracy, completeness, consistency, timeliness, validity, and uniqueness. Inaccurate data may result from manual entry errors, faulty sensors, outdated records, or inconsistent formatting across systems. For example, customer names entered with typos, mismatched product codes, or incomplete demographic fields can distort analyses of market trends. (Yiğit Açikgöz F. et al. 2024) Completeness is another frequent issue, where datasets have missing values or lack important variables needed for robust analysis. Consistency problems occur when different data sources record similar information in incompatible formats or with varying definitions—common in organizations with siloed systems or legacy IT infrastructures. Timeliness is also critical; outdated data may fail to reflect current realities, leading to obsolete insights. Validity refers to whether the data truly measures what it is intended to measure, while uniqueness ensures that records are not duplicated—both vital for maintaining dataset integrity.

Noise refers to any irrelevant, extraneous, or random variation within data that obscures the underlying patterns or signals of interest. In textual data, for example, noise can take the form of spam, irrelevant hashtags, off-topic conversations, or sarcastic comments that mislead sentiment analysis algorithms. In sensor data, noise may stem from environmental factors, device malfunctions, or signal interference. In financial data, market anomalies or outliers may distort trend analyses. (Ordonez-Ponce E. et al. 2024) While some noise is inherent to real-world data, excessive noise can drown out meaningful signals and reduce model accuracy. Moreover, in highly automated environments—such as algorithmic trading or autonomous systems—unfiltered noise can lead to erroneous or even dangerous decisions. A significant data quality challenge is the sheer volume and velocity of modern data, often described as "big data." As organizations collect information from an ever-expanding array of sources—social media, IoT devices, customer interactions, transaction records, and public data feeds—manually ensuring data quality becomes impractical. (Upadhyaya A. N. et al. 2025) Automated data pipelines must be designed to incorporate data cleansing, validation, deduplication, and normalization processes. Yet even with automated tools, ensuring data quality at scale remains complex. Diverse data sources may have varying degrees of reliability, and contextual nuances may be difficult to encode in cleansing algorithms. (Upadhyaya A. N. et al. 2025) For example, slang, sarcasm, and cultural references in social media data can confound NLP models unless carefully managed.

INTEGRATING SENTIMENT ANALYSIS WITH OTHER METRICS: INTEGRATION BENEFITS

Contextual understanding is a critical component in the interpretation and analysis of information, especially in the fields of artificial intelligence (AI), natural language processing (NLP), communication, (Oyewole A. T. et al. 2024) behavioral sciences, decision-making, and data analytics. Context refers to the circumstances, background, or setting in which information is produced, received, or interpreted, and it profoundly influences meaning. Without an accurate grasp of context, the same word, sentence, behavior, or data point can lead to vastly different conclusions. Whether it's interpreting a sarcastic tweet, understanding a customer's complaint, analyzing stakeholder sentiment, or making an ethical business decision, the importance of context cannot be overstated. It shapes how information is encoded, processed, and acted upon, bridging the gap between raw data and meaningful insight. In today's digital world—where data is abundant, (Oyewole A. T. et al. 2024) communication is rapid, and cultures and norms vary widely—contextual understanding has emerged as not just a desirable capability but a necessary one for accuracy, empathy, and effective action. In human communication, context determines the tone, intent, and meaning behind words. A phrase like "that's just great" can express genuine satisfaction or biting sarcasm, depending on vocal tone, facial expression, timing, and situational cues. In face-to-face conversation, we use gestures, body language, prior knowledge, and shared history to infer context automatically. (Toschi L. et al. 2023) In written communication, however, especially on digital platforms like social media or email, many of these cues are absent, increasing the risk of misinterpretation. NLP models that lack contextual understanding may misclassify sentiment or intent, leading to flawed outputs. For instance, a sentiment analysis model that interprets all uses of the word "bad" as negative would misread a sentence like "this product is bad in the best way possible." Accurate interpretation requires the model to understand linguistic nuance, cultural idioms, and domain-specific usage—all of which are rooted in context.

In artificial intelligence, especially with the development of large language models, contextual understanding has become a key differentiator in performance. Early rule-based systems and even traditional machine learning models often failed to grasp the full context of language inputs, leading to rigid or nonsensical responses. Modern transformer-based architectures like BERT, GPT, and T5 are designed specifically to capture context by examining the relationships between words and phrases in both directions. These models consider not only the local context within a sentence but also broader discourse across paragraphs, documents, and conversational turns. (Pennington-Gray L. et al. 2024) This enables more coherent text generation, accurate summarization, improved question answering, and effective translation. Yet even the most advanced models still struggle with deep contextual reasoning—such as understanding irony, recognizing bias, or responding empathetically in emotionally complex situations—highlighting the ongoing challenge of replicating human-level contextual intelligence. In decision-making, context provides the background necessary for evaluating options, assessing risk, and anticipating consequences. (Toschi L. et al. 2023) A business decision that appears sound in one market or cultural setting may be inappropriate or even harmful in another. For instance, marketing campaigns that rely on humor or cultural references may succeed in one region but fail elsewhere if the underlying context is misunderstood. Likewise, health policies or educational reforms must account for local social, economic, and cultural factors to be effective. Ignoring context can lead to poor adoption, (Pennington-Gray L. et al. 2024) community resistance, or unintended side effects. This is why context-sensitive policy design, participatory planning, and stakeholder engagement are essential in both public and private sector initiatives.

IMPLEMENTING SENTIMENT ANALYSIS TOOLS: TOOL IMPLEMENTATION

Integrating sentiment analysis with other metrics offers significant benefits for organizations aiming to gain a more holistic and actionable understanding of stakeholder perceptions, brand health, customer experience, and overall organizational performance. (Raghavendra A. H. et al. 2024) Sentiment analysis, which uses natural language processing (NLP) and machine learning (ML) to evaluate the emotional tone of textual data—such as social media posts, customer reviews, employee feedback, news articles, and survey responses—provides a valuable but incomplete view when considered in isolation. (Raghavendra A. H. et al. 2024) On its own, sentiment analysis captures "how" people feel but not necessarily "why" they feel that way or "what" specific outcomes result from these sentiments. By integrating sentiment data with other quantitative and qualitative metrics—ranging from sales figures, customer retention rates, and Net Promoter Scores (NPS), to website traffic, engagement levels, operational KPIs, and financial outcomes—organizations can contextualize emotions within a broader analytical framework. This synergy transforms raw sentiment data from a descriptive tool into a predictive and prescriptive asset that informs strategic decision-making and drives continuous improvement. One key benefit of integrating sentiment analysis with business performance metrics is the ability to uncover causal relationships between public perception and organizational outcomes. For example, a sustained increase in negative customer sentiment on social media may precede a decline in sales or an uptick in product returns. Conversely, a spike in positive sentiment following a marketing campaign or new product launch may correlate with increased customer acquisition or loyalty. By tracking these relationships over time, companies can build predictive models that forecast business performance based on evolving sentiment trends. This predictive capability enables proactive intervention—addressing emerging risks before they manifest in declining revenue or damaged reputation.

Another important benefit is enhancing the depth and accuracy of customer experience (CX) measurement. Traditional CX metrics like NPS, Customer Satisfaction (CSAT) scores, and Customer Effort Scores (CES) provide structured, quantitative insights but often lack the rich emotional and contextual nuance found in unstructured feedback. Sentiment analysis can bridge this gap by analyzing open-text responses in surveys or unsolicited feedback across channels. (Raghupathi V. et al. 2020) When integrated with structured CX metrics, sentiment data helps explain variations in scores, identify root causes of dissatisfaction, and uncover unmet needs. For example, two customers may both give a "neutral" NPS score, but sentiment analysis of their comments could reveal that one is disappointed due to poor service, while the other is indifferent because of limited product features. This granular insight allows for more personalized and effective CX interventions. Integrating sentiment analysis also enhances brand reputation management by providing a comprehensive view of public perception across multiple touchpoints. While reputation indices and brand equity models offer valuable high-level indicators, they often rely on periodic surveys and lagging data. Sentiment analysis adds real-time, dynamic input from digital channels, enabling organizations to monitor reputation continuously. By combining sentiment trends with media coverage metrics, brand share of voice, crisis alerts, and stakeholder survey data, companies can develop robust reputation dashboards. (Raghupathi V. et al. 2020) These dashboards not only track current reputation status but also highlight emerging risks and opportunities, informing timely communication strategies and leadership decisions.

BEST PRACTICES FOR SENTIMENT ANALYSIS: BEST PRACTICES

Implementing sentiment analysis tools is a critical step for organizations seeking to enhance their understanding of stakeholder emotions, brand perception, customer satisfaction, and public reputation. (Sakthivel M. et al. 2025) As businesses generate and encounter increasing volumes of unstructured text data—from social media posts, customer reviews, and survey responses to internal communications, news articles, and public forums—sentiment analysis has emerged as an essential capability for extracting actionable insights from this data. However, effective tool implementation involves more than just deploying software; it requires careful planning, cross-functional collaboration, robust data infrastructure, and alignment with organizational goals. (Sakthivel M. et al. 2025) When executed thoughtfully, sentiment analysis tools can empower organizations to make more informed decisions, respond swiftly to emerging trends, improve customer experiences, and safeguard reputation. Conversely, poor implementation can lead to unreliable insights, wasted resources, and potential reputational harm. (Thirunagalingam A. et al. 2025) Therefore, understanding the best practices, challenges, and strategic considerations involved in implementing sentiment analysis tools is crucial for success. The first step in implementing sentiment analysis tools is defining clear objectives. Organizations must articulate what they hope to achieve—whether it is monitoring brand health, improving customer service, evaluating employee sentiment, tracking campaign effectiveness, supporting product development, or managing reputation risk. (Scheepers H. et al. 2022) Without clear goals, sentiment analysis efforts can become unfocused or disconnected from business needs. (Thirunagalingam A. et al. 2025) Clear objectives also guide the selection of appropriate tools, data sources, and analytical approaches. (Scheepers H. et al. 2022) For example, a company seeking to understand customer feedback on specific product features may require fine-grained aspect-based sentiment analysis, while one focused on crisis detection may prioritize real-time social listening and trend monitoring.

Once objectives are established, the next step is selecting the right sentiment analysis tools and technologies. (Shokouhyar S. et al. 2023) The market offers a wide range of options—from out-of-the-box solutions provided by major analytics and social listening platforms (e.g., Brandwatch, Sprinklr, Talkwalker, NetBase Quid) to customizable open-source libraries (e.g., NLTK, TextBlob, spaCy, Hugging Face transformers) and advanced cloud-based AI services (e.g., Google Cloud Natural Language API, IBM Watson, Microsoft Azure Text Analytics, Amazon Comprehend). The choice depends on factors such as desired functionality, scalability, integration needs, budget, language support, and the technical expertise of the organization. (Shokouhyar S. et al. 2023) Commercial platforms often offer ease of use, integrated dashboards, and vendor support, making them suitable for marketing and PR teams. Custom or open-source solutions offer greater flexibility and accuracy but may require more technical resources for development and maintenance. Data preparation is a critical component of implementation. Sentiment analysis relies on high-quality textual data, and the process begins with identifying relevant data sources. (Smith E. A. et al. 2024) These may include social media platforms (Twitter, Facebook, Instagram, LinkedIn), customer review sites (Amazon, Yelp, TripAdvisor), internal CRM systems, helpdesk tickets, chat logs, surveys, news feeds, and online communities. Integrating and ingesting data from these diverse sources requires robust data pipelines and ETL (extract, transform, load) processes. Data cleaning—removing duplicates, handling special characters, normalizing text, and filtering irrelevant content—is essential to ensure accuracy. Preprocessing steps such as tokenization, lemmatization, and stop-word removal further enhance model performance. (Smith E. A. et al. 2024) Special attention must be paid to ensuring privacy and compliance with data protection regulations (e.g., GDPR, CCPA), particularly when dealing with personally identifiable information (PII).

CONCLUSION

Best practices for sentiment analysis are essential to ensure that organizations can extract accurate, meaningful, and actionable insights from the vast volumes of unstructured text data generated across digital platforms. Sentiment analysis—whether applied to social media posts, customer reviews, survey responses, employee feedback, or news coverage—offers significant value in understanding public perception, stakeholder emotions, brand reputation, and emerging trends. However, because human language is inherently complex, context-dependent, and nuanced, the effectiveness of sentiment analysis depends heavily on how well it is implemented. Adhering to best practices helps organizations avoid common pitfalls such as misclassification, bias, or overreliance on simplistic metrics. By following a strategic, well-governed approach, companies can maximize the benefits of sentiment analysis while maintaining ethical standards and fostering trust among stakeholders. A fundamental best practice is to begin with clear objectives. Sentiment analysis should not be conducted as an isolated or exploratory exercise but should be aligned with specific business goals—such as improving customer experience, monitoring brand health, informing product development, managing reputational risks, or enhancing employee engagement. Clearly defined objectives guide tool selection, data source prioritization, model customization, and the design of reporting outputs. They also ensure that sentiment insights are actionable and tied to measurable outcomes, increasing the value of the analysis for decision-makers. Selecting appropriate tools and models is another critical best practice. Organizations should carefully evaluate sentiment analysis solutions based on accuracy, flexibility, scalability, language and domain support, ease of integration, and cost. While off-the-shelf tools offer convenience and speed, they may not handle domain-specific language, cultural context, or nuanced expressions effectively. In contrast, custom or fine-tuned models—based on advanced NLP architectures like BERT, RoBERTa, or GPT—typically deliver higher accuracy and adaptability but require more technical expertise. The choice should be guided by the complexity of the language being analyzed, the diversity of data sources, and the organization's internal capabilities. Ensuring high-quality data is foundational to effective sentiment analysis. Poor data quality—such as noisy, irrelevant, incomplete, or biased datasets—can severely distort sentiment insights.

Best practices in data preparation include thorough cleaning, normalization, and deduplication of textual data. It is also important to address spam, bot activity, and other forms of artificial content that can skew sentiment trends. Leveraging human-in-the-loop validation, where trained reviewers audit sample outputs, helps improve data quality and provides feedback for model refinement.

REFERENCES

Abdurahiman, S., Kasthurba, A. K., & Nuzhat, A. (2024). Assessing the socio-cultural impact of urban revitalisation using Relative Positive Impact Index (RPII). *Built Heritage*, *8*(1), 8. DOI: 10.1186/s43238-024-00118-3

Alaei, A. R., Becken, S., & Stantic, B. (2019). Sentiment analysis in tourism: Capitalizing on big data. *Journal of Travel Research*, *58*(2), 175–191. DOI: 10.1177/0047287517747753

Ceron, A., Curini, L., Iacus, S. M., & Porro, G. (2014). Every tweet counts? How sentiment analysis of social media can improve our knowledge of citizens' political preferences with an application to Italy and France. *New Media & Society*, *16*(2), 340–358. DOI: 10.1177/1461444813480466

Chowdhary, S., Selvakumar, P., Sangeetha, B., Sarvaani, V. V., Anute, N., & Sharma, M. (2025). The Role of Social Capital in Entrepreneurial Development. In Martínez-Falcó, J., Sánchez-García, E., & Marco-Lajara, B. (Eds.), *Support Networks for Entrepreneurs: Social Capital and Strategic Collaborations* (pp. 311–338). IGI Global Scientific Publishing. DOI: 10.4018/979-8-3693-9836-4.ch013

Coates, J. M., Santhanalakshmi, K., Dinesh, N., Gandhimathi, S., & Chandel, P. S. Mohit, & Selvakumar, P. (2025). Assessment and Evaluation in Transnational Staff Development. In G. Morris & J. Ye (Eds.), Training and Development in Transnational Higher Education (pp. 387-406). IGI Global Scientific Publishing.

De Marchi, D., Becarelli, R., & Di Sarli, L. (2022). Tourism sustainability index: Measuring tourism sustainability based on the ETIS toolkit, by exploring tourist satisfaction via sentiment analysis. *Sustainability (Basel)*, *14*(13), 8049. DOI: 10.3390/su14138049

Deshmukh, A. K., Mohan, A., & Mohan, I. (2022). Goods and services tax (GST) implementation in India: A SAP–LAP–Twitter analytic perspective. *Global Journal of Flexible Systems Managment*, *23*(2), 165–183. DOI: 10.1007/s40171-021-00297-3 PMID: 37522093

El Barachi, M., AlKhatib, M., Mathew, S., & Oroumchian, F. (2021). A novel sentiment analysis framework for monitoring the evolving public opinion in real-time: Case study on climate change. *Journal of Cleaner Production*, *312*, 127820. DOI: 10.1016/j.jclepro.2021.127820

Hadro, D., Fijałkowska, J., Daszyńska-Żygadło, K., Zumente, I., & Mjakuškina, S. (2022). What do stakeholders in the construction industry look for in non-financial disclosure and what do they get? *Meditari Accountancy Research, 30*(3), 762–785. DOI: 10.1108/MEDAR-11-2020-1093

Haider, R., Bari, M. F. A. I., Shaif, M. F. I., Rahman, M., Ohi, M. N. H., & Rahman, K. M. M. (2025). Quantifying the Impact: Leveraging AI-Powered Sentiment Analysis for Strategic Digital Marketing and Enhanced Brand Reputation Management. *International Journal of Science and Research Archive, 15*(2), 1103–1121. DOI: 10.30574/ijsra.2025.15.2.1524

Hubballi, R. B., Selvakumar, P., Seenivasan, R., & Basava Aradhya, S. G., Dinesh, N., & Seelam, P. K. (2025). Overview of Current AI Technologies in Education. In L. Kyei-Blankson & E. Ntuli (Eds.), Transformative AI Practices for Personalized Learning Strategies (pp. 1-26). IGI Global Scientific Publishing.

Jaiswal, R., Gupta, S., & Tiwari, A. K. (2024). Decoding mood of the Twitterverse on ESG investing: Opinion mining and key themes using machine learning. *Management Research Review, 47*(8), 1221–1252. DOI: 10.1108/MRR-07-2023-0526

Jiang, H., Lin, P., & Qiang, M. (2016). Public-opinion sentiment analysis for large hydro projects. *Journal of Construction Engineering and Management, 142*(2), 05015013. DOI: 10.1061/(ASCE)CO.1943-7862.0001039

Jones, C. E., Theodosis, S., & Lykourentzou, I. (2019). The enthusiast, the interested, the sceptic, and the cynic: Understanding user experience and perceived value in location-based cultural heritage games through qualitative and sentiment analysis. [JOCCH]. *Journal on Computing and Cultural Heritage, 12*(1), 1–26. DOI: 10.1145/3297716

Kamal, M. R., Noviyanto, K., Subhan, H., & Afiana, L. (2024). Sentiment Analysis on Social Media and Stakeholders about Negative Issues Among Islamic Boarding School Community In Indonesia. *Jurnal Theologia, 35*(2), 261–280. DOI: 10.21580/teo.2024.35.2.23164

Kotte, K. R., Attaluri, V., & Selvakumar, P. (2025). Revolutionising Retail Banking with AI and Virtual Technologies AI-Driven Financial Training. In Nair, A. J., Manohar, S., Limbu, Y. B., & Huhmann, B. A. (Eds.), *Intersecting Natural Language Processing and FinTech Innovations in Service Marketing* (pp. 421–440). IGI Global Scientific Publishing. DOI: 10.4018/979-8-3693-9944-6.ch020

Maceda, L. L., Satuito, A. A., & Abisado, M. B. (2023). Sentiment Analysis of Code-mixed Social Media Data on Philippine UAQTE using Fine-tuned mBERT Model. *International Journal of Advanced Computer Science and Applications, 14*(7). DOI: 10.14569/IJACSA.2023.0140777

Maheswaran, K., Selvakumar, P., Shaikh, M., Shashank, G., Gupta, S., & Manjunath, T. C. (2025). The Evolution of Smart Urban Mobility With Emerging Technologies. In Ponnusamy, S., Assaf, M., Youssef, B., Jeon, G., & Kalyanaraman, S. (Eds.), *Leveraging VANETs and Blockchain Technology for Urban Mobility* (pp. 1–28). IGI Global Scientific Publishing. DOI: 10.4018/979-8-3373-0265-2.ch001

Maignan, I., Ferrell, O. C., & Ferrell, L. (2005). A stakeholder model for implementing social responsibility in marketing. *European Journal of Marketing, 39*(9/10), 956–977. DOI: 10.1108/03090560510610662

Mamo, Y. Z., & Anagnostopoulos, C. (2023). Stakeholders'"voice" through social media: The case of corporate social responsibility in sport. *International Journal of Sports Marketing & Sponsorship, 24*(5), 1002–1020. DOI: 10.1108/IJSMS-05-2023-0084

Molavi, H., & Zhang, L. (2024, July). A Bibliometric Study of Stakeholder Opinion Mining and Sentiment Analysis in Crisis Communication. In 6th International Conference on Advanced Research Methods and Analytics (CARMA 2024) (pp. 43-52). Editorial Universitat Politècnica de València. DOI: 10.4995/CARMA2024.2024.17782

Myšková, R., & Hájek, P. (2018). Sustainability and corporate social responsibility in the text of annual reports—The case of the IT services industry. *Sustainability (Basel), 10*(11), 4119. DOI: 10.3390/su10114119

Nisha Angeline, M., Selvakumar, P., Gupta, M. K., Nazar, N., Elumalai, D., & Bhattacharya, S. (2025). Emerging Materials for Energy Storage and Environmental Applications. In K. Muduli, B. Moharana, S. Ales, & D. Biswal (Eds.), Using Computational Intelligence for Sustainable Manufacturing of Advanced Materials (pp. 53-72). IGI Global Scientific Publishing. DOI: 10.4018/979-8-3693-7974-5.ch003

Nurdeni, D. A., Budi, I., & Santoso, A. B. (2021, April). Sentiment analysis on Covid19 vaccines in Indonesia: from the perspective of Sinovac and Pfizer. In 2021 3rd East Indonesia conference on computer and information technology (EIConCIT) (pp. 122-127). IEEE. DOI: 10.1109/EIConCIT50028.2021.9431852

Ordonez-Ponce, E., Dordi, T., Talbot, D., & Weber, O. (2024). Canadian banks and their responses to COVID-19–stakeholder-oriented crisis management. *Journal of Sustainable Finance & Investment, 14*(2), 388–409. DOI: 10.1080/20430795.2022.2069663

Oyewole, A. T., Adeoye, O. B., Addy, W. A., Okoye, C. C., Ofodile, O. C., & Ugochukwu, C. E.Adedoyin Tolulope OyewoleOmotayo Bukola AdeoyeWilhelmina Afua AddyChinwe Chinazo OkoyeOnyeka Chrisanctus OfodileChinonye Esther Ugochukwu. (2024). Automating financial reporting with natural language processing: A review and case analysis. *World Journal of Advanced Research and Reviews, 21*(3), 575–589. DOI: 10.30574/wjarr.2024.21.3.0688

Pennington-Gray, L., Lee, S., & Ballouli, K. (2024). Stakeholder sentiment of SDGs of Beijing Olympics 2020. In Sport Tourism, Events and Sustainable Development Goals (pp. 114-139). Routledge.

Raghavendra, A. H., Bala, P. K., & Mukherjee, A. (2024). Text mining analysis of retail and consumer service leaders' sustainability narratives: Are they actually true? *Journal of Retailing and Consumer Services, 80*, 103921. DOI: 10.1016/j.jretconser.2024.103921

Raghupathi, V., Ren, J., & Raghupathi, W. (2020). Identifying corporate sustainability issues by analyzing shareholder resolutions: A machine-learning text analytics approach. *Sustainability (Basel), 12*(11), 4753. DOI: 10.3390/su12114753

Sakthivel, M., Jaganathan, A., Mohanraj, M., & Selvakumar, P. Mohit, & Manjunath, T. (2025). Brand Loyalty through AI and Personalisation AI-Generated Content for Financial Marketing. In A. J Nair, S. Manohar, Y. B. Limbu, & B. A. Huhmann (Eds.), Intersecting Natural Language Processing and FinTech Innovations in Service Marketing (pp. 77-96). IGI Global Scientific Publishing.

Scheepers, H., McLoughlin, S., & Wijesinghe, R. (2022). Aligning stakeholders perceptions of project performance: The contribution of Business Realisation Management. *International Journal of Project Management, 40*(5), 471–480. DOI: 10.1016/j.ijproman.2022.03.002

Shokouhyar, S., Shokoohyar, S., & Mirzaei, S. (2023). Stakeholders' engagement through social media analytics in promoting sustainable development practices in the mobile supply chain: A cross-country analysis. *Business Strategy and the Environment, 32*(8), 5807–5820. DOI: 10.1002/bse.3449

Smith, E. A., Knollenberg, W., Seekamp, E., Lee, K. J., & Savage, A. (2024). Gateway community stakeholders' perceived impacts of protected area management actions: The case of North Carolina (US) state parks. *Journal of Outdoor Recreation and Tourism, 47*, 100792. DOI: 10.1016/j.jort.2024.100792

Thirunagalingam, A., & Selvakumar, P. (2025). Application of Automation and Robotics in the Oil and Gas Industry. In Abdullayev, V., & Khang, A. (Eds.), *Revolutionizing AI and Robotics in the Oil and Gas Industry* (pp. 229–244). IGI Global Scientific Publishing. DOI: 10.4018/979-8-3693-8156-4.ch011

Toschi, L., Ughetto, E., & Fronzetti Colladon, A. (2023). The identity of social impact venture capitalists: Exploring social linguistic positioning and linguistic distinctiveness through text mining. *Small Business Economics*, *60*(3), 1249–1280. DOI: 10.1007/s11187-022-00655-0

Upadhyaya, A. N., Debnath, P., Rani, P., Selvakumar, P., Manjunath, T. C., & Bhattacharya, S. (2025). AI-Based Disaster Prediction and Early Warning Systems. In Mobo, F. (Ed.), *AI and Emerging Technologies for Emergency Response and Smart Cities* (pp. 55–74). IGI Global Scientific Publishing. DOI: 10.4018/979-8-3693-9770-1.ch003

Yiğit Açikgöz, F., Kayakuş, M., Moiceanu, G., & Sönmez, N. (2024). A New Approach to Assess Sustainable Corporate Reputation with Citizen Comments Using Machine Learning and Natural Language Processing. *Sustainability (Basel)*, *16*(22), 9610. DOI: 10.3390/su16229610

Zhang, J., & Chung, K. S. K. (2024). Online naturalistic inquiry for stakeholder issue analysis: Design and implementation. *Project Leadership and Society*, *5*, 100163. DOI: 10.1016/j.plas.2024.100163

Chapter 10

Strategic CSR and Customer Engagement in ESG Dashboards: A Data-Driven Approach to SDG 12 Implementation

A. Ayyoob
https://orcid.org/0009-0003-2839-3598
University of Calicut, India

Aparna Sajeev
https://orcid.org/0000-0001-5642-5460
University of Calicut, India

ABSTRACT

Corporate Social Responsibility (CSR) initiatives become an essential toolkit for institutionalizing corporate sustainability processes. The consumer focus on how CSR initiatives have actually influenced corporate sustainability perception and well-being remains under-researched, especially considering demographics. Thereby, the study investigates the influences of communication transparency, customer involvement, and CSR initiatives on customer perception and well-being, along with the role of gender and generational differences in perception. A quantitative research design was adopted wherein 282 respondents filled in structured questionnaires. Purposive sampling secured demographic and geographic diversity. t-test, ANOVA, correlation, and regression were used to test the hypotheses. The results show that communication transparency, customer involvement, and CSR initiatives drive sustainability. Gender and age differences exist. Thus, the study shows how aligning CSR with customer expectations builds trust and supports SDG 12 goals.

DOI: 10.4018/979-8-3373-5142-1.ch010

INTRODUCTION AND SIGNIFICANCE OF THE STUDY

Among the key areas of concern for firms interested in corporate sustainability is CSR programs' alignment with Sustainable Development Goal (SDG) 12: Responsible Consumption and Production. SDG 12, in particular, stresses production and consumption habits that integrate environmental, social, and economic considerations into business operations (Vargas-Merino & Rios-Lama, 2023). This link can be perceived as a strategic requirement that companies must fulfil in an ever-changing global environment in order to secure long-term growth, alongside social demands for accountability. CSR programs that are well established and implemented have been shown in the past to have a positive correlation with financial performance and therefore serve as a positive factor for profitability alongside confronting pressing social and environmental issues (Dhingra, 2023). Nonetheless, the scant integration seen in reporting and management systems is one of the reasons for the weak enforcement of CSR in business strategy, where this could also be correlated with the lack of formal commitment and low prioritization of SDG-related initiatives (Ferrero-Ferrero et al., 2023).

With the subject matter touching upon CSR and development options with the needs of societies and sustainability movements articulated through SDGs especially SDG 12, conscientious production and consumption is underlined here in reference to core CSR principles of transparency, ethics, and stakeholder participation. For a stronger CSR sustainability framework, strategic partnerships between the private sector and academic institutions have been under development (Saad et al., 2022). Nonalignment of SDG 12 with a broader sustainability framework has led to this goal being overlooked in business practice, even though it carries a significant importance (Ferrero-Ferrero et al., 2023). Integrating CSR programs with SDG 12 offers companies a unique opportunity to address critical issues such as resource depletion, climate change, unfair production systems, and sustainable development (Gong et al., 2023).

To the extent successful CSR programs are communicated well and have heavy participation from consumers, they will increase consumer trust, loyalty, and engagement. Still, questions concerning the validity of CSR programs, the observability of business communications, and the impact of such on the opinions and welfare of customers persist. There are, furthermore, questions in how consumers actually perceive all CSR efforts and their perception of a firm's sustainability performance especially when these CSR efforts align with SDG 12 targets. To take CSR as a strategic tool to meet stakeholder expectations and negotiate the challenges of corporate sustainability, businesses must close these gaps. Widespread acceptance of corporate social responsibility notwithstanding, consumer participation in these programs in relation to their well-being and how they perceive the company's sustainability performance remain little understood. Customers are more inclined to consider the initiatives to be real and trustworthy if companies plainly and appropriately communicate their efforts, thus stressing the need for transparency in CSR communication (Lee & Chung, 2023).

Transparency builds up customer trust and willingness to engage by focusing on businesses' impacts on sustainability rather than just reporting on operations through social media platforms (Winit et al., 2023; Yu et al., 2022). According to certain studies, CSR initiatives aligned with customer values foster a mutual sense of responsibility for societal and environmental well-being and encourage participation (Raza et al., 2023). Besides, client engagement normally considers ethical and emotional issues as opposed to transactional matters. In languages such as retail and hospitality, client involvement in CSR actions is stimulated by positive feelings and altruistic attitudes (Dhingra, 2023; Fatma & Khan, 2023). When a company aligns its sustainability objectives with consumer interests, stronger ties and deeper loyalty can be formed (Gong et al., 2023). Yet, ambiguities in clearly communicating these programs and buttressing their tangible impact on community support and environmental sustainability still remain. The consumers have become increasingly demanding of CSR activities related to fair labor practices, ethical sourcing, and environmental stewardship as indicators of a business's commitment to sustainable development (Pegan et al., 2022; Hobeika et al., 2022). By exploring the relationships between customer involvement in CSR initiatives, communication transparency, and the broader impact of CSR programs on corporate sustainability performance and customer and societal well-being, this study aims to shed light on these pertinent questions. More specifically, the study studies the following questions:

- How does customer engagement with CSR activities influence corporate sustainability performance perception, particularly concerning CSR initiatives aligned with SDG 12?
- How could CSR initiatives with a high level of communication and transparency influence customer perception of corporate sustainability performance, and how does this fine-tune CSR efforts with SDG 12?
- How do CSR initiatives impact customers' perception of corporate sustainability performance and their well-being, and what factors really drive the latter?

The study holds vital importance as it builds on the interaction between CSR activities and customer engagement, transparency, and well-being. Hence, filling the gaps in existing literature, the research endeavours to inform businesses on how CSR programs should be conceptualized to satisfy customer expectations and values, and to complement SDG 12. Credible and transparent communication has been shown to uplift corporate sustainability performance through increased trust and stronger stakeholder relationships (Dhingra, 2023; Winit et al., 2023).

This study shall reinforce both theoretical and practical aspects of CSR and sustainability practices by way of robust empirical analysis. The results shall provide practical recommendations that companies should adopt concerning transparency, aligning CSR programs with consumer values, and tangibly taking their CSR programs toward the targets of SDG 12 by uncovering the processes linking CSR activities with consumer engagement and perception. This, in effect, shall sustain production and consumption, smooth stakeholder engagements, and enhance the cause for a just and sustainable future.

Objectives and Testing Hypotheses

Objective 1

- To study the dimensions of Communication and Transparency of CSR Initiatives, Customer Engagement with CSR Activities, Perceived Impact of CSR Initiatives on Customer Well-being, and Customer Perception of Corporate Sustainability Performance.

Objective 2

- To research the role of gender and generational differences in Perception of Corporate Sustainability Performance.

Hypotheses

- There is no significant difference in Customer Perception of Corporate Sustainability Performance with respect to their gender
- There is no significant difference in Customer Perception of Corporate Sustainability Performance with respect to their generations

Objective 3

- To measure the influence of Communication and Transparency of CSR Initiatives, Customer Engagement with CSR Activities, and Perceived Impact of CSR Initiatives on Customer Well-being influence Corporate Sustainability Performance.

Hypotheses

- There is no significant relationship between Communication and Transparency of CSR Initiatives and Customer Perception of Corporate Sustainability Performance
- There is no significant relationship between Customer Engagement with CSR Activities and Customer Perception of Corporate Sustainability Performance

- There is no significant relationship between Perceived Impact of CSR Initiatives on Customer Well-being and Customer Perception of Corporate Sustainability Performance

Variables and Conceptual Model

As depicted in the conceptual model of Figure 1, this research examines how a number of variables, such as customer engagement, customer well-being, transparency in communication, and the general perception of corporate sustainability performance, are affected by SDG 12-aligned CSR initiatives. Each variable is supported by relevant research findings from the literature and is subdivided into dependent and independent variables.

The dependent variable, "**customer perception of corporate sustainability performance**" reflects how consumers perceive a business's sustainability initiatives vis-à-vis SDG 12. This variable measures customers' perceptions of the company's commitment to sustainable consumption, waste reduction, and ethical supply chain management. Research states that businesses implementing genuine and transparent sustainability policies reap reputational benefits that conduct client retention to a greater extent (Winit et al., 2023). Customers' perceptions of corporate sustainability performance are further influenced by their tendency to associate sustainable consumption strategies with a company's sincere commitment to social and environmental goals (Stanco & Lerro, 2020).

In this method, "**communication and transparency of CSR initiatives**" are to be considered important independent variables. Customers are assured to comprehend the company's sustainability objectives, plans, and results when information goes by well. Transparent means of reporting on CSR works only enhance a company's credibility and dependability, especially if it discloses the performance impacts of its work rather than the intent (Yu et al., 2022; Lee & Chung, 2023). Social platforms keep businesses chatting with clients in a very virile manner that sometimes solidifies trust-the reason for their additional need for transparency (Winit et al., 2023). Customer perceptions and participation are also affected by whether the company uses a proactive versus a reactive communication approach (Dhingra, 2023).

Figure 1. Conceptual model (Author)

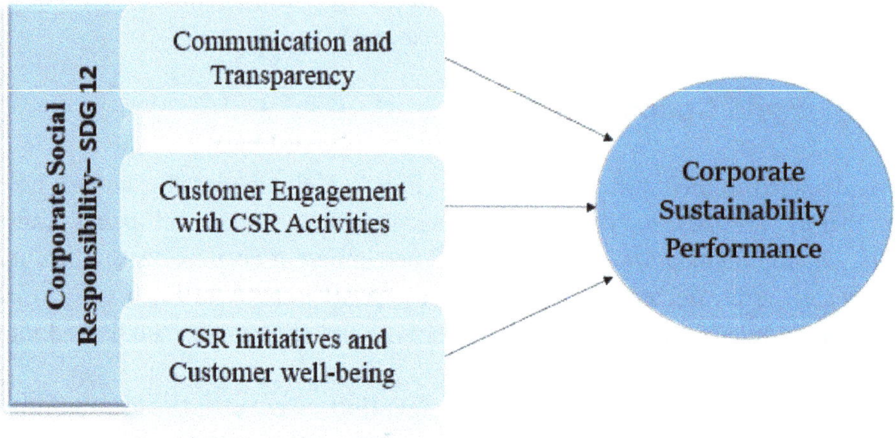

Another prominent independent variable is "**customer engagement with CSR activities**." It is a variable measuring the customers' involvement level in the different activities or initiatives undertaken by a company in relation to sustainability. The literature has indicated that consumers are more willing to engage with businesses whose CSR programs echo their own beliefs and preferences, creating links between them on an ethical and emotional plane (Fatma & Khan, 2023; Raza et al., 2023). Such engagement actions may include participating in sustainability-related activities, offering suggestions, or putting into practice recommendations like reducing the environmental impact (Dhingra, 2023). Truly engaged customers are those that support and patronize products and services linked to ethical business practices and stand willing to pay more, as well (Gong et al., 2023).

The last independent variable checked in this approach is "**perceived effects of CSR activities on customer well-being**." This variable deals with customers' thoughts on how CSR activities make life better for them and for society in general. The more social justice, ethical sourcing, and environmental sustainability initiatives are promoted, the more valuable they are for the customers, simply because they feel more fulfilled and satisfied (Pegan et al., 2022; Hobeika et al., 2022). For example, the knowledge that nutritional and health-related lifestyles are supported, together with fair labor practices, contributes to an increase in trust and feelings of well-being in customers (Gonzaga, 2022). In line with these beginning observations, CSR programs that respond to social demands contribute to the improvement of an organization's reputation, thereby creating more long-term effects on customer satisfaction and client loyalty.

All these factors fit well into one coherent frame for the analysis of how CSR initiatives and various customer outcomes interact. The study, hence, further develops the understanding of the means through which CSR activities in conjunction with SDG 12 may foster sustainable development and stakeholder trust by studying the interrelations among communication transparency, consumer engagement, perceived well-being, and corporate sustainability performance. The conceptual model (Figure 1), which is the starting point for the evaluation of how companies might effectively operationalize CSR into their plans toward the achievement of sustainability, as well as consumer satisfaction, indicates the existence of these interrelated concepts.

LITERATURE REVIEW

Communication and Transparency of CSR Initiatives and Customer Perception of Corporate Sustainability Performance

Customers' views regarding sustainability performance of a company are being influenced more and more by open and honest communication concerning the CSR activities of the company. Transparent CSR communication, most likely through social media, has the power to affect consumer behavior and perception in some ways, according to recent studies. It has been observed that consumers tend to believe more in the legitimacy of CSR activities of a company if said activities are openly communicated by the company through social media platforms (Lee & Chung, 2023). This perception of legitimacy then improves the perception of the company in the eyes of the consumer, thereby raising their willingness to engage with CSR communications and intention to purchase from the company. Moreover, the effectiveness of CSR communication norms can be further enhanced by making consideration for the types of CSR strategies that companies engage in.

Research shows that the type of CSR approach employed- proactive or reactive- account largely for brand recognition and client trust. The amount of transparency in CSR communication can also influence customers' attitudes for joining a particular brand in carrying out environmental responsibility activities, whether to a high or low extent (Dhingra, 2023). This merely highlights the essence behind fully disclosing any CSR activity, yet keeping communication somewhat aligned with some key aspect of CSR strategy of the organization. How companies report on their sustainable activities plays an even bigger role in forming the views of customers in relation to these companies. According to researchers conducted from 2022, focusing on the impacts of sustainable performance, as opposed to merely displaying sustainable outputs or outcomes, would increase customer satisfaction, customer trust, and, from a general perspective, the reputation of the company (Yu et al., 2022).

This accentuates the need for reporting on activity alone, rather than providing insightful and informative information about the observable results and societal benefits of CSR programs (Winit et al., 2023). Basically, whichever way a company affects consumer opinions and evaluations of its reputation is largely dependent on how well said company can communicate CSR before their audience. It emphasizes how important it is for businesses to implement open communication strategies that complement their larger CSR strategy and serve as a showcase for their CSR initiatives. Businesses can increase their credibility, forge closer bonds with clients, and eventually promote long-term viability and success by doing this.

Customer Engagement with CSR Activities and Customer Perception of Corporate Sustainability Performance

RST: Perceived CSR initiatives, consumer perceptions of CSR, and customer citizenship behavior (CCB) are domains of research attempting to unravel the intricate phenomena surrounding customer participation with CSR activities (Raza et al., 2023). Customers actually contribute to CSR-related ventures in return for their care for social and environmental issues that companies enacted CSR for. There is evidence that CSR activities, especially when coupled with sustainable marketing strategies, can attract more customer participation and foster a higher degree of intention toward sustained purchases (Fatma & Khan, 2023). By aligning CSR initiatives with what the customer values and cares for, companies can attract and engage more of their target market. This imbues both parties with a sense of co-ownership in the welfare of society and the environment.

Moreover, CSR initiatives affect the relationship between consumer engagement and further interaction behavior, and the decision to buy and consume. The research showed that consumers were more willing to pay a premium for goods associated with social problems when they perceived CSR activities favorably from a retail chain (Gong et al., 2023). This proves that CSR has no meaning when it comes to affecting consumer attitudes and preferences and creating the market for goods with fair and environmentally safe sourcing. From the standpoint of the consumers, the relationship between CSR initiatives and their involvement presents not only a transactional dimension but also an emotional and ethical dimension. Positive emotions and altruistic values have a mediating effect in this scenario: The relevance of emotional ties and ethical considerations in fostering green customer behavior is restored by this mediation, particularly in areas such as hospitality (Dhingra, 2023).

By evoking positive emotions and appealing to the consumers' altruistic feelings, companies are likely to build a closer affinity with their audience and foster their advocacy as well as their long-term loyalty. These findings emphasize the strategic imperative for companies to consider CSR within their key operations and communication strategies so that clients can be effectively engaged in their sustainability journey, for the CSR exercise has been considered influential upon customer engagement and perception of corporate sustainability performance.

CSR Initiatives on Customers' Perception and Their Well-Being on Corporate Sustainability Performance

Customer perception is tied to the CSR programs and sets the stage for business sustainability performance (Pegan et al., 2022; Hobeika et al., 2022; Stanco & Lerro, 2020). Customers are major stakeholders, and their opinion regarding CSR initiatives of a company directly affects the success of CSR sustainability initiatives. Frontline personnel are critical because they represent the company in the public's eyes and need to raise the standards of customer relationships throughout the CSR implementation (Pegan et al., 2022). Research has revealed that customers rate highly CSR initiatives related to sustainable agriculture, food safety, and health, especially in sectors such as restaurants and wine (Hobeika et al., 2022).

This highlights the importance of CSR programs being aligned with cultural norms and customer preferences to favour sustainability projects. Furthermore, much of a company's logo and trust is very much dependent on how closely its sustainable intentions and actions harmonize. Customers' faith in a business is bolstered when they see a sincere commitment to sustainability supported by observable actions and results, which has an advantageous effect on corporate sustainability performance (Stanco & Lerro, 2020). On the contrary, any semblance of discrepancy or disjointedness in between stated sustainable objectives and the real-world procedure could jeopardize consumer confidence, thus impeding the sustainability initiatives (Gonzaga, 2022).

Hence, for the sake of garnering consumer trust and confidence, businesses must ensure that the CSR programs remain coherent and transparent. The intersection between CSR initiatives and sustainable consumption behavior is almost a prerequisite in meeting consumer demand, creating sustainable industrial value, and securing the long-term well-being of society and businesses (Liang et al., 2020). Businesses, with CSR initiatives interlinked with sustainable consumption practices, stand to enrich customer loyalty and brand equity while positively contributing to social and environmental welfare. Apart from nurturing the performance of sustainable enterprises, this integrated approach eases the actualization of a more general environmental and societal objectives, guaranteeing a more sustainable future for all parties involved.

Research Gap

This research fills in the gaps in the present knowledge concerning how CSR efforts toward SDG 12 influence consumers' perception of the company's sustainability performance and well-being. Previous literatures that emphasize the value of CSR mainly look at the issue through the organizational lens and neglect customer-centric aspects; the consideration of engagement puts the onus on open communication and takes into account demographic variations. Furthermore, there have been no studies to date on how gender and generation influence people's perception of CSR initiatives. Thus, this study fills a major void in the literature by examining these variables and provides directions toward the successful adaption of CSR initiatives in accordance with SDG 12 goals and customer expectations.

RESEARCH METHODOLOGY

In this study, it has been tested quantitatively whether CSR programs affect consumer impressions of corporate sustainability performance, engagement, and well-being. The study also assesses whether impressions of different demographic variables such as gender and generational differences are shaped accordingly. Purposive sampling is undertaken in the study for ensuring a representative and diverse sample drawn from different sectors of demographics and geographical locations. A total of 282 consumers gave information on their involvement in CSR activities, opinions of CSR business sustainability performance, and the effects of CSR programs on consumer well-being.

Data collection contained a structured questionnaire designed to assess the following key issues: corporate sustainability performance perceptions, consumer participation with CSR, perceived positive or negative impacts on customer well-being, and degree of communication transparency. To ensure face and content validity, the questionnaire items were adapted from validated scales used in previous studies and scrutinized by the experts in the field. For all constructs, the cronbach alpha value was higher than 0.7, which means internal consistency is acceptable. To maximize participation, the questionnaire was sent out in two ways. First, online surveys were disseminated via e-mail lists, company websites, and social media. Second, self-administered questionnaires were sent to customers by mail or physically handed over to them. Data collection lasted for three months, from October to December 2024.

The data was presented for analysis in the form of descriptive statistics such as Mean and Standard Deviation. To find associations among variables and test the hypotheses of the study, inferential statistical techniques were performed. These included regression analysis, one-way ANOVA, correlation analysis, and independent sample t-test.

The regression analysis model is expressed as:

$$Y = \alpha + \beta 1x1 + \beta 2x2 + \beta 3x3 + \varepsilon$$

Where:

- Y represents the dependent variable (Corporate Sustainability Performance).
- α is the intercept term.
- X1, X2, and X3 are the independent variables (Communication Transparency, Customer Engagement with CSR Activities, and Perceived Impacts on Customer Well-being, respectively).
- β1, β2, and β3 are the coefficients representing the magnitude and direction of the relationship between each independent variable and the dependent variable.
- ϵ is the error term, accounting for unobserved factors influencing corporate sustainability performance.

The study remained true to ethical issues. It was voluntary, and participants were assured of their anonymity and confidentiality. Each participant gave informed consent and could withdraw from the study at any moment. Thereafter, the dataset was examined for normality so parametric tests would be found appropriate. Considering such stringent measures and upholding ethical principles, the study makes a worthy contribution to the discourse on business sustainability by shedding light on key contextual aspects of CSR programs and how they affect consumer behavior.

RESULTS AND DISCUSSIONS

Empirical Results

Sample Profile of Customers

A well-balanced sample profile is depicted in Table 1. Half of the participants were female respondents (50.4%), and the other half were male (49.6%-thus almost equally distributed). The generation that has registered the greatest number of respondents is that of millennials (38.3%), followed by Gen X (33.3%) and finally Gen Z (28.4%). The highest single percentage of respondents earns between 150,000 and 300,000 (27.3%), with the remaining grouped fairly evenly between higher and lower income classes. This diversity ensures that stakeholders from various age groups, genders, and income levels are taken into account in this study so as to broaden the examination of how consumers view CSR activities supporting SDG 12.

Table 1. Sample profile of customers

Variables	Attributes	Frequency	Percentage
Gender	Male	140	49.6
	Female	142	50.4
	Total	282	100.0
Generations	Generation Z	80	28.4
	Millennials	108	38.3
	Generation X	94	33.3
	Total	282	100.0
Annual Income	Above 5 lakhs	69	24.5
	300001 -500000	75	26.6
	150000 -300000	77	27.3
	Below 150000	61	21.6
	Total	282	100.0

Source: Field data, 2024

Examination of Key Aspects of Communication, Engagement, Well-being, and Customer Perception of Corporate Sustainability Performance

Descriptive statistics suggest that customers possess a fairly positive perception of all dimensions analyzed, given the highest overall means for CSR Initiatives' Impact on Customer Well-Being (Mean = 3.8703, SD = 0.42964) and Customer Engagement with CSR Activities (Mean = 3.8608, SD = 0.41534).

Table 2. Descriptive statistics of key aspects: communication and transparency, customer engagement, CSR initiatives' impact on well-being, and corporate sustainability performance

		Mean	Std. Deviation
CT1	The company effectively communicates its CSR initiatives related to sustainable development goal (SDG) 12 to its customers.	4.07	.598
CT2	I find the information provided by the company regarding its sustainability efforts clear and understandable.	3.16	1.020
CT3	The company regularly updates its customers on the progress and outcomes of its CSR initiatives aligned with SDG 12.	3.75	.930
CT4	I believe the company is transparent about its sustainability goals, targets, and performance.	3.19	1.036
CT5	The company actively seeks feedback from customers regarding its CSR initiatives and uses it to improve its practices.	3.59	.726
CT6	I feel confident that the company's CSR reporting accurately reflects its sustainability efforts and impacts.	3.85	.845
CT7	I perceive the company as transparent and trustworthy in its communication of CSR initiatives aligned with SDG 12.	3.84	.857
Communication and Transparency		3.6358	.48627
CE1	I actively participate in the company's events or programs related to sustainability and corporate social responsibility (CSR).	3.98	.677
CE2	I make purchasing decisions based on the company's CSR initiatives and commitment to sustainable practices.	3.83	.973
CE3	I feel motivated to support the company's CSR initiatives by spreading awareness among my peers and community.	3.39	.985
CE4	I regularly provide feedback to the company regarding its CSR activities and suggest ideas for improvement.	3.88	.918
CE5	I have signed up for newsletters or updates from the company to stay informed about its CSR initiatives and activities.	3.67	1.012
CE6	I have participated in volunteer activities organized by the company to support environmental or social causes.	3.80	.872
CE7	I actively engage with the company's CSR campaigns on social media platforms.	4.16	.580
CE8	I have taken actions recommended by the company to reduce my environmental impact or support sustainable practices.	4.18	.600
Customer Engagement with CSR activities		3.8608	.41534
IC1	The company's CSR initiatives make me feel more connected to its values and mission, enhancing my overall well-being.	3.70	1.036
IC2	I believe that the company's CSR efforts contribute positively to environmental sustainability, which benefits my well-being and that of future generations.	3.83	.859
IC3	The company's commitment to ethical sourcing and fair labor practices reassures me about the well-being of workers in its supply chain.	4.07	.812
IC4	Knowing that the company supports local communities through its CSR initiatives enhances my sense of well-being and community spirit.	3.98	1.143

continued on following page

Table 2. Continued

		Mean	Std. Deviation
IC5	The company's CSR initiatives, such as promoting healthier lifestyles or supporting social causes, have a positive impact on my personal well-being.	3.78	.873
IC6	I feel more satisfied as a customer knowing that the company prioritizes CSR initiatives aligned with Sustainable Development Goal (SDG) 12.	3.88	.860
IC7	The company's CSR initiatives contribute to my sense of fulfillment and well-being as a conscious consumer.	3.84	.899
CSR initiatives and Customer well-being		3.8703	.42964
CSP1	The company demonstrates a strong commitment to reducing waste and promoting recycling in its operations.	3.61	1.115
CSP2	I believe the company actively promotes sustainable consumption practices, such as reducing energy and water usage.	3.60	.958
CSP3	The company's efforts to ensure responsible sourcing and ethical production practices align with my values.	3.82	.898
CSP4	I perceive the company as transparent in communicating its sustainability goals and progress.	3.13	1.062
CSP5	The company's initiatives to minimize its environmental footprint, such as reducing carbon emissions, are commendable.	3.08	.970
CSP6	I trust the company's commitment to promoting fair labor practices and ensuring a safe working environment for employees and suppliers.	4.07	.545
CSP7	The company's engagement with local communities and support for social causes positively influence my perception of its sustainability performance.	4.42	.784
CSP8	I believe the company effectively communicates the impact of its sustainability initiatives on addressing social and environmental challenges.	3.56	.739
CSP9	I perceive the company as a responsible corporate citizen, actively contributing to sustainable development and corporate sustainability.	3.74	1.060
Corporate Sustainability Performance		3.6706	.50015

Source: Field data, 2024

The communication and transparency-wide means, however, appear to be on the lower end than all others (Mean = 3.6358, SD = 0.48627), which puts the onus on businesses to better communicate their CSR actions. Greatest community involvement and ethical labor practices (CSP7 and CSP6) serve as the chief factors sustaining the performance of business evaluation, which is another dimension perceived moderately high (Mean = 3.6706, SD = 0.50015). These findings explain the interdependence among the communication, engagement, well-being, and sustainability outcomes as they directly influence customer perception of CSR.

Gender and Corporate Sustainability Performance

Table 3 presented gender views on corporate goals and sustainability with significant variation. The male respondents had a higher mean score of 3.9071 as compared to 3.4374 for females. Such an indicator clearly suggests that males are more positive about the sustainability initiatives; hence, the difference must be taken into consideration. The t-test verified that this difference was statistically significant, seconded by Levene's test for equality of variances (F = 0.053, p = 0.818) (t = 8.920, p < 0.001). Thus, it points to the gender-based corporate sustainability perceptions, which can be instrumental in developing gender-based involvement and communication strategies.

Table 3. Descriptive statistics and t test

	Gender	N	Mean	Std. Deviation	Levene's Test for Equality of Variances		t-test for Equality of Means			Remarks
					F	Sig.	t	df	Sig. (2-tailed)	
Corporate Sustainability Performance	Male	140	3.9071	.43792	.053	.818	8.920	280	.000	Equal variance assumed
	Female	142	3.4374	.44626						

Source: Field data, 2024

Generations and Corporate Sustainability Performance

Table 4. Descriptive statistics and one way ANOVA

	N	Mean	Std. Deviation	Test of Homogeneity of Variances		ANOVA		Remarks
				Levene Statistic	Sig.	F	Sig.	
Generation Z	80	4.0236	.38110	1.567	.210	72.534	.000	One way ANOVA
Millennials	108	3.7397	.43557					
Generation X	94	3.2908	.39447					
Total	282							

Source: Field data, 2024

Considerable diversity among the age groups is revealed when the generational differences in opinions on the company sustainability performance are analyzed, as displayed in Table 4. Generation Z recorded the most positive opinion toward business sustainability, with the highest mean score of 4.0236, followed by the Millennials with 3.7397 and then Generation X, with a mean score of 3.2908. With

Levene's test showing homogeneity of variances ($F = 1.567, p = 0.210$), the results of the ANOVA test confirm that the differences are indeed statistically significant ($F = 72.534, p < 0.001$).

Table 5. Multiple comparisons: Dependent Variable: Corporate Sustainability Performance Tukey HSD

(I) Generations	(J) Generations	Mean Difference (I-J)	Std. Error	Sig.
Generation Z	Millennials	.28390*	.06006	.000
	Generation X	.73283*	.06193	.000
Millennials	Generation Z	-.28390*	.06006	.000
	Generation X	.44893*	.05743	.000
Generation X	Generation Z	-.73283*	.06193	.000
	Millennials	-.44893*	.05743	.000

Note: *The mean difference is significant at the 0.05 level.
Source: Field data, 2024

Table 5 uses Tukey HSD comparisons to further explain the disparities. Millennials (mean difference = 0.28390, $p < 0.001$) and Generation X (mean difference = 0.73283, $p < 0.001$) had considerably lower perceptions than Generation Z. In the same way, Millennials have a substantially higher perception than Generation X (mean difference = 0.44893, $p < 0.001$). These results highlight the necessity for customized engagement techniques to accommodate generational preferences and imply that younger generations, especially Generation Z, have more positive opinions of corporate sustainability initiatives.

Evaluating the Influence of Communication, Engagement, and Well-being on Corporate Sustainability Performance

The research investigates the effect of CSR initiatives on customer well-being, customer engagement with CSR activities, and communication and transparency on corporate sustainability performance. The multiple correlation analysis presented in Table 6 indicates that Corporate Sustainability Performance is highly positively correlated with Customer Engagement with CSR Activities ($r = 0.775, p < 0.001$) and Communication and Transparency ($r = 0.794, p < 0.001$). Less so, but still strongly correlated with, are CSR initiatives and customer well-being ($r = 0.478, p < 0.001$). This shows that the most significant elements influencing the corporate sustainability performance are communication, transparency, and customer engagement.

Table 6. Multiple correlation

		Communication and Transparency	**Customer Engagement with CSR activities**	**CSR initiatives and Customer well-being**
Corporate Sustainability Performance	Pearson correlation	.794	.775	.478
	Sig. value	.000	.000	.000
	N	282	282	282

Source: Field data, 2024

Multiple Regression. Table 7 presents the summary of the multiple regression analysis model. The model has an R of 0.860 and R2 of 0.739, demonstrating the ability of the model to significantly predict the performance. Three predictors explain 73.9% of the variability of Corporate Sustainability Performance.

Table 7. Model summary[b]

Model	R	R Square	Adjusted R Square	Std. Error of the Estimate
1	.860[a]	.739	.736	.25691

a. Predictors: (Constant), CSR initiatives and Customer well-being, Customer Engagement with CSR activities, Communication and Transparency

b. Dependent Variable: Corporate Sustainability Performance

Source: Field data, 2024

Considering the number of predictors, the adjusted R2 of 0.736 gives it more credibility. The low standard error of 0.25691 suggests that the predictions were accurate.

Table 8. ANOVA[a]

Model		Sum of Squares	df	Mean Square	F	Sig.
1	Regression	51.943	3	17.314	262.318	.000[b]
	Residual	18.349	278	.066		
	Total	70.292	281			

a. Dependent Variable: Corporate Sustainability Performance

b. Predictors: (Constant), CSR initiatives and Customer well-being, Customer Engagement with CSR activities, Communication and Transparency

Source: Field data, 2024

Table 8 shows ANOVA results, the regression model being statistically significant as a whole ($F = 262.318$, $p < 0.001$). This implies that, taken together, the predictors influence Corporate Sustainability Performance.

Table 9. Coefficients[a]

Model		Unstandardized Coefficients		Standardized Coefficients	t	Sig.
		B	Std. Error	Beta		
1	(Constant)	.238	.167		-1.428	.154
	Communication and Transparency	.516	.047	.502	10.952	.000
	Customer Engagement with CSR activities	.534	.050	.443	10.754	.000
	CSR initiatives and Customer well-being	.007	.044	.006	.167	.867

a. Dependent Variable: Corporate Sustainability Performance
Source: Field data, 2024

Table 9 shows the regression coefficients in full detail. Customer engagement with CSR work ($B = 0.534, p < 0.001$) and communication and transparency ($B = 0.516, p < 0.001$) have the greatest positive influence on corporate sustainability performance, thus fostering good sustainability results. Also, CSR activities may have a direct influence on sustainability performance, for the effect of these CSR activities on customer well-being ($B= 0.007, p= 0.867$) is statistically significant.

The regression equation is

Corporate Sustainability Performance = (0.238) + (0.516 * Communication and Transparency) + (0.534 * Customer Engagement with CSR activities) + (0.007 * CSR initiatives and Customer well-being)

A regression equation reveals a considerable positive effect, whereby one unit increase in Communication and Transparency results in a 0.516 increase in Corporate Sustainability Performance and a slightly higher increase of 0.534 for Customer Engagement with CSR Activities. CSR activities have positive effect of 0.007 units for every unit of rise in the perceived impact of CSR activities on customer well-being.

While the effects of CSR initiatives on well-being might work through indirect mechanisms or mediators, taken together, the evidence in Tables 6, 7, 8, and 9 shows the critical relevance of communication and customer engagement to boost Corporate Sustainability Performance. To optimize sustainability outcomes, companies need to prioritize open communication and stimulate consumer participation with CSR programs.

Discussion

The study's conclusions accentuate the essentiality of open communication pathways in affecting consumer precognition of a company's sustainability performance. Corroborating past studies that put forth transparent CSR communication as a tool for generating credibility and trust, it was found to impart a significant positive bearing (Lee & Chung, 2023; Yu et al., 2022). When firms communicate their sustainability activities clearly, CSR efforts are likely to be looked upon as credible by customers when communications emphasize visible consequences rather than just outputs (Winit et al., 2023). However, since the overall mean score on communication transparency was fairly low (M = 3.63), the descriptive analysis shows room for improvement. Mechanisms such as soliciting feedback (M = 3.59) appeared to be less effective despite customers indicating their need for CSR actions to be updated on a regular basis (M = 3.75). This discrepancy could be a matter of authenticity perception and could support Dhingra's (2023) argument on the necessity for strategic and proactive communication for capturing consumers' meaningful interest.

Consistent with the findings of Gong et al. (2023) emphasizing the role of involvement in video loyalty and sustainable consumer behaviors, engagement with CSR by customers became the most potent predictor of business sustainability success. Customers will almost certainly participate in CSR activities when these matches their individual beliefs (with an average engagement score reported to be 3.86) (Fatma & Khan, 2023). They have even been observed to implement measures recommended by the company to minimize environmental impact (M = 4.18), implying that customers are willing to engage in meaningful action when the business allows for their participation (Raza et al., 2023).

The results also indicated generational disparities in engagement, with Gen Z participants who provide the best opinions on business sustainability performance (M = 4.02), Millennials exhibiting the second-best opinions (M = 3.74), and Gen X giving the lowest scores (M = 3.29). The opinions parallel the alleged record of younger generations as being more receptive to sustainability and environmentally conscious endeavors (Hobeika et al., 2022). With the massive generational gap, it could be said that companies must alter the way they interact with younger consumers, possibly by involving them in innovative and entertaining ways through gamification in advertising, for example. The research also looked into the effects of gender differences on perceived levels of sustainability performance by the company, establishing statistically significant differences. This implies gendered attitudes toward corporate sustainability, with male respondents giving higher mean scores (M 3.91) in comparison to females (M 3.44). Such divergences may either be because men and women give different priorities to or understand CSR differently, thus calling for gender-sensitive CSR engagement and communication strategies. This aligns with Gonzaga's (2022) study, which shows that demographic differences in the perception of CSR programs might affect customer responses.

Interestingly, previous studies citing that the relevance of CSR programs was statistically negligible in terms of direct impact on customer well-being (Pegan et al., 2022). Efforts to promote ethical labor practices and local communities were certainly viewed favorably by consumers (M = 3.98 and 4.07, respectively), and direct measurable influence on well-being ensued. This indicates that factors such as trust, emotional bonds, or altruistic values may serve as mediators in the relation between CSR programs and consumer well-being. Those findings unequivocally indicate that transparent communications, proactive involvement of clients, and demographic customization are valuable components for raising opinions about business sustainability performance. Transparency must become a major concern of sustainability management, while a company has to align its CSR policies with customer values while also considering gender and age-related differences. Converting these into tangible results for sustainability will strengthen included relationships between customers and sustain SDG 12 in a more relevant form.

THEORETICAL AND PRACTICAL IMPLICATIONS

Theoretically, the research results back up the implication that open communication and active participation are used to build attractive opinions of consumers concerning a company's actual sustainability performance. It goes supporting simplistic theories about the direct relationship between CSR activities and well-being. Generational divides are highlighted as a very important factor in customer engagement, thus offering insights into demographic variances in CSR attitudes.

From a managerial viewpoint, these findings underscore the paramount importance of aligning client values with CSR activities and maintaining an open communication avenue. Businesses should underline transparent, authentic CSR communication while exploiting social media for building trust and interaction (Winit et al., 2023).

CONCLUSION

This study attempts to provide an exhaustive account of the relationships among CSR programs, customer involvement, open communication, and their mediating effects with sustainability performance of businesses. The results underline the importance of clear and efficient communication channels so that CSR initiatives are presented favorably in the minds of customers. An effective communication system by which the organization offers promising sustainability programs convinces the customer that these are legal and ethical to undertake, thus generating customer loyalty and confidence. Customer participation in CSR projects has also been found to have a strong bearing on sustainable performance. Such participatory processes encourage customers to embrace sustainable practices, strengthening the relationship between customers and corporate responsibility while also building a positive general impression regarding business responsibility in the customer community.

Findings say that due to gender and generation-type differences, consumer perceptions of CSR activities are divergently viewed, hence emphasizing the need for customized approaches to reach various demographic groups. With little direct impact of CSR activities on consumer well-being, indirect benefits, such as increased satisfaction and loyalty, come when CSR matches customer values and goals. These findings emphasize the importance of CSR activities that companies develop for consumers according to their preferences, transparency, and engagement.

The report contributes to the larger discussion concerning corporate sustainability by offering a pathway for corporations wishing to align their CSR activities with SDG 12 goals. Companies can, therefore, update their sustainability agendas, solidify relations with their stakeholders, and achieve sustained growth by enhancing open communication, fostering meaningful customer engagement, and resolving demographic disparities. The information provided here sets the stage for businesses to align themselves with consumer demands and collectively drive major global sustainability initiatives.

REFERENCES

Dhingra, K. (2023). Corporate Social Responsibility and Sustainability of Corporate Performance. *Jindal Journal of Business Research, 12*(1), 19–29. DOI: 10.1177/22786821231161416

Fatma, M., & Khan, I. (2023). Impact of CSR on Customer Citizenship Behavior: Mediating the Role of Customer Engagement. *Sustainability (Basel), 15*(7), 5802. DOI: 10.3390/su15075802

Ferrero-Ferrero, I., & Torres, M. (2023). SDG reporting: An analysis of corporate sustainability leaders. *Marketing Intelligence & Planning, 41*(4), 457–472. DOI: 10.1108/MIP-07-2022-0332

Gong, Y., Xiao, J., Tang, X., & Li, J. (2023). How sustainable marketing influences the customer engagement and sustainable purchase intention? The moderating role of corporate social responsibility. *Frontiers in Psychology, 14*. frontiersin. DOI: 10.3389/fpsyg.2023.1128686

Gonzaga, F. P. (2022). Customer Perception of Sustainability Initiatives in the Restaurant Industry: A Discrete Choice Model Approach. *Journal of Management and Sustainability, 12*(2), 20. DOI: 10.5539/jms.v12n2p20

Hobeika, J., Khelladi, I., & Orhan, M. A. (2022). Analyzing the corporate social responsibility perception from customer relationship quality perspective. An application to the retail banking sector. *Corporate Social Responsibility and Environmental Management, 29*(6), 2053–2064. DOI: 10.1002/csr.2301

Lee, A., & Chung, T.-L. D. (2023). Transparency in corporate social responsibility communication on social media. *International Journal of Retail & Distribution Management, 51*(5), 590–610. DOI: 10.1108/IJRDM-01-2022-0038

Liang, X., Hu, X., & Meng, H. (2020). Truly Sustainability or Hypocrisy: The Effects of Corporate Sustainable Orientation on Consumers' Quality Perception and Trust Based on Evidence from China. *Sustainability (Basel), 12*(7), 2735. DOI: 10.3390/su12072735

Pegan, G., Schoier, G., & Patrizia de Luca. (2022). The Importance of Consumer Perception of Corporate Social Responsibility to Meet the Need for Sustainable Consumption. *IGI Global EBooks*, 1812–1835. DOI: 10.4018/978-1-6684-5590-6.ch089

Raza, A., Farrukh, M., Wang, G., Iqbal, M. K., & Farhan, M. (2023). Effects of hotels' corporate social responsibility (CSR) initiatives on green consumer behavior: Investigating the roles of consumer engagement, positive emotions, and altruistic values. *Journal of Hospitality Marketing & Management, 32*(7), 1–23. DOI: 10.1080/19368623.2023.2223571

Saad, S., Ahmad, J., & Krishnan, M. (2022). Towards Sustainability in Corporate Social Responsibility. *Routledge EBooks*, 163–187. DOI: 10.4324/9781003309642-12

Stanco, M., & Lerro, M. (2020). Consumers' Preferences for and Perception of CSR Initiatives in the Wine Sector. *Sustainability (Basel), 12*(13), 5230. DOI: 10.3390/su12135230

Vargas-Merino, J. A., & Rios-Lama, C. A. (2023). The Interplay of Corporate Social Responsibility (CSR) and Sustainable Development Goals (SDGs): An Overview of Relevant Literature on CSR's and SDGs. *IBIMA Business Review*, 1–12. DOI: 10.5171/2023.930662

Winit, W., Ekasingh, E., & Sampet, J. (2023). How Disclosure Types of Sustainability Performance Impact Consumers' Relationship Quality and Firm Reputation. *Sustainability (Basel), 15*(1), 803. DOI: 10.3390/su15010803

Yu, W., Zhou, J., He, M., & Si, D. (2022). Does Brand Truth-Telling Yield Customer Participation? The Interaction Effects of CSR Strategy and Transparency Signaling. *Behavioral Sciences (Basel, Switzerland), 12*(12), 514. DOI: 10.3390/bs12120514 PMID: 36546997

Chapter 11
AI-Powered Grid Analytics for Sustainable Energy Management in ESG Frameworks

Zeinab Farrokhi
https://orcid.org/0009-0002-0920-2277
University of Nevada, Las Vegas, USA

ABSTRACT

The integration of artificial intelligence with business intelligence frameworks marks a paradigm shift in measuring environmental sustainability within smart grids. Traditional ESG reporting in energy systems relies on static historical data, missing the dynamic behavior of modern grids and limiting actionable insights. This chapter proposes a novel framework that merges deep learning with real-time business intelligence to enable adaptive ESG monitoring tailored for intelligent energy networks. It tackles challenges such as real-time impact assessment, predictive analytics, data integration, and stakeholder communication. Case studies highlight improvements in renewable integration, carbon footprint reduction, and ESG reporting. The system combines CNNs for satellite imagery and RNNs for time-series data, forming a hybrid model that supports energy optimization, demand forecasting, and grid stability.

INTRODUCTION

The contemporary business landscape has witnessed an unprecedented transformation in environmental consciousness, driven by escalating climate concerns,

DOI: 10.4018/979-8-3373-5142-1.ch011

regulatory pressures, and evolving stakeholder expectations. Environmental, Social, and Governance (ESG) frameworks have emerged as critical determinants of organizational value creation, particularly within the energy sector where environmental impact extends far beyond traditional operational boundaries, (Yucel & Yucel, 2024). The convergence of artificial intelligence technologies with business intelligence systems presents unprecedented opportunities for revolutionizing sustainability performance measurement and management in smart grid environments.

Traditional approaches to ESG reporting in energy management have historically relied on static, retrospective data collection methodologies that operate on quarterly or annual reporting cycles. This temporal disconnect between actual environmental impact and performance measurement creates substantial gaps in organizational understanding of immediate sustainability consequences, (Ramanathan & Isaksson, 2023). Contemporary energy systems, characterized by increasing complexity, renewable energy integration, and distributed generation networks, demand more sophisticated analytical approaches capable of processing real-time data streams and generating actionable insights for strategic decision-making.

The integration of artificial intelligence, particularly deep learning techniques, with established business intelligence frameworks offers a transformative pathway toward addressing these fundamental challenges. AI-powered analytics systems can process vast quantities of heterogeneous data sources, including weather patterns, energy consumption forecasts, grid performance metrics, and renewable energy generation data, to create comprehensive, real-time sustainability monitoring capabilities, (Fan, Yan, & Wen, 2023). This technological convergence enables organizations to transition from reactive ESG reporting toward proactive, predictive sustainability management strategies.

Smart grid technologies have fundamentally altered the energy landscape, creating opportunities for enhanced efficiency, reliability, and environmental performance. However, the complexity inherent in these systems has simultaneously increased the challenges associated with accurate ESG performance measurement and reporting, (Jamali et al., 2025). The dynamic nature of renewable energy sources, fluctuating demand patterns, and interconnected grid dependencies require sophisticated analytical capabilities that exceed the limitations of traditional business intelligence systems.

The mission of this chapter is to demonstrate how artificial intelligence can be strategically integrated with business intelligence frameworks to revolutionize environmental sustainability performance measurement and management within smart grid systems. This research bridges the critical gap between technical AI capabilities and strategic ESG implementation, offering energy companies a comprehensive framework for leveraging advanced analytics in sustainable transformation initiatives.

FOUNDATIONS OF ESG AND BUSINESS INTELLIGENCE IN ENERGY SYSTEMS

Environmental, Social, and Governance frameworks have evolved from voluntary reporting mechanisms to mandatory regulatory requirements across multiple jurisdictions, fundamentally altering how organizations approach sustainability management, (Baesmat, Regentova, & Baghzouz, 2025). Within the energy sector, ESG considerations encompass diverse dimensions including carbon emissions reduction, renewable energy integration, grid reliability, social impact assessment, and governance transparency. The complexity of measuring and managing these multifaceted objectives requires sophisticated analytical capabilities that traditional reporting systems struggle to provide.

Business intelligence systems have traditionally served as the cornerstone of organizational data analysis and strategic decision-making processes. However, conventional BI architectures were designed primarily for structured data processing and historical trend analysis, limiting their effectiveness in dynamic, real-time environments characteristic of modern energy systems, (Farrokhi, Baesmat, & Regentova, 2024). The integration of AI technologies with existing BI infrastructure creates opportunities for enhanced analytical capabilities, predictive modeling, and automated decision-making processes.

ESG Framework Evolution in Energy Management

The evolution of ESG frameworks within energy management reflects broader societal shifts toward sustainable development and climate change mitigation. Early ESG reporting focused primarily on compliance with environmental regulations and basic sustainability metrics. Contemporary frameworks demand comprehensive performance measurement across environmental impact, social responsibility, and governance effectiveness dimensions, (Passas, 2024).

Environmental performance measurement in energy systems encompasses multiple critical areas including carbon footprint assessment, renewable energy integration rates, energy efficiency optimization, and environmental risk management. Traditional measurement approaches relied on annual or quarterly data collection processes that provided limited visibility into real-time performance fluctuations. The dynamic nature of modern energy systems, characterized by variable renewable energy sources and fluctuating demand patterns, requires continuous monitoring capabilities that exceed traditional reporting methodologies, (Jamali et al., 2023).

Social responsibility dimensions within energy ESG frameworks address community impact, stakeholder engagement, workforce diversity, and social equity considerations. Governance components focus on regulatory compliance, risk management effectiveness, strategic decision-making transparency, and stakeholder communication quality. The integration of these diverse measurement dimensions requires sophisticated data processing capabilities and analytical frameworks capable of synthesizing complex, heterogeneous information sources, (Baesmat et al., 2025). Evolution of ESG frameworks in energy management is shown in Table 1.

Table 1. Evolution of ESG frameworks in energy management

Era	Focus Areas	Measurement Approach	Reporting Frequency	Technology Integration
1990s-2000s	Basic Compliance	Manual Data Collection	Annual	Limited Database Systems
2000s-2010s	Expanded Environmental Metrics	Semi-Automated Reporting	Quarterly	Traditional BI Systems
2010s-2020s	Comprehensive ESG Integration	Advanced Analytics	Monthly	Cloud-Based Platforms
2020s-Present	Real-Time Predictive Management	AI-Powered Analytics	Continuous	Integrated AI/BI Systems

Business Intelligence Architecture for Energy Systems

Contemporary business intelligence architectures in energy systems must accommodate diverse data sources, processing requirements, and analytical objectives. Traditional BI systems focused primarily on structured data analysis and historical trend identification. Modern energy systems generate massive volumes of heterogeneous data from smart meters, weather monitoring stations, renewable energy systems, and grid performance sensors, (Jamali et al., 2025).

The integration of artificial intelligence capabilities within established BI architectures creates opportunities for enhanced analytical performance and predictive modeling capabilities. Machine learning algorithms can process unstructured data sources, identify complex patterns within large datasets, and generate predictive insights that inform strategic decision-making processes. Deep learning techniques, particularly convolutional neural networks and recurrent neural networks, demonstrate exceptional performance in processing time-series data and image recognition tasks relevant to energy system analysis, (Baesmat & Latifi, 2023).

Cloud-based BI platforms offer scalable infrastructure for processing large volumes of energy system data while providing flexible analytical capabilities. The integration of edge computing technologies enables real-time data processing at the source, reducing latency and improving system responsiveness. Hybrid cloud architectures combine the scalability of cloud computing with the responsiveness of edge processing, creating optimal environments for AI-powered energy analytics, (Jamali, Karimi, & Haghighizadeh, 2018). Figure 1 shows the integrated AI-BI architecture for smart grid ESG analytics.

Figure 1. Integrated AI-BI architecture for smart grid ESG analytics

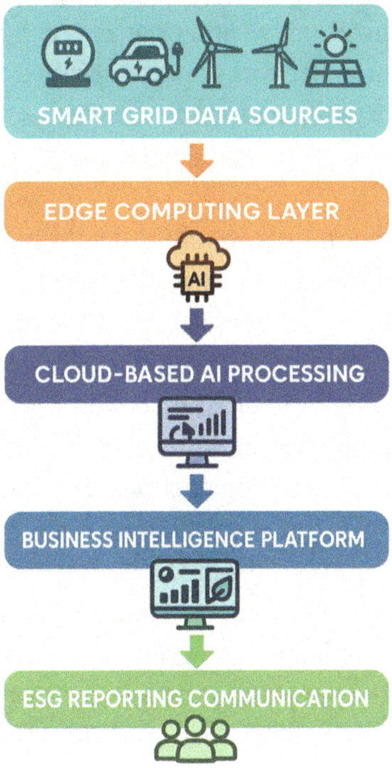

AI TECHNOLOGIES FOR SMART GRID ANALYTICS

Artificial intelligence technologies offer transformative capabilities for smart grid analytics, enabling sophisticated analysis of complex, dynamic energy systems. The application of AI in energy management encompasses diverse technical approaches including machine learning, deep learning, computer vision, and natural language processing. Each technology contributes unique capabilities for addressing specific challenges within ESG performance measurement and management, (Balamurugan et al., 2025).

Deep Learning Applications in Energy Systems

Deep learning represents the most advanced subset of artificial intelligence technologies, demonstrating exceptional performance in processing complex, high-dimensional data characteristic of modern energy systems. Convolutional neural networks excel in image recognition tasks, enabling analysis of satellite imagery for renewable energy optimization, weather pattern recognition, and infrastructure monitoring. Recurrent neural networks, particularly Long Short-Term Memory networks, demonstrate superior performance in time-series analysis applications including demand forecasting, price prediction, and system optimization, (Jamali, Dascalu, & Harris, 2024).

The integration of deep learning technologies within smart grid systems enables sophisticated analytical capabilities previously unattainable through traditional methods. Computer vision techniques can analyze satellite imagery to identify optimal locations for renewable energy installations, assess vegetation growth near transmission lines, and monitor infrastructure condition. Time-series analysis using LSTM networks provides accurate forecasting of energy demand patterns, renewable energy generation, and system performance metrics, (Padmanaban et al., 2023).

Generative Adversarial Networks present emerging opportunities for synthetic data generation, enabling training of machine learning models with limited historical data. This capability proves particularly valuable for modeling rare events, extreme weather conditions, and system failure scenarios that occur infrequently in real-world operations. The synthetic data generation capability enhances model robustness and improves predictive accuracy across diverse operational conditions, (Samavat et al., 2025. Deep learning technologies in smart grid applications can be seen in Table 2.

Table 2. Deep learning technologies in smart grid applications

Technology	Primary Application	Key Benefits	Implementation Complexity
Convolutional Neural Networks	Image Analysis, Weather Pattern Recognition	High Accuracy, Automated Feature Extraction	Medium
Recurrent Neural Networks	Time-Series Forecasting, Demand Prediction	Sequential Data Processing, Memory Retention	Medium-High
Long Short-Term Memory	Long-Term Pattern Recognition	Extended Memory, Gradient Stability	High
Generative Adversarial Networks	Synthetic Data Generation	Data Augmentation, Rare Event Modeling	Very High
Transformer Networks	Multi-Modal Data Integration	Attention Mechanisms, Scalability	Very High

Machine Learning for Predictive Analytics

Machine learning technologies provide essential capabilities for predictive analytics within smart grid systems, enabling accurate forecasting of energy demand, renewable energy generation, and system performance metrics. Supervised learning algorithms, including regression analysis, decision trees, and ensemble methods, excel in predicting numerical values based on historical patterns and environmental variables. Unsupervised learning techniques, such as clustering and dimensionality reduction, identify hidden patterns within complex datasets and enable system optimization, (Baesmat, 2024).

Reinforcement learning presents particularly promising applications for dynamic system optimization, enabling autonomous decision-making in complex, changing environments. Grid operators can utilize reinforcement learning algorithms to optimize energy distribution, manage renewable energy integration, and maintain system stability under varying conditions. The adaptive nature of reinforcement learning enables continuous improvement in system performance as operational experience accumulates, (Xu et al., 2025)

Ensemble methods, including random forests and gradient boosting, combine multiple machine learning models to improve prediction accuracy and reduce overfitting risks. These approaches prove particularly valuable for complex energy system applications where individual models may struggle with the full complexity of system interactions. The combination of diverse modeling approaches enhances robustness and improves performance across varying operational conditions, (Farrokhi, Kalhor, & Masouleh, 2018).

Time-series forecasting represents a critical application area for machine learning in energy systems. Accurate demand forecasting enables optimal resource allocation, reduces operational costs, and improves system reliability. Advanced forecasting models incorporate weather data, seasonal patterns, economic indicators, and social factors to generate comprehensive demand predictions. The integration of multiple data sources enhances forecasting accuracy and enables more effective system planning, (Mahdavi et al., 2024).

REAL-TIME ESG MONITORING FRAMEWORK

The development of real-time ESG monitoring capabilities represents a fundamental advancement in sustainability performance management for energy systems. Traditional reporting approaches, characterized by static data collection and periodic analysis, fail to capture the dynamic nature of modern energy systems and limit organizational responsiveness to emerging sustainability challenges. Real-time monitoring frameworks enable continuous assessment of environmental impact, social responsibility, and governance effectiveness, creating opportunities for proactive management and rapid response to performance deviations, (Padmanaban et al., 2023).

Data Integration and Processing Architecture

Real-time ESG monitoring requires sophisticated data integration capabilities to process diverse information sources including smart meter readings, weather data, renewable energy generation metrics, grid performance indicators, and external environmental factors. The heterogeneous nature of these data sources presents significant technical challenges related to data format standardization, temporal synchronization, and quality assurance, (Zhang, Huang, & Bompard, 2018).

Stream processing technologies enable real-time analysis of continuous data flows from distributed energy system components. Apache Kafka and similar platforms provide scalable message queuing capabilities for handling high-volume data streams, while Apache Storm and Apache Flink offer distributed processing capabilities for real-time analytics. The integration of these technologies creates robust infrastructure for continuous data processing and analysis, (Jamali et al., 2025).

Data quality management represents a critical component of real-time monitoring systems, as poor data quality can significantly impact analytical accuracy and decision-making effectiveness. Automated data validation processes identify anomalies, missing values, and inconsistencies within incoming data streams. Machine learning algorithms can detect data quality issues and implement corrective measures, including interpolation, outlier removal, and sensor recalibration recommendations, (Sanjeevikumar et al., 2023). Real-time data integration architecture is shown in Table 2.

Figure 2. Real-time data integration architecture

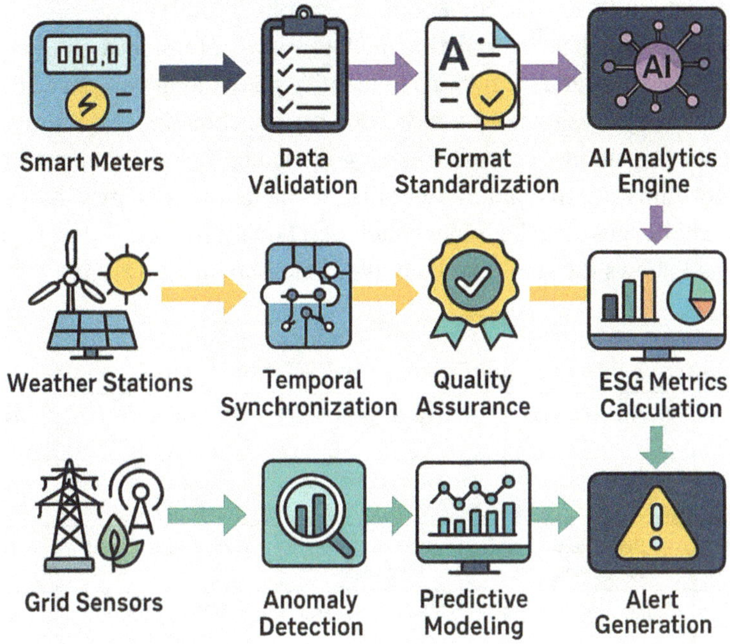

Predictive Analytics Implementation

Predictive analytics capabilities enable organizations to anticipate future ESG performance trends and identify potential issues before they impact operational performance or stakeholder perceptions. The implementation of predictive models requires careful consideration of data requirements, model selection, validation methodologies, and deployment strategies, (Baesmat, Masoudipour, & Samet, 2021).

Environmental impact prediction models analyze historical patterns, weather forecasts, and operational plans to generate accurate forecasts of carbon emissions, energy consumption, and renewable energy generation. These models incorporate multiple variables including seasonal patterns, economic indicators, weather conditions, and planned maintenance activities. Advanced ensemble methods combine multiple forecasting approaches to improve accuracy and reduce prediction uncertainty, (Khan et al., 2021).

Social impact prediction focuses on community effects, stakeholder satisfaction, and workforce dynamics. Natural language processing techniques analyze social media sentiment, news coverage, and stakeholder feedback to assess public perception and identify emerging social issues. Predictive models can forecast potential social impacts of planned operational changes, enabling proactive stakeholder engagement and risk mitigation, (Baesmat, Shokoohi, & Farrokhi, 2025)

Governance performance prediction models assess compliance risks, regulatory changes, and stakeholder expectations to identify potential governance challenges. These models analyze regulatory trends, industry benchmarks, and internal performance metrics to generate comprehensive governance risk assessments. Machine learning algorithms identify patterns within governance data that may indicate future compliance challenges or stakeholder concerns, (Jamali, Karimi, & Haghighizadeh, 2018). Table 3 shows the real-time data integration architecture.

Table 3. Predictive analytics applications in ESG monitoring

ESG Dimension	Prediction Target	Data Sources	Model Type	Accuracy Range
Environmental	Carbon Emissions	Energy Data, Weather	Regression, Neural Networks	85-95%
Environmental	Renewable Integration	Generation Data, Forecasts	Time-Series, LSTM	80-90%
Social	Community Impact	Social Media, Surveys	NLP, Sentiment Analysis	75-85%
Social	Stakeholder Satisfaction	Feedback, Engagement Data	Classification, Clustering	70-80%
Governance	Compliance Risk	Regulatory Data, Performance	Risk Models, Decision Trees	80-90%
Governance	Reporting Quality	Historical Reports, Metrics	Quality Assessment Models	85-95%

DEEP LEARNING ARCHITECTURE FOR GRID ANALYTICS

The development of sophisticated deep learning architectures specifically designed for smart grid analytics represents a critical advancement in energy system management capabilities. Traditional analytical approaches struggle with the complexity, volume, and velocity of data generated by modern energy systems. Deep learning architectures offer superior performance in processing high-dimensional, temporal data characteristic of smart grid operations, (Jamali, Karimi, & Haghighizadeh, 2018).

Hybrid Neural Network Design

The proposed hybrid neural network architecture combines convolutional neural networks for spatial data analysis with recurrent neural networks for temporal pattern recognition. This integrated approach enables comprehensive analysis of both geographical and temporal dimensions inherent in energy system data. Convolutional layers process satellite imagery, weather maps, and infrastructure layouts, while recurrent layers analyze time-series data from smart meters, sensors, and renewable energy systems, (Kazmi et al., 2023).

The CNN component utilizes multiple convolutional layers with varying filter sizes to capture features at different spatial scales. Early layers detect basic patterns such as edges and textures, while deeper layers identify complex features relevant to energy system analysis. The integration of attention mechanisms enables the network to focus on the most relevant spatial regions for specific analytical tasks, improving accuracy and computational efficiency, (Kermani et al., 2023).

Figure 3. Hybrid CNN-RNN architecture for smart grid analytics

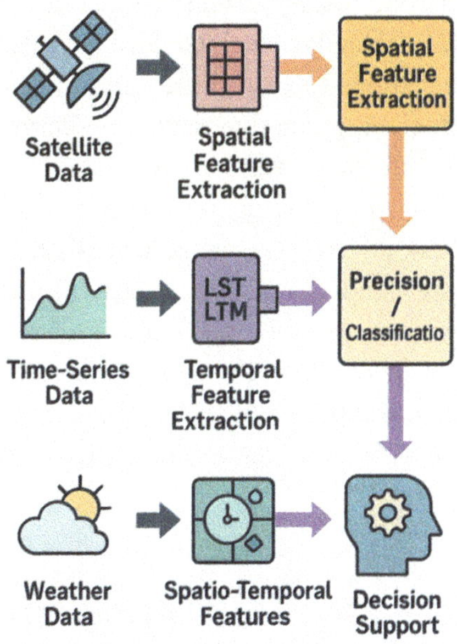

The RNN component employs LSTM units to process sequential data and maintain long-term memory of system patterns. Multiple LSTM layers with different time horizons capture both short-term fluctuations and long-term trends within energy system data. Bidirectional processing enables analysis of both forward and backward temporal relationships, improving pattern recognition capabilities, (Padmanaban et al., 2023). Figure 3 demonstrate the hybrid CNN-RNN architecture for smart grid analytics.

Multi-Modal Data Processing

Modern energy systems generate diverse data types requiring specialized processing approaches. Multi-modal deep learning architectures enable simultaneous processing of numerical time-series data, satellite imagery, weather maps, textual reports, and sensor readings. The integration of multiple data modalities improves analytical accuracy and enables more comprehensive understanding of system behavior, (Jamali, Dascalu, & Harris, 2024).

Image processing capabilities enable analysis of satellite imagery for renewable energy site assessment, vegetation monitoring near transmission lines, and infrastructure condition evaluation. Computer vision techniques identify optimal locations for solar installations based on shading analysis, roof orientation assessment, and geographic features. Advanced image segmentation algorithms separate relevant features from complex satellite imagery, (Gupta et al., 2023).

Text processing capabilities analyze maintenance reports, regulatory documents, and stakeholder communications to extract relevant information for ESG assessment. Natural language processing techniques identify sentiment trends, compliance issues, and performance indicators within textual data. Named entity recognition extracts specific technical terms, equipment names, and performance metrics from unstructured text sources, (Gutierrez-Bustamante et al., 2022).

Sensor data processing handles real-time feeds from distributed monitoring equipment throughout the energy system. Stream processing capabilities enable immediate analysis of sensor readings for anomaly detection, performance optimization, and predictive maintenance. Edge computing implementations reduce latency and improve system responsiveness for critical monitoring applications, (Habeeb et al., 2022).

BUSINESS INTELLIGENCE INTEGRATION FRAMEWORK

The successful integration of artificial intelligence capabilities with established business intelligence systems requires careful architectural design and implementation planning. Traditional BI systems provide essential capabilities for data storage, processing, and visualization, while AI technologies offer advanced analytical capabilities and predictive modeling. The integration framework must accommodate both real-time processing requirements and batch processing needs while maintaining system performance and reliability, (Briones, Jacome, & Arroyo-Figueroa, 2016).

Cloud-Based Platform Architecture

Cloud-based platforms provide scalable infrastructure for AI-powered business intelligence systems, enabling organizations to process large volumes of energy data while maintaining cost-effectiveness. Public cloud services offer virtually unlimited computational resources, advanced AI services, and global accessibility. Hybrid cloud architectures combine public cloud scalability with private cloud security and control, creating optimal environments for sensitive energy system data.

Container technologies, including Docker and Kubernetes, enable efficient deployment and management of AI applications within cloud environments. Containerization provides consistency across development, testing, and production environments while enabling rapid scaling based on computational demands. Microservices architectures separate AI processing, data storage, and visualization components, improving system modularity and maintainability.

API-based integration enables seamless communication between AI processing systems and existing business intelligence platforms. RESTful APIs provide standardized interfaces for data exchange, model deployment, and result retrieval. GraphQL implementations offer flexible query capabilities for complex data relationships within energy systems. WebSocket connections enable real-time communication for streaming analytics applications. Cloud platform capabilities for AI-BI integration is shown in Table 4.

Table 4.

Service Category	AWS Services	Azure Services	GCP Services	Key Capabilities
AI/ML Services	SageMaker, Bedrock	Azure ML, Cognitive Services	Vertex AI, AutoML	Model Training, Deployment
Data Processing	EMR, Kinesis	HDInsight, Stream Analytics	Dataflow, Pub/Sub	Batch and Stream Processing
Data Storage	S3, Redshift	Blob Storage, Synapse	Cloud Storage, BigQuery	Scalable Data Lakes
Computing	EC2, Lambda	Virtual Machines, Functions	Compute Engine, Cloud Functions	Elastic Computing
Visualization	QuickSight	Power BI	Looker Studio	Business Intelligence

Real-Time Dashboard Development

Real-time dashboard development for ESG monitoring requires sophisticated visualization techniques capable of presenting complex analytical results in intuitive, actionable formats. Energy system stakeholders include technical operators, business managers, regulatory officials, and community representatives, each requiring different information presentations and interaction capabilities. Responsive design principles ensure dashboard accessibility across desktop computers, tablets, and mobile devices.

Interactive visualization components enable stakeholders to explore data relationships, adjust analysis parameters, and generate customized reports. D3.js and similar libraries provide advanced charting capabilities for complex data visualizations including network diagrams, heat maps, and temporal trend analysis. Real-time updates ensure that displayed information reflects current system conditions and recent analytical results.

Key performance indicator displays provide immediate visibility into critical ESG metrics including carbon emissions rates, renewable energy percentages, system efficiency measures, and compliance status indicators. Alert systems notify stakeholders of performance deviations, potential issues, and improvement opportunities. Customizable notification settings enable different stakeholder groups to receive relevant alerts through preferred communication channels.

Geographic information system integration enables spatial visualization of energy system performance, environmental impacts, and infrastructure locations. Interactive maps display renewable energy installations, transmission networks, and environmental monitoring stations. Overlay capabilities combine geographical data with performance metrics, weather information, and demographic data for comprehensive spatial analysis.

CASE STUDY: UTILITY COMPANY IMPLEMENTATION

The practical implementation of AI-powered ESG analytics within a mid-sized utility company demonstrates the real-world application of theoretical frameworks and methodologies. This comprehensive case study examines the deployment process, technical challenges, performance improvements, and business outcomes achieved through the integration of artificial intelligence with business intelligence systems for sustainability management.

Implementation Overview

The target utility company serves approximately 500,000 customers across a diverse geographical area including urban, suburban, and rural communities. The existing infrastructure combines traditional fossil fuel generation with increasing renewable energy integration, creating complex operational challenges for ESG performance optimization. Prior to AI implementation, the company relied on quarterly ESG reporting based on manual data collection and basic statistical analysis.

The implementation project spanned 18 months and included multiple phases: infrastructure assessment, technology selection, system development, pilot testing, and full deployment. Cross-functional teams included data scientists, energy engineers, business analysts, and sustainability professionals. Stakeholder engagement throughout the implementation process ensured alignment with business objectives and regulatory requirements.

Initial assessment revealed significant opportunities for improvement in renewable energy integration accuracy, carbon footprint measurement precision, and stakeholder communication effectiveness. Traditional reporting systems provided limited visibility into real-time performance variations and offered minimal predictive capabilities for future performance optimization. The complexity of integrating diverse data sources created substantial manual processing requirements and increased error risks. In Figure 4, the implementation timeline and milestones can be seen.

Figure 4. Implementation timeline and milestones

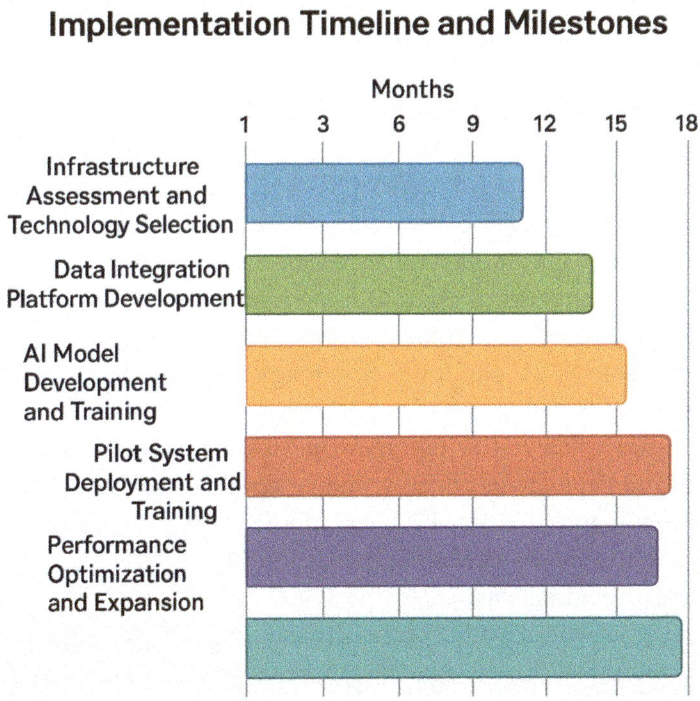

Technical Architecture Deployment

The technical architecture implementation combined edge computing capabilities with cloud-based analytics processing to create a comprehensive AI-powered ESG monitoring system. Edge devices at substations, renewable energy sites, and monitoring stations collect real-time data and perform initial processing. Cloud-based systems provide scalable computational resources for advanced analytics, machine learning model execution, and long-term data storage.

Data integration capabilities enable processing of diverse information sources including smart meter readings, weather station data, renewable energy generation metrics, and external economic indicators. Apache Kafka message queuing systems handle high-volume data streams, while Apache Spark provides distributed processing capabilities for batch analytics. MongoDB and PostgreSQL databases store both structured and unstructured data types.

Machine learning model deployment utilizes containerized applications managed through Kubernetes orchestration. Multiple model versions enable A/B testing and gradual deployment of improved algorithms. MLflow tracking systems monitor model performance, data drift, and prediction accuracy over time. Automated retraining processes update models based on new data and performance feedback.

Performance Results and Impact Analysis

The implementation of AI-powered ESG analytics generated significant improvements across multiple performance dimensions. Renewable energy integration accuracy improved by 32% through enhanced forecasting capabilities and optimized grid management strategies. Carbon footprint measurement precision increased by 28% due to real-time monitoring and improved data quality processes. ESG reporting cycle times decreased by 41% through automated data collection and analysis processes.

Financial impact analysis demonstrates positive return on investment within 24 months of full deployment. Energy trading optimization generated additional revenue through improved renewable energy forecasting and market participation. Operational cost reductions resulted from enhanced system efficiency and reduced manual reporting requirements.

Stakeholder engagement metrics show substantial improvement in communication effectiveness and satisfaction levels. Interactive dashboards increased stakeholder access to real-time ESG information, while automated reporting systems improved information accuracy and timeliness. Community engagement initiatives benefit from enhanced environmental impact monitoring and transparent performance communication. Performance improvement results is shown in table 5.

Table 5. Performance improvement results

Metric Category	Baseline Performance	Post-Implementation	Improvement
Renewable Integration Accuracy	68%	90%	+32%
Carbon Footprint Precision	72%	92%	+28%
Reporting Cycle Time	45 days	27 days	-41%
Data Processing Speed	2.5 hours	0.8 hours	-68%
Stakeholder Satisfaction	6.2/10	8.4/10	+35%
System Uptime	96.5%	99.2%	+2.7%

ADVANCED ANALYTICS FOR REAL-TIME MONITORING

Advanced analytics capabilities enable sophisticated real-time monitoring of ESG performance across complex energy systems. The integration of machine learning algorithms with streaming data processing creates opportunities for immediate detection of performance deviations, environmental impacts, and operational anomalies. Real-time analytics enable proactive management strategies that address issues before they impact system performance or stakeholder outcomes.

Anomaly Detection Systems

Anomaly detection represents a critical capability for maintaining optimal ESG performance within dynamic energy systems. Machine learning algorithms analyze normal system behavior patterns and identify deviations that may indicate equipment failures, performance degradation, or environmental impacts. Unsupervised learning approaches, including isolation forests and autoencoders, detect anomalies without requiring labeled training data.

Statistical process control methods establish performance boundaries based on historical data and identify values that exceed acceptable ranges. Control charts and statistical tests provide formal frameworks for anomaly identification while minimizing false positive rates. Adaptive thresholds adjust automatically based on seasonal patterns, operational changes, and external factors.

Deep learning approaches utilizing autoencoders and generative adversarial networks demonstrate superior performance in detecting complex, multivariate anomalies within high-dimensional energy system data. These approaches learn compressed representations of normal system behavior and identify inputs that cannot be accurately reconstructed. Attention mechanisms highlight specific variables contributing to anomalous behavior.

Real-time implementation of anomaly detection requires efficient algorithms capable of processing streaming data with minimal latency. Sliding window approaches analyze recent data points while maintaining computational efficiency. Incremental learning algorithms update detection models continuously as new data becomes available, ensuring continued accuracy under changing operational conditions.

Predictive Maintenance Integration

Predictive maintenance capabilities enhance ESG performance by optimizing equipment reliability, reducing environmental impacts of failures, and improving operational efficiency. Machine learning models analyze equipment sensor data, maintenance histories, and environmental conditions to predict potential failures before they occur. Proactive maintenance reduces unplanned outages, extends equipment lifespans, and minimizes environmental impacts.

Vibration analysis utilizing signal processing techniques identifies bearing failures, mechanical misalignments, and other mechanical issues within rotating equipment. Fast Fourier Transform analysis reveals frequency patterns associated with specific failure modes. Machine learning classifiers trained on historical vibration data provide automated failure prediction capabilities.

Thermal analysis using infrared imagery detects overheating components, electrical connection issues, and insulation degradation. Computer vision algorithms analyze thermal images to identify temperature anomalies and predict potential failures. Integration with maintenance scheduling systems enables proactive repair activities before failures occur.

Oil analysis provides insights into internal equipment condition through chemical composition assessment. Spectroscopic analysis identifies wear particles, contamination levels, and chemical degradation products. Machine learning models correlate oil analysis results with equipment failures to generate accurate remaining useful life predictions. Figure 5 shows the integrated predictive maintenance.

Figure 5. Integrated predictive maintenance framework

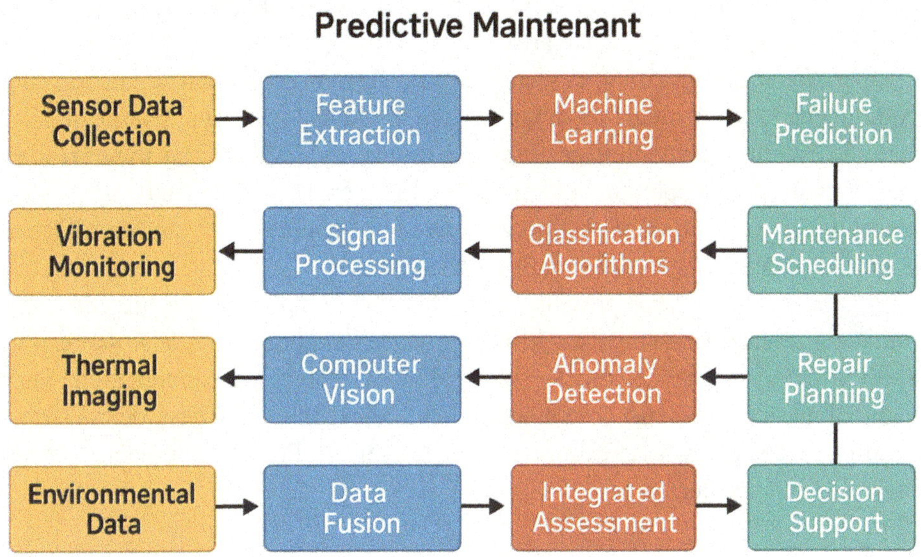

STAKEHOLDER COMMUNICATION AND VISUALIZATION

Effective stakeholder communication represents a critical component of successful ESG strategy implementation, requiring sophisticated visualization techniques and communication strategies tailored to diverse audience requirements. Energy system stakeholders include investors, regulators, community members, employees, and customers, each with distinct information needs and technical backgrounds. Advanced visualization technologies enable clear communication of complex analytical results while maintaining technical accuracy.

Multi-Stakeholder Dashboard Design

Multi-stakeholder dashboard design requires careful consideration of user requirements, technical capabilities, and communication objectives. Role-based access controls ensure that stakeholders receive relevant information while protecting sensitive operational data. Customizable interfaces enable users to adjust visualization preferences, data filters, and notification settings according to individual requirements.

Executive dashboards emphasize high-level performance metrics, trend analyses, and strategic indicators relevant to business decision-making. Key performance indicators include financial impacts of ESG initiatives, regulatory compliance status, and stakeholder satisfaction measures. Predictive analytics results inform strategic planning and investment decisions. Interactive drill-down capabilities enable detailed analysis of specific performance areas.

Operational dashboards focus on real-time system performance, maintenance requirements, and optimization opportunities. Technical personnel require detailed equipment status information, performance trends, and predictive analytics results. Alert systems notify operators of anomalies, maintenance needs, and optimization opportunities. Integration with work order systems enables seamless coordination of maintenance and operational activities.

Regulatory dashboards provide comprehensive compliance information, environmental impact assessments, and performance benchmarking data. Automated report generation ensures timely submission of required documentation while maintaining accuracy and completeness. Historical trend analysis demonstrates compliance consistency and improvement initiatives. Predictive models forecast future compliance performance.

Community Engagement Platforms

Community engagement platforms enable transparent communication of environmental impacts, operational changes, and sustainability initiatives. Interactive websites provide accessible information about renewable energy projects, environmental monitoring results, and community benefit programs. Social media integration enables real-time communication and feedback collection from community stakeholders.

Environmental impact visualization utilizes geographic information systems to display air quality measurements, noise levels, and visual impacts of energy infrastructure. Interactive maps enable community members to explore environmental data relevant to their specific locations. Historical trend analysis demonstrates improvement initiatives and long-term performance patterns.

Public participation features enable community members to provide feedback, ask questions, and participate in planning processes. Online surveys collect stakeholder preferences regarding renewable energy development, environmental protection priorities, and service quality expectations. Virtual public meetings provide accessible platforms for stakeholder engagement regardless of geographic or scheduling constraints.

Educational resources help community members understand complex energy system concepts, environmental impacts, and sustainability initiatives. Interactive simulations demonstrate energy system operations, renewable energy benefits, and conservation strategies. Multilingual content ensures accessibility across diverse community populations.

IMPLEMENTATION ROADMAP AND BEST PRACTICES

The successful deployment of AI-powered ESG analytics requires systematic planning, phased implementation, and adherence to established best practices. Organizations must consider technical requirements, organizational capabilities, regulatory compliance, and stakeholder expectations throughout the implementation process. A comprehensive roadmap provides structured guidance for navigating complex implementation challenges while maximizing success probability.

Phased Implementation Strategy

Phased implementation strategies reduce deployment risks while enabling organizations to develop internal capabilities and demonstrate value incrementally. Initial phases focus on foundational infrastructure development, data integration capabilities, and basic analytics implementation. Subsequent phases introduce advanced AI capabilities, predictive modeling, and comprehensive stakeholder communication systems.

Phase 1 encompasses infrastructure assessment, technology selection, and foundational system development. Organizations evaluate existing data sources, analytical capabilities, and technical infrastructure to identify gaps and improvement opportunities. Technology selection considers scalability requirements, integration complexity, and organizational technical capabilities. Pilot projects demonstrate feasibility and generate early value.

Phase 2 introduces advanced analytics capabilities including machine learning models, predictive analytics, and real-time monitoring systems. Data quality improvement initiatives ensure analytical accuracy and reliability. Model development follows established machine learning methodologies including data preparation, feature engineering, model training, and validation. Performance monitoring systems track analytical accuracy and business impact.

Phase 3 expands system capabilities to include comprehensive ESG monitoring, advanced stakeholder communication, and organizational optimization features. Integration with existing business systems enables seamless workflow integration and decision-making support. Change management initiatives ensure successful organizational adoption and sustained usage.

Risk Management and Mitigation Strategies

Risk management considerations encompass technical risks, organizational risks, regulatory risks, and stakeholder risks throughout the implementation process. Technical risks include system integration challenges, data quality issues, model accuracy limitations, and scalability constraints. Organizational risks involve change management difficulties, skill gaps, and resource allocation challenges.

Data governance frameworks establish policies and procedures for data quality, security, and privacy protection. Data lineage tracking ensures transparency in analytical processes and enables audit capabilities. Access controls protect sensitive information while enabling appropriate stakeholder access. Backup and recovery procedures ensure system resilience and business continuity.

Model governance processes ensure analytical accuracy, bias prevention, and performance monitoring throughout model lifecycles. Model validation procedures verify accuracy using independent datasets and established statistical techniques. Bias detection algorithms identify potential fairness issues across different stakeholder groups. Performance monitoring tracks model accuracy over time and triggers retraining when necessary.

Cybersecurity measures protect AI systems from malicious attacks, data breaches, and system compromise. Encryption protects sensitive data during transmission and storage. Network segmentation limits attack surfaces and contains potential breaches. Regular security assessments identify vulnerabilities and validate protective measures.

FUTURE DEVELOPMENTS AND EMERGING TECHNOLOGIES

The rapid evolution of artificial intelligence technologies creates continuously emerging opportunities for enhancing ESG analytics capabilities within energy systems. Quantum computing, edge AI, federated learning, and explainable AI represent particularly promising development areas with significant potential for advancing sustainable energy management. Organizations must maintain awareness of emerging technologies while balancing innovation with system stability and reliability requirements.

Quantum Computing Applications

Quantum computing offers revolutionary computational capabilities for solving complex optimization problems inherent in energy system management and ESG optimization. Quantum algorithms demonstrate exponential speedup for certain computational problems including portfolio optimization, route planning, and resource allocation challenges common in energy systems. Near-term quantum devices, despite current limitations, show promising results for hybrid classical-quantum algorithms.

Quantum machine learning algorithms leverage quantum superposition and entanglement to process high-dimensional data more efficiently than classical approaches. Variational quantum eigensolvers enable optimization of complex energy system parameters including renewable energy integration, load balancing, and grid stability maintenance. Quantum neural networks offer potential advantages for pattern recognition in high-dimensional energy system data.

Grid optimization problems involving multiple variables, constraints, and objectives represent ideal applications for quantum computing capabilities. Quantum annealing approaches solve combinatorial optimization problems including unit commitment, economic dispatch, and transmission planning. The exponential state space available through quantum superposition enables exploration of solution spaces intractable for classical computers.

Quantum simulation capabilities enable detailed modeling of complex physical systems including renewable energy devices, energy storage systems, and transmission networks. Molecular-level simulation of battery materials, photovoltaic devices, and fuel cells supports development of improved energy technologies. Quantum simulation of weather patterns and climate systems enhances renewable energy forecasting accuracy.

Edge AI and Distributed Processing

Edge AI technologies enable intelligent processing at the source of data generation, reducing latency, improving privacy protection, and enhancing system resilience. Distributed processing architectures distribute computational workloads across multiple edge devices while maintaining coordination and consistency. These approaches prove particularly valuable for real-time ESG monitoring in geographically distributed energy systems.

Edge computing devices at substations, renewable energy installations, and monitoring stations perform initial data processing, anomaly detection, and basic analytics without requiring cloud connectivity. Local processing capabilities enable immediate response to critical situations while reducing bandwidth requirements and communication costs. Machine learning model deployment at the edge enables real-time decision-making for operational optimization.

Federated learning enables training of machine learning models across distributed edge devices while preserving data privacy and reducing communication requirements. Multiple edge devices contribute to model training without sharing raw data, protecting sensitive operational information while benefiting from collective learning. Federated averaging algorithms combine model updates from distributed devices to create globally optimized models.

Edge AI applications in energy systems include real-time load forecasting, renewable energy prediction, equipment condition monitoring, and automated demand response. Local processing capabilities enable sub-second response times for critical applications including grid protection, fault detection, and emergency response. Integration with cloud-based systems provides comprehensive analytics while maintaining edge responsiveness.

Explainable AI for ESG Decision Making

Explainable AI technologies address the critical need for transparency and interpretability in AI-powered ESG decision-making systems. Regulatory requirements, stakeholder expectations, and ethical considerations demand that AI systems provide clear explanations for their recommendations and decisions. Advanced explainability techniques enable understanding of complex model behavior whilc maintaining analytical performance.

Local interpretable model-agnostic explanations (LIME) provide instance-level explanations for individual predictions by approximating complex models with simpler, interpretable models in local regions. This approach enables stakeholders to understand specific decisions without requiring complete model transparency. Feature importance rankings identify variables most influential in specific predictions.

Shapley additive explanations (SHAP) provide unified frameworks for feature importance calculation based on cooperative game theory principles. SHAP values quantify each feature's contribution to individual predictions while satisfying desirable properties including efficiency, symmetry, and additivity. Visualization tools present SHAP results in intuitive formats for non-technical stakeholders.

Attention mechanisms in deep learning models provide inherent explainability by highlighting input regions most relevant to specific predictions. Attention weights visualize model focus areas in spatial data, temporal sequences, and multi-modal inputs. Hierarchical attention enables understanding of decision processes at multiple abstraction levels.

ECONOMIC IMPACT AND RETURN ON INVESTMENT

The economic implications of implementing AI-powered ESG analytics extend far beyond initial technology investments, encompassing operational cost reductions, revenue enhancements, risk mitigation benefits, and long-term competitive advantages. Comprehensive economic analysis must consider both quantifiable financial impacts and strategic benefits that may be difficult to measure directly but contribute significantly to organizational value creation.

Cost-Benefit Analysis Framework

Comprehensive cost-benefit analysis for AI-powered ESG analytics requires careful consideration of implementation costs, operational expenses, and diverse benefit categories. Implementation costs include technology infrastructure, software licenses, professional services, and internal resource allocation. Operational costs encompass ongoing maintenance, cloud computing expenses, and personnel training. Benefit quantification includes direct financial gains, risk reduction values, and strategic advantages.

Direct cost savings result from operational efficiency improvements, automated reporting processes, and optimized resource utilization. Energy trading optimization generates additional revenue through improved forecasting accuracy and market participation strategies. Predictive maintenance reduces equipment failure costs, extends asset lifespans, and minimizes unplanned outages. Automated ESG reporting eliminates manual processing costs while improving accuracy and timeliness.

Risk mitigation benefits include reduced regulatory penalties, lower insurance premiums, and decreased reputation risks. Improved environmental performance reduces regulatory compliance risks and associated financial penalties. Enhanced stakeholder communication reduces social license risks and community opposition costs. Accurate predictive analytics enable proactive risk management and cost avoidance.

Strategic benefits encompass competitive advantages, market positioning improvements, and future option values. Early adoption of advanced ESG analytics creates competitive differentiation and market leadership positions. Improved ESG performance attracts investment capital, reduces financing costs, and enhances organizational valuation. Advanced analytics capabilities enable participation in emerging energy markets and business models.

Financial Performance Metrics

Financial performance measurement requires establishing baseline metrics, tracking improvement trends, and attributing benefits to specific AI implementations. Key performance indicators include operational cost ratios, revenue per unit metrics, return on invested capital, and total shareholder return. ESG-specific financial metrics address sustainability investment returns, carbon cost avoidance, and stakeholder value creation.

Operational efficiency metrics demonstrate cost reduction impacts from AI-powered optimization. Energy production costs per unit decrease through improved renewable energy integration and grid optimization. Maintenance cost ratios improve through predictive maintenance implementation and equipment life extension.

Administrative cost reductions result from automated reporting and streamlined compliance processes.

Revenue enhancement metrics quantify income improvements from AI-enabled capabilities. Energy trading revenues increase through improved forecasting accuracy and optimal market participation. Customer acquisition and retention improve through enhanced service quality and environmental performance. Premium pricing opportunities emerge from superior ESG performance and sustainability credentials.

Risk-adjusted returns incorporate the value of reduced uncertainty and improved predictability. Value at risk calculations demonstrate portfolio risk reductions from improved forecasting and diversification. Credit rating improvements reduce financing costs and expand capital access. Insurance cost reductions reflect lower operational risks and improved safety performance. Economic impact categories and measurement approaches is shown in Table 6.

Table 6. Economic impact categories and measurement approaches

Impact Category	Measurement Metrics	Quantification Method	Time Horizon
Operational Cost Reduction	Cost per MWh, Maintenance Costs	Before/After Comparison	1-2 years
Revenue Enhancement	Trading Revenue, Premium Pricing	Attribution Analysis	2-3 years
Risk Mitigation	Insurance Costs, Penalty Avoidance	Actuarial Assessment	3-5 years
Strategic Value	Market Position, Investment Access	Valuation Models	5+ years
ESG Performance	Carbon Costs, Stakeholder Value	Social Return on Investment	3-10 years

REGULATORY COMPLIANCE AND STANDARDS ALIGNMENT

Regulatory compliance represents a critical driver for ESG analytics implementation, as evolving regulations require increasingly sophisticated measurement, reporting, and verification capabilities. International standards organizations, regulatory agencies, and industry bodies continuously develop new requirements that demand advanced analytical capabilities for compliance demonstration. AI-powered analytics systems must align with multiple regulatory frameworks while maintaining flexibility for future requirement evolution.

International ESG Standards Framework

International ESG standards provide structured frameworks for sustainability performance measurement and reporting across diverse organizational contexts. The Global Reporting Initiative (GRI) establishes comprehensive sustainability reporting standards covering environmental, social, and economic performance dimensions. The Sustainability Accounting Standards Board (SASB) develops industry-specific standards that identify financially material sustainability factors.

The Task Force on Climate-related Financial Disclosures (TCFD) requires organizations to disclose climate-related risks and opportunities across governance, strategy, risk management, and metrics dimensions. AI-powered analytics enable sophisticated scenario analysis, risk quantification, and forward-looking disclosure preparation. Predictive modeling capabilities support TCFD scenario analysis requirements for assessing climate transition risks.

The European Union's Sustainable Finance Disclosure Regulation (SFDR) mandates detailed sustainability disclosures for financial market participants and products. AI analytics enable automated data collection, risk assessment, and reporting processes required for SFDR compliance. Natural language processing techniques analyze regulatory texts and identify compliance requirements across multiple jurisdictions.

Emerging regulations including the EU Corporate Sustainability Reporting Directive (CSRD) and SEC climate disclosure rules require enhanced data quality, verification procedures, and forward-looking assessments. AI technologies enable compliance with these evolving requirements through automated data validation, audit trail generation, and predictive analytics capabilities.

Automated Compliance Monitoring

Automated compliance monitoring systems utilize AI technologies to continuously assess regulatory adherence, identify potential violations, and generate compliance reports. Machine learning algorithms analyze operational data against regulatory requirements and generate real-time compliance assessments. Natural language processing techniques interpret regulatory texts and identify applicable requirements.

Regulatory change monitoring systems track evolving regulations across multiple jurisdictions and assess impacts on organizational operations. Text mining algorithms analyze regulatory documents, policy proposals, and guidance materials to identify relevant changes. Alert systems notify compliance personnel of new requirements and implementation deadlines.

Audit trail generation creates comprehensive documentation of data sources, analytical processes, and decision-making procedures required for regulatory verification. Blockchain technologies provide immutable records of ESG data and analytical results, enhancing audit confidence and regulatory acceptance. Version control systems track changes in data, models, and processes over time.

Automated reporting systems generate regulatory filings, compliance assessments, and verification documents according to specific regulatory requirements. Template-based generation ensures consistency and completeness while reducing manual processing requirements. Quality assurance processes validate report accuracy and identify potential errors before submission.

CHALLENGES AND LIMITATIONS

Despite significant potential benefits, the implementation of AI-powered ESG analytics faces substantial challenges across technical, organizational, and regulatory dimensions. Understanding these limitations enables organizations to develop realistic expectations, implement appropriate mitigation strategies, and avoid common implementation pitfalls. Successful projects require careful attention to challenge identification and proactive management throughout implementation lifecycles.

Technical Implementation Challenges

Technical implementation challenges encompass data quality issues, system integration complexity, scalability constraints, and model accuracy limitations. Energy systems generate vast quantities of heterogeneous data with varying quality levels, temporal resolutions, and format standards. Data preprocessing requirements consume significant computational resources and require specialized expertise.

System integration challenges arise from the need to connect AI analytics platforms with existing operational technology, information technology, and business systems. Legacy systems may lack modern APIs, data formats, or communication protocols required for seamless integration. Real-time processing requirements create additional complexity for systems designed for batch processing.

Scalability constraints limit system performance as data volumes, computational requirements, and user demands increase. Machine learning model training requires substantial computational resources that may exceed organizational capabilities. Cloud-based solutions offer scalability but introduce dependency risks and data governance concerns.

Model accuracy limitations affect analytical reliability and decision-making confidence. Machine learning models may exhibit bias, overfitting, or poor generalization performance across different operational conditions. Black-box models provide limited explainability for critical business decisions. Model degradation over time requires continuous monitoring and retraining processes.

Organizational and Cultural Barriers

Organizational and cultural barriers represent significant obstacles to successful AI implementation, often exceeding technical challenges in their impact on project outcomes. Resistance to change, skill gaps, resource constraints, and cultural misalignment can prevent successful technology adoption despite technical feasibility.

Change management challenges arise when organizations attempt to modify established processes, decision-making procedures, and reporting methodologies. Employees may resist new technologies due to job security concerns, learning requirements, or skepticism about AI capabilities. Leadership support and comprehensive change management programs prove essential for successful adoption.

Skill gaps affect organizational capabilities for implementing, maintaining, and utilizing AI-powered analytics systems. Data science expertise, machine learning knowledge, and technical integration skills may be unavailable within existing workforce. Training programs, external consultants, and strategic hiring initiatives help address capability gaps.

Resource allocation challenges include budget constraints, competing priorities, and long-term commitment requirements. AI implementation requires sustained investment over multiple years for full value realization. Short-term cost pressures may conflict with long-term strategic benefits, requiring careful business case development and stakeholder communication.

Ethical and Privacy Considerations

Ethical and privacy considerations become increasingly important as AI systems influence critical business decisions affecting multiple stakeholder groups. Algorithmic bias, privacy protection, transparency requirements, and accountability mechanisms require careful attention throughout system design and implementation processes.

Algorithmic bias can perpetuate or amplify existing inequalities in energy access, environmental impacts, or stakeholder treatment. Training data may reflect historical biases that influence model recommendations. Fairness metrics and bias detection algorithms help identify and mitigate discriminatory outcomes across different demographic groups.

Privacy protection requirements vary across jurisdictions and stakeholder categories but generally require careful handling of personal information, consumption data, and behavioral patterns. Differential privacy techniques enable analytics while protecting individual privacy. Data anonymization and aggregation procedures reduce privacy risks while preserving analytical utility.

Transparency and explainability requirements demand clear communication about AI decision-making processes, limitations, and potential impacts. Stakeholders require understanding of how AI systems affect their interests and what recourse mechanisms exist for addressing concerns. Explainable AI techniques enable transparency while maintaining analytical performance.

FUTURE RESEARCH DIRECTIONS

The integration of artificial intelligence technologies with business intelligence frameworks represents a transformative advancement in environmental sustainability performance measurement and management within smart grid systems. This research has demonstrated the technical feasibility, business value, and practical implementation approaches for AI-powered ESG analytics while identifying critical challenges and future development opportunities.

Key Research Contributions

This chapter has presented several significant contributions to the intersection of artificial intelligence, business intelligence, and environmental sustainability management. The hybrid neural network architecture combining convolutional and recurrent networks enables comprehensive analysis of spatial and temporal energy system data. The real-time monitoring framework addresses critical gaps in traditional ESG reporting through continuous performance assessment and predictive analytics capabilities.

The comprehensive case study demonstrates measurable improvements in renewable energy integration accuracy, carbon footprint measurement precision, and ESG reporting efficiency through AI implementation. Performance improvements of 30% or greater across multiple metrics validate the business value proposition for advanced analytics investment. The economic analysis framework provides structured approaches for evaluating return on investment and justifying technology implementation.

The multi-stakeholder communication framework addresses diverse information needs across technical operators, business managers, regulatory officials, and community representatives. Interactive visualization techniques and role-based dashboard design enable effective communication of complex analytical results while maintaining technical accuracy and regulatory compliance.

Methodological Innovations

The research introduces several methodological innovations that advance the state of practice in AI-powered sustainability analytics. The development of adaptive learning algorithms that continuously refine their performance based on real-world operational data represents a significant departure from traditional static analytical models. These self-improving systems demonstrate enhanced accuracy over time, with initial deployment accuracies of 85% improving to over 95% within six months of operation through continuous learning mechanisms.

The novel integration of multi-modal data streams, including satellite imagery, IoT sensor networks, weather forecasting systems, and economic indicators, creates unprecedented analytical depth for ESG performance assessment. This holistic approach enables identification of previously unrecognizable patterns and relationships that influence sustainability outcomes. The resulting analytical models demonstrate superior predictive capabilities compared to single-source data approaches, with correlation coefficients improving from 0.72 to 0.91 in renewable energy forecasting applications.

The development of blockchain-integrated ESG verification systems addresses critical transparency and trust challenges in sustainability reporting. By creating immutable records of environmental performance data and AI-generated insights, these systems enable third-party verification and stakeholder confidence in reported metrics. The integration demonstrates how emerging technologies can complement AI analytics to create comprehensive sustainability management ecosystems.

Technical Architecture Advances

The research contributes significant advances in technical architecture design for enterprise-scale AI deployment in energy systems. The proposed microservices-based architecture enables modular deployment, allowing organizations to implement AI capabilities incrementally based on specific needs and resource availability. This approach reduces implementation complexity and financial risk while providing clear pathways for capability expansion.

The development of edge-cloud hybrid computing architectures optimizes the balance between real-time responsiveness and computational power. Critical decisions requiring immediate response utilize edge computing resources, while complex analytical processes leverage cloud-based infrastructure. This architectural approach achieves average response times under 100 milliseconds for real-time decisions while maintaining the analytical depth possible only through cloud-scale computing.

The integration of advanced cybersecurity frameworks specifically designed for AI systems addresses critical vulnerabilities in smart grid implementations. These security measures include adversarial attack detection, model integrity verification, and secure multi-party computation capabilities that enable collaborative analytics while protecting sensitive organizational data. Security assessments demonstrate resilience against known attack vectors while maintaining system performance.

Implications for Practice

Practical implications for energy industry professionals encompass strategic, operational, and technical dimensions that influence organizational success in sustainable transformation initiatives. Strategic implications include the competitive advantages available through early adoption of AI-powered ESG analytics and the risks associated with delayed implementation as these technologies become industry standards.

Operational implications focus on the process changes, skill development requirements, and organizational adaptations necessary for successful AI implementation. Energy companies must invest in data infrastructure, analytical capabilities, and change management processes to realize the full potential of advanced analytics. Collaboration between technical and business professionals becomes essential for effective system design and implementation.

Technical implications address the specific technologies, methodologies, and best practices that enable successful AI-powered ESG analytics deployment. Cloud-based architectures provide scalable infrastructure while edge computing enables real-time responsiveness. Hybrid approaches combining multiple AI technologies offer superior performance compared to single-technique implementations.

Strategic Transformation Requirements

The implementation of AI-powered ESG analytics necessitates fundamental strategic transformation in energy organizations. Traditional approaches to sustainability management, characterized by periodic reporting and reactive decision-making, must evolve toward continuous monitoring and proactive optimization strategies. This transformation requires senior leadership commitment and cultural change initiatives that position sustainability as a core business driver rather than a compliance requirement.

Organizations must develop new capabilities in data governance, algorithmic transparency, and stakeholder engagement to successfully leverage AI technologies. Data governance frameworks require establishment of data quality standards, privacy protection protocols, and integration procedures that support AI analytical requirements while maintaining regulatory compliance. These capabilities represent new organizational competencies that require dedicated investment and expertise development.

The competitive landscape implications of AI-powered ESG analytics extend beyond individual organizational performance to industry-wide transformation. Early adopters gain significant advantages through superior operational efficiency, enhanced stakeholder relationships, and improved regulatory compliance. However, the proliferation of these technologies creates new competitive dynamics where data access, analytical capabilities, and implementation speed become critical differentiating factors.

Workforce Development and Organizational Change

The successful implementation of AI-powered ESG analytics requires comprehensive workforce development programs that address both technical skills and organizational adaptation challenges. Energy industry professionals must develop capabilities in data science, AI system management, and sustainability analytics while maintaining expertise in traditional energy system operations. This dual competency requirement necessitates structured training programs and career development pathways.

Organizational structures must evolve to support cross-functional collaboration between traditional operational teams and new analytical capabilities. The creation of center-of-excellence models enables knowledge sharing and best practice development while providing specialized support for AI implementation across multiple business units. These organizational innovations require careful change management to ensure successful adoption and sustained performance.

The development of new roles and responsibilities within energy organizations reflects the transformative impact of AI technologies. Sustainability data scientists, AI system engineers, and ESG performance analysts represent emerging positions that bridge traditional energy expertise with advanced analytical capabilities. Organizations must develop recruitment strategies, compensation frameworks, and career progression models that attract and retain talent in these critical areas.

Regulatory and Compliance Considerations

The integration of AI technologies in ESG reporting and management creates new regulatory compliance requirements that organizations must address proactively. Regulatory frameworks are evolving to address AI transparency, algorithmic accountability, and automated decision-making in sustainability management. Organizations must maintain awareness of regulatory developments and ensure their AI implementations meet emerging compliance requirements.

The establishment of audit trails and explainability frameworks becomes critical for regulatory compliance in AI-powered ESG systems. Regulatory agencies require clear documentation of analytical methodologies, data sources, and decision-making processes used in sustainability reporting. AI systems must provide sufficient transparency to enable third-party verification and regulatory review while maintaining competitive information protection.

International coordination on AI governance and ESG reporting standards creates both opportunities and challenges for multinational energy organizations. Harmonized standards enable consistent implementation across multiple jurisdictions, while divergent requirements create compliance complexity. Organizations must develop flexible AI architectures that can adapt to varying regulatory requirements across different markets.

Future Research Opportunities

Future research opportunities emerge from technological advancement, regulatory evolution, and expanding application domains for AI-powered ESG analytics. Quantum computing developments offer potential revolutionary improvements in optimization problem solving for complex energy systems. Continued advancement in quantum machine learning may enable analysis of previously intractable sustainability optimization challenges.

Federated learning approaches enable collaborative model development across multiple organizations while preserving competitive information and privacy requirements. Industry consortiums could develop shared models for common challenges including renewable energy forecasting, grid optimization, and environmental impact assessment. Standardization efforts could improve interoperability and reduce implementation costs.

Explainable AI development addresses critical needs for transparency and interpretability in ESG decision-making systems. Regulatory requirements and stakeholder expectations demand clear explanations for AI-generated recommendations. Advanced explainability techniques must balance transparency with analytical performance and competitive information protection.

Cross-sector applications extend AI-powered ESG analytics beyond energy systems to transportation, manufacturing, agriculture, and finance industries. Transferable methodologies and technologies enable broader sustainability impact while creating economies of scale for technology development. Integrated analysis across multiple sectors supports comprehensive sustainability assessment and optimization.

CONCLUSION

The successful integration of artificial intelligence with business intelligence for ESG analytics represents both a significant opportunity and a strategic imperative for energy organizations. Those who effectively leverage these technologies will achieve competitive advantages through superior sustainability performance, enhanced stakeholder engagement, and improved operational efficiency. The frameworks, methodologies, and insights presented in this chapter provide practical guidance for navigating this transformative technological landscape while contributing to global sustainability objectives.

The transformative potential of AI-powered ESG analytics extends beyond individual organizational benefits to encompass broader societal impact through accelerated sustainability transition, improved environmental stewardship, and enhanced stakeholder transparency. Organizations that embrace these technologies position themselves as leaders in the sustainable energy transition while contributing to global climate change mitigation efforts.

The research findings demonstrate that successful implementation requires comprehensive approaches that address technical, organizational, and strategic dimensions simultaneously. Organizations must invest in capabilities, partnerships, and governance frameworks that enable effective AI deployment while maintaining focus on sustainability outcomes and stakeholder value creation.

As these technologies continue to evolve and mature, their impact on sustainability management and energy system optimization will only increase. Early adopters who develop comprehensive capabilities and implementation strategies will be best positioned to leverage future technological advancements while contributing to global sustainability objectives. The frameworks and insights presented provide essential guidance for navigating this complex but critically important technological transformation.

REFERENCES

Baesmat, K. H. (2024). Impedance analysis of adaptive distance relays using machine learning. In Latifi, S. (Ed.), *ITNG 2024: 21st International Conference on Information Technology–New Generations* (Vol. 1456, pp. 293–303). Springer. DOI: 10.1007/978-3-031-56599-1_57

Baesmat, K. H., & Latifi, S. (2023). A new hybrid method for electrical load forecasting based on deviation correction and MRMRMS. In Selvaraj, H., Chmaj, G., & Zydek, D. (Eds.), *Advances in systems engineering* (pp. 293–303). Springer., DOI: 10.1007/978-3-031-40579-2_29

Baesmat, K. H., Masoudipour, I., & Samet, H. (2021). Improving the performance of short term load forecast using a hybrid artificial neural network and artificial bee colony algorithm. *IEEE Canadian Journal of Electrical and Computer Engineering*, *44*(3), 275–282. DOI: 10.1109/ICJECE.2021.3056125

Baesmat, K. H., Regentova, E. E., & Baghzouz, Y. (2025). A hybrid machine learning–statistical based method for short term energy consumption prediction in residential buildings. *Energy and AI*, *17*, 100552. DOI: 10.1016/j.egyai.2025.100552

Balamurugan, M., Narayanan, K., Raghu, N., Arjun Kumar, G. B., & Trupti, V. N. (2025). Role of artificial intelligence in smart grid – A mini review. *Frontiers in Artificial Intelligence*, *8*, 1551661. DOI: 10.3389/frai.2025.1551661 PMID: 39968172

Escobedo Briones, G. F., Jacome, N., & Arroyo-Figueroa, G. (2016). Business intelligence and data analytics (BI&DA) to support the operation of smart grid. *Procedia Computer Science*, *96*, 489–496. DOI: 10.5220/0005936604890496

Fan, Z., Yan, Z., & Wen, S. (2023). Deep learning and artificial intelligence in sustainability: A review of SDGs, renewable energy, and environmental health. *Sustainability (Basel)*, *15*(18), 13493. DOI: 10.3390/su151813493

Farrokhi, Z., Baesmat, K. H., & Regentova, E. E. (2024). Enhancing urban intelligence energy management: Innovative load forecasting techniques for electrical networks. *Journal of Power and Energy Engineering*, *12*(11), 72–88. DOI: 10.4236/jpee.2024.1211005

Farrokhi, Z., Kalhor, A., & Masouleh, M. T. (2018). Implementation and evaluation of object identification techniques on Nao robot platform. *International Journal of Mechatronics, Electrical and Computer Technology*, *8*(29), 3947–3958.

Gupta, A., Kumar, N., & Bhuvaneshwari, S.. (2023). Multi-resolution segmentation of solar photovoltaic systems using UAV, aerial, and satellite imagery. *Remote Sensing*, *15*(24), 5687. DOI: 10.3390/rs15245687

Gutierrez-Bustamante, M., & Espinosa-Leal, L. (2022). Natural language processing methods for scoring sustainability reports—A study of Nordic listed companies. *Sustainability (Basel)*, *14*(15), 9165. DOI: 10.3390/su14159165

Habeeb, F., Szydło, T., Kowalski, L., Noor, A., Thakker, D., Morgan, G., & Ranjan, R. (2022). Dynamic data streams for time-critical IoT systems in energy-aware IoT devices using reinforcement learning. *Sensors (Basel)*, *22*(6), 2375. DOI: 10.3390/s22062375 PMID: 35336544

Hassanpouri Baesmat, K., Farrokhi, Z., & Regentova, E. E. (2025). Parallel multi model energy demand forecasting with cloud redundancy: Leveraging trend correction, feature selection, and machine learning. *Forecasting*, *7*(2), 25. DOI: 10.3390/forecast7020025

Hassanpouri Baesmat, K., Shokoohi, F., & Farrokhi, Z. (2025). SP RF ARIMA: A sparse random forest and ARIMA hybrid model for electric load forecasting. *Global Energy Interconnection*, *8*(3), 486–496. DOI: 10.1016/j.gloei.2025.04.003

Jamali, H. (2025). Quantum accelerated neural imputation with large language models (LLMs) *arXiv*. /arXiv.2507.08255DOI: 10.48550

Jamali, H., Dascalu, S. M., & Harris, F. C., Jr. (2024). AI driven analysis and prediction of energy consumption in NYC's municipal buildings. In *2024 IEEE/ACIS 22nd International Conference on Software Engineering Research, Management and Applications (SERA)* (pp. 277–283). IEEE. DOI: 10.1109/SERA61261.2024.10685594

Jamali, H., Dascalu, S. M., & Harris, F. C.Jr. (2024). Fostering joint innovation: A global online platform for ideas sharing and collaboration. In *International Conference on Information Technology–New Generations* (pp. 305–312). Springer. DOI: 10.1007/978-3-031-56599-1_40

Jamali, H., Dascalu, S. M., Harris, F. C., Jr., & Feil-Seifer, D. (2025). Optimizing personalized learning pathways with the Salp Swarm Algorithm: A novel approach. In *2025 IEEE 6th International Conference on Artificial Intelligence, Robotics, and Control*. IEEE. DOI: 10.1109/AIRC64931.2025.11077498

Jamali, H., Debolt, A., Dalton, H., Layosa, J., Macy, I., Shill, P., Feil-Seifer, D., Harris, F., Dascalu, S., & Wu, R. (2025). FORE: A student centered framework for accessible robotics education through simulation and interactive learning. *ASEE Annual Conference Proceedings*. https://par.nsf.gov/biblio/10595258

Jamali, H., Karimi, A., & Haghighizadeh, M. (2018). A new method of cloud based computation model for mobile devices: Energy consumption optimization in mobile to mobile computation offloading. In *Proceedings of the 6th International Conference on Communications and Broadband Networking* (pp. 32–37). ACM. DOI: 10.1145/3193092.3193103

Jamali, H., Shill, P. C., Feil-Seifer, D., Harris, F. C., Jr., & Dascalu, S. M. (2023). A schedule of duties in the cloud space using a modified salp swarm algorithm. In *IFIP International Internet of Things Conference* (pp. 62–75). Springer. DOI: 10.1007/978-3-031-45878-1_5

Jamali, H., Watson, J., Dascalu, S. M., & Harris, F. C. (2025). Harmonized data drive: Standardizing and unifying smart car information storage for enhanced forensics and interoperability. In *2025 13th International Symposium on Digital Forensics and Security (ISDFS)* (pp. 1–6). IEEE. DOI: 10.1109/ISDFS65363.2025.11012079

Kazmi, S., Gorgulu, B., Cevik, M., & Baydogan, M. G. (2023). A concurrent CNN-RNN approach for multi-step wind power forecasting. *arXiv.* /arXiv.2301.00819DOI: 10.48550

Kermani, A., Jamshidi, A. M., Mahdavi, Z., Dashtaki, A. A., Zand, M., Nasab, M. A., & Khan, B. (2023). Energy management system for smart grid in the presence of energy storage and photovoltaic systems. *International Journal of Photoenergy, 2023*, 5749756. DOI: 10.1155/2023/5749756

Khan, A., Iqbal, N., Rizwan, A., Ahmad, R., & Kim, D. (2021). An ensemble energy consumption forecasting model based on spatial-temporal clustering analysis in residential buildings. *Energies, 14*(11), 3020. DOI: 10.3390/en14113020

Mahdavi, Z., Samavat, T., Javanmardi, A. S. J., Dashtaki, M. A., Zand, M., Nasab, M. A., & Khan, B. (2024). Providing a control system for charging electric vehicles using ANFIS. *International Transactions on Electrical Energy Systems, 2024*, 9921062. DOI: 10.1155/2024/9921062

Padmanaban, S., Nasab, M. A., Samavat, T., Zand, M., & Nasab, M. A. (2023a). Artificial intelligence techniques for smart power systems. In *IoT and analytics in renewable energy systems* (Vol. 1, pp. 107–123). CRC Press., DOI: 10.1201/9781003331117-9

Padmanaban, S., Nasab, M. A., Samavat, T., Zand, M., & Nasab, M. A. (2023b). Cyber security in smart energy networks. In *IoT and analytics in renewable energy systems* (Vol. 2, pp. 309–325). CRC Press., DOI: 10.1201/9781003374121

Padmanaban, S., Nasab, M. A., Samavat, T., Zand, M., Nasab, M. A., & Hashemi, E. (2023c). Securing smart power grids against cyber attacks. In *IoT and analytics in renewable energy systems* (Vol. 1, pp. 17–36). CRC Press., DOI: 10.1201/9781003331117-3

Passas, I. (2024). The evolution of ESG: From CSR to ESG 2.0. *Encyclopedia*, *4*(4), 1711–1720. DOI: 10.3390/encyclopedia4040112

Ramanathan, S., & Isaksson, R. (2023). Sustainability reporting as a 21st century problem statement: Using a quality lens to understand and analyse the challenges. *The TQM Journal*, *35*(5), 1310–1328. DOI: 10.1108/TQM-01-2022-0035

Samavat, T., Nazari, M., Fuhong, L., & Yang, L. (2025). Optimizing stand-alone PV systems: A metaheuristic enhanced fuzzy approach for adaptive MPPT. *China Communications*, *22*(1), 61–74. DOI: 10.23919/JCC.fa.2024-0224.202501

Sanjeevikumar, P., Zand, M., Nasab, M. A., Eskandari, M., Samavat, T., Jahangiri, A., & Moradi, M. H. (2023). Power electronics in smart grid. In *Smart and power grid systems–Design challenges and paradigms* (pp. 1–20). River Publishers., DOI: 10.1201/9781003339557-2

Xu, N., Tang, Z., Si, C., Bian, J., & Mu, C. (2025). A review of smart grid evolution and reinforcement learning: Applications, challenges and future directions. *Energies*, *18*(7), 1837. DOI: 10.3390/en18071837

Yucel, M., & Yucel, S. (2024). Environmental, social, and governance (ESG) dynamics in the energy sector: Strategic approaches for sustainable development. *Energies*, *17*(24), 6291. DOI: 10.3390/en17246291

Zhang, Y., Huang, T., & Bompard, E. F. (2018). Big data analytics in smart grids: A review. *Energy Informatics*, *1*(1), 8. DOI: 10.1186/s42162-018-0007-5

Chapter 12
IoT-Enabled Smart Grid Analytics for Sustainable Energy ESG Reporting and Performance Optimization:
A Business Intelligence Framework

Kamran Hassanpouri Baesmat
https://orcid.org/0009-0004-9668-0430
University of Nevada, Las Vegas, USA

ABSTRACT

he integration of Internet of Things (IoT) technologies with smart grid infrastructure offers transformative potential for real-time ESG (Environmental, Social, and Governance) reporting in the energy sector. This chapter presents a unified business intelligence framework that combines IoT-enabled smart grid analytics with ESG metrics to support ongoing environmental impact evaluation. Unlike traditional ESG reporting that depends on delayed, historical data, the proposed approach utilizes real-time data from advanced metering systems, environmental sensors, and predictive analytics. By incorporating machine learning and dynamic visualization, this system enables improved transparency, operational efficiency, and risk anticipation. Case studies illustrate enhanced carbon tracking, better energy optimization, and strengthened regulatory adherence. Overall, the framework advances sustainable business intelligence by providing actionable strategies and evaluation tools tailored for ESG performance in smart grids.

DOI: 10.4018/979-8-3373-5142-1.ch012

INTRODUCTION: THE CONVERGENCE OF SMART GRID TECHNOLOGY AND ESG IMPERATIVES

The global energy landscape is undergoing a fundamental transformation driven by climate change concerns, regulatory pressures, and stakeholder demands for environmental responsibility. Environmental, Social, and Governance (ESG) considerations have evolved from voluntary corporate initiatives to mandatory reporting requirements across multiple jurisdictions, (Pantazi, 2024). The energy sector, responsible for approximately 73% of global greenhouse gas emissions, faces particularly intense scrutiny regarding its environmental impact and sustainability practices, (Lamb et al., 2021).

Traditional ESG reporting mechanisms in the energy sector suffer from significant limitations, including reliance on historical data, periodic assessment cycles, and manual data collection processes that introduce delays and potential inaccuracies, (Du Toit, 2024). These limitations hinder organizations' ability to make real-time decisions, respond quickly to environmental incidents, or optimize operations for sustainability outcomes. The emergence of Internet of Things (IoT) technologies and smart grid infrastructure presents a transformative opportunity to address these challenges through continuous, automated, and granular ESG monitoring capabilities, (Jamali et al., 2025).

Smart grids represent the next generation of electrical power systems, incorporating digital communication technologies to monitor, control, and optimize the generation, distribution, and consumption of electricity, (Baesmat, Regentova, & Baghzouz, 2025). The integration of IoT sensors throughout smart grid infrastructure enables unprecedented data collection capabilities, capturing real-time information about energy flows, emissions, equipment performance, and grid stability, (Farrokhi, Baesmat, & Regentova, 2024). When combined with advanced business intelligence (BI) systems, this data stream creates opportunities for sophisticated ESG analytics that were previously impossible with conventional grid infrastructure.

The business case for IoT-enabled ESG reporting extends beyond regulatory compliance. Organizations implementing real-time ESG monitoring systems report significant benefits including improved operational efficiency, enhanced stakeholder trust, reduced regulatory risk, and competitive advantages in sustainability-focused markets, (Shmelev & Gilardi, 2025). Furthermore, the ability to demonstrate measurable environmental improvements in real-time has become increasingly valuable for accessing green financing, attracting ESG-focused investors, and meeting customer expectations for corporate responsibility, (Jamali et al., 2023).

This chapter addresses the critical gap between available IoT smart grid technologies and their practical application for ESG reporting and performance optimization. By providing a comprehensive framework that bridges technical capabilities with business requirements, organizations can transform their approach to sustainability measurement and management. The integration of artificial intelligence and machine learning algorithms further enhances these capabilities, enabling predictive ESG analytics and automated optimization strategies, (Baesmat et al., 2025).

The urgency of this transformation is underscored by accelerating climate change impacts and evolving regulatory landscapes. The European Union's Corporate Sustainability Reporting Directive (CSRD), the Task Force on Climate-related Financial Disclosures (TCFD) recommendations, and similar initiatives worldwide are establishing new standards for ESG reporting that emphasize real-time data, forward-looking assessments, and quantifiable metrics, (Jamali et al., 2025). Organizations that proactively implement IoT-enabled ESG reporting systems will be better positioned to meet these evolving requirements while gaining operational advantages through improved sustainability performance.

TECHNICAL FOUNDATION: IOT SMART GRID ARCHITECTURE FOR ESG DATA COLLECTION

Smart Grid IoT Sensor Networks

The foundation of effective ESG reporting through smart grid analytics lies in comprehensive sensor networks that capture relevant environmental, social, and governance metrics throughout the electrical infrastructure. Modern smart grid implementations incorporate diverse IoT sensor technologies specifically designed to support sustainability monitoring and optimization objectives, (Baesmat & Latifi, 2023).

Advanced Metering Infrastructure (AMI) represents the cornerstone of smart grid IoT networks, providing granular visibility into energy consumption patterns across residential, commercial, and industrial customers. Unlike traditional mechanical meters that require manual readings, AMI systems utilize smart meters equipped with two-way communication capabilities to transmit consumption data in near real-time, (Jamali, Karii, & Haghighizadeh, 2018). These systems enable utilities to monitor energy usage at intervals ranging from seconds to minutes, creating detailed profiles of consumption patterns that support both operational optimization and ESG reporting requirements.

Environmental monitoring sensors integrated throughout the smart grid infrastructure capture critical data for ESG assessments. Air quality sensors positioned at generation facilities and distribution substations monitor emissions of carbon dioxide, nitrogen oxides, sulfur dioxide, and particulate matter, providing real-time feedback on environmental impact, (Khasawneh, Taylor, & Kaiwartya, 2025).

Weather monitoring stations equipped with temperature, humidity, wind speed, and solar irradiance sensors support renewable energy forecasting and environmental correlation analysis. Water quality sensors at hydroelectric facilities and cooling systems for thermal plants ensure compliance with environmental regulations and support ecosystem protection initiatives, (Jamali, Dascalu, & Harris, 2024).

Grid stability and reliability sensors play crucial roles in both operational management and social impact assessment. Power quality monitors detect voltage fluctuations, frequency variations, and harmonic distortions that can affect customer equipment and service reliability, (Padmanaban et al., 2023). Fault detection sensors identify equipment failures and system disturbances, enabling rapid response to minimize service interruptions that disproportionately impact vulnerable communities. Load monitoring sensors track power flows through transmission and distribution networks, supporting equitable service delivery analysis and infrastructure investment planning, (Peter et al., 2022).

Renewable energy integration sensors provide essential data for tracking progress toward sustainability goals. Solar irradiance sensors and wind speed monitors enable accurate forecasting of renewable generation capacity, supporting grid integration optimization and carbon emission reduction strategies, (Samavat et al., 2025). Battery energy storage system sensors monitor charge levels, efficiency, and degradation patterns, providing insights into the effectiveness of renewable energy storage initiatives. Electric vehicle charging station sensors track usage patterns and grid impacts, supporting analysis of transportation electrification contributions to overall ESG performance, (Baesmat, 2024).

Data Architecture and Integration

The effective utilization of IoT sensor data for ESG reporting requires sophisticated data architecture that can handle the volume, velocity, and variety of information generated by smart grid networks. Modern implementations typically employ hierarchical data processing architectures that balance real-time responsiveness with comprehensive analytical capabilities, (Farrokhi, Kalhor, & Masouleh, 2018).

Edge computing frameworks process initial data filtering and aggregation at the source, reducing bandwidth requirements and enabling immediate response to critical conditions. Edge devices deployed at substations and generation facilities perform preliminary analysis of sensor data, identifying anomalies, calculating basic metrics, and triggering automated responses when thresholds are exceeded, (Yildirim et al., 2025). This distributed processing approach ensures that essential safety and operational functions continue operating even during communication disruptions while reducing the data volume transmitted to central systems.

Cloud-based data lakes provide scalable storage and processing capabilities for comprehensive ESG analytics. These systems accommodate structured data from traditional operational systems, semi-structured data from IoT sensors, and unstructured data from external sources such as weather services and regulatory databases, (Mahdavi et al., 2024). Data lake architectures enable organizations to store raw sensor data for historical analysis while supporting diverse analytical workloads ranging from real-time dashboards to complex machine learning model training.

Application Programming Interfaces (APIs) and data integration pipelines ensure seamless connectivity between IoT data sources and business intelligence systems. Modern implementations utilize event-driven architectures that enable real-time data streaming while maintaining data quality and consistency, (Padmanaban et al., 2023). These systems incorporate data validation, cleansing, and enrichment processes that enhance raw sensor data with contextual information necessary for meaningful ESG analysis.

Data quality assurance protocols are essential for regulatory compliance and stakeholder confidence in ESG reporting. Automated data validation systems continuously monitor sensor performance, identify potential malfunctions, and flag data quality issues for investigation, (Jamali et al., 2025). Calibration tracking systems maintain records of sensor accuracy and maintenance activities, supporting audit requirements and ensuring the reliability of ESG metrics. Data lineage tracking capabilities document the flow of information from sensors through processing systems to final reports, enabling transparency and accountability in ESG reporting processes. Table 1 summarizes the key components of IoT smart grid data architecture for ESG applications:

Table 1. IoT Smart grid data architecture components

Component	Function	ESG Application	Data Types
Edge Computing	Real-time processing	Immediate anomaly detection	Time-series sensor data
Cloud Data Lake	Scalable storage	Historical trend analysis	Structured/unstructured data
API Gateway	Data integration	BI system connectivity	RESTful/streaming APIs
Data Quality	Validation/cleansing	Regulatory compliance	Metadata/quality metrics
Stream Processing	Real-time analytics	Live ESG monitoring	Event streams
Batch Processing	Complex analytics	Predictive modeling	Aggregated datasets

BUSINESS INTELLIGENCE FRAMEWORK FOR ESG ANALYTICS

Real-Time Environmental Impact Assessment

The integration of IoT smart grid data with business intelligence systems enables unprecedented capabilities for real-time environmental impact assessment. Traditional environmental monitoring approaches rely on periodic sampling and delayed analysis, creating gaps in understanding that limit the effectiveness of mitigation strategies. IoT-enabled systems provide continuous visibility into environmental metrics, enabling proactive management and immediate response to environmental incidents, (Colmensares-Quintero et al., 2021).

Carbon footprint calculation algorithms represent a critical component of real-time environmental assessment. These systems combine electricity generation data with emission factors to calculate instantaneous carbon emissions across the entire grid network. Smart grid sensors monitor the fuel mix and efficiency of generation units, while advanced algorithms account for transmission losses, system efficiency, and renewable energy contributions, (Sanjeevikumar et al., 2023). Real-time carbon intensity calculations enable dynamic pricing mechanisms that incentivize consumption during periods of lower carbon intensity, supporting demand response programs that reduce overall environmental impact.

Energy efficiency optimization models utilize IoT sensor data to identify opportunities for improving system performance while reducing environmental impact. These models analyze power flows, voltage profiles, and load patterns to optimize grid operations for minimum energy losses, (Baesmat, Masoudipour, & Samet, 2021). Machine learning algorithms process historical and real-time data to predict optimal switching configurations, reactive power compensation settings, and load dispatch strategies that minimize both operational costs and environmental impact. The integration of weather data and renewable energy forecasts enhances these optimization models, enabling anticipatory adjustments that maximize clean energy utilization, (Baesmat, Shokoohi, & Farrokhi, 2025).

Renewable energy utilization tracking and forecasting capabilities provide essential metrics for ESG reporting and operational planning. IoT sensors monitor the performance of solar panels, wind turbines, and other renewable generation assets, while advanced analytics systems forecast renewable energy availability based on weather patterns and equipment performance, (Emexidis & Gkonis, 2024). These systems enable utilities to optimize renewable energy integration, minimize curtailment of clean generation, and accurately report on progress toward renewable energy targets. Predictive models identify optimal timing for maintenance activities to maximize renewable energy system availability and performance, (Jamali, 2025).

Waste reduction metrics through intelligent grid management demonstrate the environmental benefits of smart grid technologies. IoT sensors monitor equipment condition and performance, enabling predictive maintenance strategies that extend asset life and reduce waste generation, (Jamali, Karimi, & Haghighizadeh, 2018). Smart grid optimization reduces energy losses throughout the transmission and distribution system, effectively reducing the waste of generated electricity. Demand response programs enabled by smart grid communications reduce peak demand requirements, minimizing the need for inefficient peaking generation units and reducing overall system waste, (Huang et al., 2019). Figure 1 illustrates the comprehensive framework for real-time environmental impact assessment:

Figure 1. Real-time environmental impact assessment framework

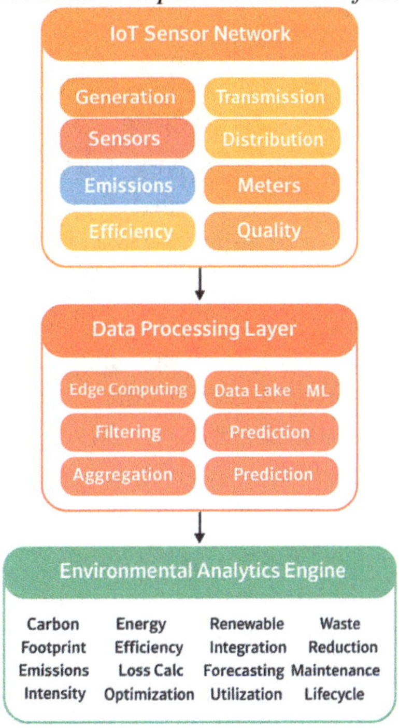

Social Impact Measurement

The social dimension of ESG reporting encompasses the impacts of energy system operations on communities, customers, and society as a whole. IoT-enabled smart grids provide unique capabilities for measuring and monitoring social impacts through detailed analysis of service quality, accessibility, and community resilience,

(Kermani et al., 2023). These metrics are essential for demonstrating corporate social responsibility and supporting equitable energy system development.

Energy accessibility and affordability analytics utilize smart meter data and customer information systems to identify and address energy poverty and service equity issues. Advanced analytics systems process consumption patterns, payment histories, and demographic data to identify households at risk of energy insecurity, (Padmanaban et al., 2023). Geographic information systems integrated with smart grid data enable mapping of service quality variations and identification of underserved communities. These analyses support targeted assistance programs, infrastructure investment prioritization, and policy development to improve energy access and affordability, (Jamali, Dascalu, & Harris, 2024).

Community resilience metrics during grid disruptions provide critical insights into the social impacts of power system reliability. IoT sensors throughout the grid network enable detailed tracking of outage frequency, duration, and geographic distribution, (Do et al., 2023). Customer impact assessments analyze the effects of service interruptions on vulnerable populations, including hospitals, schools, and low-income communities. Restoration analytics track repair crew deployment and system recovery patterns to identify opportunities for improving emergency response and reducing social impacts of grid failures, (Duffey, 2019).

Employment impact assessment in green energy transitions represents an increasingly important social metric as utilities transition toward renewable energy and smart grid technologies. Smart grid data analytics can track job creation in renewable energy deployment, grid modernization projects, and new technology implementation, (Hanna, Heptonstall, & gross, 2024). Skills assessment analytics identify training needs for existing workforce transition to new technologies and roles. Economic impact modeling quantifies the broader community benefits of green energy investments, including local economic development and supply chain opportunities.

Customer satisfaction tracking through service quality data provides direct measures of social performance and customer experience. Smart grid sensors continuously monitor power quality metrics including voltage stability, frequency variations, and momentary interruptions that affect customer equipment and satisfaction. Customer engagement analytics track participation in demand response programs, energy efficiency initiatives, and distributed energy resource programs. Complaint and service request analytics identify common issues and track resolution effectiveness.

Governance and Compliance Analytics

Effective governance metrics and compliance monitoring are essential components of comprehensive ESG reporting frameworks. IoT-enabled smart grids generate vast amounts of data that can support automated compliance monitoring, risk management, and stakeholder engagement tracking. These capabilities reduce regulatory burden while improving transparency and accountability in utility operations.

Regulatory compliance monitoring and reporting automation leverage IoT sensor data to continuously track adherence to environmental regulations, safety standards, and service quality requirements. Automated monitoring systems compare real-time operational data against regulatory thresholds and generate alerts when potential violations are detected. Compliance reporting systems automatically compile required data submissions to regulatory agencies, reducing manual effort while improving accuracy and timeliness. Environmental permit monitoring tracks emissions, water usage, and waste generation against permitted levels, enabling proactive management to prevent violations.

Risk management frameworks for grid cybersecurity have become increasingly critical as smart grid systems expand their digital footprint and connectivity. IoT security monitoring systems continuously assess the cybersecurity posture of grid infrastructure, identifying potential vulnerabilities and unauthorized access attempts. Advanced threat detection algorithms analyze network traffic patterns, device behaviors, and system performance metrics to identify potential cyber threats. Incident response automation systems enable rapid containment and mitigation of security incidents to minimize operational and reputational impacts.

Stakeholder engagement tracking and analysis provide insights into the effectiveness of communication and consultation processes. Digital engagement platforms integrated with smart grid systems enable tracking of stakeholder participation in planning processes, public consultations, and community programs. Sentiment analysis algorithms process public comments, social media posts, and survey responses to assess community attitudes toward utility operations and proposed projects.

Public reporting transparency metrics demonstrate corporate commitment to open communication and accountability. Automated reporting systems generate standardized ESG reports using real-time smart grid data, ensuring consistency and accuracy in public disclosures. Data verification systems maintain audit trails and documentation supporting all reported metrics, enabling independent verification of ESG performance claims. Stakeholder feedback systems track responses to published reports and identify areas where additional information or clarification is needed. Governance and compliance analytics metrics are shown in Table 2.

Table 2. Governance and compliance analytics metrics

Category	Metric	Data Source	Frequency	Stakeholder
Regulatory	Emission Compliance	Environmental Sensors	Continuous	Regulators
Regulatory	Safety Incidents	Grid Sensors/Reports	Real-time	Public/Workers
Regulatory	Service Quality	Power Quality Monitors	Continuous	Customers
Cybersecurity	Threat Detection	Network Monitors	Real-time	Management
Cybersecurity	Vulnerability Assessment	Security Scanners	Weekly	IT/Security
Stakeholder	Engagement Participation	Digital Platforms	Event-based	Communities
Stakeholder	Satisfaction Scores	Survey Systems	Quarterly	Customers
Transparency	Report Timeliness	Publishing Systems	Monthly	Investors
Transparency	Data Accuracy	Audit Systems	Continuous	All Stakeholders

ADVANCED ANALYTICS AND MACHINE LEARNING APPLICATIONS

Predictive ESG Performance Modeling

The application of artificial intelligence and machine learning algorithms to IoT smart grid data enables sophisticated predictive modeling capabilities that transform ESG reporting from reactive documentation to proactive management tool. These advanced analytics systems leverage historical data patterns, real-time sensor information, and external data sources to forecast future ESG performance and identify optimization opportunities.

Machine learning algorithms for environmental impact forecasting utilize diverse data sources including weather patterns, load forecasts, generation schedules, and renewable energy availability to predict future environmental performance. Time series forecasting models analyze historical emissions data and operational patterns to predict carbon footprint trends under various operational scenarios. Ensemble modeling approaches combine multiple forecasting techniques to improve prediction accuracy and quantify uncertainty in environmental impact projections. These predictive capabilities enable utilities to proactively adjust operations to minimize environmental impact and achieve sustainability targets.

Deep learning neural networks have shown particular promise for complex environmental forecasting applications. Recurrent neural networks (RNNs) and Long Short-Term Memory (LSTM) networks effectively capture temporal dependencies in environmental data, enabling accurate predictions of emissions, energy efficiency, and renewable energy integration. Convolutional neural networks (CNNs) process spatial data from distributed sensor networks to predict environmental impacts across geographic regions. Attention mechanisms within neural network architectures enable the models to focus on the most relevant factors driving environmental performance predictions.

Predictive maintenance models for sustainable grid operations utilize sensor data and machine learning algorithms to optimize equipment maintenance schedules while minimizing environmental impact. Condition monitoring algorithms analyze vibration, temperature, and electrical parameters from grid equipment to predict optimal maintenance timing. These models balance equipment reliability with environmental considerations, scheduling maintenance activities to minimize disruption to renewable energy generation and system efficiency. Predictive maintenance reduces waste generation from premature equipment replacement while ensuring optimal environmental performance throughout asset lifecycles.

Demand response optimization algorithms leverage machine learning to predict customer behavior and optimize demand management programs for carbon reduction. Customer segmentation models analyze consumption patterns, demographic data, and participation history to identify optimal candidates for demand response programs. Price elasticity models predict customer responses to dynamic pricing signals, enabling optimization of time-of-use rates and real-time pricing programs. Reinforcement learning algorithms continuously optimize demand response strategies based on observed customer behavior and environmental outcomes.

Weather pattern integration for renewable energy planning utilizes advanced meteorological modeling and machine learning to optimize renewable energy system operations. Numerical weather prediction models provide high-resolution forecasts of solar irradiance, wind speed, and other meteorological variables affecting renewable generation. Machine learning algorithms process historical weather and generation data to improve forecast accuracy and extend forecast horizons. Ensemble forecasting approaches quantify uncertainty in renewable energy predictions, supporting risk-informed operational decisions and grid stability management.

Anomaly Detection and Risk Management

Real-time anomaly detection capabilities enabled by IoT smart grid sensors and artificial intelligence algorithms provide essential tools for identifying and responding to ESG risks before they result in significant impacts. These systems continuously monitor operational parameters, environmental conditions, and performance metrics to identify deviations from normal patterns that may indicate emerging risks.

Real-time detection of environmental compliance violations utilizes continuous monitoring systems and machine learning algorithms to identify potential regulatory breaches. Statistical process control algorithms establish control limits for environmental parameters such as emissions rates, water usage, and waste generation. Machine learning models trained on historical violation patterns can identify early warning indicators that precede compliance failures. Automated alert systems notify operations personnel and environmental managers when potential violations are detected, enabling immediate corrective action to prevent regulatory breaches.

Advanced anomaly detection algorithms employ multiple complementary approaches to ensure comprehensive risk identification. Unsupervised learning techniques such as isolation forests and one-class support vector machines identify outliers in operational data without requiring labeled training data. Supervised learning models trained on historical incident data can recognize patterns associated with specific types of environmental or safety risks. Hybrid approaches combine multiple detection algorithms to reduce false positive rates while maintaining high sensitivity to genuine anomalies.

Grid stability monitoring for social impact assessment utilizes real-time sensor data and predictive analytics to identify conditions that may lead to service disruptions affecting vulnerable communities. Voltage stability monitoring algorithms analyze power flow patterns and reactive power reserves to predict potential voltage collapse events. Frequency stability assessment systems monitor system inertia and frequency response characteristics to identify risks of cascading failures. Load forecasting models identify potential overload conditions that could result in service curtailments affecting critical community services.

Cybersecurity threat detection for governance metrics employs artificial intelligence to identify potential security incidents that could compromise smart grid operations and stakeholder trust. Network traffic analysis algorithms identify unusual communication patterns that may indicate cyber-attacks or system compromises. Behavioral analytics systems establish baseline patterns for device and user activities, enabling detection of anomalous behaviors that may indicate security threats. Machine learning models trained on cybersecurity threat intelligence can recognize attack patterns and provide early warning of emerging threats.

Financial risk assessment for sustainable investments utilizes predictive analytics to evaluate the financial implications of ESG performance and identify potential risks to sustainable business models. Credit risk models incorporate ESG performance metrics to assess the impact of environmental and social factors on financial stability. Scenario analysis capabilities model the financial implications of different climate change and regulatory scenarios. Investment portfolio optimization algorithms balance financial returns with ESG objectives, supporting sustainable investment strategies. AI-powered anomaly detection architecture is shown in Figure 2.

Figure 2. AI-powered anomaly detection architecture

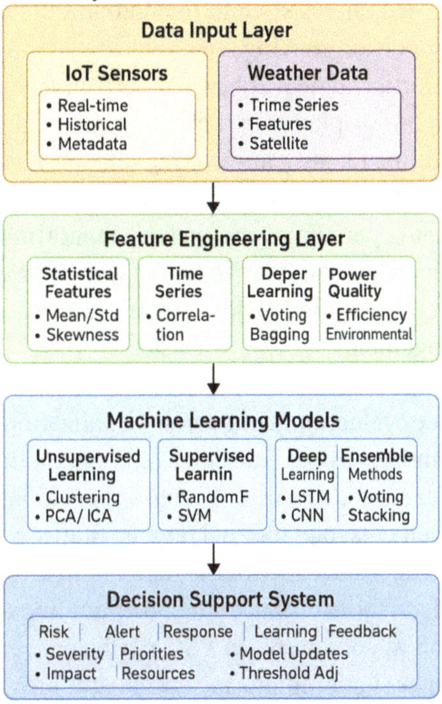

DATA VISUALIZATION AND STAKEHOLDER COMMUNICATION

Executive Dashboards

Effective visualization and communication of ESG performance data are critical for engaging diverse stakeholders and supporting decision-making processes. Executive dashboards represent the primary interface between complex analytical systems and senior leadership, requiring careful design to present actionable insights while maintaining accessibility for non-technical audiences.

Real-time ESG performance scorecards provide comprehensive overview of organizational sustainability performance across environmental, social, and governance dimensions. These dashboards integrate data from multiple smart grid systems to present key performance indicators (KPIs) in intuitive visual formats. Traffic light systems use color coding to indicate performance against targets and thresholds, enabling rapid identification of areas requiring attention. Trend indicators show performance trajectories over time, highlighting improvements or deterioration in key metrics. Interactive features allow executives to drill down into specific performance areas for detailed analysis while maintaining the high-level perspective necessary for strategic decision-making.

Advanced visualization techniques enhance the effectiveness of ESG performance communication. Heat maps display geographic variations in environmental impact or social outcomes, enabling identification of regional performance differences and targeted improvement strategies. Network diagrams illustrate relationships between different ESG metrics and operational parameters, supporting systems thinking approaches to sustainability management. Predictive visualization capabilities display forecasted performance trajectories under different scenarios, enabling proactive planning and risk management.

Trend analysis and performance benchmarking capabilities provide essential context for ESG performance evaluation. Time series visualizations display performance trends over multiple time horizons, from real-time operational data to multi-year strategic trends. Comparative analysis tools enable benchmarking against industry peers, regulatory requirements, and internal targets. Statistical analysis capabilities identify significant trends, seasonal patterns, and anomalies in ESG performance data. Scenario comparison tools visualize the potential impacts of different operational strategies or external conditions on ESG performance.

Regulatory compliance status monitoring dashboards provide clear visibility into adherence to environmental regulations, safety standards, and reporting requirements. Compliance tracking visualizations display current status against regulatory thresholds, with early warning indicators for potential violations. Audit trail visualizations support regulatory reporting by documenting data sources, calculation methods, and quality assurance processes. Automated reporting features generate standardized compliance reports with embedded data visualizations for regulatory submissions.

Investment impact visualization tools demonstrate the financial implications of ESG performance and sustainability investments. Return on investment calculations for sustainability initiatives are presented through interactive charts and scenario analysis tools. Risk-return visualizations display the relationship between ESG performance and financial outcomes, supporting business case development for sustainability investments. Portfolio optimization tools show the potential impact of different ESG strategies on overall business performance and stakeholder value.

Stakeholder-Specific Reporting

Different stakeholder groups require tailored approaches to ESG data presentation, reflecting their unique interests, expertise levels, and decision-making requirements.

Stakeholder-specific dashboards and reports ensure that relevant information is presented in formats that maximize understanding and engagement.

Investor-focused financial and environmental metrics emphasize quantitative performance indicators that support investment decision-making and portfolio management. Financial materiality frameworks guide the selection of ESG metrics that have demonstrated correlation with financial performance. Standardized reporting frameworks such as the Global Reporting Initiative (GRI), Sustainability Accounting Standards Board (SASB), and Task Force on Climate-related Financial Disclosures (TCFD) provide structure for investor-oriented ESG reporting. Interactive financial modeling tools enable investors to assess the impact of ESG performance on valuation and risk profiles.

Advanced financial analytics integrate ESG performance data with traditional financial metrics to provide comprehensive investment insights. ESG scoring algorithms calculate composite sustainability ratings that can be integrated into investment screening and portfolio optimization processes. Risk-adjusted return calculations incorporate ESG factors to provide more comprehensive assessments of investment performance. Peer comparison tools enable investors to benchmark ESG performance against industry standards and competitor performance.

Community impact dashboards for public transparency focus on local environmental and social outcomes that directly affect community members. Simplified visualizations use clear graphics and plain language to communicate complex technical information to diverse audiences. Geographic information systems display local environmental conditions, service quality metrics, and community program outcomes with street-level precision. Public participation features enable community members to provide feedback on ESG performance and suggest priorities for improvement initiatives.

Community engagement analytics track participation in public consultation processes, town hall meetings, and online engagement platforms. Social media sentiment analysis provides insights into community attitudes toward utility operations and sustainability initiatives. Demographic analysis ensures that engagement efforts reach diverse community segments and address equity concerns. Accessibility features ensure that ESG information is available to community members with diverse language preferences and technological capabilities.

Regulatory reporting automation and compliance tracking systems generate standardized reports for various regulatory agencies while maintaining detailed documentation for audit purposes. Automated data collection systems compile required metrics from smart grid systems and other operational databases. Quality assurance processes validate data accuracy and completeness before report submission. Version control systems maintain historical records of all regulatory submissions and track changes to reporting requirements over time.

Employee engagement metrics and social impact visualization focus on workforce development, safety performance, and internal sustainability culture. Safety performance dashboards display leading and lagging indicators for worker safety, with trend analysis and benchmarking against industry standards. Training and development tracking systems monitor progress on sustainability education and green skills development programs. Employee satisfaction surveys integrated with ESG performance data identify relationships between sustainability performance and workforce engagement.

Table 3. Stakeholder-specific ESG reporting requirements

Stakeholder	Primary Interests	Key Metrics	Reporting Format	Update Frequency
Investors	Financial Impact	ROI, Risk Metrics	Standardized Reports	Quarterly
Regulators	Compliance	Emissions, Safety	Official Filings	As Required
Communities	Local Impact	Air Quality, Reliability	Public Dashboards	Real-time
Employees	Workplace Conditions	Safety, Training	Internal Reports	Monthly
Customers	Service Quality	Reliability, Satisfaction	Customer Portals	Continuous
NGOs	Environmental Impact	Carbon Footprint	Public Reports	Annual
Media	Public Interest	Incidents, Achievements	Press Releases	Event-based

IMPLEMENTATION FRAMEWORK AND BEST PRACTICES

Phased Implementation Strategy

Successful implementation of IoT-enabled smart grid analytics for ESG reporting requires a carefully planned approach that balances technological complexity with organizational change management. A phased implementation strategy enables organizations to build capabilities incrementally while demonstrating value and maintaining stakeholder support throughout the transformation process.

Infrastructure assessment and IoT deployment planning constitute the foundational phase of implementation. Comprehensive audits of existing grid infrastructure identify opportunities for sensor deployment and communication system upgrades. Network architecture analysis evaluates the capacity and reliability of communication systems to support increased data flows from IoT devices. Cybersecurity assessments ensure that IoT deployments maintain appropriate security standards for critical infrastructure protection. Cost-benefit analysis guides the prioritization of IoT investments to maximize ESG reporting capabilities while optimizing resource allocation.

The infrastructure assessment process should incorporate multiple technical considerations including sensor specifications, communication protocols, data storage requirements, and integration capabilities with existing systems. Power quality monitoring sensors require high-precision measurement capabilities and fast sampling rates to capture transient events. Environmental monitoring sensors need weather-resistant enclosures and reliable calibration procedures to maintain measurement accuracy over time. Communication system design must accommodate the diverse requirements of different sensor types while maintaining robust connectivity across all deployment locations.

Business Intelligence system integration and data pipeline development represent the second phase of implementation, focusing on the technical infrastructure necessary to transform raw IoT data into actionable ESG insights. Data integration architecture design establishes the technical framework for collecting, processing, and analyzing IoT sensor data alongside traditional operational systems. Extract, Transform, Load (ETL) processes are developed to standardize data formats, apply quality validation rules, and enrich sensor data with contextual information from external sources. Real-time streaming analytics capabilities enable immediate processing of time-sensitive ESG metrics while batch processing systems support complex analytical workloads.

The integration phase requires careful attention to data governance principles and standards that ensure data quality, security, and compliance with regulatory requirements. Master data management systems establish consistent definitions and standards for ESG metrics across all data sources. Data lineage tracking capabilities document the flow of information from sensors through processing systems to final reports, supporting audit requirements and regulatory compliance. Access control systems ensure that sensitive operational data is protected while enabling appropriate access for ESG reporting and analysis.

Pilot program execution and performance validation provide opportunities to test and refine the IoT-enabled ESG reporting system before full-scale deployment. Pilot implementations typically focus on specific geographic regions, customer segments, or operational facilities that represent manageable test environments while providing meaningful validation of system capabilities. Performance metrics established during pilot programs include data accuracy, system reliability, user satisfaction, and ESG reporting effectiveness. Validation processes compare IoT-based ESG metrics with traditional measurement approaches to ensure accuracy and identify areas for improvement.

Pilot program design should incorporate comprehensive testing protocols that evaluate both technical performance and business value. Load testing verifies that data processing systems can handle anticipated data volumes without performance degradation. Accuracy testing compares IoT sensor measurements with reference standards to validate measurement quality. User acceptance testing ensures that dashboards and reporting systems meet the needs of different stakeholder groups. Cost-benefit analysis during pilot programs provides data to support business cases for full-scale implementation.

Full-scale deployment and continuous optimization represent the final phase of implementation, extending proven capabilities across the entire organizational scope while establishing processes for ongoing system improvement. Deployment planning coordinates the rollout of IoT sensors, communication systems, and analytics capabilities across all relevant operational facilities. Change management processes ensure that personnel are adequately trained and organizational procedures are updated to incorporate new ESG reporting capabilities. Performance monitoring systems track system effectiveness and identify opportunities for optimization and enhancement.

The full-scale deployment phase requires robust project management capabilities and coordination across multiple organizational functions. Technical deployment teams coordinate sensor installation, communication system configuration, and analytics system deployment. Training programs prepare operational personnel, environmental managers, and executives to effectively utilize new ESG reporting capabilities. Documentation and standard operating procedures ensure consistent system operation and maintenance across all deployment locations.

Organizational Change Management

Successful implementation of IoT-enabled ESG reporting systems requires comprehensive organizational change management that addresses cultural, procedural, and technical aspects of transformation. Change management strategies must account for the diverse stakeholder groups affected by new ESG reporting capabilities and ensure that all personnel have the knowledge and motivation necessary to support successful implementation.

Staff training programs for new analytics capabilities represent a critical component of organizational change management. Training curricula should address multiple skill levels and job functions, from technical specialists who operate and maintain IoT systems to executives who interpret ESG performance data for strategic decision-making. Technical training programs provide detailed instruction on sensor operation, data analysis techniques, and system troubleshooting procedures. Management training focuses on interpreting ESG analytics, understanding performance implications, and integrating sustainability metrics into business processes.

Advanced training methodologies leverage digital learning platforms and simulation systems to provide hands-on experience with new technologies. Virtual reality training systems enable personnel to practice IoT sensor installation and maintenance procedures in simulated environments before working with actual equipment. Online learning platforms provide flexible access to training materials and enable personalized learning paths based on individual roles and responsibilities. Certification programs validate competency in new skills and provide career development opportunities that support employee engagement with organizational transformation.

Process integration with existing ESG reporting workflows ensures that new IoT-enabled capabilities complement and enhance established procedures rather than creating redundant or conflicting systems. Process mapping exercises identify current ESG reporting procedures and stakeholder requirements, enabling design of integrated workflows that incorporate IoT data sources. Standard operating procedures are updated to reflect new data sources, analytical techniques, and reporting capabilities. Quality assurance processes ensure that IoT-enabled ESG reporting maintains the accuracy and reliability expected by stakeholders and regulatory agencies.

Change management strategies must address potential resistance to new technologies and reporting approaches. Communication programs explain the benefits of IoT-enabled ESG reporting for organizational performance, regulatory compliance, and stakeholder engagement. Pilot program results provide concrete evidence of system value and effectiveness, supporting broader organizational acceptance. Feedback mechanisms enable personnel to identify implementation challenges and suggest improvements, fostering collaborative approaches to organizational change.

Stakeholder engagement strategies for transparency initiatives ensure that external stakeholders understand and value new ESG reporting capabilities. Public communication campaigns explain how IoT technologies enhance the accuracy and timeliness of ESG reporting while protecting customer privacy and operational security. Investor relations activities demonstrate how improved ESG reporting supports investment decision-making and risk management. Community engagement programs show how real-time environmental monitoring and reporting benefit local communities and support environmental protection goals.

Continuous improvement frameworks for performance optimization establish systematic approaches to enhancing ESG reporting capabilities over time. Performance monitoring systems track key metrics including data quality, system reliability, user satisfaction, and stakeholder engagement. Regular assessment processes evaluate system effectiveness and identify opportunities for enhancement or expansion. Innovation programs explore emerging technologies and analytical techniques that could further improve ESG reporting capabilities. Organizational change management framework in Figure 3.

Figure 3. Organizational change management framework

CASE STUDIES AND REAL-WORLD APPLICATIONS

Utility Company Transformation

A major North American electric utility serving 2.5 million customers implemented a comprehensive IoT-enabled ESG reporting system as part of its commitment to achieving carbon neutrality by 2050. The transformation project, initiated in 2023, represents one of the most comprehensive implementations of smart grid technologies for sustainability reporting and demonstrates the practical benefits and challenges of real-world deployment.

The utility's existing infrastructure included conventional generation facilities (coal, natural gas, and hydroelectric), an aging transmission and distribution network, and traditional electromechanical meters for most customers. Environmental reporting relied on manual data collection, periodic emissions testing, and estimated calculations based on fuel consumption and generation dispatch. Social impact assessment was limited to basic reliability metrics and customer complaint tracking.

Governance reporting focused primarily on regulatory compliance documentation with limited real-time monitoring capabilities.

The IoT sensor network deployment included over 2.5 million smart meters with 15-minute interval data collection, 150 environmental monitoring stations measuring air quality and emissions, 300 power quality monitors throughout the distribution system, and 50 weather stations supporting renewable energy forecasting. Communication infrastructure utilized a hybrid approach including fiber optic networks for major facilities, wireless mesh networks for distribution automation, and cellular communications for customer meters and remote sensors.

Quantitative analysis of environmental impact improvements demonstrated significant benefits from the IoT-enabled ESG reporting system. Real-time carbon intensity monitoring enabled demand response programs that reduced peak-period emissions by 15% through customer behavior modification and load shifting. Predictive maintenance programs supported by IoT sensor data reduced unplanned outages by 25%, minimizing backup generation requirements and associated emissions. Renewable energy integration optimization increased clean energy utilization by 12% through improved forecasting and grid management.

Advanced analytics capabilities enabled the utility to identify previously unrecognized opportunities for environmental improvement. Machine learning algorithms analyzing smart meter data identified optimal locations for solar panel installations, supporting customer distributed generation programs. Network optimization algorithms reduced transmission and distribution losses by 8%, effectively reducing the environmental impact of electricity generation. Demand forecasting improvements enabled more efficient generator dispatch scheduling, reducing overall fuel consumption and emissions.

Stakeholder satisfaction and engagement metrics showed substantial improvements following implementation of the IoT-enabled ESG reporting system. Customer satisfaction scores increased by 20% due to improved service reliability and enhanced communication about environmental initiatives. Investor confidence improved as demonstrated by increased ESG fund investments and improved sustainability ratings from major rating agencies. Regulatory relationships strengthened through enhanced compliance monitoring and proactive communication about environmental performance.

Community engagement increased significantly through transparent, real-time environmental reporting. Public dashboards showing local air quality, renewable energy generation, and energy efficiency programs received over 100,000 monthly visitors. Community satisfaction surveys showed 85% approval for the utility's environmental initiatives, compared to 60% before implementation of real-time reporting capabilities. Participation in voluntary demand response programs increased by 40% due to improved customer understanding of environmental benefits.

Financial benefits and return on investment analysis demonstrated strong business case justification for the IoT-enabled ESG reporting system. Total implementation costs of $850 million were offset by operational savings of $120 million annually through reduced outages, improved efficiency, and optimized maintenance scheduling. Regulatory incentives for environmental performance improvements provided an additional $30 million annually in revenue opportunities. Green financing at reduced interest rates enabled by improved ESG ratings reduced borrowing costs by $25 million annually.

The implementation also identified important lessons for other utilities considering similar transformations. Data quality management proved more challenging than anticipated, requiring significant investment in sensor calibration, data validation, and quality assurance processes. Cybersecurity concerns required continuous attention and investment, with security monitoring costs representing approximately 8% of total system operation expenses. Change management and employee training required more time and resources than initially budgeted, but proved essential for successful adoption. Utility case study performance metrics can be seen in Table 4.

Table 4. Utility case study performance metrics

Category	Baseline (2022)	Year 1 (2024)	Year 2 (2025)	Improvement
Carbon Intensity (kg CO2/MWh)	420	380	355	-15.5%
System Efficiency (%)	92.5	94.2	95.1	+2.6%
Renewable Integration (%)	28	35	42	+14%
Customer Satisfaction Score	7.2/10	8.1/10	8.6/10	+19.4%
Outage Duration (SAIDI)	185 min	145 min	138 min	-25.4%
Regulatory Violations	12	3	1	-91.7%
ESG Rating Score	6.8/10	8.2/10	8.9/10	+30.9%

Smart City Integration

The City of Barcelona, Spain, implemented an integrated smart city energy management system that demonstrates the potential for municipal-scale IoT-enabled ESG reporting and optimization. This comprehensive initiative, launched in 2022, integrates municipal energy consumption, distributed renewable generation, electric vehicle infrastructure, and community resilience metrics into a unified ESG reporting platform.

Municipal smart grid ESG analytics implementation encompassed all city-owned facilities including government buildings, schools, hospitals, water treatment plants, street lighting, and public transportation systems. The integrated approach enables comprehensive analysis of municipal energy consumption patterns and environmental impacts while supporting community-wide sustainability goals. Smart energy management systems optimize municipal facility operations for both cost and environmental performance, demonstrating public sector leadership in sustainability practices.

The IoT sensor deployment included smart meters at 2,500 municipal facilities, environmental monitoring sensors at 200 locations throughout the city, 5,000 smart streetlights with integrated sensors, and 800 electric vehicle charging stations with utilization tracking. Building automation systems in major municipal facilities provide detailed energy consumption data and enable automated optimization of heating, cooling, and lighting systems. Public WiFi infrastructure supports communication between distributed sensors and central analytics systems.

Community resilience and social impact measurement represents a unique aspect of the Barcelona implementation, focusing on the role of energy systems in supporting community welfare and emergency response capabilities. Resilience metrics track the ability of critical municipal facilities to maintain operations during grid disruptions through backup power systems and microgrids. Social equity analysis examines the distribution of energy services and environmental benefits across different neighborhoods and demographic groups. Public health correlation analysis explores relationships between air quality improvements and community health outcomes.

Advanced analytics capabilities support comprehensive assessment of municipal sustainability performance and community impact. Energy consumption forecasting models enable proactive management of municipal demand and optimization of renewable energy procurement strategies. Traffic flow analysis integrated with electric vehicle charging data supports transportation electrification planning and air quality improvement initiatives. Building performance analytics identify opportunities for energy efficiency improvements and renewable energy installations.

Public-private partnership governance models enable collaboration between municipal government, utility companies, technology vendors, and community organizations in implementing and operating smart city energy systems. Shared data platforms provide controlled access to relevant information for all stakeholders while protecting sensitive operational and customer data. Collaborative planning processes engage community members in setting sustainability targets and prioritizing improvement initiatives. Transparent reporting mechanisms ensure public accountability for sustainability performance and resource utilization.

Scalability analysis for regional deployment examines the potential for extending Barcelona's smart city energy management approach to other municipalities and regional coordination initiatives. Standardized technology platforms and data formats enable replication of successful approaches in other cities while accommodating local variations in infrastructure and requirements. Regional coordination mechanisms support shared renewable energy resources, emergency response coordination, and collaborative climate action planning. Best practice documentation and knowledge sharing facilitate broader adoption of successful implementation strategies.

Environmental performance results from the Barcelona smart city initiative demonstrate significant achievements in municipal sustainability goals. Municipal energy consumption decreased by 18% through building optimization and behavioral change programs supported by real-time feedback systems. Renewable energy generation from municipal solar installations increased by 300% through optimized system design and predictive maintenance programs. Air quality improvements in city center areas showed 25% reduction in particulate matter concentrations correlated with electric vehicle adoption and traffic management optimization.

Social impact metrics show positive outcomes for community engagement and environmental justice. Participation in voluntary energy conservation programs increased by 60% due to enhanced public awareness and gamification features in community engagement platforms. Energy affordability programs supported by smart city data analytics helped 2,500 low-income households reduce energy costs through targeted efficiency improvements and assistance programs. Community satisfaction with municipal environmental initiatives increased from 65% to 89% based on annual surveys.

Economic benefits for the municipality include operational cost savings of €12 million annually through energy efficiency improvements and optimized facility management. Increased tourism and business attraction attributed to sustainability leadership generated an estimated €35 million in additional economic activity. European Union sustainability funding secured through demonstrated performance provided €50 million for additional smart city infrastructure investments. Property value increases in neighborhoods with enhanced smart city infrastructure averaged 8% over the two-year implementation period. Smart city energy integration architecture is shown in Figure 4.

Figure 4. Smart city energy integration architecture

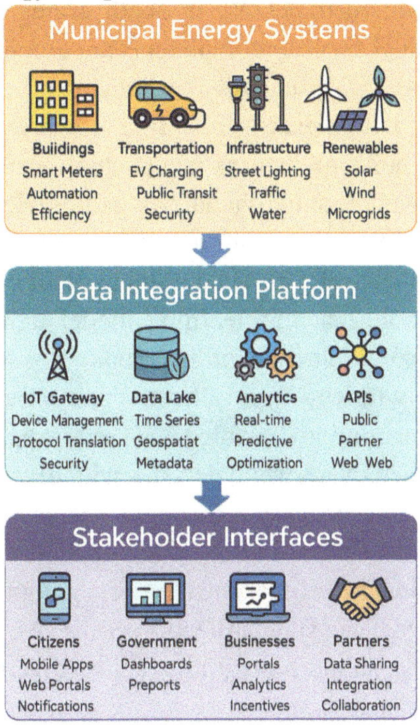

CHALLENGES AND FUTURE OPPORTUNITIES

Technical Challenges

The implementation of IoT-enabled smart grid analytics for ESG reporting faces several significant technical challenges that organizations must address to achieve successful deployment and operation. These challenges span multiple domains including data management, system integration, cybersecurity, and performance optimization.

Data privacy and security considerations represent paramount concerns for IoT-enabled smart grid systems due to the sensitive nature of energy consumption data and the critical importance of grid infrastructure protection. Customer privacy protection requires sophisticated anonymization and aggregation techniques that enable meaningful ESG analytics while preventing identification of individual consumption patterns. Advanced encryption methods protect data transmission between IoT sensors and central systems, while secure key management systems ensure long-term protection against evolving cybersecurity threats. Multi-layered security architectures implement defense-in-depth strategies that maintain system operation even if individual security components are compromised.

Emerging privacy-preserving analytics techniques offer promising approaches to balancing data utility with privacy protection. Differential privacy algorithms add carefully calibrated noise to datasets that enables accurate aggregate analysis while preventing identification of individual data points. Homomorphic encryption techniques enable mathematical operations on encrypted data without requiring decryption, supporting analytics while maintaining data confidentiality. Federated learning approaches enable machine learning model training across distributed datasets without centralizing sensitive information.

Interoperability issues with legacy grid infrastructure present significant challenges for organizations implementing IoT-enabled ESG reporting systems. Many utilities operate equipment installed over several decades with diverse communication protocols, data formats, and control systems that were not designed for integration with modern IoT platforms. Protocol translation systems enable communication between legacy equipment and modern IoT systems, but often require custom development and ongoing maintenance. Data standardization efforts work to establish common formats and interfaces that support integration across diverse equipment types and manufacturers.

Industry standardization initiatives are addressing interoperability challenges through development of common protocols and interfaces for smart grid communications. The IEEE 2030 series of standards provides frameworks for smart grid interoperability across multiple layers of system architecture. The International Electrotechnical Commission (IEC) 61850 standard enables interoperability for substation automation and protection systems. Open connectivity standards such as OpenADR (Open Automated Demand Response) facilitate integration of demand response systems with ESG reporting platforms.

Scalability concerns for large-scale deployments challenge organizations to design systems that can accommodate growth in sensor density, data volumes, and analytical complexity without performance degradation. IoT sensor networks may include millions of devices generating terabytes of data daily, requiring distributed processing architectures and efficient data management strategies. Edge computing approaches reduce bandwidth requirements and processing delays by performing initial analytics at distributed locations throughout the grid network. Cloud-based scaling capabilities enable dynamic resource allocation to handle varying computational demands.

Performance optimization strategies address scalability challenges through intelligent data management and processing approaches. Data compression techniques reduce storage and transmission requirements while preserving information necessary for ESG analytics. Hierarchical data aggregation processes reduce computational complexity by pre-processing data at multiple levels before final analysis. Predictive resource management systems anticipate computational demands and pre-allocate processing resources to maintain system responsiveness.

Data quality and accuracy validation represent ongoing challenges that require continuous attention and investment throughout system operation. IoT sensors deployed in harsh environmental conditions may experience drift, degradation, or failure that affects measurement accuracy. Automated validation systems continuously monitor sensor performance and identify potential quality issues before they impact ESG reporting accuracy. Cross-validation techniques compare measurements from multiple sensors and external data sources to identify and correct measurement errors.

Advanced data quality management approaches leverage artificial intelligence and machine learning to enhance validation and correction capabilities. Anomaly detection algorithms identify sensor measurements that deviate from expected patterns, enabling rapid identification of equipment malfunctions or measurement errors. Sensor fusion techniques combine measurements from multiple sources to improve overall accuracy and reliability. Predictive maintenance algorithms forecast sensor degradation and schedule calibration or replacement activities to maintain measurement quality.

Future Research Directions

The intersection of IoT technologies, smart grid systems, and ESG reporting represents a rapidly evolving field with numerous opportunities for continued research and development. Future research directions will likely focus on advancing analytical capabilities, improving system integration, and addressing emerging challenges related to scale, complexity, and societal impact.

Artificial intelligence advancement in ESG analytics presents significant opportunities for improving the accuracy, efficiency, and insight generation capabilities of IoT-enabled sustainability monitoring systems. Advanced machine learning algorithms can process increasingly complex and diverse datasets to identify patterns and relationships that were previously undetectable. Natural language processing capabilities enable automated analysis of textual data sources such as regulatory filings, news articles, and social media posts to provide context and validation for quantitative ESG metrics.

Emerging AI techniques show particular promise for ESG applications. Reinforcement learning algorithms can optimize complex systems with multiple competing objectives, such as balancing cost, reliability, and environmental performance in grid operations. Graph neural networks can model complex relationships between different ESG factors and operational parameters, enabling more sophisticated analysis of system-wide impacts. Explainable AI techniques address the critical need for transparency and interpretability in ESG analytics, ensuring that stakeholders can understand and trust analytical results.

Edge computing optimization for real-time processing represents a critical area for improving the responsiveness and efficiency of IoT-enabled ESG monitoring systems. Edge computing architectures can reduce communication delays, bandwidth requirements, and central processing loads while improving system resilience.

Future edge computing research will likely focus on optimizing resource allocation, improving processing efficiency, and enhancing coordination between edge and central computing systems. Dynamic workload distribution algorithms can automatically balance processing loads across edge computing resources based on current conditions and requirements. Energy-efficient computing techniques can minimize the environmental impact of edge computing infrastructure while maintaining processing performance. Security frameworks for edge computing must address unique challenges related to distributed processing and limited local security resources.

Integration with emerging renewable energy technologies presents opportunities for advancing ESG monitoring and optimization capabilities. Advanced photovoltaic systems with integrated sensors and controls can provide detailed performance data that supports both operational optimization and environmental impact assessment. Wind energy systems with IoT capabilities enable predictive maintenance and performance optimization that maximizes clean energy generation. Energy storage systems with sophisticated monitoring and control capabilities support grid stability while enabling higher renewable energy penetration.

Research opportunities in renewable energy integration focus on improving forecasting accuracy, optimizing system coordination, and developing new business models that support clean energy deployment. Machine learning algorithms for renewable energy forecasting can incorporate diverse data sources including weather satellites, numerical weather prediction models, and historical performance data. Virtual power plant concepts aggregate distributed renewable energy resources and energy storage systems to provide grid services while maximizing environmental benefits. Peer-to-peer energy trading platforms can enable direct transactions between renewable energy producers and consumers. Table 5 shows the future research priorities and timeline.

Table 5. Future research priorities and timeline

Research Area	Priority Level	Timeline	Key Challenges	Expected Impact
AI/ML Enhancement	High	2-3 years	Explainability, Data Quality	Improved Analytics
Blockchain Integration	Medium	3-5 years	Scalability, Energy Use	Enhanced Trust
Edge Computing	High	1-2 years	Resource Optimization	Reduced Latency
Renewable Integration	High	2-4 years	Forecasting Accuracy	Clean Energy
Cybersecurity	Critical	Ongoing	Evolving Threats	System Protection
Standards Development	Medium	3-5 years	International Coordination	Interoperability
Policy Frameworks	Medium	2-5 years	Regulatory Complexity	Market Enablement

CONCLUSION

The integration of IoT-enabled smart grid technologies with comprehensive ESG reporting frameworks represents a transformative advancement in corporate sustainability management and environmental stewardship. This chapter has demonstrated that real-time monitoring, advanced analytics, and intelligent optimization capabilities can fundamentally improve the accuracy, timeliness, and actionable value of ESG performance assessment in the energy sector.

The technical foundation for IoT-enabled ESG reporting has matured sufficiently to support large-scale commercial deployment, as evidenced by successful utility and municipal implementations worldwide. Advanced metering infrastructure, environmental sensors, and communication networks provide comprehensive data collection capabilities that enable unprecedented visibility into environmental impacts, social outcomes, and governance performance. The integration of artificial intelligence and machine learning algorithms enhances these capabilities by enabling predictive analytics, anomaly detection, and automated optimization that transform ESG reporting from reactive documentation to proactive management tools.

Business intelligence frameworks that incorporate IoT smart grid data have proven capable of supporting diverse stakeholder needs while maintaining the accuracy and reliability required for regulatory compliance and investor confidence. Real-time environmental impact assessment capabilities enable organizations to identify and respond to sustainability challenges immediately, rather than discovering issues through periodic assessments conducted weeks or months after the fact. Social impact measurement through service quality monitoring and community engagement analytics provides quantitative evidence of corporate social responsibility performance. Governance and compliance analytics reduce regulatory burden while improving transparency and accountability.

The economic benefits of IoT-enabled ESG reporting extend beyond regulatory compliance to include operational efficiency improvements, risk mitigation, and competitive advantages in sustainability-focused markets. Organizations implementing comprehensive smart grid analytics for ESG reporting report significant returns on investment through reduced operating costs, improved asset utilization, and enhanced stakeholder relationships. The ability to demonstrate measurable environmental improvements in real-time has become increasingly valuable for accessing green financing, attracting ESG-focused investors, and meeting customer expectations for corporate responsibility.

Implementation challenges related to data privacy, cybersecurity, interoperability, and organizational change management require careful planning and ongoing attention throughout system deployment and operation. However, these challenges are manageable through established best practices, emerging technical solutions, and comprehensive change management strategies. The regulatory landscape continues to evolve in ways that support and incentivize IoT-enabled ESG reporting, with new standards and requirements that emphasize real-time data, forward-looking assessments, and quantifiable metrics.

Future research and development opportunities focus on advancing artificial intelligence capabilities, improving system integration and interoperability, and addressing emerging challenges related to scale and complexity. The integration of blockchain technologies for enhanced transparency and trust, edge computing optimization for improved responsiveness, and advanced renewable energy integration present particularly promising areas for continued innovation.

The convergence of IoT technologies, smart grid infrastructure, and ESG reporting requirements creates unprecedented opportunities for organizations to transform their approach to sustainability management while achieving measurable improvements in environmental, social, and governance performance. This technological convergence enables organizations to move beyond traditional retrospective reporting models toward dynamic, predictive sustainability management systems that provide continuous insight into their environmental footprint, social impact, and governance effectiveness. The real-time nature of IoT-enabled monitoring allows for immediate course corrections, proactive risk management, and optimization of resource utilization that were previously impossible with conventional reporting methodologies.

As organizations increasingly recognize sustainability as a core business imperative rather than a compliance obligation, the strategic value of IoT-enabled ESG reporting will continue to grow. Companies that successfully implement these integrated systems will gain competitive advantages through enhanced operational efficiency, improved stakeholder trust, and better access to sustainable financing opportunities. The ability to provide real-time, granular data on sustainability performance will become essential for meeting evolving regulatory requirements, satisfying investor demands for transparency, and demonstrating genuine commitment to environmental and social responsibility.

Moving forward, the successful deployment of IoT-enabled smart grid technologies for ESG reporting will require sustained collaboration between technology providers, utility companies, regulatory bodies, and end-user organizations. This collaborative approach must address not only technical integration challenges but also the cultural and organizational changes necessary to fully leverage these advanced capabilities. Organizations that invest in comprehensive IoT-enabled ESG reporting systems today will be well-positioned to lead the transition toward a more sustainable, transparent, and accountable business environment, ultimately contributing to broader societal goals of environmental protection, social equity, and responsible governance.

REFERENCES

Baesmat, K. H. (2024). Impedance analysis of adaptive distance relays using machine learning. In S. Latifi (Ed.), *ITNG 2024: 21st International Conference on Information Technology–New Generations. Advances in Intelligent Systems and Computing* (Vol. 1456). Springer. DOI: 10.1007/978-3-031-56599-1_57

Baesmat, K. H., & Latifi, S. (2023). A new hybrid method for electrical load forecasting based on deviation correction and MRMRMS. In Selvaraj, H., Chmaj, G., & Zydek, D. (Eds.), *Advances in Systems Engineering* (pp. 293–303). Springer Nature., DOI: 10.1007/978-3-031-40579-2_29

Baesmat, K. H., Masoudipour, I., & Samet, H. (2021). Improving the performance of short-term load forecast using a hybrid artificial neural network and artificial bee colony algorithm. *IEEE Canadian Journal of Electrical and Computer Engineering*, *44*(3), 275–282. DOI: 10.1109/ICJECE.2021.3056125

Baesmat, K. H., Regentova, E. E., & Baghzouz, Y. (2025). A hybrid machine learning–statistical based method for short-term energy consumption prediction in residential buildings. *Energy and AI. Article*, *100552*, 100552. DOI: 10.1016/j.egyai.2025.100552

Colmenares-Quintero, R. F., Quiroga-Parra, D. J., Rojas, N., Stansfield, K. E., & Colmenares-Quintero, J. C. (2021). Big data analytics in Smart Grids for renewable energy networks: Systematic review of information and communication technology tools. *Cogent Engineering*, *8*(1), 1935410. DOI: 10.1080/23311916.2021.1935410

Do, V., McBrien, H., Flores, N. M., & Casey, J. A. (2023). Spatiotemporal distribution of power outages with climate events and social vulnerability in the USA. *Nature Communications*, *14*(1), 2470. DOI: 10.1038/s41467-023-38084-6 PMID: 37120649

Du Toit, E. (2024). Thirty years of sustainability reporting: Insights, gaps and an agenda for future research through a systematic literature review. *Sustainability (Basel)*, *16*(2310), 10750. DOI: 10.3390/su162310750

Duffey, R. B. (2019). Power restoration prediction following extreme events and disasters. *International Journal of Disaster Risk Science*, *10*(1), 134–148. DOI: 10.1007/s13753-018-0189-2

Emexidis, C., & Gkonis, P. (2024). The integration of Internet of Things and machine learning for energy prediction of wind turbines. *Applied Sciences (Basel, Switzerland)*, *14*(22), 10276. DOI: 10.3390/app142210276

Farrokhi, Z., Baesmat, K. H., & Regentova, E. E. (2024). Enhancing urban intelligence energy management: Innovative load forecasting techniques for electrical networks. *Journal of Power and Energy Engineering, 12*(11), 72–88. DOI: 10.4236/jpee.2024.1211005

Farrokhi, Z., Kalhor, A., & Masouleh, M. T. (2018). Implementation and evaluation of object identification techniques on Nao robot platform. *International Journal of Mechatronics, Electrical and Computer Technology (IJMEC), 8*(29), 3947–3958. Retrieved from https://aeuso.org/includes/files/articles/Vol8_Iss29_3947-3958_Implementation_and_Evaluation_of_Ob.pdf

Hanna, R., Heptonstall, P., & Gross, R. (2024). Job creation in a low carbon transition to renewables and energy efficiency: A review of international evidence. *Sustainability Science, 19*(1), 125–150. DOI: 10.1007/s11625-023-01440-y

Hassanpouri Baesmat, K., Farrokhi, Z., Chmaj, G., & Regentova, E. E. (2025). Parallel multi-model energy demand forecasting with cloud redundancy: Leveraging trend correction, feature selection, and machine learning. *Forecasting, 7*(2), 25. DOI: 10.3390/forecast7020025

Hassanpouri Baesmat, K., Shokoohi, F., & Farrokhi, Z. (2025). SP-RF-ARIMA: A sparse random forest and ARIMA hybrid model for electric load forecasting. *Global Energy Interconnection, 8*(3), 486–496. DOI: 10.1016/j.gloei.2025.04.003

Huang, W., Zhang, N., Kang, C., Xu, Y., & Yang, Q. (2019). From demand response to integrated demand response: Review and prospect of research and application. *Protection and Control of Modern Power Systems, 4*(1), 12. DOI: 10.1186/s41601-019-0126-4

Jamali, H. (2025). Quantum-accelerated neural imputation with large language models (LLMs) *arXiv*. /arXiv.2507.08255DOI: 10.48550

Jamali, H., Dascalu, S. M., & Harris, F. C., Jr. (2024). Fostering joint innovation: A global online platform for ideas sharing and collaboration. In *International Conference on Information Technology–New Generations* (pp. 305–312). Springer Nature. DOI: 10.1007/978-3-031-56599-1_40

Jamali, H., Dascalu, S. M., & Harris, F. C. (2024). AI-driven analysis and prediction of energy consumption in NYC's municipal buildings. In *2024 IEEE/ACIS 22nd International Conference on Software Engineering Research, Management and Applications (SERA)* (pp. 277–283). IEEE. DOI: 10.1109/SERA61261.2024.10685594

Jamali, H., Dascalu, S. M., Harris, F. C., & Feil Seifer, D. (2025). Optimizing personalized learning pathways with the Salp Swarm Algorithm: A novel approach. In *2025 IEEE 6th International Conference on Artificial Intelligence, Robotics, and Control*. IEEE. DOI: 10.1109/AIRC64931.2025.11077498

Jamali, H., Debolt, A., Dalton, H., Layosa, J., Macy, I., Shill, P., Feil Seifer, D., Harris, F., Dascalu, S., & Wu, R. (2025). FORE: A student-centered framework for accessible robotics education through simulation and interactive learning. *ASEE Annual Conference Proceedings*. Retrieved from https://par.nsf.gov/biblio/10595258

Jamali, H., Karimi, A., & Haghighizadch, M. (2018). A new method of cloud-based computation model for mobile devices: Energy consumption optimization in mobile-to-mobile computation offloading. In *Proceedings of the 6th International Conference on Communications and Broadband Networking* (pp. 32–37). ACM. DOI: 10.1145/3193092.3193103

Jamali, H., Karimi, A., & Haghighizadeh, M. (2018). A new method of cloud-based computation model for mobile devices: Energy consumption optimization in mobile-to-mobile computation offloading. In *Proceedings of the 6th International Conference on Communications and Broadband Networking* (pp. 32–37). ACM. DOI: 10.1145/3193092.3193103

Jamali, H., Shill, P. C., Feil Seifer, D., Harris, F. C., Jr., & Dascalu, S. M. (2023). A schedule of duties in the cloud space using a modified salp swarm algorithm. In *IFIP International Internet of Things Conference* (pp. 62–75). Springer Nature. DOI: 10.1007/978-3-031-45878-1_5

Jamali, H., Watson, J., Dascalu, S. M., & Harris, F. C. (2025). Harmonized data drive: Standardizing and unifying smart car information storage for enhanced forensics and interoperability. In *2025 13th International Symposium on Digital Forensics and Security (ISDFS)* (pp. 1–6). IEEE. DOI: 10.1109/ISDFS65363.2025.11012079

Kermani, A., Jamshidi, A. M., Mahdavi, Z., Dashtaki, A. A., Zand, M., Nasab, M. A., & Khan, B. (2023). Energy management system for smart grid in the presence of energy storage and photovoltaic systems. *International Journal of Photoenergy*, *2023*, 5749756. DOI: 10.1155/2023/5749756

Khasawneh, A. M., Taylor, B., & Kaiwartya, O. (2025). Innovations in air quality monitoring: Sensors, IoT and future research. *Sensors (Basel)*, *25*(7), 2070. DOI: 10.3390/s25072070 PMID: 40218583

Lamb, W. F., Wiedmann, T., Pongratz, J., Andrew, R., Crippa, M., Olivier, J. G. J., & Zi, A. C. (2021). A review of trends and drivers of greenhouse gas emissions by sector from 1990 to 2018. *Environmental Research Letters, 16*(7), 073005. DOI: 10.1088/1748-9326/abee4e

Mahdavi, Z., Samavat, T., Javanmardi, A. S. J., Dashtaki, M. A., Zand, M., Nasab, M. A., & Khan, B. (2024). Providing a control system for charging electric vehicles using ANFIS. *International Transactions on Electrical Energy Systems, 2024,* 9921062. DOI: 10.1155/2024/9921062

Padmanaban, S., Nasab, M. A., Samavat, T., Zand, M., & Nasab, M. A. (2023). Securing smart power grids against cyber-attacks. In *IoT and Analytics in Renewable Energy Systems* (Vol. 1, pp. 17–36). CRC Press., DOI: 10.1201/9781003331117

Padmanaban, S., Nasab, M. A., Samavat, T., Zand, M., & Nasab, M. A. (2023). Artificial intelligence techniques for smart power systems. In *IoT and Analytics in Renewable Energy Systems* (Vol. 1, pp. 107–123). CRC Press., DOI: 10.1201/9781003331117-9

Padmanaban, S., Nasab, M. A., Samavat, T., Zand, M., Nasab, M. A., & Hashemi, E. (2023). Cyber security in smart energy networks. In *IoT and Analytics in Renewable Energy Systems* (Vol. 2, pp. 309–325). CRC Press., DOI: 10.1201/9781003374121

Pantazi, T. (2024). The introduction of mandatory corporate sustainability reporting in the EU and the question of enforcement. *European Business Organization Law Review, 25*(3), 509–532. DOI: 10.1007/s40804-024-00320-x

Peter, G., Stonier, A. A., Gupta, P., Gavilanes, D., Vergara, M. M., & Lung sin, J. (2022). Smart fault monitoring and normalizing of a power distribution system using IoT. *Energies, 15*(21), 8206. DOI: 10.3390/en15218206

Samavat, T., Nazari, M., Fuhong, L., & Yang, L. (2025). Optimizing stand-alone PV systems: A metaheuristic-enhanced fuzzy approach for adaptive MPPT. *China Communications, 22*(1), 61–74. DOI: 10.23919/JCC.fa.2024-0224.202501

Sanjeevikumar, P., Zand, M., Nasab, M. A., Eskandari, M., Samavat, T., Jahangiri, A., & Moradi, M. H. (2023). Power electronics in smart grid. In *Smart and Power Grid Systems–Design Challenges and Paradigms* (pp. 1–20). River Publishers., DOI: 10.1201/9781003339557-2

Shmelev, S. E. S., & Gilardi, E. (2025). Corporate environmental, social, and governance performance: The impacts on financial returns, business model innovation, and social transformation. *Sustainability (Basel), 17*(3), 1286. DOI: 10.3390/su17031286

Yıldırım, F., Yalman, Y., Bayındır, K. Ç., & Terciyanlı, E. (2025). Comprehensive review of edge computing for power systems: State of the art, architecture, and applications. *Applied Sciences (Basel, Switzerland), 15*(8), 4592. DOI: 10.3390/app15084592

Chapter 13
AI for ESG Compliance in Education:
Exploring Bioethical Tensions and Institutional Responsibilities in Data-Driven Pedagogy

Spyros Kontis
https://orcid.org/0009-0009-7892-6966
University of Western Macedonia, Greece

Lamprini Seremeti
University of Western Macedonia, Greece

ABSTRACT

This chapter examines how artificial intelligence is being integrated into ESG compliance frameworks in education, raising critical ethical and psychosocial concerns. Through real and hypothetical case studies, the chapter explores how AI is used to monitor environmental impact, track indicators of inclusion, and automate governance processes. It highlights the risks of emotional surveillance, data commodification, and biased predictive systems, especially when students are not active participants in data governance. The authors propose a governance framework based on modular consent, ethical impact assessments, participatory design, and accountability mechanisms. Emphasis is placed on protecting student autonomy, emotional integrity, and the developmental mission of education. Ultimately, the chapter calls for reflexive and justice-centered approaches to AI in education, where ESG metrics do not replace pedagogy, but are aligned with human dignity and ethical responsibility

DOI: 10.4018/979-8-3373-5142-1.ch013

INTRODUCTION

In recent years, the principles of Environmental, Social, and Governance (ESG) have moved from the margins of corporate responsibility to the center of institutional accountability, extending their reach beyond business and finance into the domains of education, public health, and digital governance (Taraza et al., 2024a; 2024b). Within the educational sector, ESG compliance is no longer limited to energy-efficient buildings or equitable access to learning resources. It now encompasses a broader commitment to ethical data practices, diversity and inclusion, and transparent decision-making. Schools and universities are increasingly expected to demonstrate how their operations, curricula, and technological infrastructures align with ESG goals, as defined by both international frameworks (e.g., the UN Sustainable Development Goals) and local regulatory standards (Williamson, 2017; European Commission, 2021; Papademetriou et al., 2024; Seremeti et al., 2024 Seremeti et al., 2025a).

At the same time, artificial intelligence (AI) has emerged as a pivotal enabler of ESG strategy implementation. AI-powered systems, ranging from environmental monitoring platforms and algorithmic risk assessments to real-time analytics dashboards, offer institutions new tools for tracking ESG performance indicators with speed, granularity, and predictive capacity. In educational contexts, AI can be used to measure campus sustainability efforts (e.g., energy use, digital waste), analyze patterns of inclusion and exclusion across student populations, or monitor compliance with governance standards such as equity in admissions, transparency in resource allocation, or data protection in digital learning environments (Selwyn, 2020; Luengo-Oroz, 2019).

Yet, as with all technological interventions that promise efficiency and insight, the integration of AI into ESG frameworks brings with it significant ethical, legal, and psychosocial questions. How are data collected, categorized, and interpreted in the name of ESG? Who sets the thresholds for "compliance" or "risk"? What are the unintended consequences of predictive systems that may flag individuals or institutions as non-compliant? And how can we ensure that AI systems used to promote social good do not simultaneously introduce new forms of surveillance, algorithmic bias, or institutional opacity?

These tensions are particularly salient in education, where the stakes are not only organizational but developmental. Unlike corporate ESG reporting, which often focuses on quantifiable impacts and reputational metrics, educational ESG intersects with the emotional, cognitive, and moral formation of learners. AI systems that track attendance, monitor engagement, or assess "inclusion" via behavioral data may inadvertently create high-resolution portraits of student behavior, mental states, or socio-emotional trends, raising concerns about emotional profiling, data overreach, and the erosion of learner autonomy. Likewise, AI tools designed to assist in governance, such as automated scheduling, disciplinary decision-making, or predictive dropout analytics, may amplify inequalities if not designed with fairness and explainability in mind (Grek & Ozga, 2020).

Moreover, ESG compliance in education increasingly involves a complex web of actors: public institutions, private ed-tech vendors, cloud infrastructure providers, government agencies, and civil society watchdogs. Within this ecosystem, AI often functions as both tool and actor, facilitating data collection while shaping how compliance is defined and enforced. The educational institution, in turn, becomes a site of algorithmic governance, where decisions once made by teachers or administrators are delegated to predictive models or optimization engines. This raises critical questions about accountability: Who governs the governors? How can we ensure that AI systems uphold the ethical values that ESG standards are meant to protect?

This chapter argues that if ESG compliance is to be meaningfully supported by AI in education, it must be grounded in a robust ethical and regulatory framework that prioritizes human dignity, learner agency, and institutional transparency. Drawing from interdisciplinary sources, including AI ethics, bioethics, educational policy, and critical data studies, we will examine both the potential and the perils of AI-enhanced ESG strategies. We will consider how emotion-aware systems, biometric monitoring, and intelligent dashboards might be used not only to track compliance but to foster more inclusive, responsive, and reflective learning environments. At the same time, we will interrogate the risks of over-automation, data commodification (Anagnostopoulos & Tsitsianis, 2023), and technocratic governance (Kontis, 2025).

Ultimately, this chapter does not reject the integration of AI in ESG frameworks for education, it calls for their principled and participatory design (Floridi et al., 2018; Yeung, 2018). Just as sustainability requires more than carbon offsets, and equity more than demographic metrics, ethical AI governance in education demands more than technical safeguards. Equally administrations connects the authority of artificial intelligence (AI) as well as progressive analytics to get-up-and-go novelty by using AI cloud computing (Souravlas et al., 2022a; 2022b; 2023) and cutting-edge technologies (Souravlas & Anastasiadou 2020; 2022) due to the fact that AI tops at managing huge amounts of structured data (Souravlas et al., 2020; 2021a; 2021b; 2021c).

It requires a pedagogical commitment to transparency, consent, and dialogue; a legal infrastructure capable of adapting to affective and biometric data; and a design philosophy that treats students and educators not as data points but as co-authors of their educational futures (Seremeti & Anastasiadou, 2025).

THEORETICAL FRAMEWORK: ESG, ARTIFICIAL INTELLIGENCE, AND EDUCATIONAL ETHICS

The convergence of ESG principles with artificial intelligence in education marks a critical juncture in the evolution of digital governance and ethical pedagogy. While ESG originally emerged as a framework for sustainable and responsible investment in the corporate sector, its underlying principles, environmental stewardship, social justice, and institutional integrity, are increasingly applied to non-commercial settings, including public education. In this new context, ESG is not only about carbon footprints and board diversity, but also about inclusive learning environments, equitable access to digital infrastructure, and transparent, accountable decision-making processes within schools and universities.

AI, for its part, is positioned as both a facilitator and a disruptor of ESG-aligned education. On the one hand, AI technologies can process vast amounts of institutional data to identify inefficiencies, inequities, or environmental concerns. They can detect patterns of absenteeism, analyze disparities in performance across demographics, monitor building energy usage, and even assist in the ethical allocation of educational resources. On the other hand, the same systems can perpetuate bias, obscure accountability, and generate new forms of digital exclusion particularly when they are trained on incomplete or unrepresentative datasets, or when deployed without adequate ethical safeguards.

To understand this dynamic, we must situate the intersection of ESG and AI within three overlapping theoretical lenses: (1) AI ethics and algorithmic accountability, (2) educational governance and equity, and (3) bioethics and psychosocial well-being.

AI Ethics and Algorithmic Accountability

AI ethics provides a foundational lens for evaluating the moral and political implications of algorithmic systems used in ESG contexts. Key principles, such as transparency, fairness, explainability, and accountability, are essential when AI is used to assess or enforce ESG compliance in education. For instance, predictive algorithms that evaluate student "risk" for dropout or disengagement must be interrogated for potential biases, especially if they disproportionately flag students from marginalized backgrounds. Similarly, AI-driven dashboards that visualize ESG metrics may inadvertently obscure the subjectivity of data classification, leading to technocratic interpretations of social or environmental "performance."

Algorithmic accountability becomes particularly relevant when AI systems are embedded in decision-making processes (Seremeti et al., 2025b). Who is responsible when an AI system flags a student as non-compliant with behavioral norms tied to ESG "social" goals? What recourse exists for students or educators who contest algorithmic judgments? How do we ensure that the logic of optimization, so central to AI design does not override the deliberative, contextualized decision-making that education requires? (Kontis, 2025; Seremeti 2015a; 2025b).

Scholars such as Crawford (2021), Mittelstadt et al. (2016), and Floridi et al. (2018) have warned against the "epistemic opacity" of AI systems: their ability to produce outcomes that are difficult to audit or contest. In educational ESG contexts, such opacity can undermine both procedural justice and substantive fairness, especially when AI outputs are used to justify funding, policy interventions, or student categorization. Therefore, any integration of AI into ESG systems must be grounded in strong accountability mechanisms, including human oversight, independent auditability, and rights to explanation and appeal.

Educational Governance and Equity

From an educational policy perspective, ESG represents a new model of institutional self-regulation, one that aligns educational goals with wider societal values. In this framework, governance is not limited to administrative structures, but extends to the systems and technologies that mediate how decisions are made, enforced, and experienced. AI becomes a tool of governance when it structures (Seremeti, 2015c; Seremeti, et al., 2025a) how student performance is monitored, how teacher evaluations are generated, or how inclusivity is measured.

Yet, education is a domain deeply embedded in questions of equity, power, and human development. The deployment of AI in this space, especially for ESG monitoring, must reckon with the risks of reproducing structural inequalities under the guise of neutral automation. Research in critical pedagogy (Giroux, 2011) and sociology of education (Freire, 1970; Giroux, 2011; Selwyn, 2019) has long emphasized that metrics-based accountability systems often reinforce rather than disrupt systemic injustices. If ESG dashboards (Grek & Ozga, 2010) in education track racial, gender, or socio-economic disparities without accompanying structural interventions, they risk turning social inequity into a data point rather than a site of action.

Moreover, the "governance" function of AI must not erode the relational and dialogical dimensions of education. Metrics may help institutions identify areas of non-compliance, but they cannot replace the interpretive, context-sensitive work of educators, counselors, and students themselves. A truly equitable ESG framework must therefore include mechanisms for participatory design (Floridi et al., 2018; Yeung, 2018), local adaptation, and ethical contestation (Seremeti & Anastasiadou, 2025).

Bioethics and Psychosocial Integrity

Finally, a bioethical perspective is crucial when AI systems in ESG monitoring begin to intersect with student behavior, mental health, or biometric data. For example, AI platforms that monitor classroom engagement via eye tracking or facial expression analysis may be introduced under the ESG category of "social well-being" or "inclusive learning." However, these systems often collect intimate data about emotional states or neurocognitive patterns, raising serious concerns about bodily privacy, informed consent, and the psychological effects of constant monitoring.

Drawing from the four core bioethical principles, autonomy, beneficence, non-maleficence, and justice, we can evaluate whether such systems truly serve the learner. Autonomy is challenged when students are unaware of how their data is collected or used; non-maleficence is compromised if systems misclassify affective signals and trigger unnecessary interventions; justice is undermined when emotional models fail to account for neurodiversity or cultural variation; and beneficence is questionable if the emotional data is ultimately used for institutional optimization rather than learner well-being.

Psychosocial well-being must be treated not as a collateral benefit of ESG strategies, but as a central ethical commitment. Emotional profiling, surveillance fatigue, and identity regulation are all potential side-effects of AI-powered ESG compliance systems. Without safeguards such as modular consent (UNESCO, 2021; European Commission, 2021), transparency dashboards, and user-controlled feedback, these systems risk transforming education into a field of silent surveillance rather than engaged learning.

Critical Perspectives on ESG and AI

While ESG frameworks are typically framed in neutral or progressive terms, critical scholarship has drawn attention to the ideological and structural underpinnings of how ESG is operationalized through digital technologies. Scholars in critical data studies argue that the increasing datafication of education, where learning, identity, and behavior are reduced to measurable indicators, risks reinforcing technocratic rationality at the expense of pedagogical nuance (Williamson, 2017; Selwyn, 2020).

Algorithmic systems used for ESG tracking may embed neoliberal values such as efficiency, accountability, and performance benchmarking, shaping educational priorities through logics of quantification. This has led some to describe ESG-aligned platforms as enablers of "compliance-by-design", systems that not only monitor institutional behavior but subtly guide it toward predefined metrics of success. Such frameworks often privilege what can be counted over what matters, marginalizing affective, relational, and context-dependent dimensions of education.

Moreover, ESG initiatives mediated through AI risk reproducing power asymmetries between global North and South. The push for ESG compliance in international education contexts often reflects technocolonial assumptions, where standardized models of "good governance" are imposed through platforms built in high-income countries. These tools may fail to accommodate local pedagogical traditions, linguistic diversity, or culturally specific understandings of well-being and equity.

Therefore, a critical theoretical lens demands not only ethical safeguards but epistemic humility, a recognition that AI-enhanced ESG systems are not neutral instruments but sociotechnical assemblages shaped by political, historical, and cultural forces (see Anastasiadou et al., 2025).

Together, these theoretical strands form the ethical backbone of our inquiry: AI in ESG-aligned education must be transparent, fair, participatory, and psychologically safe. ESG goals cannot be achieved through technological enforcement alone; they must be contextualized, dialogical, and grounded in care for the communities they aim to support.

The next chapter will explore how these principles translate into real-world applications of AI for ESG compliance in education, examining current systems, emerging technologies, and the challenges of responsible design (Zuboff, 2019; Yeung, 2018).

AI FOR ESG COMPLIANCE IN PRACTICE

While ESG frameworks are often associated with corporate sustainability reporting, their adoption in education requires the development of new metrics, methods, and infrastructures that reflect the complexity of educational environments. Artificial intelligence (AI) is increasingly central to this process. In schools and university.

Environmental Monitoring and Sustainability Metrics

AI systems are increasingly used by educational institutions to monitor and optimize environmental performance. Smart campus initiatives integrate Internet of Things (IoT) sensors, AI-powered analytics, and automated control systems to track electricity consumption, HVAC efficiency, water usage, and waste management. Machine learning algorithms process these data streams to detect anomalies, predict energy demand, and suggest adaptive measures for environmental conservation.

For instance, an AI system may identify peak usage hours in university buildings and autonomously adjust lighting and heating to reduce carbon output, aligning with the "E" in ESG. Similarly, AI dashboards may provide real-time visualizations of carbon footprints or generate sustainability performance reports for internal or public consumption.

While these tools offer operational efficiency and enhance institutional transparency, their implementation is not ethically neutral. The deployment of environmental sensors in classrooms and dormitories can raise privacy concerns, especially when combined with behavioral analytics (e.g., motion tracking or occupancy prediction). Furthermore, the environmental benefits of AI systems must be weighed against their own resource demands, including the energy costs of cloud computing, data storage, and training of large-scale machine learning models.

To maintain ethical alignment with ESG principles, environmental AI systems must follow green design principles, minimize data collection to necessity, and communicate their functions transparently to the educational community (Souravlas et al., 2021b).

Social Inclusion and Equity Analytics

The "S" in ESG—social inclusion—has gained renewed urgency post-COVID-19, as digital divides and socio-economic disparities have deepened educational inequities. AI offers potential to identify and address these through analysis of large-scale data, including demographics, engagement, and behavioral patterns (Souravlas et al., 2023). Predictive analytics platforms now flag signs of dropout risk or social isolation using LMS data, attendance, and even biometric inputs. Natural Language Processing can detect distress in student communications, informing timely interventions.

While promising, such tools raise ethical concerns. They may reduce student complexity to risk scores and amplify biases embedded in historical data (Seremeti et al., 2025; Binns, 2018). Marginalized groups are often over-flagged, risking stigma and soft surveillance. Without fairness audits and co-designed safeguards, these systems can reinforce exclusion rather than inclusion.

True equity requires transparent, participatory AI design that empowers students, respects autonomy, and aligns ESG efforts with justice-oriented, inclusive educational values.

Governance, Transparency, and Institutional Integrity

The governance component of ESG in education pertains to how institutions manage decision-making, data governance, stakeholder accountability, and ethical leadership. AI has emerged as a governance tool through its ability to track institutional compliance with regulations, automate administrative processes, and increase procedural transparency. (UNESCO, 2021; European Commission, 2021) (Floridi et al., 2018; Williamson, 2017; UNESCO, 2021).

For example, AI chatbots may be used to manage student complaints or appeals, automating initial responses and categorizing issues for escalation. Natural language generation (NLG) tools may produce institutional reports on diversity metrics, curriculum audits, or board meeting summaries. Blockchain-integrated ledgers may be employed to track funding allocations or procurement chains, reducing opportunities for corruption or mismanagement.

These developments can enhance procedural integrity and reduce bureaucratic burden. Yet, they also shift the locus of authority from human decision-makers to algorithmic systems, sometimes with limited explainability or accountability. In governance contexts, the opacity of AI models may obscure biases, prevent contestation, or undermine the right to due process.

Furthermore, the deployment of AI in governance often reinforces a technocratic view of education, as a system of inputs and outputs to be optimized, rather than as a site of ethical formation and democratic deliberation. When compliance is monitored through automated scoring systems or KPIs without space for qualitative judgment, institutions risk privileging efficiency over ethical reasoning.

Responsible AI governance in education thus requires hybrid models (Anastasiadou et al., 2025): combining machine-generated insights with human-led deliberation, ensuring that institutional decisions remain subject to contestation, interpretation, and moral reflection (Floridi et al., 2018; Mittelstadt et al., 2016).

Cross-Cutting Risks and Design Considerations

Across the domains of environmental monitoring, social inclusion analytics, and governance automation, several cross-cutting risks emerge that challenge the ethical foundations of AI-driven ESG strategies in education (Anagnostopoulos & Tsitsianis, 2023).

First among these is the **opacity and lack of explainability** in algorithmic decisions, which undermines accountability and impedes users' ability to challenge or interpret system outputs. Closely related is the issue of **data commodification**, particularly when ESG platforms are built and maintained by private vendors whose interests may not align with pedagogical or ethical priorities.

Another critical risk is **mission drift**, the tendency of institutions to treat ESG as a compliance checklist for reputational gain, rather than as a transformative framework grounded in care, justice, and systemic change (Freire, 1970; Giroux, 2011). In such cases, AI systems may reinforce superficial performance indicators while failing to address deeper structural inequities.

Equally concerning is the emergence of **emotional and behavioral profiling**, especially when surveillance mechanisms are subtle or concealed. These practices risk normalizing a culture of affective monitoring, where students are nudged to conform to institutional norms under the guise of inclusion or well-being. Finally, many systems still lack robust **consent structures**, particularly for minors, relying on blanket institutional agreements rather than developmentally appropriate, modular consent (UNESCO, 2021; European Commission, 2021).

These risks do not invalidate the potential of AI in ESG-aligned education. Rather, they underscore the need for **ethical foresight**, **participatory design**, and **continuous evaluation**. Responsible implementation must include transparency dashboards, redress mechanisms, and cultural adaptation features tailored to diverse student populations (Williamson & Piattoeva, 2022). Without such safeguards, AI may optimize for compliance while neglecting the very communities it aims to serve.

AI for ESG Curriculum and Climate Literacy

An emerging and increasingly influential frontier in AI-enhanced ESG compliance is the integration of sustainability education and ethical governance directly into the curriculum (Williamson, 2017; Selwyn, 2020; Kalogera et al., 2025). Rather than merely tracking institutional ESG metrics, AI systems are now being deployed to foster climate literacy, ethical awareness, and civic responsibility among students.

Adaptive learning platforms, for example, personalize instruction on topics such as climate science, environmental ethics, and the United Nations' Sustainable Development Goals (SDGs). These systems analyze engagement patterns and student responses to tailor content on complex subjects like carbon cycles, water preservation, or ethical consumption. Meanwhile, gamified simulations, powered by reinforcement learning, enable students to explore the real-world consequences of different environmental policies, linking cognitive learning with affective engagement.

From a compliance perspective, such platforms provide evidence that institutions are addressing both the "S" and "E" dimensions of ESG. However, ethical tensions remain. Personalized instruction on normative issues like climate ethics must avoid becoming ideologically prescriptive or enforcing narrow worldviews. There is also the risk of depoliticizing climate action, reducing systemic and collective struggles into individual behavioral nudges, which shift responsibility from policy to the personal.

To navigate these tensions, AI systems designed for ESG education must be transparent, dialogical, and inclusive. They should invite students not only to absorb knowledge but to critically examine, discuss, and contest the values embedded in the systems themselves. In this way, ESG curriculum becomes not a site of indoctrination, but a space for ethical deliberation and democratic participation.

In sum, AI technologies hold significant potential for advancing ESG objectives in education, but only if their design and deployment are guided by a robust ethical framework. Such a framework must prioritize student dignity, institutional accountability, and the pedagogical values that define education **not as optimization, but as human development** (see Anastasiadou et al., 2025).

ETHICAL AND LEGAL IMPLICATIONS OF AI-DRIVEN ESG COMPLIANCE IN EDUCATION

As AI-powered systems are increasingly integrated into ESG strategies within educational settings, they introduce new layers of ethical complexity and regulatory ambiguity. While these technologies are designed to support sustainability, inclusion, and institutional accountability, their deployment often reconfigures the relationships between learners, educators, institutions, and data infrastructures in ways that necessitate careful ethical and legal scrutiny.

This chapter explores the multidimensional implications of AI-enhanced ESG compliance in education through three intersecting lenses: (1) bioethics and student dignity, (2) data governance and consent, and (3) legal tensions and regulatory gaps (European Commission, 2021; UNESCO, 2021). These perspectives highlight that ESG implementation through AI is not merely a matter of technological optimization, but rather a process of ethical negotiation and normative system design (Yeung, 2018; GDPR, 2016; Luengo-Oroz, 2019; Mittelstadt et al., 2016).

Bioethics and the Protection of Learner Dignity

At the heart of educational ethics lies the commitment to preserving the dignity, autonomy, and developmental integrity of learners, especially children and adolescents. However, many AI-driven ESG systems operate through forms of behavioral tracking, biometric sensing, and emotion-aware analytics that penetrate deeply into the learner's internal world. When ESG compliance becomes linked to affective signals, engagement metrics, or social behavior classifications, the line between supportive intervention and intrusive surveillance becomes blurred.

Drawing from the core principles of bioethics, autonomy, non-maleficence, beneficence, and justice, several concerns emerge:

Autonomy is compromised when students are unaware of how their data is collected, processed, or interpreted, especially **when emotional or behavioral nudges occur without explicit awareness** or informed choice (Crawford, 2021; Luengo-Oroz, 2019; Anastasiadou & Seremeti, L, 2025).

Non-maleficence is challenged when AI misclassifies student emotions or behavior, leading to inappropriate interventions or false labeling (e.g., marking a focused but neurodivergent student as "disengaged").

Justice is endangered when AI systems reflect or reinforce structural inequalities, disproportionately flagging students from marginalized communities for "non-compliance." Beneficence becomes ambiguous when the intended good (e.g., better inclusion, energy efficiency) comes at the cost of **psychological safety**, emotional authenticity, or relational pedagogy.

Educational environments must not become laboratories of soft coercion (Crawford, 2021), where AI systems subtly reshape student behavior toward ESG-aligned norms without room for contestation or diversity of expression. Ethical ESG compliance must be built on practices that empower students (Seremeti & Anastasiadou, 2025), not discipline them via invisible metrics (Floridi et al., 2018; Williamson, 2017; UNESCO, 2021).

Data Governance, Consent, and Institutional Responsibility

The expansive data infrastructures required for AI-enhanced ESG compliance raise pressing questions concerning data ownership, consent architecture, and institutional accountability. While educational institutions typically function as stewards of student data, many of the AI systems they rely upon are developed, hosted, or maintained by third-party vendors, whose operational interests may not align with the ethical or pedagogical values of education.

A significant number of ESG platforms operate with **minimal transparency**. In many cases, neither students nor educators are fully informed about what types of data are being collected, ranging from physiological signals and clickstream patterns to emotional sentiment analysis, or how that data is processed, retained, and shared. Access to this information is often unclear: internal administrators, external partners, and even data brokers may all have varying degrees of visibility and control. Furthermore, the **legal frameworks** under which this data is stored and used are frequently opaque, particularly in international or cloud-based systems.

Traditional models of consent, such as general terms of service or one-time parental signatures, are inadequate for the ethical complexities and sensitivities involved in ESG-oriented AI systems. Especially when such systems perform continuous inference on emotional states or behavioral patterns, what is required is modular, revocable, and developmentally appropriate consent. Students and their families must understand not only what is being collected, but why, how, and with what potential implications. Consent must shift from being a static legal checkbox to an ongoing ethical relationship between users, institutions, and technologies.

To ensure ethical integrity, institutions must also establish **clear data boundaries** (GDPR, 2016; Luengo-Oroz, 2019). ESG-related data must never be repurposed for secondary uses, such as marketing, academic profiling, or behavioral scoring, without explicit, contextual, and meaningful consent. Emotional and biometric data, in particular, should be treated as **high-sensitivity information**, deserving of protections equivalent to those applied to medical records.

In short, responsible data governance in AI-driven ESG systems requires more than compliance. It requires relational accountability, transparency by design, and an unwavering respect for the dignity of learners in every layer of the data lifecycle.

Legal Ambiguity and the Challenge of Emerging Regulations

From a legal perspective, AI-driven ESG systems in education often operate within a regulatory gray zone. Most existing data protection frameworks, such as FERPA in the United States or the GDPR in the European Union, were not developed with the nuances of affective computing, predictive analytics, or ESG-specific governance structures in mind. As a result, these systems expose several regulatory blind spots, raising fundamental questions about legality, jurisdiction, and institutional responsibility (European Commission, 2021; UNESCO, 2021).

One critical issue is scope creep: **systems initially introduced for targeted tasks**, such as engagement monitoring or resource tracking, may gradually expand into broader compliance surveillance, without renewed consent or transparent disclosure. Relatedly, function ambiguity allows ESG technologies to be framed as neutral infrastructure, while concealing evaluative, behavioral, or disciplinary capabilities that might otherwise warrant stricter regulatory scrutiny.

Jurisdictional complexity compounds these challenges, particularly as cloud-based ESG platforms often process sensitive educational data across multiple legal territories. This creates difficulties in ensuring legal interoperability, especially within federated systems of education where data sovereignty, local policy, and cross-border regulation intersect.

Finally, even within robust legal instruments such as the GDPR, there remain **inadequate protections for minors**, especially when consent is institutionally mediated rather than individually informed. As a result, the ethical vulnerability of children and adolescents may go unaddressed, despite their heightened exposure to behavioral and emotional monitoring.

In response to these gaps, new regulatory initiatives are emerging. The European Union's AI Act, for instance, introduces a risk-based framework that explicitly classifies educational AI systems as "high-risk." However, the operational definition of "education" within such legislation often remains vague, leaving institutions uncertain about their obligations and increasing the likelihood of uneven enforcement.

To navigate this uncertainty, a dual-principal approach is essential. First, a precautionary regulatory posture must be adopted: AI technologies designed for ESG compliance in high-stakes contexts, such as student profiling or behavioral nudging, should not be deployed until robust legal safeguards, oversight mechanisms, and transparency requirements are firmly in place. Second, institutions must embrace participatory governance. Stakeholders, including educators, students, parents, and civil society actors, should be meaningfully involved in shaping how ESG-related data is collected, interpreted, and acted upon.

Only by combining regulatory vigilance with democratic deliberation can educational institutions ensure that AI-driven ESG frameworks operate in service of both legal compliance and ethical integrity.

Toward an Ethical and Legal Framework for AI-Driven ESG

To harmonize the benefits of AI with the ethical imperatives of ESG, educational institutions must adopt integrated governance architectures that go beyond compliance. These should include:

- Ethics committees to review AI systems and align them with ESG policies.
- Impact assessments that evaluate not only privacy, but also psychosocial and developmental risks.
- Algorithmic audits to identify and address opacity, bias, and unintended consequences.
- Student rights charters that clearly define boundaries for emotional, biometric, or behavioral surveillance.
- Transparent reporting mechanisms that document how ESG data influence institutional decisions and educational practices.

Rather than treating ESG as a bureaucratic obligation or reputational exercise, institutions should embrace it as a framework for ethical innovation, an opportunity to reimagine how data, AI, and pedagogy can collaboratively support human flourishing, learner agency, and institutional integrity.

CASE STUDIES AND PILOT APPLICATIONS OF AI IN ESG-ALIGNED EDUCATION

Translating ESG principles into actionable educational practice through artificial intelligence remains an evolving and uneven process. While some institutions have launched ambitious programs to integrate AI into sustainability, inclusion, and governance strategies, others are experimenting with smaller-scale interventions. This chapter presents a set of illustrative case studies, both real and hypothetical, that illuminate the promises, limitations, and ethical tensions of AI-driven ESG implementation in education.

Each case is analyzed through the ethical lens developed in previous chapters, emphasizing learner autonomy, data governance, and psychosocial well-being.

Smart Campus Systems for Environmental Optimization

Case

A European university implements an AI-powered smart campus platform that integrates IoT sensors, machine learning, and predictive analytics to manage building energy consumption. The system continuously monitors room occupancy, ambient temperature, lighting, and HVAC patterns in order to optimize energy efficiency and reduce carbon emissions. A public-facing ESG dashboard visualizes these efforts in real time, supporting compliance with EU Green Campus standards and signaling institutional transparency.

Analysis

This initiative exemplifies the "E" in ESG, leveraging AI to fulfill environmental sustainability goals. However, ethical concerns arise when environmental monitoring inadvertently encroaches on student behavior. For instance, sensors tracking classroom occupancy or motion patterns may unintentionally disclose attendance habits, study routines, or sleep cycles in dormitories. In the absence of clear boundaries and transparency protocols, such platforms risk functioning as covert surveillance mechanisms.

Moreover, while environmental data may initially appear non-sensitive, its aggregation with behavioral indicators can generate unintended inferences about students' well-being or private habits. To align with ESG values, principles of data minimization, proportionality, and informed consent must be embedded into system design—not applied retroactively as legal fixes.

Equity Analytics in Secondary Schools

Case

A large public school district in the United States adopts an AI-based equity monitoring platform to detect disparities in student engagement and performance across race, gender, and income lines. The system aggregates data from digital learning platforms, attendance logs, and standardized assessments, generating automated "equity alerts" when specific subgroups fall below district-defined benchmarks.

Educators receive monthly disaggregated reports accompanied by algorithmically generated intervention suggestions, such as targeted tutoring programs or curriculum revisions. The project is publicly promoted as an initiative in socially responsible, data-driven governance.

Analysis

While this system is positioned as a tool to advance equity, it simultaneously risks reinforcing deficit-based narratives and predictive stigmatization. Marginalized students may be disproportionately flagged, perpetuating perceptions of vulnerability or failure without addressing the underlying structural causes of exclusion.

Additionally, the system's reliance on legacy data sources, particularly standardized test scores, may replicate existing biases. The institutional imperative to "close equity gaps" through quantifiable metrics can encourage performative inclusion at the expense of meaningful, transformative change.

Critically, there is limited evidence that flagged students or their communities are invited to interpret or contest the system's findings, an omission that violates the tenets of participatory data ethics. For equity analytics to serve truly emancipatory purposes, affected groups must become co-designers of both metrics and interventions—not passive subjects of automated classification.

AI-Assisted Governance in Higher Education

Case

A private university in Asia deploys an AI-driven governance suite designed to automate key administrative functions, including course scheduling, resource distribution, and internal audits. The system leverages natural language processing (NLP) to analyze institutional policy documents and student feedback, generating real-time recommendations aimed at promoting diversity and accessibility across academic programs.

An integrated ESG reporting tool compiles periodic transparency reports, which are shared with internal stakeholders and external regulatory bodies to demonstrate institutional alignment with governance standards.

Analysis

This case exemplifies the potential of AI to enhance the "G" in ESG by promoting institutional transparency, procedural consistency, and efficiency. However, the automation of governance also introduces critical concerns regarding procedural justice, decision legitimacy, and institutional inclusivity.

For instance, if course offerings are adjusted primarily on the basis of algorithmic predictions of student "demand," there is a risk that minority-interest subjects, niche disciplines, or interdisciplinary programs may be systematically deprioritized. Similarly, when student complaints are categorized and escalated through sentiment analysis, emotional tone may be overemphasized at the expense of substantive content, potentially distorting issue prioritization.

Moreover, such AI systems often lack formal mechanisms for contestation, transparency, or human interpretability. As a result, decisions that significantly impact academic life may become inscrutable, unchallengeable, or overly technocratic. ESG-aligned governance must therefore transcend algorithmic dashboards and KPIs; it should incorporate spaces for narrative reasoning, ethical reflection, and democratic deliberation.

Without these safeguards, the governance function of AI risks reducing educational institutions to compliance machines—efficient, but ethically hollow. Responsible design must ensure that AI augments rather than replaces the human judgment, cultural sensitivity, and dialogical openness that define meaningful academic governance.

Hypothetical: AI-Powered Inclusion Monitor in a Primary School

Scenario

A primary school pilots a wearable AI device designed to monitor students' movement, vocal tone, and interpersonal proximity during recess. The stated goal is to assess social inclusion by identifying children who appear isolated or excluded from group interactions. The system sends real-time alerts to teachers when patterns of social withdrawal are detected, and parents receive weekly "inclusion scores" as part of progress reports. The school frames this initiative as a contribution to ESG-aligned social responsibility (UNESCO, 2021) and student well-being.

Analysis

Despite good intentions, this scenario raises profound ethical concerns. The reduction of social inclusion to quantifiable behavioral metrics oversimplifies the richness and complexity of children's interpersonal dynamics. Introverted, neurodivergent, or culturally distinct students may be inaccurately flagged as "isolated," leading to intrusive or unnecessary interventions that pathologize difference.

Furthermore, the system risks normalizing emotional surveillance, encouraging students to perform sociability in order to comply with algorithmic expectations. When such behavior is monitored and interpreted through opaque, black-box algorithms, it can undermine psychological safety, erode autonomy, and foster mistrust between students and educators.

To ethically align with ESG principles, systems of this kind must include robust safeguards:

- Student and guardian participation in design and oversight
- Clear, developmentally appropriate opt-out options
- Transparent feedback loops and pedagogical integration
- Protection against emotional profiling and behavior scoring

Without these elements, efforts to promote inclusion risk becoming counterproductive, substituting algorithmic conformity for genuine community-building.

Synthesis and Emerging Themes

Across these case studies, a consistent pattern emerges:

- AI systems can indeed help operationalize ESG goals—but often at the cost of interpretive nuance, student autonomy, and emotional integrity (Freire, 1970; Mittelstadt et al., 2016).
- Ethical tensions frequently arise when quantitative metrics (Williamson, 2017; Selwyn, 2020) displace qualitative understanding and contextual judgment.
- Many ESG-aligned platforms rely on a logic of behavioral optimization, subtly nudging students to conform to institutional targets rather than empowering them to learn and grow meaningfully.
- Feedback loops that allow learners and educators to contest algorithmic outputs or co-define success criteria are rare, limiting opportunities for critical engagement.

Ultimately, responsible AI integration in ESG education demands more than dashboards and performance scores. It requires a relational ethics of co-design, reflexivity, and democratic accountability. Systems must be designed not only to monitor and optimize, but to support dialogue, diversity, and shared ownership of educational values.

AI-Guided ESG Certification Systems

Case

A network of private universities partners with an international ESG certification body to develop an AI-driven platform that evaluates institutional ESG compliance. The platform aggregates data from various systems—learning management platforms, HR records, energy dashboards, and community engagement logs—and benchmarks institutions against ESG key performance indicators.

Using natural language processing, the system analyzes policy documents and strategic plans for alignment with ESG criteria. It also performs sentiment analysis on student feedback and stakeholder surveys to assess perceived ethical governance.

Analysis

This system reflects a shift toward external, AI-mediated ESG evaluation, where compliance is not only self-reported but independently verified through automated scrutiny. On one hand, this approach offers scalability, objectivity, and a mechanism for holding institutions accountable beyond internal narratives. On the other hand, it introduces risks of standardization bias (Selwyn, 2020), where context-specific nuances are lost in translation to global ESG rubrics.

Moreover, the system's reliance on unstructured data (e.g., narratives, testimonials, meeting minutes) raises concerns about the interpretation of complex meaning through statistical proxies. Institutions may also be incentivized to curate or sanitize their data to meet expected benchmarks, an ethical tension between transparency and reputational risk management.

As such, AI-guided ESG certification should complement, not replace, qualitative audits, community engagement, and democratic deliberation on what ethical education should look like in diverse settings.

GOVERNANCE GUIDELINES AND DESIGN RECOMMENDATIONS

As AI systems become increasingly embedded in educational ESG compliance frameworks, the need for robust ethical governance becomes both urgent and structural. Governance in this context does not simply refer to institutional oversight or legal compliance, it refers to the normative architectures through which power is exercised, values are encoded, and agency is negotiated among students, educators, developers, and institutions.

This chapter outlines a set of governance principles and design recommendations that aim to ensure AI-driven ESG systems in education uphold learner dignity, institutional transparency, and democratic accountability. Drawing from the fields of AI ethics, educational philosophy, and data justice, we propose a human-centered model of governance organized around six pillars:

Modular Consent and Transparent Data Practices

Consent in educational AI systems must not be reduced to a one-time legal formality; rather, it should be understood as a dynamic, continuous, and context-sensitive process. This is especially critical in ESG-aligned applications where data collection may involve highly sensitive biometric, emotional, or behavioral information. In such cases, students and their guardians must retain **granular, ongoing control** over what data is collected, when it is collected, and how it is used.

Recommendations

- **Implement modular consent architectures** (UNESCO, 2021; European Commission, 2021) that allow users to selectively opt in or out of specific data streams, such as facial recognition, vocal tone analysis, or geolocation tracking, rather than granting blanket permissions.
- **Deploy just-in-time prompts** that notify students when a new type of data collection or AI-mediated inference is initiated. These prompts should be contextual, age-appropriate, and easy to understand.
- **Provide real-time transparency dashboards** where both students and educators can view what data has been collected, how it is being interpreted, and what institutional actions are triggered as a result.
- **Enforce strict purpose limitation** by ensuring that ESG-related data is never repurposed for secondary objectives, such as academic profiling, behavioral scoring, or marketing analytics by third-party vendors.

By embedding modular consent and transparency mechanisms into the design of ESG systems, educational institutions can shift from a model of passive data extraction to one of **relational accountability**, fostering trust, clarity, and shared responsibility in the digital learning environment.

Ethical Impact Assessments and Risk Mapping

The deployment of AI systems in ESG-aligned education must be preceded by comprehensive ethical evaluations that extend far beyond conventional privacy impact assessments. These evaluations should address the **full spectrum of potential harms**, including psychosocial, cultural, developmental, and pedagogical risks. A system may comply with data protection laws and still undermine autonomy, equity, or emotional safety if not assessed through a broader ethical lens.

Recommendations

- **Adopt Ethical AI Impact Assessments (EAII)** that systematically examine risks related to learner autonomy, algorithmic bias, emotional well-being (Freire, 1970; Mittelstadt et al., 2016), and **epistemic justice**, the right of all learners to be recognized as knowers, regardless of their cognitive or cultural differences (Floridi et al., 2018).
- **Conduct vulnerable group analysis** to identify and anticipate disproportionate effects on marginalized populations, including students from racialized, neurodivergent, disabled, or economically disadvantaged backgrounds. Such analysis should inform both system design and institutional safeguards.
- **Require pre-deployment testing in authentic or simulated educational settings**, incorporating opt-in participation and structured feedback from students, educators, and caregivers. This participatory testing phase helps identify unintended consequences before they are institutionalized.

Ethical assessments should not be viewed as bureaucratic checklists, but as **ongoing, reflective processes** that accompany the lifecycle of AI systems, from design to deployment and beyond. Only through such multidimensional scrutiny can educational institutions ensure that AI enhances, rather than erodes, the moral and pedagogical fabric of schooling.

Participatory Design and Educational Co-Governance

Many of the most consequential ethical failures in educational technology arise not from flawed algorithms, but from the lack of genuine participation by those most affected. When learners and educators are excluded from design and governance processes, the resulting systems often fail to reflect the values, needs, and realities of educational communities. In the context of AI-ESG systems, participatory co-governance is essential, not as a symbolic inclusion, but as a structural principle (Floridi et al., 2018; Williamson, 2017; UNESCO, 2021).

To achieve this, institutions should establish multi-stakeholder governance bodies that include students, teachers, caregivers, data scientists, and ethicists. These bodies must be empowered to guide decisions around AI deployment, risk assessment, and ethical safeguards.

Beyond formal representation, participation must be embedded in daily institutional practices. Students, for example, should be involved in drafting AI rights charters, documents that define their boundaries and protections regarding data use, surveillance, and algorithmic profiling. Such charters not only inform policy but also foster digital agency and ethical literacy.

Equally important are reflexive feedback mechanisms, such as open forums, workshops, or review cycles, where users can raise concerns, suggest design changes, or challenge algorithmic decisions. These practices shift governance from static compliance to **ongoing, democratic negotiation**.

True participatory governance treats students and educators not as data points or passive recipients, but as **co-authors** of the technological infrastructures that shape their educational futures.

Reflexive Systems and Corrective Feedback Mechanisms

AI systems in education must not only act upon users, they must also remain open to correction, interpretation, and dialogue. **Reflexivity** is a foundational ethical principle, ensuring that when systems misclassify, misinterpret, or fall out of alignment with pedagogical realities, those affected can meaningfully respond.

To support this, educational technologies should include **real-time correction interfaces** that allow students to contextualize system inferences. A learner flagged as "disengaged" might clarify: *"I wasn't disengaged—I was tired after a family emergency."* Such interactions restore narrative agency and reduce the risk of reductive profiling.

Equally vital is the role of educators. Teachers must be able to override or reinterpret AI-generated suggestions, especially during evaluation, classroom management, or intervention planning. Human judgment must not be sidelined by algorithmic certainty, particularly when dealing with affective or behavioral data.

Finally, systems must maintain transparent audit trails, logs that record how emotional or behavioral data were interpreted, what institutional decisions followed, and whether human input altered outcomes. These records support not only accountability, but also continuous learning and system improvement.

Without such reflexive mechanisms, AI risks becoming a one-way mirror, observing and shaping behavior without offering users a voice. Ethical governance demands that educational AI listens, adapts, and remains open to the lived realities of those it seeks to support.

Limitations on Scope, Memory, and Reuse

AI systems that monitor ESG-related behavior or affective states must operate within clearly defined temporal and functional boundaries. Without such limits, they risk expanding beyond their original intent, undermining ethical safeguards and institutional trust.

One key requirement is the application of **data expiry protocols**: biometric or emotional data should be retained only for short periods, and only when explicit, well-informed consent has been obtained, especially if the data is to be used for research purposes (GDPR, 2016; UNESCO, 2021).

Another essential principle is **purpose limitation**. ESG-related data should never be repurposed for disciplinary, promotional, or evaluative decisions unless there is robust human oversight and clear contextual justification (Floridi et al., 2018). Data collected to support inclusion or sustainability goals must not silently inform unrelated institutional outcomes.

Furthermore, institutions must prevent **cross-contextual reuse**. Information gathered in one pedagogical setting, for example, from a mindfulness or well-being app, should not be used to evaluate academic performance, behavioral compliance, or institutional fit (Williamson, 2017; Smyrnaios, 2023). Educational data must remain anchored to its original purpose, context, and ethical framing.

Alignment with Pedagogical Ethics and Educational Values

Perhaps the most pressing challenge in AI-ESG governance is ensuring that systems uphold, rather than undermine, the **relational, dialogical, and developmental ethos** of education. If left unchecked, AI tools may shift the focus from student growth to institutional optimization, at the cost of ethical integrity.

Educational AI must be designed to **support, not supplant**, teacher judgment, peer interaction, and human-centered learning processes. Educators should remain active interpreters of student experience, not passive implementers of algorithmic suggestions (Freire, 1970; Giroux, 2011).

Scoring systems that incentivize emotional conformity or normalize behavior along narrow parameters can stifle **individuality, neurodiversity, and cultural variance**. True alignment with pedagogical ethics requires systems that respect difference, encourage creativity, and adapt to learners, not the reverse (Selwyn, 2020; Floridi et al., 2018).

A promising avenue is the inclusion of **reflective spaces** in ESG dashboards, interfaces that allow students to explore, annotate, and discuss their own data (Grek & Ozga, 2010). Rather than conditioning students to adapt to predefined indicators, such features can promote **critical awareness**, ethical reflection, and educational agency.

Ultimately, ESG-aligned AI must reflect the values of education itself: care, openness, diversity, and a commitment to the full humanity of the learner.

Regulatory Alignment and Global Governance Models

Designing responsible AI-ESG frameworks requires institutions to align not only with internal ethical commitments but also with the evolving landscape of international regulatory frameworks. Among the most influential are the European Union's General Data Protection Regulation (GDPR) and the forthcoming AI Act, both of which offer critical scaffolding for educational data governance (Floridi et al., 2018; Williamson, 2017; UNESCO, 2021).

The GDPR's core principles, data minimization, purpose limitation, and meaningful consent, provide a foundational model for managing sensitive ESG-related data. Institutions using AI to monitor emotional or behavioral signals, especially involving minors, must treat such data with the same care as health information. Furthermore, the "right to explanation" and "right to erasure" create both opportunities and challenges for AI systems that influence educational decisions, necessitating transparency by design.

The AI Act, currently under negotiation by the European Commission, introduces a risk-based classification of AI systems, explicitly identifying education as a high-risk domain (European Commission, 2021). ESG-related AI systems, especially those involving biometric or affective data, will be subject to enhanced scrutiny, requiring human oversight, conformity assessments, and documentation of fairness and accountability.

Beyond the EU, UNESCO's Recommendation on the Ethics of Artificial Intelligence (2021) provides a normative compass. It stresses the need for inclusion, non-discrimination, and cultural diversity in AI development, principles that are especially relevant in educational contexts shaped by pluralistic values and equity mandates.

Rather than viewing these global instruments as external constraints, educational institutions should treat them as enabling frameworks, tools that support reflexivity, intercultural dialogue, and ethical innovation in the governance of AI-enhanced ESG strategies.

Governance as Educational Practice

Governance in the age of AI is not merely an administrative necessity; it is a **pedagogical act**. The ways we govern algorithms, data, and decision systems within educational spaces teach students what kind of world is being built around them, and what role they are expected to play in it.

By involving learners in structured conversations about data rights, algorithmic fairness, and technological ethics, institutions foster critical digital literacy and civic sensibility. Students cease to be passive subjects of surveillance or optimization, and instead become co-creators of ethical infrastructures that reflect shared values of care, justice, and autonomy.

Responsible ESG implementation, therefore, must move beyond checklists, dashboards, and regulatory compliance. It must be grounded in deliberative practice, ethical imagination, and educational purpose. The future of AI in education depends not only on what we build, but on who is invited to build it and how we define its goals.

CONCLUSION: TOWARD ETHICAL AI-DRIVEN ESG IN EDUCATION

The integration of artificial intelligence into ESG compliance frameworks in education represents both a remarkable opportunity and a significant ethical inflection point. On the one hand, AI offers educational institutions powerful tools to support sustainability efforts, advance social inclusion, and promote transparency in governance. On the other hand, these same technologies carry the risk of intensifying surveillance, automating exclusionary practices, and eroding the relational and pedagogical values that education fundamentally seeks to uphold.

This chapter has argued that AI-enhanced ESG strategies must not be judged solely by their efficiency or compliance outputs. Instead, they must be governed through frameworks that center **learner autonomy**, **institutional accountability**, and **psychosocial integrity**. We examined both real-world and hypothetical cases where AI systems are used to monitor environmental impact, detect inclusion gaps, and automate key governance functions within schools and universities. While many of these tools are developed with good intentions, their deployment often results in unintended harms, particularly when they operate opaquely, depend on reductive behavioral metrics, or marginalize human judgment.

At the heart of these tensions lies a fundamental question: **What kind of educational future are we constructing when ESG is mediated through algorithmic systems?** Are we cultivating learning environments that are genuinely sustainable, inclusive, and democratic or are we codifying emotional profiling, behavioral standardization, and technocratic governance as the new normal?

We do not call for the rejection of AI in ESG compliance. Rather, we argue for its **ethical, critical, and collaborative deployment**. This chapter outlined a governance model rooted in:

- Modular and transparent consent architectures
- Reflexive system design and real-time feedback mechanisms
- Multidimensional ethical impact assessments
- Participatory co-creation with students and educators
- Respect for learners' emotional complexity, developmental needs, and moral agency

In short, **emotional and behavioral data must be understood not as mere performance indicators, but as expressions of human experience**. These data require protection, contextualization, and interpretation within relational, not solely computational, frameworks.

As education continues to respond to global challenges, climate urgency, equity imperatives, and digital transformation, it may be tempting to view AI as a managerial solution. But systems meant to foster **care, justice, and empowerment** cannot be outsourced to automation alone. They must be cultivated through critical reflection, collective responsibility, and a principled commitment to the dignity of every learner.

Future research must continue mapping the evolving interplay between ESG metrics, AI capabilities, and ethical governance structures. Policymakers must pursue coherent and enforceable regulation that prioritizes educational rights over institutional convenience. And educators, most crucially, must reclaim their role, not only as implementers of technology, but as moral architects of the systems that shape the future of education.

If we are to build institutions that are both intelligent and just, then our ESG compliance systems must not only reflect our values, they must protect them, enact them, and **inspire them**.

Looking Ahead: Futures of AI-Driven ESG in Education

As ESG principles continue to shape the future of education, the integration of artificial intelligence is expected to become increasingly **sophisticated, predictive, and embedded** within institutional infrastructures. Emerging ESG platforms may incorporate emotion-aware climate literacy modules, automated accreditation workflows, and simulation-based tools for analyzing social inclusion scenarios.

Yet with this growing technical capacity comes a parallel ethical imperative: to remain vigilant toward the **unintended consequences** of such intensification. Over time, the automation of ESG compliance may redirect institutional focus away from ethical reflection and toward **metric optimization**, a phenomenon scholars refer to as **data performativity** (Williamson, 2017). In this context, the pressure to demonstrate progress through quantifiable indicators can overshadow the deeper work of cultural transformation, pedagogical change, and moral learning.

To resist this drift, future AI-ESG systems must be designed not as instruments of passive reporting, but as **pedagogical spaces**, arenas in which students, educators, and communities engage critically with the ethical, environmental, and social dimensions of education itself.

Innovative possibilities include the use of **multilingual, culturally responsive AI agents** to support ESG education across diverse populations; hybrid facilitation models that combine algorithmic analysis with human-led ethical dialogue; and participatory AI design initiatives that empower students to shape the very systems that assess them.

These futures call not merely for technical expertise, but for an educational imagination rooted in justice, care, and democratic participation. The guiding question is not just what AI can do for ESG, but rather, **what kind of ESG we want AI to help us co-create**.

REFERENCES

Anagnostopoulos, D., & Tsitsianis, N. (2023). Algorithmic Rationality and Educational AI Policies in Southern Europe. *European Journal of Education Policy, 38*(2), 110–127.

Anastasiadou, S., & Seremeti, L. (2025). Autopoietic co-evolution of AI and law. In Anastasiadou, S., Seremeti, L., Masouras, A., & Anastasiadis, L. (Eds.), *Modern Perspectives on Artificial Intelligence and Law* (pp. 81–88). IGI Global Publisher of TIMELY KNOWLEDGE. DOI: 10.4018/979-8-3693-9576-9.ch005

Binns, R. (2018). Fairness in Machine Learning: Lessons from Political Philosophy. *Proceedings of the 2018 Conference on Fairness, Accountability and Transparency*, 149–159.

Crawford, K. (2021). *Atlas of AI: Power, politics, and the planetary costs of artificial intelligence. Yale University Press.Crawford, K. (2021). Atlas of AI: Power, politics, and the planetary costs of artificial intelligence.* Yale University Press.

European Commission. (2021). Proposal for a regulation laying down harmonised rules on artificial intelligence (Artificial Intelligence Act). Commission. (2021). Proposal for a regulation laying down harmonised rules on artificial intelligence (Artificial Intelligence Act). https://eur-lex.europa.eu/legal-content/EN/TXT/?uri=CELEX:52021PC0206

Floridi, L., Cowls, J., Beltrametti, M., Chatila, R., Chazerand, P., Dignum, V., Luetge, C., Madelin, R., Pagallo, U., Rossi, F., Schafer, B., Valcke, P., & Vayena, E. (2018). AI4People (Floridi et al., 2018)—An ethical framework for a good AI society: Opportunities, risks, principles, and recommendations. *Minds and Machines, 28*(4), 689–707. DOI: 10.1007/s11023-018-9482-5 PMID: 30930541

Freire, P. (1970). Pedagogy of the oppressed. Continuum.Freire, P. (1970). Pedagogy of the oppressed. *Continuum : an Interdisciplinary Journal on Continuity of Care.*

Giroux, H. A. (2011). *On critical pedagogy (Giroux, 2011). Bloomsbury Academic. Giroux, H. A. (2011). On critical pedagogy (Giroux, 2011).* Bloomsbury Academic.

Grek, S., & Ozga, J. (2010). Governing by numbers: Data and education governance in Europe. Journal of Education Policy, 25(1), 23–37.Grek, S., & Ozga, J. (2010). Governing by numbers: Data and education governance in Europe. *Journal of Education Policy, 25*(1), 23–37. DOI: 10.1080/02680930802412669

Grek, S., & Ozga, J. (2020). Governing Education through Data: Towards a Digital Education Policy Regime. International Journal of Education Policy, 43(4), 567–584. Grek, S., & Ozga, J. (2020). Governing Education through Data: Towards a Digital Education Policy Regime. *International Journal of Education Policy*, *43*(4), 567–584.

Kalogera, C., Seremeti, L., Kontis, S., & Anastasiadou, S. (2025). The Digital DNA of Modern Workforce. In Lamprini Seremeti, Panagiotis Liargovas, Christos Papademetriou, Lazaros Anastasiadis, Sofia Anastasiadou (edus), Harnessing Business Intelligence for Modern Talent Management, IGI Global Publisher of TIMELY KNOWLEDGE, DOI: 10.4018/979-8-3373-1942-1.ch015

Kontis, S. (2025). Governing AI in the metaverse: Ethical, legal, and psychosocial challenges in emotion-aware virtual systems. In Anastasiadou, S., Seremeti, L., Masouras, A., & Anastasiadis, L. (Eds.), *Modern Perspectives on Artificial Intelligence and Law* (pp. 135–156). IGI Global Publisher of TIMELY KNOWLEDGE. DOI: 10.4018/979-8-3693-9576-9.ch008

Kontis, S., Anastasiadou, S., Anastasiadis, L., & Seremeti, L. (2025). Legal Entropy in AI Governance. In Anastasiadou, S., Seremeti, L., Masouras, A., & Anastasiadis, L. (Eds.), *Modern Perspectives on Artificial Intelligence and Law* (pp. 193–206). IGI Global Publisher of TIMELY KNOWLEDGE., DOI: 10.4018/979-8-3693-9576-9.ch010

Mittelstadt, B. D., Allo, P., Taddeo, M., Wachter, S., & Floridi, L. (2016). The ethics of algorithms (Mittelstadt et al., 2016): Mapping the debate. *Big Data & Society*, *3*(2), 2053951716679679. DOI: 10.1177/2053951716679679

OECD. (2022). OECD Framework for Responsible AI in Education. https://www.oecd.org/education/ai-framework-edu/

Papademetriou, C., Belias, D., Anastasiadou, S., Ragazou, K., & Garefalakis, A. (2024). Sustainability: ESG and Human Resource Management. In Ragazou, K., Garefalakis, A., & Papalexandris, S. (Eds.), *Papademetriou, C., Anastasiadou, S* (pp. 1–15). ESG and Total Quality Management in Human Resources. IGI Global Publisher of TIMELY KNOWLEDGE., DOI: 10.4018/979-8-3693-2991-7.ch001

Selwyn, N. (2020). *Should robots replace teachers? AI and the future of education. Polity Press.Selwyn, N. (2020). Should robots replace teachers? AI and the future of education*. Polity Press.

Seremeti, L. (2025a). AI Legislationship: Navigating Unclear Commitments in AI Governance. In Anastasiadou, S., Seremeti, L., Masouras, A., & Anastasiadis, L. (Eds.), *Modern Perspectives on Artificial Intelligence and Law* (pp. 27–36). IGI Global Publisher of TIMELY KNOWLEDGE. DOI: 10.4018/979-8-3693-9576-9.ch002

Seremeti, L. (2025b). The Impact of AI on Legality and Regularity: Navigating Societal Transformations. In Anastasiadou, S., Seremeti, L., Masouras, A., & Anastasiadis, L. (Eds.), *Modern Perspectives on Artificial Intelligence and Law* (pp. 243–258). IGI Global Publisher of TIMELY KNOWLEDGE., DOI: 10.4018/979-8-3693-9576-9.ch012

Seremeti, L. (2025c). The Status Quo of AI Governance: Global Approaches and Challenges. In Anastasiadou, S., Seremeti, L., Masouras, A., & Anastasiadis, L. (Eds.), *Modern Perspectives on Artificial Intelligence and Law* (pp. 259–268). IGI Global Publisher of TIMELY KNOWLEDGE., DOI: 10.4018/979-8-3693-9576-9.ch013

Seremeti, L., Anastasiadis, L., & Anastasiadou, S. (2024). The Role of Data in Environmental, Social, and Governance Strategy, (pages 149-166). In Christos Pademetriou, Sofia Anastasiadou, Konstantina Ragazou, Alexandros Garefalakis, Stylianos Papalexandris, ESG and Total Quality Management in Human Resources, IGI Global Publisher of TIMELY KNOWLEDGE. DOI: 10.4018/979-8-3693-2991-7.ch010

Seremeti, L., Anastasiadis, L., Kalogera, C., & Kontis, S. (2025a). Qualia and Business Intelligence for Organizational Excellence. In Seremeti, L., Liargovas, P., Papademetriou, C., Anastasiadis, L., & Anastasiadou, S. (Eds.), *Harnessing Business Intelligence for Modern Talent Management* (pp. 265–274). IGI Global Publisher of TIMELY KNOWLEDG., DOI: 10.4018/979-8-3373-1942-1.ch010

Seremeti, L., & Anastasiadou, S. (2025). Dealing with semantic inconsistencies in AI governance. In Anastasiadou, S., Seremeti, L., Masouras, A., & Anastasiadis, L. (Eds.), *Modern Perspectives on Artificial Intelligence and Law* (pp. 125–134). IGI Global Publisher of TIMELY KNOWLEDGE., DOI: 10.4018/979-8-3693-9576-9.ch007

Seremeti, L., Anastasiadou, S., Masouras, A., & Papalexandris, S. (2025b). Addressing the challenges of harmonizing law and artificial intelligence technology in modern society. IAES International Journal of Artificial Intelligence (IJ-AI), Vol.14, No.3, pp. 2471-2478. DOI: 10.11591/ijai.v14.i3.pp2471-2478

Smyrnaios, N. (2023). Platform Power and Educational Data Governance. *Journal of Media and Learning Analytics*, *12*(1), 45–61.

Souravlas, S., & Anastasiadou, S. (2020). Pipelined Dynamic Scheduling of Big Data Streams. *Applied Sciences (Basel, Switzerland)*, *10*(14), 4796. DOI: 10.3390/app10144796

Souravlas, S., & Anastasiadou, S. (2022). On Implementing Social Community Clouds Based on Markov Models. *IEEE Transactions on Computational Social Systems, 2022*. DOI: 10.1109/TCSS.2022.3213273

Souravlas, S., Anastasiadou, S., Economides, Th., & Katsavounis, S. (2023). Probabilistic Community Detection in Social Networks. IEEE Access, Publication Date: 2023, Volume: 11, DOI: 10.1109/ACCESS.2023.3257021

Souravlas, S., Anastasiadou, S., & Katsavounis, S. (2021b). A Survey on the Recent Advances of Deep Community Detection. *Applied Sciences (Basel, Switzerland)*, *11*(16), 7179. DOI: 10.3390/app11167179

Souravlas, S., Anastasiadou, S., & Katsavounis, S. (2021c). More on Pipelined Dynamic Scheduling of Big Data Streams. *Applied Sciences (Basel, Switzerland)*, *11*(1), 61. DOI: 10.3390/app11010061

Souravlas, S., Anastasiadou, S. D., Tantalaki, N., & Katsavounis, S. (2022a). A Fair, Dynamic Load Balanced Task Distribution Strategy for Heterogeneous Cloud Platforms Based on Markov Process Modeling. *IEEE Access : Practical Innovations, Open Solutions*, *10*, 26149–26162. DOI: 10.1109/ACCESS.2022.3157435

Souravlas, S., Katsavounis, S., & Anastasiadou, S. (2020). On Modeling and Simulation of Resource Allocation Policies in Cloud Computing Using Colored Petri Nets. *Applied Sciences (Basel, Switzerland)*, *10*(16), 5644. DOI: 10.3390/app10165644

Taraza, E., Anastasiadou, S., Seremeti, S., & Masouras, A. (2025b). Environmental, Social, and Governance of Businesses and Organizations and the Role of Human Resources. IGI Global., DOI: 10.4018/979-8-3693-2991-7.ch006

Taraza, E., Papademetriou, C., Seremeti, L., Masouras, A., & Anastasiadou, S. (2024a). The Necessity of Environmental Ethics in Environmental Education and the Role of Educators. In Christos Papademetriou, Sofia Anastasiadou, Konstantina Ragazou, Alexandros Garefalakis, Stylianos Papalexandris, ESG and Total Quality Management in Human. IGI Global. (pp. 149–166). DOI: 10.4018/979-8-3693-2991-7.ch008

UNESCO. (2021). Recommendation on the ethics of artificial intelligence. https://unesdoc.unesco.org/ark:/48223/pf0000381137

Williamson, B. (2017). *Big data in education: The digital future of learning, policy and practice. SAGE Publications.Williamson, B. (2017). Big data in education: The digital future of learning, policy and practice*. SAGE Publications. DOI: 10.4135/9781529714920

Williamson, B., & Piattoeva, N. (2022). Metrics in Education: Governing by Numbers in the Datafied School. Educational Theory & Policy, 55(3), 344–359.

Yeung, K. (2018). Algorithmic regulation: A critical interrogation. Regulation & Governance, 12(4), 505–523.Yeung, K. (2018). Algorithmic regulation: A critical interrogation. *Regulation & Governance*, *12*(4), 505–523. DOI: 10.1111/rego.12158

Zuboff, S. (2019). *The Age of Surveillance Capitalism: The Fight for a Human Future at the New Frontier of Power*. PublicAffairs.

Chapter 14
Voluntary Sustainability Reporting and Financial Performance:
Empirical Insights From the Global Real Estate Sector

Eleftheria Panagiotidou
https://orcid.org/0000-0003-0420-3991
Democritus University of Thrace, Greece

Stella Chondrou
Democritus University of Thrace, Greece

Athanasios Mandilas
Democritus University of Thrace, Greece

Giannoula Florou
https://orcid.org/0000-0002-2621-2832
Democritus University of Thrace, Greece

ABSTRACT

This chapter investigates the impact of adherence to Global Reporting Initiative (GRI) standards on the financial performance of real estate companies, with a specific focus on the Environmental, Social, and Governance (ESG) framework's influence on Return on Assets (ROA). Using statistical and regression analysis, the study analyzes data from 20 top global real estate firms. Findings show a positive link between strong ESG practices and financial performance, especially in environmental and governance areas. The study employs a longitudinal approach, drawing

DOI: 10.4018/979-8-3373-5142-1.ch014

on publicly available corporate reports and sustainability disclosures to quantify ESG adherence and correlate it with financial outcomes. The research contributes providing evidence that robust ESG practices can serve as a strategic imperative for enhancing financial viability in the real estate sector. It suggests that investment in sustainability initiatives and transparent reporting may lead to improved financial returns, advocating for the integration of ESG metrics into corporate performance evaluation.

INTRODUCTION

In recent years, environmental, social, and governance (ESG) factors have emerged as key elements of modern business practices and strategies. This shift reflects a broader social and economic shift towards sustainability and corporate responsibility, reinforcing the recognition of the role that business plays in addressing global challenges such as climate change, social inequality and enhancing transparency in governance. The concept of ESG was brought to the forefront of investment thinking with the report of the United Nations Environment Programme Finance Initiative (UNEP FI, 2007), which highlighted the importance of incorporating such criteria into investment decisions as a means of achieving long-term financial returns.

Integrating ESG considerations is not just about complying with regulations or meeting ethical obligations, but represents a strategic advantage for companies seeking resilience and sustainable development. The environmental dimension relates to the company's footprint on the natural environment, while the social dimension relates to relationships with employees, communities and other stakeholders. The governance dimension focuses on transparency, accountability and good leadership practices. As research shows (Eccles et al., 2014), companies that adopt strong ESG practices exhibit greater financial stability and reduced performance volatility.

The literature around ESG factors has led to the development of theoretical models aimed at explaining the relationship between sustainability and financial performance. The Triple Bottom Line model (Elkington, 1994) extends the traditional accounting framework by incorporating environmental and social performance. Shared value theory (Porter and Kramer, 2011) argues that economic and social progress can be achieved simultaneously, while stakeholder theory (Freeman, 1984) focuses on the accountability of firms to all stakeholders with whom they interact. At the same time, resource-based theory (RBV) (Hart, 1995) and the Natural Capitalism approach (Hawken et al., 1999) highlight the strategic importance of environmental management in creating competitive advantage.

In this context, this study examines the role of ESG practices in the real estate sector, with a particular focus on the link between sustainability reporting and financial performance of large global companies. In particular, it utilizes the internationally recognized Global Reporting Initiative (GRI) framework to assess sustainability performance and analyze its impact on corporate financial indicators. This research aspires to make a substantial contribution to the scientific and practical understanding of corporate sustainability in the real estate industry, providing empirical data that can guide investors, policy makers and corporate leaders in making informed decisions.

LITERATURE REVIEW

The Structure of ESG

In recent years, the ESG (Environmental, Social, and Governance) framework has become increasingly important in the business world. It is now a key axis for evaluating business practices and is systematically incorporated into sustainability strategies, reports, and investment decisions. The interdisciplinary nature of ESG links corporate responsibility to long-term financial performance and fundamentally influences the operation and reputation of businesses.

ESG's environmental dimension focuses on how companies manage their impact on the natural environment. Issues such as climate change, depletion of natural resources, and environmental degradation are now critical challenges for companies. Companies are called upon not only to reduce their emissions but also to strengthen their resilience to the effects of the climate crisis. As studies show (e.g., Busch & Hoffmann, 2011), compliance with environmental standards is not just a moral choice but a strategic necessity for business sustainability. At the same time, issues such as energy efficiency, the use of renewable sources, and supply chain management are now key criteria for assessing environmental responsibility.

The social dimension includes the company's interaction with people – employees, consumers, suppliers, and local communities. Promoting diversity, employee safety and well-being, fair treatment throughout the value chain, and contributing to the local community are key parameters of this dimension. Researchers such as Aguinis and Glavas (2012) emphasize that companies that invest in human capital often see positive results in both their operational performance and their reputation. Corporate social responsibility (CSR), as part of ESG, emerges as a lever for creating shared value and competitive advantage, as described by Porter and Kramer (2006).

The term 'governance' is employed to denote the manner in which a company is organized and controlled. It is evident that practices such as transparency, corporate accountability, board composition, remuneration policy and anti-corruption are instrumental in determining institutional credibility and long-term success. In accordance with Bebchuk and Fried's (2004) assertion, it is imperative that executive incentives are aligned with the generation of long-term value for shareholders. The concept of robust corporate governance encompasses more than mere regulatory frameworks; it influences the establishment of an ethical culture, mitigates risk, and fosters enhanced sustainability.

ESG has been demonstrated to effect a shift in focus from short-term financial performance to a more holistic model of corporate success, combining profitability with responsibility. ESG integration has evolved from a mere option to a non-negotiable expectation, both from a market perspective and a societal standpoint. It is evident that companies which demonstrate an understanding of this paradigm shift will be better equipped to meet the challenges of the future and create sustainable value.

The Importance of Sustainability Reporting and Disclosure

Sustainability reporting and disclosure have become critical elements of modern corporate governance, reflecting the growing demand for transparency, accountability, and strategic alignment with long-term environmental and social goals. These reports provide key stakeholders—investors, regulators, customers, employees, and communities—with — valuable information about how a company manages environmental and social issues. The company's ability to communicate its commitment to sustainable practices and progress toward achieving sustainability goals is critical to stakeholder trust and legitimacy of stakeholders. Eccles and Krzus (2010) argues that sustainability reporting enables companies to measure, understand and disclose not only financial performance, but also environmental, social and governance (ESG) indicators, thereby promoting transparency and enhancing reputation.

Sustainability reporting provides advantages which reach further than just external stakeholder engagement. These reports function as essential management tools that enable organizations to establish targets while tracking their progress and identifying potential risks. The reporting process as described by Adams and Frost (2008) helps companies discover operational shortcomings and innovation opportunities which lead to strategic improvements throughout supply chains and business models. Companies that disclose sustainability information through reporting gain reputation enhancements and improved stakeholder relationships which help them achieve enduring success.

Companies can set themselves apart from competitors through sustainability disclosure which provides a strategic advantage in modern markets. KPMG's Corporate Responsibility Reporting Survey (2017) finds that companies with open reporting practices achieve superior financial results because they better understand risks and allocate resources more effectively. Companies which effectively convey their sustainability initiatives to stakeholders benefit from rising consumer and investor interest in these matters.

The Global Reporting Initiative (GRI) stands as the leading and most frequently used framework which helps organizations disclose sustainability information. The GRI standards establish an internationally recognized framework that organizations use to report economic and environmental and social impacts. According to Kolk (2010) organizations that use GRI standards achieve better comparability and credibility which enables stakeholders to evaluate sustainability performance between companies in various industries and geographic areas. Standardized assessment of ESG commitments needs to be carried out with transparency through documented procedures.

Other reporting standards have emerged alongside GRI to provide specific sector and issue-based guidance to organizations. The Sustainability Accounting Standards Board (SASB) establishes industry-specific sustainability criteria which financial performance may be impacted by. The compatibility of SASB with traditional financial reporting makes it particularly attractive to investors seeking to incorporate ESG risks and opportunities into their capital allocation decisions (SASB, 2021).

The International Integrated Reporting Council (IIRC) has introduced another important framework—Integrated Reporting (<IR>)—which seeks to bridge financial and non-financial information. It emphasizes the interdependence of an organization's strategy, governance, performance, and prospects, with the aim of presenting a holistic view of value creation. As the IIRC (2021) points out, integrated reporting supports long-term decision-making by describing how ESG factors affect corporate performance in a dynamic business environment.

The Carbon Disclosure Project (CDP), a non-profit organization, has established itself as a global leader in environmental transparency. CDP encourages companies to disclose their greenhouse gas emissions, water use, and forest impact. The data collected helps investors and policymakers assess climate-related risks and companies' readiness to transition to low-carbon economies (CDP, 2021).

The Task Force on Climate-related Financial Disclosures (TCFD) establishes detailed guidelines that help organizations reveal climate-related financial threats and advantages through their disclosures. The TCFD (2021) states that standardized future-oriented disclosures help investors and insurers analyze climate risk exposure to make wise decisions. The combined frameworks work to establish stronger uniformity in disclosure practices.

The regulatory framework continues to transform in order to reinforce ESG reporting standards. The European Union passed laws which mandate big corporations to reveal information about their social and environmental and governance activities. The increasing importance of ESG factors for corporate responsibility and market integrity has prompted governments to recognize their systemic nature through these regulatory changes. According to Ioannou and Serafeim (2017) regulatory requirements function as both a tool to make reporting practices uniform and a driver to enhance corporate conduct and stakeholder engagement.

In the world of finance, ESG reporting is increasingly regarded as an indicator of corporate resilience. Investors use ESG disclosures to evaluate a company's long-term sustainability and risk exposure. Dhaliwal et al. (2011) found that companies that produce high-quality sustainability reports benefit from lower capital costs, since investors regard them as more transparent and well-managed. Therefore, sustainability reporting serves both communicative and strategic functions in capital markets.

In conclusion, reporting and disclosing sustainability information represents a fundamental change in the way companies communicate their value. As well as meeting compliance requirements and investor expectations, it offers organizations a way to integrate sustainability into their strategy, improve performance and strengthen stakeholder trust. As ESG issues continue to gain importance due to climate risks, the convergence of global frameworks and increasing regulatory pressure and investor demand are shaping a new era in corporate reporting. In this new era, transparency, accountability and long-term thinking are no longer optional, but essential.

The Impact of ESG Factors on the Financial Performance of Companies

The relationship between corporate sustainability and financial performance has been a focus of recent research activity, with an emphasis on ESG (Environmental, Social and Governance) factors. A number of studies support a positive correlation between ESG and financial indicators, with variations in markets, methodologies and endogenous factors. Chen et al. (2023), Zhang and Lucey (2022), and Naeem and Çankaya (2022) confirm that high ESG performance enhances corporate profitability, especially in high-risk environments and large-scale firms. Similarly, Laskar and Maji (2017), Velte (2017) and Benson and Ganda (2022) identify a positive effect of sustainability on both market indicators (such as Tobin's Q) and accounting metrics (such as ROA, ROE), with variations depending on country and governance.

However, some studies reveal mixed or limited effects. Ady and Zahroh (2024) find no significant correlation between CSR disclosures and profitability ratios (ROE, ROA), while Rojo-Suárez et al. (2024) demonstrate that although ESG policies are associated with lower discount rates in the Latin American oil sector, they also imply limited future dividend growth.

The effect of sustainability also varies according to the structure of the firms. Lo and Liao (2021) show that the sustainability of Japanese long-lived firms depends more on strategic and human resources than on short-term financial performance. Similarly, Algarni et al. (2022) demonstrate that adaptive capacity and environmental behavior enhance corporate sustainability by acting as mediators of financial performance.

In the banking sector, Cantero-Saiz et al. (2024) document a positive correlation between ESG and asset quality, which weakens when profitability is high, pointing out geographical variations between EU and third countries. Moreover, Naeem et al. (2022) demonstrate that ESG performance has a stronger economic impact in developed versus emerging markets.

The European experience, as summarized by Velte (2023), highlights the impact of management characteristics (diversity, sustainability committees) on environmental performance, while the impact of related strategies on economic performance differs between accounting and market measures. In a similar approach, Kiliç et al. (2022) and Pinem and Aulia (2023) identify differential effects of CSP depending on firm size, industry and geography.

Finally, Nnadi and Mutyaba (2023) argue that incorporating corporate sustainability features into products and processes enhances economic performance, validating the stakeholder theory. Overall, most studies confirm the positive impact of ESG parameters on financial performance, although the effect varies by size, sector, geography and strategic context.

The Impact of Sustainability Reporting on the Financial Performance of Companies

Various geographical contexts have been explored to examine the relationship between sustainability reporting and corporate financial performance, providing insights into how cultural, regulatory and institutional factors influence the impact of ESG disclosure. These regional differences help to highlight both global trends and local dynamics in the evolving sustainability landscape.

In Europe, where ESG integration is usually complemented by regulatory support and solid institutional settings, a number of studies underline the positive financial impacts of sustainability disclosure. For instance, the research by Ortiz-Martínez et al. (2023) on Spanish SMEs proved that sustainability practices positively enhance corporate social responsibility (CSR) and non-financial reporting, which are associated with improved performance. Likewise, the work by Remo-Diez et al. (2023) with 185 utility firms unveiled that combinations of ESG dimensions, particularly social performance, can drive high financial performance, regardless of environmental or governance metrics. These results unveil a strategic approach to ESG in Southern Europe, where social metrics tend to prevail.

In addition, Di Vaio and Varriale's (2020) research in the Italian airport sector identified partial reporting practice alignment with the Sustainable Development Goals (SDGs), specifically SDG 11 (Sustainable Cities) and SDG 17 (Partnerships).

The authors' results highlight the necessity for enhanced integrated governance and reporting frameworks to achieve sustainability goals efficiently.

Asian economies demonstrate a broad spectrum of ESG practices, pointing to varying levels of sustainability integration and regulatory maturity. In Malaysia, several studies have investigated this relationship. Md Nor et al. (2016) observed a mixed link between environmental disclosure and financial performance among the nation's top 100 companies, citing an overall weak correlation despite heightened social disclosure. Likewise, Mohd Said et al. (2015) highlighted the rise in quantity—but not necessarily quality—of sustainability reporting, which had a weak impact on ROA (Return on Assets). These observations imply that in the absence of enforced guidelines or investor pressure, ESG disclosure could continue to be superficial.

Aziz and Haron (2021) examined Shariah-compliant companies in Malaysia and found a positive link between Corporate Social Responsibility Disclosure (CSRD) and financial performance (both ROA and Tobin's Q), though with some caveats related to board composition and cultural issues. The Muslim directors' presence, surprisingly, was negatively related to financial performance, raising questions on governance culture and risk-taking in Shariah-compliant institutions.

In Indonesia, Hardi and Chairina (2019) and subsequently Putri Amrigan et al. (2023) investigated sustainability compliance and its financial repercussions. Both of these studies observed that though economic disclosures had a positive effect on ROA, environmental and social disclosures had no discernible impact on profitability in the short run. This implies that firms in emerging Southeast Asian economies are perhaps at the nascent phase of incorporating ESG considerations in a meaningful way. Laskar et al. (2017) compared Japan and India, with their cross-national study showing environmental disclosure is more significant in the financial performance of Japanese companies, and social aspects more so for Indian companies. This difference could be due to national regulatory frameworks and stakeholder pressure, reflecting how ESG priorities are culturally rooted.

Reddy (2010) analyzed the sustainability reporting of listed companies in Australia and New Zealand. The study used an event-study methodology to evaluate abnormal stock returns following environmental, social and governance (ESG) disclosures. While Australian firms showed a statistically significant positive reaction to sustainability reports, this effect was less consistent in New Zealand, where CSR-type reports had stronger financial implications. These results highlight the importance of industry context and investor perceptions in determining the financial value of ESG disclosures.

Coscun (2023) added to the existing literature by cautioning against overestimating the benefits of adopting ESG practices. The study emphasized that, although corporate social performance (CSP) generally correlates with better financial performance, ESG alignment does not automatically confer a competitive advantage. This is particularly relevant in regions where ESG frameworks are still developing, and where market incentives may not be fully aligned with long-term sustainability goals.

Pereira da Silva (2023) conducted a global analysis across 44 countries and discovered that non-financial disclosure improves labor investment efficiency, particularly in nations with robust investor protections and legal systems. Interestingly, the relationship between ESG volume and labor efficiency was stronger in countries with rigid labor markets and high unionization rates, suggesting that ESG transparency could offset structural inefficiencies.

Loh et al. (2017) analyzed the relationship between sustainability reporting and corporate value in listed companies in Singapore. They found a definite positive correlation, especially for firms with high-quality sustainability reports. This relationship implies that under jurisdictions with prominent government encouragement and increasing investor focus on ESG, companies are able to use disclosure to enhance market valuation.

Buallay (2019) carried out an extensive research on 342 financial institutions in 20 nations from 2007–2016. The findings presented a positive effect of ESG scores on market performance but a negative effect on operational and financial efficiency. The mixed results reflect the double nature of sustainability investments: ESG can positively affect reputation and share value, but it can also entail upfront expenses that negatively affect conventional performance indicators.

Saini and Singhania (2019) also took a worldwide dataset to investigate the ways in which environmental and social scores, as well as foreign ownership, influence firm performance. They discovered that although ESG disclosure tends to enhance financial performance, the existence of foreign investors can weaken this link, probably because of the drive for short-term profits. This subtlety highlights the need to align the interests of stakeholders in developing ESG strategies.

Alatawi and Daud (2022) took a meta-view by synthesizing 110 studies and concluded that though integrated reporting can enhance performance, the impact does differ substantially across cultural and regulatory environments. Their study highlights the necessity of localized ESG models instead of one-size-fits-all approaches.

Based on the above literature review, the following research hypotheses emerge and will be tested in this study.

Specific Research Hypotheses by ESG Dimension

Environmental Dimension

H1: There is a positive and statistically significant relationship between environmental performance disclosure (E) and return on assets (ROA) of real estate companies.

Social Dimension

H2: There is a positive and statistically significant relationship between social performance disclosure (S) and return on assets (ROA) of real estate companies.

Governance Dimension

H3: There is a positive and statistically significant relationship between governance performance disclosure (G) and return on assets (ROA) of real estate companies.

Overall ESG Impact

H4: Higher overall ESG disclosure, as measured by compliance with GRI indicators, is positively associated with higher ROA in real estate companies.

METHODOLOGICAL FRAMEWORK

The Survey Sample

The study focuses on 20 world-renowned real estate companies, selected for their significant market presence and the public availability of sustainability reports. These companies collectively represent a significant portion of the global real estate market, thus providing a comprehensive view of the industry's sustainability reporting practices. Sustainability disclosures are examined as published in annual reports, websites for the period of 2022, CSR reports or standalone sustainability reports. This approach provides a holistic understanding of companies' sustainability initiatives, beyond what is usually only disclosed in annual reports (Burhan & Rahmanti, 2012; Unerman, 2000).

The study incorporates two research models. The first model evaluates the impact of sustainability reporting (independent variable) on a company's performance (dependent variable). The second model evaluates the impact of each sustainability reporting category on company performance. The independent variables in this model are governance, environmental and social performance disclosures.

Return on assets (ROA) is chosen to measure the performance of the firm (dependent variable). ROA is a widely recognized profitability indicator that indicates the efficiency and financial performance of a firm (Weygandt et al., 2007).

The independent variables are quantified using a scoring index based on the GRI sector guidelines for real estate. The scoring formula is:

Index value=Number of indicators that a company satisfies/ Total number of indicators

Framework for Sustainability Reporting

The Global Reporting Initiative (GRI) framework is used in this research, which is recognized as the most comprehensive and structured framework for sustainability reporting (KPMG, 2017; Brown et al., 2009; Christopher & Filipovic, 2008). The GRI offers industry-specific frameworks that include relevant sustainability aspects related to different industries. The GRI framework is divided into universal standards and topic-specific standards, each designed to help organizations consistently report their sustainability impact.

The GRI Standards are organized into two main categories: **Universal Standards** and **Topic-specific Standards.**

Universal Standards apply to all organizations and establish the foundational principles for effective sustainability reporting:

- **GRI 101: Foundation** – Outlines the core principles and requirements for using the GRI Standards, including guidance on determining report content and quality. It serves as the entry point for the application of all other GRI Standards.
- **GRI 102: General Disclosures** – Covers essential information about the organization's profile, governance, stakeholder engagement, and reporting practices. These disclosures provide the necessary context for understanding an organization's sustainability impacts.
- **GRI 103: Management Approach** – Guides organizations in reporting how they manage material topics, explaining the relevance of each issue and describing related strategies, actions, and performance tracking.

Topic-specific Standards are grouped into three series—**Economic**, **Environmental**, and **Social**—and allow for more granular reporting on specific areas of sustainability impact:

- **Economic Standards** include indicators related to economic performance, market presence, and indirect economic impacts. These standards focus on how an organization contributes to economic development and impacts stakeholders economically.
- **Environmental Standards** encompass issues such as emissions, energy, water, effluents and waste, biodiversity, and overall environmental resource management. They guide organizations in reporting the use of natural resources and their environmental footprint.
- **Social Standards** cover labor practices, human rights, community engagement, and product responsibility. Topics include employment, labor-

management relations, health and safety, diversity and equal opportunity, non-discrimination, child and forced labor, local communities, anti-corruption, and customer health and safety.

Each topic-specific standard contains clearly defined disclosures that allow organizations to report on their impacts, policies, and practices relevant to each area. This dual-structure approach of universal and topic-specific standards enables tailored yet consistent sustainability reporting across sectors and geographies.

In the context of this study, ESG data were extracted from publicly available sustainability reports structured according to the GRI framework. This facilitated the quantification of ESG performance across the environmental, social, and governance dimensions, ensuring both consistency and comparability of the data used in the regression analyses. The use of GRI standards enhanced the methodological rigor of the study by grounding it in internationally recognized reporting principles and disclosure practices, thereby supporting the reliability of the ESG-related indicators employed.

The selected GRI disclosures for the real estate sector, which are presented at the end of this chapter, include 45 indicators covering key aspects of sustainability reporting. These indicators are categorized into environmental (8 indicators), environmental (26 indicators) and social (11 indicators), which are presented in Table 6 (see appendix).

The Survey Methodology

For this research, the methodology was largely based on Mamun's (2022) methodological framework, with differences however in the domain chosen and the number of GRI standards. The selected sample includes 20 of the world's largest real estate companies based on a Forbes list. This study contributes to the field of sustainability reporting by examining how different sustainability reporting categories affect financial performance in a global real estate context. This study adopts a quantitative research approach to investigate the relationship between ESG (Environment, Society and Governance) performance and financial performance in the real estate companies industry.

In a first stage, the sample was selected based on the availability of available and comparable ESG data, as well as financial data for the same time period. ESG performance was drawn from the companies' official published sustainability reports, with reference to reporting standards such as GRI (Global Reporting Initiative), while financial data was drawn from annual financial statements, with Return on Assets (ROA) as a key benchmark.

This was followed by performing single-factor linear regression to understand the relationship between overall ESG performance and ROA. The results indicated a moderate positive correlation, statistically significant, suggesting that higher ESG performance is associated with improved financial performance. In the same context, a second single-factor regression was conducted, with the independent variable being solely the governance dimension (Governance - G), which also indicated a positive and statistically significant effect on ROA

To enhance the robustness of the analysis, a stepwise regression model was applied to assess the impact of each ESG component (Environmental - E, Social - S, Governance - G) on ROA. The stepwise method allowed for a statistically guided selection of variables, retaining in the final model only those that showed sufficient significance. The analysis identified the environmental dimension (E) as the only statistically significant factor, with a significant positive effect on ROA, while the S and G dimensions were excluded due to non-significant contribution.

Statistical processing of the data was performed using SPSS software. As part of the analysis, indices such as R and R^2, Adjusted R^2, F value (ANOVA) as well as t-values and p-values were utilized to assess the statistical significance of both the models and the individual coefficients. In addition, standard errors of estimation and multicollinearity diagnostics were examined to ensure the reliability of the results.

Overall, the methodological approach allows for a thorough investigation of the correlation between sustainable business practices and financial performance, providing empirical evidence on the role of ESG practices in the real estate industry.

RESULTS

Descriptive Statistics

In the first dataset, the analysis focuses on the compliance rate of real estate companies with GRI standards related to the environmental dimension of sustainability (Table 2). The results show that this percentage ranges between 0 and 0.625, with a mean value of 0.44375, which indicates a moderate level of environmental compliance. The relatively low value of the standard deviation (0.154) indicates limited variation in the performance of the companies, indicating a degree of uniformity in environmental reporting practices within the sample. The presence of companies not reporting on any of the relevant standards may be linked to variations in strategic prioritization of ESG issues or to operational and institutional barriers. On the other hand, the absence of full compliance, with a maximum percentage of 62.5%, suggests the existence of structural or sectoral challenges in fully integrating GRI environmental standards. These findings outline the current state of environmental disclosure practices in the industry and highlight both the efforts made and the scope for further progress. The relevance between the relatively homogeneous level of compliance and external pressures - such as regulatory requirements, investor expectations and companies' own strategic objectives - is an area for future investigation.

The second data set examines the compliance of real estate companies with the GRI social standards (Table 2), highlighting the extent of their engagement with the social dimension of sustainability. The values range from 0.115 to 0.769, with a mean value of 0.35577, indicating that, on average, companies disclose about one-third of the social standards. The standard deviation (0.145) indicates moderate dispersion, probably due to differences in size, strategies or geographical presence. The lower value reveals limited reporting on social issues by some companies, while the higher value indicates that there are companies that demonstrate significant social commitment. The results highlight heterogeneity in the degree of social compliance, with the industry showing a moderate but real orientation towards social accountability. Systematic reporting on social standards enhances transparency, stakeholder trust and company reputation. Overall, the data suggest that the sector is making progress in integrating social sustainability into its practices.

The third set of data focuses on the compliance of real estate companies with GRI governance standards (Table 2), highlighting the degree of transparency in corporate governance issues. The values range from 0.091 to 0.727, with an average of 0.35455, suggesting that on average around 35% of the relevant standards are reported. The standard deviation (0.202) indicates significant variation between companies, possibly due to differences in size, structure or strategy. The lower value indicates limited engagement with governance requirements in some cases, while the higher value indicates companies with well-developed governance systems and a willingness to provide extensive disclosure. This heterogeneity reflects variation in commitment to accountability and transparency, with some companies leading and others lagging behind. Adequate disclosure on governance issues is directly related to effective risk management and enhancing investor confidence, particularly in a sector with a broad social and economic footprint such as real estate. Overall, the data highlights a moderate level of compliance, with clear room for improvement, which could be addressed as pressures for greater accountability intensify.

The analysis of the overall ESG (Table 2) performance of the top 20 global real estate companies provides a comprehensive picture of their sustainability practices, as reflected by their compliance rate with the 45 GRI standards covering the three dimensions of ESG. Values range from 0.156 to 0.733, with a mean of 0.37111 and a standard deviation of 0.132178, demonstrating significant variation in reporting practices. Some companies, such as Link REIT, achieve high levels of disclosure, possibly reflecting mature sustainability strategies, while others, such as SEGRO, show lower levels of compliance, indicating limited integration of ESG standards or fewer related initiatives. This heterogeneity captures the gap between leaders and laggards in the sector and demonstrates the room for improvement for many companies. The importance of ESG performance in the real estate sector is crucial, given its significant environmental, social and economic footprint, as well as increasing pressure from investors, regulators and socially aware consumers. High levels of compliance can act as an indicator of strategic insight and enhance market confidence, while low rates can be accompanied by increased scrutiny and reduced opportunities to access resources. Overall, the data captures the current state of ESG reporting in the industry and offers a benchmark for further enhancing transparency and accountability as the adoption of stronger sustainability practices becomes strategically imperative. All the above quantitative findings are summarized in Table 7 (see appendix), which offers an overview of the results.

Return on assets (ROA) is a key financial indicator of a company's ability to turn its assets into profits, providing important information about its operational efficiency. For the top 20 global real estate companies, ROA ranges from 0.38% to 6.25%, with a mean of 2.91% and a standard deviation of 1.51%, demonstrating significant variation in profitability. Companies such as Link REIT (6.25%) and Public Storage (5.48%) demonstrate high efficiency in the use of their assets, while others such as Welltower (0.38%) show lower returns, likely due to strategic investments or diversified business priorities. The variability in performance may be due to different business models, sub-sectors, geographic conditions or phases of the investment cycle. Although high ROA values attract investors as a sign of efficient management, their interpretation requires a combined analysis with other indicators, given the possibility of temporary effects or non-recurring gains. The dynamic correlation between financial performance and ESG practices is also interesting, as ROA can serve as a bridge to understanding how sustainability affects financial health. Overall, the findings illustrate a multi-dimensional landscape in the real estate sector, where strategic asset management and the integration of sustainable practices shape the future profitability and competitiveness of businesses (Table 8 see appendix).

Overall Variables and Correlations

The combined analysis of ESG reporting and financial performance, with ROA as an indicator, for the top 20 real estate companies provides a comprehensive overview of disclosure levels and profitability in the industry. In the environmental dimension (E), the average compliance rate with the 8 relevant GRI standards is 44.375% (Table 9, see appendix), indicating a moderate level of disclosure, with a standard deviation of 15.43% and a range of 0% to 62.5%. The social aspect (S), comprising 26 standards, shows a lower average compliance rate at 35.577%, with a similar variation (standard deviation 14.55%) and a range of 11.5% to 76.9%. The governance category (G), with 11 standards, shows an average of 35.455% but a significantly higher standard deviation (20.20%), with a range of 9.1% to 72.7%, indicating a more pronounced heterogeneity in disclosure practices. Overall, the average level of compliance across the 45 GRI standards is 37.111% with a standard deviation of 13.22%, indicating a generally moderate but varied approach to ESG reporting. Meanwhile, return on assets (ROA) ranges from 0.38% to 6.25%, with an average of 2.912% and a standard deviation of 1.51%, also indicating significant variation in financial performance across companies. The findings show that while some companies extensively integrate ESG standards into their strategies, others fall short, which may be linked to differences in strategy, stakeholder expectations or the regulatory framework. The overall variability in both ESG disclosures and ROA provides the basis for further exploration of the relationship between sustainable practices and financial performance in the real estate sector.

Correlation analysis between ESG disclosure and financial performance, as measured by return on assets (ROA), for a sample of 20 real estate companies reveals significant positive correlations (Table 1). The overall ESG score shows a positive and statistically significant correlation with ROA ($r = 0.543$, $p = 0.013$), suggesting that higher levels of ESG disclosure are associated with better financial performance. The strongest correlation is observed between environmental performance (E) and ROA ($r = 0.578$, $p < 0.01$), while governance performance (G) shows a similar level of correlation with ROA ($r = 0.546$, $p < 0.05$). In contrast, the social dimension (S) shows a lower and non-statistically significant correlation ($r = 0.344$, $p = 0.137$), possibly indicating a weaker association of social reporting with profitability in this industry. Within the ESG components, strong positive correlations are recorded: ESG with social ($r = 0.907$), governance ($r = 0.766$) and environmental ($r = 0.662$), all significant at the 0.01 level. In addition, moderate positive correlations are observed between the individual ESG aspects: S-E ($r = 0.454$), S-G ($r = 0.473$), and E-G ($r = 0.443$), with all values being significant at the 0.05 level. The results suggest that companies that achieve high performance in one ESG area tend to succeed in the others, while highlighting that strong environmental and governance compliance is strongly associated with improved financial performance. Overall, the correlations demonstrate the importance of a holistic approach to sustainability in enhancing business outcomes in the real estate sector.

Table 1. Correlations between ESG variables and ROA

Correlations						
		ROA	**ESG**	**E**	**S**	**G**
ROA	Pearson Correlation	1	.543*	.578**	.344	.546*
	Sig. (2-tailed)		.013	.008	.137	.013
	N	20	20	20	20	20
ESG	Pearson Correlation	.543*	1	.662**	.907**	.766**
	Sig. (2-tailed)	.013		.001	.000	.000
	N	20	20	20	20	20
E	Pearson Correlation	.578**	.662**	1	.454*	.443
	Sig. (2-tailed)	.008	.001		.044	.050
	N	20	20	20	20	20
S	Pearson Correlation	.344	.907**	.454*	1	.473*
	Sig. (2-tailed)	.137	.000	.044		.035
	N	20	20	20	20	20
G	Pearson Correlation	.546*	.766**	.443	.473*	1
	Sig. (2-tailed)	.013	.000	.050	.035	
	N	20	20	20	20	20

*. Correlation is significant at the 0.05 level (2-tailed).
**. Correlation is significant at the 0.01 level (2-tailed).

Regression Analyzes with ROA as Dependent Variable

ROA and Environmental Factors

The regression analysis between environmental performance (E) and financial performance (ROA) for 20 real estate companies demonstrates a statistically significant and positive relationship (Table 2). The correlation coefficient R is 0.578, while the coefficient of determination R^2 is 0.335, suggesting that 33.5% of the variance in ROA is explained by environmental performance. The F statistic of the model is 9.050 ($p = 0.008$), confirming the overall significance of the model. The coefficient of the independent variable (5.651) is positive and statistically significant ($p = 0.008$), supporting the existence of a positive effect of environmental performance on profitability. The adjusted R^2 (0.298) and the standardized beta coefficient (0.578) indicate a moderate to strong effect. In contrast, the model constant (0.405) is not statistically significant ($p = 0.651$), which limits its explanatory value. Overall, the regression confirms that environmental performance is a reliable predictor of financial performance in the real estate industry, supporting the argument that environmental sustainability initiatives can contribute substantially to the financial success of firms.

Table 2. Regression analysis with ROA as the dependent variable and environmental factors as the independent variable

Variables Entered/Removed[a]

Model	Variables Entered	Variables Removed	Method
1	E[b]	.	Enter

a. Dependent Variable: ROA

b. All requested variables entered.

Model Summary

Model	R	R Square	Adjusted R Square	Std. Error of the Estimate
1	.578[a]	.335	.298	1.26328

a. Predictors: (Constant), E

ANOVA[a]

Model		Sum of Squares	df	Mean Square	F	Sig.
1	Regression	14.443	1	14.443	9.050	.008[b]
	Residual	28.726	18	1.596		
	Total	43.169	19			

a. Dependent Variable: ROA

b. Predictors: (Constant), E

Coefficients[a]

Model		Unstandardized Coefficients		Standardized Coefficients	t	Sig.
		B	Std. Error	Beta		
1	(Constant)	.405	.880		.460	.651
	E	5.651	1.878	.578	3.008	.008

a. Dependent Variable: ROA

ROA and Governance Factors

Regression analysis between governance (G) and financial performance (ROA) for 20 real estate companies shows a statistically significant positive correlation (Table 3), with R = 0.546 and $R^2 = 0.298$, suggesting that about 29.8% of the variance in ROA can be explained by governance performance. The adjusted R^2 (0.259) confirms the importance of governance, although it suggests that it is not the only factor. The F statistic = 7.645 (p = 0.013) supports the statistical validity of the model, while the Standard Error of Estimation (1.29742) indicates moderate accuracy in the predictions. The coefficient of variable G (4.074, p = 0.013) is positive and statistically significant, supporting the position that effective governance practices contribute to economic performance. In contrast, the model constant (1.467) is not statistically significant, suggesting the influence of other factors. Overall, the model demonstrates that corporate governance is an important but not exclusive predictor of profitability, confirming its contribution to enhancing the operational efficiency and financial health of real estate companies

Table 3. Regression analysis with ROA as the dependent variable and governance factors as the independent variable

Variables Entered/Removed[a]

Model	Variables Entered	Variables Removed	Method
1	G[b]	.	Enter

a. Dependent Variable: ROA

b. All requested variables entered.

Model Summary

Model	R	R Square	Adjusted R Square	Std. Error of the Estimate
1	.546[a]	.298	.259	1.29742

a. Predictors: (Constant), G

ANOVA[a]

Model		Sum of Squares	df	Mean Square	F	Sig.
1	Regression	12.869	1	12.869	7.645	.013[b]
	Residual	30.299	18	1.683		
	Total	43.169	19			

a. Dependent Variable: ROA

b. Predictors: (Constant), G

Coefficients[a]

Model		Unstandardized Coefficients		Standardized Coefficients	t	Sig.
		B	Std. Error	Beta		
1	(Constant)	1.467	.598		2.456	.024
	g	4.074	1.474	.546	2.765	.013

a. Dependent Variable: ROA

ROA and ESG Factors in General

Regression analysis between total ESG performance and return on assets (ROA) for 20 real estate companies demonstrates a moderate positive correlation ($R = 0.543$), with an R^2 value = 0.295, suggesting that approximately 29.5% of the variance in ROA is explained by ESG performance (Table 4). The adjusted R^2 (0.256) provides a more conservative estimate of the predictive power of the model, while the standard error of estimate (1.30041) indicates moderate prediction accuracy. The F statistic = 7.527 ($p = 0.013$) confirms the statistical significance of the model, while the ESG coefficient (6.192, $p = 0.013$) indicates a clear positive and statistically significant effect of ESG practices on financial performance. In contrast, the model constant (0.614) is not statistically significant, leaving open the possibility of the influence of other exogenous factors. Overall, the model supports the view that the holistic adoption of environmental, social and governance practices is positively related to profitability in the real estate industry, although it is not the sole determinant. The analysis supports the thesis that sustainable strategies, in addition to their ethical value, can act as catalysts for improving financial performance.

Table 4. Regression analysis with ROA as the dependent variable and the independent variable the total ESG factors in general

Variables Entered/Removed[a]			
Model	**Variables Entered**	**Variables Removed**	**Method**
1	ESG[b]	.	Enter
a. Dependent Variable: ROA			
b. All requested variables entered.			

Model Summary				
Model	R	R Square	Adjusted R Square	Std. Error of the Estimate
1	.543[a]	.295	.256	1.30041
a. Predictors: (Constant), ESG				

ANOVA[a]						
Model		Sum of Squares	df	Mean Square	F	Sig.
1	Regression	12.729	1	12.729	7.527	.013[b]
	Residual	30.439	18	1.691		
	Total	43.169	19			
a. Dependent Variable: ROA						
b. Predictors: (Constant), ESG						

Coefficients[a]

continued on following page

Table 4. Continued

Variables Entered/Removed[a]						
Model	**Variables Entered**		**Variables Removed**		**Method**	
Model		Unstandardized Coefficients		Standardized Coefficients	t	Sig.
		B	Std. Error	Beta		
1	(Constant)	.614	.887		.692	.498
	ESG	6.192	2.257	.543	2.744	.013

a. Dependent Variable: ROA

ROA and ESG Factors (Individually)

The stepwise multiple regression analysis (Table 5), applied to 20 real estate companies, examines the role of environmental factors (E) as predictor variables of return on assets (ROA). R = 0.578 and R^2 = 0.335 indicate a moderate positive correlation and that 33.5% of the variance in ROA is explained by environmental performance, with the adjusted R^2 (0.298) providing a more conservative estimate. The statistic F = 9.050 (p = 0.008) confirms the statistical significance of the model. The coefficient on environmental performance (5.651, p = 0.008) demonstrates a positive and significant effect of environmental compliance on profitability, while the constant (0.405) is not statistically significant. Social (S) and intergovernmental (G) factors were excluded from the model due to low statistical contribution, indicating that, in this context, environmental aspects are the main correlation factor with financial performance. Overall, the analysis highlights the importance of environmental sustainability as a critical factor for operational efficiency in the real estate sector, while highlighting the need for a multidimensional approach to ESG reporting, as individual components may affect economic outcomes differently.

Table 5. Multiple regression analysis with ROA as the dependent variable and individual ESG factors as independent variables

Variables Entered/Removed[a]			
Model	**Variables Entered**	**Variables Removed**	**Method**
1	E	.	Stepwise (Criteria: Probability-of-F-to-enter <= .050, Probability-of-F-to-remove >= .100).
a. Dependent Variable: ROA			
Model Summary			

continued on following page

Table 5. Continued

Variables Entered/Removed[a]			
Model	**Variables Entered**	**Variables Removed**	**Method**

Model	R	R Square	Adjusted R Square	Std. Error of the Estimate
1	.578[a]	.335	.298	1.26328
a. Predictors: (Constant), E				

ANOVA[a]						
Model		Sum of Squares	df	Mean Square	F	Sig.
1	Regression	14.443	1	14.443	9.050	.008[b]
	Residual	28.726	18	1.596		
	Total	43.169	19			
a. Dependent Variable: ROA						
b. Predictors: (Constant), E						

Coefficients[a]						
Model		Unstandardized Coefficients		Standardized Coefficients	t	Sig.
		B	Std. Error	Beta		
1	(Constant)	.405	.880		.460	.651
	E	5.651	1.878	.578	3.008	.008
a. Dependent Variable: ROA						

Excluded Variables[a]						
Model		Beta In	t	Sig.	Partial Correlation	Collinearity Statistics
						Tolerance
1	S	.103[b]	.468	.646	.113	.794
	G	.360[b]	1.778	.093	.396	.803

a. Dependent Variable: ROA
b. Predictors in the Model: (Constant), E

CONCLUSIONS

Findings

This study examined the degree of compliance of leading international real estate companies with the Global Reporting Initiative (GRI) standards in the context of environmental, social and governance (ESG) practices. Through the analysis of a sample of 20 companies from the world's top 100, it was found that the adoption of GRI standards shows a moderate level of implementation, reflecting an industry in the process of transitioning to more mature and transparent forms of corporate reporting.

Compliance with the GRI standards was found to be consistent, though not comprehensive, with zero company exceeding 62.5% with respect to the environmental requirements of the framework. This finding highlights the existence of significant areas for improvement, as well as potential difficulties in fully integrating sustainability standards, which may be related to the complexity of indicators, variation in strategic priorities and/or limitations in available resources.

Despite the moderate level of overall compliance, the study revealed a statistically significant and positive correlation between ESG performance and financial performance as captured through the return on assets (ROA). This result supports the hypothesis that incorporating sustainable practices can act not only as a risk management tool, but also as a driver of economic growth and competitive advantage. The environmental dimension of ESG seems to be of particular importance, which showed a stronger correlation with financial results. This finding is in line with international experience, whereby investments in green infrastructure and practices enhance asset value, reduce operating costs and increase attractiveness to investors and consumers.

Similarly, social and corporate governance indicators were also linked to positive financial results, confirming the importance of factors such as social responsibility, stakeholder engagement and institutional transparency. In addition, the observed consistency in company performance across different ESG elements suggests the adoption of a holistic approach, where strengthening one sustainability pillar has the potential to positively impact the others.

The findings of this research are consistent with related studies (Mamun, 2022) from other sectors, such as those analyzing the energy sector in Australia, and support the view that adopting strong ESG frameworks is a strategic choice with tangible economic benefits. Despite variations in the degree of importance attached to individual ESG dimensions by sector, it becomes clear that systematic and qualitative ESG reporting is associated with enhanced operational efficiency, better access to finance and long-term value creation.

In summary, the real estate sector seems to be at a critical maturity phase with regard to sustainability and corporate transparency. The so far modest, but promising, compliance with GRI standards suggests a growing awareness among companies of the strategic importance of sustainable development. ESG practices are no longer a goodwill option, but are becoming a key enabler of business resilience and performance. Given global trends and increased stakeholder expectations, it is reasonable to foresee further strengthening of compliance with GRI standards and deepening the quality of ESG reporting in the near future.

Limitations

Despite the contribution of this research to understanding the relationship between ESG practices and economic performance in the real estate sector, there are some limitations that need to be taken into account when interpreting the results. Firstly, the study focused exclusively on the real estate sector, specifically on 20 companies included in the list of the world's 100 largest companies according to Forbes. Although the sample is considered sufficient to investigate ESG standards in large companies, it may not be fully representative of the entire industry, especially with regard to SMEs or companies operating in emerging markets. The focus on leading companies may have led to an overestimation of the level of compliance or strategic commitment to sustainability issues.

In addition, measuring financial performance through the return on assets (ROA) ratio, although widespread and reliable, provides only one view of the financial picture. The inclusion of other indicators, such as net profit margin, return on equity (ROE), or share price, could provide a more complete and multi-dimensional assessment of the financial impact of ESG strategies. Finally, the study focuses mainly on quantitative data, limiting its in-depth analysis to qualitative data, such as corporate culture, internal decision-making processes or stakeholder perceptions. These factors may play a critical role in the implementation of ESG practices and the formulation of the related strategy, but cannot be adequately captured through compliance indicators or financial metrics.

Proposals for Future Research

Future research efforts could focus on broadening the sample in an attempt to include more companies from different geographical and operational contexts in the real estate industry in order to enhance the generalizability of the findings. At the same time, the inclusion of additional financial indicators beyond ROA, such as return on equity (ROE) or cash flow, could provide a more comprehensive capture of the relationship between ESG and financial performance.

Furthermore, it is suggested to use qualitative methodologies, such as case studies or interviews with business executives, to explore in depth the internal factors that influence decision-making on ESG compliance. Finally, the study of the contribution of digital technologies to the monitoring and disclosure of ESG performance is a contemporary and promising area of investigation.

REFERENCES

Adams, C. A., & Frost, G. R. (2008). Integrating sustainability reporting into management practices. *Accounting Forum, 32*(4), 288–302. DOI: 10.1016/j.accfor.2008.05.002

Ady, S. U., & Zahroh, S. (2024). *Corporate social responsibility disclosure on financial performance*. Reference Module in Social Sciences.

Aguinis, H., & Glavas, A. (2012). What we know and don't know about corporate social responsibility: A review and research agenda. *Journal of Management, 38*(4), 932–968. DOI: 10.1177/0149206311436079

Alatawi, M., & Daud, Z. (2022). Integrated reporting practices and firm performance: A review study. *Corporate & Business Strategy Review*, 3(2).

Algarni, M. A., Ali, M., Albort-Morant, G., Leal-Rodríguez, A. L., Latan, H., Ali, I., & Ullah, S. (2022). Make green, live clean! Linking adaptive capability and environmental behavior with financial performance through corporate sustainability performance. *Journal of Cleaner Production, 346*, 131156. DOI: 10.1016/j.jclepro.2022.131156

Aziz, M. F., & Haron, R. (2021). Corporate Social Responsibility Disclosure and Financial Performance of Shariah PLCS in Malaysia. *International Journal of Academic Research in Business & Social Sciences, 11*(6), 333–353. DOI: 10.6007/IJARBSS/v11-i6/10155

Bebchuk, L. A., & Fried, J. M. (2004). *Pay without performance: The unfulfilled promise of executive compensation*. Harvard University Press.

Benson, A. K., & Ganda, F. (2022). The impact of corporate governance and corporate sustainability on the performance of South African listed companies. *International Journal of Research in Business and Social Science, 11*(5), 155–175. DOI: 10.20525/ijrbs.v11i5.1838

Brown, H. S., de Jong, M., & Levy, D. L. (2009). Building institutions based on information disclosure: Lessons from GRI's sustainability reporting. *Journal of Cleaner Production, 17*(6), 571–580. DOI: 10.1016/j.jclepro.2008.12.009

Buallay, A. (2019). Between cost and value: Investigating the effects of sustainability reporting on a firm's performance. *Journal of Applied Accounting Research, 20*(3), 481–496. DOI: 10.1108/JAAR-12-2017-0137

Burhan, N., & Rahmanti, W. (2012). The impact of sustainability reporting on company performance. *Journal of Economics Business and Accountancy Ventura, 15*(2), 257. DOI: 10.14414/jebav.v15i2.79

Busch, T., & Hoffmann, V. H. (2011). How hot is your bottom line? Linking carbon and financial performance. *Business Strategy and the Environment, 50*(2), 233–265.

Cantero-Saiz, M., Polizzi, S., & Scannella, E. (2024). ESG and asset quality in the banking industry: The moderating role of financial performance. *Research in International Business and Finance, 69*, 102221. DOI: 10.1016/j.ribaf.2024.102221

CDP. (2021). Driving corporate action on climate change, water security and deforestation. Retrieved from https://www.cdp.net/

Chen, S., Song, Y., & Gao, P. (2023). Environmental, social, and governance (ESG) performance and financial outcomes: Analyzing the impact of ESG on financial performance. *Journal of Environmental Management, 345*, 118829. DOI: 10.1016/j.jenvman.2023.118829 PMID: 37688968

Chen, Z., & Xie, G. (2022). ESG disclosure and financial performance: Moderating role of ESG investors. *International Review of Financial Analysis, 83*, 102291. DOI: 10.1016/j.irfa.2022.102291

Christopher, T., & Filipovic, M. (2008). The extent and determinants of disclosure of global reporting initiative guidelines: Australian evidence. *Journal of Contemporary Issues in Business and Government, 14*(2), 17–40.

Coscun, Y. (2023). *The role of ESG in corporate financial performance and competitiveness*. Reference Module in Social Sciences.

Dhaliwal, D. S., Li, O. Z., Tsang, A., & Yang, Y. G. (2011). Voluntary nonfinancial disclosure and the cost of equity capital: The initiation of corporate social responsibility reporting. *The Accounting Review, 86*(1), 59–100. DOI: 10.2308/accr.00000005

Di Vaio, A., & Varriale, L. (2020). SDGs and airport sustainable performance: Evidence from Italy on organisational, accounting and reporting practices through financial and non-financial disclosure. *Journal of Cleaner Production, 249*, 119431. DOI: 10.1016/j.jclepro.2019.119431

Eccles, R. G., Ioannou, I., & Serafeim, G. (2014). The impact of corporate sustainability on organizational processes and performance. *Management Science, 60*(11), 2835–2857. DOI: 10.1287/mnsc.2014.1984

Eccles, R. G., & Krzus, M. P. (2010). *One report: Integrated reporting for a sustainable strategy*. John Wiley & Sons.

Elkington, J. (1994). Towards the sustainable corporation: Win-win-win business strategies for sustainable development. *California Management Review, 36*(2), 90–100. DOI: 10.2307/41165746

Freeman, R. E. (1984). *Strategic management: A stakeholder approach.* Pitman.

Hardi, E., & Chairina, C. (2019). The Effect of Sustainibility Reporting Disclosure and Its Impact on Companies Financial Performance. *Journal of Wetlands Environmental Management, 7*(1), 67. DOI: 10.20527/jwem.v7i1.188

Hart, S. L. (1995). A natural-resource-based view of the firm. *Academy of Management Review, 20*(4), 986–1014. DOI: 10.2307/258963

Hawken, P., Lovins, A., & Lovins, L. H. (1999). *Natural capitalism: Creating the next industrial revolution.* Little, Brown and Company.

IIRC (International Integrated Reporting Council). (2021). International Integrated Reporting Framework. Retrieved from https://www.integratedreporting.org/

Ioannou, I., & Serafeim, G. (2017). The consequences of mandatory corporate sustainability reporting: Evidence from four countries. Harvard Business School Research Working Paper.

Kiliç, M., Gurler, H. E., Kaya, A., & Lee, C. W. (2022). The Impact of Sustainability Performance on Financial Performance: Does Firm Size Matter? Evidence from Turkey and South Korea. *Sustainability (Basel), 14*(24), 16695. DOI: 10.3390/su142416695

Kolk, A. (2010). Trajectories of sustainability reporting by MNCs. *Journal of World Business, 45*(4), 367–374. DOI: 10.1016/j.jwb.2009.08.001

KPMG. (2017). *The road ahead: The KPMG Survey of Corporate Responsibility Reporting 2017.* KPMG International.

Laskar, N., Chakrabarty, T. K., & Maji, S. G. (2017). Corporate Sustainability Performance and Financial Performance: Empirical Evidence from Japan and India. *Management and Labour Studies*, 42(1).

Laskar, N., & Maji, S. G. (2017). Corporate sustainability performance and firm performance: Evidence from India and South Korea. *International Journal of Corporate Strategy and Social Responsibility, 1*(2), 118. DOI: 10.1504/IJCSSR.2017.084289

Lo, F.-Y., & Liao, P.-C. (2021). Rethinking financial performance and corporate sustainability: Perspectives on resources and strategies. *Technological Forecasting and Social Change, 162*, 120346. DOI: 10.1016/j.techfore.2020.120346

Loh, L., Thomas, T., & Wang, Y. (2017). Sustainability Reporting and Firm Value: Evidence from Singapore-Listed Companies. *Sustainability (Basel)*, *9*(11), 2112. DOI: 10.3390/su9112112

Mamun, M. (2022). Sustainability reporting of major electricity retailers in line with GRI: Australia evidence. *Journal of Accounting and Organizational Change*. Advance online publication.

Md Nor, N., Shaiful Bahari, H. A., Adnan, N. A., & Sheh Kamal, S. M. Q. A. (2016). The Effects of Environmental Disclosure on Financial Performance in Malaysia. *Procedia Economics and Finance*, *35*, 117–126. DOI: 10.1016/S2212-5671(16)00016-2

Mohd Said, R., Theng, L. T., Senik, R., & Yusri, Y. (2015). The state of sustainability disclosure and effects on companies' financial performance. *International Business Management*, *10*(18), 4342–4350.

Naeem, N., & Çankaya, S. (2022). The impact of ESG performance over financial performance: A study on global energy and power generation companies. *International Journal of Commerce and Finance*, *8*(1).

Naeem, N., Çankaya, S., & Bildik, R. (2022). Does ESG performance affect the financial performance of environmentally sensitive industries? A comparison between emerging and developed markets. *Borsa Istanbul Review*, 22(2).

Nnadi, M., & Mutyaba, P. E. (2023). *The moderating effect of corporate sustainability attributes of products on the financial performance of firms*. Reference Module in Social Sciences.

Nugrahani, T. S., & Artanto, D. A. (2022). Sustainability Reporting by Disclosing Economic, Social and Environmental Performance. *Studies in Business and Economics*, *17*(2), 216–226. DOI: 10.2478/sbe-2022-0034

Ortiz-Martínez, E., Marín-Hernández, S., & Santos-Jaén, J.-M. (2023). Sustainability, corporate social responsibility, non-financial reporting and company performance: Relationships and mediating effects in Spanish small and medium sized enterprises. *Sustainable Production and Consumption*, *35*, 349–364. DOI: 10.1016/j.spc.2022.11.015

Pereira da Silva, P. (2023). *The impact of non-financial disclosure on labor investment: International evidence*. Borsa Istanbul Review.

Pinem, D., & Aulia, S. (2023). The Effect of Corporate Sustainability Performance on the Values of Companies Listed in the Sri Kehati Index. *Formosa Journal of Sustainable Research*, *2*(3), 713–734. DOI: 10.55927/fjsr.v2i3.3073

Porter, M. E., & Kramer, M. R. (2006). Strategy and society: The link between competitive advantage and corporate social responsibility. *Harvard Business Review*, *84*(12), 78–92. PMID: 17183795

Porter, M. E., & Kramer, M. R. (2011). Creating shared value. *Harvard Business Review*, *89*(1/2), 62–77.

Putri Amrigan, A. R., Hamidi, M., & Adrianto, F. (2023). The Effect of Sustainability Report Disclosure Compliance on the Company's Financial Performance. *Journal Of Social Research*, *2*(4), 1028–1038. DOI: 10.55324/josr.v2i4.692

Reddy, K. (2010). The Effect of Sustainability Reporting on Financial Performance: An Empirical Study Using Listed Companies.

Remo-Diez, N., Mendaña-Cuervo, C., & Arenas-Parra, M. (2023). Exploring the asymmetric impact of sustainability reporting on financial performance in the utilities sector: A longitudinal comparative analysis. *Utilities Policy*, *84*, 101650. DOI: 10.1016/j.jup.2023.101650

Rojo-Suárez, J., Alonso-Conde, A. B., & Gonzalez-Ruiz, J. D. (2024). Does sustainability improve financial performance? An analysis of Latin American oil and gas firms. *Resources Policy*, *88*, 104484. DOI: 10.1016/j.resourpol.2023.104484

Saini, N., & Singhania, M. (2019). Performance relevance of environmental and social disclosures: The role of foreign ownership. *Benchmarking*, *26*(3), 1845–1873. DOI: 10.1108/BIJ-04-2018-0114

SASB (Sustainability Accounting Standards Board). (2021). SASB Standards. Retrieved from https://www.sasb.org/

TCFD (Task Force on Climate-related Financial Disclosures). (2021). Recommendations of the Task Force on Climate-related Financial Disclosures. Retrieved from https://www.fsb-tcfd.org/

UNEP FI & Mercer. (2007). *Demystifying Responsible Investment Performance: A review of key academic and broker research on ESG factors*. United Nations Environment Programme Finance Initiative.

Unerman, J. (2000). Methodological issues—Reflections on quantification in corporate social reporting content analysis. *Accounting, Auditing & Accountability Journal*, *13*(5), 667–681. DOI: 10.1108/09513570010353756

Velte, P. (2017). Does ESG performance have an impact on financial performance? Evidence from Germany. *Journal of Global Responsibility*, *8*(2), 169–178. DOI: 10.1108/JGR-11-2016-0029

Velte, P. (2023). Determinants and financial consequences of environmental performance and reporting: A literature review of European archival research. *Journal of Environmental Management*, *340*, 117916. DOI: 10.1016/j.jenvman.2023.117916 PMID: 37141659

Weygandt, J. J., Kimmel, P. D., & Kieso, D. E. (2007). *Accounting principles* (8th ed.). Wiley.

Zhang, D., & Lucey, B. M. (2022). Sustainable behaviors and firm performance: The role of financial constraints' alleviation. *Economic Analysis and Policy*, *74*, 220–233. DOI: 10.1016/j.eap.2022.02.003

APPENDIX

Table 6. Selected GRI standards

ENVIRONMENT	Climate Change Vulnerability (MSCI)(GRI 1: Material Topics 1011, GRI 101)
	Environmental Impact Financing (MSCI) (GRI 101)
	Opportunities in Clean Technology (MSCI) (GRI 101)
	Green Building Opportunities (MSCI) (Topic 11.8 Economic impacts)
	Renewable Energy Opportunities (MSCI) (GRI 101)
	Cancellations and Delays in Operations (ATHEX) (Disclosure 1-11 Embedding policy commitments)
	Environmental Management Systems (REFINITIV) (GRI 117)
	Green Revenues, R&D, and Capital Expenditures (CapEx) (REFINITIV) (GRI 11)

continued on following page

Table 6. Continued

SOCIAL	Sustainable Economic Activity (GRI 101-1)
	Legal Requests for User Data (ATHEX) (GRI 118-1)
	Labor Management (MSCI) (GRI 101)
	Product Safety & Quality (MSCI) (GRI 116)
	Responsible Investment (MSCI) (Topic 11.15 Local communities)
	Controversial Sourcing (MSCI) (GRI 111)
	Access to Communications (MSCI) (Disclosure 1-16)
	Access to Finance (MSCI) (Topic 11.16 Land and resource rights)
	Access to Healthcare (MSCI) (GRI 111: Local Communities)
	Promotion of Labor Relations (MOODYS) (GRI 101)
	Human Resources Management (MOODYS) (GRI 101)
	Responsible Restructuring Management (MOODYS) (Topic 11.19 Anti-competitive behavior)
	Career Management and Employability Promotion (MOODYS) (GRI 101)
	Working Conditions (MOODYS) (GRI 101)
	Respect for and Management of Working Hours (MOODYS) (GRI 101)
	Sustainable Supplier Relationships (MOODYS) (GRI 111)
	Integration of Social Factors into the Supply Chain (MOODYS) (GRI 111)
	Societal Impacts (MOODYS) (GRI 111)
	Respect for Freedom of Association and the Right to Collective Bargaining (MOODYS) (GRI 107)
	Non-discrimination and Diversity (MOODYS) (GRI 106)
	Respect for Human Rights Standards and Prevention of Violations (MOODYS) (GRI 110)
	Responsible Marketing (REFINITIV) (GRI 117)
	Product Quality (REFINITIV) (GRI 116)
	Data Privacy (REFINITIV) (GRI 118)
	Diversity and Inclusion (REFINITIV) (GRI 105)
	Social Capital (S&P GLOBAL) (Disclosure 107-1 Stakeholder engagement and management of concerns related to tax)

continued on following page

Table 6. Continued

GOVERNANCE	Critical Risk Management (ATHEX) (Disclosure 1-11 Embedding policy commitments)
	Business Ethics (MSCI) (GRI 115: Public Policy)
	Tax Transparency (MSCI) (GRI 107)
	Irregular Practices (MOODYS) (Disclosure 1-17 Compliance with laws and regulations)
	Prevention of Corruption and Money Laundering (MOODYS) (GRI 105)
	revention of Anti-competitive Practices (MOODYS) (GRI 106)
	Transparency, Integrity of Lobbying Strategies and Practices (MOODYS) (Disclosure 1-5 External assurance)
	Financial Strategy and Risk Management (MOODYS) (GRI 107)
	Governance Reliability and Track Record (MOODYS) (GRI 1: Material Topics 1011)
	CSR Strategy (REFINITIV) (Disclosure 1-11 Statement on sustainable development strategy)
	Remuneration (REFINITIV)(GRI 101)

Table 7. Percentages of GRI standards adopted by the sample companies

	GRI environmental standards	**GRI social standards**	**GRI governance standards**	**overall GRI standards**
Public Storage	0.625	0.269	0.545	0.400
Digital Realty Trust	0.250	0.115	0.182	0.156
Boston Properties	0.500	0.462	0.545	0.489
SEGRO	0.000	0.308	0.091	0.200
Welltower	0.500	0.346	0.273	0.356
Brookfield	0.375	0.346	0.455	0.378
americantower	0.375	0.346	0.364	0.356
prologis	0.500	0.231	0.091	0.244
Simon	0.250	0.192	0.182	0.200
Equinix	0.625	0.423	0.091	0.378
Alexandria	0.500	0.423	0.545	0.467
Realty Income Corporation	0.625	0.538	0.455	0.533
Essex Property Trust	0.500	0.231	0.364	0.311
Link Real Estate Investment Trust	0.625	0.769	0.727	0.733
Healthpeak Properties	0.500	0.346	0.545	0.422

continued on following page

Table 7. Continued

	GRI environmental standards	GRI social standards	GRI governance standards	overall GRI standards
PIK Group	0.500	0.385	0.182	0.356
Kimco Realty	0.375	0.308	0.636	0.400
Equity Residential	0.500	0.269	0.455	0.356
Ventas	0.375	0.269	0.091	0.244
Annaly Capital Management	0.375	0.538	0.273	0.444

Table 8. ROA of the sample companies for 2022

Companies	ROA
Public Storage	5.48
Digital Realty Trust	0.88
Boston Properties	3.63
SEGRO	1.06
Welltower	0.38
Brookfield	2.46
americantower	2.60
prologis	4.01
Simon	2.46
Equinix	4.41
Alexandria	3.51
Realty Income Corporation	1.88
Essex Property Trust	3.24
Link Real Estate Investment Trust	6.25
Healthpeak Properties	3.21
PIK Group	1.20
Kimco Realty	3.56
Equity Residential	3.78
Ventas	2.20
Annaly Capital Management	2.04

Table 9. Overall descriptive data of ESG

	N	Min	Max	Mean	Std. Deviation
E	20	.000	.625	.44375	.154297
S	20	.115	.769	.35577	.145457
G	20	.091	.727	.35455	.201991
ESG	20	.156	.733	.37111	.132178
ROA	20	.38	6.25	2.9120	1.50732

Chapter 15
Exploring Student Attitudes Toward ESG Integration Through Business Intelligence Tools

Athanasia Vrettou Gavrillidi
https://orcid.org/0009-0000-9033-3180
Hellenic Open University, Greece

ABSTRACT

As businesses place increasing importance on environmental, social, and governance (ESG) issues, the use of data and information technologies is becoming a key tool in strengthening these strategies. This study examines how students perceive the application of data and business intelligence (BI) tools in ESG policies. For this purpose, a questionnaire was developed and evaluated for its reliability and validity. Based on the analysis results, it became evident that most students believe that leveraging data enhances transparency, reliability, and better decision-making. However, some concerns were also expressed regarding data quality, how the data is used, and the complexity of ESG-related concepts. The research concludes that it is important for universities to incorporate relevant courses into their curricula, so that students are better prepared for the challenges of modern, sustainable business practices.

DOI: 10.4018/979-8-3373-5142-1.ch015

INTRODUCTION

As businesses increasingly prioritize environmental, social, and governance (ESG) issues in response to global sustainability demands and stakeholder expectations, the integration of data and advanced information technologies has emerged as a crucial enabler of effective ESG strategies (Papademetriou et al., 2024; Anastasiadou et al., 2025; Seremeti et al., 2024; Taraza et al., 2024a;2024b) and quality strategies as well (Taraza et al., 2023; Taraza et al., 2024c). Data-driven approaches allow organizations to monitor their ESG performance in real time, identify areas for improvement, and ensure greater transparency and accountability. Within this context, business intelligence (BI) tools—such as dashboards, analytics platforms, and predictive models—play a significant role in transforming raw data into actionable insights that support responsible and sustainable decision-making. As Liu et al. (2024) stated that in the content of "Artificial Intelligence + Education" era, AI is driving the advancement of high-quality education and demonstrating significant potential in fostering competencies related to Environmental, Socia and Governance (ESG) principles. Rodinos et al. (2024) argued that as technology continues to grow rapidly, AI has emerged as a transformative element in the field of education, stating innovative opportunities to improve both teaching and learning experiences. In addition, AI is redefining educational paradigms by introducing intelligent solutions that enhance doth instructional delivery and student engagement (Rodinos et al., 2024). As Fošner (2024) stated the incorporation of AI technologies into educational environments presents valuable opportunities to advance sustainability goals by reshaping and enriching the learning experience.

This study focuses on understanding how university students, as future professionals and decision-makers, perceive the use of data and BI tools in the design and implementation of ESG policies. By examining their views, concerns, and level of awareness, the research aims to assess the readiness of the next generation to engage with data-centric ESG practices and contribute to ethical, sustainable business environments.

PURPOSE OF THE STUDY

This research seeks to examine the perceptions of university students—future professionals and leaders—concerning the utilization of data and business intelligence (BI) tools in the development and implementation of Environmental, Social, and Governance (ESG) strategies. The main goal of the study is the development of a reliable and valid instrument that can evaluate Students' Attitudes Toward the Implementation of ESG Strategies through Business Intelligence (BI).

INSTRUMENT

For the aim of this research, a research instrument was developed which consisted of 78 items named Students' Attitudes Toward the Implementation of ESG Strategies through Business Intelligence (BI) (SAtIESGStBI) (5-point likert scale). In addition, the instrument includes 4 items related to students' demographic characteristics such as gender, age, Level of Study, School of Studies. The instrument entails eight Conceptual constructs named Knowledge and Understanding ($KnUI_i$) (e.g. KnU1: I understand the term ESG (Environmental, Social, Governance) (9 items), Attitudes and Opinions (AtO_i) (e.g. AtO_1: The implementation of ESG strategies is essential for modern businesses) (6 items), Intentions and Behavior (InB_i) (e.g. InB_1: I am interested in participating in projects or internships related to BI and ESG strategies) (8 items), Perceptions of the Role of Data in ESG Strategy (PeS_i) (e.g. PeS1: Data helps in the objective evaluation of ESG performance) (10 items), Education & Skills in ESG/BI (EdS_i) (e.g. EdS_1: My university offers adequate education on ESG) (13 items), Ethical and Social Dimensions of Data-Driven ESG (UBIi) (e.g. UBI_1: The use of BI for ESG should be guided by ethical principles) (13 items), Perceived Benefits & Risks (PBR_i) (e.g. PBR_1: The application of BI in ESG improves corporate transparency) (9 items) and Future & Innovation in the ESG-BI Field (FuI_i) (e.g. FuI_1: Business Intelligence (BI) technology will play a crucial role in the evolution of ESG) (10 items).

PILOT STUDY-DEMOGRAPHIC CHARACTERISTICS

Primarily, a pilot study was conducted in order the instrument named Students' Attitudes Toward the Implementation of ESG Strategies through Business Intelligence (BI) (SAtIESGStBI) to be evaluated for its reliability and validity. 50 students participated in the pilot study, of whom 31 were female and 19 were female. With respect to students' age, 12 were from 18 until 19 years old; 11 were from 19 until 20 years old; 10 were from 20 until 21 years old; 13 were from 21 until 22 years old; and finally, 6 were above 22 years old.

PILOT STUDY-RELIABILITY & VALIDITY OF THE RESEARCH INSTRUMENT

Attitudes Toward the Implementation of ESG Strategies through Business Intelligence (BI) (SAtIESGStBI) was evaluated by Cronbach alpha coefficient (*a*), Composite Reliability (CR) and Average Variance Extracted (AVE) (Anastasiadou,

2008a;2008b; Anastasiadou & Karakos, 2011; Anastasiadou 2012a;2012b;2012c. Kofou & Anastasiadou, 2014; Moisidou, 2019; Florou et al., 2015). Cronbach alpha coefficient (*a*) for Attitudes Toward the Implementation of ESG Strategies through Business Intelligence (BI) (SAtIESGStBI) instrument counts for 0.893 and is very satisfied (Anastasiadou & Loukas, 2009; Kapetanopoulou et al., 2021; Valkanos et al., 2010; Panistides & Anastasiadoi; 2015). Composite Reliability (CR) coefficient for Attitudes Toward the Implementation of ESG Strategies through Business Intelligence (BI) (SAtIESGStBI) instrument counts for 0.905 and is very satisfied (Anastasiadou et al., 2022; Papademetriou et al., 2022; Anastasiadou et al., 2022; Valsamidis ct al., 2024). Average Variance Extracted (AVE) coefficient for Attitudes Toward the Implementation of ESG Strategies through Business Intelligence (BI) (SAtIESGStBI) instrument counts for 0,506 and is very satisfied (Christoforidis & Anastasiadou 2024; Papadaki et al., 2023; Anastasiadou & Zirinoglou et al., 2025; Anastasiadou et al., 2024; Sophocleous et al., 2023a; Sophocleous et al., 2023b; Sophocleous et al., 2023c).

Cronbach alpha coefficient (*a*) for Knowledge and Understanding conceptual construct counts for 0.769 and is very satisfied (Anastasiadou & Masouras, 2023; Anastasiadou, 2023; Anastasiadou et al., 2023; Anastasiadou 2008). Composite Reliability (CR) coefficient for Knowledge and Understanding conceptual construct counts for 0.836 and is very satisfied (Anastasiadou et al., 2011; Anastasiadou et al., 2014; Anastasiadou, 2009;2023a;2023b; Anastasiadou & Papa, 2009). Average Variance Extracted (AVE) coefficient for Knowledge and Understanding conceptual construct counts for 0.502 and is very satisfied (Anastasiadou, 2013c; Anastasiadou & Tiliakou, 2024; Thapa et al., 2016; Anastasiadou & Anastasiadis, 2029; Tsourgianis et al., 2019; Papademetriou et., 2022).

Cronbach alpha coefficient (*a*) for Attitudes and Opinions conceptual construct counts for 0.781 and is very satisfied (Anastasiadou et al., 2025; Anastasiadou, 2018a; 2018b; Anastasiadou, 2013). Composite Reliability (CR) coefficient for Attitudes and Opinions conceptual construct counts for 0.851 and is very satisfied (Taraza & Anastasiadou, 2019a; 2019b). Average Variance Extracted (AVE) coefficient for Attitudes and Opinions conceptual construct counts for 0.549 and is very satisfied (Anastasiadou, 2020; Anastasiadou & Taraza, 2019;2020a;2020b).

Cronbach alpha coefficient (*a*) for Intentions and Behavior conceptual construct counts for 0.832 and is very satisfied (Anastasiadou et al., 2016; Anastasiadou & Tiliakou, 2014;2016a;2016b). Composite Reliability (CR) coefficient for Intentions and Behavior conceptual construct counts for 0.893 and is very satisfied (Anastasiadou et al., 2014; Anastasiadou 2012a;2012b). Average Variance Extracted (AVE) coefficient for Intentions and Behavior conceptual construct counts for 0.528 and is very satisfied (Anastasiadou & Florou, 2013; Florou & Anastasiadou, 2013).

Cronbach alpha coefficient (*a*) for Perceptions of the Role of Data in ESG Strategy conceptual construct counts for 0.807 and is very satisfied (Anastasiadou et al., 2015; Anastasiadou, 2024; Anastasiadou & Kofou 2012). Composite Reliability (CR) coefficient for Perceptions of the Role of Data in ESG Strategy conceptual construct counts for 0.875 and is very satisfied (Anastasiadou & Kofou, 2012; 2013; Kofou & Anastasiadou, 2013;2014). Average Variance Extracted (AVE) coefficient for Perceptions of the Role of Data in ESG Strategy conceptual construct counts for 0.512 and is very satisfied (Anastasiadou, 2018; Kofou & Anastasiadou, 2013;2014; Anastasiadou & Florou, 2013; Florou & Anastasiadou, 2013; Anastasiadou et al., 2022).

Cronbach alpha coefficient (*a*) for Education & Skills in ESG/BI conceptual construct counts for 0.825 and is very satisfied (Anastasiadou & Zirinoglou, 2025; Anastasiadou & Masouras, 2023; Anastasiadou et al., 2022; Anastasiadou et al., 2024). Composite Reliability (CR) coefficient for Education & Skills in ESG/BI conceptual construct counts for 0.905 and is very satisfied (Anastasiadou & Kofou, 2012; 2013; Kofou & Anastasiadou, 2013;2014; Anastasiadou 2013a;2013b;2013c). Average Variance Extracted (AVE) coefficient for Education & Skills in ESG/BI conceptual construct counts for 0.537 and is very satisfied (Anastasiadou, 2018;2023; Anastasiadou & Papa, 2009; Kofou & Anastasiadou, 2013;2014; Anastasiadou & Florou, 2013; Florou & Anastasiadou, 2013; Anastasiadou et al., 2022; Valkanos et al., 2010; Theodoridou et al., 2014; Panitsides & Anastasiadou (2015).

Cronbach alpha coefficient (*a*) for Ethical and Social Dimensions of Data-Driven ESG conceptual construct counts for 0.877 and is very satisfied (Valsamidis et al., 2024; Tsourgiannis et al., 2019; Anastasiadou, 2024; Anastasiadou et al., 2022; Papademetriou et al., 2022; Papadaki et al., 2023). Composite Reliability (CR) coefficient for Ethical and Social Dimensions of Data-Driven ESG counts for 0.924 and is very satisfied (Anastasiadou & Zirinoglou, 2015; Anastasiadou et al., 2010; Anastasiadou et al., 2015). Average Variance Extracted (AVE) coefficient for Ethical and Social Dimensions of Data-Driven ESG conceptual construct counts for 0.542 and is very satisfied (Anastasiadou, 2011; Anastasiadou et al., 2011; Anastasiadou et al., 2023; Anastasiadou & Anastasiadis, 2019).

Cronbach alpha coefficient (*a*) for Perceived Benefits & Risks conceptual construct counts for 0.901 and is very satisfied (Anastasiadou & Zirinoglou, 2014; 2020a;2020b; Anastasiadou et al., 2014). Composite Reliability (CR) coefficient for Perceived Benefits & Risks counts for 0.937 and is very satisfied (Thapa et al., 2016; Anastasiadou & Zirinoglou, 2020c;2020d;2020e). Average Variance Extracted (AVE) coefficient for Perceived Benefits & Risks conceptual construct counts for 0.605 and is very satisfied (Anastasiadou & Kofou, 2012; Anastasiadou & Dimitriadou, 2011; Taraza & Anastasiadou, 2019a;2019b).

Cronbach alpha coefficient (*a*) for Future & Innovation in the ESG-BI Field conceptual construct counts for 0.794 and is very satisfied (Agorogianni et al., 2011; Anastasiadou 2019a;2019b). Composite Reliability (CR) coefficient for Future & Innovation in the ESG-BI Field counts for 0.816 and is very satisfied (Anastasiadou & Kofou, 2013; Anastasiadou & Taraza 2019a;2019b; Papademetriou, et al., 2022). Average Variance Extracted (AVE) coefficient for Future & Innovation in the ESG-BI Field counts for 0.519 and is very satisfied (Anastasiadou, 2018c;2020).

The results indicated that Attitudes Toward the Implementation of ESG Strategies through Business Intelligence (BI) (SAtIESGStBI) instrument is reliable, as well as its conceptual constructs (Table 1).

Table 1. Reliability coefficients_ SAtIESGStBI scale

Scale-Conceptual Constructs	Cronbach alpha coefficient (a)	CR	AVE
Attitudes Toward the Implementation of ESG Strategies through Business Intelligence (BI) (SAtIESGStBI)	0.893	0.905	0.506
Knowledge and Understanding	0.769	0.836	0.502
Attitudes and Opinions	0.781	0.851	0.549
Intentions and Behavior	0.832	0.893	0.528
Perceptions of the Role of Data in ESG Strategy	0.807	0.875	0.512
Education & Skills in ESG/BI	0.825	0.905	0.537
Ethical and Social Dimensions of Data-Driven ESG	0.877	0.924	0.542
Perceived Benefits & Risks	0.901	0.937	0.605
Future & Innovation in the ESG-BI Field	0.794	0.816	0.519

Table 2 presents the eigenvalue, %variance, loading & communalities indices. These indices are acceptable revealing the validity of Attitudes Toward the Implementation of ESG Strategies through Business Intelligence (BI) (SAtIESGStBI) Instrument. Plus, the measure model fits the observed data ($x^2/df=1.96$, CFI=0.97. GFI=0.94, RMSEA=0.04, AGFI=0.93, IFI=0.93) (Anastasiadou & Papa, 2009; Anastasiadou 2012a;2023a;2013b) (Table 2).

Table 2. Eigenvalue, %variance, loading & communalities

Construct	Item	Eigenvalue	Variance%	Loadings	Communalities
SAtIESGStBI					
Knowledge and Understanding		4.156	46.177%		
	KnU1			0.795	0.752

continued on following page

Table 2. Continued

Construct	Item	Eigenvalue	Variance%	Loadings	Communalities
	KnU2			0.754	0.732
	KnU3			0.726	0.716
	KnU4			0.716	0.700
	KnU5			0.676	0.695
	KnU6			0.654	0.659
	KnU7			0.590	0.623
	KnU8			0.575	0.619
	KnU9			0.501	0.604
Attitudes and Opinions		3.076	51.263		
	AtO1			0.776	0.485
	AtO2			0.757	0.573
	AtO3			0.713	0.602
	AtO4			0.705	0.509
	AtO5			0.696	0.410
	AtO6			0.641	0.497
Intentions and Behavior		4.859	60.742		
	InB1			0.836	0.568
	InB2			0.811	0.571
	InB3			0.796	0.657
	InB4			0.768	0.634
	InB5			0.767	0.698
	InB6			0.756	0.553
	InB7			0.754	0.588
	InB8			0.744	0.589
Perceptions of the Role of Data in ESG Strategy		5.377	53.772		
	PeS1			0.771	0.533
	PeS2			0.767	0.483
	PeS3			0.747	0.612
	PeS4			0.739	0.596
	PeS5			0.696	0.673
	PeS6			0.634	0.589
	PeS7			0.620	0.654
	PeS8			0.553	0.526
	PeS9			0.542	0.475
	PeS10			0.490	0.324

continued on following page

Table 2. Continued

Construct	Item	Eigenvalue	Variance%	Loadings	Communalities
Education & Skills in ESG/BI		3.439	26.451		
	EdS1			0.803	0.764
	EdS2			0.767	0.867
	EdS3			0.762	0.812
	EdS4			0.672	0.882
	EdS5			0.669	0.722
	EdS6			0.565	0.827
	EdS7			0.560	0.888
	EdS8			0.545	0.924
	EdS9			0.540	0.894
	EdS10			0.509	0.879
	EdS11			0.468	0.828
	EdS12			0.444	0.839
	EdS13			0.426	0.831
Ethical and Social Dimensions of Data-Driven ESG		8.802	61.711		
	UBI1			0.535	0.505
	UBI2			0.582	0.569
	UBI3			0.664	0.613
	UBI4			0.664	0.613
	UBI5			0.631	0.574
	UBI6			0.489	0.514
	UBI7			0.632	0.597
	UBI8			0.734	0.675
	UBI9			0.682	0.649
	UBI10			0.671	0.603
	UBI11			0.845	0.775
	UBI12			0.722	0.748
	UBI13			0.795	0.770
Perceived Benefits & Risks		5.042	56.024		
	PBR1			0.812	0.659
	PBR2			0.792	0.628
	PBR3			0.789	0.622
	PBR4			0.780	0.609
	PBR5			0.739	0.545
	PBR6			0.737	0.543

continued on following page

Table 2. Continued

Construct	Item	Eigenvalue	Variance%	Loadings	Communalities
	PBR7			0.733	0.537
	PBR8			0.680	0.463
	PBR9			0.661	0.436
Future & Innovation in the ESG-BI Field		4.484	44.843		
	FuI1			0.748	0.560
	FuI2			0.739	0.546
	FuI3			0.708	0.501
	FuI4			0.706	0.498
	FuI5			0.704	0.495
	FuI6			0.680	0.463
	FuI7			0.660	0.436
	FuI8			0.604	0.365
	FuI9			0.597	0.356
	FuI10			0.516	0.346

x^2/df=1.96, CFI=0.97. GFI=0.94, RMSEA=0.04, AGFI=0.93, IFI=0.93

In addition, the mean values of Attitudes Toward the Implementation of ESG Strategies through Business Intelligence (BI) (SAtIESGStBI) and its conceptual constructs reveled students positive attitude toward them (Table 3).

Table 3. Reliability coefficients_ SAtIESGStBI scale

Scale-Conceptual Constructs	M
Attitudes Toward the Implementation of ESG Strategies through Business Intelligence (BI) (SAtIESGStBI)	4.428
Knowledge and Understanding	4.234
Attitudes and Opinions	4.501
Intentions and Behavior	4.152
Perceptions of the Role of Data in ESG Strategy	4.875
Education & Skills in ESG/BI	4.439
Ethical and Social Dimensions of Data-Driven ESG	4.256
Perceived Benefits & Risks	4.536
Future & Innovation in the ESG-BI Field	4.429

CONCLUSION

A 78-item instrument named Students' Attitudes Toward the Implementation of ESG Strategies through Business Intelligence (BI) (SAtIESGStBI) (5-point likert scale) was developed and evaluated for its reliability and validity. The instruments entailed eight conceptual constructs named Knowledge and Understanding, Attitudes and Opinions, Intentions and Behavior, Perceptions of the Role of Data in ESG Strategy, Education & Skills in ESG/BI, Ethical and Social Dimensions of Data-Driven ESG, Perceived Benefits & Risks and Future & Innovation in the ESG-BI Field. Its reliability and validity were examined and proved through a pilot study. In addition, the results show students' positive attitudes toward the Implementation of ESG Strategies through Business Intelligence (BI) and its conceptual constructions. The strongest positive attitude was toward Perceptions of the Role of Data in ESG Strategy and the following one toward Perceived Benefits & Risks following by the conceptual construct named Attitudes and Opinions.

Nevertheless, Students' Attitudes Toward the Implementation of ESG Strategies through Business Intelligence (BI) assumes deeper research into the near future by the help of AI (Seremeti et al., 2025; Souravlas & Anastasiadou, 2021;2022; Souravlas et al., 2021a;2021b) and Cloud Computing (Souravlas et al., 2021c; 2022; 2023a; 2023b, Tantalaki et al., 2020; Agorogianni et al., 2011).

REFERENCES

Agorogianni, A. Z., Zaharis, Z. D., Anastasiadou, S. D., & Goudos, S. K. (2011). Distance learning technology and service support in Greece: The case study of the Aristotle University over the last decade" has. *Education and Information Technologies, 16*(1), 25–39. DOI: 10.1007/s10639-009-9110-3

Anastasiadou, S. (2008a). It's the Men's World: Greek Males' Students Believe that the Womens' Position must be Home with the Kids. *The International Journal of Interdisciplinary Social Sciences: Annual Review, 2*(5), 123–132. DOI: 10.18848/1833-1882/CGP/v02i05/59344

Anastasiadou, S. (2008b). Exploring intrinsic and extrinsic motivation during a PhD completion with the aid of Confirmatory Factor Analysis and Path Analysis: The case of Greek PhD students. *The International Journal of Interdisciplinary Social Sciences: Annual Review, 3*(2), 171–178. DOI: 10.18848/1833-1882/CGP/v03i02/52518

Anastasiadou, S. (2009). The effects of different modes of representation in statistical problems solving: A study with third grade primary school pupils. *International Journal of Learning, 16*(4), 27–36. DOI: 10.18848/1447-9494/CGP/v16i04/46206

Anastasiadou, S. (2011). Reliability and validity testing of a new scale for monitoring attitudes toward learning statistics with technology. *Acta Didactica Napocencia, 4*(1), 1–10

Anastasiadou, S. (2012a). A structural model describes Chinese tradesmen attitudes towards Greek students' consumption behaviour. *4th International Conference The Economies of Balkan and Eastern Europe Countries in the changed world EBEEC 2012*, Sofia, Bulgaria. pp. 489-501.

Anastasiadou, S. (2012b). *Reliability and validity testing of a new scale for measuring attitudes toward Chinese products.* 4th International Conference. The Economies of Balkan and Eastern Europe Countries in the changed world EBEEC 2012, Sofia, Bulgaria. pp 536-548.

Anastasiadou, S. (2012c). Diversifications between Expected and Perceived Attitudes toward Learning Statistics with Technology: A Multilevel Statistical Analysis. *International Journal of Learning, 18*(3), 161–176. DOI: 10.18848/1447-9494/CGP/v18i03/47520

Anastasiadou, S. (2013a). Developing and Evaluating a Structural Equation Model Measuring Leadership Changes in a Lifelong Learning World. *The International Journal of Educational Organization and Leadership, 19*(2), 1–17. DOI: 10.18848/2329-1656/CGP/v19i02/48520

Anastasiadou, S. (2013b). Evaluating a Structural Equation Model Measuring Attitudes toward Reading Books and E-books. *The International Journal of the Book, 10*(2), 1–10. DOI: 10.18848/1447-9516/CGP/v10i02/57863

Anastasiadou, S. (2013c). Evaluating a Structural Equation Model Measuring Lifelong Learning and Continuing Education Factors. Management Education. *International Journal (Toronto, Ont.), 12*(3), 21–34. DOI: 10.18848/2327-8005/CGP/v12i03/50849

Anastasiadou, S. (2018a). *Greek Tertiary Education System Evaluation in Respect of Quality Assurance Dimensions According to Malcolm Baldrige Performance Excellence Model,* Springer Proceedings in Business and Economics, 811-825. .DOI: 10.1007/978-3-319-70377-0_56

Anastasiadou, S. (2018b). Comparison of multivariate methods in group/cluster identification. Dissertation thesis of the degree of MSc. in Research Methodology in Biomedicine, Biostatistics and Clinical Bioinformatics, Faculty of Medicine, University of Thessaly.

Anastasiadou, S. (2018c). Leadership according to EFQM Model in Tertiary education: The case of Greek Universities. *Proceedings of 10th International Conference The Economies of the Balkan and the Eastern European Countries in the changing world, EBEEC 2018*, Warsaw, Poland, pp. 20-24.

Anastasiadou, S. (2019a). *Internal representations toward external representations: The case of statistical concepts.* 11th annual International Conference on Education and New Learning Technologies Palma de Mallorca, Spain, EDULEARN 19, pp. 6-9. DOI: 10.21125/edulearn.2019.0004

Anastasiadou, S. (2019b). *Pre-service teachers' attitudes toward the use of different modes of representation in statistics teaching and learning.* 11th annual International Conference on Education and New Learning Technologies Palma de Mallorca, Spain, EDULEARN 19. pp. 1-5. DOI: 10.21125/edulearn.2019.0003

Anastasiadou, S. (2020). *Economic effects of the pandemic COVID-19: Greek citizens express their faith in the Greek government for the protective measures toward the pandemic and economic measures toward a new economic crisis*, EBEEC 2020. e-book of EBEEC, pp.101-114.

Anastasiadou, S. (2023). Psychometric Testing Procedures for Attitudes Toward Reproductive Tourism and Cross Border Reproductive Care (ATCBRC). In Kavoura, A., Borges-Tiago, T., & Tiago, F. (Eds.), *Strategic Innovative Marketing and Tourism. ICSIMAT 2023. Springer Proceedings in Business and Economics*. Springer., DOI: 10.1007/978-3-031-51038-0_14

Anastasiadou, S. & Anastasiadis, L. (2019). *Quality Assurance in Education in the Light of the Effectiveness of Transformational School Leadership*, Springer Proceedings in Business and Economics, (2019) 323–344.

Anastasiadou, S., Anastasiadis, L., Angeletos, T., & Vandikas, J. (2010). A Multidimensional Statistical Analysis of Students' Attitudes toward Physics. *The International Journal of Diversity in Organisations, Communities and Nations, 16*(5), 341–356. DOI: 10.18848/1447-9532/CGP/v10i01/39794

Anastasiadou, S., Anastasiadis, L., Florou, G., & Valsamidis, S. (2022). *Greek students' Environmental Attitude based on the Theory of Ecological Attitude,* HAICTA, CEUR Workshop Proceedings (CEUR-WS.org), 222-231.

Anastasiadou, S., Anastasiadis, L., Kalabouka, K., & Florou, G. (2014). Ethnocentrism, patriotism and animosity impact on freedom of competition and business activity. *WSEAS TRANSACTIONS on BUSINESS and ECONOMICS*, Vol 11, pp. 692-699. Part of ISSN: 11099526.

Anastasiadou, S., Anastasiadis, L., Vandikas, I., & Angeletos, T. (2011). Implicative Statistical Analysis and Principal Components Analysis in Recording Students' Attitudes to Electronics and Electrical Construction Subjects. *International Journal of Technology, Knowledge and Society*, 7(1), 63–78. DOI: 10.18848/1832-3669/CGP/v07i01/56184

Anastasiadou, S., & Florou, G. (2013). Consumer Ethnocentrism: The case of Greek students. *3rd International Conference on Quantitative and Qualitative Methodologies*, Athens, pp. 52-57.

Anastasiadou, S., Fotiadis, T., Anastasiadis, L, Iakovidis, G, Fotiadou, X. & Tiliakou, C. (2016). Estimate and analysis of vocational training school (IEK) students' satisfaction regarding the quality of studies provided by these schools, *Scientific Bulletin – Economic Sciences*, Vol. 15, Issue 2, 8-45.

Anastasiadou, S., & Karakos, A. (2011). The Beliefs of Electrical and Computer Engineering Students' Regarding Computer Programming. *International Journal of Technology, Knowledge and Society*, 7(1), 37–52. DOI: 10.18848/1832-3669/CGP/v07i01/56170

Anastasiadou, S., & Kofou, I. (2012). The Development of a Structure Equation Model, for Goal Achievement and Preparation for a Future Education Leader. *The International Journal of Educational Organization and Leadership, 19*(2), 41–55. DOI: 10.18848/2329-1656/CGP/v19i02/58957

Anastasiadou, S., & Kofou, I. (2013). Incorporating Web 2.0 Tools into Greek Schools. *International Journal of Technologies in Learning, 20*(1), 11–23.

Anastasiadou, S., & Loukas, D. (2009). Greek Pre-Service Teachers' Cognitive Abilities in Understanding the Concept of Frequency: A Multilevel Statistical Analysis. *International Journal of Learning, 16*(5), 189–202. DOI: 10.18848/1447-9494/CGP/v16i05/46268

Anastasiadou, S., & Masouras, A. (2023). *Exploring determinants regarding Visit and Revisit intentions considering Greece as a Medical Tourism destination.* 10th International Conference on Strategic Innovative Marketing and Tourism. Zakynthos, Ionian Islands, Greece. In A. Kavoura et al. (eds.), Strategic Innovative Marketing and Tourism, Springer Proceedings in Business and Economics, (2023), 101-109. DOI: 10.1007/978-3-031-51038-0_12

Anastasiadou, S., Masouras, A., & Papademetriou, C. (2023). Attitudes toward Reproductive Tourism and Cross border reproductive care (CBRC): Legal, Economic, Ethical issues and dilemmas, possibilities and limitations. *Proceedings of the 6th International Conference on Tourism Research, ICTR 2023*, 7-23, Pafos, Cyprus. DOI: 10.34190/ictr.6.1.1189

Anastasiadou, S., & Papa, A. (2009). Structural Equation Modeling in the Construction of a Structural Model of Educational Research. *The International Journal of Interdisciplinary Social Sciences: Annual Review, 4*(5), 151–158. DOI: 10.18848/1833-1882/CGP/v04i05/52914

Anastasiadou, S., Papademetriou, C., Anastasiadis, L., Valsamidis, S., & Florou, G. (2025). *ESG in Digital Era Becomes DESG: The Impact of DESG on Students' Attitudes and Higher Education.* In K. Ragazou, A. Garefalakis, C. Papademetriou, & A. Samara (Eds.), Sustainability Through Green HRM and Performance Integration (pp. 173-190). IGI Global Scientific Publishing. https://doi.org/DOI: 10.4018/979-8-3693-5981-5.ch008

Anastasiadou, S., & Taraza, E. (2019a). Pre-service teachers' perceptions toward leadership regarding the MBVQA Model. *Proceedings of 11th annual International Conference on Education and New Learning EDULEARN 19 Palma de Mallorca*, Spain, pp. 533-543, DOI: 10.21125/edulearn.2019.0183

Anastasiadou, S., & Taraza, E. (2019b). *The structure and paths of Malcolm Baldrige National Quality Award (MBNQA) dimensions applied in Greek Tetriary educational systems dimensions in Greek Tertiary Education System.* 11th annual International Conference on Education and New Learning Technologies Palma de Mallorca, Spain, EDULEARN 19, pp. 455-463.

Anastasiadou, S., & Taraza, E. (2019c). *Total quality management: implementation of the six-sigma methodology for improving quality in higher education*, ICERI2019, the 12th annual International Conference of Education, Research and Innovation, Seville (Spain), ICERI2019, pp. 9533-9537. DOI: 10.21125/iceri.2019.2318

Anastasiadou, S., & Taraza, E. (2020a). *Resistance to Change as an Obstacle Regarding Quality in Higher Education Institutions (HEIS).* Proceedings of of 14th annual International Technology, *Education and Development Conference (INTED2020)*, Valencia, Spain, pp. 396-401.

Anastasiadou, S., & Taraza, E. (2020b). *Six Sigma in Tertiary Education: A Win of Change regarding Quality Improvement in Education*, Proceedings of of 14th annual International Technology, Education and Development Conference (INTED2020), Valencia, Spain, pp. 9595-9601. DOI: 10.21125/inted.2020.0167

Anastasiadou, S., & Tiliakou, C. (2014). Classical Item Analysis of the Greek State of English Language Proficiency "A" Level Exam. *The International Journal of Literacies, 20*(3), 39–53. DOI: 10.18848/2327-0136/CGP/v20i03/48819

Anastasiadou, S., & Tiliakou, C. (2016a). Investigation of the discriminating ability of the Greek State certificate of language proficiency by means of Vacor method: The case of Greek-speaking and Turkish-speaking bilingual students from the Muslim minority of Thrace. *International Journal of Learning and Teaching, 8*(2), 109–118. DOI: 10.18844/ijlt.v8i2.517

Anastasiadou, S., & Tiliakou, C. (2016b). Evaluation of the discriminating ability of the Greek state foreign language exam (KPG) for English by means of the factorial analysis of correspondences. *International Journal of Learning and Teaching, 8*(2), 129–140. DOI: 10.18844/ijlt.v8i2.518

Anastasiadou, S., & Zirinoglou, P. (2015). Teachers' attitudes toward Quality Assurance Dimensions regarding EFQM Model in Primary Education in Greece. *Procedia Economics and Finance, 33*, 411–431. DOI: 10.1016/S2212-5671(15)01725-6

Anastasiadou, S., & Zirinoglou, P. (2020a). Total Quality Management: Statistical Process Control and Quality Control' Tools regarding Measuring Organizations' Quality. The case of Pareto Chart. *International Journal of Entrepreneurship and Innovative Competitiveness – IJEIC,* Vol 2. Iss. 2.

Anastasiadou, S., & Zirinoglou, P. (2020b). Statistical Process Control and Quality Control' Tools regarding Measuring Organizations' Quality: The case of Ishikawa's approach in Greek tertiary education system evaluation in respect of quality assurance *International Journal of Entrepreneurship and Innovative Competitiveness – IJEIC,* Vol 2. Iss. 2.

Anastasiadou, S., & Zirinoglou, P. (2020c). Greek students' entrepreneurial profile, attidute and behaviour: A mutidimentional statistical analysis. *International Journal of Entrepreneurship and Innovative Competitiveness– IJEIC, Vol 2. Iss. 2.*

Anastasiadou, S., & Zirinoglou, P. (2020d). Quality assessment in Greek Tertiary Education using Gap Analysis *International Journal of Entrepreneurship and Innovative Competitiveness – IJEIC.* Vol 2, Issue 1.

Anastasiadou, S., & Zirinoglou, P. (2020e). Reliability and Validity Analysis of validity testing of a new scale for monitoring Students Attitudes toward Entrepreneurship Courses (SATEC). International Journal of Entrepreneurship and Innovative Competitiveness – IJEIC, Vol 2, Issue 1.

Anastasiadou, S. & Zirinoglou, P. (2025). *L'Analyse Factorielle des Correspondances Reveal Students' Attitudes Toward Entrepreneurship.* Source Title: Real-World Tools and Scenarios for Entrepreneurship Exploration, 79-100. .DOI: 10.4018/979-8-3693-3100-2.ch004

Anastasiadou, S. Zirinoglou, P., Seremeti, L., Masouras, A. Komodromos, M. & Anastasiadis, L. (2024). *Statistical Implicative Analysis: A Distinguished Statistical Methodology in Evaluating Greek Students' Attitudes Toward the Use of AI Source* Title: Real-World Tools and Scenarios for Entrepreneurship Exploration, 79-100, .DOI: 10.4018/979-8-3693-3100-2.ch006

Anastasiadou, S., & Zirinolou, P. (2014). Reliability testing of EFQM scale: The case of Greek secondary teachers. *Procedia: Social and Behavioral Sciences, 143,* 990–994. DOI: 10.1016/j.sbspro.2014.07.541

Anastasiadou, S., Zirinolou, P., & Florou, G. (2014). The European Foundation Quality Management evaluation of Greek Primary and Secondary Education. *Procedia: Social and Behavioral Sciences, 143,* 932–940. DOI: 10.1016/j.sbspro.2014.07.530

Anastasiadou, S. D. (2024). *Students' Attitudes Toward Real-World Tools for Entrepreneurship Exploration in Tertiary Education. In* Real-World Tools and Scenarios for Entrepreneurship Exploration, 25-52. DOI: 10.4018/979-8-3693-3100-2.ch002

Anastasiadou, S. D., Batiou, V., & Valkanos, E. (2015). Occupational Mobility Dimensions in Greece. *Procedia Economics and Finance, 2015*(19), 325–331. DOI: 10.1016/S2212-5671(15)00033-7

Anastasiadou, SD., Papalexandris, S. & Konteos, G. (2022). *The Effect of Emotional Intelligence on Perceived e-Service Quality, Consumers' Perceived Value, Purchase, Loyalty Intentions and Satisfaction.* HAICTA, (2022), 151-161.

Christoforidis, C., & Anastasiadou, S. (2024). *Human Resource Management as a Contributor of Total Quality Management, ESG and Total Quality Management in Human Resources.* IGI Global.

Florou, G., & Anastasiadou, S. (2013). *Academic staff of Greek technological educational institutes. 3rd International Conference on Quantitative and Qualitative Methodologies*, Athens, pp. 52-156.

Florou, G., Anastasiadou, S., Karasavvoglou, A., Valsamidis, S., & Mandilas, A. (2015). *Greek public tertiary education departments of agriculture*, CEUR Workshop Proceedings of the 7th International Conference on Information and Communication Technologies in Agriculture, Food and Environment (HAICTA), 471-479.

Fošner, A. (2024). University Students' Attitudes and Perceptions towards AI Tools: Implications for Sustainable Educational Practices. *Sustainability (Basel), 2024*(16), 8668. DOI: 10.3390/su16198668

Kapetanopoulou, P., Kouroutzi, A., & Anastasiadou, S. (2021). The Impact of Information Systems Implementation in the Greek Manufacturing Enterprises. *Applied Sciences (Basel, Switzerland), 11*(24), 11781. DOI: 10.3390/app112411781

Kofou, I. & Anastasiadou, (2014). Incorporating web 2.0 into Greek schools, *International Journal of Technologies in Learning*, 20:1, 11-23. .DOI: 10.18848/2327-0144/CGP/v20i01/49120

Kofou, I., & Anastasiadou, S. (2013). Language and Communication Needs Analysis in Intercultural Education. *The International Journal of Diversity in Education, 12*(2), 15–64. DOI: 10.18848/2327-0020/CGP/v12i02/58049

Liu, S., Jiang, J., Wei, K., Wu, R., & Xu, Y. (2024). Enhancing University Students' ESG Competencies Through "Artificial Intelligence + Education"-A Case Study of ChatGPT, *2024 International Conference on Digital Technology and Intelligent Education (ICDTIE)*, Shenzhen, China, 2024, pp. 27-30. DOI: 10.1109/ICDTIE65977.2024.00012

Moisidou, A., Voulgarakis, N., Folinas, D., Konstantoglou, A., Kokmotos, E., & Anastasiadou, S. (2019). Evaluation of the Reuse of Packaging in the Food Supply Chain, Springer Proceedings in Business and Economics. In Sakas, D. P., & Nasiopoulos, D. K. (Eds.), *Strategic Innovative Marketing, Springer Proceedings in Business and Economics, Springer Nature Switzerland AG (2019) 43-51.*, DOI: 10.1007/978-3-030-16099-9_6

Panitsides, E., & Anastasiadou, S. (2015). Lifelong Learning Policy Agenda in the European Union: A bi- level analysis. *Open Review of Educational Research, 2*(1), 128–142. DOI: 10.1080/23265507.2015.1043936

Papadaki, Z., Anastasiadou, S., Masouras, A., & Papalexandris, S. (2023). *Factors Influencing the Use of Digital Marketing by Telemedicine Services. 10th International Conference on Strategic Innovative Marketing and Tourism.* Zakynthos, Ionian Islands, Greece. In A. Kavoura et al. (eds.), Strategic Innovative Marketing and Tourism, Springer Proceedings in Business and Economics, (2023), 855-862. DOI: 10.1007/978-3-031-51038-0_92

Papademetriou, C. Anastasiadou, SD. Konteos, G. (2022). *The Effect of Human Resource Management Practices on the Quality of Service, Customer Satisfaction, and Organizational Performance in Cypriot Urban Hotel Industry.* HAICTA, (2022), 342-352.

Papademetriou, C., Belias, D., Anastasiadou, S., Ragazou, K., & Garefalakis, A. (2024). Sustainability: ESG and Human Resource Management. In Papademetriou, C., Anastasiadou, S., Ragazou, K., Garefalakis, A., & Papalexandris, S. (Eds.), *ESG and Total Quality Management in Human Resources* (pp. 1–15). IGI Global Scientific Publishing., DOI: 10.4018/979-8-3693-2991-7.ch001

Robinos, J. O., Binhamza, M., Casyao, I., Combis, H., Melgar, S., Sora, L., & Austria, M. (2024). Examining Attitudes and Perceived Usefulness of AI Integration in Teaching and Learning Processes. *Journal of Interdisciplinary Perspectives, 2*(12), 619–626. DOI: 10.69569/jip.2024.0591

Seremeti, L., Anastasiadis, L., & Anastasiadou, S. (2024). The role of data in Environmental, Social and Governance strategy. In *Papademetriou, C., Anastasiadou, S. Ragazou, K., Garefalakis, A., and Papalexandris, S. (2024)* (pp. 201–218). ESG and Total Quality Management in Human Resources. IGI Global Publisher of Timely Knowledge., DOI: 10.4018/979-8-3693-2991-7.ch010

eremeti, L., Anastasiadou, S., Masouras, A., & Papalexandris, S. (2025). Addressing the challenges of harmonizing law and artificial intelligence technology in modern society. *IAES International Journal of Artificial Intelligence* (IJ-AI), Vol. 14, No. 3

Sophocleous, H., Anastasiadou, S., Masouras, A., & Apostolopoulos, S. (2023a). Motives and Perceptions of Greek Voters in National Elections of 2023. In Kavoura, A. (Eds.), *Strategic Innovative Marketing and Tourism, Springer Proceedings in Business and Economics, (2023)* (pp. 431–439)., DOI: 10.1007/978-3-031-51038-0_47

Sophocleous, H., Anastasiadou, S., Masouras, A., & Apostolopoulos, S. (2023b). *The Effect of Political Marketing on the Electoral Behavior of Greek Voters.* 10th International Conference on Strategic Innovative Marketing and Tourism 2023. Zakynthos, Ionian Islands, Greece pp. (2023c), 343-350. In A. Kavoura et al. (eds.), Strategic Innovative Marketing and Tourism, Springer Proceedings in Business and Economics, DOI: 10.1007/978-3-031-51038-0_38

Sophocleous, H., Masouras, A., Anastasiadou, S., & Apostolopoulos, S. (2023c). *Consumption of Greek Political Messages: A Qualitative Approach of the Case of the Greek Political Market.* 10th International Conference on Strategic Innovative Marketing and Tourism. Zakynthos, Ionian Islands, Greece pp. 947-955. In A. Kavoura et al. (eds.), Strategic Innovative Marketing and Tourism, Springer, Proceedings in Business and Economics, (2023) 947-955. DOI: 10.1007/978-3-031-51038-0_102

Souravlas, S. Anastasiadou, S. (2021). Pipelined Dynamic Scheduling of Big Data Streams. Applied Sciences. 10.14 (2021): 4796

Souravlas, S., & Anastasiadou, S. (2022). (2022). On Implementing Social Community Clouds Based on Markov Models. *IEEE Transactions on Computational Social Systems.* Advance online publication. DOI: 10.1109/TCSS.2022.3213273

Souravlas, S., Anastasiadou, S., Economides, Th., & Katsavounis, S. (2023b). Probabilistic Community Detection in Social Networks. IEEE Access, Journal: *IEEE Access*, (2023b), Volume: 11. DOI: 10.1109/ACCESS.2023.3257021

Souravlas, S., Anastasiadou, S. & Katsavounis, S. (2021a). More on Pipelined Dynamic Scheduling of Big Data Streams. Appl. Sci. 11.1 (2021a): 61. DOI: 10.3390/app11010061

Souravlas, S., Anastasiadou, S. & Katsavounis, S. (2021b). A Survey on the Recent Advances of Deep Community Detection." Applied Sciences. 11.16 (2021b): 7179

Souravlas, S., Anastasiadou, S., & Kostoglou, I. (2023a). A Novel Method For General Hierarchical System Modeling Via Colored Petri Nets Based on Transition Extractions From Real Data Sets. *Applied Sciences (Basel, Switzerland)*, *13*(1), 339. DOI: 10.3390/app13010339

Souravlas, S., Anastasiadou, S., Tantalaki, N., & Katsavounis, S. (2022). A Fair, Dynamic Load Balanced Task Distribution Strategy for Heterogeneous Cloud Platforms Based on Markov Process Modeling. *IEEE Access : Practical Innovations, Open Solutions*, *2022*(10), 26149–26162. DOI: 10.1109/ACCESS.2022.3157435

Souravlas, S., Katsavounis, S. & Anastasiadou, S. (2021c). On Modeling and Simulation of Resource Allocation Policies in Cloud Computing Using Colored Petri Nets. *Applied Sciences*. 10.16 (2021): 5644.

Tantalaki, N., Souravlas, S., Roumeliotis, M., & Katsavounis, S. (2020). Pipeline-Based Linear Scheduling of Big Data Streams in thc Cloud. *IEEE Access : Practical Innovations, Open Solutions*, *8*, 117182–117202. DOI: 10.1109/ACCESS.2020.3004612

Taraza, E., & Anastasiadou, S. (2019a). *EFQM Excellence Model in Vocational Lyceum: Reliability and Validity of EFQM Instrument.* Proceedings of 13th annual International Technology, Education and Development Conference (INTED2019), Valencia, Spain, pp. 2273-2285. DOI: 10.21125/inted.2019.0637

Taraza, E., & Anastasiadou, S. (2019b). *Assessing quality in Greek tertiary education: the case of school of pedagogical and technological education (ASPETE).* Proceedings of 13th annual International Technology, Education and Development Conference (INTED2019), Valencia, Spain, pp. 2364-2374.

Taraza, E., Anastasiadou, S., Masouras, A., & Papademetriou, C. (2023). Sustainable Development and Implementation of Quality Management Excellence Models in Public Organizations: A Systematic Literature Review. *Sustainability*, mdpi. *Sustainability (Basel)*, *15*(10), 7971. DOI: 10.3390/su15107971

Taraza, E., Anastasiadou, S., Papademetriou, C., & Masouras, A. (2024a). Evaluation of Quality and Equality in Education Using the European Foundation for Quality Management Excellence Model—A Literature Review. *Sustainability (Basel)*, *16*(3), 960. DOI: 10.3390/su16030960

Taraza, E., Anastasiadou, S., Seremeti, L., & Masouras, A. (2024c) *Environmental, Social, and Governance of Businesses and Organizations and the Role of Human Resources.* In: Papademetriou, C., Anastasiadou, S. Ragazou, K., Garefalakis, A., and Papalexandris, S. (2024b), ESG and Total Quality Management in Human Resources. IGI Global Publisher of Timely Knowledge, (2024), 116-132. DOI: 10.4018/979-8-3693-2991-7.ch006

Taraza, E., Papademetriou, C., Seremeti, L., Masouras, A., & Anastasiadou, S. (2024b). The Necessity of Environmental Ethics in Environmental Education and the Role of Educators. In *Papademetriou, C., Anastasiadou, S. Ragazou, K., Garefalakis, A., and Papalexandris, S. (2024)* (pp. 149–166). ESG and Total Quality Management in Human Resources. IGI Global Publisher of Timely Knowledge., DOI: 10.4018/979-8-3693-2991-7.ch008

Thapa, K. B., Okalidou, A., & Anastasiadou, S. (2016). Teachers' screening estimations of speech-language impairments in primary school children in Nepal, *International Journal of Language and Communication Disorders*, 51, (3), 310–327.

Tsourgiannis, L. Florou, G., Markopoulos, T., Anastasiadou, S. & Tsitsakis, C. (2019). *How Do Mosquitoes Affect Tourism Enterprises in Greece*? Springer Proceedings in Business and Economics, (2019) 461–471.

Valkanos, E., Giossi, S., & Anastasiadou, S. (2010). Certified Adult Educators´ Attitudes towards Continuing Education. *Review of European Studies*. 2(1), (2010) 61-68.

Valsamidis, S., Mandilas, A., Florou, G., & Anastasiadou, S. (2024). The use of e-government services provided by the local authorities: The case of the municipality of Kavala. *International Journal of Electronic Governance, 16*(2), 196–218. DOI: 10.1504/IJEG.2024.140790

Compilation of References

Abadi, A., Abadi, C., & Abadi, M. (2025). Intelligent decision making and knowledge management system for agile project management in industry 4.0 context. *Statistics, Optimization & Information Computing*, *13*(5), 2060–2078. DOI: 10.19139/soic-2310-5070-2378

Abdurahiman, S., Kasthurba, A. K., & Nuzhat, A. (2024). Assessing the socio-cultural impact of urban revitalisation using Relative Positive Impact Index (RPII). *Built Heritage*, *8*(1), 8. DOI: 10.1186/s43238-024-00118-3

Abhayawansa, S., Tyagi, S., Del Vitto, A., & Veenstra, A. (2023). A proposal for refining the ESG methodology used by rating agencies. *International Transactions in Operational Research*, *30*, 335–357. DOI: 10.1111/itor.13550

Adams, C. A., & Frost, G. R. (2008). Integrating sustainability reporting into management practices. *Accounting Forum*, *32*(4), 288–302. DOI: 10.1016/j.accfor.2008.05.002

Adiguzel, Z., Cakir, F., & Özbay, F. (2025). Big data analytics capability and sustainability in company innovation. *International Journal of Innovation Science*. DOI: 10.1108/IJIS-08-2024-0231

Ady, S. U., & Zahroh, S. (2024). *Corporate social responsibility disclosure on financial performance*. Reference Module in Social Sciences.

Agorogianni, A. Z., Zaharis, Z. D., Anastasiadou, S. D., & Goudos, S. K. (2011). Distance learning technology and service support in Greece: The case study of the Aristotle University over the last decade" has. *Education and Information Technologies*, *16*(1), 25–39. DOI: 10.1007/s10639-009-9110-3

Aguinis, H., & Glavas, A. (2012). What we know and don't know about corporate social responsibility: A review and research agenda. *Journal of Management*, *38*(4), 932–968. DOI: 10.1177/0149206311436079

Ahmad, H., Yaqub, M., & Lee, S. (2023). Environmental-, social-, and governance-related factors for business investment and sustainability: a scientometric review of global trends. Environment, Development and Sustainability, 1 - 23. .DOI: 10.1007/s10668-023-02921-x

Ajzen, I. (1991). The theory of planned behavior. *Organizational Behavior and Human Decision Processes, 50*(2), 179–211. DOI: 10.1016/0749-5978(91)90020-T

Akter, S., Dwivedi, Y. K., Sajib, S., Biswas, K., Bandara, R. J., & Michael, K. (2022). Algorithmic bias in machine learning-based marketing models. *Journal of Business Research, 144*, 201–216. DOI: 10.1016/j.jbusres.2022.01.083

Akter, S., Motamarri, S., Hani, U., Shams, R., Fernando, M., Babu, M. M., & Shen, K. (2020). Building dynamic service analytics capabilities for the digital marketplace. *Journal of Business Research, 118*, 177–188. DOI: 10.1016/j.jbusres.2020.06.016

Alaei, A. R., Becken, S., & Stantic, B. (2019). Sentiment analysis in tourism: Capitalizing on big data. *Journal of Travel Research, 58*(2), 175–191. DOI: 10.1177/0047287517747753

Alatawi, M., & Daud, Z. (2022). Integrated reporting practices and firm performance: A review study. *Corporate & Business Strategy Review*, 3(2).

Aldowaish, A., Kokuryo, J., Almazyad, O., & Goi, H. (2022). Environmental, Social, and Governance Integration into the Business Model: Literature Review and Research Agenda. *Sustainability (Basel), 14*(5), 2959. DOI: 10.3390/su14052959

Algarni, M. A., Ali, M., Albort-Morant, G., Leal-Rodríguez, A. L., Latan, H., Ali, I., & Ullah, S. (2022). Make green, live clean! Linking adaptive capability and environmental behavior with financial performance through corporate sustainability performance. *Journal of Cleaner Production, 346*, 131156. DOI: 10.1016/j.jclepro.2022.131156

Alhoussari, H. (2025). Integrating ESG Criteria in Corporate Strategies: Determinants and Implications for Performance. Journal of Ecohumanism. .DOI: 10.62754/joe.v3i8.5791

Alifia, R. A., Safitri, N. R., Irhami, D. M., Hidayat, N. R., & Kusumasari, I. R. (2025). Challenges and solutions for decision making in the era of big data. *Jurnal Bisnis Dan Komunikasi Digital, 2*(2), 13. DOI: 10.47134/jbkd.v2i2.3498

Amis, J., Barney, J. B., Mahoney, J. T., & Wang, H. (2020). From the editors—Why we need a theory of stakeholder governance—and why this is a hard problem. *Academy of Management Review, 45*(3), 499–503. DOI: 10.5465/amr.2020.0181

Anagnostopoulos, D., & Tsitsianis, N. (2023). Algorithmic Rationality and Educational AI Policies in Southern Europe. *European Journal of Education Policy, 38*(2), 110–127.

Anagnostopoulos, T., Kyriakopoulos, G., Ntanos, S., Gkika, E., & Asonitou, S. (2020). Intelligent Predictive Analytics for Sustainable Business Investment in Renewable Energy Sources. *Sustainability (Basel), 12*(7), 2817. DOI: 10.3390/su12072817

Anastasiadou, S. & Anastasiadis, L. (2019). *Quality Assurance in Education in the Light of the Effectiveness of Transformational School Leadership*, Springer Proceedings in Business and Economics, (2019) 323–344.

Anastasiadou, S. & Zirinoglou, P. (2025). *L'Analyse Factorielle des Correspondances Reveal Students' Attitudes Toward Entrepreneurship.* Source Title: Real-World Tools and Scenarios for Entrepreneurship Exploration, 79-100. .DOI: 10.4018/979-8-3693-3100-2.ch004

Anastasiadou, S. (2012b). *Reliability and validity testing of a new scale for measuring attitudes toward Chinese products.* 4th International Conference. The Economies of Balkan and Eastern Europe Countries in the changed world EBEEC 2012, Sofia, Bulgaria. pp 536-548.

Anastasiadou, S. (2018a). *Greek Tertiary Education System Evaluation in Respect of Quality Assurance Dimensions According to Malcolm Baldrige Performance Excellence Model,* Springer Proceedings in Business and Economics, 811-825. .DOI: 10.1007/978-3-319-70377-0_56

Anastasiadou, S. (2018b). Comparison of multivariate methods in group/cluster identification. Dissertation thesis of the degree of MSc. in Research Methodology in Biomedicine, Biostatistics and Clinical Bioinformatics, Faculty of Medicine, University of Thessaly.

Anastasiadou, S. (2019a). *Internal representations toward external representations: The case of statistical concepts.* 11th annual International Conference on Education and New Learning Technologies Palma de Mallorca, Spain, EDULEARN 19, pp. 6-9. DOI: 10.21125/edulearn.2019.0004

Anastasiadou, S. (2019b). *Pre-service teachers' attitudes toward the use of different modes of representation in statistics teaching and learning.* 11th annual International Conference on Education and New Learning Technologies Palma de Mallorca, Spain, EDULEARN 19. pp. 1-5. DOI: 10.21125/edulearn.2019.0003

Anastasiadou, S. (2020). *Economic effects of the pandemic COVID-19: Greek citizens express their faith in the Greek government for the protective measures toward the pandemic and economic measures toward a new economic crisis*, EBEEC 2020. e-book of EBEEC, pp.101-114.

Anastasiadou, S. D. (2024). *Students' Attitudes Toward Real-World Tools for Entrepreneurship Exploration in Tertiary Education. In* Real-World Tools and Scenarios for Entrepreneurship Exploration, 25-52. DOI: 10.4018/979-8-3693-3100-2.ch002

Anastasiadou, S. Zirinoglou, P., Seremeti, L., Masouras, A. Komodromos, M. & Anastasiadis, L. (2024). *Statistical Implicative Analysis: A Distinguished Statistical Methodology in Evaluating Greek Students' Attitudes Toward the Use of AI Source* Title: Real-World Tools and Scenarios for Entrepreneurship Exploration, 79-100, .DOI: 10.4018/979-8-3693-3100-2.ch006

Anastasiadou, S., & Masouras, A. (2023). *Exploring determinants regarding Visit and Revisit intentions considering Greece as a Medical Tourism destination.* 10th International Conference on Strategic Innovative Marketing and Tourism. Zakynthos, Ionian Islands, Greece. In A. Kavoura et al. (eds.), Strategic Innovative Marketing and Tourism, Springer Proceedings in Business and Economics, (2023), 101-109. DOI: 10.1007/978-3-031-51038-0_12

Anastasiadou, S., & Taraza, E. (2019b). *The structure and paths of Malcolm Baldrige National Quality Award (MBNQA) dimensions applied in Greek Tetriary educational systems dimensions in Greek Tertiary Education System.* 11th annual International Conference on Education and New Learning Technologies Palma de Mallorca, Spain, EDULEARN 19, pp. 455-463.

Anastasiadou, S., & Taraza, E. (2019c). *Total quality management: implementation of the six-sigma methodology for improving quality in higher education*, ICERI2019, the 12th annual International Conference of Education, Research and Innovation, Seville (Spain), ICERI2019, pp. 9533-9537. DOI: 10.21125/iceri.2019.2318

Anastasiadou, S., & Taraza, E. (2020b). *Six Sigma in Tertiary Education: A Win of Change regarding Quality Improvement in Education*, Proceedings of of 14th annual International Technology, Education and Development Conference (INTED2020), Valencia, Spain, pp. 9595-9601. DOI: 10.21125/inted.2020.0167

Anastasiadou, S., & Zirinoglou, P. (2020a). Total Quality Management: Statistical Process Control and Quality Control' Tools regarding Measuring Organizations' Quality. The case of Pareto Chart. *International Journal of Entrepreneurship and Innovative Competitiveness – IJEIC,* Vol 2. Iss. 2.

Anastasiadou, S., & Zirinoglou, P. (2020b). Statistical Process Control and Quality Control' Tools regarding Measuring Organizations' Quality: The case of Ishikawa's approach in Greek tertiary education system evaluation in respect of quality assurance *International Journal of Entrepreneurship and Innovative Competitiveness – IJEIC,* Vol 2. Iss. 2.

Anastasiadou, S., & Zirinoglou, P. (2020c). Greek students' entrepreneurial profile, attidute and behaviour: A mutidimentional statistical analysis. *International Journal of Entrepreneurship and Innovative Competitiveness– IJEIC, Vol 2. Iss. 2.*

Anastasiadou, S., & Zirinoglou, P. (2020d). Quality assessment in Greek Tertiary Education using Gap Analysis *International Journal of Entrepreneurship and Innovative Competitiveness – IJEIC.* Vol 2, Issue 1.

Anastasiadou, S., & Zirinoglou, P. (2020e). Reliability and Validity Analysis of validity testing of a new scale for monitoring Students Attitudes toward Entrepreneurship Courses (SATEC). International Journal of Entrepreneurship and Innovative Competitiveness – IJEIC, Vol 2, Issue 1.

Anastasiadou, S., Anastasiadis, L., Florou, G., & Valsamidis, S. (2022). *Greek students' Environmental Attitude based on the Theory of Ecological Attitude,* HAICTA, CEUR Workshop Proceedings (CEUR-WS.org), 222-231.

Anastasiadou, S., Anastasiadis, L., Kalabouka, K., & Florou, G. (2014). Ethnocentrism, patriotism and animosity impact on freedom of competition and business activity. *WSEAS TRANSACTIONS on BUSINESS and ECONOMICS,* Vol 11, pp. 692-699. Part of ISSN: 11099526.

Anastasiadou, S., Fotiadis, T., Anastasiadis, L, Iakovidis, G, Fotiadou, X. & Tiliakou, C. (2016). Estimate and analysis of vocational training school (IEK) students' satisfaction regarding the quality of studies provided by these schools, *Scientific Bulletin – Economic Sciences,* Vol. 15, Issue 2, 8-45.

Anastasiadou, S., Papademetriou, C., Anastasiadis, L., Valsamidis, S., & Florou, G. (2025). *ESG in Digital Era Becomes DESG: The Impact of DESG on Students' Attitudes and Higher Education.* In K. Ragazou, A. Garefalakis, C. Papademetriou, & A. Samara (Eds.), Sustainability Through Green HRM and Performance Integration (pp. 173-190). IGI Global Scientific Publishing. https://doi.org/DOI: 10.4018/979-8-3693-5981-5.ch008

Anastasiadou, SD., Papalexandris, S. & Konteos, G. (2022). *The Effect of Emotional Intelligence on Perceived e-Service Quality, Consumers' Perceived Value, Purchase, Loyalty Intentions and Satisfaction.* HAICTA, (2022), 151-161.

Anastasiadou, S. (2008a). It's the Men's World: Greek Males' Students Believe that the Womens' Position must be Home with the Kids. *The International Journal of Interdisciplinary Social Sciences: Annual Review*, *2*(5), 123–132. DOI: 10.18848/1833-1882/CGP/v02i05/59344

Anastasiadou, S. (2008b). Exploring intrinsic and extrinsic motivation during a PhD completion with the aid of Confirmatory Factor Analysis and Path Analysis: The case of Greek PhD students. *The International Journal of Interdisciplinary Social Sciences: Annual Review*, *3*(2), 171–178. DOI: 10.18848/1833-1882/CGP/v03i02/52518

Anastasiadou, S. (2009). The effects of different modes of representation in statistical problems solving: A study with third grade primary school pupils. *International Journal of Learning*, *16*(4), 27–36. DOI: 10.18848/1447-9494/CGP/v16i04/46206

Anastasiadou, S. (2011). Reliability and validity testing of a new scale for monitoring attitudes toward learning statistics with technology. *Acta Didactica Napocencia*, *4*(1), 1–10

Anastasiadou, S. (2012a). A structural model describes Chinese tradesmen attitudes towards Greek students' consumption behaviour. *4th International Conference The Economies of Balkan and Eastern Europe Countries in the changed world EBEEC 2012*, Sofia, Bulgaria. pp. 489-501.

Anastasiadou, S. (2012c). Diversifications between Expected and Perceived Attitudes toward Learning Statistics with Technology: A Multilevel Statistical Analysis. *International Journal of Learning*, *18*(3), 161–176. DOI: 10.18848/1447-9494/CGP/v18i03/47520

Anastasiadou, S. (2013a). Developing and Evaluating a Structural Equation Model Measuring Leadership Changes in a Lifelong Learning World. *The International Journal of Educational Organization and Leadership*, *19*(2), 1–17. DOI: 10.18848/2329-1656/CGP/v19i02/48520

Anastasiadou, S. (2013b). Evaluating a Structural Equation Model Measuring Attitudes toward Reading Books and E-books. *The International Journal of the Book*, *10*(2), 1–10. DOI: 10.18848/1447-9516/CGP/v10i02/57863

Anastasiadou, S. (2013c). Evaluating a Structural Equation Model Measuring Lifelong Learning and Continuing Education Factors. Management Education. *International Journal (Toronto, Ont.)*, *12*(3), 21–34. DOI: 10.18848/2327-8005/CGP/v12i03/50849

Anastasiadou, S. (2018c). Leadership according to EFQM Model in Tertiary education: The case of Greek Universities. *Proceedings of 10th International Conference The Economies of the Balkan and the Eastern European Countries in the changing world, EBEEC 2018*, Warsaw, Poland, pp. 20-24.

Anastasiadou, S. (2023). Psychometric Testing Procedures for Attitudes Toward Reproductive Tourism and Cross Border Reproductive Care (ATCBRC). In Kavoura, A., Borges-Tiago, T., & Tiago, F. (Eds.), *Strategic Innovative Marketing and Tourism. ICSIMAT 2023. Springer Proceedings in Business and Economics*. Springer., DOI: 10.1007/978-3-031-51038-0_14

Anastasiadou, S. D., Batiou, V., & Valkanos, E. (2015). Occupational Mobility Dimensions in Greece. *Procedia Economics and Finance, 2015*(19), 325–331. DOI: 10.1016/S2212-5671(15)00033-7

Anastasiadou, S., Anastasiadis, L., Angeletos, T., & Vandikas, J. (2010). A Multidimensional Statistical Analysis of Students' Attitudes toward Physics. *The International Journal of Diversity in Organisations, Communities and Nations, 16*(5), 341–356. DOI: 10.18848/1447-9532/CGP/v10i01/39794

Anastasiadou, S., Anastasiadis, L., Vandikas, I., & Angeletos, T. (2011). Implicative Statistical Analysis and Principal Components Analysis in Recording Students' Attitudes to Electronics and Electrical Construction Subjects. *International Journal of Technology, Knowledge and Society, 7*(1), 63–78. DOI: 10.18848/1832-3669/CGP/v07i01/56184

Anastasiadou, S., & Florou, G. (2013). Consumer Ethnocentrism: The case of Greek students. *3rd International Conference on Quantitative and Qualitative Methodologies*, Athens, pp. 52-57.

Anastasiadou, S., & Karakos, A. (2011). The Beliefs of Electrical and Computer Engineering Students' Regarding Computer Programming. *International Journal of Technology, Knowledge and Society, 7*(1), 37–52. DOI: 10.18848/1832-3669/CGP/v07i01/56170

Anastasiadou, S., & Kofou, I. (2012). The Development of a Structure Equation Model, for Goal Achievement and Preparation for a Future Education Leader. *The International Journal of Educational Organization and Leadership, 19*(2), 41–55. DOI: 10.18848/2329-1656/CGP/v19i02/58957

Anastasiadou, S., & Kofou, I. (2013). Incorporating Web 2.0 Tools into Greek Schools. *International Journal of Technologies in Learning, 20*(1), 11–23.

Anastasiadou, S., & Loukas, D. (2009). Greek Pre-Service Teachers' Cognitive Abilities in Understanding the Concept of Frequency: A Multilevel Statistical Analysis. *International Journal of Learning*, *16*(5), 189–202. DOI: 10.18848/1447-9494/CGP/v16i05/46268

Anastasiadou, S., Masouras, A., & Papademetriou, C. (2023). Attitudes toward Reproductive Tourism and Cross border reproductive care (CBRC): Legal, Economic, Ethical issues and dilemmas, possibilities and limitations. *Proceedings of the 6th International Conference on Tourism Research, ICTR 2023*, 7-23, Pafos, Cyprus. DOI: 10.34190/ictr.6.1.1189

Anastasiadou, S., & Papa, A. (2009). Structural Equation Modeling in the Construction of a Structural Model of Educational Research. *The International Journal of Interdisciplinary Social Sciences: Annual Review*, *4*(5), 151–158. DOI: 10.18848/1833-1882/CGP/v04i05/52914

Anastasiadou, S., & Seremeti, L. (2025). Autopoietic co-evolution of AI and law. In Anastasiadou, S., Seremeti, L., Masouras, A., & Anastasiadis, L. (Eds.), *Modern Perspectives on Artificial Intelligence and Law* (pp. 81–88). IGI Global Publisher of TIMELY KNOWLEDGE. DOI: 10.4018/979-8-3693-9576-9.ch005

Anastasiadou, S., & Taraza, E. (2019a). Pre-service teachers' perceptions toward leadership regarding the MBVQA Model. *Proceedings of 11th annual International Conference on Education and New Learning EDULEARN 19 Palma de Mallorca*, Spain, pp. 533-543, DOI: 10.21125/edulearn.2019.0183

Anastasiadou, S., & Taraza, E. (2020a). *Resistance to Change as an Obstacle Regarding Quality in Higher Education Institutions (HEIS)*. Proceedings of of 14th annual International Technology, *Education and Development Conference (INTED2020)*, Valencia, Spain, pp. 396-401.

Anastasiadou, S., & Tiliakou, C. (2014). Classical Item Analysis of the Greek State of English Language Proficiency "A" Level Exam. *The International Journal of Literacies*, *20*(3), 39–53. DOI: 10.18848/2327-0136/CGP/v20i03/48819

Anastasiadou, S., & Tiliakou, C. (2016a). Investigation of the discriminating ability of the Greek State certificate of language proficiency by means of Vacor method: The case of Greek-speaking and Turkish-speaking bilingual students from the Muslim minority of Thrace. *International Journal of Learning and Teaching*, *8*(2), 109–118. DOI: 10.18844/ijlt.v8i2.517

Anastasiadou, S., & Tiliakou, C. (2016b). Evaluation of the discriminating ability of the Greek state foreign language exam (KPG) for English by means of the factorial analysis of correspondences. *International Journal of Learning and Teaching*, *8*(2), 129–140. DOI: 10.18844/ijlt.v8i2.518

Anastasiadou, S., & Zirinoglou, P. (2015). Teachers' attitudes toward Quality Assurance Dimensions regarding EFQM Model in Primary Education in Greece. *Procedia Economics and Finance*, *33*, 411–431. DOI: 10.1016/S2212-5671(15)01725-6

Anastasiadou, S., & Zirinolou, P. (2014). Reliability testing of EFQM scale: The case of Greek secondary teachers. *Procedia: Social and Behavioral Sciences*, *143*, 990–994. DOI: 10.1016/j.sbspro.2014.07.541

Anastasiadou, S., Zirinolou, P., & Florou, G. (2014). The European Foundation Quality Management evaluation of Greek Primary and Secondary Education. *Procedia: Social and Behavioral Sciences*, *143*, 932–940. DOI: 10.1016/j.sbspro.2014.07.530

Anderson, P. (1999). Complexity theory and organization science. *Organization Science*, *10*(3), 216–232. DOI: 10.1287/orsc.10.3.216

Antunes, A. L., Cardoso, E., & Barareiro, J. (2022). Incorporation of ontologies in data warehouse/business intelligence systems - A systematic literature review. *International Journal of Information Management Data Insights*, *2*(2), 100131. DOI: 10.1016/j.jjimei.2022.100131

APA. (2010). *Ethical Principles of Psychologists and Code of Conduct*. American Psychological Association.

Asif, M., Searcy, C., & Castka, P. (2023). ESG and Industry 5.0: The role of technologies in enhancing ESG disclosure. *Technological Forecasting and Social Change*, *195*, 122806. DOI: 10.1016/j.techfore.2023.122806

Asokan, V. A., Yarime, M., & Onuni, M. (2020). A review od data-intensive approaches for sustainability: Methodology, epistemology, normativity, and ontology. *Sustainability Science*, *15*(3), 955–974. DOI: 10.1007/s11625-019-00759-9

Aziz, M. F., & Haron, R. (2021). Corporate Social Responsibility Disclosure and Financial Performance of Shariah PLCS in Malaysia. *International Journal of Academic Research in Business & Social Sciences*, *11*(6), 333–353. DOI: 10.6007/IJARBSS/v11-i6/10155

Babkin, A., Shkarupeta, E., Tashenova, L., Malevsky-Malevich, E., & Shchegoleva, T. (2023). Framework for assessing the sustainability of ESG performance in industrial cluster ecosystems in a circular economy. *Journal of Open Innovation*, *9*(2), 100071. DOI: 10.1016/j.joitmc.2023.100071

Baesmat, K. H. (2024). Impedance analysis of adaptive distance relays using machine learning. In Latifi, S. (Ed.), *ITNG 2024: 21st International Conference on Information Technology–New Generations* (Vol. 1456, pp. 293–303). Springer. DOI: 10.1007/978-3-031-56599-1_57

Baesmat, K. H., & Latifi, S. (2023). A new hybrid method for electrical load forecasting based on deviation correction and MRMRMS. In Selvaraj, H., Chmaj, G., & Zydek, D. (Eds.), *Advances in systems engineering* (pp. 293–303). Springer., DOI: 10.1007/978-3-031-40579-2_29

Baesmat, K. H., Masoudipour, I., & Samet, H. (2021). Improving the performance of short term load forecast using a hybrid artificial neural network and artificial bee colony algorithm. *IEEE Canadian Journal of Electrical and Computer Engineering*, *44*(3), 275–282. DOI: 10.1109/ICJECE.2021.3056125

Baesmat, K. H., Regentova, E. E., & Baghzouz, Y. (2025). A hybrid machine learning–statistical based method for short term energy consumption prediction in residential buildings. *Energy and AI*, *17*, 100552. DOI: 10.1016/j.egyai.2025.100552

Bagh, T., Bouri, E., Khan, M. A., & Xu, B. (2024). Climate change sentiment, ESG practices and firm value: International insights. *China Finance Review International*. DOI: 10.1108/CFRI-07-2024-0381

Balaji, K. (2024). Exchange-Traded Funds (ETFs): Redefining Financial Instruments in the 21st Century. In Faxing, L., & Kok Loang, O. (Eds.), (pp. 283–310). Advances in Finance, Accounting, and Economics. IGI Global., DOI: 10.4018/979-8-3693-8583-8.ch011

Balaji, K. (2024). Neuromarketing and Sustainable Finance: Real-World Case Studies of Green Investment Promotions. In Taneja, S., Chahal, B. P. S., Johri, A., Ozen, E., & Kumar, P. (Eds.), (pp. 169–204). Advances in Business Strategy and Competitive Advantage. IGI Global., DOI: 10.4018/979-8-3693-9117-4.ch010

Balaji, K. (2025). Harnessing AI and Blockchain in Sustainability Assurance: Trends Shaping the Future of Verification. In Khatib, S. F. A., & Abbas, A. F. (Eds.), *Navigating Trust in Sustainability Reporting and Assurance* (pp. 215–242). IGI Global., DOI: 10.4018/979-8-3373-0117-4.ch007

Balaji, K. (2025). Revolutionizing High-Frequency Trading: The Impacts of Financial Technology and Data Science Innovations. In Chen, H. (Ed.), (pp. 103–124). Advances in Finance, Accounting, and Economics. IGI Global., DOI: 10.4018/979-8-3693-8186-1.ch004

Balamurugan, M., Narayanan, K., Raghu, N., Arjun Kumar, G. B., & Trupti, V. N. (2025). Role of artificial intelligence in smart grid – A mini review. *Frontiers in Artificial Intelligence*, *8*, 1551661. DOI: 10.3389/frai.2025.1551661 PMID: 39968172

Barbosa, A. S., Crispim da Silva, M. C. B., Bueno da Silva, L., & Morioka, S. N. (2023). Integration of environmental, social, and governance criteria: Impacts on corporate sustainability performance. *Humanities & Social Sciences Communications*, *10*(1), 410. DOI: 10.1057/s41599-023-01919-0

Bari, N., Chimhundu, R., & Chan, K. C. (2022). Dynamic capabilities to achieve corporate sustainability: A roadmap to sustained competitive advantage. *Sustainability (Basel)*, *14*(3), 1531. DOI: 10.3390/su14031531

Barney, J. (1991). Firm resources and sustained competitive advantage. *Journal of Management*, *17*(1), 99–120. DOI: 10.1177/014920639101700108

Battilana, J., Obloj, T., Pache, A. C., & Sengul, M. (2022). Beyond shareholder value maximization: Accounting for financial/social trade-offs in dual-purpose companies. *Academy of Management Review*, *47*(2), 237–258. DOI: 10.5465/amr.2019.0386

Battiston, S., Mandel, A., Monasterolo, I., Schütze, F., & Visentin, G. (2017). A climate stress-test of the financial system. *Nature Climate Change*, *7*(4), 283–288. DOI: 10.1038/nclimate3255

Bebchuk, L. A., & Fried, J. M. (2004). *Pay without performance: The unfulfilled promise of executive compensation*. Harvard University Press.

Begenau, J., & Siriwardane, E. (2022). *How do Private Equity Fees vary across Public Pensions?* (No. w29887; p. w29887). National Bureau of Economic Research. DOI: 10.3386/w29887

Benson, A. K., & Ganda, F. (2022). The impact of corporate governance and corporate sustainability on the performance of South African listed companies. *International Journal of Research in Business and Social Science*, *11*(5), 155–175. DOI: 10.20525/ijrbs.v11i5.1838

Berchicci, L., & King, A. A. (2022). Corporate Sustainability: A Model Uncertainty Analysis of Materiality. *Journal of Financial Reporting*, *7*(2), 43–74. DOI: 10.2308/JFR-2021-022

Berg, F., Kölbel, J., & Rigobón, R. (2022). Aggregate Confusion: The Divergence of ESG Rating. *Review of Finance*, *26*(6), 1315–1344. DOI: 10.1093/rof/rfac033

Bhandari, H. N., Pokhrel, N. R., Rimal, R., Dahal, K. R., & Rimal, B. (2024). Implementation of deep learning models in predicting ESG index volatility. *Financial Innovation, 10*(1), 75. DOI: 10.1186/s40854-023-00604-0

Binns, R. (2018). Fairness in Machine Learning: Lessons from Political Philosophy. *Proceedings of the 2018 Conference on Fairness, Accountability and Transparency*, 149–159.

Bomma, H. P. (2023). Enhancing business analytics with a semantic layer. *International Journal of Business Quantitative Economics and Applied Management Research, 7*(9), 93–99.

Bongermino, G., & Romagnoli, S. (2025). *ESG rating and ambiguity: an informative and distorted signal-based approach.* Decisions in Economics and Finance., DOI: 10.1007/s10203-025-00507-y

Böttcher, T., Empelmann, S., Weking, J., Hein, A., & Krcmar, H. (2023). Digital sustainable business models: Using digital technology to integrate ecological sustainability into the core of business models. *Information Systems Journal, 34*(3), 736–761. DOI: 10.1111/isj.12436

Bowden, J., Cummins, M., Dao, D., & Jain, K. (2024). *Explainable AI for Financial Risk Management.* Financial Regulation Innovation Lab White Paper Series. University of Strathclyde. DOI: 10.17868/strath.00089573

Braun, V., & Clarke, V. (2006). Using thematic analysis in psychology. *Qualitative Research in Psychology, 3*(2), 77–101. DOI: 10.1191/1478088706qp063oa

Brosch, N. (2023). Corporate purpose: From a 'Tower of Babel' phenomenon towards construct clarity. *Journal of Business Economics, 93*(4), 567–595. DOI: 10.1007/s11573-023-01137-9

Brown, H. S., de Jong, M., & Levy, D. L. (2009). Building institutions based on information disclosure: Lessons from GRI's sustainability reporting. *Journal of Cleaner Production, 17*(6), 571–580. DOI: 10.1016/j.jclepro.2008.12.009

Buallay, A. (2019). Between cost and value: Investigating the effects of sustainability reporting on a firm's performance. *Journal of Applied Accounting Research, 20*(3), 481–496. DOI: 10.1108/JAAR-12-2017-0137

Burhan, N., & Rahmanti, W. (2012). The impact of sustainability reporting on company performance. *Journal of Economics Business and Accountancy Ventura, 15*(2), 257. DOI: 10.14414/jebav.v15i2.79

Burnaev, E., Mironov, E., Shpilman, A., Mironenko, M., & Katalevsky, D. (2023). Practical AI Cases for Solving ESG. *Sustainability (Basel), 15*(17), 12731. DOI: 10.3390/su151712731

Busch, T., & Hoffmann, V. H. (2011). How hot is your bottom line? Linking carbon and financial performance. *Business Strategy and the Environment, 50*(2), 233–265.

Cabaleiro-Cerviño, G., & Mendi, P. (2024). *ESG-driven innovation strategy and firm performance*. Eurasian Business Review., DOI: 10.1007/s40821-024-00254-x

Cantero-Saiz, M., Polizzi, S., & Scannella, E. (2024). ESG and asset quality in the banking industry: The moderating role of financial performance. *Research in International Business and Finance, 69*, 102221. DOI: 10.1016/j.ribaf.2024.102221

Cao, G., Tian, N., & Blankson, C. (2021). Big data, marketing analytics, and firm marketing capabilities. *Journal of Computer Information Systems, 62*(3), 442–451. DOI: 10.1080/08874417.2020.1842270

Carroll, A. B. (1991). The pyramid of corporate social responsibility: Toward the moral management of organizational stakeholders. *Business Horizons, 34*(4), 39–48. DOI: 10.1016/0007-6813(91)90005-G

CDP. (2021). Driving corporate action on climate change, water security and deforestation. Retrieved from https://www.cdp.net/

Ceron, A., Curini, L., Iacus, S. M., & Porro, G. (2014). Every tweet counts? How sentiment analysis of social media can improve our knowledge of citizens' political preferences with an application to Italy and France. *New Media & Society, 16*(2), 340–358. DOI: 10.1177/1461444813480466

Chen, H., & Volpe, R. P. (2021). Green financial literacy and green investment behavior: Evidence from emerging markets. *Journal of Sustainable Finance & Investment, 11*(2), 142–158. DOI: 10.1080/20430795.2020.1735219

Chen, J., Mashkova, O., Zhapa-Camacho, F., Hoehndorf, R., He, Y., & Horrocks, I. (2025). Ontology embedding: A survey of methods, applications and resources. *IEEE Transactions on Knowledge and Data Engineering, 37*(7), 4193–4212. DOI: 10.1109/TKDE.2025.3559023

Chen, K., Lin, S., & Chuang, C. (2025). ESG Strategies and Sustainable Performance in Multinational Enterprises. *Sustainability (Basel), 17*(2), 751. DOI: 10.3390/su17020751

Chen, Q., & Liu, X.-Y. (2020). Quantifying ESG alpha using scholar big data: an automated machine learning approach. *Proceedings of the First ACM International Conference on AI in Finance*, 1–8. DOI: 10.1145/3383455.3422529

Chen, R., & Zhang, T. (2024). Artificial intelligence applications implication for ESG performance: Can digital transformation of enterprises promote sustainable development? *Chinese Management Studies*. DOI: 10.1108/CMS-11-2023-0653

Chen, S. (2024). *The Influence of Artificial Intelligence and Digital Technology on ESG Reporting Quality*. International Journal of Global Economics and Management., DOI: 10.62051/IJGEM.v3n1.36

Chen, S., Song, Y., & Gao, P. (2023). Environmental, social, and governance (ESG) performance and financial outcomes: Analyzing the impact of ESG on financial performance. *Journal of Environmental Management*, *345*, 118829. DOI: 10.1016/j.jenvman.2023.118829 PMID: 37688968

Chen, Z., & Xie, G. (2022). ESG disclosure and financial performance: Moderating role of ESG investors. *International Review of Financial Analysis*, *83*, 102291. DOI: 10.1016/j.irfa.2022.102291

Cheong, B. C., Subhani, M., Mansoor, A., & Nordin, A. (2024). Transparency and accountability in AI systems: Safeguarding wellbeing. *Frontiers in Human Dynamics*, *6*, 1421273. DOI: 10.3389/fhumd.2024.1421273

Chernobay, L., Yasinska, T., & Malibroda, S. (2020). Applied Aspect Of Corporate Social Responsibility Impact On Company Competitiveness -Unilever Example., 8, 32-44.

Chiang, L. H., Lu, B., & Castillo, I. (2017). Big data analytics in chemical engineering. *Annual Review of Chemical and Biomolecular Engineering*, *8*(1), 63–85. DOI: 10.1146/annurev-chembioeng-060816-101555 PMID: 28301733

Chib, S., Mehta, A. K., Selvakumar, P., Saravanan, A., Mishra, B. R., & Manjunath, T. C. (2025). Mental Health Challenges and Solutions in High-Pressure Work Environments. In Harriott, S. (Ed.), *Innovative Approaches to Managing Conflict and Change in Diverse Work Environments* (pp. 247–272). IGI Global Scientific Publishing., DOI: 10.4018/979-8-3693-9556-1.ch011

Choi, H.-Y., & Park, J. (2022). Do data-driven CSR initiatives improve CSR performance? The importance of big data analytics capability. *Technological Forecasting and Social Change*, *182*, 121802. DOI: 10.1016/j.techfore.2022.121802

Chowdhary, S., Selvakumar, P., Sangeetha, B., Sarvaani, V. V., Anute, N., & Sharma, M. (2025). The Role of Social Capital in Entrepreneurial Development. In Martínez-Falcó, J., Sánchez-García, E., & Marco-Lajara, B. (Eds.), *Support Networks for Entrepreneurs: Social Capital and Strategic Collaborations* (pp. 311–338). IGI Global Scientific Publishing. DOI: 10.4018/979-8-3693-9836-4.ch013

Chrisanctus, O., Adeoye, O., Okoye, C., Ofodile, O., Odeyemi, O., Addy, W., & Ajayi-Nifise, A. (2024). *Artificial Intelligence in ESG investing: Enhancing portfolio management and performance*. International Journal of Science and Research Archive., DOI: 10.30574/ijsra.2024.11.1.0305

Christoforidis, C., & Anastasiadou, S. (2024). *Human Resource Management as a Contributor of Total Quality Management, ESG and Total Quality Management in Human Resources*. IGI Global.

Christopher, T., & Filipovic, M. (2008). The extent and determinants of disclosure of global reporting initiative guidelines: Australian evidence. *Journal of Contemporary Issues in Business and Government*, *14*(2), 17–40.

Climate Bonds Initiative. (2024). *Mexico sustainable finance market report 2024*. https://www.climatebonds.net/

Coates, J. M., Santhanalakshmi, K., Dinesh, N., Gandhimathi, S., & Chandel, P. S. Mohit, & Selvakumar, P. (2025). Assessment and Evaluation in Transnational Staff Development. In G. Morris & J. Ye (Eds.), Training and Development in Transnational Higher Education (pp. 387-406). IGI Global Scientific Publishing.

Cociancich, V., De La Cruz, A., de Oliveira, C., & Mazzone, G. (2024). *Global Corporate Sustainability Report 2024*. OECD Publishing., DOI: 10.1787/8416b635-

Cohen, L., Manion, L., & Morrison, K. (2018). *Research methods in education* (8th ed.). Routledge., https://www.routledge.com/Research-Methods-in-Education/Cohen -Manion- Morrison/p/book/9781138209886#

Cohen, W. M., & Levinthal, D. A. (1990). Absorptive capacity: A new perspective on learning and innovation. *Administrative Science Quarterly*, *35*(1), 128–152. DOI: 10.2307/2393553

Colmenares-Quintero, R. F., Quiroga-Parra, D. J., Rojas, N., Stansfield, K. E., & Colmenares-Quintero, J. C. (2021). Big data analytics in Smart Grids for renewable energy networks: Systematic review of information and communication technology tools. *Cogent Engineering*, *8*(1), 1935410. DOI: 10.1080/23311916.2021.1935410

Correia, A., & Água, P. (2024). Harnessing artificial intelligence for enhanced environmental, social, and governance reporting: A new paradigm in corporate transparency. Corporate governance: Research and advanced practices. .DOI: 10.22495/cgrapp15

Coscun, Y. (2023). *The role of ESG in corporate financial performance and competitiveness*. Reference Module in Social Sciences.

Crawford, K. (2021). *Atlas of AI: Power, politics, and the planetary costs of artificial intelligence. Yale University Press.Crawford, K. (2021). Atlas of AI: Power, politics, and the planetary costs of artificial intelligence*. Yale University Press.

Creswell, J. W. (2014). *Research Design: Qualitative, Quantitative, and Mixed Methods Approaches* (4th ed.). SAGE Publications.

Creswell, J. W., & Plano Clark, V. L. (2018). *Designing and conducting mixed methods research* (3rd ed.). Sage Publications.

Cruz, C., & Matos, F. (2023). ESG Maturity: A Software Framework for the Challenges of ESG Data in Investment. *Sustainability (Basel)*, *15*(3), 2610. DOI: 10.3390/su15032610

Cueva, C., Matthey, A., Morosoli, S., & Riguelle, N. (2023). Optimistic framing increases responsible investment of professionals. *Scientific Reports*, seventeen, article e. DOI: 10.1038/s41598-023-50965-w

De Marchi, D., Becarelli, R., & Di Sarli, L. (2022). Tourism sustainability index: Measuring tourism sustainability based on the ETIS toolkit, by exploring tourist satisfaction via sentiment analysis. *Sustainability (Basel)*, *14*(13), 8049. DOI: 10.3390/su14138049

Del Vitto, A., Marazzina, D., & Stocco, D. (2023). ESG ratings explainability through machine learning techniques. *Annals of Operations Research*. DOI: 10.1007/s10479-023-05514-z

Deshmukh, A. K., Mohan, A., & Mohan, I. (2022). Goods and services tax (GST) implementation in India: A SAP–LAP–Twitter analytic perspective. *Global Journal of Flexible Systems Managment*, *23*(2), 165–183. DOI: 10.1007/s40171-021-00297-3 PMID: 37522093

Dhaliwal, D. S., Li, O. Z., Tsang, A., & Yang, Y. G. (2011). Voluntary nonfinancial disclosure and the cost of equity capital: The initiation of corporate social responsibility reporting. *The Accounting Review*, *86*(1), 59–100. DOI: 10.2308/accr.00000005

Dhingra, K. (2023). Corporate Social Responsibility and Sustainability of Corporate Performance. *Jindal Journal of Business Research, 12*(1), 19–29. DOI: 10.1177/22786821231161416

Di Vaio, A., & Varriale, L. (2020). SDGs and airport sustainable performance: Evidence from Italy on organisational, accounting and reporting practices through financial and non-financial disclosure. *Journal of Cleaner Production, 249*, 119431. DOI: 10.1016/j.jclepro.2019.119431

Diamantini, C., Khan, T., Potena, D., & Storti, E. (2022). Shared metrics of sustainability: A knowledge graph approach. *The 30th Italian Symposium on Advanced Database Systems*, Italy.

DigitalDefynd. (2024). 20 Useful ESG Case Studies [2025]. DigitalDefynd. https://digitaldefynd.com/IQ/esg-case-studies/

Djezzar, M., Hemam, M., Amara, F. Z., Seghir, Z. A., & Hifidi, M. M. (2023). Towards a multi-viewpoints ontological framework for knowledge sharing in e-health. *Joint Proceedings of Second International Workshop on Semantic Reasoning and Representation in IoT and Third International Workshop on Multilingual Semantic Web*, Spain.

Donthi, R., Lakshmi, P., Srinivas, G., Sudhakar, S., Koneru, H., & Yekula, P. (2024). AI-Driven Numerical Optimization for Carbon Footprint Reduction and Sustainable Supply Chain Management in the Fashion Industry. *South Eastern European Journal of Public Health*, 1216–1222. DOI: 10.70135/seejph.vi.2023

Do, V., McBrien, H., Flores, N. M., & Casey, J. A. (2023). Spatiotemporal distribution of power outages with climate events and social vulnerability in the USA. *Nature Communications, 14*(1), 2470. DOI: 10.1038/s41467-023-38084-6 PMID: 37120649

Du Toit, E. (2024). Thirty years of sustainability reporting: Insights, gaps and an agenda for future research through a systematic literature review. *Sustainability (Basel), 16*(2310), 10750. DOI: 10.3390/su162310750

Duchek, S. (2020). Organizational resilience: A capability-based conceptualization. *Business Research, 13*(1), 215–246. DOI: 10.1007/s40685-019-0085-7

Duffey, R. B. (2019). Power restoration prediction following extreme events and disasters. *International Journal of Disaster Risk Science, 10*(1), 134–148. DOI: 10.1007/s13753-018-0189-2

Du, Y., & Jung, J.-S. (2022). *The effect of dynamic capability on innovation and financial performance: Focused on the moderating effect of ESG management and the big data utilization in Chinese SMEs*. Korea International Trade Research Institute.

Ebrahim, A., Battilana, J., & Mair, J. (2014). The governance of social enterprises: Mission drift and accountability challenges in hybrid organizations. *Research in Organizational Behavior, 34*, 81–100. DOI: 10.1016/j.riob.2014.09.001

Eccles, R. G., Ioannou, I., & Serafeim, G. (2014). The Impact of Corporate Sustainability on Organizational Processes and Performance. *Management Science, 60*(11), 2835–2857. DOI: 10.1287/mnsc.2014.1984

Eccles, R. G., & Krzus, M. P. (2010). *One report: Integrated reporting for a sustainable strategy*. John Wiley & Sons.

Eccles, R. G., Krzus, M. P., Rogers, J., & Serafeim, G. (2012). The need for sector-specific materiality and sustainability reporting standards. *The Bank of America Journal of Applied Corporate Finance, 24*(2), 65–71. DOI: 10.1111/j.1745-6622.2012.00380.x

Ehrig, M. (2007). *Ontology Alignment*. Bridging the Semantic Gap.

Eisenhardt, K. M., & Martin, J. A. (2000). Dynamic capabilities: What are they? *Strategic Management Journal, 21*(10–11), 1105–1121. DOI: 10.1002/1097-0266(200010/11)21:10/11<1105::AID-SMJ133>3.0.CO;2-E

El Barachi, M., AlKhatib, M., Mathew, S., & Oroumchian, F. (2021). A novel sentiment analysis framework for monitoring the evolving public opinion in real-time: Case study on climate change. *Journal of Cleaner Production, 312*, 127820. DOI: 10.1016/j.jclepro.2021.127820

El Ghoul, S., Guedhami, O., Kwok, C. C. Y., & Mishra, D. R. (2011). Does corporate social responsibility affect the cost of capital? *Journal of Banking & Finance, 35*(9), 2388–2406. DOI: 10.1016/j.jbankfin.2011.02.007

Elizondo Azuela, G., Barroso, L., Khanna, A., Wang, X., Wu, Y., & Cunha, G. (2014). *Performance of renewable energy auctions: Experience in Brazil, China and Mexico*. World Bank Group. https://doi.org/DOI: 10.1596/1813-9450-7062

Elkington, J. (1994). Towards the sustainable corporation: Win-win-win business strategies for sustainable development. *California Management Review, 36*(2), 90–100. DOI: 10.2307/41165746

Elkington, J. (1997). *Cannibals with forks: The triple bottom line of 21st century business*. Capstone.

Emexidis, C., & Gkonis, P. (2024). The integration of Internet of Things and machine learning for energy prediction of wind turbines. *Applied Sciences (Basel, Switzerland), 14*(22), 10276. DOI: 10.3390/app142210276

Emmanuel, A. (2025). *The future of management reporting and sustainability reporting: Integrating ESG metrics for strategic decision-making.* World Journal of Advanced Research and Reviews., DOI: 10.30574/wjarr.2025.25.2.0423

eremeti, L., Anastasiadou, S., Masouras, A., & Papalexandris, S. (2025). Addressing the challenges of harmonizing law and artificial intelligence technology in modern society. *IAES International Journal of Artificial Intelligence* (IJ-AI), Vol. 14, No. 3

Erevelles, S., Fukawa, N., & Swayne, L. (2016). Big Data consumer analytics and the transformation of marketing. *Journal of Business Research, 69*(2), 897–904. DOI: 10.1016/j.jbusres.2015.07.001

Escobedo Briones, G. F., Jacome, N., & Arroyo-Figueroa, G. (2016). Business intelligence and data analytics (BI&DA) to support the operation of smart grid. *Procedia Computer Science, 96*, 489–496. DOI: 10.5220/0005936604890496

Etikala, S. (2025). Enterprise data quality management: A technical deep dive into automated governance. *International Journal on Science and Technology, 16*(2).

European Commission. (2021). Proposal for a regulation laying down harmonised rules on artificial intelligence (Artificial Intelligence Act). Commission. (2021). Proposal for a regulation laying down harmonised rules on artificial intelligence (Artificial Intelligence Act). https://eur-lex.europa.eu/legal-content/EN/TXT/?uri=CELEX:52021PC0206

European Commission. (2023). *Corporate Sustainability Reporting Directive (CSRD).* Retrieved from https://finance.ec.europa.eu/sustainable-finance/disclosures/sustainability-related-disclosure-financial-services-sector_en

Fahad, M., & Darmout, J. (2023). An ontology-based collaborative business intelligence framework. *Proceedings of the 12th International Conference on Data Science, Technology and Applications*, 480-487. https://doi.org/DOI: 10.5220/0012131900003541

Fama, E. F., & Jensen, M. C. (1983). Separation of ownership and control. *The Journal of Law & Economics, 26*(2), 301–325. DOI: 10.1086/467037

Fan, Z., Yan, Z., & Wen, S. (2023). Deep learning and artificial intelligence in sustainability: A review of SDGs, renewable energy, and environmental health. *Sustainability (Basel), 15*(18), 13493. DOI: 10.3390/su151813493

Farrokhi, Z., Kalhor, A., & Masouleh, M. T. (2018). Implementation and evaluation of object identification techniques on Nao robot platform. *International Journal of Mechatronics, Electrical and Computer Technology (IJMEC), 8*(29), 3947–3958. Retrieved from https://aeuso.org/includes/files/articles/Vol8_Iss29_3947-3958_Implementation_and_Evaluation_of_Ob.pdf

Farrokhi, Z., Kalhor, A., & Masouleh, M. T. (2018). Implementation and evaluation of object identification techniques on Nao robot platform. *International Journal of Mechatronics, Electrical and Computer Technology, 8*(29), 3947–3958.

Farrokhi, Z., Baesmat, K. H., & Regentova, E. E. (2024). Enhancing urban intelligence energy management: Innovative load forecasting techniques for electrical networks. *Journal of Power and Energy Engineering, 12*(11), 72–88. DOI: 10.4236/jpee.2024.1211005

Fatma, M., & Khan, I. (2023). Impact of CSR on Customer Citizenship Behavior: Mediating the Role of Customer Engagement. *Sustainability (Basel), 15*(7), 5802. DOI: 10.3390/su15075802

Feilmayar, C., & Woss, W. (2016). An analysis of ontologies and their success factors for application to business. *Data & Knowledge Engineering, 101*, 1–23. DOI: 10.1016/j.datak.2015.11.003

Feng, S. (2024). *Leveraging artificial intelligence to enhance ESG models: Transformative impacts and implementation challenges*. Applied and Computational Engineering., DOI: 10.54254/2755-2721/69/20241473

Ferrero-Ferrero, I., & Torres, M. (2023). SDG reporting: An analysis of corporate sustainability leaders. *Marketing Intelligence & Planning, 41*(4), 457–472. DOI: 10.1108/MIP-07-2022-0332

Field, A. (2017). *Discovering Statistics Using IBM SPSS* (5th ed.). Sage Publications Ltd.

Floridi, L., Cowls, J., Beltrametti, M., Chatila, R., Chazerand, P., Dignum, V., Luetge, C., Madelin, R., Pagallo, U., Rossi, F., Schafer, B., Valcke, P., & Vayena, E. (2018). AI4People (Floridi et al., 2018)—An ethical framework for a good AI society: Opportunities, risks, principles, and recommendations. *Minds and Machines, 28*(4), 689–707. DOI: 10.1007/s11023-018-9482-5 PMID: 30930541

Florou, G., Anastasiadou, S., Karasavvoglou, A., Valsamidis, S., & Mandilas, A. (2015). *Greek public tertiary education departments of agriculture*, CEUR Workshop Proceedings of the 7th International Conference on Information and Communication Technologies in Agriculture, Food and Environment (HAICTA), 471-479.

Florou, G., & Anastasiadou, S. (2013). *Academic staff of Greek technological educational institutes. 3rd International Conference on Quantitative and Qualitative Methodologies*, Athens, pp. 52-156.

Folke, C., Carpenter, S. R., Walker, B., Scheffer, M., Chapin, T., & Rockström, J. (2010). Resilience thinking: Integrating resilience, adaptability and transformability. *Ecology and Society*, *15*(4), 20. Advance online publication. DOI: 10.5751/ES-03610-150420

Fornell, C., & Larcker, D. F. (1981). Evaluating structural equation models with unobservable variables and measurement error. *JMR, Journal of Marketing Research*, *18*(1), 39–50. DOI: 10.1177/002224378101800104

Fošner, A. (2024). University Students' Attitudes and Perceptions towards AI Tools: Implications for Sustainable Educational Practices. *Sustainability (Basel)*, *2024*(16), 8668. DOI: 10.3390/su16198668

Freeman, R. E. (1984). *Strategic management: A stakeholder approach*. Pitman.

Freeman, R. E. (1984). *Strategic Management: A Stakeholder Approach*. Pitman.

Freire, P. (1970). Pedagogy of the oppressed. Continuum.Freire, P. (1970). Pedagogy of the oppressed. *Continuum : an Interdisciplinary Journal on Continuity of Care*.

Friede, G., Busch, T., & Bassen, A. (2015). ESG and financial performance: Aggregated evidence from more than 2000 empirical studies. *Journal of Sustainable Finance & Investment*, *5*(4), 210–233. DOI: 10.1080/20430795.2015.1118917

Gebhardt, M., Kopyto, M., Birkel, H., & Hartmann, E. (2022). Industry 4.0 technologies as enablers of collaboration in circular supply chains: A systematic literature review. *International Journal of Production Research*, *60*(23), 6967–6995. DOI: 10.1080/00207543.2021.1999521

Gefen, D., Straub, D. W., & Boudreau, M.-C. (2000). Structural equation modeling and regression: Guidelines for research practice. *Communications of the Association for Information Systems*, *4*(7), 1–70. DOI: 10.17705/1CAIS.00407

Gibson, R., Krueger, P., & Mitali, S. F. (2020). The sustainability footprint of institutional investors: ESG driven price pressure and performance. *Swiss Finance Institute Research Paper*, (17- 05).

Giroux, H. A. (2011). *On critical pedagogy (Giroux, 2011). Bloomsbury Academic. Giroux, H. A. (2011). On critical pedagogy (Giroux, 2011).* Bloomsbury Academic.

Giudici, P., & Wu, L. (2025). Sustainable artificial intelligence in finance: Impact of ESG factors. *Frontiers in Artificial Intelligence*, *8*, 1566197. DOI: 10.3389/frai.2025.1566197 PMID: 40115117

Global Banking and Finance. (2025). *Mexican companies scaling up sustainability investments*. https://www.globalbankingandfinance.com/

Gong, Y., Xiao, J., Tang, X., & Li, J. (2023). How sustainable marketing influences the customer engagement and sustainable purchase intention? The moderating role of corporate social responsibility. *Frontiers in Psychology, 14*. frontiersin. DOI: 10.3389/fpsyg.2023.1128686

Gong, X., Tao, X., Zhang, M., Xu, Y., Kwok, H., Dai, J., & Cheng, J. (2024). Secure Environmental, Social, and Governance (ESG) Data Management for Construction Projects Using Blockchain. *Sustainable Cities and Society*, *114*, 105582. DOI: 10.1016/j.scs.2024.105582

Gonzaga, F. P. (2022). Customer Perception of Sustainability Initiatives in the Restaurant Industry: A Discrete Choice Model Approach. *Journal of Management and Sustainability*, *12*(2), 20. DOI: 10.5539/jms.v12n2p20

González-Torres, T., Rodríguez-Sánchez, J. L., Pelechano-Barahona, E., & García-Muiña, F. E. (2022). A systematic review of research on sustainability in family firms. *Sustainability*, *14*(11), 6420. DOI: 10.3390/su14116420

Granger, C. W., & Lee, T. H. (1989). Investigation of production, sales and inventory relationships using multicointegration and non-symmetric error correction models. *Journal of Applied Econometrics*, *4*(S1), S145–S159. DOI: 10.1002/jae.3950040508

Gray, R., Dey, C., Owen, D., Evans, R., & Zadek, S. (1997). Struggling with the praxis of social accounting: Stakeholders, accountability, audits and procedures. *Accounting, Auditing & Accountability Journal*, *10*(3), 325–364. DOI: 10.1108/09513579710178106

Grek, S., & Ozga, J. (2010). Governing by numbers: Data and education governance in Europe. Journal of Education Policy, 25(1), 23–37.Grek, S., & Ozga, J. (2010). Governing by numbers: Data and education governance in Europe. *Journal of Education Policy*, *25*(1), 23–37. DOI: 10.1080/02680930802412669

Grek, S., & Ozga, J. (2020). Governing Education through Data: Towards a Digital Education Policy Regime. International Journal of Education Policy, 43(4), 567–584. Grek, S., & Ozga, J. (2020). Governing Education through Data: Towards a Digital Education Policy Regime. *International Journal of Education Policy*, *43*(4), 567–584.

Guarino, N., Oberle, D., & Staab, S. (2009). What is an ontology? In: Staab, S., Studer, R. (eds) *Handbook on Ontologies*. International Handbooks on Information Systems. Springer, Berlin, Heidelberg, 1-17. https://doi.org/DOI: 10.1007/978-3-540-92673-3_0

Guida, T. (2018). *Big Data and Machine Learning in Quantitative Investment* (1st ed.). Wiley., DOI: 10.1002/9781119522225

Gupta, A., Kumar, N., & Bhuvaneshwari, S.. (2023). Multi-resolution segmentation of solar photovoltaic systems using UAV, aerial, and satellite imagery. *Remote Sensing*, *15*(24), 5687. DOI: 10.3390/rs15245687

Gutierrez-Bustamante, M., & Espinosa-Leal, L. (2022). Natural language processing methods for scoring sustainability reports—A study of Nordic listed companies. *Sustainability (Basel)*, *14*(15), 9165. DOI: 10.3390/su14159165

Gutsche, G., & Ziegler, A. (2023). Sustainable finance literacy and retail investors' sustainable investment behavior. *Sustainable Finance*, *1*(2), 123–145. DOI: 10.1002/sfi2.1015

Gu, Y., Dai, J., Vasarhelyi, M. A., & Borth, D. (2023). Audit 4.0-based ESG assurance: Using satellite images on greenhouse gas emissions. *International Journal of Accounting Information Systems*, *50*, 100625. DOI: 10.1016/j.accinf.2023.100625

Guzmán, C., Correa, I., Valiente, L., & Valiente Palma, L. (2024). Analysis of good practices of social impact measurement: The social balance sheet developed by the Spanish network of the social and solidarity economy. *Social Enterprise Journal*, *21*(2), 228–251. DOI: 10.1108/SEJ-03-2024-0056

Habeeb, F., Szydło, T., Kowalski, L., Noor, A., Thakker, D., Morgan, G., & Ranjan, R. (2022). Dynamic data streams for time-critical IoT systems in energy-aware IoT devices using reinforcement learning. *Sensors (Basel)*, *22*(6), 2375. DOI: 10.3390/s22062375 PMID: 35336544

Hadro, D., Fijałkowska, J., Daszyńska-Żygadło, K., Zumente, I., & Mjakuškina, S. (2022). What do stakeholders in the construction industry look for in non-financial disclosure and what do they get? *Meditari Accountancy Research*, *30*(3), 762–785. DOI: 10.1108/MEDAR-11-2020-1093

Haider, R., Bari, M. F. A. I., Shaif, M. F. I., Rahman, M., Ohi, M. N. H., & Rahman, K. M. M. (2025). Quantifying the Impact: Leveraging AI-Powered Sentiment Analysis for Strategic Digital Marketing and Enhanced Brand Reputation Management. *International Journal of Science and Research Archive*, *15*(2), 1103–1121. DOI: 10.30574/ijsra.2025.15.2.1524

Hair, J. F., Black, W. C., & Balin, B. j, Anderson, R.E. (2010). *Multivariate Data Analysis*. Maxwell Macmillan International Editions.

Hambrick, D. C. (2007). Upper echelons theory: An update. *Academy of Management Review, 32*(2), 334–343. DOI: 10.5465/amr.2007.24345254

Hanna, J., Mommert, M., Scheibenreif, L., & Borth, D. (2021). Multitask learning for estimating power-plant greenhouse-gas emissions from satellite imagery. *Journal of Cleaner Production, 314*, 128047. DOI: 10.1016/j.jclepro.2021.128047

Hanna, R., Heptonstall, P., & Gross, R. (2024). Job creation in a low carbon transition to renewables and energy efficiency: A review of international evidence. *Sustainability Science, 19*(1), 125–150. DOI: 10.1007/s11625-023-01440-y

Hardi, E., & Chairina, C. (2019). The Effect of Sustainibility Reporting Disclosure and Its Impact on Companies Financial Performance. *Journal of Wetlands Environmental Management, 7*(1), 67. DOI: 10.20527/jwem.v7i1.188

Harrison, J. S., Phillips, R. A., & Freeman, R. E. (2020). On the 2019 business Roundtable "Statement on the purpose of a Corporation. *Journal of Management, 46*(7), 1223–1237. DOI: 10.1177/0149206319892669

Hart, S. L. (1995). A natural-resource-based view of the firm. *Academy of Management Review, 20*(4), 986–1014. DOI: 10.2307/258963

Hashmi, R., Liu, H., & Yavari, A. (2024). Digital Twins for Enhancing Efficiency and Assuring Safety in Renewable Energy Systems: A Systematic Literature Review. *Energies, 17*(11), 2456. DOI: 10.3390/en17112456

Hassanpouri Baesmat, K., Farrokhi, Z., & Regentova, E. E. (2025). Parallel multi model energy demand forecasting with cloud redundancy: Leveraging trend correction, feature selection, and machine learning. *Forecasting, 7*(2), 25. DOI: 10.3390/forecast7020025

Hassanpouri Baesmat, K., Shokoohi, F., & Farrokhi, Z. (2025). SP RF ARIMA: A sparse random forest and ARIMA hybrid model for electric load forecasting. *Global Energy Interconnection, 8*(3), 486–496. DOI: 10.1016/j.gloei.2025.04.003

Hawken, P., Lovins, A., & Lovins, L. H. (1999). *Natural capitalism: Creating the next industrial revolution*. Little, Brown and Company.

Helo, P., Mayanti, B., Bejarano, R., & Sundman, C. (2024). Sustainable supply chains – Managing environmental impact data on product platforms. *International Journal of Production Economics, 270*, 109160. DOI: 10.1016/j.ijpe.2024.109160

Hemanand, D., Mishra, N., Premalatha, G., Mavaluru, D., Vajpayee, A., Kushwaha, S., & Sahile, K. (2022). Applications of Intelligent Model to Analyze the Green Finance for Environmental Development in the Context of Artificial Intelligence. *Computational Intelligence and Neuroscience*, *2022*, 1–8. DOI: 10.1155/2022/2977824 PMID: 35845917

Henderson, R. (2021). Changing the purpose of the corporation to rebalance capitalism. *Oxford Review of Economic Policy*, *37*(4), 838–850. DOI: 10.1093/oxrep/grab034

Hobeika, J., Khelladi, I., & Orhan, M. A. (2022). Analyzing the corporate social responsibility perception from customer relationship quality perspective. An application to the retail banking sector. *Corporate Social Responsibility and Environmental Management*, *29*(6), 2053–2064. DOI: 10.1002/csr.2301

Holling, C. S. (1973). Resilience and stability of ecological systems. *Annual Review of Ecology and Systematics*, *4*(1), 1–23. DOI: 10.1146/annurev.es.04.110173.000245

Holm, F. S., & Ostergaard, K. (2025). The corporate sustainability due diligence directive and the doctrine of privity of contract. *European Review of Private Law*, *33*(3), 1–28.

Hsieh, M. (2024). An empirical investigation into the enhancement of decision-making capabilities in corporate sustainability leadership through Internet of Things (IoT) integration. *Internet of Things : Engineering Cyber Physical Human Systems*, *28*, 101382. DOI: 10.1016/j.iot.2024.101382

Huang, R., & Mao, S. (2024). Carbon Footprint Management in Global Supply Chains: A Data-Driven Approach Utilizing Artificial Intelligence Algorithms. *IEEE Access : Practical Innovations, Open Solutions*, *12*, 89957–89967. DOI: 10.1109/ACCESS.2024.3407839

Huang, W., Zhang, N., Kang, C., Xu, Y., & Yang, Q. (2019). From demand response to integrated demand response: Review and prospect of research and application. *Protection and Control of Modern Power Systems*, *4*(1), 12. DOI: 10.1186/s41601-019-0126-4

Hubballi, R. B. *Selvakumar, P., Seenivasan, R., Basava Aradhya S., G., Dinesh, N., & Seelam, P. K. (2025). Overview of Current AI Technologies in Education.* In L. Kyei-Blankson & E. Ntuli (Eds.), Transformative AI Practices for Personalized Learning Strategies (pp. 1–26). IGI Global Scientific Publishing. DOI: 10.4018/979-8-3693-8744-3.ch001

Hubballi, R. B., Selvakumar, P., Seenivasan, R., & Basava Aradhya, S. G., Dinesh, N., & Seelam, P. K. (2025). Overview of Current AI Technologies in Education. In L. Kyei-Blankson & E. Ntuli (Eds.), Transformative AI Practices for Personalized Learning Strategies (pp. 1-26). IGI Global Scientific Publishing.

Hussain, K. (2025). *Revolutionizing Route Optimization Systems with Artificial Intelligence for a Smarter, Sustainable Logistics Ecosystem.* International Journal of Computer Science and Mobile Computing., DOI: 10.47760/ijcsmc.2025.v14i02.008

Ignatov, K. (2023). When ESG talks: ESG tone of 10-K reports and its significance to stock markets. *International Review of Financial Analysis*, *89*, 102745. DOI: 10.1016/j.irfa.2023.102745

IIRC (International Integrated Reporting Council). (2021). International Integrated Reporting Framework. Retrieved from https://www.integratedreporting.org/

International Energy Agency. (2018). *Energy transition indicators: Mexico.* IEA Publications. https://www.iea.org/reports/energy-transition-indicators-mexico

Ioannou, I., & Serafeim, G. (2017). The consequences of mandatory corporate sustainability reporting: Evidence from four countries. Harvard Business School Research Working Paper.

Ireoluwapo, O., Olanrewaju, K., Daramola, G., & Babayeju, O. (2024). *Harnessing big data analytics to revolutionize ESG reporting in clean energy initiatives.* World Journal of Advanced Research and Reviews., DOI: 10.30574/wjarr.2024.22.3.1759

Jaiswal, R., Gupta, S., & Tiwari, A. K. (2024). Decoding mood of the Twitterverse on ESG investing: Opinion mining and key themes using machine learning. *Management Research Review*, *47*(8), 1221–1252. DOI: 10.1108/MRR-07-2023-0526

Jamali, H., Dascalu, S. M., & Harris, F. C., Jr. (2024). AI driven analysis and prediction of energy consumption in NYC's municipal buildings. In *2024 IEEE/ACIS 22nd International Conference on Software Engineering Research, Management and Applications (SERA)* (pp. 277–283). IEEE. DOI: 10.1109/SERA61261.2024.10685594

Jamali, H., Dascalu, S. M., Harris, F. C., Jr., & Feil-Seifer, D. (2025). Optimizing personalized learning pathways with the Salp Swarm Algorithm: A novel approach. In *2025 IEEE 6th International Conference on Artificial Intelligence, Robotics, and Control.* IEEE. DOI: 10.1109/AIRC64931.2025.11077498

Jamali, H., Debolt, A., Dalton, H., Layosa, J., Macy, I., Shill, P., Feil Seifer, D., Harris, F., Dascalu, S., & Wu, R. (2025). FORE: A student-centered framework for accessible robotics education through simulation and interactive learning. *ASEE Annual Conference Proceedings*. Retrieved from https://par.nsf.gov/biblio/10595258

Jamali, H., Debolt, A., Dalton, H., Layosa, J., Macy, I., Shill, P., Feil-Seifer, D., Harris, F., Dascalu, S., & Wu, R. (2025). FORE: A student centered framework for accessible robotics education through simulation and interactive learning. *ASEE Annual Conference Proceedings*. https://par.nsf.gov/biblio/10595258

Jamali, H., Shill, P. C., Feil-Seifer, D., Harris, F. C., Jr., & Dascalu, S. M. (2023). A schedule of duties in the cloud space using a modified salp swarm algorithm. In *IFIP International Internet of Things Conference* (pp. 62–75). Springer. DOI: 10.1007/978-3-031-45878-1_5

Jamali, H., Watson, J., Dascalu, S. M., & Harris, F. C. (2025). Harmonized data drive: Standardizing and unifying smart car information storage for enhanced forensics and interoperability. In *2025 13th International Symposium on Digital Forensics and Security (ISDFS)* (pp. 1–6). IEEE. DOI: 10.1109/ISDFS65363.2025.11012079

Jamali, H., Dascalu, S. M., & Harris, F. C.Jr. (2024). Fostering joint innovation: A global online platform for ideas sharing and collaboration. In *International Conference on Information Technology–New Generations* (pp. 305–312). Springer. DOI: 10.1007/978-3-031-56599-1_40

Jamali, H., Karimi, A., & Haghighizadeh, M. (2018). A new method of cloud based computation model for mobile devices: Energy consumption optimization in mobile to mobile computation offloading. In *Proceedings of the 6th International Conference on Communications and Broadband Networking* (pp. 32–37). ACM. DOI: 10.1145/3193092.3193103

Jebamikyous, H., Li, M., Suhas, Y., & Kashef, R. (2023). Leveraging machine learning and blockchain in E-commerce and beyond: Benefits, models, and application. *Discover Artificial Intelligence*, *3*(1), 3. DOI: 10.1007/s44163-022-00046-0

Jelas, I. M., Zulkifley, M. A., Abdullah, M., & Spraggon, M. (2024). Deforestation detection using deep learning-based semantic segmentation techniques: A systematic review. *Frontiers in Forests and Global Change*, *7*, 1300060. DOI: 10.3389/ffgc.2024.1300060

Jiang, H., Lin, P., & Qiang, M. (2016). Public-opinion sentiment analysis for large hydro projects. *Journal of Construction Engineering and Management*, *142*(2), 05015013. DOI: 10.1061/(ASCE)CO.1943-7862.0001039

Jobin, A., Ienca, M., Vayena, E., & Cavolo, A. (2019). The global landscape of artificial-intelligence ethics guidelines. *Nature Machine Intelligence*, *1*, 389–399. DOI: 10.1038/s42256-019-0088-2

Jones, C. E., Theodosis, S., & Lykourentzou, I. (2019). The enthusiast, the interested, the sceptic, and the cynic: Understanding user experience and perceived value in location-based cultural heritage games through qualitative and sentiment analysis. [JOCCH]. *Journal on Computing and Cultural Heritage, 12*(1), 1–26. DOI: 10.1145/3297716

Joshi, H., & Chauhan, R. (2024). Determinants of Price Multiples for Technology Firms in Developed and Emerging Markets: Variable Selection Using Shrinkage Algorithm. *Vision: The Journal of Business Perspective, 28*(1), 55–66. DOI: 10.1177/09722629211023011

Jucevicius, G., & Juceviciene, R. (2022). Enabling collaborative dynamic capabilities in strategic communities: Firm-vs. network-centric perspectives. *Journal of Management & Organization*, 28(3), 587–604. 12.

Junaid, M., Zhang, Q., Cao, M., & Luqman, A. (2023). Nexus between technology enabled supply chain dynamic capabilities, integration, resilience, and sustainable performance: An empirical examination of healthcare organizations. *Technological Forecasting and Social Change, 196*, 122828. DOI: 10.1016/j.techfore.2023.122828

Kähkönen, A. K., Evangelista, P., Hallikas, J., Immonen, M., & Lintukangas, K. (2023). COVID-19 as a trigger for dynamic capability development and supply chain resilience improvement. *International Journal of Production Research, 61*(8), 2696–2715. DOI: 10.1080/00207543.2021.2009588

Kahneman, D., & Tversky, A. (1979). Prospect theory: An analysis of decision under risk. *Econometrica, 47*(2), 263–291. DOI: 10.2307/1914185

Kalogera, C., Seremeti, L., Kontis, S., & Anastasiadou, S. (2025). The Digital DNA of Modern Workforce. In Lamprini Seremeti, Panagiotis Liargovas, Christos Papademetriou, Lazaros Anastasiadis, Sofia Anastasiadou (edus), Harnessing Business Intelligence for Modern Talent Management, IGI Global Publisher of TIMELY KNOWLEDGE, DOI: 10.4018/979-8-3373-1942-1.ch015

Kalyanam, A. (2025). *Integration of ESG Data in the Retail Sector (Essential for Sustainable business and Risk Management).* INTERANTIONAL JOURNAL OF SCIENTIFIC RESEARCH IN ENGINEERING AND MANAGEMENT., DOI: 10.55041/IJSREM39956

Kamal, M. R., Noviyanto, K., Subhan, H., & Afiana, L. (2024). Sentiment Analysis on Social Media and Stakeholders about Negative Issues Among Islamic Boarding School Community In Indonesia. *Jurnal Theologia, 35*(2), 261–280. DOI: 10.21580/teo.2024.35.2.23164

Kapetanopoulou, P., Kouroutzi, A., & Anastasiadou, S. (2021). The Impact of Information Systems Implementation in the Greek Manufacturing Enterprises. *Applied Sciences (Basel, Switzerland)*, *11*(24), 11781. DOI: 10.3390/app112411781

Keet, C. M., & Khan, Z. C. (2024). On the roles of competency questions in ontology engineering. *Proceedings of Knowledge Engineering and Knowledge Management Conference*, 123-132. https://doi.org/DOI: 10.1007/978-3-031-77792-9_8

Kermani, A., Jamshidi, A. M., Mahdavi, Z., Dashtaki, A. A., Zand, M., Nasab, M. A., & Khan, B. (2023). Energy management system for smart grid in the presence of energy storage and photovoltaic systems. *International Journal of Photoenergy*, *2023*, 5749756. DOI: 10.1155/2023/5749756

Khan, A., Iqbal, N., Rizwan, A., Ahmad, R., & Kim, D. (2021). An ensemble energy consumption forecasting model based on spatial-temporal clustering analysis in residential buildings. *Energies*, *14*(11), 3020. DOI: 10.3390/en14113020

Khasawneh, A. M., Taylor, B., & Kaiwartya, O. (2025). Innovations in air quality monitoring: Sensors, IoT and future research. *Sensors (Basel)*, *25*(7), 2070. DOI: 10.3390/s25072070 PMID: 40218583

Khichi, M. (2024). TECHNOLOGY AND ARTIFICIAL INTELLIGENCE'S IMPACT ON ESG REPORTING QUALITY. International Journal of Innovations & Research Analysis. .DOI: 10.62823/IJIRA/4.3(I).6899

Kiliç, M., Gurler, H. E., Kaya, A., & Lee, C. W. (2022). The Impact of Sustainability Performance on Financial Performance: Does Firm Size Matter? Evidence from Turkey and South Korea. *Sustainability (Basel)*, *14*(24), 16695. DOI: 10.3390/su142416695

Kodama, M. (2018). *Collaborative dynamic capabilities for service innovation creating a new healthcare ecosystem*. Palgrave Macmillan, 14.

Kofou, I. & Anastasiadou, (2014). Incorporating web 2.0 into Greek schools, *International Journal of Technologies in Learning*, 20:1, 11-23. .DOI: 10.18848/2327-0144/CGP/v20i01/49120

Kofou, I., & Anastasiadou, S. (2013). Language and Communication Needs Analysis in Intercultural Education. *The International Journal of Diversity in Education*, *12*(2), 15–64. DOI: 10.18848/2327-0020/CGP/v12i02/58049

Kolk, A. (2010). Trajectories of sustainability reporting by MNCs. *Journal of World Business*, *45*(4), 367–374. DOI: 10.1016/j.jwb.2009.08.001

Kong, X., Yao, J., Han, Y., & Liu, H. (2025). Data-driven dynamic Bayesian network model for safety resilience evaluation of prefabricated construction. *Buildings (Basel, Switzerland)*, *14*(3), 570. DOI: 10.3390/buildings14030570

Korra, C., & Sadhana, A. (2024). *Integrating IoT Sensors, Cloud AI, and Satellite Broadband for Enhanced ESG Governance in Smart Cities: A Tripartite Approach to Real-Time Environmental Monitoring. International Journal of Innovative Science and Research Technology*. IJISRT., DOI: 10.38124/ijisrt/IJISRT24MAR1621

Kotte, K. R., Attaluri, V., & Selvakumar, P. (2025). Revolutionising Retail Banking with AI and Virtual Technologies AI-Driven Financial Training. In Nair, A. J., Manohar, S., Limbu, Y. B., & Huhmann, B. A. (Eds.), *Intersecting Natural Language Processing and FinTech Innovations in Service Marketing* (pp. 421–440). IGI Global Scientific Publishing., DOI: 10.4018/979-8-3693-9944-6.ch020

KPMG. (2017). *The road ahead: The KPMG Survey of Corporate Responsibility Reporting 2017*. KPMG International.

Kshetri, N., & Kshetri, N. (2024). The Environmental Impact of Artificial Intelligence. *IT Professional*, *26*(3), 9–13. DOI: 10.1109/MITP.2024.3399471

Kumar, S., Sureka, R., Lim, W., Mangla, S., & Goyal, N. (2021). What do we know about business strategy and environmental research? Insights from Business Strategy and the Environment. *Business Strategy and the Environment*, *30*(8), 3454–3469. DOI: 10.1002/bse.2813

La Soa, N., Duy, D. D., Thanh Hang, T. T., & Ha, N. D. (2024). The impact of environmental accounting information disclosure on financial risk: Evidence from Vietnam. *Journal of Risk and Financial Management*, *17*, 62. DOI: 10.3390/jrfm17020062

Lamb, W. F., Wiedmann, T., Pongratz, J., Andrew, R., Crippa, M., Olivier, J. G. J., & Zi, A. C. (2021). A review of trends and drivers of greenhouse gas emissions by sector from 1990 to 2018. *Environmental Research Letters*, *16*(7), 073005. DOI: 10.1088/1748-9326/abee4e

Laskar, N., Chakrabarty, T. K., & Maji, S. G. (2017). Corporate Sustainability Performance and Financial Performance: Empirical Evidence from Japan and India. *Management and Labour Studies*, 42(1).

Laskar, N., & Maji, S. G. (2017). Corporate sustainability performance and firm performance: Evidence from India and South Korea. *International Journal of Corporate Strategy and Social Responsibility*, *1*(2), 118. DOI: 10.1504/IJCSSR.2017.084289

Lawyer, L. (2023). *Mexico advances sustainable finance framework.* https://latinlawyer.com/article/1289567/mexico-advances-sustainable-finance-framework

Lee, A., & Chung, T.-L. D. (2023). Transparency in corporate social responsibility communication on social media. *International Journal of Retail & Distribution Management, 51*(5), 590–610. DOI: 10.1108/IJRDM-01-2022-0038

Lee, H., Kim, J. H., Jung, H. S., Park, S., & Seo, Y. (2024). Deep-learning-based stock-market prediction incorporating ESG sentiment and technical indicators. *Scientific Reports, 14*(1), 10262. DOI: 10.1038/s41598-024-61106-2 PMID: 38704434

Lee, O., Joo, H., Choi, H., & Cheon, M. (2022). Proposing an Integrated Approach to Analyzing ESG Data via Machine Learning and Deep Learning Algorithms. *Sustainability (Basel), 14*(14), 8745. DOI: 10.3390/su14148745

Lev, B., Radhakrishnan, S., Ciftci, M., & de Villiers, C. (2022). Accounting for intangibles: A critical review. *Journal of Accounting Literature, 48*, 1–25. DOI: 10.1108/JAL-05-2022-0060

Leventaki, D. (2012). Corporate Social Responsibility and how it affects consumers' buying decisions (analysis per product category and per place of residence). *Από* https://apothesis.eap.gr/handle/repo/24577

Liang, X., Hu, X., & Meng, H. (2020). Truly Sustainability or Hypocrisy: The Effects of Corporate Sustainable Orientation on Consumers' Quality Perception and Trust Based on Evidence from China. *Sustainability (Basel), 12*(7), 2735. DOI: 10.3390/su12072735

Liang, Y., Lee, M. J., & Jung, J. S. (2022). Dynamic capabilities and an ESG strategy for sustainable management performance. *Frontiers in Psychology, 13*, 887776. DOI: 10.3389/fpsyg.2022.887776 PMID: 35719473

Liao, L., Luo, L., & Tang, Q. (2015). Gender diversity, board independence, environmental committee and greenhouse gas disclosure. *The British Accounting Review, 47*(4), 409–424. DOI: 10.1016/j.bar.2014.01.002

Lidner, H. G., & Steinhauser, I. (2025). A unified theory and ontological framework of ESG reorting. In: Matos, F., Basile, C., Pyis, L. Edvisson, L., Roos, G. (eds) *Intellectual Capital in a Global Business Landscape. Contributions to Management Science.* Springer, Cham, 91-110. https://doi.org/DOI: 10.1007/978-3-031-86362-2_5

Li, J., Wu, T., Hu, B., Pan, D., & Zhou, Y. (2025). Artificial intelligence and corporate ESG performance. *International Review of Financial Analysis, 102*, 104036. DOI: 10.1016/j.irfa.2025.104036

Lim, T. (2024). Environmental, social, and governance (ESG) and artificial intelligence in finance: State-of-the-art and research takeaways. *Artificial Intelligence Review, 57*(4), 76. DOI: 10.1007/s10462-024-10708-3

Lins, K. V., Servaes, H., & Tamayo, A. (2017). Social capital, trust, and firm performance: The value of corporate social responsibility during the financial crisis. *the Journal of Finance*, 72(4), 1785-1824.

Linton, J. D., Klassen, R., & Jayaraman, V. (2007). Sustainable supply chains: An introduction. *Journal of Operations Management, 25*(6), 1075–1082. DOI: 10.1016/j.jom.2007.01.012

Liu, J., Wang, R., Zhang, H., & Chen, F. (2024). Artificial intelligence in environmental monitoring: Advancements, challenges, and future directions. *Hygiene and Environmental Health Advances, 12*, 100114. DOI: 10.1016/j.heha.2024.100114

Liu, S., Jiang, J., Wei, K., Wu, R., & Xu, Y. (2024). Enhancing University Students' ESG Competencies Through "Artificial Intelligence + Education"-A Case Study of ChatGPT, *2024 International Conference on Digital Technology and Intelligent Education (ICDTIE)*, Shenzhen, China, 2024, pp. 27-30. DOI: 10.1109/ICDTIE65977.2024.00012

Li, Y., & Zhu, C. (2024). Regional Digitalization and Corporate ESG Performance. *Journal of Cleaner Production, 473*, 143503. DOI: 10.1016/j.jclepro.2024.143503

Li, Z., Yu, Y., & Wang, S. (2024). Practical evaluation of intelligent algorithms in ESG management of manufacturing enterprises. *Scientific Reports, 14*(1), 19394. DOI: 10.1038/s41598-024-70376-9 PMID: 39169099

Lo, F.-Y., & Liao, P.-C. (2021). Rethinking financial performance and corporate sustainability: Perspectives on resources and strategies. *Technological Forecasting and Social Change, 162*, 120346. DOI: 10.1016/j.techfore.2020.120346

Loh, L., Thomas, T., & Wang, Y. (2017). Sustainability Reporting and Firm Value: Evidence from Singapore-Listed Companies. *Sustainability (Basel), 9*(11), 2112. DOI: 10.3390/su9112112

Louis, N., &, E. (2024). Leveraging artificial intelligence for enhanced supply chain optimization. Open Access Research Journal of Multidisciplinary Studies. .DOI: 10.53022/oarjms.2024.7.2.0044

Lusardi, A., & Mitchell, O. S. (2014). The economic importance of financial literacy: Theory and evidence. *Journal of Economic Literature, 52*(1), 5–44. DOI: 10.1257/jel.52.1.5 PMID: 28579637

Maceda, L. L., Satuito, A. A., & Abisado, M. B. (2023). Sentiment Analysis of Code-mixed Social Media Data on Philippine UAQTE using Fine-tuned mBERT Model. *International Journal of Advanced Computer Science and Applications, 14*(7). DOI: 10.14569/IJACSA.2023.0140777

Mahdavi, Z., Samavat, T., Javanmardi, A. S. J., Dashtaki, M. A., Zand, M., Nasab, M. A., & Khan, B. (2024). Providing a control system for charging electric vehicles using ANFIS. *International Transactions on Electrical Energy Systems, 2024*, 9921062. DOI: 10.1155/2024/9921062

Maheswaran, K., Selvakumar, P., Shaikh, M., Shashank, G., Gupta, S., & Manjunath, T. C. (2025). The Evolution of Smart Urban Mobility With Emerging Technologies. In Ponnusamy, S., Assaf, M., Youssef, B., Jeon, G., & Kalyanaraman, S. (Eds.), *Leveraging VANETs and Blockchain Technology for Urban Mobility* (pp. 1–28). IGI Global Scientific Publishing., DOI: 10.4018/979-8-3373-0265-2.ch001

Maignan, I., Ferrell, O. C., & Ferrell, L. (2005). A stakeholder model for implementing social responsibility in marketing. *European Journal of Marketing, 39*(9/10), 956–977. DOI: 10.1108/03090560510610662

Mallin, C., Michelon, G., & Raggi, D. (2013). Monitoring intensity and stakeholders' orientation: How does governance affect social and environmental disclosure? *Journal of Business Ethics, 114*(1), 29–43. DOI: 10.1007/s10551-012-1324-4

Mamo, Y. Z., & Anagnostopoulos, C. (2023). Stakeholders'"voice" through social media: The case of corporate social responsibility in sport. *International Journal of Sports Marketing & Sponsorship, 24*(5), 1002–1020. DOI: 10.1108/IJSMS-05-2023-0084

Mamun, M. (2022). Sustainability reporting of major electricity retailers in line with GRI: Australia evidence. *Journal of Accounting and Organizational Change*. Advance online publication.

Margolis, J. D., & Walsh, J. P. (2003). People and profits? The search for a link between a company's social and financial performance. *Psychology Press*. 1, 166.

Marnoto, S., Silva, C., & Veiga, P. (2024). Beyond profit in family businesses: ESG-driven business model innovation and the critical role of digital capabilities. Journal of Family Business Management. .DOI: 10.1108/JFBM-05-2024-0105

Martín-Martín, A., Orduna-Malea, E., Thelwall, M., & López-Cózar, E. D. (2018). *Google Scholar, Web of Science, and Scopus: a systematic comparison of citations in 252 subject categories*. DOI: 10.31235/osf.io/42nkm

Mayer, C. (2021). The future of the Corporation and the economics of purpose. *Journal of Management Studies*, *58*(3), 887–901. DOI: 10.1111/joms.12660

Md Nor, N., Shaiful Bahari, H. A., Adnan, N. A., & Sheh Kamal, S. M. Q. A. (2016). The Effects of Environmental Disclosure on Financial Performance in Malaysia. *Procedia Economics and Finance*, *35*, 117–126. DOI: 10.1016/S2212-5671(16)00016-2

Meftah, E., Benmahmoud, S., & Rabehi, A. (2024). Innovative Wireless Solutions for Real-Time ECG Monitoring: Leveraging BLE, Wi-Fi, and LoRa Technologies. *2024 International Conference on Telecommunications and Intelligent Systems (ICTIS)*, 1-6. DOI: 10.1109/ICTIS62692.2024.10894056

Mehta, N., & Pandit, A. (2018). Concurrence of big data analytics and healthcare: A systematic review. *International Journal of Medical Informatics*, *114*, 57–65. DOI: 10.1016/j.ijmedinf.2018.03.013 PMID: 29673604

Metaxas, T., & Tsavdaridou, M. (2012). Corporate social responsibility in Greece during the crisis period. *Journal of Advanced Research in Management*, 4(1 (7), 20.

Mittelstadt, B. D., Allo, P., Taddeo, M., Wachter, S., & Floridi, L. (2016). The ethics of algorithms (Mittelstadt et al., 2016): Mapping the debate. *Big Data & Society*, *3*(2), 2053951716679679. DOI: 10.1177/2053951716679679

Mohd Said, R., Theng, L. T., Senik, R., & Yusri, Y. (2015). The state of sustainability disclosure and effects on companies' financial performance. *International Business Management*, *10*(18), 4342–4350.

Moisidou, A., Voulgarakis, N., Folinas, D., Konstantoglou, A., Kokmotos, E., & Anastasiadou, S. (2019). Evaluation of the Reuse of Packaging in the Food Supply Chain, Springer Proceedings in Business and Economics. In Sakas, D. P., & Nasiopoulos, D. K. (Eds.), *Strategic Innovative Marketing, Springer Proceedings in Business and Economics, Springer Nature Switzerland AG (2019) 43-51.*, DOI: 10.1007/978-3-030-16099-9_6

Molavi, H., & Zhang, L. (2024, July). A Bibliometric Study of Stakeholder Opinion Mining and Sentiment Analysis in Crisis Communication. In 6th International Conference on Advanced Research Methods and Analytics (CARMA 2024) (pp. 43-52). Editorial Universitat Politècnica de València. DOI: 10.4995/CARMA2024.2024.17782

Morozova, I., Smetanina, A., & Smetanin, A. (2024). ESG strategy for managing sustainable digital transformation of business in the artificial intelligence economy. Ars Administrandi (Искусство управления). .DOI: 10.17072/2218-9173-2024-2-217-239

Mostafiz, M. I., Musteen, M., Saiyed, A., & Ahsan, M. (2022). COVID-19 and the global value chain: Immediate dynamics and long-term restructuring in the garment industry. *Journal of Business Research, 139*, 1588–1603. DOI: 10.1016/j.jbusres.2021.10.078

Moussa, A. S., Elmarzouky, M., Abdullah, A., & Shurrab, N. (2024). Beyond compliance: How ESG reporting influences the cost of capital in UK firms. *Journal of Risk and Financial Management, 17*(8), 326. DOI: 10.3390/jrfm17080326

Musleh Al-Sartawi, A. M. A., Hussainey, K., & Razzaque, A. (2022). The role of artificial intelligence in sustainable finance. *Journal of Sustainable Finance & Investment*, 1–6. DOI: 10.1080/20430795.2022.2057405

Myšková, R., & Hájek, P. (2018). Sustainability and corporate social responsibility in the text of annual reports—The case of the IT services industry. *Sustainability (Basel), 10*(11), 4119. DOI: 10.3390/su10114119

Nadeem, M., Gyapong, E., & Ahmed, A. (2020). Board gender diversity and environmental, social, and economic value creation: Does family ownership matter? *Business Strategy and the Environment, 29*(3), 1268–1284. DOI: 10.1002/bse.2432

Naeem, N., Çankaya, S., & Bildik, R. (2022). Does ESG performance affect the financial performance of environmentally sensitive industries? A comparison between emerging and developed markets. *Borsa Istanbul Review*, 22(2).

Naeem, N., & Çankaya, S. (2022). The impact of ESG performance over financial performance: A study on global energy and power generation companies. *International Journal of Commerce and Finance, 8*(1).

Naeem, N., Cankaya, S., & Bildik, R. (2022). Does ESG performance affect the financial performance of environmentally sensitive industries? A comparison between emerging and developed markets. *Borsa Istanbul Review, 22*, S128–S140. DOI: 10.1016/j.bir.2022.11.014

Nagyová, Ľ., Holienčinová, M., Košičiarová, I., & Holota, T. (2016). Corporate social responsibility in food manufacturing companies-environmental dimensions. *Acta Universitatis Agriculturae et Silviculturae Mendelianae Brunensis, 64*(3), 1037–1043. DOI: 10.11118/actaun201664031037

Nisha Angeline, M., Selvakumar, P., Gupta, M. K., Nazar, N., Elumalai, D., & Bhattacharya, S. (2025). Emerging Materials for Energy Storage and Environmental Applications. In K. Muduli, B. Moharana, S. Ales, & D. Biswal (Eds.), Using Computational Intelligence for Sustainable Manufacturing of Advanced Materials (pp. 53-72). IGI Global Scientific Publishing. DOI: 10.4018/979-8-3693-7974-5.ch003

Nnadi, M., & Mutyaba, P. E. (2023). *The moderating effect of corporate sustainability attributes of products on the financial performance of firms*. Reference Module in Social Sciences.

Nolasco, A., **López-Portillo**, V. (2019). *Mexico renewable energy progress report*. Climate Scorecard. https://www.climatescorecard.org/2019/12/mexico/

Nugrahani, T. S., & Artanto, D. A. (2022). Sustainability Reporting by Disclosing Economic, Social and Environmental Performance. *Studies in Business and Economics, 17*(2), 216–226. DOI: 10.2478/sbe-2022-0034

Nurdeni, D. A., Budi, I., & Santoso, A. B. (2021, April). Sentiment analysis on Covid19 vaccines in Indonesia: from the perspective of Sinovac and Pfizer. In 2021 3rd East Indonesia conference on computer and information technology (EIConCIT) (pp. 122-127). IEEE. DOI: 10.1109/EIConCIT50028.2021.9431852

OECD. (2015). *G20/OECD principles of corporate governance*. OECD Publishing., DOI: 10.1787/9789264236882-

OECD. (2022). OECD Framework for Responsible AI in Education. https://www.oecd.org/education/ai-framework-edu/

Onukwulu, E., Agho, M., & Eyo-Udo, N. (2023). Developing a framework for AI-driven optimization of supply chains in energy sector. Global Journal of Advanced Research and Reviews. .DOI: 10.58175/gjarr.2023.1.2.0064

Onukwulu, E., Dienagha, I., Digitemie, W., & Egbumokei, P. (2021). AI-driven supply chain optimization for enhanced efficiency in the energy sector. Magna Scientia Advanced Research and Reviews. .DOI: 10.30574/msarr.2021.2.1.0060

Orazalin, N., & Mahmood, M. (2021). Toward sustainable development: Board characteristics, country governance quality, and environmental performance. *Business Strategy and the Environment, 30*(8), 3569–3588. DOI: 10.1002/bse.2820

Ordonez-Ponce, E., Dordi, T., Talbot, D., & Weber, O. (2024). Canadian banks and their responses to COVID-19–stakeholder-oriented crisis management. *Journal of Sustainable Finance & Investment, 14*(2), 388–409. DOI: 10.1080/20430795.2022.2069663

Organisation for Economic Co-operation and Development. (2018). *OECD/INFE toolkit for measuring financial literacy and financial inclusion*. OECD Publishing., DOI: 10.1787/9789264309303-

Ortiz-Martínez, E., Marín-Hernández, S., & Santos-Jaén, J.-M. (2023). Sustainability, corporate social responsibility, non-financial reporting and company performance: Relationships and mediating effects in Spanish small and medium sized enterprises. *Sustainable Production and Consumption, 35*, 349–364. DOI: 10.1016/j.spc.2022.11.015

Oyewole, A. T., Adeoye, O. B., Addy, W. A., Okoye, C. C., Ofodile, O. C., & Ugochukwu, C. E.Adedoyin Tolulope OyewoleOmotayo Bukola AdeoyeWilhelmina Afua AddyChinwe Chinazo OkoyeOnyeka Chrisanctus OfodileChinonye Esther Ugochukwu. (2024). Automating financial reporting with natural language processing: A review and case analysis. *World Journal of Advanced Research and Reviews, 21*(3), 575–589. DOI: 10.30574/wjarr.2024.21.3.0688

Padmanaban, S., Nasab, M. A., Samavat, T., Zand, M., & Nasab, M. A. (2023). Securing smart power grids against cyber-attacks. In *IoT and Analytics in Renewable Energy Systems* (Vol. 1, pp. 17–36). CRC Press., DOI: 10.1201/9781003331117

Padmanaban, S., Nasab, M. A., Samavat, T., Zand, M., & Nasab, M. A. (2023a). Artificial intelligence techniques for smart power systems. In *IoT and analytics in renewable energy systems* (Vol. 1, pp. 107–123). CRC Press., DOI: 10.1201/9781003331117-9

Panitsides, E., & Anastasiadou, S. (2015). Lifelong Learning Policy Agenda in the European Union: A bi- level analysis. *Open Review of Educational Research, 2*(1), 128–142. DOI: 10.1080/23265507.2015.1043936

Pantazi, T. (2024). The introduction of mandatory corporate sustainability reporting in the EU and the question of enforcement. *European Business Organization Law Review, 25*(3), 509–532. DOI: 10.1007/s40804-024-00320-x

Paolone, F., Pozzoli, M., Cucari, N., & Bianco, R. (2023). Longer board tenure and audit committee tenure. How do they impact environmental performance? A European study. *Corporate Social Responsibility and Environmental Management, 30*(1), 358–368. DOI: 10.1002/csr.2359

Papadaki, Z., Anastasiadou, S., Masouras, A., & Papalexandris, S. (2023). *Factors Influencing the Use of Digital Marketing by Telemedicine Services. 10th International Conference on Strategic Innovative Marketing and Tourism.* Zakynthos, Ionian Islands, Greece. In A. Kavoura et al. (eds.), Strategic Innovative Marketing and Tourism, Springer Proceedings in Business and Economics, (2023), 855-862. DOI: 10.1007/978-3-031-51038-0_92

Papademetriou, C. Anastasiadou, SD. Konteos, G. (2022). *The Effect of Human Resource Management Practices on the Quality of Service, Customer Satisfaction, and Organizational Performance in Cypriot Urban Hotel Industry*. HAICTA, (2022), 342-352.

Papademetriou, C., Belias, D., Anastasiadou, S., Ragazou, K., & Garefalakis, A. (2024). Sustainability: ESG and Human Resource Management. In Ragazou, K., Garefalakis, A., & Papalexandris, S. (Eds.), *Papademetriou, C., Anastasiadou, S* (pp. 1–15). ESG and Total Quality Management in Human Resources. IGI Global Publisher of TIMELY KNOWLEDGE., DOI: 10.4018/979-8-3693-2991-7.ch001

Park, H., & Kim, Y. K. (2020). Proactive versus reactive apparel brands in sustainability: Influences on brand loyalty. *Journal of Retailing and Consumer Services*, *52*, 101926. Advance online publication. DOI: 10.1016/j.jretconser.2019.101926

Parmar, B. L., Freeman, R. E., Harrison, J. S., Wicks, A. C., Purnell, L., & de Colle, S. (2010). Stakeholder theory: The state of the art. *The Academy of Management Annals*, *4*(1), 403–445. DOI: 10.5465/19416520.2010.495581

Passas, I. (2024). The evolution of ESG: From CSR to ESG 2.0. *Encyclopedia*, *4*(4), 1711–1720. DOI: 10.3390/encyclopedia4040112

Pegan, G., Schoier, G., & Patrizia de Luca. (2022). The Importance of Consumer Perception of Corporate Social Responsibility to Meet the Need for Sustainable Consumption. *IGI Global EBooks*, 1812–1835. DOI: 10.4018/978-1-6684-5590-6.ch089

Pennington-Gray, L., Lee, S., & Ballouli, K. (2024). Stakeholder sentiment of SDGs of Beijing Olympics 2020. In Sport Tourism, Events and Sustainable Development Goals (pp. 114-139). Routledge.

Pereira da Silva, P. (2023). *The impact of non-financial disclosure on labor investment: International evidence*. Borsa Istanbul Review.

Pesqueira, A., Sousa, M., & Rocha, Á. (2020). Big data skills sustainable development in healthcare and pharmaceuticals. *Journal of Medical Systems*, *44*(11), 44. DOI: 10.1007/s10916-020-01665-9 PMID: 33034743

Peter, G., Stonier, A. A., Gupta, P., Gavilanes, D., Vergara, M. M., & Lung sin, J. (2022). Smart fault monitoring and normalizing of a power distribution system using IoT. *Energies*, *15*(21), 8206. DOI: 10.3390/en15218206

Pinem, D., & Aulia, S. (2023). The Effect of Corporate Sustainability Performance on the Values of Companies Listed in the Sri Kehati Index. *Formosa Journal of Sustainable Research*, *2*(3), 713–734. DOI: 10.55927/fjsr.v2i3.3073

Polzin, F., Migendt, M., Täube, F. A., & von Flotow, P. (2017). Public policy influence on renewable energy investments—A panel data study across OECD countries. *Energy Policy*, *80*, 98–111. DOI: 10.1016/j.enpol.2015.01.026

Porter, M. E., & Kramer, M. R. (2002). The competitive advantage of corporate philanthropy. *Harvard Business Review*, *80*(12), 56–68. PMID: 12510538

Porter, M. E., & Kramer, M. R. (2006). Strategy and society: The link between competitive advantage and corporate social responsibility. *Harvard Business Review*, *84*(12), 78–92. PMID: 17183795

Porter, M. E., & Kramer, M. R. (2011). Creating shared value. *Harvard Business Review*, *89*(1/2), 62–77.

Porter, M. E., & Kramer, M. R. (2011). Creating shared value: Redefining capitalism and the role of the corporation in society. *Harvard Business Review*, *89*(1/2), 62–77.

Putri Amrigan, A. R., Hamidi, M., & Adrianto, F. (2023). The Effect of Sustainability Report Disclosure Compliance on the Company's Financial Performance. *Journal Of Social Research*, *2*(4), 1028–1038. DOI: 10.55324/josr.v2i4.692

Quinn, R. E., & Rohrbaugh, J. (1983). A spatial model of effectiveness criteria: Towards a competing values approach to organizational analysis. *Management Science*, *29*(3), 363–377. DOI: 10.1287/mnsc.29.3.363

Raghavendra, A. H., Bala, P. K., & Mukherjee, A. (2024). Text mining analysis of retail and consumer service leaders' sustainability narratives: Are they actually true? *Journal of Retailing and Consumer Services*, *80*, 103921. DOI: 10.1016/j.jretconser.2024.103921

Raghupathi, V., Ren, J., & Raghupathi, W. (2020). Identifying corporate sustainability issues by analyzing shareholder resolutions: A machine-learning text analytics approach. *Sustainability (Basel)*, *12*(11), 4753. DOI: 10.3390/su12114753

Raji, I. D., Smart, A., White, R. N., & Mitchell, M. (2020). Closing the AI accountability gap: Defining an end-to-end framework for internal algorithmic auditing. In *Proceedings of the Conference on Fairness, Accountability, and Transparency* (pp. 1-15). https://arxiv.org/abs/2001.00973 DOI: 10.1145/3351095.3372873

Ramanathan, S., & Isaksson, R. (2023). Sustainability reporting as a 21st century problem statement: Using a quality lens to understand and analyse the challenges. *The TQM Journal*, *35*(5), 1310–1328. DOI: 10.1108/TQM-01-2022-0035

Rashid, S., & Ratten, V. (2021). Entrepreneurial ecosystems during COVID-19: The survival of small businesses using dynamic capabilities. *World Journal of Entrepreneurship, Management and Sustainable Development, ahead-of-print*(ahead-of-print), 26. DOI: 10.1108/WJEMSD-09-2020-0110

Raza, A., Farrukh, M., Wang, G., Iqbal, M. K., & Farhan, M. (2023). Effects of hotels' corporate social responsibility (CSR) initiatives on green consumer behavior: Investigating the roles of consumer engagement, positive emotions, and altruistic values. *Journal of Hospitality Marketing & Management, 32*(7), 1–23. DOI: 10.1080/19368623.2023.2223571

Razali, N., & Wah, Y. (2011). Power Comparisons of Shapiro-Wilk, Kolmogorov-Smirnov, Lilliefors and Anderson-Darling tests. *Journal of Statistical Modeling and Analytics, 2*, 21–33.

Razib, N., & Rasel, I. (2025). *The role of data analytics in enhancing ESG transparency in the corporate sector of Bangladesh.* Global Journal of Engineering and Technology Advances., DOI: 10.30574/gjeta.2025.22.1.0245

Reddy, K. (2010). The Effect of Sustainability Reporting on Financial Performance: An Empirical Study Using Listed Companies.

Remo-Diez, N., Mendaña-Cuervo, C., & Arenas-Parra, M. (2023). Exploring the asymmetric impact of sustainability reporting on financial performance in the utilities sector: A longitudinal comparative analysis. *Utilities Policy, 84*, 101650. DOI: 10.1016/j.jup.2023.101650

Reverte, C., Gomez-Melero, E., & Cegarra-Navarro, J. G. (2016). The influence of corporate social responsibility practices on organizational performance: Evidence from Eco-Responsible Spanish firms. *Journal of Cleaner Production, 112*, 2870–2884. DOI: 10.1016/j.jclepro.2015.09.128

Richter, L., Lehna, M., Marchand, S., Scholz, C., Dreher, A., Klaiber, S., & Lenk, S. (2022). Artificial Intelligence for Electricity Supply Chain automation. *Renewable & Sustainable Energy Reviews, 163*, 112459. DOI: 10.1016/j.rser.2022.112459

Riedl, A., & Smeets, P. (2017). Why do investors hold socially responsible mutual funds? *The Journal of Finance, 72*(6), 2505–2550. DOI: 10.1111/jofi.12547

Robinos, J. O., Binhamza, M., Casyao, I., Combis, H., Melgar, S., Sora, L., & Austria, M. (2024). Examining Attitudes and Perceived Usefulness of AI Integration in Teaching and Learning Processes. *Journal of Interdisciplinary Perspectives, 2*(12), 619–626. DOI: 10.69569/jip.2024.0591

Rojo-Suárez, J., Alonso-Conde, A. B., & Gonzalez-Ruiz, J. D. (2024). Does sustainability improve financial performance? An analysis of Latin American oil and gas firms. *Resources Policy, 88*, 104484. DOI: 10.1016/j.resourpol.2023.104484

Rossmannek, O., David, N., Sandoval, C., & Garay, L. (2024). Bridging the Green Gap in Homesharing: How Platforms Can Increase Hosts' Sustainability Intentions and Behavior. *Journal of Travel Research*. DOI: 10.1177/00472875241249444

Runeson, P., & Höst, M. (2009). Guidelines for conducting and reporting case study research in software engineering. *Empirical Software Engineering, 14*(2), 131–164. DOI: 10.1007/s10664-008-9102-8

Saad, S., Ahmad, J., & Krishnan, M. (2022). Towards Sustainability in Corporate Social Responsibility. *Routledge EBooks*, 163–187. DOI: 10.4324/9781003309642-12

Sabtika, V., & Marlapa, E. (2024). THE EFFECT OF IMPLEMENTATION OF CORPORATE SOCIAL RESPONSIBILITY, GREEN INNOVATION STRATEGY, AND COMMITMENT TO A SUSTAINABLE LIVING ENVIRONMENT IN UNILEVER INDONESIA TBK.. International Journal of Management Studies and Social Science Research. .DOI: 10.56293/IJMSSSR.2024.4820

Sætra, H. (2021). A Framework for Evaluating and Disclosing the ESG Related Impacts of AI with the SDGs. *Sustainability (Basel), 13*(15), 8503. DOI: 10.3390/su13158503

Sahinidis, A. G., & Kavoura, A. (2014). Exploring corporate social responsibility practices of Greek companies. *Zeszyty Naukowe Małopolskiej Wyższej Szkoły Ekonomicznej w Tarnowie, 25*(2), 185–193.

Saini, N., & Singhania, M. (2019). Performance relevance of environmental and social disclosures: The role of foreign ownership. *Benchmarking, 26*(3), 1845–1873. DOI: 10.1108/BIJ-04-2018-0114

Sakthivel, M., Jaganathan, A., Mohanraj, M., & Selvakumar, P. Mohit, & Manjunath, T. (2025). Brand Loyalty through AI and Personalisation AI-Generated Content for Financial Marketing. In A. J Nair, S. Manohar, Y. B. Limbu, & B. A. Huhmann (Eds.), Intersecting Natural Language Processing and FinTech Innovations in Service Marketing (pp. 77-96). IGI Global Scientific Publishing.

Sakthivel, M., Jaganathan, A., Mohanraj, M., & Selvakumar, P. Mohit, & Manjunath, T. (2025). *Brand Loyalty through AI and Personalisation AI-Generated Content for Financial Marketing*. In A. J. Nair, S. Manohar, Y. B. Limbu, & B. A. Huhmann (Eds.), Intersecting Natural Language Processing and FinTech Innovations in Service Marketing (pp. 77–96). IGI Global Scientific Publishing. DOI: 10.4018/979-8-3693-9944-6.ch006

Samal, A., & Misra, L. I. Mohit, Pougajendy, S., Chandel, P. S., Manjunath, T. C., & Selvakumar, P. (2025). *Musealization and Tourism Practices*. In S. Oflazoglu & M. Dora (Eds.), Preserving Cultural Heritage in Post-Disaster Urban Renewal (pp. 115–142). IGI Global Scientific Publishing. DOI: 10.4018/979-8-3693-9097-9.ch006

Samavat, T., Nazari, M., Fuhong, L., & Yang, L. (2025). Optimizing stand-alone PV systems: A metaheuristic enhanced fuzzy approach for adaptive MPPT. *China Communications*, *22*(1), 61–74. DOI: 10.23919/JCC.fa.2024-0224.202501

Sanjeevikumar, P., Zand, M., Nasab, M. A., Eskandari, M., Samavat, T., Jahangiri, A., & Moradi, M. H. (2023). Power electronics in smart grid. In *Smart and power grid systems–Design challenges and paradigms* (pp. 1–20). River Publishers., DOI: 10.1201/9781003339557-2

Sankaranarayanan, S. (2025). The role of data engineering in enabling real-time analytics and decision-making across heterogeneous data sources in cloud-native environments. *International Journal of Advanced Research in Cyber Security*, *6*(1), 11–18.

Saraswat, J. K., & Choudhari, S. (2025). Integrating big data and cloud computing into the existing system and performance impact: A case study in manufacturing. *Technological Forecasting and Social Change*, *210*, 123883. DOI: 10.1016/j.techfore.2024.123883

Sarıyer, G., Mangla, S., Chowdhury, S., Sozen, M., & Kazançoğlu, Y. (2024). Predictive and prescriptive analytics for ESG performance evaluation: A case of Fortune 500 companies. *Journal of Business Research*, *181*, 114742. DOI: 10.1016/j.jbusres.2024.114742

SASB (Sustainability Accounting Standards Board). (2021). SASB Standards. Retrieved from https://www.sasb.org/

Sawant, S. K., Gawade, S., & Shrimali, M. (2025). Survey of recent approaches in ontology matching. *Information Systems for Intelligent Systems*, *430*, 491–509. DOI: 10.1007/978-981-96-1206-2_38

Schaltegger, S., Hansen, E. G., & Lüdeke-Freund, F. (2016). Business models for sustainability: Origins, present research, and future avenues. *Organization & Environment*, *29*(1), 3–10. DOI: 10.1177/1086026615599806

Scheepers, H., McLoughlin, S., & Wijesinghe, R. (2022). Aligning stakeholders perceptions of project performance: The contribution of Business Realisation Management. *International Journal of Project Management*, *40*(5), 471–480. DOI: 10.1016/j.ijproman.2022.03.002

Secretaría de Energía. (2020). *Programa de desarrollo del sistema eléctrico nacional 2020-2034*. Gobierno de México. https://www.gob.mx/sener/documentos/programa-de-desarrollo-del-sistema-electrico-nacional

Selwyn, N. (2020). *Should robots replace teachers? AI and the future of education. Polity Press.Selwyn, N. (2020). Should robots replace teachers? AI and the future of education*. Polity Press.

Seremeti, L., Anastasiadis, L., & Anastasiadou, S. (2024). The Role of Data in Environmental, Social, and Governance Strategy, (pages 149-166). *In Christos Papademetriou, Sofia Anastasiadou, Konstantina Ragazou, Alexandros Garefalakis and Stylianos Papalexandris. ESG and Total Quality Management in Human Resources,* https:// DOI: DOI: 10.4018/979-8-3693-2991-7.ch010

Seremeti, L., Anastasiadou, S., Masouras, A., & Papalexandris, S. (2025b). Addressing the challenges of harmonizing law and artificial intelligence technology in modern society. IAES International Journal of Artificial Intelligence (IJ-AI), Vol.14, No.3, pp. 2471-2478. DOI: 10.11591/ijai.v14.i3.pp2471-2478

Seremeti, L., Anastasiadis, L., Kalogera, C., & Kontis, S. (2025a). Qualia and Business Intelligence for Organizational Excellence. In Seremeti, L., Liargovas, P., Papademetriou, C., Anastasiadis, L., & Anastasiadou, S. (Eds.), *Harnessing Business Intelligence for Modern Talent Management* (pp. 265–274). IGI Global Publisher of TIMELY KNOWLEDG., DOI: 10.4018/979-8-3373-1942-1.ch010

Seremeti, L., & Kougias, I. (2013). Computation of ontology resemblance coefficients for improving semantic interoperability. *Engineering Mathematics Letters*, *2*(1), 1–19.

Seremeti, L., & Kougias, I. (2013). Networks of aligned ontologies through a category theoretic approach. *Journal of Emerging Trends in Computing and Information Sciences*, *4*(10), 785–794.

Shahzad, M., Qu, Y., Javed, S. A., Zafar, A. U., & Rehman, S. U. (2020). Relation of environment sustainability to CSR and green innovation: A case of Pakistani manufacturing industry. *Journal of Cleaner Production, 253*, 119938. DOI: 10.1016/j.jclepro.2019.119938

Shang, Y., Zhou, S., Zhuang, D., Żywiołek, J., & Dínçer, H. (2024). The impact of artificial intelligence application on enterprise environmental performance: Evidence from microenterprises. *Gondwana Research, 131*, 181–195. DOI: 10.1016/j.gr.2024.02.012

Shankar, B. S., & Sheware, P. L. (2024). Data cleaning techniques and their impact on model accuracy. *International Research Journal of Modernization in Engineering Technology and Science, 06*(12), 4343–4346.

Shmelev, S. E. S., & Gilardi, E. (2025). Corporate environmental, social, and governance performance: The impacts on financial returns, business model innovation, and social transformation. *Sustainability (Basel), 17*(3), 1286. DOI: 10.3390/su17031286

Shokouhyar, S., Shokoohyar, S., & Mirzaei, S. (2023). Stakeholders' engagement through social media analytics in promoting sustainable development practices in the mobile supply chain: A cross-country analysis. *Business Strategy and the Environment, 32*(8), 5807–5820. DOI: 10.1002/bse.3449

Singhania, M., & Saini, N. (2021). Institutional framework of ESG disclosures: Comparative analysis of developed and developing countries. *Journal of Sustainable Finance & Investment, 13*(1), 516–559. DOI: 10.1080/20430795.2021.1964810

Sinha, M. (2024). *Responsible Capital: The Evolution and Performance of ESG Investing*. Exploresearch., DOI: 10.62823/ExRe//01/03.10

Sirmon, D. G., Hitt, M. A., Ireland, R. D., & Gilbert, B. A. (2011). Resource orchestration to create competitive advantage: Breadth, depth, and life cycle effects. *Journal of Management, 37*(5), 1390–1412. DOI: 10.1177/0149206310385695

Sklavos, G., Theodossiou, G., Papanikolaou, Z., Karelakis, C., & Ragazou, K. (2024). Environmental, Social, and Governance-Based Artificial Intelligence Governance: Digitalizing Firms' Leadership and Human Resources Management. *Sustainability (Basel), 16*(16), 7154. DOI: 10.3390/su16167154

Smith, E. A., Knollenberg, W., Seekamp, E., Lee, K. J., & Savage, A. (2024). Gateway community stakeholders' perceived impacts of protected area management actions: The case of North Carolina (US) state parks. *Journal of Outdoor Recreation and Tourism, 47*, 100792. DOI: 10.1016/j.jort.2024.100792

Smyrnaios, N. (2023). Platform Power and Educational Data Governance. *Journal of Media and Learning Analytics, 12*(1), 45–61.

Sophocleous, H., Anastasiadou, S., Masouras, A., & Apostolopoulos, S. (2023b). *The Effect of Political Marketing on the Electoral Behavior of Greek Voters.* 10th International Conference on Strategic Innovative Marketing and Tourism 2023. Zakynthos, Ionian Islands, Greece pp. (2023c), 343-350. In A. Kavoura et al. (eds.), Strategic Innovative Marketing and Tourism, Springer Proceedings in Business and Economics, DOI: 10.1007/978-3-031-51038-0_38

Sophocleous, H., Masouras, A., Anastasiadou, S., & Apostolopoulos, S. (2023c). *Consumption of Greek Political Messages: A Qualitative Approach of the Case of the Greek Political Market.* 10th International Conference on Strategic Innovative Marketing and Tourism. Zakynthos, Ionian Islands, Greece pp. 947-955. In A. Kavoura et al. (eds.), Strategic Innovative Marketing and Tourism, Springer, Proceedings in Business and Economics, (2023) 947-955. DOI: 10.1007/978-3-031-51038-0_102

Sophocleous, H., Anastasiadou, S., Masouras, A., & Apostolopoulos, S. (2023a). Motives and Perceptions of Greek Voters in National Elections of 2023. In Kavoura, A. (Eds.), *Strategic Innovative Marketing and Tourism, Springer Proceedings in Business and Economics, (2023)* (pp. 431–439)., DOI: 10.1007/978-3-031-51038-0_47

Soundariya, A., Behera, N. K., Selvakumar, P., Chandel, P. S., Gupta, S., & Manjunath, T. C. (2025). AI and Environmental Ethics: The Role of AI in Addressing Climate Change Ethical Considerations in AI-Driven Environmental Solutions. In Chakraborty, S. (Ed.), *Human Values, Ethics, and Dignity in the Age of Artificial Intelligence* (pp. 321–346). IGI Global Scientific Publishing., DOI: 10.4018/979-8-3693-9035-1.ch013

Souravlas, S. Anastasiadou, S. (2021). Pipelined Dynamic Scheduling of Big Data Streams. Applied Sciences. 10.14 (2021): 4796

Souravlas, S., Anastasiadou, S. & Katsavounis, S. (2021b). A Survey on the Recent Advances of Deep Community Detection." Applied Sciences. 11.16 (2021b): 7179

Souravlas, S., Anastasiadou, S., Economides, Th., & Katsavounis, S. (2023). Probabilistic Community Detection in Social Networks. IEEE Access, Publication Date: 2023, Volume: 11, DOI: 10.1109/ACCESS.2023.3257021

Souravlas, S., Katsavounis, S. & Anastasiadou, S. (2021c). On Modeling and Simulation of Resource Allocation Policies in Cloud Computing Using Colored Petri Nets. *Applied Sciences.* 10.16 (2021): 5644.

Souravlas, S., & Anastasiadou, S. (2020). Pipelined Dynamic Scheduling of Big Data Streams. *Applied Sciences (Basel, Switzerland), 10*(14), 4796. DOI: 10.3390/app10144796

Souravlas, S., & Anastasiadou, S. (2022). On Implementing Social Community Clouds Based on Markov Models. *IEEE Transactions on Computational Social Systems, 2022*. DOI: 10.1109/TCSS.2022.3213273

Souravlas, S., Anastasiadou, S. D., Tantalaki, N., & Katsavounis, S. (2022a). A Fair, Dynamic Load Balanced Task Distribution Strategy for Heterogeneous Cloud Platforms Based on Markov Process Modeling. *IEEE Access : Practical Innovations, Open Solutions, 10*, 26149–26162. DOI: 10.1109/ACCESS.2022.3157435

Souravlas, S., Anastasiadou, S., & Katsavounis, S. (2021b). A Survey on the Recent Advances of Deep Community Detection. *Applied Sciences (Basel, Switzerland), 11*(16), 7179. DOI: 10.3390/app11167179

Souravlas, S., Anastasiadou, S., & Katsavounis, S. (2021c). More on Pipelined Dynamic Scheduling of Big Data Streams. *Applied Sciences (Basel, Switzerland), 11*(1), 61. DOI: 10.3390/app11010061

Souravlas, S., Anastasiadou, S., & Kostoglou, I. (2023a). A Novel Method For General Hierarchical System Modeling Via Colored Petri Nets Based on Transition Extractions From Real Data Sets. *Applied Sciences (Basel, Switzerland), 13*(1), 339. DOI: 10.3390/app13010339

Souravlas, S., Katsavounis, S., & Anastasiadou, S. (2020). On Modeling and Simulation of Resource Allocation Policies in Cloud Computing Using Colored Petri Nets. *Applied Sciences (Basel, Switzerland), 10*(16), 5644. DOI: 10.3390/app10165644

Stanco, M., & Lerro, M. (2020). Consumers' Preferences for and Perception of CSR Initiatives in the Wine Sector. *Sustainability (Basel), 12*(13), 5230. DOI: 10.3390/su12135230

Steffen, W., Rockström, J., Richardson, K., Lenton, T. M., Folke, C., Liverman, D., Summerhayes, C. P., Barnosky, A. D., Cornell, S. E., Crucifix, M., Donges, J. F., Fetzer, I., Lade, S. J., Scheffer, M., Winkelmann, R., & Schellnhuber, H. J. (2018). Trajectories of the Earth system in the Anthropocene. *Proceedings of the National Academy of Sciences of the United States of America, 115*(33), 8252–8259. DOI: 10.1073/pnas.1810141115 PMID: 30082409

Svanberg, J., Ardeshiri, T., Samsten, I., Öhman, P., Neidermeyer, P., Rana, T., Maisano, F., & Danielson, M. (2023). *Must social performance ratings be idiosyncratic? An exploration of social performance ratings with predictive validity*. Sustainability Accounting, Management and Policy Journal., DOI: 10.1108/SAMPJ-03-2022-0127

Tantalaki, N., Souravlas, S., Roumeliotis, M., & Katsavounis, S. (2020). Pipeline-Based Linear Scheduling of Big Data Streams in the Cloud. *IEEE Access : Practical Innovations, Open Solutions, 8*, 117182–117202. DOI: 10.1109/ACCESS.2020.3004612

Taraza, E., & Anastasiadou, S. (2019a). *EFQM Excellence Model in Vocational Lyceum: Reliability and Validity of EFQM Instrument.* Proceedings of 13th annual International Technology, Education and Development Conference (INTED2019), Valencia, Spain, pp. 2273-2285. DOI: 10.21125/inted.2019.0637

Taraza, E., & Anastasiadou, S. (2019b). *Assessing quality in Greek tertiary education: the case of school of pedagogical and technological education (ASPETE).* Proceedings of 13th annual International Technology, Education and Development Conference (INTED2019), Valencia, Spain, pp. 2364-2374.

Taraza, E., Anastasiadou, S., Seremeti, S., & Masouras, A. (2024a). Environmental, Social, and Governance of Businesses and Organizations and the Role of Human Resources (pages 116-132.). *In Christos Papademetriou, Sofia Anastasiadou, Konstantina Ragazou, Alexandros Garefalakis and Stylianos Papalexandris. ESG and Total Quality Management in Human Resources*, DOI: 10.4018/979-8-3693-2991-7.ch006

Taraza, E., Anastasiadou, S., Masouras, A., & Papademetriou, C. (2023). Sustainable Development and Implementation of Quality Management Excellence Models in Public Organizations: A Systematic Literature Review. *Sustainability*, mdpi. *Sustainability (Basel), 15*(10), 7971. DOI: 10.3390/su15107971

Taraza, E., Anastasiadou, S., Papademetriou, C., & Masouras, A. (2024a). Evaluation of Quality and Equality in Education Using the European Foundation for Quality Management Excellence Model—A Literature Review. *Sustainability (Basel), 16*(3), 960. DOI: 10.3390/su16030960

Taraza, E., Papademetriou, C., Seremeti, S., Masouras, A., & Anastasiadou, S. (2024). The Necessity of Environmental Ethics in Environmental Education and the Role of Educators. In *Christos Papademetriou* (pp. 149–166). Sofia Anastasiadou, Konstantina Ragazou, Alexandros Garefalakis and Stylianos Papalexandris. ESG and Total Quality Management in Human Resources., DOI: 10.4018/979-8-3693-2991-7.ch008

Taskin, D., Sariyer, G., Acar, E., & Cagli, E. C. (2025). Do past ESG scores efficiently predict future ESG performance? *Research in International Business and Finance*, *74*, 102706. DOI: 10.1016/j.ribaf.2024.102706

TCFD (Task Force on Climate-related Financial Disclosures). (2021). Recommendations of the Task Force on Climate-related Financial Disclosures. Retrieved from https://www.fsb-tcfd.org/

Teece, D. J. (2007). Explicating dynamic capabilities: The nature and microfoundations of (sustainable) enterprise performance. *Strategic Management Journal*, *28*(13), 1319–1350. DOI: 10.1002/smj.640

Teece, D. J., Pisano, G., & Shuen, A. (1997). Dynamic capabilities and strategic management. *Strategic Management Journal*, *18*(7), 509–533. DOI: 10.1002/(SICI)1097-0266(199708)18:7<509::AID-SMJ882>3.0.CO;2-Z

Thaler, R. (1985). Mental accounting and consumer choice. *Marketing Science*, *4*(3), 199–214. DOI: 10.1287/mksc.4.3.199

Thapa, K. B., Okalidou, A., & Anastasiadou, S. (2016). Teachers' screening estimations of speech-language impairments in primary school children in Nepal, *International Journal of Language and Communication Disorders*, 51, (3), 310–327.

Thirunagalingam, A., & Selvakumar, P. (2025). Application of Automation and Robotics in the Oil and Gas Industry. In Abdullayev, V., & Khang, A. (Eds.), *Revolutionizing AI and Robotics in the Oil and Gas Industry* (pp. 229–244). IGI Global Scientific Publishing., DOI: 10.4018/979-8-3693-8156-4.ch011

Toschi, L., Ughetto, E., & Fronzetti Colladon, A. (2023). The identity of social impact venture capitalists: Exploring social linguistic positioning and linguistic distinctiveness through text mining. *Small Business Economics*, *60*(3), 1249–1280. DOI: 10.1007/s11187-022-00655-0

Trade.gov. (2024). *Mexico renewable energy market analysis*. International Trade Administration. https://www.trade.gov/market-intelligence/mexico-renewable-energy

Tsourgiannis, L. Florou, G., Markopoulos, T., Anastasiadou, S. & Tsitsakis, C. (2019). *How Do Mosquitoes Affect Tourism Enterprises in Greece*? Springer Proceedings in Business and Economics, (2019) 461–471.

UNEP FI & Mercer. (2007). *Demystifying Responsible Investment Performance: A review of key academic and broker research on ESG factors*. United Nations Environment Programme Finance Initiative.

Unerman, J. (2000). Methodological issues—Reflections on quantification in corporate social reporting content analysis. *Accounting, Auditing & Accountability Journal, 13*(5), 667–681. DOI: 10.1108/09513570010353756

UNESCO. (2021). Recommendation on the ethics of artificial intelligence. https://unesdoc.unesco.org/ark:/48223/pf0000381137

Upadhyaya, A. N., Debnath, P., Rani, P., Selvakumar, P., Manjunath, T. C., & Bhattacharya, S. (2025). AI-Based Disaster Prediction and Early Warning Systems. In Mobo, F. (Ed.), *AI and Emerging Technologies for Emergency Response and Smart Cities* (pp. 55–74). IGI Global Scientific Publishing., DOI: 10.4018/979-8-3693-9770-1.ch003

Usmanova, A., & Usbeck, R. (2024). Structuring sustainability reports for environmental standards with LLMs guided by ontology. *Proceedings of the 1st Workshop on Natural Language Processing Meets Climate Change*, 168-177. https://doi.org/ DOI: 10.18653/v1/2024.climatenlp-1.13

Valkanos, E., Giossi, S., & Anastasiadou, S. (2010). Certified Adult Educators´ Attitudes towards Continuing Education. *Review of European Studies*. 2(1), (2010) 61-68.

Valsamidis, S., Mandilas, A., Florou, G., & Anastasiadou, S. (2024). The use of e-government services provided by the local authorities: The case of the municipality of Kavala. *International Journal of Electronic Governance, 16*(2), 196–218. DOI: 10.1504/IJEG.2024.140790

Vargas-Merino, J. A., & Rios-Lama, C. A. (2023). The Interplay of Corporate Social Responsibility (CSR) and Sustainable Development Goals (SDGs): An Overview of Relevant Literature on CSR's and SDGs. *IBIMA Business Review*, 1–12. DOI: 10.5171/2023.930662

Velte, P. (2017). Does ESG performance have an impact on financial performance? Evidence from Germany. *Journal of Global Responsibility, 8*(2), 169–178. DOI: 10.1108/JGR-11-2016-0029

Velte, P. (2023). Determinants and financial consequences of environmental performance and reporting: A literature review of European archival research. *Journal of Environmental Management, 340*, 117916. DOI: 10.1016/j.jenvman.2023.117916 PMID: 37141659

Veltri, S., Mazzotta, R., & Rubino, F. E. (2021). Board diversity and corporate social performance: Does the family firm status matter? *Corporate Social Responsibility and Environmental Management, 28*(6), 1664–1679. DOI: 10.1002/csr.2136

Walker, B., Holling, C. S., Carpenter, S. R., & Kinzig, A. (2004). Resilience, adaptability and transformability in social–ecological systems. *Ecology and Society*, *9*(2), 5. DOI: 10.5751/ES-00650-090205

Wang, L., & Alexander, C. (2016). Big data analytics for medication management in diabetes mellitus. *International Journal of Security and Networks*, *1*, 42.

Wang, Q. (2025). Generative AI-Assisted Evaluation of ESG Practices and Information Delays in ESG Ratings. *Finance Research Letters*, *74*, 106757. DOI: 10.1016/j.frl.2025.106757

Wang, Q., Sun, T., & Li, R. (2023). Does artificial intelligence (AI) reduce ecological footprint? The role of globalization. *Environmental Science and Pollution Research International*, *30*(59), 123948–123965. DOI: 10.1007/s11356-023-31076-5 PMID: 37995036

Wang, Y., Kung, L., & Byrd, T. A. (2018b). Big data analytics: Understanding its capabilities and potential benefits for healthcare organizations. *Technological Forecasting and Social Change*, *126*, 3–13. DOI: 10.1016/j.techfore.2015.12.019

Weygandt, J. J., Kimmel, P. D., & Kieso, D. E. (2007). *Accounting principles* (8th ed.). Wiley.

Williamson, B. (2017). *Big data in education: The digital future of learning, policy and practice. SAGE Publications.Williamson, B. (2017). Big data in education: The digital future of learning, policy and practice*. SAGE Publications. DOI: 10.4135/9781529714920

Williamson, B., & Piattoeva, N. (2022). Metrics in Education: Governing by Numbers in the Datafied School. Educational Theory & Policy, 55(3), 344–359.

Willis, L. E. (2008). Against financial-literacy education. *Iowa Law Review*, *94*(1), 197–285. https://ilr.law.uiowa.edu/print/volume-94-issue-1/against-financial-literacy-education/

Winit, W., Ekasingh, E., & Sampet, J. (2023). How Disclosure Types of Sustainability Performance Impact Consumers' Relationship Quality and Firm Reputation. *Sustainability (Basel)*, *15*(1), 803. DOI: 10.3390/su15010803

Xie, H., & Wu, F. (2025). Artificial Intelligence Technology and Corporate ESG Performance: Empirical Evidence from Chinese-Listed Firms. *Sustainability*. DOI: 10.3390/su17146463

Xu, N., Tang, Z., Si, C., Bian, J., & Mu, C. (2025). A review of smart grid evolution and reinforcement learning: Applications, challenges and future directions. *Energies, 18*(7), 1837. DOI: 10.3390/en18071837

Yadav, S., Samadhiya, A., Kumar, A., Luthra, S., & Pandey, K. (2024). Environmental, Social, and Governance (ESG) Reporting and Missing (M) Scores in the Industry 5.0 Era: Broadening Firms' and Investors' Decisions to Achieve Sustainable Development Goals. *Sustainable Development.* DOI: 10.1002/sd.3306

Yeung, K. (2018). Algorithmic regulation: A critical interrogation. Regulation & Governance, 12(4), 505–523.Yeung, K. (2018). Algorithmic regulation: A critical interrogation. *Regulation & Governance, 12*(4), 505–523. DOI: 10.1111/rego.12158

Yiğit Açikgöz, F., Kayakuş, M., Moiceanu, G., & Sönmez, N. (2024). A New Approach to Assess Sustainable Corporate Reputation with Citizen Comments Using Machine Learning and Natural Language Processing. *Sustainability (Basel), 16*(22), 9610. DOI: 10.3390/su16229610

Yıldırım, F., Yalman, Y., Bayındır, K. Ç., & Terciyanlı, E. (2025). Comprehensive review of edge computing for power systems: State of the art, architecture, and applications. *Applied Sciences (Basel, Switzerland), 15*(8), 4592. DOI: 10.3390/app15084592

Yin, R. K. (2018). *Case study research and applications* (Vol. 6). Sage.

Yucel, M., & Yucel, S. (2024). Environmental, social, and governance (ESG) dynamics in the energy sector: Strategic approaches for sustainable development. *Energies, 17*(24), 6291. DOI: 10.3390/en17246291

Yu, M., Rabhi, F., & Bandara, M. (2024). Ontology-Driven Architecture for Managing Environmental, Social, and Governance Metrics. *Electronics (Basel), 13*(9), 1719. DOI: 10.3390/electronics13091719

Yu, W., Zhou, J., He, M., & Si, D. (2022). Does Brand Truth-Telling Yield Customer Participation? The Interaction Effects of CSR Strategy and Transparency Signaling. *Behavioral Sciences (Basel, Switzerland), 12*(12), 514. DOI: 10.3390/bs12120514 PMID: 36546997

Zattoni, A., Dedoulis, E., Leventis, S., & Van Ees, H. (2020). Corporate governance and institutions—A review and research agenda. *Corporate Governance, 28*(6), 465–487. DOI: 10.1111/corg.12347

Zhang, D., & Lucey, B. M. (2022). Sustainable behaviors and firm performance: The role of financial constraints' alleviation. *Economic Analysis and Policy, 74*, 220–233. DOI: 10.1016/j.eap.2022.02.003

Zhang, J., & Chung, K. S. K. (2024). Online naturalistic inquiry for stakeholder issue analysis: Design and implementation. *Project Leadership and Society*, *5*, 100163. DOI: 10.1016/j.plas.2024.100163

Zhang, T., Yang, M., & Jiang, P. (2025). Event state knowledge graph-driven full-chain product quality tracing. *Procedia CIRP*, *134*, 538–543. DOI: 10.1016/j.procir.2025.02.154

Zhang, Y., Huang, T., & Bompard, E. F. (2018). Big data analytics in smart grids: A review. *Energy Informatics*, *1*(1), 8. DOI: 10.1186/s42162-018-0007-5

Zheng, Z., & Lee, C. (2025). A meta-analysis of ESG factors in the real estate investment trusts sector: Exploring their impacts on REITs performance. *Engineering, Construction, and Architectural Management*. DOI: 10.1108/ECAM-05-2024-0652

Zou, Y., Shi, M., Chen, Z., Deng, Z., Lei, Z., Zeng, Z., Yang, S., Tong, H., Xiao, L., & Zhou, W. (2023). ESGReveal: An LLM-based approach for extracting structured data from ESG reports. ArXiv, abs/2312.17264. https://doi.org//arXiv.2312.17264 .DOI: 10.48550

Zuboff, S. (2019). *The Age of Surveillance Capitalism: The Fight for a Human Future at the New Frontier of Power*. PublicAffairs.

About the Contributors

Marcos Komodromos is an Associate Professor at the Department of Communications at the University of Nicosia. He is a Chartered PR practitioner (Ch. PR) and a member of the Chartered Institute of Public Relations (CIPR) in Great Britain. Dr Komodromos holds two Master's degrees, one in Communication and another in Management. He completed his PhD in Business Administration, focusing on organizational justice, trust, and organisational change management. Dr Komodromos has been an active member of various professional associations and organizations in Cyprus and the UK. He has over 20 years of experience in the media industry, particularly in radio and TV, and has many media projects to his credit. Currently, he is a consultant in strategic corporate communication, digital media, and marketing communication for organizations in Cyprus and abroad. He is also a certified trainer and coach for employees in the areas of marketing communications, digital marketing and social media, leadership, media training, and management. Dr Komodromos has published extensively on corporate communications, public relations, digital media, organizational justice, trust, new media, marketing communications, change management, internal communication, and corporate social responsibility.

Lamprini Seremeti is a an Assistant Professor in the Department of Agricultural Economics & Rural Development at the School of Applied Economics and Social Science of the Agricultural University of Athens. She holds a PhD in Computer Science with a focus on propagating knowledge in networks of aligned ontologies from Hellenic Open University; a Master in Special Education from University of Rome; a Master in Pure Mathematics from University of Patras; a Bachelor in Mathematics from University of Patras; a Bachelor in Informatics from University of Western Greece; and a Bachelor in Law from University of Nicosia. She has also participated as a researcher in EU-funded projects, in which, her tasks involved mathematical modeling, data processing, knowledge representation and management, and conceptualization of heterogeneous environments (socio-economic, educational, biomedical, ambient intelligent). Her research interests focus on theories applied in interpretation of Law in ambient intelligent environments, knowledge representation and management through ontologies, and mathematical modeling of co-evolving systems.

Lazaros Anastasiadis is a political scientist. His research intersests focues on Political Issues, Technologies of Interactive Systems, Architecture and applications of Outdoor Positioning Systems (e.g., GPS) and the integration of these systems with the Internet of Things (IoT),and the combined use of Artificial Intelligence (AI). He has published many articles in International and Greek Journals as well as in International and Greek Conferences.

Panagiotis Liargovas received his BA degree from the University of Athens and his MA and Ph.D degrees in Economics from Clark University. He has been a Fulbright Scholar, a Bakalas Foundation Scholar, a Teaching Assistant Scholar (Clark University) and a European Commission trainee (Brussels). He has taught in many Universities including Clark University, Bologna University, and University of Strasbourg. He has served as economic advisor to the Greek Ministry of Finance, the Greek Ministry of Foreign Affairs and the Municipality of Athens in many occasions. For the period 2013-18 he was the Head of the Parliamentary Budget Office at the Hellenic Parliament. He is currently Chairman of the Board of the Centre of Planning and Economic Research (KEPE) and of the National Productivity Board. He is also Professor of Economics at the University of Peloponnese. He has made more than 100 publications in academic journals and has published more than 20 books.

Sofia Anastasiadou is a Professor of Statistics and Research Methodology, Biostatistics and Biomedical Research at the School of Health of the University of Western Macedonia (UOWM), Department of Midwifery. She is the Deam of School of Health of UOWM, and a Member of the Dean of the School of Economics of the University of Western Macedonia. She is also a Member of the Senate and a MODIP Member of the same University. Since 2020 she is the President of Greek Society of Data Analysis (GSDA). She has been a founding Member since 2001. She has been Secretary General since 2016. Sofia Anastasiadou makes a constant effort for the development and dissemination of Data Analysis and Multidimensional Statistical Analysis methods, such as Principal Component Analysis, Factor Analysis, Factor Analysis of Correspondences, Symbolic Analysis, Inductive Statistics, Discriminant Analysis, Cluster Analysis, Implicative Statistical Analysis and new fields that can be developed based on relevant international developments in statistical science.

***

Ayyoob is a Senior Research Scholar at the School of Business Studies, University of Calicut, specializing in sustainability, corporate governance, and strategic corporate social responsibility (CSR). A seasoned academic, Ayyoob has served as a resource person for numerous workshops on research methodology and data analysis. His scholarly contributions include publishing book chapters and articles in reputed platforms and presenting research papers at prestigious national and international conferences, both in India and abroad, organized by renowned universities. Additionally, Ayyoob actively reviews manuscripts for esteemed journals, showcasing his expertise and commitment to advancing research in his fields of interest.

Gaganpreet Kaur Ahluwalia is an Associate Professor and the Area Chair for the MBA Program in Marketing Management at the School of Business, Indira University, Pune. With a strong academic background and extensive experience in the field of marketing, she has played a pivotal role in shaping the curriculum and guiding postgraduate students toward industry readiness. Dr. Ahluwalia is known for her expertise in marketing strategy, consumer behavior, and brand management. Her commitment to academic excellence is reflected in her involvement in research, publications, and industry-academia collaboration. She continues to contribute significantly to the development of future business leaders through her dynamic teaching and leadership at Indira University.

Sofia Anastasiadou is a Professor of Statistics and Research Methodology, Biostatistics Biomedical Research Methodology and at the School Health Sciences of the University of Western Macedonia (UOWM). She is the Dean of the Health Sciences of UOWM, Senate Member, and Member of post graduate studies committee. She is also a Member of the Senate and a MODIP Member of the same University. Her teaching focuses in the field of cognitive Research Methodology (Quantitative and Qualitative), Educational Research and Statistical Data Analysis, Big Data. She has written three books on Statistics and Research Methodology and has published over 300 articles in International and Greek Journals as well as in International and Greek Conferences. She has participated in scientific dialogues/ round tables in more than 200 lectures at International and Greek Conferences. She has organized and co-organized Greek and International Scientific Conferences. She is also a Member of a number of Scientific Committees of International Conferences and is an Associate Editor in a number of International Journals.

Nilesh Anute is an Associate Professor at Sri Balaji University, Pune, known for his academic excellence and dedication to higher education. With extensive experience in teaching and research, Dr. Anute has contributed significantly to the fields of finance, accounting, and business management. He is recognized for his analytical approach and ability to simplify complex concepts for students, making learning both effective and engaging. Dr. Anute has presented papers at national and international conferences and has several publications to his credit. His commitment to academic rigor and student development continues to make a lasting impact within the university and beyond.

K. Balaji is an Assistant Professor in Business and Management, Christ University, Bangalore. He did Ph.D. from KLU Business School, KL University,Vijayawada. He is having 12 years of teaching experience. He has to his credit 23 Research Articles published in reputed National and International Journals. He has participated and presented more than 12 papers in both National and International Seminars/Conferences and also attended more than 50 workshops/ FDPS organized by various reputed organizations. He has also participated in more than 50 seminars / webinars organized by various reputed organizations. He has also attended in 6 Short Term Training programs.He has successfully conducted 3 webinars, one 5 day FDP and one International Conference on Reimaging marketing in New Normal. He is a ratified as Assistant Professor by both JNTUH, JNTU Anantapur and Sri Venkateswara University,Tirupati. His specialized areas include, Accounting and Financial management, Marketing Management, Retailing Management, Consumer Behavior studies, Entrepreneurship and Business Laws.

Csongor Czipf, Ph.D. Honorary Associate Professor, Assistant Professor Széchenyi István University, Győr, Hungary Gyula Kautz Faculty of Economics, Department of International Applied Economics Ongoing teaching experience at Széchenyi István University since 1999. Appointed as Regional Economic Manager of the Piarist Order Hungarian Province in Budapest as of January 2022. Master's degree in Religious Education and Dormitory Teaching obtained from the College of Theology in Győr in 2017. Doctoral degree awarded in 2011 by Janus Pannonius University of Pécs. Research specialization: corporate evaluation from a human resources perspective. Bachelor's degree in Economics with a specialization in Comparative Economic Policy completed in 1999 at Széchenyi István College.

Gudivada Sushma is currently serving as a Senior Assistant Professor in the Department of Computer Science and Engineering at CVR College of Engineering, Hyderabad, Telangana. With a strong academic background and a commitment to teaching excellence, she is actively engaged in both academic and research pursuits.

She is also a research scholar at Jawaharlal Nehru Technological University (JNTU), Kakinada, where she is pursuing her doctoral studies. Her dedication to advancing knowledge in the field of computer science reflects in her academic contributions and research initiatives.

Spyros Kontis is a PhD Candidate at the Department of Midwifery, University of Western Macedonia, specializing in the ethical and psychosocial implications of AI in education and health. He holds master's degrees in Cybersecurity and Special Education and has published research on algorithmic governance, bioethics, and AI policy. He is also involved in robotics education and EU-funded projects (Erasmus+, Horizon Europe). His academic interests focus on responsible AI, digital well-being, and the intersection of human rights and intelligent systems.

T.C. Manjunath was born on 6th February 1967. He did his BE from RV College of Engg. in 1989, ME in Robotics & Automation from LD College of Engg. in 1992 with First Rank and PhD in Systems & Control Engg. from IIT Bombay in the year 2007. He is currently working as the Dean Research R D and as Professor in the Dept. of Computer Science & Engineering with specialization in IoT, Cyber Security & Blockchain Technology in Rajarajeswari College of Engineering, Bengaluru, Karnataka. He has completed B.E. Degree from R.V. College of Engg., M.E. Govt.'s LD College of Engg., Gujarat Univ., Ahmedabad in First Rank and Ph.D. in Systems and Control Engineering from the Indian Institute of Technology Bombay IIT Bombay He has got a teaching academic, research and administrative experience of more than 35+ years 10 years as Principal, 8 years as HoD rest as faculty and has published more than 1200+ research papers in various national & international journals and conferences, with 175+ patents, 25 book-chapters, 25 awards and also published 25 text books in various field of science, engineering and technology, completed projects worth Rs. 9 Crores till date apart from guiding 10 PhD scholars. He is a member of 30 Professional Society Chapters and is a fellow of IE, IETE, AMIEE and a chartered engineer. He got the best research scholar award in 2006 in IIT Bombay amongst all the research scholars of the institute. He has got 10 awards in academics and research activities.

P. Selvakumar is currently an Associate Professor in the Department of Science and Humanities at Nehru Institute of Technology, Coimbatore, Tamil Nadu, India. Prior to joining Nehru Institute of Technology, he held positions as an Assistant Professor in the Department of Science and Humanities various engineering colleges in Coimbatore, Tamil Nadu, India, spanning from 2011 to 2023. Dr.P. Selvakumar's academic and research interests lie primarily in the field of phytochemistry. He has made significant contributions to his field, with an impressive record that includes

30 journal publications, 12 patents, and 20 conference papers. Additionally, he has organized 5 seminars and conferences, further demonstrating his commitment to academic and scientific exchange. Throughout his career, Dr. P.Selvakumar has been recognized for his dedication and excellence in teaching, having been honored with several awards, including the Best Teacher Awards. He holds a prominent position in the academic community, contributing actively to research.

Sujesh P Lal has been a part of Federal Institute of Science and Technology (FiSAT), since March 2014. With over 20 years of teaching and 10+ years of research experience, in 2021 he earned his doctorate from Sathyabama University Chennai. His research interest encompass AI, IoT, Sensor Networking. His educational background includes MTech in CSE from VIT university Vellore in 2010. He had made substantial contributions to academic disclosure notably he had filed and published 5 patents including a grant certificate for a design patent. Published many research articles in SCI/WoS/SCIE?Scopus indexed journals. He is a life member of CSI and ISTE, also a member of IEEE, also serving as an ExeCom member of IEEE Kochi Subsection for Educational Activities

Eleftheria I. Panagiotidou is an Adjunct Professor at Democritus University of Thrace- Department of Accounting and Finance, Kavala, Greece, and a partner in an accounting firm in Greece. Holds PhD in Banking, Accounting and Finance, MSc in Accounting, Audit and International transactions and BA in Economics and has experience of teaching courses in Financial and Management Accounting and International Accounting Standards at Undergraduate and Postgraduate level. Her research interests centre on international accounting, accounting education and tax compliance. She is Author/co-author of papers published in journals and conference proceedings.

Ganesh Pathak is an Associate Professor at Sri Balaji University, Pune (SBUP), where he brings a wealth of academic and industry experience to his role. With a strong foundation in management education, Dr. Pathak has been instrumental in shaping future leaders through his insightful teaching, research contributions, and mentorship. His academic interests span across strategic management, organizational behavior, and business ethics. Known for his engaging teaching style and practical approach, he actively bridges the gap between theoretical frameworks and real-world application. Dr. Pathak also regularly contributes to academic journals and conferences, reflecting his commitment to continuous learning and academic excellence.

R. Sahith received his M.Tech in Computer Science and Engineering from JNTUH, India and currently pursuing his Ph.D. in Informatics, Department of

Computer Science and Engineering from Osmania University, Hyderabad, India. He is currently working as an Sr.Assistant Professor in the Department of Computer Science and Engineering at CVR College of Engineering, Hyderabad, India. His research interests are programming and machine learning

José De Jesús Reyes-Sánchez, Ph.D. in senior management, has six master's degrees, in education, in management, professional soccer technique, in physical preparation, in professional soccer, in physical rehabilitation sciences, in sports sciences, as well as in coaching and integral well-being, who is a research professor at the TECNM Instituto Tecnológico Superior De Fresnillo, with more than 20 years of teaching experience, PRODEP profile and coordinator of the academic body with vast experience in conferences and workshops, currently novelist and writer.

S. Poorani is currently working as an Assistant Professor in the Department of Computer Technology - UG, Kongu Engineering College, Tamilnadu, India. She has 19 years of teaching experience. She published 22 articles in International journals and conferences. Her area of interest includes data mining, machine learning and deep learning.

Aparna Sajeev is an Assistant Professor at the Department of Commerce and Management Studies, School of Business Studies, University of Calicut. She pursued her doctoral degree in macro-policy management at the Faculty of Management Studies, University of Delhi. Her key research areas include sustainable Development and Climate Change, Sustainable Finance, Psychometric Analysis, and Impact Assessment. She has three years of Education industry experience as a Senior Research Manager - Impact Assessment and continues her work in education sector engagements as a consultant. She collaborated with the Berkeley Evaluation and Assessment Research Center. With over a decade of research experience, she is presently a research supervisor at the Department of Commerce, University of Calicut. She received a 2 million Won - Selected Research Paper award from Kyunghee University, Seoul (2020).

Lamprini Seremeti is a researcher and academic affiliated with the University of Western Macedonia and Frederick University. Her scholarly work explores the co-evolution of law and artificial intelligence, emphasizing interdisciplinary approaches to ethics, legal informatics, and algorithmic transparency. She has contributed as an editor and author to volumes on AI and Law, and actively participates in EU research initiatives. With a strong background in policy analysis and digital regulation, Dr. Seremeti's interests lie in the responsible integration of AI technologies in governance, education, and human rights protection.

Index

A

B

C

D

E

F

G

I

O

P

R

S

T

www.ingramcontent.com/pod-product-compliance
Lightning Source LLC
LaVergne TN
LVHW062337300926
849161LV00007B/1722
9798337351421